THE PRENTICE HALL SERIES IN MARKETING

Philip Kotler, Series Editor

THIRD EDITION

Marketing Channels

Louis W. Stern

John D. Gray Distinguished Professor of Marketing
Northwestern University

Adel I. El-Ansary

Professor and Chairman, Department of Business Administration
The George Washington University

Prentice Hall, *Englewood Cliffs, New Jersey 07632*

Library of Congress Cataloging-in-Publication Data

STERN, LOUIS W. (date)
    Marketing channels.

    (The Prentice-Hall series in marketing)
    Bibliography.
    Includes index.
    1. Marketing channels. I. Ansary, Adel I. II. Title.
III. Series.
HF5415.129.S75 1988   658.8'4   87–17396
ISBN 0-13-557158-8

Editorial/production supervision and
   interior design: Joan Stone
Cover design: Lundgren Graphics
Manufacturing buyer: Barbara Kelly Kittle

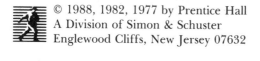

© 1988, 1982, 1977 by Prentice Hall
A Division of Simon & Schuster
Englewood Cliffs, New Jersey 07632

Printed in the United States of America

10 9 8 7 6 5 4 3 2 1

ISBN 0-13-557158-8 01

Prentice-Hall International (UK) Limited, *London*
Prentice-Hall of Australia Pty. Limited, *Sydney*
Prentice-Hall Canada Inc., *Toronto*
Prentice-Hall Hispanoamericana, S.A., *Mexico*
Prentice-Hall of India Private Limited, *New Delhi*
Prentice-Hall of Japan, Inc., *Tokyo*
Simon & Schuster Asia Pte. Ltd., *Singapore*
Editora Prentice-Hall do Brasil, Ltda., *Rio de Janeiro*

To

My wife, Rhona, with love
Louis W. Stern

To

My wife, Nawal, with love
Adel I. El-Ansary

Contents

3 Wholesaling: Structure and Strategy, *101*

4 Physical Distribution: Structure and Strategy, *144*

PART THREE

Channel Management: Planning, Coordinating, Organizing, and Controlling, *195*

5 Channel Planning: Strategy and Design, *200*

6 Mechanisms for Achieving Channel Coordination, *260*

7 Organizational Patterns in Marketing Channels, *315*

8 Legal Constraints on the Interorganization Management of Marketing Channels, *370*

9 Channel Management by Channel Participants, *410*

Preface

Similar to the second edition, the third edition of *Marketing Channels* continues to adopt the *managerial* frame of reference. Emphasis is on how to *plan, organize,* and *control* the relationships among the institutions and agencies involved in the process of making certain that products and services are available for consumption by industrial, commercial, and household consumers. The end result of effective marketing channel management is the assurance of adequate levels of time, place, and possession utilities in all items of value to consumers. Therefore, the focus of the text is on channel *performance*.

Channel members can achieve high yield performance primarily through their demand stimulation and delivery activities. But performance requirements at one level of the marketing channel imply performance requirements and expectations at other levels. Retailers, for example, often measure their productivity by employing such criteria as sales per square foot, sales per employee, and sales per transaction. Generation of a high level of sales per square foot may necessitate heavy advertising by manufacturers and the maintenance of high inventory levels by wholesalers. These large promotion and storage burdens may, in turn, reduce the return on investment available to manufacturers and wholesalers. The interface among the various performance requirements, policies, and practices at different levels of marketing channels dictates the need for systemwide communication and coordination.

While the major thrust of the text is centered on developing means for securing systemwide coordination and, thereby, satisfactory marketing channel performance, we have spent the first two parts of the text laying the groundwork for the managerial processes introduced later. Thus, Part I explores theories that describe why channels have emerged and why they assume the various structures that they do. It provides an essential backdrop to any discussion of channel management. Introduced in Part I are such concepts as service output levels and marketing flows, on which we rely heavily in the remainder of the book. Part II is devoted to a strategic analysis of retailing, wholesaling, and physical distribution management. Because retailers, wholesalers, and logistic institutions comprise some of the foremost "actors" in channel networks, we believe that it is imperative that the reader have more than a nodding acquaintance with their orientations so that when the discussion turns to the question of interrelationships among channel members, everyone can be on an equal footing relative to the degree of knowledge about how the "actors" operate. We have not devoted a separate chapter to manufacturers because we assume that most readers have some knowledge of how manufacturers market their products, especially via previous course work or readings in marketing management.

Part III comprises the "core" of the text. It contains seven chapters in total. Chapter 5, the first chapter in Part III, deals with the planning and designing of channels. Chapter 6 focuses on how to organize and coordinate channel member behavior generally. Chapter 7 provides examples of specific ways in which channels have been organized, building on the principles laid out in Chapters 1 and 6. Chapter 8 indicates the various constraints present in federal U.S. law on the coordination and control of channel activities. Chapter 9 examines channel management strategies practiced by institutions located on different levels in the channel. The specific focus is on the question of channel leadership and a discussion of which institutions are likely to be in the best positions to allocate resources within channels. In Chapter 10, we examine communications problems and the development of information systems, given the critical nature of effective communications within channels. The final chapter in Part III, Chapter 11, is devoted to an assessment of the performance of channels and the institutions comprising them. It incorporates a broad, social viewpoint, but its main focus, like the previous chapters, is on managerial issues in marketing channels. It is in this chapter that instruments for monitoring performance—such as the strategic profit model, the channel audit, direct product profit analysis (DPP), and distribution cost analysis—are described.

Part IV of the text deals with channel management in other contexts, i.e., in the international arena and in service industries. Exploring marketing channels in other countries enriches the analysis. It underscores the generalizability of channel management processes while recognizing the importance of cultural factors in adjusting the process. Because services constitute over 60 percent of the GNP in the U.S. and because the marketing of services is not always clearly understood, the final chapter in the text looks at marketing channels in the service sector. As with the international arena, the channel management process appears to be generic but in need of adjustments from time to time because of the significant nuances apparent in the marketing of services.

Because case analysis is frequently used as a pedagogical tool in courses dealing with marketing channels, we have included in the *Instructor's Manual* of the third edition a list of over 50 cases of varying length and orientation suitable for use with this text. The list has been keyed to the four separate parts of the text described above.

Although this edition retains the same organization and managerial framework adopted in the second edition, the contents have changed in several ways. First, the analytic thrust of the text is more strategic in orientation. Channel management is viewed as the implementation of interorganization management strategies designed to render "high performing" technical and behavioral channel structures. This strategic management orientation is best illustrated by the integrative framework presented in the first figure in the chapter dealing with Channel Management, Chapter 9.

Second, the latest research findings, theoretical developments, and managerial trends have been incorporated and interwoven throughout the fabric of all chapters. In fact, Chapter 4 on Physical Distribution and Chapter 10 on Channel Communication and Information Systems have been completely rewritten. The advancements in materials requirements planning (MRP), just-in-time (JIT), and strategic physical distribution management have made physical distribution institutions and their management an even more critical factor in competitive strategy. Similarly, the new and emerging information systems and communication technologies have permanently altered the technical and behavioral communication structures in marketing channels. Channel members adopting the new technologies are enhancing their power positions and, subsequently, their potential to gain channel control and to assume the role of the Channel Captain or Channel Manager.

Third, the volume of research on marketing channels has increased by leaps and bounds since the second edition. Equally significant is the deployment of robust research methodologies leading to richer interpretation of the new research findings and reassessment of previous ones. New research findings are incorporated into Chapters 6 and 9 dealing with channel coordination and channel management by channel participants.

Finally, we increased the number of technical and professional appendices from nine in the second edition to fifteen in the third edition. A number of the second edition's appendices have been eliminated or revised and new ones added. These include appendices on "Continuous–Review Reorder–Point Models," "Insights into Channel Coordination from Management Science," "Square D and Its Distributors: A Discussion of Policy and Procedure," "Insights into Channel Planning from Management Science," "Common Industrial Channel Offerings, Categorized by Distributor Requirements," "IBM's View of Channel Value-Added Elements," "The 7-ELEVEN Store Franchise," and "Selected Literature on Channel Management."

Acknowledgments

There are three sets of individuals who have deeply influenced the structure and content of this book. Although there is some overlap in the sets, one group has operated primarily in support and encouragement of the first author, another has aided the second author, and the third has been important to both authors.

The first author is deeply indebted to his marvelous colleagues at Northwestern University for their stimulation and interest. Being in the scholarly but warm and friendly atmosphere provided by them has been a source of considerable inspiration and pleasure. Most particularly, he is thankful for and appreciative of the contributions to his thinking made by the doctoral students he has come in contact with over the years. Although all of the students are too numerous to mention here, special thanks for unique contributions to this and previous editions of the text must go to Lynn W. Phillips, Torger Reve, Ravi Achrol, C. M. Sashi, and Shumeet Banerji. Thanks also go to Marion Davis and Laura Kingsley for their typing assistance. All of these people, and many more, are owed a great deal for their contributions.

The second author would like to acknowledge the encouragement and support of his colleagues at The George Washington University. Special thanks to James H. Perry for his review, editorial assistance, and content contributions to JIT, MRP, and inventory models sections in Chapter 4. This book could not have been possible without the inspiring work and contributions of a number of marketing scholars. Many thanks to all, particularly those who have been personally supportive and encouraging over a number of years. A special debt is owed to the first author, Louis W. Stern; William R. Davidson; Bert C. McCammon, Jr.; and Robert F. Lusch. The third edition would not have been possible without the capable typing assistance of Erin Jones. Her dedication, attention to detail, and patience could not have been surpassed. It is with deep affection that the support, encouragement, and love of his wife, Nawal, is acknowledged. The exciting personal growth and career progress at the World Bank of his son, Waleed, have been inspirational. The deep affection, artistic touches, and the prospects of a bright future of his son, Tarik, have provided the source of renewed energy and enthusiasm at difficult times. Their contributions transcended the three editions.

Finally, both authors owe a great deal to Orville Walker, Robert Lusch, Brian Harris, James R. Brown, John Nevin, Ernest R. Cadotte, and Robert W. Ruekert, who reviewed either one, two, or all three editions of the text. We are especially indebted to the large number of authors whose work we cite throughout the text. Without their efforts, we could not have written this book.

Louis W. Stern
Evanston, Illinois

Adel I. El-Ansary
Washington, D.C.

PART ONE

THE EMERGENCE OF MARKETING CHANNELS

Many U.S. consumers like to purchase foreign products because of their reputation for high quality and low cost compared with domestic products. These products, which include cameras, watches, and even crystal, are typically available in specialty electronics stores, catalog showrooms, and discount stores at 20 to 40 percent below their normal prices. However, when consumers try to have such products serviced or repaired they may be in for an unpleasant surprise. When a product is sent for repairs under warranty, it is usually mailed back with a repair estimate.[1]

This type of problem is common when consumers purchase *gray-market* merchandise. Gray-market goods are foreign products purchased by U.S. retailers from a manufacturer's distributor overseas. Through the use of this distribution channel, the manufacturer's U.S. subsidiary or authorized importer is omitted and so are the warranties and other authorized dealer services. The problem just recounted occurs frequently because retailers aren't required to tell consumers that gray-market merchandise does not come with a U.S. factory warranty.

Distribution channels for the delivery of goods and services such as appliances, automobiles, food, governmental services (e.g., garbage collection, mass transit), and

[1] Hank Gilman, "No Guarantees for Guarantees in Gray Market," *Wall Street Journal,* February 5, 1985, p. 33.

financial services (e.g., mortgage loans) are often managed ineffectively and inefficiently, a situation resulting not only in an enormous loss of resources but in disgruntled and disaffected consumers seemingly put upon by forces they cannot control. The solution lies, it appears, not only in adopting consumer-oriented objectives and programs but in managing the systems responsible for the delivery of the objectives and programs in a more satisfactory manner.

The need for effective management of distribution systems is especially crucial as economies move into periods of stunted growth. As new market opportunities decrease for many industries, numerous companies shift their marketing strategies away from expanding total market demand and toward building market share within their existing markets.[2] Such a situation forces, in turn, a reassessment of many corporate functions, particularly distribution. Although marketing strategies and tactics have traditionally been developed by management on the basis of a study of ultimate consumer or end-user needs, environmental contingencies are likely to compel deeper attention to distribution problems. For example, it has been predicted that in periods of low economic growth there is likely to be "a shift away from what the consumer wants and more critical emphasis on establishing a relationship with the jobber, wholesaler, and retailer. . . . Instead of asking what kind of toothbrushes the consumer wants, one must go to Kresge, Sears, and the drug stores and find out what kind of packaging, display cases, delivery, pay terms, and buying incentives they need."[3]

Managerial analyses of marketing channels are required to find solutions to these and other types of problems. These analyses dissect and examine the past, present, and prospective efforts that channel members make to organize, coordinate, influence, direct, and control relationships within the entire channel. Specifically, channel management seeks to improve overall distribution-system performance through forging more effective and efficient linkages among the organizations responsible for the delivery of a particular product or service to its predetermined points of consumption. The linkages or relationships among channel members are, however, greatly influenced by the basic structure of the channel itself. That is, it is important to know why certain types of structures emerge before we can turn to an in-depth analysis of channel member relations, because these relations take place within a specific structure, not apart from it. Therefore, Part One of this text deals with the emergence of channel structures.

[2] "Marketing When the Growth Slows," *Business Week* (April 14, 1975), pp. 44–50.
[3] *Ibid.,* p. 48.

CHAPTER ONE

Marketing Channels: Structure and Functions

Consumers are aware that literally thousands of goods and services are available through a very large number of diverse retail outlets. What consumers may not be as well aware of is the fact that the *channel structure,* or the set of institutions, agencies, and establishments through which the product must move to get to them, can be amazingly complex. Consider, for example, the marketing channel structure existing in 1984 for the International Business Machines (IBM) Personal Computer (Fig. 1–1). The success of IBM's marketing effort depends to a large extent upon the coordination of the efforts of the internal and external marketing organizations that constitute the structure of its marketing channel.

Usually, combinations of institutions specializing in manufacturing, wholesaling, retailing, and many other areas join forces in marketing channel arrangements to make possible the delivery of goods to industrial users or customers and to final consumers. The same is true for the marketing of services. For example, in the case of health care delivery, hospitals, ambulance services, physicians, laboratories, insurance companies, and drugstores combine efforts in an organized channel arrangement to ensure the delivery of a critical service. All these institutions depend on each other to cater effectively to consumer demand. Therefore, marketing channels can be viewed as *sets of interdependent organizations involved in the process of making a product or service available for use or consumption.* From the outset, it should be recognized that not only do marketing channels *satisfy demand* by supplying goods and services at the right place, quantity, quality, and price, but they also *stimulate demand* through the promotional activities of the units (e.g., retailers, manufacturers' representatives, sales offices, and wholesalers) comprising them. Therefore, the channel should be viewed as an orches-

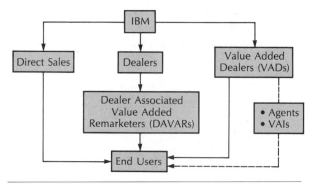

Figure 1–1 Marketing channels for the IBM personal computer

Source: Future Computing/Datapro

trated network that creates value for the user or consumer through the generation of form, possession, time, and place utilities.[1]

A major focus of marketing channel management is *delivery.* It is only through distribution that public and private goods can be made available for consumption.[2] Producers of such goods (including manufacturers of industrial and consumer goods, legislators framing laws, educational administrators conceiving new means for achieving quality education, and insurance companies developing unique health insurance coverage, among many others) are individually capable of generating only form or structural utility for their "products." They can organize their production capabilities in such a way that the products they have developed can, in fact, be seen, analyzed, debated, and, by a select few perhaps, digested. But the actual large-scale delivery of the products to the consuming public demands different types of efforts which create time, place, and possession utilities. In other words, the consumer cannot obtain a finished product unless the product is transported to where he[3] can gain access to it, stored until he is ready for it, and eventually exchanged for money or other goods or services so that he can gain possession of it. In fact, the four types of utility (form, time, place, and possession) are inseparable; there can be no "complete" product without incorporating all four into any given object, idea, or service.

---

[1] Robert F. Lusch, "Erase Distribution Channel from Your Vocabulary and Add Marketing Channels," *Marketing News* (July 27, 1979), p. 12.

[2] The term *goods* is being used in its broadest sense to encompass all things of value. For an enlightening discussion of the distinction between public and private goods (broadly defined), see Mancur Olson, Jr., *The Logic of Collective Action* (Cambridge, Mass.: Harvard University Press, 1965).

[3] We of course acknowledge the equal status of the female. However, we continue to use the traditional *he* to avoid unwieldy construction.

THE EMERGENCE OF MARKETING
CHANNEL STRUCTURES

In order to gain an appropriate base for understanding the marketing channel, it is important to understand at the outset the underlying reasons for the emergence of channel structures. Here, emphasis is placed on the economic rationale for the existence of channels, because economic reasons are the foremost determinants of channel structures. Later, it will be possible to introduce other determinants, including key technological, political, and social factors, and to examine how these factors influence the makeup of channel systems.

The emergence and arrangement of the wide variety of distribution-oriented institutions and agencies, typically called *intermediaries* because they stand between production on the one hand and consumption on the other, can be explained in terms of four logically related steps in an economic process:[4]

1. Intermediaries arise in the process of exchange because they can improve the efficiency of the process.
2. Channel intermediaries arise to adjust the discrepancy of assortments through the performance of the sorting processes.
3. Marketing agencies hang together in channel arrangements to provide for the routinization of transactions.
4. Channels facilitate the searching process.

Each of these steps is examined in the following pages.

The Rationale for Intermediaries

In primitive cultures, most household needs are *produced* within the household. However, at an early stage in the development of economic activities, *exchange* replaced production as a means of satisfying individual needs. The development of exchange is facilitated when there is a surplus in production over current household requirements and when this surplus cannot be held for future consumption because of the perishable nature of the products or the lack of storage facilities. Thus, if numerous households are able to effect small surpluses of different products, a basis for exchange is developed.

Alderson and Martin formulated the following law of exchange, which specifies the conditions under which an exchange will take place:[5]

Given that x is an element of the assortment A_1 and y is an element of the assortment A_2, x is exchangeable for y if, and only if, these three conditions hold:

(a) x is different from y.
(b) The potency of the assortment A_1 is increased by dropping x and adding y.

---

[4] The following discussion is based on Wroe Alderson, "Factors Governing the Development of Marketing Channels," in Richard M. Clewett (ed.), *Marketing Channels for Manufactured Products* (Homewood, Ill.: Richard D. Irwin, 1954), pp. 5–22.

[5] Wroe Alderson and Miles W. Martin, "Toward a Formal Theory of Transactions and Transvections," in Bruce E. Mallen (ed.), *The Marketing Channel: A Conceptual Viewpoint* (New York: John Wiley & Sons, Inc., 1967), pp. 50–51.

(c) The potency of the assortment A_2 is increased by adding x and dropping y.

These conditions of exchange are more easily met when production becomes specialized and the assortment of goods is broadened. As households find their needs satisfied by an increased quantity and variety of goods, the mechanism of exchange increases in importance.

However, as the importance of exchange increases, so does the difficulty of maintaining *mutual* interactions among *all* households. For example, a small village of only five specialized households would require ten transactions to carry out *decentralized* exchanges (i.e., exchanges at each production point). In order to reduce the complexity of this exchange system and thus facilitate transactions, intermediaries appear in the process. Through the operation of a central market, one dealer can considerably reduce the number of transactions. In the preceding example, only five transactions would be required to carry out a *centralized* exchange. This conception of decentralized versus centralized exchange is illustrated in Fig. 1–2.

Implicit in the preceding example is the notion that a decentralized system of exchange is less efficient than a centralized network employing intermediaries. The same rationale can be applied to direct selling from manufacturers to retailers relative to selling through wholesalers. Figure 1–3 shows that, given four manufacturers and ten retailers who buy goods from each manufacturer, the number of contact lines amounts to 40. If the manufacturers sell to these retailers through one wholesaler, the number of necessary contacts is reduced to 14.

However, the number of necessary contacts increases dramatically as more wholesalers are added. For example, if the four manufacturers in our example use two wholesalers, the number of contacts rises from 14 to 28, and if four wholesalers are used, the number of contacts will be 64. Thus, employing more and more intermediaries is subject to diminishing returns simply from a *contactual* efficiency perspective.

It should also be noted in this simple illustration that the cost of any two contact lines of transaction—i.e., manufacturer–wholesaler, wholesaler–retailer, manufacturer–retailer—is assumed to be the same. Also, it is assumed that whenever more than one wholesaler is employed by a manufacturer, each retailer will avail himself of the services of each of these wholesalers. Obviously, accounting must be made for differences between direct and indirect communication costs, in the effectiveness and efficiency of the institutions involved in the transaction, and in the quality of the contact between the various channel members.

The Discrepancy of Assortment and Sorting

In addition to increasing the efficiency of transactions, intermediaries smooth the flow of goods and services by creating possession, place, and time utilities. These utilities enhance the potency of the consumer's assortment. One aspect of this *smoothing* process requires that intermediaries engage in the performance of a *sorting* function. This procedure is necessary in order to bridge the *discrepancy* between the assortment of goods and services generated by the producer and the assortment demanded by the consumer. The discrepancy results

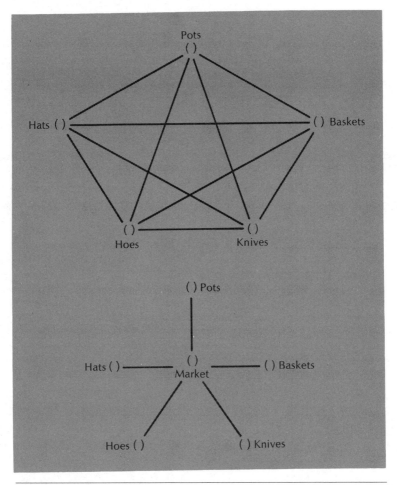

Figure 1–2   Decentralized versus centralized exchange

Source: Wroe Alderson, "Factors Governing the Development of Marketing Channels," in Richard M. Clewett (ed.), *Marketing Channels for Manufactured Products* (Homewood, Ill.: Richard D. Irwin, 1954), p. 7.

from the fact that manufacturers typically produce a large quantity of a limited variety of goods, whereas consumers usually desire only a limited quantity of a wide variety of goods.

The sorting function performed by intermediaries includes the following activities:

1. *Sorting out.* Breaking down a heterogeneous supply into separate stocks that are relatively homogeneous. (Sorting out is typified by the grading of agricultural products, such as grading eggs according to size and grading beef as either choice or prime.)
2. *Accumulation.* Bringing similar stocks from a number of sources together into a larger homogeneous supply. (Wholesalers accumulate varied goods for retailers, and retailers accumulate goods for their customers.)

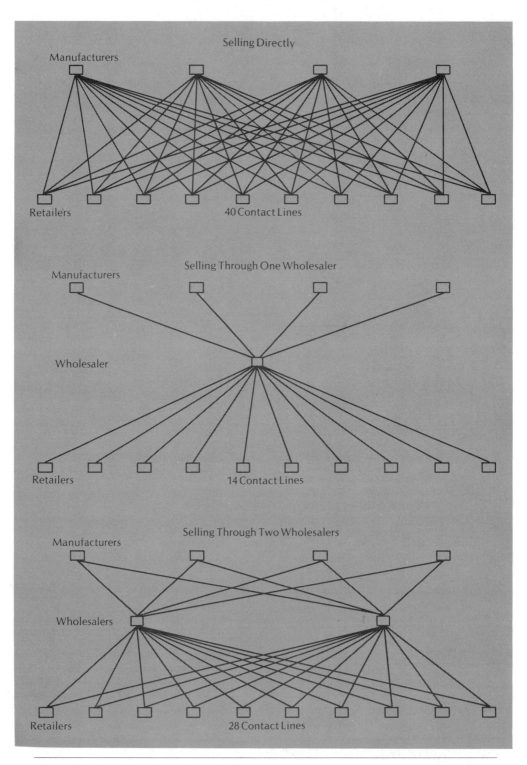

Figure 1–3 Rationale for intermediaries

3. *Allocation.* Breaking a homogeneous supply down into smaller and smaller lots. (Allocating at the wholesale level is referred to as *breaking bulk.*) Goods received in carloads are sold in case lots. A buyer of case lots in turn sells individual units. The allocation processes generally coincide with geographical dispersal and successive movement of products from origin to end consumer.

4. *Assorting.* Building up the assortment of products for resale in association with each other. (Wholesalers build assortments of goods for retailers, and retailers build assortments for their customers.)[6]

While sorting out and accumulation predominate in the marketing of agricultural and extractive products, allocation and assorting predominate in the marketing of finished manufactured goods. It should be noted that the discrepancy of assortment induces specialization in the exchange process, and the need for such specialization may impede the vertical integration of marketing agencies. For example, a manufacturer of a limited line of hardware items could open his own retail outlets only if he were willing to accumulate the wide variety of items generally sold through those outlets. In general, hardware wholesalers can perform such services more efficiently than individual manufacturers. Assortment discrepancy also explains why Bethlehem Steel has told its small-volume customers not to buy from it directly but rather to obtain from wholesalers the assortments of the wide variety of steel products they require. On the other hand, large-volume buyers who need homogeneous supplies of steel in large lots have been urged to deal directly with Bethlehem's steel mills.[7]

Routinization

Each transaction involves ordering of, valuation of, and payment for goods and services. The buyer and seller must agree to the amount, mode, and timing of payment. The cost of distribution can be minimized if the transactions are routinized; otherwise, every transaction is subject to bargaining, with a concomitant loss of efficiency.

Moreover, routinization facilitates the development of the exchange system. It leads to standardization of goods and services whose performance characteristics can be easily compared and assessed. It encourages production of items that are more highly valued. In fact, exchange relationships between buyers and sellers are standardized so that lot size, frequency of delivery and payment, and communication are routinized. Because of routinization, a sequence of marketing agencies can hang together in a channel arrangement or structure.

Automatic ordering is a prime illustration of routinization. It eliminates the cost of placing orders when retail inventory levels reach the reordering point. For example, supplies of cereals and canned goods at Safeway and A&P supermarkets are automatically replenished from distribution warehouses. These warehouses have direct on-line computers to communicate orders to manufacturers and other suppliers. Kellogg has direct on-line communication capabilities with the distribution warehouses of major retail supermarket chains. Similar

---

[6] Other authors have described the sorting processes as "concentration, equalization, and dispersion" and "collecting, sorting, and dispersing." See Rayburn D. Tousley, Eugene Clark, and Fred E. Clark, *Principles of Marketing* (New York: Macmillan Company, 1962), pp. 7 and 8; and Roland S. Vaile, E. T. Grether, and Reavis Cox, *Marketing in the American Economy* (New York: Ronald Press, 1952), pp. 134–50, respectively.

[7] Robert E. Weigand, "Fit Your Products to Your Markets," *Harvard Business Review* (January-February 1977), p. 102.

ordering systems have been established in the marketing channels for medical supplies and industrial abrasives by American Hospital Supply and Norton Company. Thus, hospitals and manufacturing firms that deal with these companies are able to achieve high transactional efficiency in their purchasing of medical supplies and abrasives. Without routinization, the cost of distribution can increase dramatically.

Searching

Buyers and sellers are engaged in a double search process in the marketplace. The process of search involves uncertainty because producers are not certain of consumers' needs, and consumers are not certain that they will be able to find what they are looking for. Marketing channels facilitate the process of searching, as when, for example:

- Wholesale and retail institutions are organized by separate lines of trade, such as drug, hardware, and grocery
- Products such as over-the-counter drugs are widely available through thousands of drug stores, supermarkets, convenience stores, and even gasoline stations
- Hundreds of thousands of parts are supplied to automotive repair facilities from local jobbers within hours of the placement of orders

COMPOSITION OF MARKETING CHANNELS

A marketing or distribution channel comprises a set of interdependent institutions and agencies involved with the task of moving anything of value from its point of conception, extraction, or production to points of consumption. As an example, some of the institutions and agencies involved in the distribution of canned fruits are portrayed in Fig. 1–4. Included in Fig. 1–4 are the business firms that are primarily responsible for the flow of title to the merchandise from manufacturer to consumer. Although excluded from Fig. 1–4 are the numerous agencies and institutions that *facilitate* the passage of title and the physical movement of the goods, such as common carriers, financial institutions, and advertising agencies, they too are members of the channel for this particular product.

Even though it is incomplete, Fig. 1–4 permits at least a beginning conceptualization of the various channels of distribution that can be utilized to deliver a product to consumers. It shows the range of channel alternatives from direct to indirect methods, using various types of middlemen. It also illustrates the options at each channel level of using proprietary representation (retailer's own distribution center), full-function wholesalers, or limited-function wholesalers (cash-and-carry). Each of these channels may be designed to cater to the needs of a different market, market segment, and/or operational requirement of the wholesalers and retailers involved.

Functions and Flows in Marketing Channels

Manufacturers, wholesalers, and retailers as well as other channel members exist in channel arrangements to perform certain functions. For example, in the medical instrument industry, distributors perform four functions: (1) carrying

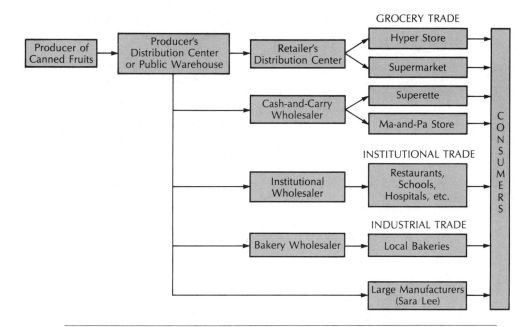

Figure 1–4 Channel mapping for a manufacturer of canned fruits

Source: Reprinted, by permission of the publisher, from "Shifting Shoals in Marketing Channels: The MIDAS Approach to Channel Systems," by E. W. Smykay and M. A. Higby, *Management Review* (July 1981), p. 19. © 1981 American Management Association, New York. All rights reserved.

inventory and physical distribution, (2) selling, (3) providing after-sale service, and (4) extending credit to their customers. If a manufacturer in the industry opts to sell directly to dealers and other customers, he will have to either assume all functions performed by his distributors or shift part of them to his dealers and other customers.[8]

The above discussion underscores three important principles in the structure of marketing channels:

1. One can eliminate or substitute institutions in the channel arrangement.
2. However, the functions these institutions perform cannot be eliminated.
3. When institutions are eliminated, their functions are shifted either forward or backward in the channel and, therefore, are assumed by other members.

It is a truism that "you can eliminate the middleman but you cannot eliminate his functions."

To the extent that the same function is performed at more than one level of the marketing channel, the work load for the function is shared by members at these levels. For example, manufacturers, wholesalers, and retailers may all carry inventory. This duplication may increase distribution cost. However, the increase in cost is justifiable to the extent that it may be necessary to provide goods to customers at the right quantity, quality, time, and place.

[8] Benson P. Shapiro, "Improve Distribution with Your Promotional Mix," *Harvard Business Review* (March-April 1977), pp. 116–17.

In this text, we will refer frequently to *flows* in channels. A *flow* is *identical* to a *function*. However, the term *flow* is somewhat more descriptive of movement, and, therefore, we tend to prefer it. Figure 1–5 depicts eight universal flows or functions. Physical possession, ownership, and promotion are typically forward flows from producer to consumer. Each of these moves "down" the distribution channel—a manufacturer promotes his product to a wholesaler, who in turn promotes it to a retailer, and so on. The negotiation, financing, and risking flows move in both directions, whereas ordering and payment are backward flows.

It is interesting and useful to note that any time inventories are held by one member of the channel system, a financing operation is under way. Thus, when a wholesaler takes title and assumes physical possession of a portion of the output of a manufacturer, the wholesaler is financing the manufacturer. Such a notion is made clear when one examines the carrying costs of inventory. The largest component of carrying cost is the cost of the capital tied up when inventories are held in a dormant state. (Other carrying costs are obsolescence, depreciation, pilferage, breakage, storage, insurance, and taxes.) The reason for the significance of capital costs is relatively obvious—if money were not tied up in inventory, a firm would be able to invest those funds elsewhere. In effect, capital costs are opportunity costs of holding inventory. Thus, when one member of a channel has been "freed" from holding inventory—when his inventories have been exchanged for cash—he may reinvest these funds. In the furniture industry, traditional furniture retailers operating on a sold-order basis choose not to participate in the backward financing flow. On the other hand, "warehouse"

Figure 1–5 Marketing flows in channels

Source: Adapted from R. S. Vaile, E. T. Grether, and R. Cox, *Marketing in the American Economy* (New York: The Ronald Press, 1952), p. 113.

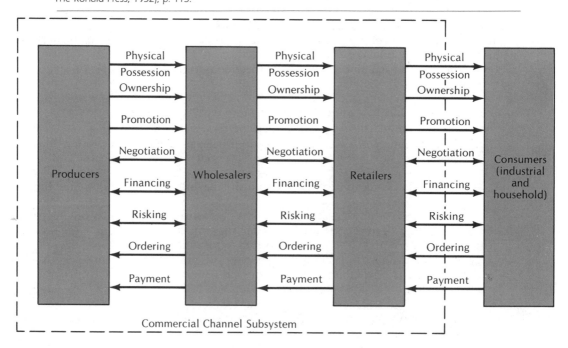

furniture retailers do participate in this flow directly and thereby receive benefits from manufacturers in the form of lower prices and preferential treatment.

Many other examples of the backward flow of financing can be found beyond those associated with the holding of inventory. Thus, when a department store buyer commits himself to purchasing a large volume of a particular fashion good prior to the mass production and shipment of the item, the commitment may be factored and the funds used by the garment manufacturer to finance his production process. Prepayment for merchandise is another example of the backward financing flow.

The forward flow of financing is even more common. General Motors Acceptance Corporation is a specific institution established by the manufacturer to finance not only ultimate consumers of its automobiles but also inventories held by dealers. In fact, all terms of sale, with the exception of cash on delivery and prepayment, may be viewed as elements of the forward flow of financing.

Channel Member Specialization

All of the flows or functions are indispensable—at least one institution or agency within the system must assume responsibility for each of them if the channel is to operate at all. But it is not necessary that every institution participate in the furtherance of all of the flows. In fact, it is for this reason that the channel of distribution is an example of a division of labor on a macro scale. Certain institutions and agencies specialize in one or more of the flows, as indicated in Fig. 1–6. The use of these and other intermediaries largely boils down

Figure 1–6 *Channel institutions particular to selected marketing flows*

Source: Reprinted by permission of the publisher from "Telemarketing in Distribution Channels," by Ray Vorhees and John Coppett, *Industrial Marketing Management,* Vol. 12, p. 107. Copyright 1983 by Elsevier Science Publishing Co., Inc.

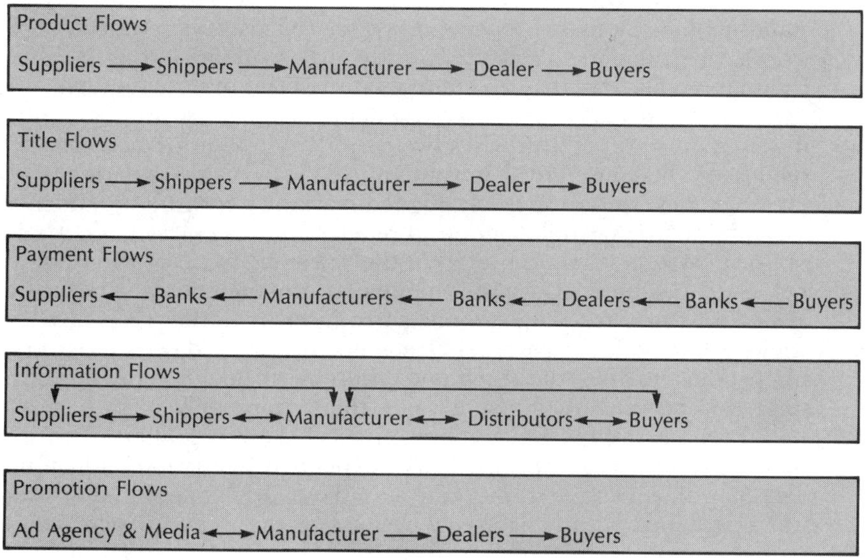

Product Flows

Suppliers ⟶ Shippers ⟶ Manufacturer ⟶ Dealer ⟶ Buyers

Title Flows

Suppliers ⟶ Shippers ⟶ Manufacturer ⟶ Dealer ⟶ Buyers

Payment Flows

Suppliers ⟵ Banks ⟵ Manufacturers ⟵ Banks ⟵ Dealers ⟵ Banks ⟵ Buyers

Information Flows

Suppliers ⟷ Shippers ⟷ Manufacturer ⟷ Distributors ⟷ Buyers

Promotion Flows

Ad Agency & Media ⟷ Manufacturer ⟶ Dealers ⟶ Buyers

to their superior efficiency in the performance of basic marketing tasks and functions. Marketing intermediaries, through their experience, their specialization, their contacts, and their scale, offer other channel members more than they can usually achieve on their own.

In reality, participation by channel members in different flows renders them members of a number of different channels, such as an ownership or title channel, a negotiations channel, a physical distribution channel, a financing channel, and a promotional channel. The task of channel member coordination should be extended to the coordination of these different channels. Often, new product introduction by manufacturers fails as a result of lack of synchronization of physical and promotional flows or channels. While national promotion may vigorously proceed on schedule, delays in transportation and lack of distribution warehouse space may delay the availability of the product at retail outlets.

ANALYZING MARKETING CHANNEL STRUCTURES

The basic economic rationale for the emergence of channel intermediaries and institutional arrangements can be understood in terms of the need for exchange and exchange efficiency, minimization of assortment discrepancies, routinization, and the facilitation of search procedures. But such rationale provides little information as to why channels, such as the one depicted in Fig. 1–7, are structured one way or another to satisfy this need. More specifically, how can one account for the variations in channel structure in terms of the number of levels and the extent of specialization of functions or flows?

Channels as a Network of Systems

Perhaps most important to the analysis of channel structure is an understanding that channels consist of *interdependent* institutions and agencies, in other words, that their members are interdependent relative to task performance. A channel can be viewed as a system because of this interdependency—it is a set of *interrelated* and *interdependent* components engaged in producing an output. A distribution channel comprises two major subsystems or sectors: *commercial* and *consumer*. The commercial subsystem (to which major attention is given in this text) includes a set of vertically aligned marketing institutions and agencies, such as manufacturers, wholesalers, and retailers. The *consumer* (industrial and household) subsystem is incorporated in the *task environment* of the commercial channel. Each commercial channel member is dependent on other institutions for achieving its goal(s). For example, a producer (manufacturer, physician, welfare agency) is dependent on others (retailers, hospitals, day care centers) in getting his product to the consumer and, thereby, in gaining his objectives (profits, improved health care, a reduction in the welfare rolls).

Perhaps the most glaring example of the recognition of this interdependency in recent years was the effort expended by the Credit Committee of the Toy Manufacturers Association to save Toys "R" Us. This major retailer of toys was threatened with bankruptcy because of the weak financial condition of its parent company, Interstate Stores, Inc. The TMA Credit Committee worked

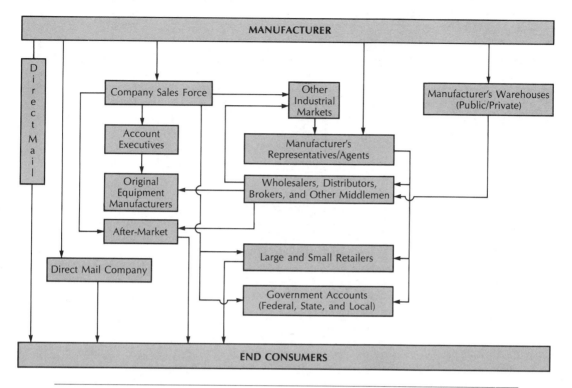

Figure 1–7   Channel alternatives for a manufacturer of industrial and consumer goods

Source: Reprinted, by permission of the publisher, from "Shifting Shoals in Marketing Channels: The MIDAS Approach to Channel Systems," by E. W. Smykay and M. A. Higby, *Management Review* (July 1981), p. 23. © 1981 American Management Association, New York. All rights reserved.

directly with banks in devising a plan that not only kept Toys "R" Us healthy but also prevented toy manufacturers, in the aggregate, from losing $80 million in sales. The decision of the banks to grant credit to Toys "R" Us was, to a large extent, based on the fact that six of the largest toy manufacturers were willing to extend credit to Toys "R" Us on their own.[9] Clearly, the six manufacturers and the members of the TMA Credit Committee realized the importance of adopting a systems perspective in the marketing channel for toys. As a result of these and other actions, Toys "R" Us has become an even more significant and successful force in toy retailing with sales amounting to over $1.7 billion.

The marketing channel has boundaries, as all systems do. These include geographic (market area), economic (capability to handle a certain volume of goods or services), and human (capability to interact) boundaries. Furthermore, a channel, like other systems, is part of a larger system that provides it with inputs and imposes restrictions on its operation. A channel exists as part of an economy's distribution structure that encompasses other channels. The economy's distribution structure is a subsystem of the national environment, which is a subsystem of the international environment. Both the national and interna-

[9] "How the TMA Saves Toys 'R' Us," *Toys* (May 1975), pp. 45–47.

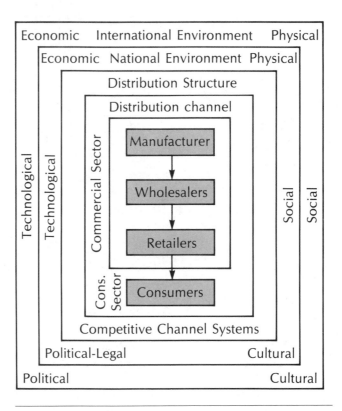

Figure 1–8 *The channel as a processing subsystem within the environment*

tional environments encompass physical, economic, social, cultural, and political subsystems that influence the development of and impose constraints on the focal channel system. This configuration of systems is portrayed in Fig. 1–8. The impact of these environments on individual channel members and on channel organization and design is discussed throughout later chapters.

It is important here to recognize that marketing channels evolve and function in dynamic environments. A channel structure is determined in part by the environment in which the channel operates. For example:

- As a result of high domestic labor costs, many U.S. footwear manufacturers were displaced by international competitors from Brazil, Italy, and Spain. In response, Congress held hearings in 1985 on footwear import quotas. The impact of this action on American consumer welfare, on U.S. footwear importers, and on the economy of leading footwear-exporting countries had to be taken into account.

- New computer-technology applications combined with the capabilities of a vast communication network are changing consumer shopping behavior. Sales volume of direct "to-consumer" marketing channels exceeded $200 billion in 1984. For every dollar spent in a retail store, 37.5 cents were spent ordering goods by mail, phone, or computer. Soon the computer will take over a much larger percentage of that market, as evidenced by the rapid growth of computer shopping service companies such as Comp-U-Card International and Comp-U-Mail.[10]

- New communication technologies are changing merchandise presentation methods. Videodisk Monitor Magazine reports that 66 companies are experimenting with interactive videodisks to supplement sales clerks by providing detailed information about products. For example, the Dayton Hudson department stores chain has joined with Thomasville Furniture to show the Thomasville product line using interactive videodisks. Using a touch screen, customers can select the style and type of furniture they want to see on the screen in model rooms or standing alone.[11]
- Changing consumer life styles including the increased emphasis on leisure time, physical fitness, health maintenance, and/or growth of specialty sporting goods, supermarkets, health spas, and HMO's and convenience 24-hour grocery stores.

The survival and growth of certain channel members and the demise of others is best explained by viewing the channel as an *open system*. The evolution of channel systems is an ongoing adaptation of organizations to economic and sociopolitical forces both within the channel and in the external environment.[12] A systems theory framework for conceptualizing distribution channels can be useful in understanding the growth, survival, or demise of channel members and systems. One such framework has been proposed by Morris and Sirgy. It can be summarized in terms of the following propositions:

Proposition 1. A channel member is more likely to adapt and grow . . . [if] the channel member defines its role and objectives in the context of the channel network and more specifically as a function of the dominant (or its superordinate) channel member.

Proposition 2. A channel member is more likely to adapt and grow . . . [if] the channel member closely monitors changes in its environment that are directly related to its role expectations.

Proposition 3. A channel member is more likely to adapt and grow . . . [if] it undertakes corrective action . . . when significant deviations are detected between role expectations and role outcomes.

Proposition 4. A channel member is more likely to adapt and grow . . . [if when] alternative and repeated corrective actions fail to meet the role expectations of the channel member, these role expectations change in the direction of role outcomes.

Proposition 5. A channel system is more likely to adapt and grow . . . [if] the behaviors of its channel members are fully coordinated with one another in a hierarchy of controls.

Proposition 6. A channel system is more likely to adapt and grow . . . [if] it achieves balance between channel members' role expectations that are internally derived and those that are imposed upon them by their superordinate members.

Proposition 7. A channel system is more likely to adapt and grow . . . [if] it achieves a high level of market performance with a high level of channel members' satisfaction.

[10] Judith Rosenfeld, "Revolutionizing Retail," *Marketing Communications* (February 1985), pp. 66–71; and remarks by Stan Rapp at the Direct Marketing Association's 67th Annual Conference, Chicago, 1985.
[11] Reported in William Nickels, "Technomarketing's Macro Implications," A paper presented before the 10th Annual Macromarketing Conference, 1985.
[12] Louis W. Stern and T. Reve, "Distribution Channels as Political Economies: A Framework for Comparative Analysis," *Journal of Marketing*, Vol. 44 (Summer 1980), pp. 52–64.

- *Proposition 8.* Channel systems that are . . . vertically integrated have the ability to be more impactful on the environment, but are less responsive to environmental demands. Conversely, channel systems that are nonintegrated . . . are less able to impact upon their environment, but are highly responsive to the demands of the environment.[13]

Channel Structures and Channel Outputs

To explain the key elements determining how channels are structured, Bucklin has developed a rather elaborate theory, the rudiments of which are outlined briefly here.[14] In essence, Bucklin argues that the separation of production from consumption, because of the economic rules of specialization, necessitates the performance of the various marketing functions or flows to meet expressed demand for service outputs. Marketing channels that provide higher levels of service outputs reduce consumers' search, waiting time, storage, and other costs by lessening their involvement with the accomplishment of these necessary activities. Other things being equal (especially price), consumers will prefer to deal with a marketing channel that provides a higher level of service outputs.

Bucklin has specified four service outputs: (1) spatial convenience (or market decentralization), (2) lot size, (3) waiting or delivery time, and (4) product variety (or assortment depth and breadth).[15] Spatial convenience provided by market decentralization of wholesale and/or retail outlets increases consumers' satisfaction by reducing transportation requirements and search costs. Community shopping centers and neighborhood supermarkets, convenience stores, vending machines, and gas stations are but a few examples of satisfying consumers' spatial convenience.

Similarly, the number of units to be purchased at each transaction can obviously affect the industrial or household consumer's welfare. When the marketing channel system allows consumers to buy in small units, purchases may move directly into the consumption process. If, however, consumers must purchase in larger lots, some disparity between purchasing and consumption patterns will emerge, burdening consumers with product storage and mainte-

[13] Michael Morris and M. Joseph Sirgy, "Applications of General Systems Theory Concepts to Marketing Channels," in Robert F. Lusch et al. (eds.), *1985 Educators Conference Proceedings* (Chicago: American Marketing Association, 1985), pp. 336, 337, 338.

[14] Louis P. Bucklin, *A Theory of Distribution Channel Structure* (Berkeley, Calif.: IBER Special Publications, 1966). Much of the paraphrasing of Bucklin's model has been drawn from Michael Etgar, "An Empirical Analysis of the Motivations for the Development of Centrally Coordinated Vertical Marketing Systems: The Case of the Property and Casualty Insurance Industry," unpublished Ph.D. dissertation, The University of California at Berkeley, 1974, pp. 95–97.

[15] Bucklin, *op. cit.,* pp. 7–10; and Louis P. Bucklin, *Competition and Evolution in the Distributive Trades* (Englewood Cliffs, N.J.: Prentice-Hall, Inc., 1972), pp. 18–31. Clearly, the list of service outputs provided to consumers by a channel can be expanded to include provision of credit, maintenance of product quality, availability of information, stability of supply, availability of personal service and attention, and risk reduction, among others. For exposition purposes, however, the discussion here is limited to the four major service outputs suggested by Bucklin in the monograph and book just cited. For further elaboration of this subject, see Louis P. Bucklin and James M. Carman, "Vertical Market Structure Theory and the Health Care Delivery System," in Jagdish N. Sheth and Peter L. Wright (eds.), *Marketing Analysis for Societal Problems* (Urbana, Ill.: University of Illinois Bureau of Economic and Business Research, 1974), pp. 7–21; Lee E. Preston and Norman R. Collins, *Studies in a Simulated Market* (Berkeley, Calif.: University of California Institute of Business and Economic Research, 1966); and Christina Fulop, *Competition for Consumers* (London: Allen and Unwin, 1964), Chapter 2.

nance costs. Consequently, the smaller the lot size allowed by a channel, the higher the channel's output and, normally, the price to the consumer.

Waiting time, the third service output isolated by Bucklin, is defined as the period that the industrial or household consumer must wait between ordering and receiving goods. Again, the longer the waiting time, the more inconvenient it is for the consumer, who is required to plan his/her consumption far in advance. Usually, when customers are willing to wait, they are compensated in terms of lower prices, as when ordering through a Sears catalog. Finally, the wider the breadth of assortment—the greater the product variety—available to the consumer, the higher the output of the marketing channel and the higher the distribution cost, since greater assortment entails carrying more inventory. For example, while A&P supermarkets carry, on average, an assortment of 8000 product line items or stockkeeping units (SKUs), Basics stores carry a limited assortment of 800 SKUs at substantially lower prices.

These service outputs are achieved through the performance of the marketing functions or flows. The decisions on the amount of output to be delivered by channel members are obviously directly influenced by the resource base and capabilities of channel members to perform various marketing functions and by the kind of service outputs desired by consumers. The result of the interaction between channel member resources and consumer requirements is a channel structure or arrangement that is capable of satisfying the needs of both channel members and consumers. Under reasonably competitive conditions and low barriers to entry, the channel structure that evolves over the long run should comprise a group of institutions so well adjusted to that structure's task and environment that no other type of arrangement could create greater returns (e.g., profits or other goals) or more consumer satisfaction per dollar of product cost.[16] This arrangement is called the *normative structure.* The determination of channel structure by service outputs is illustrated in Fig. 1–9.

The more service outputs required by consumers, the more likely it is that intermediaries will be included in the channel structure. Thus, if consumers wish to purchase in small lots, then there are likely to be numerous middlemen performing sorting operations between mass producers and the final users. If

[16] Bucklin, *A Theory of Distribution Channel Structure, op. cit.,* p. 5.

Figure 1–9   The determination of channel structure

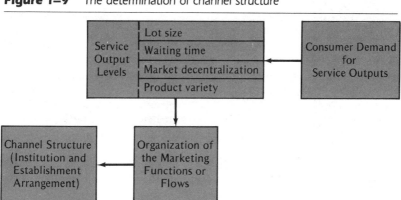

waiting time is to be reduced, then decentralization of outlets must follow, and, therefore, more middlemen will be included in the channel structure. The same type of reasoning can be applied to all of the service outputs. However, as service outputs increase, costs will undoubtedly increase, and these higher costs will tend to be reflected in higher prices to consumers. Consumers are usually faced with a choice between channel structures that provide few service outputs but relatively low prices and structures where both service outputs and prices are high. The more the consumer or end-user participates in the marketing flows (in terms of search, physical possession, financing, and the like), the more he should be compensated for his efforts. Where channel service outputs are low, consumers are supposedly compensated for their additional efforts through the lower relative prices provided by such channel structures. Thus, when construction machinery manufacturers, such as Caterpillar or J. I. Case, purchase brake parts in carload quantities from firms like Bendix and are willing to wait several months for delivery from distant plants, they can expect to pay lower prices than if they were to order the same parts from a local warehouse distributor who is willing to ship in smaller quantities and to deliver the parts much more quickly. The lower the level of service outputs provided, the greater are the economies of scale that can be achieved by channel members, and vice versa.

The final structure that emerges is, therefore, a function of the desire of channel members to achieve scale economies relative to each of the marketing flows and the demand of consumers for various service outputs. An optimal structure is one that minimizes the total costs of the system (both commercial and consumer) by appropriately adjusting the level of the service outputs.[17] Within a channel, members can attempt to shift the degree of their participation in each flow in order to provide the greatest possible service output at the lowest possible cost. But such shifting calls for a tremendous amount of coordination and cooperation. This is one reason the management of channel systems is so critical.

Postponement-Speculation and Channel Structure

The way in which channels are structured is, to a significant extent, determined by where inventories should best be held in order to provide appropriate service levels, fulfill the required sorting processes, and still deliver an adequate return to channel members. To explain the process involved in the determination of inventory locations, Bucklin, using Alderson's original scheme,[18] developed the principle of *postponement-speculation*.[19] According to Bucklin, efficiency in marketing channels is promoted by the postponement of changes in (1) the form and identity of a product to the latest possible point in the marketing process and (2) inventory location to the latest possible point in time. Risk and uncertainty costs increase as the product becomes more differentiated. Postponement promotes efficiency by moving differentiation nearer to the time of purchase when demand is more certain, thus reducing risk and uncertainty costs. Also, the cost of physical distribution of goods is reduced by sorting products in large lots and in relatively undifferentiated states. For example, some

[17] Bucklin and Carman, *op. cit.*, p. 12.

[18] Wroe Alderson, "Marketing Efficiency and the Principle of Postponement," *Cost and Profit Outlook*, Vol. 3 (September 1950).

[19] Louis P. Bucklin, "Postponement, Speculation and the Structure of Distribution Channels," in Mallen (ed.), *op. cit.*, pp. 67–74.

bicycle manufacturers carry large inventories of unassembled bicycle parts. As they receive orders, they assemble the bicycles for direct delivery to distributors and dealers. This way, they do not need to hold finished-good inventories.

Postponement is a tool used by a channel member to shift the risk of owning goods to another channel member. For example:

- Manufacturers of special industrial machinery postpone by refusing to produce except upon receipt of orders.
- Middlemen postpone by buying from sellers who offer faster delivery, thus shifting inventory backward.
- Consumers postpone by buying from retail outlets, where goods are available directly from the store shelf.

Speculation is the *opposite* of postponement. The speculation concept holds that "changes in form, and the movement of goods to forward inventories, should be made at the earliest possible time in the marketing process in order to reduce the costs of the marketing system."[20] Thus risk is shifted to or assumed by a channel institution rather than shifted away from it. Speculation makes possible cost reductions through (1) economies of large-scale production runs; (2) the elimination of frequent orders, which increase the costs of order processing and transportation; and (3) the reduction of stockouts and their attendant cost of consumer dissatisfaction and possible subsequent brand switching. An accurate sales forecast is essential in marketing channels dominated by speculation. Otherwise, the increase in the cost of carrying speculative inventories will outweigh cost-reduction benefits emanating from long production runs and infrequent orders.

The variables in the postponement-speculation theory are shown in Fig. 1–10. The vertical axis represents the average cost of performing some function, or set of functions, for one unit of any given commodity. The horizontal axis measures the time required to deliver the commodity to the buyer after an order has been placed. If these two elements are taken together, the coordinates measure the cost of certain marketing functions or flows performed in a channel with respect to delivery time.

Three basic sets of flows are shown in Fig. 1–10. The curve labeled C represents the costs incurred by the buyer in holding an inventory. The curve AD' shows the costs of those flows necessary to supply the buyer directly from a manufacturing point some specified distance away. Curve DB reveals the costs incurred by flows utilized to ship the commodity from this same production point through a speculative inventory (e.g., a stocking intermediary, such as a manufacturer's distribution center, public warehouse, merchant wholesaler, or retailer) to the buyer.

The postponement-speculation theory holds that channel structure is determined by the interrelationships of curves C, AD', and DB, as follows:

1. The minimal cost of supplying the buyer for every possible delivery time is derived from curves AD' and DB. As may be seen in Fig. 1–10, especially fast delivery service can be provided only by the indirect channel (i.e., by using a stocking intermediary). However, at some delivery time, I', the cost of serving the consumer directly from the producer will intersect and fall below the cost of indirect shipment. The minimal costs derived from both curves are designated DD'. From the

[20] *Ibid.*, p. 68.

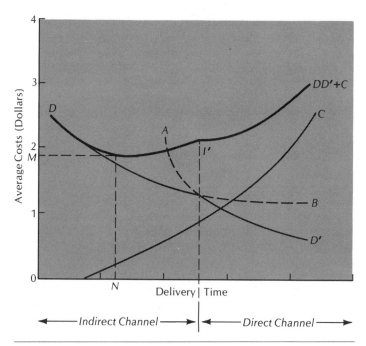

Figure 1–10 Using the postponement-speculation concept to determine channel structure

Source: Reprinted from Louis P. Bucklin and Leslie Halpert, "Exploring Channels of Distribution for Cement with the Principle of Postponement-speculation," in Peter D. Bennett (ed.), *Marketing and Economic Development* (Chicago: American Marketing Association, 1965), p. 698.

perspective of channel cost, it will be cheaper to service the buyer from a speculative inventory if delivery times shorter than I' are demanded. If the consumer is willing to accept delivery times longer than I', then direct shipment will be the least expensive.

2. The minimal *total* cost curve for the channel with respect to delivery time is derived by summing the cost of moving goods to the buyer, DD', and the buyer's costs of holding inventory, C. The curve is represented in Fig. 1–10 by $DD' + C$. Total channel costs initially fall as delivery time lengthens, because increased buyer expenses are more than made up for by savings in other parts of the channel. However, the savings from these sources gradually diminish and buyer costs begin to rise more rapidly. A minimal cost point is reached and expenses for the channel rise thereafter. *Channel structure is controlled by the location of this minimum point.* If, as in the present case, it falls to the left of I', then goods would be expected to flow through the speculative inventory (i.e., an intermediary). If, on the other hand, the savings of the buyer from postponement were not as great as those depicted, the minimum point would fall to the right of I' and shipments would be made directly from producer to consumer.[21]

[21] Louis P. Bucklin and Leslie Halpert, "Exploring Channels of Distribution for Cement with the Principle of Postponement-speculation," in Peter D. Bennett (ed.), *Marketing and Economic Development* (Chicago: American Marketing Association, 1965), p. 699. Note that the type of cost behavior discussed above and depicted in Fig. 1–10 excludes from consideration any potential savings from sorting in the channel. Such savings, derived from the possibility of economies in large-scale trans-

In the situation portrayed in Fig. 1–10, the costs of postponement are minimized by the use of a speculative inventory, because the minimal cost point, M, falls to the left of I'. If, however, the risk costs to the customer were less, or the general cost of holding inventories at the customer's home (or warehouse, as the case may be) were lower, then C would be farther to the right. Point M would also shift to the right. With sufficient reduction in consumer cost, M would appear to the right of I', indicating that direct shipment in the channel would be the means to minimize postponement cost.

The theory of postponement-speculation provides a useful basis for understanding channel structure. It is possible to assert that speculative inventories create the opportunity for new institutions to hold title in the channel. The existence of speculative inventories leads to the use of indirect channels; the economic need to have such inventories opens the door to middlemen to demonstrate whether they are capable of reducing the costs of inventory risk-taking (that is, the costs associated with participating in the flows of physical possession and ownership). On the other hand, postponement creates an opportunity for different institutions in the channel—freight forwarders, drop shippers, and agent middlemen who do not take title to merchandise but who, in the absence of speculative inventories, facilitate the use of more direct channels of distribution.

It is also possible to apply the principle of postponement-speculation to an understanding of the differences between household and industrial buying. Much household buying is fragmented, involves small lots, and is undertaken frequently, especially with regard to convenience and some shopping goods. The costs to households of holding large inventories tend to be relatively high. Thus, longer and more indirect channels often exist for convenience goods. Speculation is an important determinant of the channel structure for such goods, because there are more points in the channel where inventory may be held. In industrial purchasing, however, the opposite generally holds, and thus the desire to postpone has led to the development of a different type of institutional arrangement where there are more direct, shorter channels.

As mentioned, the accuracy of sales forecasting is a critical feature of speculation. This fact is underscored by the troubles that have frequently plagued the residential real estate development industry. Most speculative builders merely follow current market trends without understanding the dynamics of future demand. Therefore, during economic downturns they are caught with excessive inventories of unsold houses, which often lead them to bankruptcy. Some of the larger and more sophisticated home builders, such as Ryan Homes, reduce their vulnerability by using national, regional, and local sales forecasts as well as postponing home interior finishing, including fixtures, floors, and wallpaper, to suit the requests of the home buyer.

Channel Structure and Functional Spinoff

It is possible to expand Bucklin's analysis beyond physical possession, ownership, and risk-taking to other flows associated with marketing channels. In fact, each marketing flow may be thought to have a differently shaped cost

---

port to the speculative inventory point, are, as mentioned in the preceding section, a fundamental characteristic of channels and must be introduced into the analysis before a final structure can be determined.

curve, which may include increasing, decreasing, or constant returns. Thus, savings can be affected if the activities or flows subject to increasing returns are performed at a higher output level. A firm with limited resources in a competitive industry will normally delegate these increasing return activities to enterprises that specialize in them. Through such delegation (or shifting of the flows), the firm is able, as Stigler observes, to lower its average and marginal costs and thereby to improve its competitive position.[22] In essence, specialized channel intermediaries provide external economies to firms employing them. Eventually, however, reintegration of the delegated flows may be warranted as a firm's output expands or as technology changes, because the firm may then find itself capable of performing them at an optimum scale.[23]

Such a pattern of vertical disintegration followed by vertical reintegration can be observed in the case of small manufacturers who rely heavily on agent middlemen to represent them in the market and on specialized storage, transportation, and financing institutions to perform these respective functions in their channels. As these small manufacturers expand, they tend to develop their own sales forces, perform their own storage, transportation, and financing, and thus dispense with the services of agent middlemen and other specialized institutions. Similar analyses can be applied to wholesalers and retailers. For example, Sears started as a mail-order retailer and expanded horizontally. As its operations grew, Sears integrated backward by operating its own warehousing and other wholesaling facilities and then owning or controlling manufacturing facilities. Thus, when a firm's output and its market are limited, it will likely find itself shifting flows onto others in its channel, if it can, in fact, convince others to accept responsibility for these flows.[24] As market size expands, it becomes increasingly economical to vertically integrate, a pattern fully evident among the largest manufacturing and distributive organizations.[25]

It is important to note that there may be considerable problems associated with shifting flows or, as Mallen has put it, "spinning off" functions.[26] It may be exceedingly difficult to separate the joint costs associated with the performance of many marketing flows (e.g., physical possession and ownership). Furthermore, most companies deal with multiple products and services for which costs are shared. There is also a time horizon involved as well as a host of noneconomic considerations. Nevertheless, the concept of shifting flows is a viable one; like so many management decisions, it demands appropriate accounting procedures to be implemented correctly.

[22] George J. Stigler, "The Division of Labor Is Limited by the Extent of the Market," *Journal of Political Economy,* Vol. 59 (June 1951), pp. 185–193.

[23] Control as well as economic considerations are crucial here. In fact, control may override economics in many situations. This factor is discussed in detail in later chapters.

[24] This is not always a foregone conclusion. Very small firms often find it difficult to secure needed services from agents, advertising agencies, and financial institutions, for example, and therefore must integrate these flows, even though it would be more economical to pass them along to someone else.

[25] For a useful analytical perspective on this issue, see Stanley F. Stasch, "A Method of Dynamically Analyzing the Stability of the Economic Structure of Channels of Distribution," unpublished Ph.D. dissertation, Northwestern University, 1964.

[26] Bruce E. Mallen, "Functional Spin-Off: A Key to Anticipating Change in Distribution Structure," *Journal of Marketing,* Vol. 37 (July 1973), pp. 18–25. Also see William P. Dommermuth and R. Clifton Andersen, "Distribution Systems: Firms, Functions and Efficiencies," *MSU Business Topics,* Vol. 17 (Spring 1969), pp. 51–56.

Additional Factors
Determining Channel Structure

Added to these economics-oriented explanations of why channels take on certain structural properties must be technological, cultural, physical, social, and political factors.[27] For example, the emergence of the supermarket in the structure of food distribution was contingent upon the availability of technologies such as the mass media and mass communications, the cash register, packaging and refrigeration, and the automobile. However, the introduction of the supermarket in developing countries is impeded by cultural variables, such as high rates of illiteracy, the habit of tasting food products before buying, and the delegation of buying to domestic help. Vending and dollar-change machines provide an example of technological and cultural influences on the distribution structure of candy, snack foods, beverages, and other items. Thus, in affluent societies with convenience-oriented cultures, consumers are willing to pay the extra cost associated with buying from vending machines. And the advent and continuous development of electronic data-processing systems have enabled manufacturers and middlemen to accurately assess their distribution costs and redesign their respective channels.

Geography, size of market area, location of production centers, and concentration of population, among other physical factors, also play important roles in determining the structure of channels. Distribution channels tend to be longer (i.e., include more intermediaries) when production is concentrated and population and markets are dispersed. Furthermore, we find that urban areas are served by a wide variety of retail outlets, including department stores, discount houses, and supermarkets, while rural areas may be served solely by a general store.

In addition, local, state, and federal laws can influence channel structure in both direct and indirect ways. There are laws that circumscribe territorial restrictions in distribution, price discrimination, full-line forcing, and unfair sales practices. And there are licensing boards that screen entrants to particular channels.

Social and behavioral variables can also influence the makeup of a channel. For example, Galbraith has advanced the concept of countervailing power as a tentative explanation of channel structure and practices.[28] His theory emphasizes that (1) private economic power is held in check by the countervailing power of those who are subject to it; (2) economic power begets countervailing power; (3) countervailing power is a self-generating force that complements competition as a regulatory force in the economy; and (4) countervailing power can take many forms, the most important of which is threatened or actual vertical integration. Manifestations of the effect of countervailing power on distribution channel structure are provided by the following examples.

- The emergence of the mass retailer to countervail the power of large manufacturers

[27] For example, Preston believes that channel structure is a function of population density and cluster, per capita income, geographic setting and resource endowment, volume and variety of goods, and managerial capabilities. See Lee E. Preston, "Marketing Organization and Economic Development: Structure, Products, and Management," in Louis P. Bucklin (ed.), *Vertical Marketing Systems* (Glenview, Ill.: Scott, Foresman and Co., 1970), pp. 116–33.

[28] John K. Galbraith, *American Capitalism*, rev. ed. (Boston: Houghton Mifflin Co., 1956), pp. 110–14, 117–23.

- The utilization of private brands by chain retailers to countervail the power of large manufacturers having popular national brands
- The emergence of voluntary and retailer cooperative chains to countervail the power of the large corporate chains
- Trade association activities by small retailers (pharmacies, independent service stations, and independent grocery stores) in an attempt to countervail the power of chains and manufacturers

Admittedly, more could be said about each of these factors; it is hoped that readers will be able to develop additional examples of their influence on the structure of channels with which they are familiar. The main point to be remembered here, however, is that explanations of channel structure in terms of economic variables alone are obviously insufficient, even though such economic models provide an appropriate starting point for understanding why specific structures emerge. The necessity for going beyond economic variables is made especially clear when one attempts to answer the question of why uneconomic channel structures persist over time. In other words, why is it that all channels do not gravitate to or obtain the normative structure specified by Bucklin? The answer comes from examining the myriad social, cultural, and political, as well as economic, variables. As McCammon points out, uneconomic channels may persist for the following reasons:[29]

1. *Reseller solidarity.* Channel participants organize and function as groups that tend to support traditional trade practices and long-established institutional relationships. Trade association actions, attempts by independent retailers to outlaw chain stores, and department store operators' efforts to block discount store operations attest to the role of reseller solidarity in determining channel structure.
2. *Entrepreneurial values.* Large resellers are growth-oriented, tend to adopt economic criteria for decision-making purposes, and use new, efficient technologies. On the other hand, small resellers have limited expectations, tend to maintain the status quo, view their demand curve as relatively fixed, and resist growth beyond their limited growth expectations.
3. *Organizational rigidity.* Firms respond incrementally to innovations because of organizational rigidities. Thus, the process of change takes a long time.
4. *The firm's channel position.* Kriesberg grouped channel intermediaries into insiders, who are members of the dominant channel; strivers, who want to become members of the channel; complementors, who perform functions complementary to functions performed by insiders; and transients, who take advantage of temporary opportunities and are not interested in becoming members.[30] Whereas transients usually disrupt the status quo by engaging in deviant competitive behavior, insiders, strivers, and complementors are more interested in maintaining the status quo. Thus, firms completely outside the channel are most likely to introduce basic and enduring innovations in the channel structure.
5. *Market segmentation.* New institutions do not appeal to all market segments. Traditional institutions seem to have loyal segments that they appeal to. Thus, these institutions are not compelled to change.

[29] Bert C. McCammon, Jr., "Alternative Explanations of Institutional Change and Change Evolution," in William G. Moller, Jr., and David L. Wilemon (eds.), *Marketing Channels* (Homewood, Ill.: Richard D. Irwin, 1971), pp. 136–41.

[30] Louis Kriesberg, "Occupational Controls Among Steel Distributors," in Louis W. Stern (ed.), *Distribution Channels: Behavioral Dimensions* (Boston: Houghton Mifflin Co., 1969), pp. 50–60.

Indeed, to have a goal of moving toward a normative channel structure, one must meet the assumptions of low barriers to entry and competitive conditions. In many of the preceding examples, entry is purposely inhibited through group action, product differentiation, industrial norms, and the like. In addition, the concept of a normative channel structure is long-run in nature; in a dynamic environment, such a structure cannot be reached at any one point in time. Change must always take place according to an assessment of future requirements, and thus there will always be a gap between the actual and the ideal. In fact, it is probably best to adopt an evolutionary view of structure, because what exists always seems to be a compromise among past structure, present requirements, and predictions about the future.

CHANNEL MANAGEMENT AND COMPETITION

Economic battles involving producers versus producers or middlemen versus middlemen will not, in the long run, determine the ultimate victors in the marketplace. Rather, the relevant unit of competition is an entire distribution system comprising an entire network of interrelated institutions and agencies. For example, in the passenger tire industry, Firestone's system of distributors and dealers is in competition with Goodyear's entire system. The long-term standing of either company will depend in large measure on how well each company manages the relations among the institutions and agencies involved in the distribution task so as best to satisfy the needs of the end-users of tires.

Exactly the same point applies to other industries as well. In the auto industry the continuing slump in auto sales in 1984–85 began to have harsh repercussions on suppliers and dealers as well as manufacturers. Manufacturers, such as General Motors and Ford, asked their suppliers to cut their prices by 2 to 3.3 percent. In return, they were given the opportunity to participate in future model programs or were signed to multiyear contracts instead of the traditional one-year agreements. Suppliers said these demands reflected GM and Ford's efforts to emulate their Japanese competitors' practice of dealing with a small network of efficient suppliers, which work closely with the auto companies in improving productivity and cutting costs.[31]

Similarly, in the computer industry Apple has tried to strengthen its ties with companies that produce software and computer accessories by improving intercompany communications. Apple has also tried to smooth relationships with its dealers by offering incentives such as wholesale discounts of approximately 4 percent on bulk orders of certain Apple products and by making substantial contributions to marketing programs for dealers who order six or more Macintosh computers. These incentives put some pressure on Apple's profits but in turn eased strained relations with some of its dealers.[32]

[31] Amal Nag, "Ford's Suppliers Appear Cool to Request That New Prices Exclude Labor Cost Rise," *Wall Street Journal*, January 10, 1983, p. 8, and "GM Wants Cut in Prices from Suppliers," *Wall Street Journal*, May 2, 1984, p. 3.
[32] Patricia A. Bellew, "Apple Computer Intensifies Marketing," *Wall Street Journal*, August 2, 1985, p. 4.

Viewing channels as competitive units is significant for all companies, including those that market their products through a number of different channels and those that develop assortments of goods and services by purchasing from a variety of suppliers. The way individual manufacturers coordinate their activities with the various intermediaries with whom they deal, and vice versa, will determine the viability of one type of channel alignment versus other channel alignments made up of different institutions and agencies handling similar or substitutable merchandise.

If, within a given marketing channel, an institution or agency does not see fit to coordinate effectively and efficiently with other members of the same network, but rather pursues its own goals in an independent, self-serving manner, it is possible to predict the eventual demise of the channel alignment of which it is a part as a strong competitive force. Ideally, then, channel members should attempt to coordinate their objectives, plans, and programs with other members in such a way that the performance of the total distribution system to which they belong is enhanced. However, it has been argued that such integrated action up and down a marketing channel is actually a rarity. The following comments by a consumer goods marketer are illustrative:

> If I could gain more help from my distribution channels, we could substantially increase volume and have even greater impact on profits. But when I press the button which says, "Get the distributors to increase sales of product A immediately," all too often I get a push on product C in three months. Our channels are so long and complex that we have little effect on them.[33]

Fortunately, there are exceptions to this attitude. For example, when Coca-Cola introduced "new" Coke, bottlers who are Coke's front-line contact with consumers were the first to feel the heat. They expressed their frustrations and Coca-Cola responded by publicly apologizing for discontinuing the 99-year-old product and later revived it as Coca-Cola Classic.[34]

Channel participants are often not concerned with all the transactions that occur between each of the various links in the channel, however. Middlemen, in particular, are most concerned about the dealings that take place with those channel members immediately adjacent to them from whom they buy and to whom they sell.[35] In this sense, channel intermediaries are not, in fact, functioning as enlisted member components of a distribution system, but rather are acting individually as *independent markets,* with each one choosing those products and suppliers that best help him serve the target groups for whom he acts as a purchasing agent. From this perspective, the middleman's method of operation—the functions he performs, the clients he serves, and the objectives, policies, and programs he adopts—is the result of his own independent decisions.

This notion of each channel intermediary acting as an independent market must be qualified and analyzed with regard to total channel performance. Although an "independent" orientation on the part of any channel member may indeed be operational at times, it is put into effect only at the risk of sacrificing

---

[33] Shapiro, *op. cit.,* p. 115.

[34] John Koten and Scott Kilman, "Marketing Classic: How Coke's Decision to Market Two Versions Undid over Four Years of Planning," *Wall Street Journal,* July 15, 1985, p. 1.

[35] Philip McVey, "Are Channels of Distribution What the Textbooks Say?" *Journal of Marketing,* Vol. 24 (January 1961), pp. 61–65.

the levels of coordination necessary for overall channel effectiveness, efficiency, growth, and long-run survival. Thus, a high degree of independent, suboptimizing behavior on the part of individual channel participants serves as a detriment to the viability of the total channel network. The problem for actors within any distribution network is, therefore, to cooperate in developing an interorganization system that will minimize suboptimization so that a high degree of channel coordination is still attainable.

APPROACH OF THE TEXT

The preceding discussion underscores the critical importance of channel member coordination in ensuring channel system viability. The approach of this text is *managerial*. It focuses on *planning, organizing, coordinating, directing,* and *controlling the efforts of channel members.*

The task of channel management is complex and taxing. Most businesses sell a number of products under different labels, and operate in a number of different markets. Products and services are marketed through several channels to a wide range of customers. Channel intermediaries differ in type, volume purchased, location, and many other operating characteristics. This *multimarketing*[36] phenomenon poses difficult channel management issues, which will be dealt with in the remainder of this text.

ORGANIZATION OF THE TEXT

The organization of this text emanates from the framework for understanding channel management shown in Fig. 1–11. The framework specifies channel management systems in terms of interrelated sets of structural and managerial variables. The various chapters in the text discuss these sets of variables, as denoted in Fig. 1–11. The remainder of this section is devoted to an explanation of the organization of the text as outlined in the framework.

A prerequisite to the effective management of marketing channels is a knowledge of the reasons channels exist, the functions they perform, and the factors that account for the way they are structured. In this first chapter, key theoretical concepts have been examined. These concepts explain why specialized institutions and agencies have emerged to assist in the task of making goods and services available to industrial, institutional, and household consumers. The need for efficient exchange via sorting processes, routinization of marketing activities, and reasonably rapid search procedures compels the existence of a large variety of intermediaries. The way in which these intermediaries are linked together depends on the service outputs demanded by consumers. The higher the output demanded, the greater the number of institutions and agencies that will likely be required to bridge the gap between production and consumption. Service outputs are generated through the organization of the marketing functions or flows—physical possession, ownership, promotion, negotiation, financ-

---

[36] See Robert Weigand, "Fit Products to Your Markets," *Harvard Business Review* (January-February 1977), pp. 95–105.

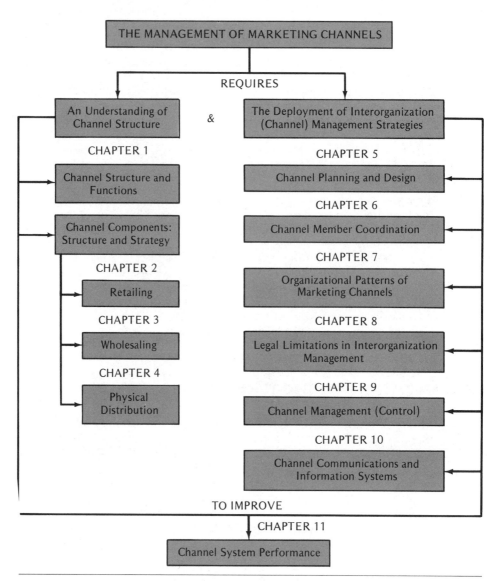

Figure 1–11   A framework for understanding channel management

Chapters 12 and 13 dealing with international marketing channels and marketing channels for services are not noted here. These chapters deal with channel management in special contexts. Therefore, they incorporate all variables in the framework.

ing, risking, ordering, and payment. The actual levels of performance of these functions depend, in turn, on the *economics* of distribution, which requires balancing the needs of channel members to achieve profitability and manage risk, on the one hand, and the desires of consumers to receive the highest possible amount of service output at the lowest possible price, on the other hand. Therefore, there are pressures on channel members to both postpone and to speculate. In addition to these pressures, there are a host of social, political, and cultural factors impinging on channel members. These factors influence and, in some cases, dictate how a channel will be structured.

All of the concepts introduced in this chapter provide relevant background information that can be employed in the management of marketing channels. Without an understanding of each of them and their interaction with one another, any attempts at channel management are likely to be shortsighted and superficial.

Against this backdrop, it is now possible to uncover some of the specific attributes of the intermediaries constituting marketing channels in order to gain a deeper comprehension of their roles within channels and their potential for meeting the needs of the customers they serve. Part Two of this text describes some of the key components of marketing channels—retailers, wholesalers, transportation agencies, public and private warehouse facilities, and distribution centers. Each of these institutions and agencies has its own structure, performance requirements, and management styles. Because channel members tend to focus on their own goals and performance, these features must be understood before any attempts are made to plan, organize, coordinate, and control the channel as a system. In essence, it is imperative to develop an understanding of the internal management of these component institutions before trying to manage the relationships among them. Therefore, Chapters 2, 3, and 4 deal with the structure, management, and performance requirements of retailing, wholesaling, and physical distribution institutions, respectively.

It should be clearly noted at the outset that manufacturers and consumers are also significant components of marketing channels. However, specific chapters on manufacturer marketing strategy and on consumer behavior are not included in this text because these topics are extensively covered in almost all basic marketing and marketing management texts. In contrast, retailer, wholesaler, and physical distribution agency strategies are subjects of a special nature. Not many readers have had experience and/or training in these areas. Those who do have an adequate background in them may wish to proceed from this chapter directly to Part Three.

Part Three focuses on the management of the marketing channel—on planning, organizing, coordinating, and controlling. Careful selection of channel members and planning of channel arrangements are essential if firms are to survive severe competition in the marketplace. Therefore, Chapter 5 examines channel design strategies and considers different policies necessary for the orderly functioning of channels.

Marketing channels can be organized differently to reach similar or different market segments. Forms of channel organization vary. Channels may be organized as loose coalitions of independently owned manufacturers, wholesalers, retailers, and other institutions. Alternatively, they may be organized as closely aligned marketing systems. In the latter instance, channels may be fully integrated corporate vertical marketing systems, contractual systems, or administered systems. Also, channels may be simple (direct to the consumer) or complex (involving a number of levels and engaging a large number of intermediaries). The marketing channel is a complex technical and behavioral system. Different forms of channel organization and management necessitate an understanding of channel member behavior. Chapter 6 examines the marketing channel as a behavioral system. It focuses on the development of an understanding of channel member behavioral tendencies and responses to attempts to manage and coordinate the system. In turn, Chapter 7 discusses organizational patterns of marketing channels in the light of the behavioral tendencies and responses described in Chapter 6.

Naturally, marketers are not free to organize channels and deploy measures of channel management without any restrictions. The design, organization, and specification of policies guiding organizational relationships between channel members are governed by legal restrictions and constraints, which are the subject of Chapter 8.

The implementation of channel planning and organization cannot be effectively achieved without instituting channel coordination through (1) the exercise of leadership, (2) the application of various motivational methods to induce channel members to cooperate, and (3) the development of an appropriate network for communication and exchange of vital information among channel members. Chapter 9 deals with issues related to channel leadership and the direction of channel member effort through appropriate motivation. It discusses channel management by manufacturers, wholesalers, and retailers, explores the methods for dominance and motivation deployed by each, and, finally, discusses who should lead the channel.

Chapter 10 examines channel communication problems and the institution of effective channel information systems. Manufacturers, wholesalers, retailers, transportation agencies, and other participants in the marketing channel system need to communicate and share information in order to function effectively. Forecasting sales, controlling and managing inventories, tracking orders and shipments, launching cooperative advertising campaigns, introducing new products, and putting into effect price changes all require information sharing through a carefully planned and designed communication and information system.

The process of managing a channel system is incomplete without the design and activation of a performance control and audit system. Systematic assessment of channel member and channel system performance, the provision of feedback, and the institution of corrective action mechanisms are necessary to maintain channel control. The final chapter of Part Three, Chapter 11, deals with the assessment of the performance of channel institutions and the channel system. Performance can be assessed from a macro or a micro viewpoint. Both views are considered in Chapter 11. Performance issues such as system output, profitability, growth, distribution cost analysis, and equity in serving various markets are examined.

Part Four of the text examines channel management in other contexts— the international arena and the marketing of services. Exploring distribution channels in other countries enriches our managerial analysis. It enables us to examine the impact of different environments and managerial problems on channel system performance. Chapter 12 deals with international marketing channels.

Whether marketing channels for services are drastically different from marketing channels for goods is debatable. Some contend that they are structurally different and require different analyses and sets of strategies. Others indicate that although different in form and type, the structures for the distribution of goods and services encompass the same technical, behavioral, and managerial variables. Therefore, analyses and strategies for management of marketing channels for goods are adaptable and applicable to marketing channels for services. We subscribe to this viewpoint. But because services constitute over 40 percent of total consumer expenditures in the U.S., they warrant special attention. Furthermore, marketing channels for services are less understood. A discussion of such channels is, therefore, presented in Chapter 13.

DISCUSSION QUESTIONS

1. What are some approaches to the study of distribution channels besides the interorganization systems approach?

2. In a low-growth economy, many strategists emphasize *demand management* rather than *demand stimulation*. How might this affect a firm's marketing mix, particularly as it relates to distribution? If there is a continued deemphasis of demand stimulation in the future, will the role of channel management in marketing become more or less important as an influence on overall corporate performance?

3. Peter F. Drucker, a well-known management scholar, recently described the distribution function as the "economy's dark continent," implying that this aspect of organizational activity has long been ignored as a potential area for strategic development. Why, do you feel, was there such neglect for so long a period?

4. Consider these examples of contemporary marketing channels:

   Avon's distribution system delivering cosmetics direct from manufacturer to consumer through a sales force of 400,000 saleswomen.

   Levitz's warehouse-showroom method of furniture distribution, which stocks large quantities of furniture at each warehouse-showroom at considerable savings, thus enabling Levitz to pass lower prices on to the consumer.

   Hanes Corporation's consignment marketing channel for its L'eggs pantyhose, wherein retailers take no title for the goods, make no financial investment, and perform no delivery service or display maintenance, but receive only a certain percentage of the pantyhose sales for their allocation of space to the L'eggs display.

   a. Select one of these channels and speculate who the other channel participants are and to what extent each member participates in the eight universal marketing flows.

   b. How might these flows be shifted, either among the members now in the channel or to different agencies or institutions not presently included? What do you think would be the implications of such shifts?

   c. Within each of these distribution systems, specify what the consumer's role is from a flow-absorption perspective. How, in turn, does this affect the consumer's level of "compensation"?

5. Do you think a channel management approach is useful and applicable to all types of distribution channel systems? Which types of distribution channels would seemingly need it the most? Which would find it the least applicable?

6. Should advertising agencies and financial institutions be considered channel members? Why? Why not?

7. Is it more useful, from a managerial perspective, to think of consumers (end-users) as members of a channel or as elements in the task environment of the channel? Can consumers be "manipulated" and/or incorporated by channel management?

8. According to Alderson, "the number of intervening marketing agencies tends to go up as distance increases." Distance, in his conception, is measured in terms of "the time and cost involved in communication and transportation." What factors, then, would tend to increase (or decrease) distance?

9. Explain the tradeoffs between the number of available product alternatives *and* search and information costs; between spatial convenience *and* seller costs. Apply your answer to the health care delivery system and to the distribution channel for stainless steel.

10. Bucklin and Carman state that "an optimal structure is one which minimizes the total cost (both commercial and consumer) of the system by the appropriate adjustment of the level of . . . service outputs." Can you apply this statement to each of the marketing flows?

11. Is it likely that vertical disintegration is typical in growing industries while vertical integration is typical in declining industries? Explain.

PART TWO

COMPONENTS
OF
MARKETING CHANNELS

Marketing channels comprise a host of different institutions and agencies. Among the most prominent of these are retailers, wholesalers, common and contract carriers, distribution centers, and public warehouses. To gain a perspective on how all of these various institutions might best be put together to form channels, it is necessary to start with some fundamentals by examining what is going on in each of these various aspects of the so-called distributive trades. Without the fundamentals, it is impossible to design, select, and motivate a "winning" combination.

To some readers of this text, the material in the next three chapters will be "old hat." After all, previous work experience or course work in retailing, wholesaling, and/or physical distribution activities should be sufficient grounding for going directly to a discussion of the planning, organizing, and controlling of channels. We agree. Therefore, the already educated might wish to skim the next several chapters and selectively read parts of them. For others, and even for those who merely will undertake a healthy skimming, here is a brief preview of coming attractions.

Chapter 2 deals with retailing, mainly from a strategic perspective. That is, after a very brief look at the structure of retailing, we turn to the operational orientations that retailers adopt in differentiating their offerings from those of their competitors. The dimensions addressed are margins and turnover, assortments, location, and customer services. Then, the strategic environment of retailing is examined. Specifically, the impact on retailing of changes in consumer and resource markets as well as among competitors is explored in some detail. The basic reason for all of this attention to environmental factors is quite simple: the environment of retailing is the environment for all consumer goods marketing channels, because retailers are the gatekeepers to the market. If manufacturers or wholesalers are to deal with retailers, they had better have a thorough knowledge of the factors that impinge on retailing, both operationally and environmentally. For example, some of Sears's massive problems in the late 1970s and early 1980s can be traced to operational factors, such as its move to shopping mall anchor stores (malls have an intense fashion orientation; Sears is not known as a fashion merchant), the costs of developing a consumer franchise in private brands, the continued dependence on salespeople, and internal power struggles between field territories and headquarters merchandisers; *and* to environmental factors, such as the demise of vendor price-fixing (the umbrella under which Sears priced its private label merchandise), the developing force of specialist chains, and the social upheavals of the 1960s, which affected shopping patterns into the 1970s and beyond.[1] Suppliers to Sears who did not watch these developments very closely were hurt very badly as Sears's sales started to stagnate.

The chapter on wholesaling (Chapter 3) takes a slightly different tack. A great deal of time is spent getting the reader to understand the structure of wholesaling—the kinds of agencies and institutions that make up this often misunderstood and confusing line of trade. Then the discussion turns to an examination of just what it is that wholesalers can be expected to accomplish for their customers and their suppliers. This examination is more or less what one might expect to find in most textbooks that deal with wholesaling. It is followed, however, by a critical (what we call "hard-nosed") assessment of what wholesalers *actually do* accomplish for others. Finally, we discuss some of the managerial concerns of wholesalers. These revolve mainly around asset management, because inventories and accounts receivable make up an enormous percentage of the total assets of any wholesaler's operation. We have devoted a whole chapter to wholesaling, because wholesalers, especially those involved with the distribution of industrial goods, play very important roles in many lines of trade.

Whether one is talking about retailing, wholesaling, or manufacturing, it is impossible to ignore the critical physical distribution functions involved with moving products from points of production to points of consumption. In fact, opportunities and problems associated with the management of physical distribution are, to some, what the marketing channel is all about. While there is no doubt that dealing effectively with issues surrounding the marketing flows of physical possession (storage and transportation) and ownership (inventory) is essential to the successful management of channels, it is probably better to think of marketing channels as encompassing *both* transaction and physical distribution channels. As Bowersox and his colleagues state:

> The *transaction channel* consists of specialized intermediaries such as manufacturing agents, sales personnel, jobbers, wholesalers, and retailers engaged in negotiation, contracting, and post-transaction administration of sales on a continuing basis. The *physical*

---

[1] See the excellent article "Sears Is So Big," *Chain Store Age*, General Merchandise Edition (January 1980), pp. 93–116.

distribution channel contains a network of intermediaries engaged in the functions of physical movement. Participants are physical distribution specialists concerned with solving problems involved in product transfer.[2]

Chapter 4 explores physical distribution management, in general, and provides a description of physical distribution specialists, in particular. The latter are concerned with meeting customer service objectives of availability, speed and consistency, and quality.

All told, the next three chapters provide the foundation for the construction of marketing channels. Any attempt to manage a channel would be futile without at least a rudimentary knowledge of their contents.

[2] Donald J. Bowersox, M. Bixby Cooper, Douglas M. Lambert, and Donald A. Taylor, *Management in Marketing Channels* (New York: McGraw-Hill Book Company, 1980), p. 199.

CHAPTER TWO

Retailing: Structure and Strategy

Modern retailing has emerged as a fiercely competitive and innovation-oriented industry populated by an ever-growing variety of institutions and constantly buffeted by a highly fluid environment. The purpose of this chapter is to describe the complex phenomena affecting the retail end of the marketing channel so that managers can more fully account for "bottom-up" pressures when forming distribution strategies and designing channel systems.

THE STRUCTURE OF RETAILING

Retailing consists of the activities involved in selling goods and services to ultimate consumers. Thus, a retail sale is one in which the buyer is an ultimate consumer, as opposed to a business or institutional purchaser. In contrast with purchases for resale or for business, industrial, or institutional use, the buying motive for a retail sale is always personal or family satisfaction stemming from the final consumption of the item being purchased.[1]

Retailing is one of the major industries in the United States. It consists of over 1½ million single-unit and over 340 thousand multiunit establishments and accounts for approximately 10 percent of total national income.[2] Transacted sales for store and nonstore retailing were $1297 billion in 1984.[3]

[1] William R. Davidson, Daniel J. Sweeney, and Ronald W. Stampfl, *Retailing Management*, 5th ed. (New York: John Wiley and Sons, 1984), p. 14.
[2] U.S. Bureau of the Census, *Statistical Abstract of the United States, 1986* (Washington, D.C.: U.S. Government Printing Office, 1985), pp. 772–75.
[3] *Ibid.*, p. 775.

While the commonly accepted conduits of retailing are stores, the mail, house-to-house sales agents, and vending machines, it is logical to include under the retailing rubric all "outlets" that seek to serve ultimate consumers. These would include service establishments such as motels and hotels, as shown in Table 2–1. Under this broadened concept of marketing, such "outlets" as hospitals, day-care centers, churches, and perhaps even public schools might also be

Table 2–1   Retail sales of store, nonstore, and service institutions, 1983

	Billions of Dollars	Percentage of:			
		Store Sales	Store and Nonstore Sales	Service Sales	Store, Nonstore, and Service Sales
Store, Nonstore, and Service Sales	$1254.9				100.0%
Store Retailing	1067.1	100.0%	97.8%		85.0
Food stores	259.4	24.3			
Automobile dealers	221.7	20.8			
General merchandise group stores[a]	143.0	13.4			
Eating and drinking places	115.7	10.8			
Gasoline service stations	103.1	9.7			
Apparel stores	54.0	5.1			
Lumber and building materials stores	59.9	5.6			
Drugstores	38.8	3.6			
Furniture and home furnishings stores	51.8	4.9			
Liquor stores	19.7	1.8			
Nonstore Retailing[b]	23.6.		2.2		1.9
Services	164.2			100.0%	13.1
Hotels, motels, tourist courts, camps	33.4			20.3	
Personal services (laundry, dry cleaning, beauty shops, barber shops, photography, shoe repair, funeral, alteration, etc.)	32.7			20.0	
Automobile repair and other auto services	39.1			23.8	
Miscellaneous repair services (electrical, watch, jewelry, furniture)	16.6			10.1	
Amusement, recreation, motion pictures	42.4			25.8	

[a] Includes department stores, discount department stores, miscellaneous general merchandise stores, variety stores, and jewelry stores.

[b] Includes sales by mail-order catalog desks in department stores of some mail-order firms, sales by vending machines, and sales by direct-selling establishments (house-to-house canvassing, party planning, telephone selling, etc.)

Sources: U.S. Bureau of the Census, *Statistical Abstract of the United States, 1985* (Washington, D.C.: U.S. Government Printing Office, 1984), pp. 782, 792; and authors' calculations.

included. These latter institutions, as well as banks and financial institutions (the "retailers" of money), have been omitted from Table 2–1 for a simple reason: it is difficult to quantify their output in terms of dollar sales.

Over the past 50 years, retail sales have grown approximately nine times as fast as population and at about the same rate as income. In contrast with this phenomenal growth, the total number of retail outlets has increased only marginally, from about 1½ million to 2 million, during this period, reflecting the increased importance of large-scale, high-volume operations in all fields of retailing and the significant application of managerial expertise that accompanied expansion.

Of the various categories of retailing institutions listed in Table 2–1, store retailing is by far the most significant, accounting for 85 percent of total retail sales. Within this category, food stores obtain the greatest share, accounting for 24 percent of total store retailing sales in 1983. If one adds receipts from eating and drinking places to food store sales, then food-oriented purchases consume over one-third of retail expenditures—an indication of the emphasis Americans place on eating and drinking. The automotive group (auto dealers, gas stations) transacted about 21 percent of store sales, while general merchandise stores accounted for approximately 13 percent.[4]

To a significant extent, however, statistics do not reveal the underlying dynamics of the exciting developments that have occurred over the past century. There has been a veritable revolution in retailing, even though small shopkeepers are still local landmarks in every community. Specific details of the revolution that highlight broad, secular trends can be found in the writings of Bucklin[5] and McNair and May.[6] Many of the strategic changes have been cataloged by McCammon and Bates.[7] In this chapter, attention is given to current trends. The focus is on the implications of recent environmental changes for strategic planning in retailing. Without such knowledge on the part of the individuals concerned with marketing consumer goods, channel management is destined to be shortsighted and ineffective.

[4] There are significant problems in using and analyzing the Census Bureau's Census of Business data to portray movements and shifts over time. As Dalrymple and Thompson point out, merchandise groupings are not necessarily descriptive of the type of merchandise sold, largely because of scrambled merchandising. Three religious goods stores studied by Dalrymple and Thompson reported sales of packaged alcoholic beverages, cigars, cigarettes, curtains, draperies, hardware, footwear, furniture, and major appliances. In addition, there are changes in Census classifications from one enumeration to another, as well as reclassifications of establishments to reflect changes in the character of their operations. Also, each merchandise group encompasses several components, and changes in one or several of these are masked by the aggregation process. Thus, the category *food stores* includes grocery stores, meat markets, fish markets, fruit and vegetable markets, and candy, nut, and confectionery stores. Within this category, only grocery stores have fared remarkably well over time. Finally, the Census defines a retail establishment as one that makes at least 51 percent of its sales to retail customers. Under such a system, up to 49 percent of a store's sales could be misclassified. Although such misclassification might not affect drugstore sales significantly, since most sales are made to the consumer in such outlets, they might have an important effect on sales by lumberyards. ᶜ ᵎ Douglas J. Dalrymple and Donald L. Thompson, *Retailing: An Economic View* (New York: Free Press, 1969), p. 17.

[5] See Louis P. Bucklin's careful study *Competition and Evolution in the Distributive Trades* (Englewood Cliffs, N.J.: Prentice-Hall, 1972).

[6] Malcolm P. McNair and Eleanor G. May, *The Evolution of Retail Institutions in the United States* (Cambridge, Mass.: Marketing Science Institute, 1976).

[7] Bert C. McCammon, Jr., and Albert D. Bates, "Reseller Strategies and the Financial Performance of the Firm," in Hans B. Thorelli (ed.), *Strategy +Structure = Performance* (Bloomington, Ind.: Indiana University Press, 1977), pp. 146–78.

Before examining the environment of retailing and its impact on strategy, we must first understand the operating dimensions common to all retailing institutions. It is these dimensions that management can manipulate in response to environmental change. From a strategic perspective, retail management can attempt to secure a competitive advantage by combining the dimensions in different ways. Therefore, we now turn to a discussion of these generic dimensions. Then we shall explore the strategic environment of retailing, carrying these dimensions along in our analytical kit.

THE OPERATIONAL DIMENSIONS
OF RETAIL INSTITUTIONS

The character of almost all retail institutions is determined by the choices management makes, in light of marketplace pressures, relative to margin and inventory goals, assortments of merchandise to be carried, location of outlets, and customer services to be offered.[8] Thus, the typical definitions of a number of highly familiar retail institutions shown in Exhibit 2–1 are generally couched in terms of these dimensions. The ultimate operating dimensions adopted by management are the result of two major forces: (1) consumer demand for service outputs[9] and (2) internal financial requirements. The latter directly affect the margin and turnover dimensions, and the former the assortment, location, and customer services dimensions. Each operating dimension is discussed briefly in the following pages.

Margin and Turnover

The fundamental point of departure between traditional and modern retailing systems might best be conceptualized by contrasting institutions characterized by high margin, low turnover, and numerous personal services with those characterized by low margin, high turnover, and minimum services. Both sets of institutions continue to exist, but in the twentieth century, the spotlight has focused on the revolutionary volume efficiencies flowing out of the latter style of operation. This has been especially true in grocery retailing, where such mass merchandising outlets as superstores, warehouse stores, and combination stores (see Exhibit 2–2) continue to evolve.

Essentially, the low-margin/high-turnover model is oriented towards generating maximal operational efficiency and passing on the savings generated to the customer. However, many of the savings "passed on to the customer" must be seen as involving a *transfer* of cost (opportunity cost as well as actual "effort" cost) rather than a clear elimination of it. Thus, reductions in service output levels, such as those associated with product selection opportunity, convenience of location, "atmosphere," personal services, financial and delivery accommodations, and the like, accompany the typical retail package offered by the low-

[8] Our discussion of major operational dimensions is based on Ronald R. Gist, *Retailing: Concepts and Decisions* (New York: John Wiley & Sons, 1968), pp. 37–79. It is possible to expand the list considerably by dividing the various concepts, thereby highlighting such variables as layout, atmospherics, and promotion.

[9] The concept of service outputs was introduced in Chapter 1.

EXHIBIT 2–1 Characteristics of selected major retailing institutions and forms of organization

Department Stores are retail organizations that (1) sell a wide variety of merchandise, including piece goods, home furnishings, and furniture; (2) are organized by departments; (3) have large sales; (4) sell mainly to women; (5) are located typically in downtown shopping districts or in suburban shopping centers; (6) frequently establish branch operations; and (7) usually offer a large amount of "free" service.

Specialty Stores retail a broad selection of a restricted class of goods. While there are departmentalized specialty stores of considerable size (e.g., Filene's and I. Magnin), the term *specialty store* is most commonly applied to small and medium-sized establishments or boutiques handling limited lines of soft (clothing, linens, etc.) or hard (kitchen utensils, appliances, etc.) goods.

Chain Store Systems are characterized by: (1) central ownership or control; (2) central management; (3) similarity of stores; and (4) two or more units. (Census classification has expanded the number of stores constituting a chain to 11 or more.) Buying power combined with managerial efficiencies characterize effective chain store system operations.

Supermarkets are generally low-margin, high-turnover retail organizations. In the food industry, a supermarket can be defined as a large, departmentalized retail establishment offering a relatively broad and complete stock of dry groceries, fresh meat, perishable produce, and dairy products, supplemented by a variety of convenience, nonfood merchandise and operated on a self-serve basis.

Planned Shopping Centers are integrated developments, under single ownership, with coordinated and complete shopping facilities and adequate parking space. The stores in the centers are leased to various retailers. Frequently, the stores in the centers engage in joint advertising, promotional, and public relations programs.

Discount Houses are retail establishments that generally feature: (1) a broad merchandise assortment, including both soft and hard goods; (2) price as the main sales appeal; (3) relatively low operating cost ratios; (4) relatively inexpensive buildings, equipment, and fixtures; (5) an emphasis on self-service operations; (6) limited customer services; (7) an emphasis on rapid turnover of merchandise; (8) large stores and parking areas; (9) carnival-like atmospheres; and (10) frequent use of leased departments.

Nonstore Retailers are typified by three general types of organizations:

1. *Automatic merchandisers* utilize vending machines. The assortment offered is limited to stable products of low unit value and certain other convenience goods. Costs of operations are usually high due to the expense of these machines, which require considerable stocking time and repair labor. Thus, both prices and margins are typically high.

2. *Mail-order houses* are establishments that receive their orders by mail and make their sales (deliveries) by mail, parcel post, express, truck, or freight. Retail mail-order houses are of three main types: the department store merchandise house (Sears, Roebuck and Spiegel); the smaller general merchandise firm that carries lines far less broad than would be found in a department store (L. L. Bean); and the specialty house (e.g., Franklin Mint Corporation). Generally, installment credit is used extensively. Other commonly offered services include telephone ordering, convenient pickup depots, catalog stores, strong guarantees, and liberal return policies. Prices are supposedly lower than at conventional retailers' outlets, although postal and delivery charges tend to bring them closer to those existing elsewhere.

3. *House-to-house selling* is typified by organizations, such as Avon and Tupperware, that engage in direct sales to ultimate consumers in the latter's homes. Demonstration and return after trial are among the various services offered by house-to-house sellers; cash, rather than credit, is the usual mode of transaction. In general, overhead costs are relatively low, the major expense being travel costs and salesperson turnover.

EXHIBIT 2–2   Grocery store formats

COMBINATION STORES

Concept: A substantially larger-than-average supermarket, offering an extensive selection of non-food items, including all categories typically found in a super drug store.

- Selling area of at least 30,000 sq. ft.
- Annual sales of at least $12,000,000
- Sells prescriptions through a full-line drug store within a store
- Handles more OTC drug and HBA items than other supermarket formats

Examples: Kroger-Sav-On; Jewel/Osco; Albertson-Southco; Skagg's/Alpha Beta; Pathmark
Size of Universe: Approximately 950 stores in 1984

SUPERSTORES

Concept: A larger-than-average supermarket handling an unusually wide range of grocery and non-food items, but without the emphasis on all drug store items seen in combination stores.

- Selling area of at least 20,000 sq. ft.
- Annual sales of at least $8,000,000
- More grocery SKU's than stores with any other format
- Handles more OTC drug items than the average supermarket
- May have a pharmacy—about 15% at present

Examples: Selected stores operated by Safeway; Kroger; Shop Rite; Publix; Jewel
Size of Universe: Approximately 4,600 in 1984

WAREHOUSE STORES

Concept: A supermarket characterized by offering lower prices attained by reduced services. A no-frills type of operation with lower SKU counts than found in comparably sized conventional stores—typically 1,500 to 7,500 items.
Examples: Grand Union's Basics; Migram's Save Mart; Tradewell's Prairie Markets; Roundy's Pick & Save; Supervalue's Cub Markets; Finast's Edwards; Purity Supreme's Heartland
Size of Universe: Approximately 3,250 in 1984

margin/high-turnover operation. In essence, then, this operational philosophy is founded on the costs (represented by marketing functions or flows) that certain segments of consumers are willing to absorb in certain classes of purchasing behavior.

What this means in terms of comparative, visible characteristics of the two polar prototypes is indicated in Exhibit 2–3. Exhibit 2–4 illustrates how specific stores may be positioned along these dimensions. Clearly, real-world retailing organizations may fall anywhere in the space described by the two axes. Sometimes, as Mason and Mayer point out, an outlet is forced by price competition to maintain low margins, but because of a poor location, incompetent management, or undercapitalization, it is unable to generate a sufficient volume of business.[10] Such an outlet might be described as operating in the low-margin/low-turnover quadrant. Obviously, this quadrant does not represent an institutional prototype in the sense of a class of organizations demonstrating a unique functional viability.

Of critical importance in determining which path to follow—low margin/high turnover or high margin/low turnover—are management's perceptions of the organization's financial requirements. The appropriate pathway can be highlighted by using the strategic profit model (SPM). The specifics of this model are spelled out in detail in Chapter 11. However, a brief description of the SPM is

[10] Joseph B. Mason and Morris L. Mayer, *Modern Retailing: Theory and Practice,* 3rd ed. (Dallas: Business Publications, 1984), p. 21.

EXHIBIT 2–3   Characteristics of low-margin/high-turnover
retailing strategies
vs. high-margin/low-turnover strategies

LOW MARGIN HIGH TURNOVER	HIGH MARGIN LOW TURNOVER
Merchandise presold or self-sold	Merchandise sold in store
Few services or "optional charge" services	Many services
Isolated locations	Cluster locations
Simple organizational characteristics	Complex organization
Variety large, assortments small	Variety smaller, assortments larger
Prices below the market	Prices above the market
Promotional emphasis on price	Promotion institutional and merchandise-oriented
	Located near other institutions

Source: Joseph B. Mason and Morris L. Mayer, *Modern Retailing: Theory and Practice,* 3rd ed. (Dallas: Business Publications, Inc., ©1984), p. 22.

---

introduced here so that the reader can gain some appreciation of its influence on the margin and turnover dimensions of retail strategy.

Basically, the SPM can be laid out as follows:

$$\frac{\dfrac{\text{Net profit}}{\text{Net sales}}}{\times} \times \dfrac{\text{Net sales}}{\text{Total assets}} = \dfrac{\text{Net profit}}{\text{Total assets}} \times \dfrac{\text{Total assets}}{\text{Net worth}} = \dfrac{\text{Net profit}}{\text{Net worth}}$$

EXHIBIT 2-4   The margin-turnover classification

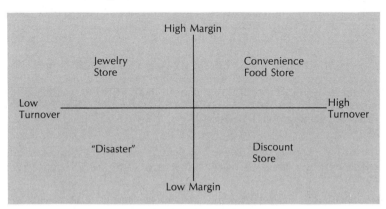

Source: Joseph B. Mason and Morris L. Mayer, *Modern Retailing: Theory and Practice,* 3rd ed. (Dallas: Business Publications, Inc., ©1984), p. 22.

Management can pursue margin management (net profit/net sales), asset turnover (net sales/total assets), *and/or* financial management via financial leverage (total assets/net worth) in order to secure a target return on net worth. If there is tremendous downward pressure on margins, because of competitive forces and economic conditions generally, then a likely path for management to pursue is asset turnover. These sets of conditions have led management to emphasize such criteria as sales per square foot (which reflects space and location productivity), sales per employee (which reflects labor productivity), and sales per transaction (which reflects merchandising program productivity).

Increasingly, retailers have turned to an evaluation of the gross margin return on inventory (GMROI) in line with their desire to improve asset turnover, specifically, and overall profitability, generally.[11] The components of GMROI are as follows:

$$\frac{\text{Gross margin}}{\text{Net sales}} \times \frac{\text{Net sales}}{\text{Average inventory}} = \frac{\text{Gross margin}}{\text{Average inventory}}$$
$$\text{(at cost)} \qquad \text{(at cost)}$$

GMROI allows the retailer to evaluate inventory on the return on investment it produces and not just on the gross margin percentage. As Bates observes, this means that GMROI often considers items with widely varying gross margin percentages as equally profitable, as in the following example:[12]

Item	Gross margin	× Sales to inventory	= GMROI
A	50%	3	150%
B	30%	5	150%
C	25%	6	150%

According to Bates:

> By using GMROI approaches the firm expands its alternatives in exploring methods for improving inventory results. There are many product categories where price competition prevents raising the gross margin. In this instance, improved inventory performance can be used to raise GMROI. If the firm were just using gross margin percentage, this flexibility would not be so obvious.
>
> GMROI also allows the firm to consciously consider the tradeoff between gross margin and inventory utilization. There might be instances in which the firm would knowingly lower its gross margin in an effort to produce a higher sales to inventory ratio and a higher GMROI. Only a concept such as GMROI can provide a basis for making such a decision.[13]

Another major criterion used by retailers, especially supermarkets, to select items that enhance asset turnover while providing an adequate return is gross

---

[11] See Daniel J. Sweeney, "Improving the Profitability of Retail Merchandising Decisions," *Journal of Marketing*, Vol. 37 (January 1973), pp. 60–68.

[12] Albert D. Bates, *Retailing and Its Environment* (New York: D. Van Nostrand Company, 1979), p. 155.

[13] *Ibid.*, pp. 155–56.

margin dollars generated per linear or cubic foot of shelf space assigned to the item, as calculated by the following formula:

$$\frac{\text{Gross margin per unit (\$)} \times \text{Number of units sold}}{\text{Linear (cubic) feet of shelf space assigned to the unit}}$$

Such a measure permits assessment of performance and serves as a guide for determining which merchandise items to add or delete. Retailers' use of measures such as this one, GMROI, and direct product profit (discussed in Chapter 11) places pressures on suppliers. Not only do the gross margins offered by suppliers have to be adequate, but the suppliers are often forced to engage in extensive promotion of the items in order to generate the sales volume (in units) required by the retailers. In addition, suppliers are forced to give more attention to the amount of shelf or floor space consumed by their items. Furthermore, any systems designed by suppliers to speed up the replenishment of inventory on the shelf can be helpful in generating the numbers for adequate performance. Faster replenishment rates mean less need for shelf space and less inventory investment, and therefore a reduction in the denominator in the formulas.

In order to secure consistent approaches in the margin and turnover dimensions and thus achieve targeted rates of return, some retailers, such as Radio Shack, Petrie Stores, and Target Stores, are adopting totally rationalized programs. These involve a high degree of centralized management control combined with rigorous operating procedures for each phase of the retail operation.[14] In this way, every aspect of the company's operation is performed in an identical manner in every store. The implications for suppliers to such retailers are, again, profound:

> For manufacturers, rationalized retailing could lead to more formalized relationships with retail accounts as retailers develop sophisticated supplier evaluation programs, make greater use of buying committees and other centralized management techniques, and purchase a greater share of their requirements on a contractual, programmed basis.[15]

Assortment

The three terms *general, variety,* and *specialty* are commonly used to describe retail stores based on the *extent* of product lines carried, i.e., the extent of consumer selection offered. However, while the specialty store has demonstrated a remarkable upswing in recent history, the concepts of general and variety stores have been so drastically overhauled that they have little defining power in the modern world of U.S. retailing. With the bankruptcy of W. T. Grant in 1975, Woolworth is the last *national* variety store chain. The strategic problem for variety chains is that supermarkets and drugstore chains are selling more and more variety-store-type merchandise. Traditional trade distinctions are rapidly evaporating in a very fluid market.

Therefore, rather than cling to old-hat definitions, it is better to use the term *variety* to describe generically different classes of goods making up the product offer, i.e., the *breadth* of product lines. The term *assortment,* on the other

[14] Albert D. Bates, "The Troubled Future of Retailing," *Business Horizons* (August 1976), p. 27.
[15] *Ibid.,* p. 28.

hand, refers to the *depth* of product brands or models offered within each generic product category. Typically, a discount department store like K-Mart has a limited assortment of fast-moving, low-priced items across a wide variety of household goods, ready-to-wear, cosmetics, sporting goods, electric appliances, auto accessories, and the like. In contrast, a specialty store dealing only, or primarily, in home audio-visual electronic goods, such as Radio Shack or Team Electronics, would have a very large and complete line of radios, tape recorders, and high-fidelity equipment, offering the deepest selection of models, styles, sizes, prices, etc.

With many modern retail operations diversifying their traditional lines of generically "related" products into unrelated lines and with traditional concepts of what constitutes a retail line of trade being freely trampled upon, it may be more appropriate to focus here on the practice of general merchandising and to discuss the principles that underlie *generalization* as a strategy. For example, from a strategic perspective, there is a major tradeoff between providing one-stop shopping convenience and offering locational convenience. The size of operations required to carry a wide variety of products that permit one-stop shopping militates against locational convenience. On the other hand, there is also a direct, and equally vital, tradeoff between selection convenience and delivered price. Carrying slower-moving models to complete the product assortment militates against price discounting. Consumer markets comprise numerous segments with differing sets of shopping needs. Normatively speaking, retailing institutions design and evolve their product-mix strategies to suit changing shopping patterns.

At the macro level, generalization takes the form of substantial integration of whole lines of trade. The strategic opportunity here lies in enhancing one-stop shopping convenience and, as a spillover, increasing exposure of the store's entire offer to impulse purchasing. Taken to its extreme, generalization can result in institutional diversification. All of these strategies are highly visible in today's fluid retail markets.

Across-the-board diversification by many leading retail chains has led to the emergence of what some authors describe as the *conglomerchant*,[16] and the trade literature continuously reports takeover bids, acquisitions, and mergers. For example, in 1984 (prior to spinning off its specialty stores), Carter Hawley Hale Stores, Inc., owned and operated The Broadway (50 stores in Southern California and the Southwest), Emporium Capwell (22 stores), Thalhimers (25 stores), John Wanamaker (16 stores), Weinstock's (12 stores), Bergdorf Goodman (1 store), Contempo Casuals (105 stores), Holt Renfrew (16 stores), and Neiman-Marcus (21 stores). Melville Corporation owns and operates Meldisco (in K-Mart stores), Thom McAn, Marshall's, CVS, Foxmoor, Chess King, Open Country, and Kay-Bee Toy and Hobby Shops. Dayton Hudson owns and operates Target, Mervyn's, Hudson's, Dayton's, and Lechmere. And, before it was acquired in 1986, Allied Stores Corporation owned and operated Jordan Marsh, Stern's, Maas Brothers, Miller Rhoads, Joske's, The Bon, Brooks Brothers, Bonwit Teller, Garfinkel's, and Ann Taylor, among others.

Two tactical concepts related to variety and assortment strategies are creaming and scrambling. The *creaming* approach incorporates largely presold,

---

[16] See, for example, Rollie Tillman, "Rise of the Conglomerchant," *Harvard Business Review*, Vol. 49 (November–December 1971), pp. 44–51. Also see Richard Miller, "Strategic Pathways to Growth in Retailing," *Journal of Business Strategy*, Vol. 1 (Winter 1981), pp. 16–29.

fast-moving items picked from some other line of retailing. For example, a specialty store adding some lines of impulse goods, such as candy bars, would typically offer only a small number of the fastest-selling brands among the scores of brands available for display. Creaming is a low-risk ("small but sure") profits tactic, because brands with strong consumer preferences typically allow only small retail margins.[17] Generalization strategies of supermarkets and drug chains have the appearance of creaming when compared with the more systematic departmentalization of discounter product mixes. Drugstores carry *selected* cameras, auto accessories, and even camping equipment and lawn furniture, but they certainly do not set up whole departments in these lines.

Retailers generalizing with an eye to larger profit contributions tend to turn to *scrambling*. Scrambling typically carries the retailer into a much more diverse and unrelated mix of product lines. The brands involved offer higher margins, are slower moving, and do not have as strong consumer preferences. Scrambling is a "large but unsure" profit tactic with a greater measure of risk. It will likely involve the retailer in promotional activity to support the line. Scrambling is a widely practiced growth and profit strategy of mass retailers, and its impact on the structure of retailing has been far-reaching. As Gist observes, "the logic of 'scrambling' is such that we might expect the types of institutions that operate [exclusively] on a high-margin, low-stock-turnover philosophy to fall prey through 'scrambling' to the institutions that feature the low-margin, high-stock-turnover philosophy."[18] Nonprescription drugs and watches were among the first products to fall prey to scrambling by the new high-volume retailers.

The assortment dimension of retailing operations is clearly a matter that demands the attention of top management, for decisions in this area will color the entire character of the enterprise. However, once the general strategy is established for the organization, the tactical task of choosing specific products or brands usually falls to functionaries called *buyers*. Buyers play a central role in retailing; unlike their counterparts in manufacturing concerns, their status within their home organizations is very high. Because buying is such a critical aspect of retailing, it is important to understand the evaluative processes and procedures that take place in vendor selection. The appendixes to this chapter are geared to that end. Appendix 2A discusses the choice strategies employed by retail buyers; Appendix 2B is a glossary of pricing and buying terms commonly used by retailers; and Appendix 2C briefly describes some of their merchandise planning and control procedures.

Location

In a general sense, products are classified on the basis of consumer purchasing patterns. That is, they are thought of as being convenience, shopping, or specialty goods. Implicit in this conceptualization is the extent of *search-shopping* activity the consumer is willing to undertake. Consequently, there are strategic location implications in the product line variety and assortment strategies the retailer pursues. In addition, there are extremely critical environmental impacts deriving from shifts and trends in intracity and interregional residence patterns.

As discussed in Chapter 5, which deals with marketing channel strategy

[17] Gist, *op. cit.*, p. 102.
[18] *Ibid.*, p. 103. For an analysis of these and related issues, see Edgar A. Pessemier, *Retail Assortments*, Marketing Science Institute Report No. 80-111 (Cambridge, Mass., 1980).

and design, Bucklin has suggested a matrix classification of convenience, shopping, and specialty *stores* against convenience, shopping, and specialty *goods*.[19] With such a cross-classification as a guide, retailers can first select their target markets and then develop appropriate strategies to reach them. For example, to appeal to the convenience store–specialty good segment, retailers would include two important elements in their marketing mix: (1) a highly accessible location and (2) a good selection of widely accepted brands. Depth of assortment, price, store promotion, facilities, and personal selling are less important when specialty goods are sold through convenience stores.

Consumer search-shopping behavior varies between consumer segments as well as between product categories. It also varies over time as demographic and life-style changes occur across market segments. For example, the tendency in recent times has been toward a pattern of decreased search-shopping activity. The typical consumer visits only one store and rarely more than two. Significantly, such patterns seem to be true even for a variety of *shopping* goods.[20] As the section of this chapter on the retailing environment will develop more fully, time saved is becoming as important as money saved. This factor, along with widespread access and exposure to mass media, is reducing both shopping frequency as well as the necessity of information search.

The implications of these observations are profound, because they mean that location decisions are becoming even more critical to retailer viability. Once a retailer has selected a specific region of the country that he wishes to enter (e.g., the Southwest) and a specific metropolitan or rural market within that region that he wishes to serve (e.g., Austin), he must delineate the relevant trading area for the type of retailing establishment he wishes to erect and then pick a specific location within the trading area as a store site. Because these decisions are so crucial, we now turn to a brief discussion of the major factors involved in each.

Trading Area Measurement and Evaluation. A trading area is the area from which a retailer draws or expects to draw the vast majority of his customers. Retailing is a localized activity, and the bulk of any establishment's sales may be traced to persons within the immediate area. Basically, the extent of a trading area is determined by (1) the nature of the product(s) or service(s) offered, including price, availability from other sources, and extent to which the merchandise or service reflects the user's taste; and (2) the consumer's perception of the shopping task or attitude toward the buying process. (Some consumers consider shopping a pleasure, while others see it as a chore. Obviously, the greater the number in the former category, the larger the trading area is likely to be.)

In operational terms, a *trading area* can be defined from a buyer's, seller's, and/or sales volume standpoint.

- From a *buyer's standpoint,* a trading area is the region inside which the buyer may reasonably expect to find goods and services at competitive and prevailing prices.

[19] Louis P. Bucklin, "Retail Strategy and the Classification of Consumer Goods," *Journal of Marketing,* Vol. 27 (January 1963), pp. 50–55. For an extension of Bucklin's scheme, see Morris L. Mayer, J. Barry Mason, and Morris Gee, "A Reconceptualization of Store Classification as Related to Retail Strategy Formulation," *Journal of Retailing,* Vol. 47 (Fall 1971), p. 35.

[20] Joseph B. Mason and Morris L. Mayer, "Empirical Observations of Consumer Behavior in the Marketplace: Implications for a Classification of Goods System and Retail Strategy Formulation," *Journal of Retailing,* Vol. 48 (Fall 1972), pp. 22–23.

- From a *seller's standpoint*, a trading area is a district whose size is usually determined by boundaries within which it is economical in terms of volume and cost for a marketing unit or group to sell and/or deliver a good or service.
- From a *sales volume standpoint*, a trading area is the area surrounding the community from which a retailer secures approximately 90 percent of his sales of a representative group of commodities. Sometimes the trading area is classified in terms of primary and secondary areas. The primary area includes 75 percent of the customers, the secondary area 15 percent. The remaining 10 percent represents the fringe or tertiary trading area.

Trading area determination is a complex process, since an area's size is a function of an individual store's character and mode of operation as well as the cluster of stores surrounding that store. For example, if the store sells unique and exclusive merchandise, its trading area definitely becomes larger. The increased popularity of mail-order selling, telemarketing, and, concomitantly, in-home purchasing has also served to expand trading areas for a wide variety of organizations.

Dalyrmple and Thompson have observed that trading areas result from the collective responses people make in balancing the attractiveness of near and distant retail outlets against the cost, time, and energy that must be spent in overcoming distance.[21] Studies have shown that style and fashion goods produce significantly greater consumer travel and search activity than do low-value, bulky items such as lumber, or convenience items such as food.[22] For existing stores and shopping centers, the geographic extent of trading areas can be established through the use of automobile license checks, charge account records, mail-order lists, check clearings, automobile traffic flow, and newspaper circulation. For example, Sears uses an optical scanner to read customer addresses off credit records; the addresses are then plotted by computer on maps.[23] An analysis of customer demographic characteristics can be obtained from these same records in order to develop a profile of each store's trading area within the Sears organization.

Selecting a Specific Site.   Once potential trading areas are defined, a description of several specifically proposed sites within each is developed with respect to such factors as accessibility and traffic flow, extent of trading area, population and its distribution, income, economic stability, and competition.[24] Evidence that can be used as a first approximation of the value of a site includes (1) consumer preference for an existing store or cluster of stores, and (2) natural or artificial barriers to the free movement of customers in the direction of the proposed site. Even though retail location analysis is characterized by its experts as an art rather than a science,[25] it is possible to go well beyond this first approximation in assessing a potential site. For example, Victory Markets, a chain of over 90 supermarkets operating out of Norwich, N.Y., uses a computer-

[21] Dalrymple and Thompson, *op. cit.,* p. 98.
[22] *Ibid.*
[23] Computer graphics are becoming extremely useful in trading area and site location analysis. See "The Spurt in Computer Graphics," *Business Week* (June 16, 1980), pp. 104–6.
[24] See Saul B. Cohen and William Applebaum, "Evaluating Store Sites and Determining Store Rents," *Economic Geography,* Vol. 36 (January 1960), pp. 1–35.
[25] See William Applebaum, "Methods for Determining Store Trade Areas, Market Penetration and Potential Sales," *Journal of Marketing Research,* Vol. 3 (May 1966), pp. 127–41.

ized evaluation model to predict the weekly retail sales of a potential site. The predictions generated by Victory have been within 2 percent of actual sales.[26]

Over the years, a number of attempts have been made to bring more rigorous approaches to retail site selection problem solving, including the development of checklist methods, analog methods,[27] gravity models,[28] environmental models,[29] regression analysis,[30] sectogram techniques,[31] and microanalytic modeling, such as the multiplicative competitive interactive choice model.[32] A brief summary of each of these methods is provided in Exhibit 2–5. Most of these methods are, however, plagued with theoretical, operational, or practical difficulties such that, irrespective of the approach taken in the store location decision process, the retailer's judgment must enter into the final analysis.[33] This is so because of the great many variables affecting the utility of a location beyond those employed in the various models or techniques, as specified in Exhibit 2–5. It is essential to evaluate factors related to the nature and strength of competition, the socioeconomic pattern of the area, trading area growth potential, the availability of the site, and the existence of facilitating agencies (e.g., mass transit) before a decision is made.[34] For example, in many cases, retailers evaluate cur-

[26] "Site Selection by Computer Model," *Chain Store Age—Executive Edition* (September 1971), p. E77. For another example of computerized site selection, see the approach that the Rayco Company has employed with considerable success, in "Can a Computer Tell You Where to Locate Stores?" *Chain Store Age—Executive Edition* (December 1964), p. E28.

[27] See William Applebaum, "The Analog Method for Estimating Potential Store Sales," in Curt Kornblau (ed.), *Guide to Store Location Research with Emphasis on Supermarkets* (Reading, Mass.: Addison-Wesley, 1968), pp. 232–43.

[28] See, for example, David L. Huff, "Ecological Characteristics of Consumer Behavior," *Papers and Proceedings of the Regional Science Association,* Vol. 7 (1961), pp. 19–21; David L. Huff, "Defining and Estimating a Trading Area," *Journal of Marketing,* Vol. 28 (July 1964), pp. 34–38; and David L. Huff, "A Probabilistic Analysis of Consumer Spatial Behavior," in William S. Decker (ed.), *Emerging Concepts in Marketing* (Chicago: American Marketing Association, 1963), pp. 443–61. Huff's gravitation model appears to be the most widely quoted site selection approach in marketing textbooks. Unfortunately, it suffers from severe operational and practical difficulties. For a discussion of these difficulties, see David B. MacKay, "Consumer Movement and Store Location Analysis," unpublished Ph.D. dissertation, Northwestern University, 1971, pp. 40–43.

[29] See William R. Kinney, Jr., "Separating Environmental Factor Effects for Location and Facility Decisions," *Journal of Retailing,* Vol. 48 (Spring 1972), pp. 67–75.

[30] See, for example, G. I. Heald, "Application of the Automatic Interaction Detector (AID) Programme and Multiple Regression Technique to the Assessment of Store Performance and Site Selection," *Operations Research Quarterly,* Vol. 23 (December 1972), pp. 445–57.

[31] See J. B. Schneider, "Retail Competition Patterns in a Metropolitan Area," *Journal of Retailing,* Vol. 45 (Winter 1969–70), pp. 67–74.

[32] See David B. MacKay, "A Microanalytic Approach to Store Location Analysis," *Journal of Marketing Research,* Vol. 9 (May 1972), pp. 134–40; Vijay Mahajan, Arun Jain, and Brian T. Ratchford, "Use of Binary Attributes in the Multiplicative Competitive Interactive Choice Model," *Journal of Consumer Research,* Vol. 5 (December 1978), pp. 210–15. A useful extension of the gravitational model suggested by Huff, op. cit., is the multiplicative competitive interactive (MCI) model. The MCI model explicitly incorporates the competitive environment in the evaluation of store sites. Furthermore, it has been demonstrated that the MCI model can be calibrated using least squares and simulation procedures. See Arun K. Jain and Vijay Mahajan, "Evaluating the Competitive Environment in Retailing Using Multiplicative Competitive Interactive Models," in Jagdish N. Sheth (ed.), *Research in Marketing,* Vol. 2 (Greenwich, Conn.: Jai Press, 1979), pp. 217–35.

[33] For a summary of the difficulties associated with many of these methods and models, see MacKay, *Consumer Movement,* pp. 29–67. Also see Willard R. Bishop, Jr., "An Application of the Intra-Urban Gravity Model to Store Location Research," unpublished Ph.D. dissertation, Cornell University, 1969.

[34] Robert F. Zaloudek, "Practical Location Analysis in New Market Areas," *Stores,* Vol. 53 (November 1971), pp. 15, 40–41.

EXHIBIT 2–5 Several quantitative approaches to retail store location analysis

TYPE	DESCRIPTION
Checklist methods	These methods list all factors that must be considered in site selection. Factors are given subjective weights by the retailer, and each potential site is rated on each factor. Numerical ratings for each site on each factor and factor rankings for each site are then combined to yield an overall evaluation for each location.
Analog models	Sales or volume projections of new stores are based directly on the sales or volume estimates of existing stores.
Gravity models	Sales at a potential site are estimated on the basis of the site's size and its spatial relationship to the market it serves.
Environmental models	The performance of a retail outlet is described as the sum of the effects of various quantifiable location and facility factors (such as local population characteristics—income, ages, occupational class—competition, and nature and condition of outlet facilities) and the effect of managerial actions. A linear statistical model scans the proposed locations and computes the expected contributions of all location and facility factor combinations.
Regression analysis	Annual store sales are predicted on the basis of a set of independent variables that record the demographic and physical characteristics of stores and their neighborhoods.
Sectogram techniques	The spatial relationship between a set of retail facilities and the consumers who utilize them is analyzed on a metropolis-wide basis. These techniques determine how well the spatial pattern of retail outlets and population are matched, identifying underserved areas as high-potential locations.
Microanalytic modeling	Recognizes the multistop facet of shopping behavior. Evaluates potential retail locations using a spatial model defined by discriminant analysis, Monte Carlo simulation, multidimensional scaling, and other statistical techniques.

---

rent demand and ignore future demand, even though the economic growth potential of an area is critical. In fact, the location decision is a dynamic one because of shifts in population concentration and the continuous development of the structure of retailing.

Customer Service

Virtually all major retail innovations of the twentieth century have relied to greater or lesser degrees on manipulating the services variable to contribute to their strategic operational offer. The principle is easy to appreciate when we consider such services as in-store sales help. When retailers drop the "friendly" behind-the-counter sales assistant who helps customers locate and compare merchandise and is available for "expert" advice, the whole locate-compare-select process is being shifted to the consumer.

Retailing is one of the few remaining industries that is highly labor-intensive. Labor costs are estimated to exceed 50 to 60 percent of a store's total expenses and are even higher than this for a "full-service" organization.[35] Hence, the economies that can be passed on to the consumer by eliminating certain kinds of in-store assistance are usually substantial. The same is true for delivery functions, but the principle is not immediately apparent for services like customer credit. The fact is that, besides the cost of risk and the cost of administering credit plans, the retailer also incurs the cost of holding (in a financial sense) the consumer's purchases for the duration of the credit period. It takes little imagination to visualize the considerable savings it would mean for operations like Sears to be able to reduce the period for which credit is allowed without charge. However, successful operations are built not on transferring "savings" for the sake of savings, but on being able to identify the functions that customers are willing to assume and the cost in time, money, effort, and convenience at which the assumption becomes attractive to them.

Because customers and products differ in their service requirements, successful retail operations can be designed around different levels of service offers. Thus, self-service outlets, such as warehouse retailers, supermarkets, and discount stores, provide very few services, emphasize price appeals, and generally focus on staple goods. Full-service outlets, such as specialty stores and department stores, provide a wide variety of services and tend to be oriented towards fashion or specialty merchandise. (Nordstrom on the West Coast is an excellent example.) The most dramatic innovations in retailing over the past 40 years have hinged primarily on reducing customer services, though for certain services, like credit cards, competitive pressures have often made the innovators backtrack a little. Discount houses, warehouse retailers, and catalog showrooms belong to this group. On the other hand, mail-order selling, numerous specialty stores (e.g., The Limited, The Gap, Crate & Barrel), and retailing through vending machines have also demonstrated robust growth. These latter institutions represent situations where services have been maintained or increased.[36] Overall, the range of choice available to consumers, especially in general merchandising (see Exhibit 2–6), is incredibly wide.

Although the four operational dimensions just discussed are critical to an understanding of why retailing institutions run the gamut from small "mom and pop" stores to enormous hypermarkets, many others play an important role in determining the character of retailing enterprises. The totality of retailing variables is portrayed in Exhibit 2–7. These variables permit retailers to map effective strategies for meeting consumer expectations.

THE STRATEGIC ENVIRONMENT OF RETAILING

Retailers are the only channel members who come face-to-face *on a regular basis* with the most important elements of a commercial channel's environment—consumers. Due to their strategic position, it is not surprising that retailers are

---

[35] Larry D. Redinbaugh, *Retailing Management: A Planning Approach* (New York: McGraw-Hill Book Co., 1976), pp. 12 and 14.

[36] Even though vending machines rely on self-service, such operations are not low in service. Except for in-home shopping, "automatic" retailers offer the highest delivery and convenience service of all institutions.

EXHIBIT 2–6 Components of general merchandise retailing

STORE TYPE	EXAMPLES
Quality Specialty Stores	Saks Fifth Avenue, I. Magnin
Targeted Specialty Stores	The Limited, County Seat
Traditional Department Stores	
Upper Moderate	Bloomingdale's, Macy's
Moderate	Foley's, Jordan Marsh
Lower Moderate	Alexander's, The Boston Store,
Value-oriented Specialty Stores	Mervyn's, Main Street
National Brands for Less (off-price)	Loehmann's, Marshall's
Traditional Department Stores	
Upscale	Target, Caldor
Downscale	K-Mart, Zayre
Very Downscale	Dollar General, Family Dollar
Mass Merchandisers	Sears, Ward's
Catalog Showrooms	Service Merchandise, McDade's
Warehouse Stores	The Price Club, Pick'N'Save
Hypermarkets*	Bigg's, Meier's
Variety Stores	Woolworth, Ben Franklin
Drugstores	Long's, Walgreen
Mail-Order	L.L. Bean, Spiegel

* Hypermarkets are enormous stores (over 150,000 square feet with in excess of 60 checkout lanes) which sell food and nonfood items on a self-service, discount basis. The store type originated in Europe. France has over 550 hypermarkets, accounting for nearly 12 percent of the country's retail trade. See Roger Ricklefs, "French Hypermarkets Check Out the U.S.," *Wall Street Journal*, May 20, 1986, p. 34.

immediately and acutely affected by changes and shifts in the interface between the commercial channel and the marketplace.[37] The forces impinging on retailers will directly and significantly affect the performance of the entire channel system. Therefore, it is imperative to examine in some detail the various components of the retailing environment.[38]

The Consumer Environment

Population Shifts.   Among the most widely documented impacts on the structure of retailing has been the so-called flight to the suburbs, which was made possible by the growth of automobile usage, road-building programs, and the deterioration of public transportation services to downtown business districts.[39] The suburban flight initially dealt a severe blow to downtown retailing centers in general and department stores in particular. On the other hand, the emergence and increasing viability of planned regional shopping centers and malls were prime factors in the recovery of department stores. In 1954, depart-

[37] The conceptualization of the retailing environment used here follows the excellent discussion found in Bates, *Retailing and Its Environment.*

[38] If uncertainty in the retailing environment is very high, there are likely to be strains toward vertical integration in the channel (see Chapters 5 and 7).

[39] Sears was among the first to take advantage of these shifts. Montgomery Ward was extremely slow. This in part accounts for the difference in their performances since World War II.

EXHIBIT 2–7   Building a retail marketing strategy

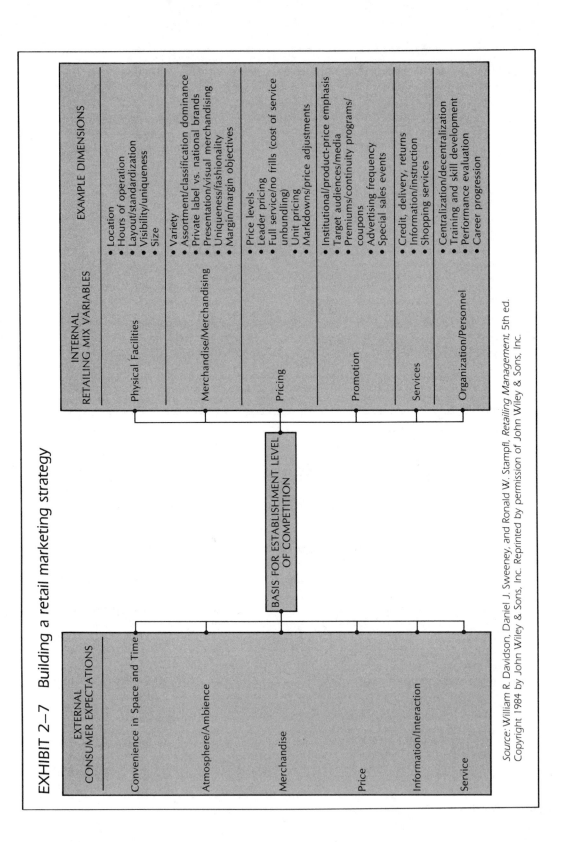

Source: William R. Davidson, Daniel J. Sweeney, and Ronald W. Stampfl. *Retailing Management*, 5th ed. Copyright 1984 by John Wiley & Sons, Inc. Reprinted by permission of John Wiley & Sons, Inc.

ment store sales as a percentage of retail sales dipped to 6.2, down from 8.9 percent in 1929. However, by 1983 the department stores' share had risen to 10 percent.[40]

The same forces that crippled the downtown central business districts—suburbanization and traffic congestion, parking headaches, and increasing crime in downtown areas—were responsible for nurturing the shopping centers. In addition, the shopping center provided more convenient and longer shopping hours and highly integrated one-stop shopping. Nevertheless, after years of unprecedented growth, the shopping center industry has been slowing down, with little hope of enjoying a quick recovery.[41] Stricter zoning laws, Environmental Protection Agency (EPA) regulations, escalating land value, capital and construction costs, overstored markets, slower population growth, and more expensive energy sources are among the factors contributing to the industry's problems. There is simply no longer any major incentive to continue to build large shopping centers, especially of the superregional mall variety. The oversaturation of markets is reflected in the fact that in 1982, shopping center space per capita was 13.9 square feet compared with 5.3 in 1964.[42] Nevertheless, the nation's approximately 25,000 shopping centers account for over 60 percent of retail sales.

In contrast with suburban malls, there has been increased shopping center construction in downtown areas as part of revitalization programs. The Rouse Co. has been instrumental in this development. Some of its more notable successes have been Baltimore's Harborplace, Boston's Faneuil Hall Marketplace, Milwaukee's Grand Avenue, New York's South Street Seaport, Toledo's Portside, Norfolk's Waterside, and Philadelphia's Gallery at Market Street East.

The slowdown in construction of large regional shopping malls has also renewed investors' and builders' interest in small community shopping centers—the so-called strip centers anchored by a supermarket or a discount retailer. Rents are lower than at malls ($4 to $15 per square foot for strips, $14 to $35 per square foot for malls), as are operating costs and purchase prices.[43]

Another major population trend has been the pronounced migration to sunbelt states such as Florida, Texas, California, and Arizona. Among national retail chains, a very large portion of new construction money is being funneled in this direction. However, population density is very important to retailers, and the 10 most densely populated states are in the Northeast. These states produce a higher dollar volume of retail sales per square mile than any of the other 40 states.[44]

Positioning stores in smaller towns and in exurbia (metropolitan fringe communities) reflects another important demographic development. It appears that such small towns, usually not more than four hours away from major cities,

[40] U.S. Bureau of the Census, *op. cit.*, p. 784.

[41] See, for example, "Shopping Centers: What's Ahead?" *Chain Store Age—Executive Edition* (May 1975), p. 23; and Donald M. Schwartz, "End of Era? Shopping Centers," *Chicago Sun-Times*, September 14, 1975, Real Estate Section, p. 15.

[42] Davidson, Sweeney, and Stampfl, *op. cit.*, p. 49.

[43] Robert Guenther, "Now That Nation is 'Malled,' Can 'Stripping' Be Far Off?" *Wall Street Journal*, July 31, 1985, p. 19. Rents at Trump Tower on New York's Fifth Avenue run as high as $400 per square foot. See Robert Guenther, "Some Doubt Stores Will Find Rents at Trump Worthwhile," *Wall Street Journal*, May 25, 1983, p. 25.

[44] Eugene Carlson, "Population Density Remains Primary Factor for Retailers," *Wall Street Journal*, November 6, 1984, p. 31.

are enjoying explosive growth because of changes in life styles and values, especially the search for simplicity, lower crime rates, cleaner environments, less congestion, and lower costs of living.[45] A discounter that has become very successful by positioning itself in smaller communities is Wal-Mart. Conventional retail yardsticks have generally based the minimum population for sustaining a full-line discount store at 100,000. Wal-Mart, with more than 80 percent of its units in towns of fewer than 15,000 residents, has exploded this myth. Founded in 1962, the chain consisted of 817 stores achieving $6.4 billion in sales in 1985.[46] In addition to Wal-Mart, chains such as Bi-Lo (discount supermarkets), Ames, Duckwall-Alco, and Family Dollar have been able to achieve positions of competitive dominance at a relatively low cost by focusing on secondary markets.[47]

Mobility is another important population variable. About 20 percent of the population moves every year, although two-thirds of these moves are within the same county. The high mobility rate means that most retail outlets turn over their customer base and must constantly attract new customers. It also means that multiple-outlet firms have a decided advantage in the marketplace.

The New American Family.   The American household is undergoing a major transformation. Less marriage, later marriage, fewer children, more divorce, one-parent families, and a dramatic increase in working-wife households are the new social realities. The average American home was 2.7 persons in 1985, down from 3.3 in 1960, and is expected to be 2.4 by 1990.[48] These divorce and marriage trends, coupled with a significant gap in life expectancy between men and women, are the principal factors behind the increase in single-person households, which accounted for 25 percent of all households in 1985, compared with 17 percent in 1960.[49]

The most widely discussed phenomenon affecting the American family and its life style is the working wife. Women's participation in the labor force rose from 25 percent to 53 percent from the early 1950s to the mid 1980s.[50] It is projected to reach 60 percent by 1995. The total implications of the working wife are yet to be experienced, because, so far, much of female employment has been in traditionally low-pay jobs. But barriers are crumbling, and less sex discrimination, combined with more education and professionalism, are increasingly changing the nature of the jobs women are receiving. In general, the working-wife phenomenon has been largely responsible for what has been termed a growing "poverty of time."[51] Together with other changes in cultural values, notably a remarkable increase in leisure pursuits and physical fitness activities, it has radically reduced the amount of time households are willing to devote to "running the home" or shopping.

[45] Leonard L. Berry, "The New Consumer," in Ronald W. Stampfl and Elizabeth C. Hirschman (eds.), *Competitive Structure in Retail Markets: The Department Store Perspective* (Chicago: The American Marketing Association, 1980), p. 1. See also Steve Weiner, "With Many Cities Full of Stores, Chains Open Outlets in Small Towns," *Wall Street Journal,* May 28, 1981, p. 1.

[46] "Sam Walton of Wal-Mart: Just Your Basic Homespun Billionaire," *Business Week* (October 14, 1985), p. 142.

[47] Hank Gilman, "Rural Retailing Chains Prosper by Combining Service, Sophistication," *Wall Street Journal,* July 2, 1984, p. 1.

[48] U.S. Bureau of the Census, *op. cit.,* p. 40.

[49] *Ibid.,* p. 39.

[50] *Ibid.,* p. 392.

[51] William Lazer and John E. Smallwood, "Consumer Environments and Life Styles of the Seventies," *MSU Business Topics,* Vol. 20 (Spring 1972), p. 15.

The impact of these trends has been far-reaching. On the one hand, they represent the opportunity behind the boom in convenience store retailing for "fill-in" purchases. On the other hand, they are fueling the ever-increasing demand for fast-food outlets, prepared meals, and faster kitchen appliances, while cutting into the traditional supermarket business.

The delivery of convenience is likely to become highly sophisticated in the future, especially via in-home shopping through interactive telecommunication systems.[52] The forerunners of such systems already exist. For example, the 700,000 members of Comp-U-Card International, a buyers' club, can purchase name-brand appliances, furniture, fine china, silver, and even automobiles at prices 20 to 40 percent below retail simply by calling a toll-free telephone number. Members provide basic product-requirement information to operators, who scan their electronic listings (which are updated daily) and quote the best available prices, delivery times, etc. Comp-U-Card has no showrooms, warehouses, or catalogs, but deals with over 100 vendors around the country.[53] Going Comp-U-Card one step better is Home Shopping Network of Clearwater, Florida. In 1985, HSN began national cablecasts of its 24-hour network, in which sales agents market merchandise from garden tools to crystal bowls at discount prices. The network shows nothing but commercials. Consumers call a toll-free number listed on the screen and charge their purchases to their credit cards. In its first eight months of national operation, HSN had sales of $63.9 million and profits of $6.8 million.[54]

An equally dramatic consequence of the poverty-of-time phenomenon is that Americans are, in record numbers, eating away from home. Eighteen percent of their meals are coming from restaurants, and 48 percent of their food dollars are going to this industry.[55] Of the $131 billion spent in eating places in 1985, 35 percent went to franchised restaurant outlets, such as McDonald's, Kentucky Fried Chicken, Red Lobster, and Pizza Hut.[56] However, the impact of eating out as a sociological phenomenon should not be underestimated or characterized as a purely time- and labor-saving expedient of a time-conscious society, because there appears to be a discernible *preference* pattern, especially for the type of foods available through fast-food outlets.[57]

Age, Income, and Education.   Clearly the biggest news from a demographic perspective is the coming of age of the baby boomers (the 73 million people born between 1946 and 1964). They have spawned the yuppies (young, urban, upwardly mobile professionals) as well as others less well heeled. During the decade ending in 1990, the total U.S. population will have grown no more than 10

[52] See, for example, F. Kelley Shuptrine, "The Distribution/Retailing Institute of Tomorrow," *Journal of Retailing*, Vol. 51 (Spring 1975), p. 20; Eleanor G. May, "Nontraditional Retailing," in Stampfl and Hirschman (eds.), *op. cit.*, pp. 124–31; and Larry J. Rosenberg and Elizabeth C. Hirschman, "Retailing without Stores," *Harvard Business Review*, Vol. 58 (July-August 1980), pp. 103–12.

[53] "The Man Who Computerized Bargain Hunting," *Fortune* (July 9, 1984), p. 137; "Comp U Card Helps Millions Shop by Phone," *Business Week* (September 10, 1979), p. 58.

[54] "Hot Times for Home Shopping," *Fortune* (July 7, 1986), p. 10.

[55] "Supermarkets Realize That Usual Food Items Won't Sustain Profits," *Wall Street Journal*, July 18, 1977, p. 1 and *1986 Nielsen Review of Retail Grocery Store Trends* (Northbrook, Ill.: A. C. Nielsen, 1986), pp. 5 and 6.

[56] *1986 Nielsen Review of Retail Grocery Store Trends*, p. 6.

[57] See "Want to Cook Meals Just Like Mother Used to Take Out?" *Wall Street Journal*, October 12, 1978, p. 1.

percent (less than 1 percent per year, on average); the age group constituting the baby boomers (25 to 45 years old) will have grown by 30 percent.

The baby boomers are the most educated generation in U.S. history: 85 percent completed high school and 46 percent went on to college. By 1990, the entire group (college or no college) will dominate the labor force, accounting for 54 percent of all workers.

Life-style issues abound in discussions about the boomers. Apparently, they want stronger family and religious ties and have greater respect for authority than their predecessors, but they are also more tolerant of diversity. They are bringing a new work ethic to corporate America, insisting on such benefits as flextime, maternity and paternity leave, and day-care services when they are ready to start families. They also have entrepreneurial orientations, and even though they want to have children, they will have fewer of them. They represent a curious blend of me-generation attitudes and old-fashioned family values. And they have a simple criterion in selecting products and services: quality. Boomers are far less concerned than their parents with bargain hunting.[58]

Many boomers are well off. For example, in 1983, households headed by people 25 to 34, the center of the baby boomers in terms of age, had median incomes of $21,746—slightly higher than the national median.[59] Nearly 25 percent of them earned at least $35,000 and more than 60 percent were homeowners by 1983. By 1995, 26 percent of households headed by people 35 to 44 will have incomes greater than $50,000 (in constant 1982 dollars), versus only 12 percent for similar households in 1980. In fact, the boomers should be a formidable market for four more decades. The year 2000 should be a high-water mark for marketers because the boomers will be in their prime spending years.[60]

Not all baby boomers are well off, and certainly not all of them are yuppies. According to a study by J. Walter Thompson U.S.A., there is a rich segment, a poor segment, and a would-be segment.[61] The last of these groups would be yuppies if they had the money. While they have the same amount of higher education, they do not have the financial resources. Thompson also isolates "elite workers," who have the money but not the education, and "workers," who have neither the education nor the high incomes. In 1985, there were 3.1 million yuppies, 2.3 million elite workers, 11.8 million would-be's, and 41.9 million workers. Median annual incomes were as follows:

Yuppies	$39,100
Elite workers	$34,852
Would-be's	$15,000
Workers	$10,036

[58] See Geoffrey Colvin, "What the Baby-Boomers Will Buy Next," *Fortune* (October 15, 1984), pp. 28–34; "Baby Boomers Push for Power," *Business Week* (July 2, 1984), pp. 52–56; and Abigail Trafford and Susanna McBee, "America's Middle-Age Spread," *Review (Eastern Airlines)* (March 1985), pp. 35ff (reprinted from *U.S. News & World Report*).

[59] Colvin, *op. cit.*, p. 31.

[60] Baby boomers are, however, caught in a financial squeeze between spiraling costs and stagnating salaries, which has caused them to postpone homeownership and children. See Betsy Morris, "Many Baby Boomers Find They Are Caught in a Financial Squeeze," *Wall Street Journal*, December 17, 1985, p. 1.

[61] Philip H. Dougherty, "More Than Yuppies in Baby Boom," *New York Times*, August 2, 1985, p. 37.

While Yuppies are heavy users of L.L. Bean and Sears catalogues, style-conscious would-be's can only be found following L.L. Bean, while the elite workers thumb loyally through the Sears entry.[62]

In terms of income alone, the extremes (those making less than $15,000 or more than $35,000) are growing as a percentage of all families. To a large extent, this is due to the explosive growth of the service economy, because the gap between managerial and nonmanagerial salaries is much wider in services than in manufacturing. For example, in the health-services industry, doctors, dentists, and health administrators averaged over $43,000 per year in 1980 while nonsupervisory workers—orderlies, nurse's aides, most nurses, and health technicians—averaged a meager $9700. Retailers can fine-tune their appeals to cater to this polarity.

> Neiman-Marcus and K-Mart are good examples. The Neiman-Marcus customer has a median income of between $50,000 and $65,000 a year. "Some people think we're positioned for an elitist customer base, and to some extent that's true," says Ferdinand Hauslein Jr., vice president for marketing. "But we offer merchandise in all price levels—we have shirts as low as $30 or $35." For most customers at K-Mart, . . . a $30 shirt sounds like a cruel joke. "The typical customer has more demands on income than income," according to Michael G. Wellman, director of planning and research.[63]

The poorest 40 percent of households—those that earn an average of $9500 per year and account for 20 percent of total retail sales—have been severely squeezed by the sharp rise in food and fuel prices. These households spend 40 percent of their income on food and fuel, up from 33 percent in the 1972–74 period.[64] In contrast, the top income tier spends only about 25 percent on food and fuel. It is little wonder that the bottom tier continues to shop at K-Mart, Family Dollar, Dollar General, and Stuart's Department Stores.

Another highly significant demographic phenomenon is the "graying of America." In 1985, households headed by persons over 50 outnumbered those headed by persons under 35 by a substantial margin. Those 50 and beyond accounted for half of all discretionary spending power, compared with a fifth of the total for those under 35. During the period 1985–90, the nation's adult population will grow by 14 percent, but the number of people over 50 will increase by some 23 percent. The implications for marketers have been pointed out by Fabian Linden, executive director of the Conference Board's Consumer Research Center:

> Generally, the categories of goods and services that the family buys in its passage through time remain the same. The basics remain basic. There can be significant differences, however, in *how much* is spent for each type of product or service. Young people with low income confronted with rapidly expanding demands are more disposed toward lower- and medium-priced lines, while the elderly, with diminishing needs but still sturdy incomes, may be more likely to reach out for higher quality and the more expensive end of the price spectrum.[65]

[62] *Ibid.*
[63] Bruce Steinberg, "The Mass Market Is Splitting Apart," *Fortune* (November 28, 1983), p. 82.
[64] Hank Gilman, "Retailers That Target Low-Income Shoppers Are Growing Rapidly," *Wall Street Journal,* June 24, 1985, p. 1.
[65] Fabian Linden, "New Money and the Old," *Across the Board* (July/August 1985), p. 49.

Table 2–2   Ranking of 12 different factors in choosing a store to shop

| | Importance | | | |
| | High | Middle | Low | |
Factors		(percentage of respondents)		Mean Rating [Scale: 1 (low) to 9 (high)]
Quality of merchandise	21%	66%	13%	5.37
Prices	15	60	25	4.76
Location of store	14	56	30	4.58
Looks of the merchandise	8	64	28	4.34
How much enjoy shopping there	11	56	33	4.28
Sales and specials	7	55	38	4.05
How clean the store is	4	60	35	4.04
Return or exchange policy	7	53	40	4.00
Assortment	6	54	40	3.94
How well stocked	3	59	38	3.85
Sales help	5	52	43	3.82
Advertising	2	34	64	2.93

Source: Chain Store Age/Leo J. Shapiro & Associates, Chain Store Age, General Merchandising Trends (May 1985), p. 15.

There is also evidence that the elderly exhibit unique shopping, credit, and media habits.[66] Sociologically and politically, there has been a growing mood of conservatism in the United States resulting from a waning youth culture and a generally more mature population.[67]

An increased emphasis on quality and value is bound to be spurred by the baby boomers and by the increased number of working wives. Because of the "poverty of time" and the dual incomes available to numerous households, the amount of "frivolous," time-consuming purchasing will be reduced, but the ability to purchase higher-quality goods and services may be enhanced. Because neither wife nor husband will wish to be saddled with the service problems that may attend questionable but inexpensive merchandise, both will insist on buying highly scrutinized brands, particularly in durables, from "reputable" merchants. For example, a survey sponsored by *Chain Store Age* in 1984 asked over 1000 respondents in five major cities to rank the relative importance of 12 different factors that go into the decision of choosing a store to shop for general merchandise.[68] The results, reported in Table 2–2, indicate, as one might expect, that value is multidimensional. According to the survey, Sears was the clear winner in the competition for the consumer's value vote.

[66] William O. Bearden and J. Barry Mason, "Elderly Use of In-Store Information Sources and Dimensions of Product Satisfaction/Dissatisfaction," *Journal of Retailing* (Spring 1979), p. 80. For an excellent review of studies, see Lynn W. Phillips and Brian Sternthal, "Age Differences in Information Processing: A Perspective on the Aged Consumer," *Journal of Marketing Research,* Vol. 74 (November 1977), pp. 444–57.

[67] See Peter Petre, "Marketers Mine for Gold in the Old," *Fortune* (March 31, 1986), pp. 70–78; and Hank Gilman, "Marketers Court Older Consumers as Balance of Buying Power Shifts," *Wall Street Journal,* April 23, 1986, p. 37.

[68] "Value Is a Complex Equation," *Chain Store Age, General Merchandise Trends* (May 1985), pp. 14–59.

In terms of education, 34 percent of persons 25 and older had a minimum of four years of high school in 1950. In 1983, the figure was 72 percent.[69] By 1983, approximately 43 percent of the *under*-30 population had attended college. Almost one-quarter of those 25 to 45 (the baby boomers) have college degrees. Supposedly, educated consumers are more rational in consumption behavior, are less susceptible to emotional appeals and brand-institutional loyalties, and demand more product information.[70]

While the foregoing factors are likely to have highly diverse impacts on individuals and market segments, two broad developments can be traced to the joint effect of the trends in income, dominant age groups, and education. On the one hand, there seems to be a trend away from frills, flash, and planned obsolescence. The booming discount industry and the growth of generic brands in both the food and drug markets are indicative of the consumer's willingness to absorb some service functions, shop in austere surroundings, and deflate advertisers' claims in order to secure better prices.[71] On the other hand, although there are many indications that the new mood of the American consumer is more utilitarian and that consumers are willing to sacrifice some quality when the increment in quality is not worth the additional price, it does not follow that there is a general mood of price consciousness. Rather, as mentioned, it is a value consciousness. For example, in fields other than foods and drugs, there is a dramatic swing toward more expensive, higher-quality goods. The attitude seems to be that if one brand costs $20 or $30 more than another one but will last twice as long, the premium is well spent. Consumers are spending more, even splurging, on quality, even if this means scrimping on other purchases.[72]

The demographic shifts just enumerated underscore the significance of retailing in marketing. Retailing is the final link in the commercial sector of marketing channels. Since retailers are in direct and constant contact with final consumers, they are more sensitive and respond more quickly to shifting market segments and consumers' changing demands for service outputs. Because of the multitude of market segments and the need to consider nontraditional bases for market segmentation, retailers have had to continually adjust their offerings and the ways in which they make their offerings available. For example, to serve segments characterized by the "poverty of time," mail-order houses, direct marketing schemes, and in-home and in-office selling have emerged and flourished. In 1984, direct marketing—which includes catalogs, direct-mail, and direct-response advertising on television, on radio, and in magazines, as well as tele-

    [69] U.S. Bureau of the Census, *op. cit.,* p. 134.
    [70] Bates, *Retailing and Its Environment,* p. 13.
    [71] See "Plain Labels Challenge the Supermarket Establishment," *Fortune* (March 26, 1979), p. 70. By the fall of 1979, generics had captured market shares of 10 percent or greater in such product categories as peanut butter, salad and cooking oils, fabric softeners, liquid detergents, paper towels, and toilet tissue in stores handling generics in 1978 and 1979: "A Source of Generic Share Changes," *Nielsen Researcher,* No. 2 (1980), p. 13. Excellent discussions of the impact of generics and limited-service stores can be found in "No-Frills Food: New Power for the Supermarkets," *Business Week* (March 23, 1981), pp. 70–80; Meg Cox, "Food Stores with Few Services Spring Up to Lure Increasingly Frugal Consumers," *Wall Street Journal,* January 23, 1981, p. 36; and Steve Weiner, "Many Stores Abandon 'Service with a Smile,' Rely on Signs, Displays," *Wall Street Journal,* March 16, 1981, p. 1. But also see Bill Abrams, "Reports of Generics' Success May Be Greatly Exaggerated," *Wall Street Journal,* May 7, 1981, p. 27.
    [72] "Buyers Swing to Quality," *Time* (December 3, 1979), p. 82. See also "Dual Incomes Will Lift More Families to Middle-Class Affluence in the Decade," *Wall Street Journal,* June 27, 1980, p. 21.

EXHIBIT 2–8   Contrast between traditional and new values

TRADITIONAL VALUES	NEW VALUES
Self-denial	Self-fulfillment
Higher standard of living	Better quality of life
Distinctive sex roles	Blurred sex roles
Accepted definition of success	Individualized definition of success
Traditional family life	Alternate families
Faith in industry, institutions, leaders	Self-reliance
Live to work	Work to live
Heroes	Idea people
Expansionism	Pluralism
Patriotism	Less nationalism
Unparalleled growth	Growing sense of limits
Industrial growth	Information/service growth
Receptive to technology	More technological

Source: Joseph T. Plummer, "The Changing American Consumer: Identifying Tomorrow's Franchise," Young & Rubicam Presentation to Executive Committee of Grandmet USA, February 1984.

phone sales—accounted for $150 billion in sales, compared with $98.8 billion five years earlier.

Time-poor consumers are attracted by broad and deep assortments and therefore find specialty retailers such as The Limited, The Gap, and Crate & Barrel particularly appealing. These specialty shopping attractions are designed to reduce search time. Simultaneously, discount houses, catalog showrooms, limited-assortment grocery stores, and other institutions emerge to satisfy the needs of market segments anxious over the declining value of money. These segments are willing to trade off service outputs for lower prices, and the retailing sector has adapted accordingly.

Consumer Values.   There appears to have emerged a new set of consumer values, which emphasizes people first and things second, as opposed to the things-first, people-second culture that has basically dominated the United States since the end of World War II. Studies show that 80 percent of consumers are concerned with "being good to myself" and "improving myself."[73] The ramifications of the new values are many, including less pressure to conform, tolerance of diversity, personalization, customization, permissiveness, instant gratification, a need for more enjoyment, a concern for ecology, and an emphasis on doing rather than having. Contrasts between traditional and new values are shown in Exhibit 2–8. As Berry and Wilson observe,

> more and more people are deciding that the quality of life is more important than the quantity of life, that human beings are more important than things.

[73] Rodger D. Blackwell, "Successful Retailers of 80's Will Cater to Specific Lifestyle Segments," *Marketing News* (March 7, 1980), p. 3.

Significantly, the new values are not a refutation of money and the possessions and services that money can buy. Rather, what is occurring is a reordering of priorities, a growing awareness that a big income can't necessarily be equated with personal happiness, and that a fast-increasing GNP doesn't necessarily reflect a sound and healthy society.[74]

The continued growth of the "new values" will undoubtedly affect life styles dramatically. The emphasis on health and fitness management, diverse family relationships, job switching, dual-career families, continuing education, and the blurring of traditional roles is already evident. To use the terminology of the Values and Lifestyles Program (VALS) developed by SRI International (see Table 2–3), the marketplace of 1990 won't be dominated by the middle-class, family-oriented "belongers" who are motivated mostly to fit in with their peers. Instead, the most influential group is likely to be the "inner-directed" consumers who are more self-reliant and less status-conscious. Inner-directed consumers will grow to 30 percent of the population by 1990 from 22 percent in 1980 and will account for 27 percent of consumer spending. Inner-directed consumers want high-quality products, exhibit less brand loyalty, and are more willing to experiment. They are, therefore, a more difficult group than belongers for marketers to reach.[75]

It is obvious that behavioral trends impinge heavily on consumer shopping habits and patronage patterns. However, as Bates points out, behavioral analysis is particularly useful for detailed studies of specific stores but is difficult to generalize to more global statements.[76] To illustrate how consumer attitudes affect retail opportunity, the implications of six widely held consumer values have been laid out in Table 2–4.

In line with the emerging demographic patterns, the new values, and the growing poverty of time, some major department stores are actually remodeling parts of their stores into mall-like clusters of specialty shops. Macy's (New York) was the first to succeed with such a plan, in 1976. More recently, similar changes have been implemented by such stores as Bloomingdale's, Marshall Field's, Carson Pirie Scott, and Jordan Marsh.[77] The "specialty" clustering is not simply a question of better-defined departments. The major opportunity in clustering is that instead of a single image for the whole store, a life-style type of segmentation within the store might evolve.

Mass merchandisers are increasingly faced with the problems of *image projection* and *positioning* in the market. K-Mart, known for its low prices, has been stressing quality; Sears, known for its quality, has been stressing price; and Penney's, a retailer with a solid but conservative "bargain basement" image, is stressing a fashion image. The rapidly changing demographic and sociocultural composition of middle America is responsible for the traditional mass merchandiser's dilemma. Image positioning is increasingly becoming the crux of retail

[74] Leonard L. Berry and Ian H. Wilson, "Retailing: The Next Ten Years," *Journal of Retailing,* Vol. 53 (Fall 1977), p. 10.

[75] "Inner-Directed Consumers," *Wall Street Journal,* May 5, 1983, p. 31; Arnold Mitchell, *The Nine American Lifestyles: Who We Are and Where We're Going* (New York: Warner Books, 1983).

[76] Bates, *Retailing and Its Environment,* p. 14.

[77] See "Department Stores Fight for Their Life," *Chicago Tribune,* September 17, 1979, section 4, p. 11; "Many Department Stores Are Converting Open Floors into Varied Specialty Shops," *Wall Street Journal,* October 10, 1978, p. 40; and Anthony Ramirez, "Department Stores Shape Up," *Fortune* (September 1, 1986), pp. 50–52.

Table 2–3   Characteristics of the VALS™ lifestyles

Lifestyle	Characteristics	Number (millions)	Age	% Female	Median Income	Education	Buying Patterns
Survivors	Old; intensely poor; fearful; depressed; despairing; far removed from the cultural mainstream; misfits	7	Most over 65	73	$7500	8th–9th Grade	Price dominant; buy for immediate needs; focused on basics
Sustainers	Living on the edge of poverty; angry and resentful; streetwise; some involved in the underground economy	12	67% under 35	57	$9000	11th Grade	Price and warranty important; cautious buyers; some buy on impulse
Belongers	Aging; traditional and conventional; contented; intensely patriotic; sentimental; deeply stable	64	Median—57	58	$18,000	High School Graduate	Buy for family and home; buy fads; middle and low mass markets
Emulators	Youthful and ambitious; macho; show-off; trying to break into the system, to make it big	17	Median—28	47	$24,000	High School Graduate	Conspicuous consumption; imitative; buy "in" items and popular fashions
Achievers	Middle-aged and prosperous; able leaders; self-assured; materialistic; builders of the American "dream"	34	Median—42	42	$43,500	32% at least College Graduates	Give evidence of success; luxury and gift markets; buy "top of the line" and "new and improved" products
I-Am-Me's	Transition state; exhibitionist and narcissistic; young; impulsive; dramatic; experimental; active; inventive	5	94% under 25	49	<$6000	Some College	Display one's tastes; clique buying; experiment with fads; source of far-out fads
Experientials	Youthful; seek direct experience; person-centered;	8	28	53	$30,500	38% at least College Graduates	Process over product; vigorous outdoor sports;

Table 2–3   (Continued)

Lifestyle	Characteristics	Number (millions)	Age	% Female	Median Income	Education	Buying Patterns
	artistic; intensely oriented toward inner growth						introspective; crafts
Societally Conscious	Mission-oriented; leaders of single-issue groups; mature; successful; some live lives of voluntary simplicity	19	37	50	$36,000	66% College Graduates; 39% some Graduate	Conservation emphasis; environmental concerns; frugality; simplicity; buy high-quality items
Integrateds	Psychologically mature; large field of vision; tolerant and understanding; sense of fittingness	3					Varied self-expression; aesthetically oriented; ecologically aware; one-of-a-kind items

Sources: Adapted from Arnold Mitchell, *Consumer Values: A Typology* (Menlo Park, Calif.: SRI International, 1976); Arnold Mitchell, *The Nine American Lifestyles: Who We Are and Where We're Going* (New York: Warner Books, 1983), pp. 176–79; and the Values and Lifestyles (VALS™) Program at SRI International, Menlo Park, California. Adapted with permission of Macmillan Publishing Company for *The Nine American Lifestyles* by Arnold Mitchell. Copyright © 1983 by Arnold Mitchell.

strategy. Pure demographics are becoming less accurate as segment definers, and life-style indicators are becoming more appropriate.[78] The increased emphasis on positioning in retailing is significant for manufacturers as well as for retailers:

> For retailers it could mean a strong increase in nonprice competition which will be difficult if not impossible for unpositioned firms to counter. In particular, firms with very broad target markets, such as conventional department stores and discount stores, will have great difficulty in competing with positioned firms. For manufacturers, positioning could necessitate the use of multiple market programs to meet the buying requirements of retail firms positioned in a variety of different ways.[79]

[78] See Melvin R. Crask, "Department Stores vs. Discount Stores," in Stampfl and Hirschman (eds.), *op. cit.,* pp. 33–42. With regard to specific positioning methodologies, see Lawrence J. Ring, Charles W. King, and Douglas J. Tigert, "Market Structure and Retail Position," in Stampfl and Hirschman (eds.), *op. cit.,* pp. 149–60. The multi-attribute decision models or choice strategies discussed in Appendix 2A of this chapter are appropriate to employ as a starting point for perceptual mapping purposes.

[79] Bates, "The Troubled Future of Retailing," *op. cit.,* p. 28.

Table 2–4   Several widely held consumer attitudes and their implications for marketing channels

Consumer Attitude	Examples of Channel Implications	Examples of Channels Capitalizing on the Attitude
More casual life styles—a desire to live in a more relaxed, informal style with regard to dress, home environment, etc.	• Need to maintain a current assortment of life-style-oriented merchandise • Need to monitor changing tastes at the retail level	• Jeans West—casual apparel • Pier I—casual home furnishings
Instant gratification—desire for immediate access to goods and services	• Need for easier credit availability to facilitate purchasing • Reductions of in-store waiting time • Reductions of stock-out levels	• Levitz—availability of furniture on an instant take-home basis • Caterpillar—worldwide availability of spare parts within 24 hours
Energy/ecological/environmental orientation—gradual proliferation of resource conservation ethic	• Need for demonstrated energy/ecological/environmental concern	• Coors—aluminum can recycling program • Amoco—premium gasoline blended with grain alcohol
Time conservation—growing recognition that time is a critical resource and constraint in many consumers' lives	• Need to develop products requiring a minimum of care and easy repair • Need to develop operating hours consistent with consumers' discretionary time	• General Electric—service contracts for major appliances • Citicorp—24-hour, seven-day-a-week, 800-number transaction line
Naturalism—a revolt against artificial, plastic, "mass-produced" characteristics of society in favor of more natural ones	• More natural-product displays, using woods, bricks, etc. • Adding a greater variety of products to the product line to satisfy consumers' individual tastes	• Perkins Pancakes—upgraded decor featuring natural wood fixtures and softer incandescent light • Wendy's—providing hamburgers in a couple of hundred different combinations
Blurring of male–female roles—men and women performing roles stereotypically performed by the opposite sex	• Need to assist men and women in performing nontraditional roles	• Friedman's Microwave Ovens—offering microwave cooking classes to both men and women

Sources: Adapted from Albert D. Bates, *Retailing and Its Environment* (New York: D. Van Nostrand Company, 1979), p. 15; and James F. Engel and Roger D. Blackwell, *Consumer Behavior,* 4th ed. (Chicago: Dryden Press, 1982), pp. 208–13.

The Competitive Environment

Broadly speaking, the structure of competition in retailing is described in Table 2–5. The nature of each of the types of competition listed in Table 2–5 is qualitatively different and poses different strategic implications. Furthermore, in recent years the competitive environment of retailing has become more difficult to decipher. A slow-growth economy and escalating costs of capital, construction, energy, and labor are squeezing profits on the one side while, on the other, increasingly saturated markets, new aggressive forms of innovative retailing, and generally more sophisticated management approaches are placing mar-

Table 2–5 Competition in the retailing sector

Type of Competition	Scope of Competition	Corporate Illustrations
Intratype	Between the *same* type of outlets	Thrifty vs. Walgreen
Intertype	Between *different* types of outlets	Kroger vs. K-Mart
Systems	Between *different* types of vertically integrated systems, including voluntary groups, cooperative groups, franchise networks, and corporate chains	Sears vs. True Value
Free-form	Between free-form corporations, each of which operates multiple types of outlets to serve multiple market segments	Edison Bros. vs. Melville

Source: Bert C. McCammon, Jr., "Future Shock and the Practice of Management," a paper presented at the Fifth Annual Attitude Research Conference of the American Marketing Association, Madrid, 1973, p. 8.

gins under continuous assault in most product categories. Most retailers operate fairly close to their break-even volumes; therefore, they are exceedingly vulnerable to new entrants siphoning off even a modest part of their sales.[80] Given this picture, it is important to concentrate on understanding where the greatest threats seem to be coming from—increasing intertype competition and polarization; the growth of vertical marketing systems, including free-form corporations; and the acceleration of institutional life cycles.

Increasing Intertype Competition and Polarization. Some decades ago it might have been reasonable to think of supermarkets competing primarily with supermarkets, department stores with department stores, and so on. But in the modern world of distribution, the fastest-growing form of competition is intertype. Supermarkets compete against convenience stores, warehouse stores, combination food and drug stores, and restaurants (especially fast-food outlets) for the consumer's food dollar. Likewise, in many lines of general merchandise and apparel, the struggle for patronage is increasingly among specialty store chains, department stores, discount department stores, and family centers.[81] An idea of the extent of intertype competition emerges when the sales for three product categories—health and beauty aids, hardware, and machine-made glassware—are tracked. At one time, each of these was virtually the exclusive domain of a single type of outlet. Now, as shown in Table 2–6, sales come from a wide spectrum of retailing establishments.

The intensity of intertype competition has been heightened by the appearance of specialty store chains like The Limited, Toys "R" Us, and Radio Shack. Carrying extremely deep and broad assortments (like Toys "R" Us) and sharply focused on well-defined segments (like The Limited, which aims directly at the

[80] Supermarkets have a break-even point that ranges between 94 and 96 percent of their current sales, while general merchandise retailers' break-even points approach 85 to 92 percent of their current sales. Bert C. McCammon, Jr., Jack J. Kasulis, and Jack A. Lesser, "The New Parameters of Retail Competition: The Intensified Struggle for Market Share," in Stampfl and Hirschman (eds.), *op. cit.*, p. 110.

[81] For some useful insights into the structure of retail markets, see Elizabeth C. Hirschman, "A Descriptive Theory of Retail Market Structure," *Journal of Retailing*, Vol. 54 (Winter 1978), pp. 29–48.

Table 2–6 Sales of health and beauty aids, hardware products, and machine-made glassware by type of outlet

Health and Beauty Aids		Hardware Products		Machine-made Glassware	
Type of Outlet	Percentage of Total Sales	Type of Outlet	Percentage of Total Sales	Type of Outlet	Percentage of Total Sales
Grocery stores	32.2%	Hardware and building materials stores	31.0%	Discount stores	27.8%
Drugstores	32.1	General merchandise and variety stores	23.8	General merchandise and variety stores	24.6
Discount stores	12.0	Discount stores	17.7	Department stores	18.2
General merchandise and variety stores	8.4	Home improvement centers	16.4	Grocery stores	11.8
Nonstore retailers	8.2	Department stores	4.9	Specialty stores	7.9
Department stores	5.7	Nonstore retailers	2.0	Drugstores	4.3
All other	1.4	Grocery stores	2.0	All other	5.4
		All other	2.2		
Total	100.0%	Total	100.0%	Total	100.0%

Source: Albert D. Bates, *Retailing and Its Environment* (New York: D. Van Nostrand Company, 1979), p. 25.

18-to-35-year-old style-and-fashion-conscious woman), these specialty chains have been highly successful and have posed an especially significant threat to traditional department stores.

The intensity of intertype competition has also been heightened by the appearance of new mass merchandisers, particularly the warehouse-type operations, such as Home Depot (home centers), Price Club (general merchandise), and Wal-Mart. As shown in Table 2–7, a number of these merchants have been extremely successful. All of the organizations depicted in Table 2–7 are particularly well positioned for future growth because they enjoy unusually strong consumer franchises, being perceived as places where a purchaser can receive "good value for money expended."[82] Indeed, some of these retailers are a new breed, called *category killers*. Essentially the ultimate in specialty stores, the category killer gets its name from its marketing strategy: carry such a large amount of merchandise at such good prices that the competition is destroyed.[83] Prime examples are Toys "R" Us and Trak Auto. Emerging on the horizon is Ikea, a Swedish home furnishings and housewares retailer that stocks more than 15,000 items.

[82] McCammon, Kasulis, and Lesser, *op. cit.,* p. 111.
[83] Steve Weiner, "With Big Selection and Low Prices, 'Category Killer' Stores Are a Hit," *Wall Street Journal,* June 17, 1986, p. 33. See also "Shopping Swedish Style Comes to the U.S.," *Fortune* (January 20, 1986), p. 63.

Table 2—7 Financial profiles of selected retailing companies

	Net Profits/ Net Sales (percentage)	Net Sales/ Total Assets (times)	Net Profits/ Total Assets (percentage)	Total Assets/ Net Worth (times)	Net Profits/ Net Worth (percentage)	Year
Bruno's Inc.	2.5	4.5	11.3	1.9	21.8	1983
Burlington Coat Factory	5.3	2.0	10.7	2.7	29.3	1982
The ClothesTime, Inc.	2.5	5.0	12.2	3.4	41.6	1983
The Computer Factory	3.7	4.0	14.8	1.6	24.0	1983
The Crown Books Corporation	3.8	2.3	8.7	5.6	49.2	1983
The Jack Eckerd Corporation	3.1	2.7	8.3	1.5	12.6	1983
Fuddruckers, Inc.	4.9	2.5	12.2	4.8	58.8	1983
The Gap Stores, Inc.	4.5	2.4	11.0	1.6	17.8	1984
The Heckinger Company	5.2	1.8	9.1	1.8	16.2	1984
The Home Depot	4.0	2.4	9.8	1.6	15.7	1984
The Limited, Inc.	4.7	2.3	10.5	2.6	27.4	1983
Longs Drug Stores, Inc.	3.0	3.8	11.3	1.4	16.2	1984
R.H. Macy & Co., Inc.	5.4	1.8	9.9	2.0	19.2	1983
The Melville Corporation	4.4	2.6	11.4	1.8	20.2	1983
Payless Cashways, Inc.	4.0	2.4	9.4	1.8	16.9	1983
The Petrie Stores Corporation	7.6	1.4	10.6	1.5	16.0	1984
The Pic 'N' Save Corporation	16.0	1.4	21.8	1.2	26.7	1983
Pier 1 Imports	6.5	2.0	13.3	2.0	26.5	1983
The Price Company	2.3	4.6	10.4	2.0	21.3	1983
Revco D.S., Inc.	3.7	3.0	11.1	1.6	17.9	1983
The Standard Brands Paint Co.	6.3	1.7	10.7	1.2	13.2	1984
The Syms Corp.	5.1	3.4	17.2	1.4	24.5	1983
The Tandy Corporation	11.1	1.6	17.6	1.4	24.8	1983
Toys "R" Us, Inc.	6.2	1.9	11.5	1.7	19.8	1983
The Trak Auto Corporation	8.8	5.9	52.1	1.9	99.0	1983
The United States Shoe Corp.	5.0	2.3	11.2	1.7	19.3	1984
Wal-Mart Stores, Inc.	4.2	2.8	11.9	2.2	26.6	1984

Source: Bert C. McCammon, Jr., *The New Strategic Era in Retailing: Appendices and Exhibits* (Norman, Okla.: Distribution Research Program, Center for Economic and Management Research, College of Business Administration, University of Oklahoma, 1984).

EXHIBIT 2–9   Polarization of retail trade

High Tech,
Mass
Merchandisers

Traditional
Retailers

High Touch,
Specialty
Stores

No-frills stores
Warehouse stores
Generic products
Convenience stores

SUPERMARKETS

Macy's Cellar
Byerly's
Food Emporium

Discounters

DEPARTMENT STORES

Boutiques
Bloomingdale's

Source: Adapted from Stephen P. Arbeit, "Confronting the Crisis in Mass Marketing," Ogilvy and Mather's Viewpoint, Vol. 2 (1982), p. 5.

The most successful retailers can be dichotomized into (1) those operating highly targeted stores averaging between 5000 and 15,000 square feet in space, typified by classification dominance (e.g., all sizes, brands, and kinds of running, tennis, and basketball shoes are likely to be found at Athlete's Foot and Foot Locker stores), and (2) those operating very large mass merchandising operations with stores 100,000 square feet and up (Bigg's in Cincinnati is 200,000 square feet) carrying tens of thousands of items (Bigg's carries 60,000) and selling them at low margins across a wide variety of merchandise lines.[84] This phenomenon (portrayed in Exhibit 2–9) has been called the *polarization of retailing*.

To some extent, the polarity has come about as a result of life-style changes. Consumers are choosing outlets that are congruent with the decision they have to make. Some decisions are "high-touch": the consumer needs ego gratification and personal attention in order to make a choice, because of a high sense of personal involvement in the decision itself. Other decisions are "high-tech": everything is spelled out very explicitly, the consumer needs to be involved very little, and technology replaces effort.[85] In food retailing, supermarkets are losing business to high-tech outlets (e.g., box and warehouse stores, such as Aldi and Cub Foods) on the one hand and high-touch outlets (e.g., Macy's Cellar, Byerly's in Minnesota, Dierberg's in St. Louis, Lofino's in Dayton, and Treasure Island in Chicago) on the other. Department stores are facing similar competition. The result is that, on average, targeted specialists and warehouse technology retailers are experiencing high rates of growth and attractive returns on their investments while traditional retailers are facing stagnant rates of growth and low yields.

[84] See "Boom Times in a Bargain-Hunter's Paradise," *Business Week* (March 11, 1985), pp. 116, 120.

[85] Stephen P. Arbeit, "Confronting the Crisis in Mass Marketing," *Ogilvy and Mather's Viewpoint*, Vol. 2 (1982), p. 4.

The Growth of Vertical Marketing Systems and Free-Form Corporations. The significance of this fact of retailing life is evidenced by the attention it is given in this text: an entire chapter (Chapter 7) is devoted to vertical marketing systems. A highly dynamic environment is placing enormous demands for increasingly sophisticated management of manufacturer-wholesaler-retailer relations. The new technologies and the need for fine-tuning assortments, controlling inventories, and monitoring and adapting the retailer's position in the market require specialized and skilled staffs. Larger and more complex organizations are necessary to house the specialists who will take responsibility for managing the marketing channel all the way from point of production to point of consumption. Thus, the McDonalds, Super Valus, Safeways, Sears, K-Marts, and Federateds of this world will continue to dominate the retailing scene largely because they administer, through franchising, vertical integration, or simply the use of their massive power, the marketing channels in which they are found. The result is a strong and positive impact on the ultimate consumer.

To a large extent, the growth of vertical marketing systems has spawned the growth of free-form corporations, or, as discussed earlier, "conglomerchants." One way of looking at the growth of such companies as Dayton-Hudson; Edison Brothers; Melville Corporation; and United States Shoe Corporation is to think of them as differentiating themselves to serve increasingly fragmented market segments. Another, complementary, way to look at their growth is to portray their acquisitions and internal developments as a hedge against increasingly shorter retail life cycles and intensifying intertype competition. With the pace of innovation seeming always to accelerate, it makes a lot of sense to invest in a variety of distributive modes rather than in a single type.

The result of the growth of vertical market systems and free-form corporations is that the fully independent small store is likely to be squeezed even further. Also, market penetration by new forms of retailing and the maturing of these forms will occur much faster, because the larger organizations will be quick to spot potential ideas (e.g., generic brands) and bring their huge resources to bear in developing them. Finally, the larger organizations will be less vulnerable to attack, because they will be serving a wide number of market segments with a variety of store types (e.g., department, discount, and specialty).[86] Stores will be tailored in image, size, location, merchandise, and services to fit specific consumer segments and will be deliberately managed to retain this fit for as long as the segments remain opportune. Indeed, future changes in patterns of distribution and retailing form are likely to involve a more prominent element of managerial *intervention* rather than just environmental *determinism*.

The Acceleration of Institutional Life Cycles. A number of theoretical schemes have been suggested as descriptive of institutional evolution in retailing. The best-known theory is the Wheel of Retailing. It hypothesizes that retail innovations emerge as low-cost, low-price, high-volume operations because of the void created in the marketplace as older institutions trade up. But, like the innovations before them, the new institutions proliferate, and in order to differentiate themselves from one another, they also find themselves trading up in

---

[86] See Dillard B. Tinsley, John R. Brooks, Jr., and Michael d'Amico, "Will the Wheel of Retailing Stop Turning?" *Akron Business and Economic Review* (Summer 1978), p. 26.

facilities, assortments, customer services, promotions, and the like. The vast majority of retail innovations in this century fit this principle of low-cost entry, and most of these have been dogged by the trading-up phenomenon.[87] But there are exceptions: automatic vending, suburban shopping centers, and specialty chains do not conform to the low-cost principle.

Ronald Gist, drawing on Hegel's philosophy of dialectical evolution, suggests a pattern of synthesis: when a "thesis" (the original institution) is challenged by the inevitable "antithesis" (the innovator), there is a merging of the two.[88] The warehouse grocery store might be viewed as a synthesis of the supermarket and the discount food store modes of retailing, for example. Fast-food outlets have been described as a combination of the early drive-ins (which had extensive menus and order-prepared food) and the later take-out operations featuring precooked food and very limited menus.[89]

Another popular descriptive model is the general-specific-general cycle, or the retail "accordian" theory.[90] The theory describes discernible cycles of alternation between general wide-assortment merchandising and specialty narrow-line operations. A number of other theories exist, including the crisis-change model introduced in Chapter 5, that provide a reasonable fit with some of the evolutionary phenomena in retailing. However, none of the theories, including those mentioned above, generalizes across all situations or provides any predictive leverage.[91] Despite their weaknesses, though, the theories do have a very useful role to play, because they focus on the fact that change is a way of life in retailing and provide speculative frameworks for trying to interpret the direction of change implied by current events.

One of the more intriguing theories of institutional change to emerge in recent years is the concept of the institutional life cycle.[92] Like the product life cycle concept, the argument here is that retail institutions go through anthropomorphic life cycles that can be partitioned into stages of *early growth, accelerated development, maturity,* and *decline.* As illustrated in Fig. 2–1, new retail institutions generate high rates of growth and attractive profitability ratios during their initial stages of development. Illustrative of institutions that achieved extraordinary results during their formative years are the department store in the late 1800s, the supermarket in the 1930s, and the discount department store in the late 1950s and early 1960s. However, as retail institutions mature, they are increasingly confronted by new forms of competition and forced to compete in overstored or saturated markets.[93] As a result, price competition for these institutions intensifies, accompanied by declines in market share and profitability. Ultimately, mature institutions enter the decline stage of their life cycle and become disadvantaged participants in the marketplace. From this perspective,

[87] McNair and May, *op. cit.* See also McNair and May's "The Next Revolution of the Retailing Wheel," *Harvard Business Review,* Vol. 56 (September-October 1978), pp. 81–91.

[88] Gist, *op. cit.,* p. 106.

[89] Mason and Mayer, *Modern Retailing,* pp. 45, 52.

[90] Stanley C. Hollander, "Notes on the Retail Accordian," *Journal of Retailing,* Vol. 42 (Summer 1966), pp. 29–40.

[91] For a critique, see Stanley C. Hollander, "Oddities, Nostalgia, Wheels and Other Patterns in Retail Evolution," in Stampfl and Hirschman (eds.), *op. cit.,* pp. 78–87.

[92] William R. Davidson, Albert D. Bates, and Stephen J. Bass, "The Retail Life Cycle," *Harvard Business Review* (November-December 1976), pp. 89–96.

[93] See Bert C. McCammon, Jr., "The Future of Catalog Showrooms: Growth and Its Challenges to Management," Marketing Science Institute Working Paper, 1973, pp. 2–3.

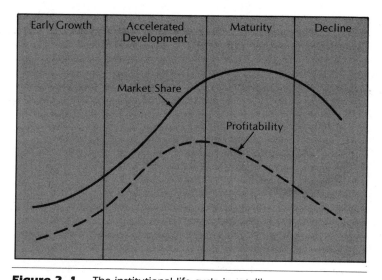

| Early Growth | Accelerated Development | Maturity | Decline |

Figure 2–1   The institutional life cycle in retailing

Source: Bert C. McCammon, Jr., "The Future of Catalog Showrooms: Growth and Its Challenges to Management," *Marketing Science Institute Working Paper*, April 1983, p. 2.

department stores, variety stores, and supermarkets are already mature and/or declining retail institutions. That is, they represent methods of doing business that no longer regularly produce high rates of growth or rates of return on investment.[94]

More important for managers, however, is the knowledge that institutional life cycles within retailing have accelerated over the years. For example, it has been estimated that the time to reach maturity has declined from approximately 100 years, in the case of department stores, to approximately 5 years, in the case of off-price apparel stores (see Table 2–8). Implicit is the point that contemporary institutions now in their initial stages of development will soon be faced with problems and challenges that confront department stores and supermarkets today. Indeed, an accelerating technological environment, more fluid consumer behavioral patterns (e.g., falling brand loyalties), crumbling "line-of-trade" barriers, a more acute appreciation of change as a way of life among managements, and a high level of awareness served by the booming trade journals industry are all contributing to the pace of the life cycle and to the tense competitive environment of retailing.

In a detailed elaboration of the life cycle concept, Davidson, Bates, and Bass have highlighted some of the management activities that become important in different stages (see Table 2–9). They have pointed out that, given the inevitability of the life cycle, management's responsibility in any one company is to anticipate changes in the stages and to adapt the organization to them as effectively as possible.[95]

[94] *Ibid.*, p. 3. As indicated in Table 2–8 of the present text, catalog showrooms are also entering maturity. See "No Christmas Cheer for Catalog Showrooms," *Business Week* (November 24, 1980), pp. 137, 141.
[95] Davidson, Bates, and Bass, *op. cit.*, p. 93.

Table 2–8   The accelerating pace of institutional life cycles

Institutional Type	Period of Fastest Growth	Period from Inception to Maturity (years)	Stage of Life Cycle	Representative Firms[a]
General store	1800–40	100	Declining	A local institution
Single-line/specialty store	1820–40	100	Mature	Hickory Farms
Department store	1860–1940	80	Mature	Marshall Field's
Variety store	1870–1930	50	Declining	Morgan-Lindsay
Mail-order house	1915–50	50	Mature	Spiegel
Corporate chain	1920–30	50	Mature	Sears
Discount store	1955–75	20	Mature	K-Mart
Supermarket	1935–65	35	Mature	A&P
Shopping center	1950–65	40	Mature	Paramus
Cooperative	1930–50	40	Mature	Ace Hardware
Gasoline station	1930–50	45	Mature	Texaco
Convenience store	1965–75	20	Mature	7-Eleven
Fast-food operation	1960–75	15	Mature	Shoney's
Home improvement center	1965–80	15	Late growth	Lowes
Superspecialist	1975–85	10	Late growth	The Limited
Warehouse retailing	1970–80	10	Late growth	Levitz
Catalog-showroom	1970–80	10	Mature	Service Merchandise
Off-price apparel store	1980–85	5	Mature	T.J. Maxx

[a] These firms are representative of institutional types and are not necessarily in the stage of the life cycle specified for the institutional group as a whole.

Source: Adapted from Joseph B. Mason and Morris L. Mayer, *Modern Retailing: Theory and Practice,* 3rd ed. (Dallas: Business Publications, Inc., © 1981), p. 93.

Furthermore, the concept has been applied to individual *stores* (in addition to institutional types) through the development of a consumer segment/profile interface along the time horizon, as shown in Fig. 2–2. Applying much the same theory that applies to the diffusion of product innovations, one might argue that the composition of a store's consumer segment will undergo natural change as the store matures.[96] In fact, as implied in Fig. 2–2, the same reasoning could be used to explain changes in consumer segments for products, brands, firms, and enterprises as well as for stores, locations, and institutions. To ensure their success, retailers must adapt their operating dimensions (margins, assortments, services, etc.) to best suit their shifting consumer bases. And it may be necessary for firms to radically reposition themselves at appropriate times to stay in touch with a chosen segment. Such retailers as Montgomery Ward and A&P have been very slow to learn this lesson. Unfortunately, W.T. Grant never did.

The Resource Environment[97]

The economic bonanza of the post–World War II years, which demonstrated a remarkable degree of continuity between 1947 and 1973, is being replaced by a more sobering set of realities: the higher cost of energy, lower real

[96] William R. Davidson and John E. Smallwood, "An Overview of the Retail Life Cycle," in Stampfl and Hirschman (eds.), *op. cit.,* p. 56.
[97] This section is based largely on Bates, *Retailing and Its Environment,* pp. 14–20 and Chapter 2.

Table 2–9 Management activities in the life cycle

Area or Subject of Concern		Stage of Life Cycle Development			
		1. Innovation	2. Accelerated development	3. Maturity	4. Decline
Market characteristics	Number of competitors	Very few	Moderate	Many direct competitors Moderate indirect competition	Moderate direct competition Many indirect competitors
	Rate of sales growth	Very rapid	Rapid	Moderate to slow	Slow or negative
	Level of profitability	Low to moderate	High	Moderate	Very low
	Duration of new innovations	3 to 5 years	5 to 6 years	Indefinite	Indefinite
Appropriate retailer actions	Investment/ growth/risk decisions	Investment minimiza- tion—high risks accepted	High levels of investment to sustain growth	Tightly controlled growth in untapped markets	Minimal capital expenditures and only when essential
	Central management concerns	Concept refinement through adjustment and experimentation	Establishing a preemptive market position	Excess capacity and "overstoring" Prolonging maturity and revising the retail concept	Engaging in a "runout" strategy
	Use of management control techniques	Minimal	Moderate	Extensive	Moderate
	Most successful management style	Entrepreneurial	Centralized	"Professional"	Caretaker
Appropriate supplier actions	Channel strategy	Develop a preemptive market position	Hold market position	Maintain profitable sales	Avoid excessive costs
	Channel problems	Possible antagonism of other accounts	Possible antagonism of other accounts	Dealing with more scientific retailers	Servicing accounts at a profit
	Channel research	Identification of key innovations	Identification of other retailers adopting the innovation	Initial screening of new innovation opportunities	Active search for new innovation opportunities
	Trade incentives	Direct financial support	Price concessions	New price incentives	None

Source: Reprinted by permission of the *Harvard Business Review.* An exhibit from "The Retail Life Cycle," by William Davidson, Albert Bates, and Stephen Bass (November-December 1976), p. 92. Copyright © 1976 by the President and Fellows of Harvard College; all rights reserved.

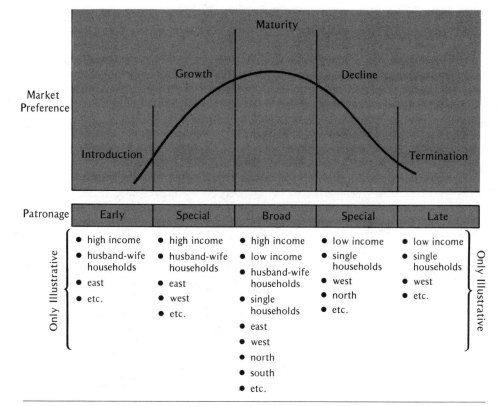

Figure 2–2   Life cycle analysis for consumer focus

Source: William R. Davidson and John E. Smallwood, "An Overview of the Retail Life Cycle." Reprinted from Ronald W. Stampfl and Elizabeth C. Hirschman (eds.), *Competitive Structure in Retail Markets: The Department Store Perspective* by the American Marketing Association (Chicago, 1980), p. 56.

growth in the GNP, erosion of consumer confidence, the growing entanglement of resource availabilities with international politics, uncertain capital availability, and a growing ethic of resource conservation and environmental protection.[98] Bates has identified five major sources of resource turbulence that underlie the productivity and profitability squeeze on retailers that became increasingly apparent during the late 1970s and early 1980s.[99] Each of these sources—capital costs, labor productivity, construction costs, merchandise availability, and the new technologies—is discussed briefly in this section.

Capital Costs.   Capital acquisition is an extremely critical strategic dimension for large-scale retailers. With the vast majority operating on relatively thin profit margins, even a small increase in interest rates can spell disaster for the balance sheet. This stark reality is compounded by the fact that retailing is not considered a very desirable investment field in financial circles. Analyzing 163 large-scale retailers and 746 similar-sized manufacturers, Bates found that be-

[98] Berry and Wilson, *op. cit.,* p. 11.
[99] See Chapter 11 of this text for a discussion of performance by retailing institutions.

tween 1970 and 1976 the retailers faced effective interest rates about half a percentage point above those charged the manufacturers.[100]

Labor Productivity. As shown in Chapter 11, labor productivity in retailing can be characterized, in the aggregate, as downright sluggish. Retailing is a labor-intensive industry; it has traditionally experienced greater productivity problems than more capital-intensive industries. Even in self-service operations payroll is over half of the expense account, and for conventional department stores it is almost two-thirds.[101] Furthermore, as McCammon and Hammer point out,

> lagging productivity at some point results in lagging wages. Lagging wages, in turn, eventually result in the recruitment of marginal personnel, which further depresses productivity. The ultimate consequence of this iterative process is a stagnant and depressed industry.[102]

Construction Costs. Rentals account for the second largest chunk of operating expenses. For example, sharply rising construction costs pushed rental charges in new regional shopping malls from $5 per square foot in 1970 to over $15 per square foot in 1985. Indeed, many retailers, like K-Mart, actually prefer to use free-standing locations rather than shopping centers and malls. Another resulting trend has been the recycling of facilities, such as abandoned supermarkets, variety stores, discount department stores, warehouses, and even train stations. Other retailers are experimenting with new low-cost construction techniques as well as with less elaborate interior designs and with modular construction, which allows rapid dismantling and rearrangement of display spaces. Given the pressures they face, retailers can increasingly be expected to turn to their suppliers for more direct investment assistance. In particular, the financing of inventory and fixtures could become integral parts of some suppliers' marketing programs.

Merchandise Availability. Peacetime product shortages were largely unknown to U.S. retailers until the 1970s. The oil embargo of 1974 had a widespread impact on retailing far beyond the effect it had on retail service stations. Petroleum-based industries, particularly plastics, and highly energy-dependent industries witnessed acute supply problems and rapidly escalating prices. Other shortages, such as the coffee shortage of 1976–77, affected profits in other industries.[103] Although these specific instances are things of the past, the future of raw material resources in general remains highly uncertain, and their availability is increasingly tangled with international politics. Retailers may have to increase the length of their contracts with suppliers or even reduce the number of suppliers with whom they deal so as to assure themselves of needed goods. Clearly, this will increase retailers' dependency on their suppliers and thus alter relationships within the marketing channel. The importance of such dependencies within the channel is examined in detail in Chapter 6.

[100] Bates, *Retailing and Its Environment*, p. 16.
[101] *Ibid.*, p. 17. Labor productivity is discussed more fully in Chapter 11 of the present text.
[102] Bert C. McCammon, Jr., and William L. Hammer, "A Frame of Reference for Improving Productivity in Distribution," *Atlanta Economic Review* (September-October 1974), p. 10.
[103] See, for example, "Fast Food Chains Take a Beating on Breakfast," *Business Week* (February 21, 1977), p. 30.

The New Technologies. Recent technological innovations have created a dilemma for retailers. On the one hand, they provide a major opportunity for improved operational and managerial efficiency. On the other, they involve major investments at a time when the short-run return picture is grim, and the long-run cost-benefit opportunity is very difficult to gauge.

Two general areas of technological innovation have been particularly influential over the past decade. One is totally automated warehousing,[104] whose applications at the retail level have resulted in the emergence of retail-warehouse institutions such as home improvement centers, grocery warehouse stores,[105] general merchandise warehouses (e.g., Price Club), and home furnishings "warehouse" retailers (e.g., Levitz), as well as the hypermarche (hypermarket) in Europe.[106] The other innovation is the use of electronic point-of-sale (POS) machinery. The new POS electronic cash registers are often tied to sophisticated computerized information and inventory control systems. The "front end" of a store is responsible for the bulk of labor expenses for many forms of retailing. When the adoption of the Universal Product Code (UPC) for packaged groceries and other codes for general merchandise (such as the Standard Merchandise Classification) is combined with the automation of the checkout procedure and detailed inventory monitoring, opportunities for increased efficiency are enhanced.[107] In addition, the impact of this technology on the relations between retailers and their suppliers, due to the significance of the data generated by such systems, is likely to be enormous, as discussed in Chapter 10.

A host of electronic media for in-home or nonstore shopping, some of which are described in Exhibit 2–10, are in the testing phase. There is considerable controversy over the long-term impact of these new technologies. On the pro side are individuals who point out that one of the thorniest challenges to mail-order houses is the rising cost of catalogs.[108] For example, in 1980 it cost Spiegel over three dollars to print and distribute a single issue of its catalog. The cost today is closer to ten dollars. It is now possible to store catalogs on a videodisc that provides fast random access, improved color reproduction, sound, and either still or moving pictures. These video catalogs can be distributed directly to customers for use on videodisc players. Orders can be entered from the home via telephone or special terminals. The advantages are more convenient shopping, less travel, and (supposedly) merchandise priced below that found in high-overhead stores. According to Rosenberg and Hirschman, a sufficient base of consumers is emerging to support telecommunication merchandising, especially because of the poverty of time faced by consumers.[109] In support of the likely diffusion of videotext, it has been pointed out that (1) the infrastructure is being built to carry the communications, (2) standards are being estab-

---

[104] For a particularly striking example, see "How Giant Food Harnesses High Tech to Fatten Supermarket Profits," *Business Week* (December 5, 1983), p. 120.

[105] See Steve Weiner and Betsy Morris, "Bigger, Shrewder, and Cheaper Cub Leads Food Stores into the Future," *Wall Street Journal,* August 8, 1985, p. 17.

[106] Hypermarkets have come to the U.S. in the form of Bigg's in Cincinnati and Meier's in Grand Rapids, Michigan. See Steven Greenhouse, "Hypermarkets Come to U.S.," *New York Times,* February 7, 1985, p. D1. See also Roger Ricklefs, "French Hypermarkets Check Out the U.S.," *Wall Street Journal,* May 20, 1986, p. 34.

[107] See "Scanning Gains More Ground," *Chain Store Age—Executive Edition* (February 1977), p. 21.

[108] Joseph S. Mallory, "Paperless Retailing," *Booz-Allen's Outlook* (Fall/Winter 1980), p. 59.

[109] Rosenberg and Hirschman, *op. cit.,* p. 105.

EXHIBIT 2–10 New technologies for in-home and/or nonstore retailing

TELETEXT

Teletext is a system that combines computer and communications technologies for the widespread dissemination of textual and graphic information by electronic means, for display on low-cost terminals (e.g., suitably equipped TV receivers) under selective control of the recipient. It is a simple, one-way transmission as opposed to a two-way interactive system, such as videotext. Teletext first emerged in Europe in the mid 1970s with substantial government support. Information services include stock market reports, weather, news, sports, leisure information, games, and recipes. More than a million Britons are teletext users.

VIDEOTEXT

Videotext is a two-way, interactive electronic information system in which the viewer has direct access, by telephone or cable TV lines, to masses of data from a central computer. Users can summon up the information they need; and make transactions such as travel reservations, home banking, and teleshopping; send electronic mail; and take educational courses. The big advantage of videotext over teletext is that the number of pages it can deliver to the screen is virtually limitless, since the information is sent through wires rather than on the broadcast spectrum teletext uses. Any information, from encyclopedias to catalogs, can be committed to a videotext system for instant retrieval. Customers can access the information by telephone or by a two-way cable system. The desired information appears on the home television screen, which is connected to the telephone system through a decoder. By operating a keypad, a consumer can control the information appearing on the screen. Videotext subscribers pay more for the information they access than teletext subscribers because of on-line computer costs as well as hardware expenses.

VIDEODISC

Videodisc is an interactive electronic system that uses flat optical discs capable of storing vast amounts of information—in the form of moving pictures, still pictures, printed pages, and sound—for display on a TV screen. Videodisc technology allows the user to access data randomly and manipulate images for instruction, testing, game playing, and data storage. A single optical disc can store 108,000 individual still frames, the equivalent of 900 slide carousels.

INTERACTIVE CABLE TELEVISION

An interactive cable system, such as the Warner-Amex Cable Communications QUBE service in Columbus, Ohio, permits viewers to purchase merchandise displayed on their television screens and charge the cost to a credit card or bank account by punching a keypad. The system offers viewers the convenience of making impulse purchases from an armchair without having to make even a telephone call.

lished (by AT&T) that would ensure that any home terminal could operate with any videotext system, (3) the public is becoming more receptive to such space-age systems and is accelerating its purchases of electronic products for the home, and (4) dozens of major corporations are convinced that videotext offers great potential and are investing heavily in programs to make it work.[110]

On the con side, Quelch and Takeuchi have argued that,

> catalog programming on interactive cable television is unlikely to supplant the printed catalogs used by direct marketers or to emerge in the near future as a significant source of sales revenue for them.[111]

Their skepticism is based on the implied negative replies to the following questions:

- Will people watch catalog programs?
- Will consumers be willing to pay more than the regular monthly cable charge for an opportunity to view such programming?
- For those people who do watch, what advantages, if any, will it offer them over a printed catalog?[112]

And even if consumers are inclined to purchase a cable-advertised item, can they be certain that the price of the item is reasonable relative to store prices? Quelch and Takeuchi also find similar problems with interactive information retrieval systems (e.g., the graphics are unsophisticated; dresses look like they are made out of Lego blocks) and videocassettes and videodiscs (e.g., production costs greater than those of print media; incompatibility of equipment). Other critics point out that information providers have had difficulty identifying the services for which users would pay. But perhaps the most apt reason for the slow progress of the new technologies listed in Exhibit 2–10 is that in each instance the technological achievement exceeds the consumer demand.[113] As one observer has put it in discussing teletext and videotext, "they simply do not offer enough value to really take off."[114]

When all of these developments on the technological front are put together with all of the other environmental shifts already mentioned, the problems *and* the opportunities confronting retailers seem overwhelming. The need for increasingly sophisticated marketing management in retailing has never been more acute.

THE FUTURE OF RETAILING

Despite the existence of a number of highly successful and highly profitable companies in the retailing industry, it would be a serious mistake to conclude that the future of retailing is bright. With few exceptions, retailers can look

[110] "The Home Information Revolution," *Business Week* (June 29, 1981), p. 74.
[111] John A. Quelch and Hirotaka Takeuchi, "Nonstore Marketing: Fast Track or Slow?" *Harvard Business Review*, Vol. 59 (July-August 1981), p. 80.
[112] *Ibid.*
[113] Erik Sandberg-Diment, "When Technology Outpaces Needs," *New York Times*, June 9, 1985, p. F13.
[114] *Ibid.*

forward to very slow growth in sales and relatively low returns on their investments. The profitability of retailing is described in Chapter 11; a discussion of that topic is deferred until then. However, it is important to lay out here the reasons for this pessimistic outlook.

First, as May, Ress, and Salmon point out, annual growth in retail sales, measured in real dollars, will average only 2.3 percent.[115] While this is higher than the 1.73 percent growth rate from the mid 1970s to the mid 1980s,[116] it is not a very comforting figure. Second, there are just too many stores relative to the demand for goods and services.[117] This overstoring has led to poor space productivity and severe price-cutting in order to maintain existing levels of sales. (Retailers refer to price-cutting as "heavy promotional activity.") Until a major shake-out is completed, this condition is bound to exist for a considerable period. Third, with the exception of computer stores, optical stores (due to the graying of America), home improvement centers (which cater to do-it-yourselfers), toy stores (serving wealthy, indulgent yuppies and bountiful grandparents), and direct response marketing (particularly mail-order), all store types are expected to suffer. This is because the merchandise lines carried by most stores will not enjoy rapid growth. For example, sales of convenience goods and apparel are expected to be below average, while other goods' sales will grow at a faster rate but be nothing to write home about.[118]

Despite this gloomy picture, some important advice can be offered to retailers seeking to survive and even to prosper as the industry approaches the twenty-first century:

> The conventional retailers who truly deliver what many consumers expect from them, namely outstanding assortments, appropriate ambience, good service, and reasonable prices, will continue to prosper. Similarly, low-margin retailers who provide satisfactory assortments, good in-stock positions, and reduced transaction time will also flourish. The losers will be conventional retailers who charge traditional margins for marginal shopping experiences, and the low-margin retailers who raise margins while emasculating assortments and front-end service. . . . Effective execution of a sensible, coherent strategy will be more important than whether a retailer belongs to the conventional or low-margin fraternity.[119]

CONSEQUENCES FOR MARKETING CHANNEL RELATIONSHIPS

The consequences for marketing channel relationships of the various environmental factors facing retailers are profound and far-reaching. Many of the consequences have already been enumerated or implied in this chapter. Others will become evident in later chapters as issues relevant to marketing channel

---

[115] Eleanor G. May, C. William Ress, and Walter J. Salmon, *Future Trends in Retailing*, Marketing Science Institute Report No. 85–102 (Cambridge, Mass., 1985), p. 1.

[116] Davidson, Sweeney, and Stampfl, *op. cit.*, p. 47.

[117] See Jeremy Main, "Merchants' Woe: Too Many Stores," *Fortune* (May 13, 1985) pp. 62–72; and Hank Gilman and Steve Weiner, "Oversupply of Retail Outlets Is Seen as Big Cause of Holiday Price Cuts," *Wall Street Journal*, December 18, 1984, p. 37.

[118] May, Ress, and Salmon, *op. cit.*, pp. 8–95.

[119] *Ibid.*, p. 97.

management are analyzed. Rather than talk in abstractions, we provide here two brief examples of how some of the factors we have discussed are having important effects on channel relations. The first example concerns the food industry, and the second deals with the growth of off-price retailing in the apparel industry.

The Food Industry[120]

Inflation has changed the balance of power in the food industry. Food retailers who once relied mainly on customer service and wide assortments to secure differential advantages are now struggling to maintain profits while attempting to price below their competitors. Supermarket advertisements and in-store displays increasingly tend to feature generic or private-label products as opposed to name brands. The result of these pressures on food retailers is that supermarket operators are assuming more responsibility for marketing while trying to get manufacturers to absorb more of their costs.

Specifically, food chains are becoming more selective when it comes to choosing new products, especially size and flavor variations. They are also becoming more selective about the manufacturer promotions they will support with advertising and special displays. According to one observer,

> the amount and depth of temporary reduced-price deals has escalated to the point where manufacturers are losing control of their brands. They are "used" when the price is right—that is, when they are "on deal"—and pushed aside when they are not.[121]

Most of the merchandise sold by warehouse stores is bought "on deal," and these stores are growing in number and in market share, as shown in Exhibit 2–11. Food chains are also pressuring suppliers to improve credit terms and distribution methods in order to reduce expenses.

Manufacturers once held the balance of power in the food industry because of the tremendous advertising and promotion budgets they deployed to pull consumers into stores. Supermarkets deferred to suppliers' merchandising suggestions and relied on their data to determine what products to stock. Now supermarkets are collecting their own data and are resisting suppliers' efforts to force distribution. To a significant extent, generic and private brands awakened food retailers to their power. Because of the availability of these brands, companies like General Foods now find themselves competing with their own customers for shelf space and promotional support; e.g., they are competing with Safeway's generic brands. One study, funded by the Federal Trade Commission, went so far as to predict the following scenario for the year 1990:

> Each chain will have established its role as the store where one can buy with confidence. This will be backed by a combination of stores to service segmented markets, or by combinations of different store labels offering varying quality and/

[120] This example is drawn from Bill Abrams, "Food Chains Pressure Suppliers, Altering Industry Balance of Power," *Wall Street Journal*, August 21, 1980, p. 25. See also "No-Frills Food"; "New Worry for Manufacturers: Growth of Warehouse Outlets," *Wall Street Journal*, May 28, 1981, p. 23.

[121] Ronald C. Curhan, "Deals: Time for a Reshuffle?" *Progressive Grocer* (January 1982), p. 94. See also John A. Quelch, "It's time to Make Trade Promotion More Productive," *Harvard Business Review*, Vol. 61 (May-June 1983), pp. 130–36.

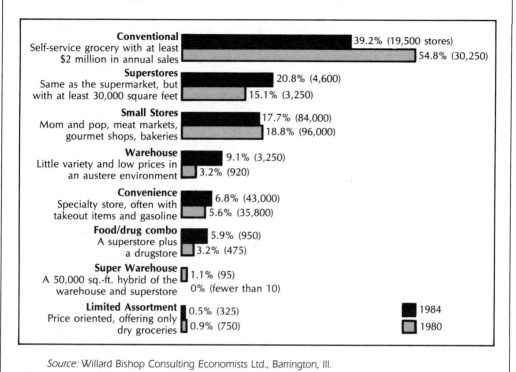

EXHIBIT 2–11   Where Americans shop for groceries
Market Share in 1984 and 1980

Conventional
Self-service grocery with at least
$2 million in annual sales
39.2% (19,500 stores)
54.8% (30,250)

Superstores
Same as the supermarket, but
with at least 30,000 square feet
20.8% (4,600)
15.1% (3,250)

Small Stores
Mom and pop, meat markets,
gourmet shops, bakeries
17.7% (84,000)
18.8% (96,000)

Warehouse
Little variety and low prices in
an austere environment
9.1% (3,250)
3.2% (920)

Convenience
Specialty store, often with
takeout items and gasoline
6.8% (43,000)
5.6% (35,800)

Food/drug combo
A superstore plus
a drugstore
5.9% (950)
3.2% (475)

Super Warehouse
A 50,000 sq.-ft. hybrid of the
warehouse and superstore
1.1% (95)
0% (fewer than 10)

Limited Assortment
Price oriented, offering only
dry groceries
0.5% (325)
0.9% (750)

■ 1984
▨ 1980

Source: Willard Bishop Consulting Economists Ltd., Barrington, Ill.

or price relationships along the entire competitive spectrum, or by a combination of these two approaches. Thus, the store and its store brands will become the equivalent in the consumers' eyes of the current national branded products.

The majority of shelf space in the store will be occupied by store labels, which carry maximum profitability to the retail operator. . . . Selected national brands may be carried. They will be selected largely by the determination of margin return per square foot.[122]

Nevertheless, even though manufacturers have lost some of their power, they still have a considerable amount left over. When they "blitz" products with advertisements and promotion, retailers find themselves under enormous pressure to carry the items. The FTC-funded study just cited amplified this point, but highlighted the investment required by manufacturers:

For the national processor to acquire needed shelf space allocations . . . , he will either have to have extraordinarily successful consumer pull, i.e., a significant

[122] Charles W. Williams, Inc., *Future Developments in the Food Industry: Probable Efforts at Vertical Integration by Food Retailers,* prepared for Office of Policy Planning, Federal Trade Commission (Washington, D.C.: Federal Trade Commission, 1981), pp. 65–66. See also a paraphrasing of this study, "Who Will Control the Food Industry," *Food Engineering* (January 1982), pp. 19–23.

number of consumers will be known not to shop in the store unless they carry the item, or he will have to offer trade discounts in exchange for the shelf space exposure. Another option may be in the leasing of specific amounts of shelf space which guarantee the retailer his target profit per square foot.[123]

The battle for shelf space contributed to the wave of food-company mergers and acquisitions during the 1980s. The larger the number of brand-name products a company has and the more money it can devote to advertising, customer coupons, and retailer discounts, the more shelf space it can command.[124] Even if they are "forced" to carry new products, supermarkets are more likely than ever to remove those that do not sell. And vigilant attention to sales performance will increase as more retailers install electronic checkout scanners that provide quick, detailed sales information.

Another major issue for food retailers facing high interest and labor costs is the expense of holding and handling inventory. Many stores are urging their suppliers to liberalize the typical 2 percent discount for bills paid within ten days. To reduce their inventories, some supermarkets also ask for faster delivery from supplier warehouses.

Retailer demands are starting to get a response from manufacturers. Pillsbury and its Green Giant subsidiary frequently are praised for their efforts. They hold rap sessions with stores, sometimes preprice merchandise, and "tray-pack" canned goods that can go to store aisles without much handling. Pillsbury's sales force helps stores build displays and plan advertisements. Price changes are sent to stores by Mailgram. Pillsbury also provides a rack (which it developed at its own expense but which does not bear its name) that retailers use to organize their refrigerated dough cases. Even Procter & Gamble, a company not known for its retailer-oriented perspective, has made a major response. In 1980, it led the food industry when it raised to seven cents from five cents the fee paid to stores for handling cents-off coupons.

Ironically, retailers might not benefit from the change in balance of power. Many industry experts believe that the stores will likely pass the savings along to consumers in the form of lower prices. The new innovations will merely increase competition in what is already an exceedingly competitive industry.

Off-Price Apparel Stores

Starting in the 1970s and continuing into the early 1980s, garment industry executives and the media focused much attention and energy on the growth of off-price stores, such as Loehmann's, T.J. Maxx, Marshall's, and Syms. Some retailing analysts were predicting that "off-price" would account for 25 percent of retail apparel sales by the end of the 1980s. Off-price retailing is characterized by (1) regular, everyday sale of medium- to high-quality products at deep discounts; (2) opportunistic purchase of closeout, late-season, overstocked, or slightly damaged merchandise at extremely favorable merchandise cost; and (3) conventional gross margins and high inventory turnover. Off-pricers differ from ordinary discounters (e.g., Venture, Target, K-Mart), who buy at regular wholesale prices and simply accept a lower-than-usual markup. The off-pricers

---

[123] *Ibid.*, p. 66.
[124] See Robert Johnson and Betsy Morris, "Food Companies Fight to Display More Products on Less Shelf Space," *Wall Street Journal*, April 10, 1986, p. 27.

keep their selling expenses down to the discounters' level, but they buy brand-name and designer-label merchandise at lower-than-normal wholesale.

Most sales by off-price stores are made at the expense of the traditional department stores. Paradoxically, the department stores were largely responsible for the rapid growth of off-price retailing. Bloomingdale's, Macy's, Shillito's, Rich's, Foley's, and all the rest of the traditional merchants brought on off-price by

- maintaining the same merchandise as one another (e.g., every major retailer carried Calvin Klein jeans) and differentiating themselves only on the basis of site selection and in-store ambience
- keystone pricing and keystone pricing plus additional markups ("keystone" pricing means that the retail price is arrived at by doubling the wholesale price)
- reducing services by having fewer salespeople, dropping free delivery, instituting charges for gift wrapping, etc.
- maintaining low backroom stocks[125]

The consumers who flocked to the off-price stores in the early 1980s had grown to realize that the "high touch" they were supposed to be receiving from the traditional stores wasn't worth the price those stores were asking. In other words, by substituting their own labor for what the department stores were promising but not delivering, they could save 30 to 50 percent on merchandise nearly identical to what the department stores were offering or had offered a season earlier.

But most important from a marketing channel perspective were the relationships between the stores and their vendors before and during the rapid growth of the off-pricers. The department stores had increasingly shifted business risks to their vendors by expecting them to share the costs of advertising and markdowns and insisting on returning merchandise. Also, given the high cost of money (especially during the late 1970s), the department stores looked for maximum credit extension from their sources of supply. They also asked to receive their orders in small installments so that if the first shipment sold poorly, they could cancel later shipments.[126] In contrast, the off-pricers were willing to buy in large lots, take any colors and sizes available, dispose of all goods that didn't sell (i.e., no returns to the vendor), have all goods shipped to one location, and pay on time, sometimes immediately upon delivery.

Although most designers and brand-name manufacturers would have preferred to deal with department and specialty stores exclusively, the contrast between the traditional retailers and the off-price merchants became too stark for them to ignore. When a retailer trims his assortment and orders only a fraction of the manufacturer's full line, places his orders later, and pays later, the manufacturer is forced to explore alternate avenues of distribution. Traditional retailers unwittingly pushed both the consumer and the manufacturer out the door, aiding the rise of what they wanted least: off-price retailers of quality merchandise.

[125] Ann M. Morrison, "The Upshot of Off-Price," *Fortune* (June 13, 1983), p. 124. See also Jack G. Kaikati, "Don't Discount Off-Price Retailers," *Harvard Business Review,* Vol. 63 (May-June 1985), pp. 58–92; and "This Business Is Anything but Threadbare," *Business Week* (August 18, 1986), pp. 98–99. The latter article chronicles the spectacular rise of Clothestime, one of the few success stories in the competitive and fickle off-price junior apparel business.

[126] Morrison, *op. cit.,* p. 124.

Off-pricers' willingness to take large quantities of merchandise was especially important to suppliers. Modern technology and multinational manufacturing arrangements have made it possible for manufacturers to produce more high-quality goods than ever before, often at lower cost. The existing retail accounts could no longer handle the manufacturers' normal capacity, much less their increased capacity.

By and large, the off-price tempo slowed considerably during the mid 1980s.[127] There were several reasons for this. First, traditional retailers began to bring their prices more in line with those of the off-pricers by engaging in frequent price promotions. Second, many department stores began to engage in opportunistic purchases to support special events. Third, traditional retailers developed or reemphasized major private-label programs (e.g., Bloomingdale's Bloomies, Dayton-Hudson's Boundary Waters, Federated's Allen Solly, and Neiman-Marcus's Competitive Edge)[128] thereby reducing their dependency on branded and/or designer items. Probably the most significant reason for the resurgence of the department stores versus the off-pricers was the improvement in the economy, which meant that traditional retailers could order most of the output of their vendors. However, whether relationships in the marketing channel have really changed for the better is uncertain. By and large, the atmosphere in the apparel industry is one of apprehension, anxiety, and mistrust. Strong, effective, and equitable interorganizational management among channel members is more the exception than the rule.

SUMMARY AND CONCLUSIONS

Retailing involves the direct sale of goods and services to ultimate household consumers. The overwhelming majority of retail sales are consummated in stores or retail establishments as opposed to other conduits, such as the mail, house-to-house selling, or vending machines.

The primary strategies available to retailers revolve around four operational dimensions. The first is concerned with margins and inventory turnover rates. During the twentieth century, a heavy emphasis has been placed on low-margin, high-turnover, minimum-service operations. Such operations have traded off between the services they perform for consumers and the prices they charge. Consumers have been increasingly willing to participate more heavily in the marketing flows.

The second dimension is concerned with assortments, whereby retailing institutions design and evolve product-mix strategies to suit changing shopping patterns. The third dimension is location. Decreased search-shopping patterns are making the location decision, particularly site selection, even more impor-

[127] See Janet Key, "Plums Stores Go Sour for Retail Giant," *Chicago Tribune*, March 5, 1984, Section 3, p. 1; Ed Leefeldt, "Off-Price Apparel Retailers' Rapid Growth Seems to Be Slowing, with Shakeout Likely," *Wall Street Journal*, January 23, 1984, p. 41; "Off-Price Apparel's Slip Is Showing," *Business Week* (April 8, 1985), p. 42; and "Why Designer Labels Are Fading," *Business Week* (February 21, 1983), p. 70.

[128] Hank Gilman, "Retailers Bet Their Designer Wear Can Lure You Past Calvin Klein," *Wall Street Journal*, February 1, 1985, p. 25; and Janet Key, "Retailers Hunt for Distinction," *Chicago Tribune*, December 18, 1983, Section 7, p. 1. See also Steve Weiner, "Caught in a Cross-Fire, Brand-Apparel Makers Design Their Defenses," *Wall Street Journal*, January 24, 1984, p. 1.

tant. While the emphasis is on convenience, there is a difficult tradeoff between one-stop shopping convenience and spatial convenience for many lines of retail trade. The fourth dimension is customer service. Large-scale retailers are becoming increasingly sophisticated at dividing their markets into segments with high, moderate, and low service requirements and have developed different means (through acquisition or internal growth) to serve each segment.

Retailers face an exceedingly complex and difficult set of environments. The consumer environment is marked by population shifts, the emergence of the "new" American family, changes in the age, income, and education levels of the population, and alterations in consumer values. Particularly notable and consequential for retailers have been the flight to the suburbs, the migration to the Sunbelt, the importance of smaller towns as markets, continued mobility, the increase in single-person households and in working wives, and the growing poverty of time. In addition, such factors as the graying of America, the significance of the baby boomers, and the increase in inner-directedness demand that significant emphasis be placed on life-style segmentation and positioning.

The competitive environment is exceedingly threatening. Increasing inter-type competition, polarization, vertical marketing systems, and free-form corporations combined with the acceleration of institutional life cycles mean that no retailer's market is secure from competitive incursions. Also, problems in securing capital, high labor productivity, facilities and real estate, and merchandise are likely to be a part of the retailer's landscape for some time. Adoption of new technologies will help considerably, but the risk is high because of the enormous investment required in purchasing and using such systems. Clearly, the need to employ sophisticated and effective management practices in retailing is critical for survival, not to mention growth.

While it is certain that new retailing institutions will continue to emerge and that existing institutions will continue to evolve during the remainder of the twentieth century, there is considerable room for innovative management within the present institutional mix. For example, as Bucklin observes,

> there are substantial frontiers yet to be conquered in tying together the wholesale and retail sectors of the business, improving logistics and inventory control.[129]

The next two chapters focus, respectively, on the wholesaling institutions comprising channels and on the management of logistical or physical distribution. Then, in Part Three, we focus on marketing channel strategy and design and on effective interorganization management of channel systems—the means by which the "frontiers" will be "conquered."

DISCUSSION QUESTIONS

1. The poet Paul Valéry once remarked, "Once destiny was an honest game of cards which followed certain conventions, with a limited number of cards and values. Now the player realizes in amazement that the hand of his future contains cards never seen before and that the rules of the game are modified by each play." Relate Valéry's statement to the problems facing high-level retail executives today.
2. One author has described the revolution in retailing as a process of "creative

---

[129] Bucklin, *Competition and Evolution*, p. 168.

destruction," because of the many new institutions that have appeared in this industry over the years. If, as McCammon suggests, institutional life cycles have shortened to approximately ten years, what types of institutional forms do you predict will arise in the 1990s to "creatively destroy" the institutions that are emerging as powers in retail trade today (e.g., warehouse technologies and organizations, and extensions of the supermarket concept)?

State fully the reasons behind your answer, including environmental factors you believe will help to bring about these changes.

3. Consider these environmental factors in answering the following questions:

    a. Assume that you are a high-level retail executive for a major chain of super-markets. Given your assumptions about the future, what strategies would you initiate to adapt your organization to the impending environment?
    b. If you were a manufacturer of household consumer durables, what action would you take relative to future retail distribution outlets for your products?

4. In your opinion, what kind of competition exists in retailing—perfect, monopolisti-cally competitive (atomistic), oligopolistic, or monopolistic? Explain in full, using a variety of lines of retail trade to illustrate.

5. With the continuing trend of scrambled merchandising and the proliferation of "me too" retail establishments, differences between competing outlets are often perceived as superficial by the consumer, with the result that a firm's advertising and promotion may often be attributed to a competitor. Consequently, many ana-lysts believe that store positioning will become the most important retail marketing strategy of the 1990s. Describe what you believe to be the various positioning strategies of

    a. Burger King
    b. Cadillac

Enumerate both the advantages and the disadvantages that seem to be associated with each of these strategies.

6. Assume that you are planning on establishing a major department store operation with several nearby branches somewhere in the United States. Outline the general steps you would undertake in conducting both an *inter-* and an *intraregional* location analysis for your store. Included in your outline should be a list of all the factors (population, buyer power, etc.) that you would consider for each type of analysis.

What types of locational assistance might you seek from manufacturers and wholesalers whose products you planned to carry?

7. Why is an understanding of the retail buying process important from an *interorgani-zational* perspective? If, through market research, a manufacturer determined that a retail buyer was using a linear choice model in making his merchandise selection, what general promotional tactics might he employ to help insure his product's selection? How would his tactics differ if the retail buyer were instead using:

    a. a conjunctive model
    b. a lexicographic model
    c. a disjunctive model

On an *a priori* basis, what situational factors might prompt the retail buyer to use one choice model instead of another? (*Hint:* Consider, for example, such situational factors as *perceived risk attached to the buyer's decision* and *amount of time available to make the decision.*) An answer to this question requires a reading of Appendix 2A.

8. What is meant by merchandising variety and assortment? What are the dimensions of assortment? What purposes does the merchandising budget serve? (See Appendix 2C.)

9. As the retailing environment becomes more turbulent, which of the following policy decision areas—location, merchandise selection, or inventory control—do you believe becomes more important, as well as more difficult for the retailer? Offer at least *three* compelling reasons in support of your position.

10. One of the important trends in retailing is increased intertype competition. Explain how Goodyear Tire & Rubber Co. has attempted to accommodate this trend through its distribution strategy for passenger tires. What kinds of retail outlets does Goodyear market its tires through?

Appendix 2A

Evaluative Procedures (Choice Strategies) Used by Retail Buyers

The evaluative procedures employed by retail buyers can be classified as particular types of decision rules or *choice strategies*.[1] The actual choice strategy that retail buyers use is a direct result of the type of decision problem they face when making their merchandise selection.[2] Because buyers must generally select merchandise from among a number of competing brands, all of which can be described in terms of their various attributes, the situation confronting the buyer can be accurately described as a *multiple-attribute decision problem*.[3] In general, evaluating individual brands and their respective sources of supply involves rating alternative sources along some or all of the following ten product attributes or performance parameters:[4]

- Demonstrated consumer demand (or projected demand, if a new product)
- Projected gross margin
- Expected volume

[1] Development of the choice strategy concept is found in Peter Wright, "Consumer Choice Strategies: Simplifying vs. Optimizing," *Journal of Marketing Research*, Vol. 7 (February 1975), pp. 60–67.

[2] The authors wish to acknowledge the significant contribution of Lynn W. Phillips to the development of the following discussion.

[3] For an overview of this type of decision problem see Kenneth R. MacCrimmon, "An Overview of Multiple Objective Decision Making," in J. L. Cochrane and M. Zeleny (eds.), *Multiple Criteria Decision Making* (Columbia, S.C.: University of South Carolina Press, 1973), pp. 18–44.

[4] This list is not necessarily in order of importance. Furthermore, the number of attributes considered by the buyer obviously varies from situation to situation. Doyle and Weinberg, for example, in a study of supermarket buyers' decisions, found that buyers examined only 8 dimensions, while Montgomery, in a similar study, reported that 18 factors were taken into consideration. See Peter Doyle and Charles B. Weinberg, "Effective New Product Decisions for Supermarkets," *Operations Research Quarterly*, Vol. 24 (March 1973), pp. 45–54; and David B. Montgomery, "New Product Distribution: An Analysis of Supermarket Buyer Decision," *Journal of Marketing Research*, Vol. 12 (November 1975), pp. 255–64.

- Merchandise suitability
- Prices and terms
- Service level offered
- Manufacturer reputation
- Quality of the brand
- Promotional assistance
- Vendor's distribution policy (national, regional, or local; exclusive, selective, or intensive)

The choice strategy, then, is the method by which the retail buyer evaluates each multi-attribute brand alternative and discriminates it from the others in order to arrive at a merchandise selection.

There are numerous choice strategies that a buyer might adopt.[5] To illustrate the application of multi-attribute decision models, consider the situation of a retail buyer choosing among potential suppliers of wristwatches. The buyer employing a *linear additive* choice strategy would first assign subjective weights to each of the ten product attributes according to the importance he places on each. For example, in the case of wristwatches, manufacturer's reputation and demonstrated consumer demand might be deemed more important by some retailers than a factor such as promotional assistance. Second, the buyer would judge each alternative according to the extent to which it seemingly possessed each of the attributes. One brand, for example, might be perceived as being of higher quality than the other brands under consideration. After assessing each alternative relative to each attribute, the retail buyer would then combine each of these unidimensional judgments according to a simple linear rule. This rule would dictate the selection, through a process similar to the one depicted in Table 2A–1, of the supply source offering the highest global utility index. In the wristwatch example, the buyer would choose brand 4 because of its superior overall evaluation.

On the other hand, the retail buyer might use a *conjunctive* choice strategy in making a selection. The results in this case could be different from those arrived at through application of the linear strategy.[6] Using a conjunctive model, the buyer would establish minimum cutoff values for each attribute and then compare competing brands against these values. If any of the brands were rated below the cutoff value on any of the attributes, it would be rejected as a choice

[5] All choice strategies may be carried out overtly, such as by pencil and paper calculation, or cognitively. In fact, most investigations of choice strategy paradigms involve an examination of how well they approximate actual cognitive processes. Although retail buyers could use either approach, their evaluations of potential suppliers often are done quickly and judgmentally because of their workload. See, for example, Doyle and Weinberg, *op. cit.*, p. 51. One possible strategy is the *linear additive* method of evaluation. For a review of this choice model, see William L. Wilkie and Edgar A. Pessemier, "Issues in Marketing's Use of Multi-Attribute Attitude Models," *Journal of Marketing Research*, Vol. 10 (November 1973), pp. 428–41. Empirical evidence indicating that retail buyers may cognitively use a linear additive method of evaluation has been marshaled by Roger M. Heller, Michael J. Kearney, and Bruce J. Mehaffey in "Modeling Supermarket Product Selection," *Journal of Marketing Research*, Vol. 10 (February 1973), pp. 34–37.

[6] Both Wright and Russ offer extended discussions of the nonlinear models presented here. See Peter Wright, "The Simplifying Consumer: Perspectives on Information Processing Strategies," a paper presented at the American Marketing Association Doctoral Consortium, East Lansing, Michigan, 1973; and Frederick Russ, "Consumer Evaluation of Alternative Product Models," *Combined Proceedings of the 1971 Spring and Fall Conferences* (Chicago: American Marketing Association, 1972), pp. 664–68.

Table 2A–1 Hypothetical application of a linear additive choice strategy for choosing among alternative brands of wristwatches

Attribute Considered	Importance of the Attributes to the Retail Buyer (A)	Judgments about Individual Brands of Wristwatches across All Attributes			
		Brand 1 (B_1)	Brand 2 (B_2)	Brand 3 (B_3)	Brand 4 (B_4)
Demonstrated consumer demand (or projected demand, if a new product)	0.9	0.5	0.9	0.4	0.8
Projected gross margin	0.8	0.6	0.6	0.4	0.6
Expected volume	0.7	0.6	0.7	0.3	0.7
Merchandise suitability	0.6	0.5	0.4	0.4	0.4
Prices and terms	0.5	0.5	0.4	0.6	0.5
Service level offered	0.5	0.5	0.3	0.4	0.5
Manufacturer reputation	0.6	0.5	0.6	0.3	0.8
Quality of the brand	0.7	0.6	0.5	0.3	0.8
Promotional assistance	0.3	0.5	0.4	0.5	0.5
Vendor's distribution policy	0.4	0.5	0.3	0.4	0.7
Global utility index for each alternative					
$$U = \sum_{i=1}^{n} A_i B_{ij}$$		3.22	3.32	2.33	3.90

where

U = overall judged utility of a brand alternative

A_i = numerical weight assigned to the ith dimension

B_{ij} = a numerical value for the jth brand alternative on the ith dimension

possibility. For example, in Table 2A–1, if the retail buyer established a minimum cutoff value of *0.5* for each of the ten dimensions, brand 1 would be selected as the best choice, because it is the only brand that meets or surpasses the established cutoff on each attribute.

Another approach that the retail buyer might use is a *lexicographic* choice strategy. Here, the buyer first orders the different attribute according to importance. Then the buyer compares all the alternative sources of supply on the single most important dimension. If one brand offers a noticeably better outcome on that dimension, it is selected. If, however, a number of alternative brands qualify, so that the buyer still cannot discriminate among the various available choices, he then drops down to the second most important attribute and repeats the procedure. This one-dimension-at-a-time process is followed until a choice is identified. In the wristwatch example depicted in Table 2A–1, brand 2 would now be selected, since it is perceived as surpassing all the other alternatives on the most important dimension—demonstrated consumer demand.

There are other choice strategies available to the retail buyer. These, as well as those already mentioned, are summarized in Exhibit 2A–1. Not presented are the hybrid or modified versions that some of these strategies may take

EXHIBIT 2A–1 Possible choice strategies a retail buyer may employ when selecting sources of supply

CHOICE STRATEGY MODEL	SPECIFIC STRATEGIES	STRATEGY DESCRIPTION
Linear	Linear additive	Weights are assigned to each attribute according to its perceived importance. Each supplier/brand alternative then receives a rating on each dimension. These are combined linearly to form an overall judgment for each supplier/brand alternative that can be compared in making the final selection.
	Linear averaging	Same as linear additive, except that the evaluative weights must sum to one to connote a dependency among the dimensions.[a]
Lexicographic	Regular lexicography	All supplier/brand alternatives are compared on the single most important dimension. If one surpasses all others on that dimension, it is selected. If not, the process continues along the other dimensions until the supplier(s)/brand(s) is (are) selected.
	Lexicographic semiorder	Same as regular lexicography, except that, even when a supplier/brand alternative surpasses other alternatives on the single most important dimension, if the difference is not a significant one, the comparison continues along the other dimensions until the supplier(s)/brand(s) is (are) selected.
Multiple Cutoff	Conjunctive	All suppliers/brands are compared against some minimum cutoff on each dimension. Those supplier/brand alternatives *below* the cutoff on any dimension are rejected.
	Disjunctive	Same as conjunctive, except that any supplier/brand alternative *above* the cutoff on any single dimension is accepted.
	Elimination by aspects	Minimum cutoffs are established for each attribute. Supplier/brand alternatives are eliminated that fail to surpass the cutoff on the most discriminating dimension, then the second most discriminating, etc., until all dimensions are exhausted or the supplier(s)/brand(s) is (are) selected. The most discriminating dimension is the one that will eliminate the most alternatives from further consideration.
	Sequential elimination	Minimum cutoffs are established for each dimension. Supplier/brand alternatives are eliminated that fail to surpass the cutoff on the most important dimension, then the second most important, etc., until all dimensions are exhausted or the supplier(s)/brand(s) is (are) selected.[b]

[a] For example, the weights, or A_i's in the utility index of Table 2A–1, would have to sum to one in order to indicate the *relative* importance of the dimensions, if it were to be an averaging model. An illustration of this choice strategy is presented in Chapter 5 in the discussion of how to choose among alternative channel strategies.

[b] An application of this choice model is also illustrated in Chapter 5.

Source: Lynn W. Phillips, "Evaluation Process Models: An Overview," an unpublished doctoral seminar paper, Northwestern University, 1975.

on.[7] For example, since it is possible for several alternatives to exceed all established cutoff values when a conjunctive strategy is used, a further discrimination procedure may be necessary to identify a final choice for the retail buyer. One such mode of discrimination is to combine the conjunctive strategy with a satisficing first-choice rule, whereby the brand chosen is the first one that meets all standards. Another mode of discrimination would be a multistage use of strategies, whereby the retail buyer might employ a conjunctive scheme to narrow the number of brand alternatives and then apply a lexicographic or linear strategy in making the final choice.

As mentioned, the choice strategy the retail buyer uses in judging brand alternatives has significant implications for the planning of marketing efforts on the part of suppliers seeking to serve the buyer. For example, if the buyer is using a lexicographic strategy, a supplier would do best to focus promotional efforts on what the buyer perceives as the product's most important attribute, because the supplier's brand will be chosen if it surpasses all other alternatives on this dimension. However, such an approach may not prove effective if the buyer is instead employing a conjunctive decision rule. Convincing the buyer that a supplier's brand is outstanding on one dimension will not be sufficient if the brand falls below standards set for the other dimensions considered. When a linear additive choice strategy is used, marketing efforts could be directed by a supplier at increasing his brand's rating on any dimension, because in light of the additive nature of the choice process the increase would positively affect the overall evaluation of the brand.

[7] See Hillel Einhorn, "The Use of Nonlinear, Noncompensatory Models in Decision Making," *Psychological Bulletin*, Vol. 73 (1970), pp. 221–30.

Appendix 2B

A Glossary of Pricing and Buying Terms Commonly Used by Retailers

Original Retail. The first price at which the merchandise is offered for sale.

Sales Retail. The final selling price.

Merchandise Cost. The billed cost of merchandise less any applicable trade or quantity discounts plus inbound transportation costs, if paid by the buyer. Cash discounts are not deducted to arrive at merchandise cost. Usually, they are either deducted from "aggregate cost of goods sold" at the end of an accounting period or added to net operating profits. If cash discounts are added to net operating profit, the amount added is treated as financial income with no effect on gross margins.

Markup. The difference between merchandise cost and the retail price.

Initial Markup or Mark-on. The difference between merchandise cost and the original retail value.

Maintained Markup or Margin. The difference between the *gross* cost of goods sold and net sales.

Gross Margin of Profit. The dollar difference between the *total* cost of goods sold and net sales.

Gross Margin Return on Inventory (GMROI). Gross margin divided by average inventory (at cost). GMROI is used most appropriately in measuring the performance of products within a single merchandise category. The measure permits the buyer to look at products with different gross margin percentages and different rates of inventory turnover and make a relatively quick evaluation as to which are the best performers. The components of GMROI are

Gross Margin Percentage		Sales-to-Inventory Ratio		GMROI
$\dfrac{\text{Gross margin}}{\text{Net sales}}$	$\times$	$\dfrac{\text{Net sales}}{\text{Average inventory (at cost)}}$	$=$	$\dfrac{\text{Gross margin}}{\text{Average inventory (at cost)}}$

Total Cost. Total cost of goods sold = Gross cost of goods sold + Workroom costs − Cash discounts

Markdown. A reduction in the original or previous retail price of merchandise. The *markdown percentage* is the ratio of the dollar markdown during a period to the net sales for the same period.

Off-Retail. Designates specific reductions off the original retail price. Retailers can express markup in terms of retail price or cost. Large retailers and progressive small retailers express markups in terms of retail for several reasons. First, other operating ratios are expressed in terms of percentage net sales. Second, net sales figures are available more frequently than cost figures. Finally, most trade statistics are expressed in terms of sales.

Markup on retail can be converted to cost base by using the following formula:

$$\text{Markup \% on cost} = \frac{\text{Markup \% on retail}}{100\% - \text{Markup \% on retail}}$$

On the other hand,

$$\text{Markup \% on retail} = \frac{\text{Markup \% on cost}}{100\% + \text{Markup \% on cost}}$$

F.O.B. The seller places the merchandise "free on board" the carrier at the point of shipment or other predesignated place. The buyer assumes title to the merchandise and pays all freight charges from this point.

Delivered Sale. The seller pays all freight charges to the buyer's destination and retains title to the goods until they are received by the buyer.

Freight Allowances. F.O.B. terms can be used with freight allowances to transfer the title to the buyer at the point of shipping, while the seller absorbs the transportation cost. The seller ships F.O.B. and the buyer deducts freight costs from his invoice payment.

Trade Discount. Vendors usually quote a list price and offer a trade discount to provide the purchaser a reasonable margin to cover his operating expenses and provide for net profit margin. Trade discounts are sometimes labeled *functional discounts*. They are usually quoted in a series of percentages, such as list price less 33 percent, 15 percent, 5 percent, for different channel intermediaries. Therefore, if a list price of $100 is assumed, the discount applies as follows for different channel members:

List price	$100.00	
Less 33%	33.00	retailer
	$ 67.00	
Less 15%	10.05	wholesaler
	56.95	
Less 5%	2.85	manufacturer's representative
	$ 54.10	

Quantity Discounts. Vendors offer two types of quantity discounts: noncumulative and cumulative. While noncumulative discounts are offered on volume of each order, cumulative discounts are offered on total volume for a specified period. Quantity discounts are offered to encourage volume buying. Legally, they should not exceed production and distribution cost savings to the seller owing to volume buying.

Seasonal Discounts. Discounts offered to buyers of seasonal products who place their orders before the season's buying period. This enables the manufacturer to use his equipment more efficiently by spreading production throughout the year.

Cash Discount. Vendors selling on credit offer a cash discount for payment within a specified period. The cash discount is usually expressed in the following format: 2/10, net 30. This means that the seller extends credit for 30 days. If payment is made within 10 days, a 2 percent discount is offered to the buyer. The 2 percent interest rate for 10 days is equivalent to a 36 percent effective interest rate per year. Therefore, the passing up of cash discounts can be very costly. Some middlemen who operate on slim margins simply cannot realize a profit on a merchandise shipment unless they take advantage of the cash discount. Channel intermediaries usually maintain a line of credit at low interest rates to pay their bills within the cash discount period.

Cash Datings. Cash datings include C.O.D. (cash on delivery), C.W.O. (cash with order), R.O.G. (receipt of goods), S.D.–B.L. (sight draft–bill of lading). S.D.–B.L. means that a sight draft is attached to the bill of lading and must be honored before the buyer takes possession of the shipment.

Future Datings. Future datings include:
1. ordinary dating, such as "2/10, net 30."
2. end-of-month dating, such as "2/10, net 30, E.O.M.," where the cash discount and the net credit periods begin on the first day of the following month rather than on the invoice date.
3. proximo dating, such as "2 percent, 10th proximo, net 60," which specifies a date in the following month on which payment must be made in order to take the cash discount.
4. extra dating, such as "2/10—30 days extra," which means that the buyer has 70 days from the invoice date to pay his bill and benefit from the discount.
5. advance or season dating, such as "2/10, net 30 as of May 1," which means that the discount and net periods are calculated from May 1. Sometimes extra dating is accompanied with an anticipation allowance. For example, if the buyer is quoted "2/10, 60 days extra," and he pays in 10 days, or 60 days ahead, an additional discount is made available to him.

Appendix 2C

Merchandise Planning and Control

Merchandise planning and control start with decisions about merchandise variety and assortment. Variety decisions involve determination of the different kinds of goods to be carried or services to be offered. For example, a department store carries a wide variety of merchandising ranging from men's clothing and women's fashions to sports equipment and appliances. On the other hand, assortment decisions involve determination of the range of choice (e.g., brands, styles or models, colors, sizes, prices) offered to the customer within a variety classification. The more carefully and wisely decisions on variety and assortment are made, the more likely the retailer is to achieve a satisfactory rate of *stockturn*.

The rate of stockturn (stock turnover) is the number of times during a given period in which the average amount of stock on hand is sold. It is most commonly determined by dividing the average inventory at cost into the cost of the merchandise sold.[1] To achieve a high rate of stockturn, retailers frequently attempt to limit their investment in inventory, which, in turn, reduces storage space as well as such expenses as interest, taxes, and insurance on merchandise. "Fresher" merchandise will be on hand, thereby generating more sales. Thus, a rapid stockturn can lead to greater returns on invested capital.[2]

While the retailing firms with the highest rates of turnover tend to realize the greatest profit-to-sales ratios,[3] significant problems may be encountered by adopting high-turnover goals. For example, higher sales volume can be generated through lower margins, which in turn reduce profitability; lower inventory levels may result in lost sales due to out-of-stock conditions; purchasing in small quantities may result in additional ordering (clerical) costs and the loss of quantity discounts; and greater expense may be involved in receiving, checking, and marking merchandise. Merchandise budget planning provides the means by which the appropriate balance can be achieved between retail stock and sales volume.

MERCHANDISE BUDGETING

The merchandise budget plan is a forecast of specified merchandise-related activities for a definite period. Although the usual period is one season of six months, in practice it is often broken down into monthly or even shorter periods. Merchandise budgeting requires the retail decision maker to make forecasts and plans relative to five basic variables: sales, stock levels, reductions, purchases, and

---

[1] It is also computed by dividing average inventory at retail into the net sales figure or by dividing average inventory in physical units into sales in physical units.

[2] Delbert J. Duncan, Charles F. Phillips, and Ronald Savitt, *Modern Retailing Management*, 10th ed. (Homewood, Ill.: Richard D. Irwin, 1983), p. 266.

[3] *Ibid.*, pp. 266–67.

gross margin and operating profit.[4] Each of these variables will be addressed briefly.

Planned Sales and Stock Levels

The *first step* in budget determination is the preparation of the *sales forecast* for the season and for each month in the season for which the budget is being prepared. The *second step* involves the determination of the *beginning-of-the-month* (B.O.M.) *inventory* (stock on hand), which necessitates specification of a desired rate of stockturn for each month of the season. If, for example, the desired stock-sales ratio for the month of June is 4 and forecasted (planned) sales during June are $10,000, then the planned B.O.M. stock would be $40,000.[5] It is also important, for budgeting purposes, to calculate the stock available at the end of the month (E.O.M. stock). This figure is identical to the B.O.M. stock for the following month. Thus, in our example, May's E.O.M. stock is $40,000 (or June's B.O.M. stock).

Planned Reductions

This *third step* in budget preparation involves accounting for markdowns, shortages, and employee discounts. Reduction planning is critical because any amount of reductions has exactly the same effect on the value of stock as an equal amount of sales. Markdowns vary from month to month, depending upon special and sales events. In addition, shortages are becoming an increasing problem to retailers. Shortages result from shoplifting, employee pilferage, miscounting, and pricing and checkout mistakes. Generally, merchandise managers can rely on past data in forecasting both shortages and employee discounts.

Planned Purchases

When figures for sales, opening (B.O.M.) and closing (E.O.M.) stocks, and reductions have been forecast, the *fourth step*, the *planning of purchases* in dollars, becomes merely a mechanical mathematical operation. Thus, planned purchases are equal to planned stock at the end of the month (E.O.M.) + planned sales + planned reductions − stock at the beginning of the month (B.O.M.). Suppose, for example, that the planned E.O.M. stock for June was $67,500[6] and that reductions for June were forecast to be $2500. Then,

Planned E.O.M. stock (June 30)	$67,500
Planned sales (June 1–June 30)	10,000
Planned reductions	2500
Total	$80,000

---

[4] All of these variables have been treated more fully elsewhere, should the reader desire more detail. See Duncan, Hollander, and Savitt, *op. cit.*

[5] There are numerous variations used to determine B.O.M. stock. See Duncan, Hollander, and Savitt, *op. cit.*, p. 229.

[6] Derived from a desired stock–sales ratio for July of 4.5 and projected sales for July of $15,000. Remember, June's E.O.M. is the same as July's B.O.M.

Less
Planned B.O.M. stock (June 1)   40,000

Planned purchases $40,000

The planned-purchases figure is, however, based on *retail prices*. To determine the financial resources needed to acquire the merchandise, it is necessary to determine planned purchases at *cost*. The difference between planned purchases at retail and at cost represents the initial markup goal for the merchandise in question. This goal is established by determining the amount of operating expenses necessary to achieve the forecasted sales volume, as well as the profits desired from the specific operation, and combining this information with the data on reductions. Thus,

$$\text{Initial markup goal} = \frac{\text{Expenses} + \text{Profit} + \text{Reductions}}{\text{Net sales} + \text{Reductions}}$$

A term frequently used in retailing is *open-to-buy*. It refers to the amount, in terms of retail prices or at cost, that a buyer is open to receive into stock during a certain period on the basis of the plans formulated.[7] Thus, planned purchases and open-to-buy may be synonymous where forecasts coincide with actual results. However, adjustments in inventories, fluctuations in sales volume, unplanned markdowns, and goods ordered but not received all serve to complicate the determination of the amount that a buyer may spend.[8]

Planned Gross Margin and Operating Profit

The *gross margin* is the initial markup adjusted for price changes, stock shortages, and other reductions. The difference between gross margin and expenses required to generate sales will yield either a contribution to profit or a *net operating profit* (before taxes), depending, of course, on the sophistication of a retailer's accounting system and the narrowness of his merchandise budgeting.

[7] Duncan, Hollander, and Savitt, *op. cit.*, p. 234.
[8] *Ibid.*

CHAPTER THREE

Wholesaling: Structure and Strategy

WHOLESALING DEFINED

One of the most confusing aspects of marketing channels is wholesaling. There are so many different types of wholesaling establishments that it is difficult to get a fix on just what wholesaling is. The nomenclature of the distributive trades adds to this confusion. Wholesalers are called jobbers, distributors, and middlemen, among other names. (Some of the names are unprintable, because of the antagonism towards wholesalers which has been built up over the years due to their alleged role in increasing the overall cost of distribution.) This problem of terminology is confounded by the fact that manufacturers' agents, rack jobbers, food brokers, commission merchants, and a host of other functionaries are also members of the wholesaling "industry." Therefore, any attempt to define just what a wholesaler is is bound to apply in some situations but miss the mark in others.

Nevertheless, to avoid semantic debates and to at least attempt a beginning, we can adopt the U.S. Bureau of the Census's definition for starters:

> Wholesaling is concerned with the activities of those persons or establishments which sell to retailers and other merchants, and/or to industrial, institutional, and commercial users, but who do not sell in significant amounts to ultimate consumers.

Of course, accepting this definition as the gospel truth means that every sale made by every organization to anyone but an ultimate consumer is a "wholesale sale." This would include every manufacturing firm (with the exception of the small amount of sales made through factory outlets to household consumers) as well as sales made by such diverse organizations as hotels, insurance companies, and accounting firms when they deal with "industrial, institutional, and commercial" users in booking rooms, arranging pension plans, or preparing annual reports.

In actuality, then, almost all organizations (except those dealing with ultimate consumers) are engaged in wholesale transactions. Taking such a broad perspective in this chapter would force us to consider every form of marketing at every level in a channel other than retailing. Our intention here is not to provide a global view of marketing practices but to take a brief look at some of the structural and strategic dimensions of wholesale trade—defined quite narrowly to encompass only the operations of specialized, independently owned and operated wholesaling institutions and establishments engaged primarily in domestic marketing. About 50 percent of the total output marketed "at wholesale" passes through such institutions and establishments. In addition, the focus in this chapter is largely on "merchant" wholesalers—independently owned firms that purchase goods from suppliers for their own account, operate one or more warehouses in which they receive and take title to goods, store them, and later reship them.[1] By assuming such a narrow focus, it will be possible to become more fully exposed to and examine more thoroughly those channel members normally referred to as wholesalers. This way, when we turn to specific approaches to channel management in later chapters, we may take account of the unique contributions, characteristics, and orientations of these institutions in forming the most beneficial systemwide strategies for the channel.

RATIONALE FOR THE EMERGENCE OF MODERN WHOLESALERS

The wholesaler's functions are shaped by the vast economic task of coordinating production and consumption, or, in Alderson's words, of matching heterogeneous demands for assortments at various levels within distribution.[2] Thus, wholesalers aid in bridging the gap between periods and places in which goods are produced and those in which they are consumed or used.

The sorting process of wholesalers is the key to their economic viability. It frequently happens that the quantities in which goods are produced or the characteristics with which they are endowed by nature do not match either the quantities in which they are demanded or the characteristics desired by those who use or consume them. Channel intermediaries (e.g., wholesalers and retailers) essentially solve the problem of the discrepancy between the various assortments of goods and services required by industrial and household consumers *and* the assortments available directly from individual producers. In other words, manufacturers usually produce a large quantity of a limited number of products, whereas consumers purchase only a few items of a large number of diverse products. Middlemen reduce this *discrepancy of assortments,* thereby en-

---

[1] Richard S. Lopata, "Faster Pace in Wholesaling," *Harvard Business Review,* Vol. 47 (July-August 1969), p. 131.

[2] Wroe Alderson, "Factors Governing the Development of Marketing Channels," in William G. Moller, Jr., and David L. Wilemon (eds.), *Marketing Channels: A Systems Viewpoint* (Homewood, Ill.: Richard D. Irwin, 1971), p. 20.

abling consumers to avoid dealing directly with individual manufacturers in order to satisfy their needs.

The rationale for a wholesaler's existence boils down to the functions he performs for the suppliers and customers he serves. That is, his economic justification is based on just what it is that he can do for his clientele, whether they be retailers, institutions (e.g., hospitals, schools, restaurants), manufacturers, or any other type of business enterprise. For example, with respect to his customers, a wholesaler can often provide the following services:

- *Physical possession.* A wholesaler can store goods in anticipation of customer needs and can provide quick delivery when the goods are desired because he is usually located closer to customers than more centralized manufacturing facilities.

- *Ownership.* Many wholesalers take title to the goods they store; therefore, they absorb inventory carrying costs for their customers. Customers can purchase from wholesalers in small lots; if they purchase directly, they generally must assume a larger inventory burden.

- *Information.* Wholesalers maintain sales forces, issue catalogs, advertise in trade journals, originate or participate in a wide variety of sales promotions, and provide technical assistance. As they engage in all of these activities, they provide valuable information to their customers about the products they carry as well as about market conditions affecting demand. The most sophisticated wholesalers also maintain on-line purchasing and inventory control information systems.

- *Financing.* A wholesaler finances the exchange process by investing in inventory and by extending credit to customers.

- *Risk-taking.* A wholesaler assumes risk when he takes possession and ownership of products that can deteriorate or become obsolete. In some circumstances, he assumes partial responsibility for product failures, warranties, and price fluctuations. He obviously takes risks by granting credit. In some instances, a wholesaler will even guarantee the sale of products or accept returns for full credit.

- *Negotiating.* Wholesalers generally bring together an *assortment* of merchandise, usually of related items, by negotiating with a number of different sources. Wholesalers generally negotiate terms and conditions with their customers, but in some cases these are set by suppliers.

- *Ordering.* A wholesaler can anticipate his customers' needs and thereby simplify their buying tasks. Rather than having to negotiate and purchase from a large number of sources, a customer can order from one source the assortment of products required. In addition, a wholesaler may inspect, test, or judge the products he receives for quality, thereby assuming an even greater role in the ordering process for his customers.

Thus, in the case of industrial goods needed in the assembly of a given product (e.g., transistors for radios), it may be less costly for the purchasing organization to place the burden of handling, owning, storing, delivering, and ordering the goods on a wholesaler rather than having to order in very large lots directly from the manufacturer, especially if the goods will have to be held for a considerable period before they are used up in the production process. Similar economies are available to purchasers of certain consumer goods, such as toys. For instance, almost 80 percent of all retail toy sales are made during November and December. Although thousands of toys are marketed every Christmas season, probably less than a hundred are best sellers. Because of the fickleness of consumers, retailers cannot accurately predict the demand for toys too far in advance. Therefore, they place numerous reorders of popular toys during the peak selling season. Wholesalers maintain large speculative inventories close to retail markets, thus permitting speedy delivery of toys on short notice.

As is pointed out later in this chapter, the preponderance of firms engaged in wholesale distribution are small, making under $5 million in annual sales. The typical wholesaler establishes the market connection between hundreds of manufacturers and end-users. Many of these manufacturers are themselves small businessmen who must rely on wholesalers to establish, maintain, and nurture markets for their products. The majority of customers are also small businessmen who look to wholesalers for many of the services just listed.

Pressure on Wholesalers

Wholesalers have been under increasing pressure, however, to prove and improve their economic viability. Several forces are threatening their standing in distribution. The most significant of these forces are, according to Bucklin, (1) the decline of the role and importance of wholesalers in importing and exporting; (2) the fact that manufacturers have expanded the scale of their factories, broadened their product lines, and integrated forward into distribution; and (3) the growth of chain stores.[3] These pressures started building during the late nineteenth century and have not abated since. In addition, the wholesaler's unique position in the middle of channels subjects him to the impact of the constant changes and innovations in the whole marketplace.

> Technological advances, product line proliferation, changing retail structures, and social adjustments are only a few of the real problems that complicate the wholesaler's life. Each improved product passing through the wholesale level generates a new demand for investments in warehouse space, market analysis, and sales training, and for myriad adjustments in the wholesaler's information systems. Each major retailing shift designed to satisfy customer needs obliges him to adjust his selling patterns, to review his customer service levels, to study product assortments, and to revise his strategies.[4]

The structure of wholesaling must, therefore, be capable of parrying or absorbing these changes.

THE STRUCTURE OF WHOLESALING

Wholesaling may be characterized as an industry in which the degree of specialization has constantly increased as a response to the waves of change just mentioned. In fact, as depicted in Exhibit 3–1, as well as in the appendix to this chapter, the amount of institutional variety in wholesaling is almost overwhelming. Such a variety offers buyers and sellers many channel choices, as dictated by such considerations as size, market segmentation, financial strength, services offered, and chosen method of operation. It also makes possible a high degree of

[3] Louis P. Bucklin, *Competition and Evolution in the Distributive Trades* (Englewood Cliffs, N.J.: Prentice-Hall, 1972), p. 203.
[4] Lopata, *op. cit.*, p. 131.

MERCHANT WHOLESALERS

Wholesale merchants or jobbers
Industrial distributors
Voluntary group wholesalers
Importers
Exporters
Cash-and-carry wholesalers
Retailer cooperative warehouses
Terminal and country grain elevators
Farm products assemblers
Wholesale cooperative associations
Petroleum bulk plants and terminals

MANUFACTURERS' SALES BRANCHES AND OFFICES

Sales branches (with stocks)
Sales offices (without stocks)

AGENTS, BROKERS, AND COMMISSION MERCHANTS

Auction companies
Import agents
Export agents
Selling agents
Merchandise brokers
Commission merchants
Manufacturers' agents

Source: U.S. Department of Commerce, Bureau of the Census, *1982 Census of Wholesale Trade, Industry Series,* Report No. WC82-1-1 (Washington, D.C.: U.S. Government Printing Office, 1985), Appendix A, p. A-9.

marketing flow or functional shiftability, whereby all wholesaling functions or a small part thereof may be shifted from one type of agency to another.

From a channel analysis perspective, it is important to understand what specific roles the various wholesaling institutions and agencies assume, so that when a channel is designed or adjusted, the appropriate kind of organization can be included. An essential piece of information in this regard is whether a wholesaler participates in all or only a few of the marketing flows (physical possession, ownership, promotion, negotiation, financing, risking, ordering, and payment). That is, assuming a manufacturer's or a retailer's perspective for the moment, what is it that one could expect to receive from a wholesaler in the way of services performed? Clearly, the more services performed, the higher the wholesaler's compensation will have to be from the channel as a whole. The appendix to this chapter provides a rather detailed, but not exhaustive, listing of the flows participated in by a variety of wholesaling enterprises. Table 3–1 provides a bare-bones summary of the appendix.

An examination of Table 3–1 indicates that full-function merchant wholesalers participate in all the flows while brokers and manufacturers' agents partici-

Table 3–1 Summary of wholesalers' participation in the marketing flows

	Physical Possession	Ownership	Promotion	Negotiation	Financing	Risking	Ordering	Payment
A. Merchant Wholesalers								
1. Full-function or service wholesalers	High	High	High	High	High	High	High	High
2. Limited-function wholesalers								
a. Drop shipper (desk jobber)	None	High	Low	High	High	High	High	High
b. Cash-carry wholesalers	High	High	Low	High	None	Low	High	High
c. Wagon (truck) jobbing	Low	Low	Low	High	Low	Low	High	High
d. Rack jobbers (service merchandisers)	High	High	High	High	High	High	High	High
e. Converters	Low	High	Low	High	High	High	High	High
f. Wholesaler-sponsored (voluntary) chains	High	High	High	High	High	High	High	High
B. Retailer-sponsored Cooperatives	High	High	High	High	High	High	High	High
C. Function Middlemen (Agents and Brokers)								
1. Brokers	None	None	High	Low	None	None	High	Low
2. Manufacturers' agents	None	None	High	None	None	None	High	Low
3. Selling agents	None	None	High	High	None	None	High	Low
4. Commission merchants	High	None	High	High	High	High	High	High

pate in only a few of them. Therefore, if a manufacturer were to "employ" full-function merchant wholesalers, the discount granted to these wholesalers would have to be considerably more than the commission he would have to pay to manufacturers' agents or brokers for selling his products to end-users. But when a manufacturer does not use a full-function wholesaler, he does not "save" the discount, because he must assume all of the services the wholesaler would have provided.

To provide some order and analysis to what must appear to the onlooker as a chaotic structure, scholars, merchants, and the U.S. Bureau of the Census have divided all of the various wholesaling institutions and establishments into the three major types shown in Table 3–2.[5] Several salient facts can be gleaned about wholesaling in general and about specific types in particular directly from this table or from computations based on its data. First, the volume of wholesale trade in *constant dollars* was almost half again as large in 1982 as in 1967.[6] Second, merchant wholesalers continue to hold the largest share of wholesale trade, and their share appears to be growing.

Third, there has been a substantial rise in the number of wholesale establishments: between 1967 and 1982, they increased by over 33 percent. Over the same period, the number of retail establishments remained relatively constant while retail sales grew at a rate comparable to that for wholesaling. This means that the differential in size between the typical wholesale and retail establishment has been continually declining. If size can be taken as an indicator of vertical market power, such a change may have vast implications for channel leadership.

What Table 3–2 does not show is another phenomenon similar to that taking place in retailing—the growing polarity of the wholesale trade. According to the *1982 Census of Wholesale Trade*, only 11 percent of the 321,410 firms in wholesaling in 1982 maintained multiple locations or, as the Census calls them, establishments. But these firms accounted for 68 percent of wholesalers' sales. Furthermore, for multi-establishment firms, sales averaged $10 million at *each* location compared with $2 million for single-establishment firms. Even though there seems to be a trend toward larger size, the average wholesaling firm is still very small. For example, 80 percent of merchant wholesalers employ less than 20 people.

Because of their obvious importance in the wholesaling structure, some additional developments within merchant wholesaling, among manufacturers' sales branches and offices, and among agents and brokers are mentioned in the remainder of this section.

Merchant Wholesalers

The sales of merchant wholesalers rose significantly over the period covered in Table 3–2. Likewise, the proportion of merchant wholesaler establishments increased rather dramatically over this period relative to the increase in the number of establishments of other wholesaler types. However, while overall

---

[5] Definitions of the various types of wholesalers can be found in the appendix to this chapter.

[6] Nationally, aggregate sales by wholesalers are larger than sales by retailers because of the large product flow to industrial markets that does not pass through the retail trade *and* because some products are sold two or more times by wholesale institutions.

Table 3–2 Trends in wholesaling establishments and sales, by type of wholesaler

	Establishments (number)					Sales (billions of dollars)				
	1963	1967	1972	1977	1982	1963	1967	1972	1977	1982
Total	308,177	311,464	369,791	382,837	415,829	358.4	459.5	728.5	1250.4	1997.9
	(percentage of total)					(percentage of total)				
Merchant-wholesalers	72.4	72.0	73.4	80.3	81.3	49.3	49.5	50.8	56.8	62.8
Manufacturer sales branches and offices	9.4	9.9	11.9	10.6	9.2	34.5	36.0	36.8	37.9	34.0
Sales branches (with stock)	5.3	5.4	8.4	7.0	5.3	16.2	15.4	18.0	18.6	16.9
Sales offices (without stock)	4.1	4.5	3.5	3.6	3.9	18.2	20.7	18.8	19.3	17.0
Agents and brokers	8.2	8.5	8.4	9.1	9.5	15.8	14.0	10.9	11.0	11.5

Some of the columns do not add up to 100 percent because of rounding or lack of data.

Source: U.S. Department of Commerce, Bureau of the Census, *Census of Wholesale Trade,* various years; and authors' calculations.

Table 3–3 Sales of selected durable and nondurable goods
by U.S. merchant wholesale groups

	Sales ($ billions)		% Growth
	1977	1982	1977–82
Durable Goods			
Total	296.0	476.8	61.1
Motor vehicles and automotive parts and supplies	55.1	91.4	65.9
Furniture and home furnishing	11.1	17.7	54.1
Lumber and other construction materials	27.6	33.1	19.1
Sporting, recreational, photographic, and hobby goods, toys, and supplies	8.1	13.7	69.1
Metals and minerals, except petroleum	32.8	49.0	49.4
Electrical goods	30.4	55.8	83.6
Hardware and plumbing and heating equipment and supplies	19.9	29.3	47.2
Machinery, equipment, and supplies	85.7	140.9	64.4
Nondurable Goods			
Total	380.1	682.5	79.6
Paper and paper products	15.1	25.9	71.5
Drugs, drug properties, and druggists' sundries	10.1	18.6	84.2
Apparel, piece goods, and notions	17.9	29.6	65.4
Groceries and related products	111.6	174.7	56.5
Chemicals and allied products	9.9	19.5	97.0
Petroleum and petroleum products	59.5	167.1	180.8
Beer, wines, and distilled alcoholic beverages	22.4	36.5	62.9
Tobacco and tobacco products	9.6	12.7	32.3
All Lines of Trade			
Total	676.1	1159.3	71.5

Sources: U.S. Department of Commerce, Bureau of the Census, *1977 Census of Wholesale Trade, Vol. II, Geographic Area Statistics, Part I, U.S. Summary* (Washington, D.C.: U.S. Government Printing Office, 1981); U.S. Department of Commerce, Bureau of the Census, *1982 Census of Wholesale Trade, Industry Series,* Report No. WC82-1-1 (Washington, D.C.: U.S. Government Printing Office, 1985); and authors' calculations.

growth—in sales and establishments—has been strongly positive, the success of merchant wholesalers has varied widely from the standpoint of individual commodity lines. (Sales of selected nondurable and durable goods by merchant wholesale groups are shown in Table 3–3.)[7]

Some merchant wholesalers have found considerable success by restricting their activities to a limited range of products within a product grouping. In groceries, drugs, hardware, and jewelry, specialty wholesalers have been able to aid retail chains in expanding their product lines in directions unfamiliar to chain buyers and merchandisers (e.g., nonfood items in grocery stores).

[7] Besides product class groupings, wholesalers can also be broken down into customer categories. Thus, one broad class of wholesalers sells retailers such diverse commodities as food, drugs, tobacco, hardware, dry goods, and appliances. Another class sells such items as food, paper products, and medical goods and supplies to restaurants and institutions. A third class sells building materials to builders and contractors. A fourth class sells manufacturing supplies such as tools, chemicals, and abrasives to manufacturers. In the complex automotive parts aftermarket, there are even warehouse distributors who sell only to other jobbers. However, growth generalities are difficult to make here because of the diversity of products included within each class.

Manufacturers' Sales Branches and Offices

Branches are captive wholesaling operations owned and operated by a manufacturer. Branch operations are common, for example, in electrical supplies (e.g., General Electric Supply Company) and in plumbing (e.g., Crane Supply Company and Arnstan–American Standard). Captive branch operations are also employed heavily by truck manufacturers, full-line farm equipment manufacturers, and large producers of major appliances.[8]

Manufacturers' sales branches are of two types: those that carry inventories and those that do not. As shown in Table 3–2, the growth of the former type has stopped, indicating that manufacturers are finding the cost of maintaining inventory-carrying branches increasingly prohibitive, especially given the interest rates prevailing in the late 1970s and early 1980s. With the average cost of closing an industrial sale approaching $600, it is little wonder that manufacturers are turning more frequently to merchant wholesalers for help, especially in tapping markets comprising smaller businesses.

Agents and Brokers

The resurgence of agents and brokers shown in Table 3–2 masks the decline in the relative importance of certain categories within this segment. Most particularly, as seen in Table 3–4, the share of manufacturers' agents (or representatives) has fallen dramatically. Manufacturers' agents sell noncompeting product lines for a commission; the primary marketing flows in which they participate are promotion and ordering. The economics of manufacturers' agents make them very attractive, especially because they don't get paid until they make a sale, and a supplier sustains little or no overhead burden associated with their upkeep, compared with the enormous drain associated with maintaining a company-employed sales force. For small or medium-sized manufacturers, the agent plays an increasingly important role. Only the heaviest hitters among manufacturers can sustain a string of field offices strategically situated around the country. Also, manufacturers' agents often offer other advantages, such as market knowledge, established customer relationships, and complementary lines of products.

If these are facts of life, then why is it that the shares of manufacturers' agents declined rather than increased between 1977 and 1982? The answer is relatively straightforward.[9] Bluntly put, manufacturers and their customers prefer to deal with company sales agents over manufacturers' agents. According to several studies, factory sales representatives are viewed in both consumer and industrial goods channels as direct links to the manufacturer, as providers of fast service and in-depth product knowledge, as experts in training others in the use of their products, and as loyal employees.[10] Clearly, there is considerable variance associated with each of these assertions, but by and large, it isn't that manufacturers' representatives are disliked;[11] it's that company sales agents are strongly preferred by most channel members.

[8] Lopata, *op. cit.*, p. 131.

[9] The answer can be derived analytically by employing transaction cost economics to "make versus buy" situations (e.g., vertical integration). This approach is discussed in Chapters 5 and 7.

[10] See Isadore Barmash, "Sales Reps under Pressure," *New York Times*, April 16, 1981; and "How Good Are Manufacturers' Agents?" *Industrial Distributor* (May 1982), pp. 119–25.

[11] Some *are* disliked. See "How Good Are Manufacturers' Agents?" *op. cit.*, p. 117.

Table 3–4 Sales by agent wholesalers (in millions of dollars), 1977 and 1982

Type of Operation	1977		1982	
	Volume of Trade	Percentage of Total	Volume of Trade	Percentage of Total
Auction companies	10,826	8.3	15,781	7.5
Brokers	30,585	23.4	71,750	33.9
Commission merchants	27,996	21.4	34,995	16.5
Import agents	3,920	3.0	11,860	5.6
Export agents	8,822	6.8	9,957	4.7
Manufacturers' agents[a]	48,369	37.1	67,232	31.8
Total	130,488	100.0	211,575	100.0

[a] Includes selling agents.

Source: U.S. Department of Commerce, Census of Business, *Wholesale Trade, Summary Statistics* (Washington, D.C.: U.S. Government Printing Office, 1977 and 1982).

How, then, can one explain the almost phenomenal share growth of brokers? This growth is due almost entirely to the growing importance of brokers in the food industry. Like manufacturers' agents, brokers market primarily noncompeting products, but these products are not complex. In other words, it is difficult for a company sales agent to gain a differential advantage in product knowledge over a broker, given the nature of the commodities a broker sells. Brokers have gained respect for themselves at headquarters (with buyers) as well as at the store level (with store managers) because of the range of services they offer. They follow products from point of entry into a customer's warehouse to point of exit from a customer's store, performing planogram, resetting, and shelf-detailing tasks as well as lending labor for special assignments (e.g., building aisle-end displays) when needed. Also, they have incorporated sophisticated computer programs that allow them to maintain on-line linkups with their customers and suppliers. In other words, they have added considerable value to the marketing channel, and their growth is evidence of their achievement.

SELECTING AND USING WHOLESALERS

It is an old axiom of marketing that it is possible to eliminate wholesalers (or any middlemen, for that matter) but impossible to eliminate their functions. The major question facing a manufacturer is whether, by vertically integrating (that is, by establishing his own sales branches and warehouse facilities), he can perform the functions more efficiently and effectively than a wholesaler. This question is a cause of considerable controversy in formulating marketing channel strategy.

The likelihood is that the cost of marketing through wholesalers is not going to be *vastly* different from the funds a firm would have to expend on its own to obtain the same services. If this is so, then what accounts for the large amount of direct selling that goes on? Why is vertical integration of wholesaling functions so popular, especially among large manufacturing and retailing firms?

The answer lies not only in *efficiency* considerations but mainly in *effectiveness* considerations. The fact that a given type of wholesaling firm participates in a number of marketing flows gives some idea about the *potential* for a division of labor in the channel. But the crucial question from a management perspective is to what extent (i.e., how *heavily*) and with what level of quality does the firm participate? To answer this question, we must first examine what it is that wholesalers can, ideally, provide. Then, we will juxtapose this description against a hard-nosed assessment of the orientation of many wholesalers.

How Can Wholesalers Serve Suppliers?

Ideally, wholesalers have a great deal of potential as channel partners for suppliers. From an operational perspective, suppliers of both industrial and consumer goods may rely on wholesalers for several key reasons:[12]

1. Wholesalers have continuity in and intimacy with local markets. Being close to customers, they are in a position to take the initial steps in the sale of any product—identifying prospective users and determining the extent of their needs.
2. Wholesalers make possible local availability of stocks and thereby relieve suppliers of small-order business, which the latter can seldom conduct on a profitable basis. Also, they tend to have an acute understanding of the costs of holding and handling inventory in which they have made major commitments.
3. Within their territories, wholesalers can provide suppliers with a sales force that is in close touch with the needs of customers and prospects. Also, because a wholesaler represents a number of suppliers, he can often cover a given territory at a lower cost than the manufacturer's own sales representative.
4. Wholesalers perform financial services for suppliers by providing volume cash markets through which they can recover capital that would otherwise be invested in inventories.

In its literature detailing some of its views on supplier-distributor management, Frank Lynn & Associates, a consulting firm specializing in distributor/dealer marketing, insightfully observes that the economic role of the distributor (or wholesaler) is to transfer marketing costs from the manufacturer into his own business.

In a well-run distributor marketing program, distributors assume some of the marketing functions (and the costs associated with performing these functions), which manufacturers would otherwise be responsible for:

- Carrying inventory
- Selling efforts
- Handling orders
- Extending credit

Distributors incur these marketing costs because the costs are integrally tied to the service requirements of their customers:

- Ordering flexibility
- Inventory support

[12] Many of these points have been made in more detail by Richard M. Hill, *Wholesaling Management* (Homewood, Ill.: Richard D. Irwin, 1963), pp. 10–14. See also Frederick E. Webster, Jr., *Industrial Marketing Strategy*, 2nd ed. (New York: John Wiley & Sons, 1984), pp. 194–204.

- Service and delivery
- Production scheduling
- Credit terms
- Single-source convenience[13]

Lynn points out that the sum of the marketing costs that distributors transfer into their businesses should determine the compensation they receive from their suppliers. Similar to the position taken in Chapter 1, Lynn argues that

> the discount that distributors receive compensates them for performing [the] marketing functions. . . . The mechanism that effectively transfers marketing costs to distributors is the distributor discount pricing structure.[14]

From the point of view of the manufacturer, the several salient factors shown in Exhibit 3–2 must be evaluated in determining the type of wholesaling establishment to use. These factors must always be conditioned by the nature of the ultimate market for the goods in question.

How Can Wholesalers Serve Retailers?

Manufacturers are generally self-centered and myopic. Their interest is to encourage retailers to promote and sell their own lines of products. On the other hand, wholesalers have a strong vested interest in building up their retail customers as merchants, since it is quite likely that, particularly in the case of smaller retail establishments, an individual wholesaler will be able to supply a large part of the retailer's requirements for merchandise. It is in the wholesaler's interest to spend considerable effort and resources training, stimulating, and helping retailers to become better managers. Therefore, wholesalers sometimes become highly knowledgeable in retail merchandise management. In this respect, the benefits to the retailer derived from relying on wholesalers may be described as follows:[15]

1. Wholesalers can give their retail customers a great deal of direct selling aid in the form of price concessions on featured items, point-of-sale material, and cooperative advertising, all of which are frequently generated by specific suppliers for wholesalers to pass along to retailers.
2. Wholesalers often can provide assistance in planning store layout, building design, and material specifications.
3. Wholesalers can offer retailers guidance and counsel in public relations, housekeeping and accounting methods, administrative procedures, and the like.

In the toy industry, for instance, many retailers prefer to make a significant proportion of their total annual toy purchases from wholesalers rather than from manufacturers, because, as one retail executive has indicated:[16]

1. In many instances reorders are filled more quickly.
2. Wholesalers guarantee the sale (any items not sold can be returned for full credit).

[13] Frank Lynn & Associates, Inc., *Is Your Distributor Discount Pricing Structure Costing You Money?* (Chicago: Frank Lynn & Associates, 1983), p. 2.
[14] *Ibid.*
[15] See Hill, *op. cit.*, pp. 16–21, for more explanation and details.
[16] Richard N. Cardozo and James E. Haefner, *Note on the Toy Industry,* Intercollegiate Case Clearinghouse, No. ICH 14M60 (Boston, 1970), p. 9.

EXHIBIT 3–2   Criteria of choice in the decision of what
type of wholesaling establishment to use—
point of view of the manufacturer

1. Evaluation of sales efforts of wholesaler
   a. Extent and activity of sales force of wholesaler
   b. Does sales force *sell*, or does it just take orders?
   c. Extent to which manufacturer must supplement wholesaler's sales efforts with own promotion, sales force, and/or detail men
   d. Number of lines handled by wholesaler
      (1) Does wholesaler handle too many lines to give sufficient attention to manufacturer's line?
         (a) Use of heavy advertising, good margins, realistic pricing to stimulate attention on part of wholesaler
         (b) Preference, sometimes, for more attention to individual line by use of specialty or limited-line wholesalers
      (2) Does wholesaler handle competing lines?
         (a) Use of sales or manufacturers' agents sometimes indicated
         (b) May necessitate creation of exclusive distributorships
2. Evaluation of relationship of wholesaler to channel of distribution for the product
   a. Type of wholesaler that can give widest distribution and assurance of sufficient retail outlets for line
   b. When particular types of retail outlets are desired, and what type of wholesaler can best handle them
   c. Quality and continuity of relationships maintained between wholesaling and retailing firms
   d. Degree to which wholesaler cooperates in promotion, pricing, financing, and other marketing activities
   e. Willingness of wholesaler to maintain continuous relationship with manufacturer

Source: Department of Marketing, Wharton School, University of Pennsylvania.

3. Defective products are replaced promptly.
4. The wholesaler extends long-term credit.
5. The percentage of markup by working through a wholesaler is more than offset by decreased inventory costs and improved service.

Obviously, the foremost advantage for many retailers in relying on wholesalers is the fact that the latter buy in large quantities, break bulk to suit the convenience of their customers, and then pass along the savings effected both in cost and transportation. These savings are frequently very favorable when compared with the costs of obtaining merchandise directly in small lots from distant points. Thus, by using wholesalers, independent retailers can avoid diluting the energies of their often overtaxed executive staffs. Furthermore, these retailers obtain access through wholesalers to a large group of products of small manufacturers that might not otherwise be available to them. Even for larger establishments, reliance on wholesalers allows conversion of dead-weight store space, formerly devoted to merchandise storage, into profit-making selling or customer service space. For example, although supermarket and discount chains can buy at the same price as a rack jobber or service merchandiser, the latter's hold on the market comes from knowing precisely what to buy and minimizing the handling and inventory costs of a variety of nonfood products, such as health and beauty aids, phonograph records, hardware, and sporting goods. And even for more mainstream grocery items, managers of large chains operating in widely scattered areas, such as Albertson's and Safeway, have found it beneficial to get some of their supplies from wholesalers.[17]

Some of the significant criteria retailers use in evaluating what type of wholesaler to "employ" are listed in Exhibit 3–3. As in the case of the manufacturer or supplier, these criteria are conditioned by the nature of the products the retailer carries and the market he serves.

How Can Wholesalers Serve the Business User?

Merchant wholesaler sales are divided about equally between retailers and business or industrial users. Although many of the advantages to the business user from relying on wholesalers are exactly the same as those mentioned for retailers, some additional factors are briefly discussed here.

[17] Ford S. Worthy, "Wall Street Warms to Supermarkets," *Fortune* (November 29, 1982), p. 146.

The short lead times on deliveries made available through wholesalers are especially important to industrial users. Flexibility in production scheduling can generally be achieved if production planners know that speedy local deliveries can be forthcoming. This factor is especially important for just-in-time (JIT) inventory scheduling, a development addressed in Chapter 4. Just-in-time is requiring industrial distributors to work more closely with manufacturing customers in planning inventory needs. The manufacturers are paring the number of distributors from which they buy in order to make closer planning more workable. And the introduction of just-in-time is requiring distributors to hold larger inventories, thus pressuring profit margins. However, just-in-time represents a great opportunity for many distributors who are capable of capitalizing on it. For example, Continental Glass & Plastic, a Chicago distributor, supplies containers to Walgreen Laboratories on a JIT basis; the laboratory uses the containers to package health and beauty aids for its parent, the Walgreen drugstore chain. Executives of Continental and Walgreen project Walgreen's container needs six months in advance. Four weeks before delivery, Continental is locked into a firm delivery date, though it has a three-day leeway on either side. While the seven-day margin is not exactly down-to-the-minute planning (as dictated by many JIT systems), it is a vast improvement over the past, when delivery dates were highly variable.[18]

Demands by customers for rapid delivery account for why industrial distributors, perhaps more than most types of wholesale firms, are plagued with small orders. One steel warehouse reported that 31.7 percent of the orders it received averaged $7.50 per order, created 32 percent of its administration cost, and contributed only 6 percent to its total sales.[19] A study of maintenance, repair, and operating supply distributors found that 80 percent of the orders placed by purchasers amounted to $100 or less. In many cases, 50 percent of the orders were for less than $40. Yet, that same 80 percent seldom exceeded 20 percent of the total dollar purchases.[20]

In addition, many types of wholesalers provide unique forms of technical assistance that are relatively costly to duplicate elsewhere, except in situations where a buyer can purchase in very large quantities. For example, machine tool and accessories wholesalers often have specialists on their staffs who are available to help customers with problems pertaining to the selection and use of tools and parts. It is not unusual to find such technically trained persons as metallurgists, chemists, draftsmen, and mechanical and civil engineers employed by wholesalers for this purpose.[21] And in data processing, wholesalers called *value added resellers* (VAR) have emerged who package computer software with computing equipment to solve specific problems for specific industries (e.g., inventory control for auto parts dealers).[22] Even managerial assistance is being increasingly provided to business users by wholesalers. Thus,

> an electronics distributor . . . analyzed the stockkeeping methods of one of his industrial customers and recommended revised delivery schedules, prearranged

[18] Steven P. Galante, "Distributors Bow to Demands of 'Just-in-Time' Delivery," *Wall Street Journal*, June 30, 1986, p. 23.

[19] J. Irwin Peters, "Industrial Distributors Solve Management, Cost Problems with 'Systems Contracting,'" *Marketing News* (May 1, 1981), p. 12

[20] Richard M. Hill, Ralph S. Alexander, and James S. Cross, *Industrial Marketing*, 4th ed. (Homewood, Ill.: Richard D. Irwin, 1975), p. 231.

[21] Hill, *op. cit.*, pp. 22–23.

[22] See Bro Uttal, "Pitching Computers to Small Business," *Fortune* (April 1, 1985), pp. 95–104.

items, packs suitable for assembly line use, and standardized item identification. The customer was able to reduce the possession costs on his stock by 15% of its value.[23]

Business users and retailers alike must be concerned with the overall or *ultimate cost* of the goods they purchase, handle, and store—not merely with the price at which such goods are obtained. When adequate accounting is made, it can often be found that the ultimate cost of dealing with wholesalers is less than the ultimate cost of dealing directly with manufacturers, even though the quantity discounts made available by the latter are not generally available when wholesalers are used as suppliers. This ultimate cost concept can justify the use of wholesalers in situations where they might not otherwise appear to be economical.[24]

Recognition of the ultimate cost concept by both wholesalers and their customers has led to a phenomenon called *systems selling*.

> Systems selling is a broad, inconclusive term that may be used to describe any form of cooperative contracting relationship between an industrial distributor and his customer for the ordering and distribution of low-value, repetitively used items for maintenance, repair, or operating (MRO) purposes, or for use in manufacturing original equipment.[25]

Wholesalers offer such purchasing systems in order to alleviate the high cost and paperwork facing firms seeking to acquire a wide variety of items, ranging from power tools and welding supplies to lamps, electronic equipment, and hardware. The major means employed by wholesalers' system selling arrangements to solve these problems include (1) shifting the bulk of the customer's on-premises MRO inventory back to the stocking wholesaler, (2) providing for automatic and semi-automatic ordering of these items on an as-needed basis, and (3) providing one-day delivery of the ordered items.[26] Customer benefits from the arrangement may include:

1. A reduction of the time spent in purchasing low-value items
2. A reduction in purchasing paperwork
3. Simplified requisitioning
4. More free in-plant storage space
5. Greater harmony and closer ties between customer and wholesaler

As Hannaford points out,

> A system selling arrangement changes the roles of supplier and customer as traditional channel autonomy is supplanted by the cooperative meshing of resources. Instead of the fragmented purchase of individual items, the system provides complete solutions to the product and service needs/problems of industrial customers.[27]

[23] Lopata, *op. cit.*, p. 140.
[24] The term *ultimate cost concept* was introduced to the authors by Richard S. Lopata and Richard E. Peterson, Principals, SAM Associates, Chicago.
[25] William J. Hannaford, "Systems Selling: Problems and Benefits for Buyers and Sellers," *Industrial Marketing Management*, Vol. 5 (June 1976), p. 139.
[26] *Ibid.*, p. 139.
[27] *Ibid.*, p. 141.

Indeed, the notion of system selling ranges far beyond applications to items used to support or maintain manufacturing processes. For example, a drug wholesaler in Columbus, Ohio, has provided a systems selling arrangement for a major discount chain relative to the chain's needs for health, beauty, and pharmaceutical items. The chain retains very little warehouse or backroom stock of the items; rather, the wholesaling firm provides all of the services required to maintain an adequate assortment of the items on the shelves of each of the chain's stores within its assigned territory. Similar arrangements exist between medical supply companies, such as American Hospital Supply Company, and a number of hospitals. Hospital employees have generally done a poor job of managing inventories on their own, and thus the increasing need to shift such functions back onto wholesalers.[28]

There are dozens of varieties of systems selling programs in operation. Exhibit 3–4 depicts two types of programs currently used by wholesalers—systems contracting and blanket ordering. While both involve contractual agreements that usually specify the vendor (i.e., the wholesaler) as the sole source of the designated items over the life of the contract, systems contracting goes further by providing a total system of solutions for customer purchasing problems.

[28] P. Ronald Stephenson, "Strategic Analysis of Wholesaler Distribution: A Study of the Medical Supply Industry," *Industrial Marketing Management*, Vol. 5 (March 1976), p. 39.

EXHIBIT 3–4 Characteristics of systems contracting and blanket ordering

SYSTEMS CONTRACTING	BLANKET ORDERING
1. Contract terms are relatively loose, founded on distributor–buyer trust and mutual cooperation:	1. Contracts are usually firm and relatively inflexible. Less cooperation and trust is required:
a. One contract can cover the distributor's entire product line of different MRO items.	a. Precise and specific single products (or closely related families of items) are specifically named in separate contracts.
b. Buyer does not specify quantities to be carried by seller and is not committed to buy any specific quantity.	b. Buyers specify quantities to be carried by seller and agree to buy that quantity over the life of the contract.
c. No specific termination date is necessarily required; contract is often subject only to periodic review rather than renegotiation.	c. Most contracts have six-month to one-year specified termination date. Contracts up for renegotiation are easily lost to competitors who bid lower prices.
d. Prices are not tied to duration of contract. Escalator clauses allow for price changes after notification and waiting period.	d. Prices are fixed for life of contract—a necessity because of fixed expiration date.
2. Vendor assumes financial and warehousing responsibility for contract inventories, guaranteeing specific standards of performance:	2. Responsibility for providing materials inventory remains with buyer. No standards of performance are guaranteed or imposed:
a. Sufficient stocking of contract items on distributor's premises, based on forecast of usage provided by buyer.	a. Vendor does not assume customer's stores functions.
b. 95% item availability at all times.	b. 95% in-stock item availability not guaranteed at all times.
c. Guaranteed 48-hour delivery or better; emergency deliveries immediately.	c. Delivery times not a critical factor: customer has storeroom.

3. Users of MRO items requisition stocks directly from Systems vendor. Purchasing department is not involved, except for general overseeing.
4. One billing transaction (invoice) sent monthly or semi-monthly; covers all requisitions for that time period.
5. All items under contract are listed in supplier's "catalog" (or tab report, printed list, card file) showing item descriptions, stock numbers, order quantities.
6. Separate cost-reducing services can be provided by the supplier as part of the total package, including:
   a. Information compiled on item usage.
   b. Consultation or technical seminars to educate users.
   c. Constant maintenance and servicing by supplier's salesmen.
7. Entire program and negotiations are often vendor-initiated and center upon the buyer's top financial, accounting, or purchasing management.

8. Program is sold on the basis of improving customer's total cost of procurement. Price is secondary consideration and is frequently *not* the lowest bid.
9. The cooperative relationship is characterized by a spirit of faith, trust, and harmony. Parties liken it to a marriage or true partnership.

3. Blanket Order releases do not go directly to vendor, but must first be approved by Purchasing Department.
4. Each requisition/delivery requires a separate invoicing procedure. No summary tally sheets for a period's orders.
5. No catalog of several items is needed; each contract is for a single, specific item or narrowly defined class of items.
6. No separate services are offered as part of the contract. Major means of cost reduction is through negotiation of lowest possible prices.

7. Program and negotiations are frequently customer-initiated and consist of an invitation to bid on a year's contract. Negotiations center around purchasing agents.
8. Purchasing agents insist upon price as the focal point. Total cost of procurement is not the basis of the contract, even if vendor would like it to be so.
9. The relationship is characterized by a short-term feeling of caution and distrust. Suspicion replaces faith and trust.

Source: William J. Hannaford, "Systems Selling: Problems and Benefits for Buyers and Sellers," *Industrial Marketing Management,* Vol. 5 (June 1976), p. 142.

This discussion of systems selling is included here not because we believe that systems purchasing is always an appropriate arrangement for customers of wholesalers,[29] but because it illustrates in a specific way the potential scope of a wholesaler's functions. In particular, it illustrates the ultimate cost concept. Wholesalers will rarely offer the lowest prices, but employing them as channel partners may provide *total cost* savings in the area of supplies procurement through reductions in costs associated with paperwork, vendor analysis, requisitioning, inefficient central stores operations, and the like.

A Hard-Nosed Assessment

Most of the preceding descriptions of what a wholesaler can do for suppliers, retailers, and business users provide optimistic pictures. However, the channel analyst should approach the selection of wholesalers as channel partners with a great deal of caution. Although wholesalers can spread the costs of participating in the marketing flows over an entire commodity line (e.g., groceries, electri-

[29] In a survey of 500 wholesalers, Hannaford found that 70 percent claimed to be involved in systems selling but that their systems accounted for 19 percent of their total sales or less. Hannaford, *op. cit.,* p. 140.

cal supplies, plumbing and heating equipment) and thereby have the potential for reducing the overall cost of distribution, they are not, for the most part, aggressive marketers because of their size, their managerial capacity and ability, and their traditional orientations. In fact, wholesaling firms are, in general, much more preoccupied with logistics and credit and collection functions than they are with marketing strategy. This preoccupation has meant that they have been severely out of position as major changes take place within certain industries, and have had to scramble to maintain viability within them.

While there are many significant exceptions to this generalization, merchant wholesalers—the dominant group among wholesalers both in numbers and in dollar volume—are, for the most part, very small family-owned companies (80 percent have sales of less than $5 million annually and employ less than 20 people) that rely on their contacts with other small companies, either suppliers or clients, for survival. These companies frequently lack management expertise and an infrastructure capable of putting into practice sophisticated marketing methods. They exist because the suppliers and/or customers with whom they are linked simply cannot afford to integrate the wholesaling functions and therefore must rely on such intermediaries to reach markets or obtain supply. Often the link between wholesalers and their clientele is more personal (e.g., family ties) than economic.

Over the past 40 years, the position of wholesalers has been significantly threatened with regard to the marketing of consumer goods. Relatively few wholesalers have been successful in meeting the challenges head on. Although there have been changes in the marketing of industrial goods too, it appears that wholesalers have, from a managerial perspective, shown greater adaptability and innovativeness in their approaches to industrial goods suppliers and markets than they have in their approach to consumer goods. To obtain a realistic perspective of wholesaling, it is important to delve briefly into developments in both sectors of the economy as they have affected wholesalers.

Consumer Goods.   Retailers have been particularly active in revolutionizing physical distribution practices. They have taken advantage of large-volume purchasing, warehousing, and delivery operations by forming mass merchandising chain organizations, as discussed in Chapter 2. To a large extent, as the chains grew and prospered, numerous wholesalers selling consumer goods continued to be order takers rather than developing expertise in marketing strategy and tactics. They relied on manufacturers to stimulate demand for brand-name products among ultimate consumers via advertising and waited for the generated demand to pull the brands through the channel. Indeed, many wholesalers were easily replaceable by retailers, because they no longer offered an economical or effective alternative to achieving sales or logistical services. What mass retailers could not obtain from the manufacturers directly, they could supply to themselves on their own. Wholesalers were quickly relegated to meeting the needs of small businesses. Because there are still tens of thousands of small manufacturers and retailers in existence, many wholesalers of consumer goods have continued to serve an economic purpose, but to a shrinking portion of the market.

On the other hand, those few wholesalers who saw the handwriting on the wall and tried to secure the marketing and physical distribution advantages of large-scale retail chain operations while permitting local ownership of individual retail units have succeeded handsomely. They formed voluntary (wholesaler-sponsored) chains (e.g., Super Valu Stores, Fleming, and Malone & Hyde in groceries), franchised systems (e.g., Midas International and Western Auto in the automotive aftermarket), and administered systems (e.g., Genuine Parts's NAPA jobber network for automotive parts) in order to gain efficiencies in purchasing, advertising, warehousing, accounting, inventory control, and virtually every other business function. They also permitted themselves to become part of retailer-sponsored cooperatives (e.g., Cotter's True Value and Ace Hardware). For example, almost 40 percent of total full-line hardware wholesaler sales are accounted for by so-called dealer-owned wholesalers. The return on investment of many of these various systems organized around wholesalers is frequently above 20 percent. Given that the average return for wholesaling corporations for which public data are available is around 14 percent, as shown in Chapter 11, the performance of these wholesalers is well above the norm. In fact, their effect on marketing channels is so important that a discussion of their activities is saved for Chapter 7, where we examine a number of vertical marketing systems, including those built around wholesalers, in which purposive interorganization management is being practiced.

Beyond those consumer goods wholesalers who have formed vertical marketing systems, there are others who have been successful without changing their corporate organization. Some have restricted their activities to a limited range of products and have sought market niches that do not require high sales volume to be competitive. In groceries, drugs, hardware, and jewelry, specialty wholesalers have been able to develop a substantial volume of business. For example, in the grocery trade, such firms supply such products as frozen food, dairy products, fancy or gourmet foods, bread and baked goods, and beverages. As Bucklin points out,

> they exist only to the extent that the inventory, handling, and transport requirements are so specialized that they cannot be duplicated by the chain (or general-line wholesaler) or that their product line is such that these competing organizations cannot attain sufficient volume to offset the costs of handling desirable assortments.[30]

Service merchandisers or rack jobbers have been particularly effective, because they generally supply the value-added services listed in Exhibit 3–5. The more successful specialty wholesalers, like rack jobbers, have been able to serve both large suppliers and large buyers, thus severing the wholesalers' traditional dependence on small-scale retailing.[31]

On the other hand, there have also been a number of general- or full-line consumer goods wholesalers who have achieved viability. Their route to success has been to improve their management and marketing practices, particularly by creatively utilizing advanced information-processing technology. McKesson Cor-

[30] Bucklin, *op cit.,* pp. 233–34.
[31] *Ibid.,* p. 235. For an excellent example in the magazine and paperback book industry, see Paul Doebler, "Charles Levy–Spawned Company Computerizes the Problems Out of Distribution and Sales," *Publishers Weekly,* Vol. 205 (February 4, 1974). See also "Napco: Seeking a National Network as a Nonfood Supermarket Supplier," *Business Week* (November 8, 1982), p. 70.

EXHIBIT 3–5　Services offered by service merchandisers
(rack jobbers)

MERCHANDISING SERVICES

Recommend type, brand, and amount of merchandise to stock
Design a plan for the rotation of goods, especially high-risk seasonal items
Develop merchandise "planograms" for stores
Prepare ad mats that customers can use in local newspapers

COMPUTER SERVICES

Track customers' sales and gross profit by category
Print price labels and conduct other paperwork
Provide tailor-made information upon request

SALESPERSON'S SERVICES

Check merchandise at the back of the store after it arrives from the warehouse to insure that the
customer receives exactly what has been ordered
Serve as a store consultant by helping managers plan and execute promotions
Plan the rotation of merchandise
Advise on in-store display techniques
Conduct in-store order writing
Stock shelves and keep them orderly

WAREHOUSE AND DELIVERY SERVICES

Receive shipments from manufacturers
Separate and warehouse shipments
Select, label, and box merchandise for individual stores
Deliver merchandise to stores

Source: From Hirotaka Takeuchi, *A Note on Wholesale Institutions,* 9-581-011. Boston, Harvard Business
School, 1980. p. 12. Adapted and reprinted by permission.

poration and Bergen Brunswig Corporation are excellent examples.[32] These
companies sell pharmaceuticals, over-the-counter drugs, and toiletries to small,
independently owned drugstores. While McKesson is highly diversified, over 40
percent of its sales revenues comes from its drug distribution business. Both
McKesson and Bergen Brunswig have adopted innovative electronic data-processing procedures that have brought efficiencies to pharmacists' handling of
inventories. For example, a clerk in a drugstore can alert a hand-held computer
to a product's identity by simply waving a small wand across a code on a shelf
label. Then the clerk can feed the computer an order for that particular item,
and the machine relays it over telephone lines directly to McKesson's or Bergen's

[32] This discussion of McKesson and Bergen is based on the following sources: Aimee L.
Morner, "Discovering the Drug Distributors," *Fortune* (February 8, 1982), pp. 99, 102; "Foremost-
McKesson: The Computer Moves Distribution to Center Stage," *Business Week* (December 7, 1981),
pp. 115–20; "McKesson's New Freedom Spurs a Shopping Spree," *Business Week* (October 24, 1983),
p. 172; "For Drug Distributors, Information Is the Rx for Survival," *Business Week* (October 14,
1985), p. 116; and Jennifer Bingham Hull, "Bergen Brunswig Is Ready to Expand Following National Intergroup Accord," *Wall Street Journal,* October 11, 1984, p. 8.

warehouses. Electronic systems have helped drugstores not only eliminate errors and reduce clerical expenses but also keep inventories down, because McKesson and Bergen can deliver within 24 hours. McKesson and Bergen also sell customized shelf labels and stickers for each product, priced to the druggist's specifications. And they can pack items in the order in which the merchandise will be placed on shelves. Both companies also provide retailers with management information reports, which measure sales and markups for groups of products in each store.

McKesson and Bergen have set up computerized accounts-receivable programs that enable pharmacists to offer charge accounts to preferred customers—something most small businesses cannot handle without investing in processing equipment of their own. The pharmacists can also check a patient's drug allergies or provide customers with records of drug purchases for submission with their tax returns.

McKesson has developed a pharmaceutical card system in which it plays the middleman between corporations and their employees in servicing medical insurance claims. Participating companies give their employees cards that are honored at 41,000 U.S. drugstores; employees can fill any prescription for a two-dollar charge. The pharmacist then sends a form to a McKesson clearinghouse, where computers forward bills to corporate benefits offices. Those offices then ship their payments to McKesson, which funnels them back to the druggists. McKesson receives a fee for the service, but its real benefit is tying itself all the more closely to its current drugstore customers.

In addition, McKesson operates a rack-jobbing service by setting up displays of cosmetics and jewelry in drugstores. It has built up a 1000-person rack-jobbing corps that operates from all of its 52 distribution centers. By relying on this service, drugstores can reduce their own, more expensive labor forces while securing more effective in-store displays of high-margin items.

On the supply side, McKesson and Bergen have established direct computer links with over 30 pharmaceutical manufacturers. These links permit electronic order processing. Because of this electronic data interchange (EDI) system, McKesson has been able to reduce its purchasing staff from 140 people to 13. By using computers to process information, McKesson and Bergen help manufacturers manage inventories, collect and analyze market data, and even plan sales campaigns and new product development. Some pharmaceutical manufacturers claim that electronic systems such as McKesson's and Bergen's have allowed them to cut down order turnaround time from 10–14 days to 1–3 days.[33]

According to a study conducted in the early 1980s for drug wholesalers by Booz Allen, there are strong expectations that drugstore chains will grow twice as fast as independent pharmacies, and increase their share of the retail drug market to 65 percent by 1990 (compared with 53 percent in 1979). As in other areas of retailing, more chains could decide to build their own warehouses rather than use distributors. (In 1983, for example, a subsidiary of Kroger, a major

[33] "For Drug Distributors, Information Is the Rx for Survival," *op. cit.*, p. 116. See also E. Raymond Corey, "The Role of Information and Communications Technology in Industrial Distribution," in Robert D. Buzzell (ed.), *Marketing in an Electronic Age* (Boston: Harvard Business School Press, 1985), pp. 29–51. For more information about EDI systems, see Louis W. Stern and Patrick J. Kaufmann, "Electronic Data Interchange in Selected Consumer Goods Industries: An Interorganizational Perspective," in Buzzell (ed.), *op. cit.*, pp. 52–73.

chain store customer of McKesson, decided to service its retail outlets itself.) In addition, supermarkets and mass merchandisers such as K-Mart are anticipated to lure more and more customers for prescription drugs. Therefore, the threat to wholesalers is likely to intensify. Only innovators, such as McKesson and Bergen, will continue to thrive in what is clearly an increasingly competitive environment.[34]

Neither McKesson nor Bergen is typical of wholesaling firms that sell items for resale. Both are significantly more advanced in their management practices than the norm. And yet neither McKesson nor Bergen could be described as a marketing giant. That is, while they have certainly developed systems for their retail customers, their major emphasis is on physical distribution—good inventory control and speedy ordering and delivery systems. Indeed, marketing for most wholesalers is equivalent to selling: the focus is on conversion of inventory into cash, on generation of sales volume, on short-run solutions, on the problems of individual customers, and on the importance of field work (e.g., selling or distribution). There are very few wholesalers who are preoccupied with profit planning, with analyzing long-run trends, threats, and opportunities, with studying customer types and market segment differences, and with developing strong systems for market analysis, planning, and control.[35]

Industrial Goods.   Manufacturers of many types of industrial goods tend to be more engineering-oriented than marketing-oriented. They prefer to allocate resources to research and production rather than to distribution, which they know has historically delivered a much lower return on investment. Given this orientation, it is not surprising that they frequently turn "troublesome" marketing problems over to distribution specialists. This is one of the reasons that industrial distribution, in contrast with consumer goods, has been a particularly viable sector of wholesaling over the years.

The situation involving industrial distribution is particularly intriguing because in some respects it is a microcosm of the dynamics of distribution generally. Industrial distributors are frequently viewed as a special class of merchant wholesaler. According to Frederick Webster, who has performed an extensive study of industrial distributors, this middleman

> sells primarily to manufacturers. He stocks the products he sells, has at least one outside salesperson as well as an inside telephone and/or counter salesperson, and performs a broad variety of marketing channel functions. . . . The products stocked include: *maintenance, repair, and operating* supplies (MRO items); *original equipment* (OEM) supplies, such as fasteners, power transmission components, fluid power equipment, and small rubber parts, which become part of the manufacturer's finished product; *equipment* used in the operation of a business, such as hand tools, power tools, and conveyors; and *machinery* used to make raw materials and semi-finished goods into finished products.[36]

[34] Another innovator is Alco Standard. See "Alco Standard: Getting Out of Manufacturing to Become a Big-Time Distributor," *Business Week* (March 26, 1984), p. 126.

[35] For an excellent discussion distinguishing selling from marketing, see Philip Kotler, "From Sales Obsession to Marketing Effectiveness," *Harvard Business Review,* Vol. 55 (November-December 1977), pp. 67–75.

[36] Frederick E. Webster, Jr., "The Role of the Industrial Distributor in Marketing Strategy," *Journal of Marketing,* Vol. 40 (July 1976), p. 11.

On average, industrial distributors are as small as the wholesalers serving retailers, but the median size is increasing as the number of distributors declines and as the market expands. The increase in size means that more firms are able to adopt electronic data processing for inventory control, order processing, and other administrative controls.

The distributor's importance in the marketing channel for industrial goods is growing for a variety of reasons, including the desire of manufacturers to shift more physical distribution responsibilities to distributors as a result of inflationary cost pressures; the tendency of a number of products (e.g., bearings) to become commodities, which permits distributors more control over the relationship with the customer because of the diminishing importance of brand names for such products; and the increased value that distributors are adding to products by performing special services, such as assembly and submanufacturing, for their customers.[37] For example, estimates by Joseph T. Ryerson & Son, a major metal distributor, indicate that the marketing of processed steels (steel that is cut or fabricated by the distributor) could go as high as 90 percent of its sales in the near future. The metals "service center" is no longer a "warehouse" where a buyer may go for small lots; it now adds value to the generic products it carries by performing such operations as welding, bending, shearing, and stamping.

From the supplier's perspective, industrial distributors have become more capable in fulfilling their major responsibility in the channel. That is, their job has been primarily to contact present and potential customers and to make the product available—with the necessary supporting services, such as delivery, credit, and technical advice—as quickly as is economically feasible.[38] In this respect, they may have discouraged the kind of integration of wholesaling functions so prevalent in consumer goods channels. In fact, it is much easier for the industrial goods manufacturer to go "direct" than it is for the consumer goods manufacturer, a point expanded upon in Chapter 5. It would, for example, be virtually impossible for General Foods Corporation to sell its products directly to thousands of individual retail stores, but it is feasible for Monsanto to sell its products directly to hundreds of industrial end-users. Thus, in consumer goods the major problem for wholesalers is the backward vertical integration of retailers into wholesaling. In industrial goods, the problem is one of manufacturers integrating forward. While such integration is occurring, the problem for wholesalers appears to be more acute relative to consumer goods.

One of the ways industrial distributors have maintained and even increased their importance in the marketing channel is by doing something some of their counterparts selling consumer goods have also done: they have specialized their operations. Product specialists represent more than 70 percent of all industrial distributors, up from 23 percent in 1964.[39] Although specialists carry fewer product lines than the general-line distributor, the inventory is usually deeper. As Webster points out,

> the trend toward specialization has generally been associated with increased technical competence and product knowledge. The specialist can offer greater depth,

[37] Webster, *Industrial Marketing Strategy*, p. 198.

[38] Webster, "The Role of the Industrial Distributor," p. 13.

[39] Tom O'Boyle, "Industrial Distributors Eye '80's Boom, but Shakeout Could Peril Smaller Firms," *Crain's Chicago Business* (October 29, 1979), p. 18.

including multiple brands, in a given product area. Some general line distributors have agreed to set up specialist departments as a condition for obtaining a leading product line. In other cases, manufacturers report that they are being forced to go to the specialist distributors, because of their wide acceptance in certain product areas.[40]

For example, more than 90 percent of Semiconductor Specialists' sales come from semiconductors and microprocessors alone. A. M. Castle, a metals distributor, sells more nickel, alloys, and specialty metals than its competitors. And Premier Industrial has 14 completely separate divisions, each with its own sales force, serving distinct markets, from J. L. Holcomb Manufacturing, which sells cleaning agents, brushes, insecticides, and the like, to Certanium Alloys & Research, which sells welding electrodes, brazing alloys, solders, and other welding aids. In addition to specializing their product lines, a number of distributors have hired technical experts, and this development has led to instances where distributor salesmen are more knowledgeable about a given technological area than the manufacturer's own salesmen. An outstanding example of these trends is Anixter Bros., a $650 million distributor of telephone, cable television, and other communicating products as well as electrical and electronic wire and cable (see Exhibit 3–6).

Another way in which industrial distributors have enhanced their role in

[40] Webster, *Industrial Marketing Strategy*, p. 199.

the marketing channel is the formation of distributor chains. Individual entrepreneurs have either acquired or established multiple outlets. As a result, they have been able to secure significant economies of scale by establishing one highly sophisticated inventory, purchasing, and distribution system. The merger trend is particularly strong among bearing and power transmission distributors. Mergers are often preferred to internal development because personal service in wholesaling is such a strong marketing factor: established distributors have an existing clientele that often can be retained after the merger. For example, Sysco Corporation, by acquiring over 40 small wholesalers, has become the largest American food distributor for restaurants, hospitals, and other institutions.[41] It has been able to amass economies of scale, power with food processors, and the ability to provide consistent quality in some 8000 items ranging from catsup to caviar to chef's hats. The company serves more than 100,000 customers in 139 of the nation's 150 leading metropolitan centers from its 64 distribution centers. Contrary to its effect on many smaller-scale wholesalers, the proliferation of large fast-food chains, such as Wendy's and Kentucky Fried Chicken, has helped Sysco grow, because most large chains prefer to use as few distribution companies as possible in order to keep better track of costs. The systems Sysco has put in place have met the chains' needs to such a degree that its customers engage in relatively little backward vertical integration.

Some of the advantages that distributor chains have over small, privately owned, single-warehouse firms are as follows:[42]

1. Inventory power. Chain inventories are not only deeper and cheaper but also broader and more diversified.
2. Large, linked warehouses. Such warehouses permit adding highly sophisticated computerized systems, purchasing in quantity, and stocking in depth, and result in lower warehousing costs per outlet.
3. Quantity discounts
4. Multiple brand coverage
5. Private labeling. This movement is particularly strong for such product lines as bearings, electrical motors and equipment, and MRO supplies. (For example, private labels account for almost 100 percent of Associated Spring's sales; 55 percent of W. W. Grainger's sales; and 90 percent of Lawson Products' sales.)

Selected operating data for six major industrial distribution chains are given in Table 3–5.

From a potential customer's perspective, the chains incorporate many of the attributes that are important to industrial customers in choosing a source of supply. They are able to keep delivery promises, offer a better discount structure, maintain an efficient phone order system, provide stock breadth and depth, offer technical services, enact appropriate sales procedures (e.g., regular sales calls), maintain a strong assortment of brand names, offer quick delivery time, and provide quality assurance. Indeed, because of their capabilities, they have created serious policy questions for manufacturers seeking to employ *both*

[41] See "Food Distribution: The Leaders Are Getting Hungry for More," *Business Week* (March 24, 1986), pp. 106–8; and John Gorman, "Food-Service Growth Fills Out Sysco Menu," *Chicago Tribune*, November 14, 1985, section 3, p. 1.
[42] "The Chain of Events in Industrial Distribution," *Marketing News* (January 30, 1976), p. 7.

Table 3–5 Selected data for six wholesale distributors

Company	Sales ($)	# of SKUs[a]	# of SKLs[b]	# of Salesmen	$ per SKU	$ per Salesman	Pages per Catalog	Geography	Return on Sales (%)	Return on Equity (%)
W. W. Grainger, Inc.	1160M	14,000+	196	650	82,850	1,785,000	1540	National	6.5	16
Lawson	140M	20,000+	5	1100[c]	7600	110,000	500	National	5.6	16
McMaster Carr	300M	140,000	3	None	2150	N/A	2005	National	N/A	N/A
Bearings, Inc.	500M	190,000	275	600	2630	835,000	2500	National[d]	2.2	10
United Stationers	550M	25,000	39	225	22,000	2,450,000	768	National	2.6	22
Syracuse Supply	105M	40,000	12	100	2625	105,000	1100	East Coast	.8	13

[a] SKL = stockkeeping location.
[b] SKU = stockkeeping unit.
[c] Manufacturers' reps—30 percent commission
[d] 35 States.

Sources: Presentation of Wiley N. Caldwell, President, W. W. Grainger, Inc., at Northwestern University J. L. Kellogg Graduate School of Management, April 14, 1987. Published data or best estimates. All figures are for 1984, 1985, or 1986.

independent and chain distributors in their channels. Some of these questions are as follows:[43]

1. Can we afford to offer exclusives to independents? to chains? If we offer them to independents, is there any way to protect existing exclusives and still sell to chains?
2. How do we sell to chains? Do we need separate sales forces, one for chains and one for independents?
3. Is our volume to chains large enough to permit us to withdraw our branch warehousing support to independents?
4. Should we help independents to pool?
5. How large a reduction in price are we willing to grant chains for assuming the entire warehousing burden?
6. Do we want to sell for private label sales?
7. What kind of discounting structure should we employ?

Despite the significant changes in industrial distribution just cataloged, manufacturers frequently remain frustrated by the low level of management competence among distributors and their lack of management depth, as well as by distributors' inadequate financial management and the frequent absence of provision for management succession.[44] In fact, industrial goods distributors, like their counterparts in consumer goods wholesaling, are viewed as basically noninnovative and unsophisticated, especially from a marketing perspective. Their sales agents are seen more as order takers than as creative individuals who are interested in finding new accounts and aggressively promoting new products. They are perceived by manufacturers to have little interest in market research and an inadequate source of information about the markets in which they operate.[45] Therefore, though there have been important improvements, industrial distributors, on average, appear to have a long way to go before they can be counted on to perform in accordance with the modern marketing concept.

Wholesalers have, however, been particularly strong in medical supply channels and in channels whose characteristics are similar to those found in the distribution of medical supplies. Several factors account for the importance of medical supply wholesalers:[46]

1. The large number of potential customers (There are over 7000 hospitals and approximately 330,000 physicians in the U.S.)
2. The small average manufacturer size (Average manufacturer sales volume is low. Even the largest firms can obtain only limited market coverage with a direct sales/distribution strategy.)
3. The small average transaction size (Even in the largest hospitals, average transaction size for one manufacturer's product line is likely to be relatively small. Therefore, selling costs per transaction would be extremely high if products were sold on a direct basis.)
4. The high inventory/service requirements (Substantial inventories must be carried locally, frequently adequate to support mandatory zero out-of-stock poli-

---

[43] *Ibid*, p. 7.
[44] Webster, *Industrial Marketing Strategy*, p. 200.
[45] *Ibid.*, pp. 200–201; and Webster, "The Role of the Industrial Distributor," p. 14.
[46] Stephenson, *op. cit.*, pp. 38–40.

cies. Also, logistics services must be available to support emergency delivery requests.)

By far the major player in this field is American Hospital Supply Corporation (AHS), now part of Baxter Travel, which distributes products from 8500 manufacturers to more than 100,000 health-care providers.[47] AHS saw its market share soar in the 1970s after it set up computer links to its customers and suppliers. The computer system that put the company in front of its competitors is called ASAP (Analytical Systems Automated Purchasing). ASAP is a network of computer terminals that allows approximately 3000 hospitals to order directly from AHS's distribution centers. The technology permits AHS to cut inventories, improve customer service, and obtain better terms from suppliers for higher volumes. Even more important from a strategic viewpoint, it often locks out rival distributors that do not have similar linkups to hospitals.

In contrast with the specialist trend mentioned earlier, AHS is a general-line supply house. It offers a wider variety of products than any of its competitors. Furthermore, it has more warehouses (over 120) and more company-owned delivery trucks than any other company in its industry. This distribution network combined with (and connected with) its computer network means that AHS's ability to respond to its customers' needs (especially in life-and-death situations) is unparalleled.

Some of AHS's major customers have begun to group themselves into formal affiliations (e.g., Voluntary Hospitals of America) or corporations (e.g., Humana, Hospital Corporation of America). Through central purchasing and warehouse arrangements (i.e., backward vertical integration), these groups could achieve considerable savings for themselves, thereby eliminating AHS from its supply channel. AHS diminished this possibility by establishing, in 1979, a corporate marketing program. The program offers participants rebates and price freezes when they reach volume purchasing goals. Corporate customers also qualify for low-cost consulting and management programs. The agreements all but eliminate the usual adversarial relationship between buyer and seller. The linkage becomes a "partnership," with hospital cost containment as a common goal. Within six years of its introduction, the program had secured agreements with hospitals representing 10 percent of U.S. hospital beds and had achieved, by itself, an annual sales revenue of $400 million for AHS. AHS's total sales revenue is more than $3 billion.

One of the major reasons for the continued prominence of wholesalers of industrial goods is the push-type marketing strategies adopted by industrial goods manufacturers. That is, rather than relying upon consumer-directed promotion, such as advertising and coupons, to stimulate demand at the end-user level and thereby pull the product through the marketing channel, industrial goods manufacturers place considerable weight on personal selling. Because wholesalers maintain large "inside" and "outside" sales forces and can spread the costs of their sales forces over a number of manufacturers' product lines, it

[47] This discussion of AHS was drawn from the following sources: "Information Power," *Business Week* (October 14, 1985), p. 109; Anne B. Pillsbury, "The Hard-Selling Supplier to the Sick," *Fortune* (July 26, 1982), pp. 56–61; Hal Lancaster, "American Hospital's Marketing Program Places Company atop a Troubled Industry," *Wall Street Journal*, August 24, 1984, p. 19; and Michael L. Millenson, "American Hospital Supply Stays Way Ahead of the Pack," *Chicago Tribune*, January 20, 1982, business section, p. 1.

frequently is more economical for manufacturers to look to wholesalers to provide the "push," especially for small accounts.[48] In addition, it is very expensive to maintain a series of distribution centers around the country that specialize in making a single manufacturer's product available to widely dispersed end-users in a variety of industries. Therefore, the selling and the physical distribution functions performed by wholesalers provide them with a differential advantage in the marketing of many types of industrial goods. Unfortunately, wholesalers have not, on average, fully capitalized on this advantage, primarily because of some of their managerial weaknesses alluded to previously.

THE STRATEGIC MANAGEMENT
OF WHOLESALING INSTITUTIONS

The two major *financial* factors determining the success of wholesalers, defined in terms of achieving target rates of return on investment or on assets, are the net profit margin and the asset turnover attained.

Margin Management

Net profit margin is a function of gross margin achieved and operating expenses incurred. Net profit is extremely sensitive to the level of gross margin. In wholesaling, a small change in gross margin (either positive or negative) will carry directly through to net profit, producing a disproportionately large change. As a result, gross margin is widely used as a critical decision variable at the wholesale level of distribution. Likewise, net profits are extremely sensitive to expense changes.

The margins that wholesalers receive are highly dependent upon the prices they are able to negotiate with suppliers, the prices they charge their customers, the mix of products they carry (their assortments), the market segments they choose to serve, and their desired growth rates. In the long run, strategic decisions surrounding these critical variables commit individual firms to specific gross margin and operating cost characteristics. For example, Stephenson has observed that in the medical supply industry,

> a high growth strategy . . . involves commitment (on the part of wholesalers) to the hospital market with relatively low gross margins and the need for highly streamlined operating characteristics producing low average operating costs. On the other hand, emphasis on the physician segment means relatively high available gross margins, but commitment to a high operating cost strategy—high sales/service requirements, increased logistical demands, and relatively small average transaction size.[49]

Margins vary widely by line of trade served, depending, of course, on the needs and requirements of customers served. Thus, gross margins of electrical supply distributors vary from over 25 percent for MRO items sold to industrial accounts

---

[48] See James A. Narus and James C. Anderson, "Industrial Distributor Selling: The Roles of Outside and Inside Sales," *Industrial Marketing Management*, Vol. 15 (1986), pp. 55–62.

[49] Stephenson, *op. cit.,* p. 41.

Table 3–6 Gross margins achieved by leading industrial distributors

Company	Gross Margin (Percent)
Lawson Products	70.2%
Premier Industrial	45.2
Barnes Group	34.8
Vallen Corp.	34.5
W. W. Grainger	29.0
Bearings, Inc.	28.7
Columbia General	26.1
Anixter Bros.	25.4
Kaman Corp.	24.3

Source: Bert C. McCammon, Jr., *Investment Opportunities in the Distribution Industry: A Strategic Analysis* (Norman, Okla.: Distribution Research Program, Center for Economic and Management Research, University of Oklahoma, 1981), Exhibit 10.

to less than 10 percent for household appliances sold to retailers. Leading industrial distributors can usually generate gross margins exceeding 25 percent (see Table 3–6).

Asset Management

In addition, wholesalers can generate high rates of asset turnover through intense asset management. Typically, a very high proportion of total assets (over 60 percent, as shown in Table 3–7) are invested in the current category, primarily in accounts receivable and inventory. Unlike the manufacturer who has heavy

Table 3–7 Composition of assets for wholesaling corporations

Assets	Percentage
Current assets	
Cash or its equivalent	6.9
Accounts receivable	25.3
Inventory	26.5
All other	3.8
Total	62.5
Fixed assets	
Property, plant, and equipment	22.8
All other	14.7
Total	37.5
Total assets	100.0%

Source: U.S. Bureau of the Census, *Quarterly Financial Report for Manufacturing, Mining, and Trade Corporations,* First Quarter 1985, Series QFR-85-1 (Washington, D.C.: U.S. Government Printing Office, 1985), p. 139.

investments in fixed plant and equipment, the wholesaler is in a position to exercise strong short-term credit and inventory controls in an effort to achieve desirable asset turnover levels. Furthermore, the overall liquidity of wholesaling operations means that it is very difficult for a wholesaler to go bankrupt. Three factors seem to account for the average wholesaler's buoyancy, irrespective of his marketing failings. First, the typical wholesaler has a multiplicity of suppliers and customers; therefore, he is not dependent on any one source of supply or sales. Second, many wholesalers are able to turn over their inventories about six times a year, on average, which means that they are a maximum of 60 days away from a cash position. Third, they are generally only 50 days away from cash relative to accounts receivable. The question then is not usually how to achieve appropriate asset management for survival purposes, but rather how to generate a high rate of return.

Accounts Receivable.   With regard to accounts receivable, it is often the case that 90 percent or more of a wholesaler's sales are made on a credit basis. Proper use of credit in building sales, as well as effective employment of the capital invested, therefore requires careful attention to the management of the credit function. Achieving an adequate cash flow is critical to a wholesaler's operation and demands careful attention to the evaluation and selection of credit risks, collection of accounts, and overall control of credit. For example, the average collection period varies considerably among different kinds of wholesale business, depending in part on the customary terms of sale. (The average collection period for certain grocery wholesalers is only 14 days, compared with 45 to 50 days in dry goods, footwear, and floor coverings.)

Inventory.   In wholesaling as well as in retailing, achieving a reasonably high inventory turnover rate is one of the prime prerequisites to obtaining an adequate rate of return on invested capital. Higher profits on investment are gained both through the effect that a high turnover rate has on operating expenses (as turnover increases, the costs of possession—interest on capital invested in inventory, insurance, property taxes, and warehousing space—decline) *and* on the amount of capital invested in inventory. However, various surveys and trade conferences suggest that the merchant wholesaler's major problem is inventory control and management.[50] Such a heavy investment in inventory is made necessary by the large number of items that wholesalers must carry in order to serve the needs of their clients. Compounding the problem is the fact that suppliers are generating enormous quantities of new products. For example, the automotive distributor carries over 70,000 identifiable items, compared with 40,000 ten years ago. Furthermore, many of the items wholesalers must carry are slow-moving articles that are required infrequently but, when needed, are vital to the operations of the wholesaler's customer.

Some of the wholesaler's reactions to his inventory problems have been (1) to demand that suppliers reduce the size and variety of the lines they offer; (2) to select only popular items from among a supplier's line (a practice called *cherry picking*); or (3) to select items and set stock levels according to item demand and item movement.[51] In the last case, wholesalers are dropping many slow-moving and/or low-revenue-producing supply items from their assortments while plac-

[50] Lopata, *op. cit.,* p. 138.
[51] *Ibid.*

Table 3–8 Benefits derived by selected wholesalers from developing management information systems

Performance Measurement	Results Achieved with	
	Conventional Data Processing System	Management Information System
Inventory service level	84.6%	89.6%
Gross margin/net sales	17.3%	20.6%
Average inventory (number of weeks supply)	14.8	13.0
Gross margin/average inventory	73.6%	103.9%
Contribution margin/average inventory	49.6%	79.9%

Source: Management Horizons Data Systems, as reported in Bert C. McCammon, Jr., and James W. Kenderine, "Mainstream Developments in Wholesaling," a paper presented at the 1975 Conference of the Southwestern Marketing Association, p. 7.

ing stronger sales efforts behind higher-priced product lines with larger dollar volumes. Concomitantly, these wholesalers are retraining sales agents as equipment demonstrators and discouraging them from merely taking small orders.

Clearly, improved management practices are a prerequisite to improved performance in the inventory control area. Such practices must not only encompass the setting of minimum order policies but must include the broader aspect of developing effective management information systems based on up-to-date electronic data processing. Some of the potential benefits available to wholesalers who adapt more sophisticated methods are shown in Tables 3–8 and 3–9. Indeed, the discussion of inventory control in Chapter 4 is exceedingly pertinent to wholesaling; without appropriate management of the marketing flows of ownership and physical possession, the wholesaler will not only derive lower rates of return but will also lose a significant amount of his value to the channel as a whole.

Table 3–9 Benefits derived by selected wholesalers from adopting improved management practices

Management Practice	Number Order Lines per Manhour
Minimum order policy	9.3
No minimum order policy	8.8
Out-of-stocks deleted before orders are picked	13.1
Out-of-stocks deleted after orders are picked	8.2
Item location shown on order or pick ticket	9.3
Item location not shown on order or pick ticket	8.6
Picking sequence specified on order or pick ticket	9.4
Picking sequence not specified on order or pick ticket	8.7

Source: Hardware Institute for Research and Development, as reported in Bert C. McCammon, Jr., and James W. Kenderine, "Mainstream Developments in Wholesaling," a paper presented at the 1975 Conference of the Southern Marketing Association, p. 7.

FUTURE TRENDS
IN WHOLESALE DISTRIBUTION

In 1982, Arthur Andersen and Company completed a Delphi forecast of the wholesale distribution industry. The study was sponsored by the Distribution Research and Education Foundation of the National Association of Wholesaler-Distributors. Among the conclusions of the study were the following predictions:[52]

- The size of individual wholesale distribution companies will increase significantly in real terms. By 1990, companies with sales of more than $20 million will account for nearly 80 percent of total volume.
- Acquisition and merger will be a major growth strategy.
- Geographic expansion will be a major growth strategy as companies use technology to reach new market areas at relatively low costs.
- Wholesaler-distributors will compete over an increasingly diverse geographic area. By 1990, the number of companies servicing a radius of 100 to 300 miles will increase by 20 percent while those servicing a more-than 300-mile radius will increase by 35 percent.

Regarding functions performed by wholesalers, the study specifically addressed likely changes in the flows of promotion, information, physical possession, and ownership. Among its predictions were these:[53]

- By 1990, there will be as many inside as outside sales agents in the average wholesale distribution firm. The roles of the inside and outside sales forces will change. Inside sales personnel will perform more of a selling role, as distinct from order-taking, while the outside sales force will perform more of a promotional and marketing function.
- Computer information systems will make possible important changes in marketing strategy and growth in sales. Seventy-five percent of all wholesaler-distributors will use on-line order entry systems by 1990; 83 percent will use computer systems for internal marketing and sales analysis.
- Sales shipped by wholesaler-distributors in their own delivery vehicles will drop from 59 percent in 1980 to 38 percent in 1990. Common and private carriers not owned by the wholesaler-distributor delivered an estimated 20 percent of sales in 1980. This is expected to increase to 40 percent by 1990.
- The number of companies using on-line information systems for purchasing and inventory control will more than triple current levels. Seventy percent of all wholesaler-distributors will use these systems by 1990. (Table 3–10 shows the relative increases in the use of purchasing and inventory control information systems.)

Overall, the study results are bullish on the future of wholesaling. For example, the panelists predicted that total sales by wholesaler-distributors will grow in real terms by 4.9 percent per year between 1986 and 1990, a rate higher than that forecasted for the gross national product. The upbeat nature of the findings must be tempered by the fact that the 250 panelists may have been

[52] Arthur Andersen & Co., *Future Trends in Wholesale Distribution: A Time of Opportunity* (Washington, D.C.: Distribution Research and Education Foundation, 1982), pp. 7–8.
[53] *Ibid.*, pp. 8–9.

Table 3–10 *Projected use of purchasing and inventory control information systems*

Projected Use	Percentage of Wholesalers			
	1970	1980	1985	1990
On-line order entry	5%	15%	40%	75%
Order processing systems	4	15	35	55
On-line inventory control	5	20	40	70
Automatic reordering	5	10	25	50

Source: Arthur Andersen and Co., *Future Trends in Wholesale Distribution: A Time of Opportunity* (Washington, D.C.: Distribution Research and Education Foundation, 1982), p. 33.

closely associated with the wholesale-distribution industry in one way or another and, therefore, potentially favorably disposed towards it. Not enough information is given in the published report of the study about the composition of the sample to enable one to assess the degree of possible bias. Nevertheless, even if the study reflects the views of those who are friends of the industry, it provides a useful perspective on where they believe wholesaling is headed.

CHANNEL MANAGEMENT ISSUES IN USING WHOLESALERS

With the exception of the large, professionally managed wholesaling firms, such as Genuine Parts Company in the automotive industry, McKesson Corporation and Bergen Brunswig Corporation in the drug industry, Anixter Brothers in the wire and cable industry, W. W. Grainger in industrial supply, Sysco in food service, Graybar Electric Company in electrical supply, Fleming Companies in groceries, American Hospital Supply Corporation in medical supplies, and Earl M. Jorgensen Company in metals, most wholesaling firms can, as indicated, be categorized as small, entrepreneurially oriented, relatively unsophisticated, and generally risk-averse businesses. Therefore, when a manufacturer turns to a wholesaler for assistance in making his products available for sale and for stimulating demand among industrial, institutional, or commercial end-users or among retailers, he cannot give up his own responsibility for effective marketing, nor can he expect the wholesaler to respond to all his suggestions. For example, Frank Lynn & Associates argues that

> the manufacturer is responsible for establishing his brand's identity with the end-user, and for pulling his product through the marketing channel. The distributor only supplies the product; the manufacturer must create the demand for it.[54] Distributor marketing. . .presents a. . .different set of market conditions:
>
> - The distributor is an independent business that "sits" between the manufacturer and the end-user thereby filtering the manufacturer's perspective of what is happening in the marketplace

[54] Frank Lynn & Associates, Inc., *Distributor/Dealer Marketing* (Chicago: Frank Lynn & Associates, 1982), p. 9.

- The distributor operates his business to maximize his own best interests which may or may not coincide with the best interests of the manufacturer
- The distributor controls where his sales force goes, who they call on, how frequently they call, and which products they "push"

As a result, the manufacturer has a very limited ability to exercise *control* over a distributor marketing program—it has to be managed! This "managing" versus "controlling" requirement is one of the reasons why many companies find distributor marketing to be so difficult and so distasteful.[55]

Hlavacek and McCuistion warn that manufacturers should not assume that distributors will get their products specified.[56] They point out that only in unusual cases does an engineering type of distributor get the specifying job done, and that a solution for manufacturers is to designate a company person to perform the task. If the required specification work is not done for him, the distributor will not get the order. W. C. Howard, vice-president of the Norton Company, a manufacturer of abrasives committed to distributing its products through wholesalers, has supported this view but gone even farther. He has said that distributors do not do well in establishing new accounts or in missionary selling of new products or concepts to established accounts. Their forte is selling existing products to existing accounts (i.e., maintenance selling).[57]

Given these realities, manufacturers must assume new responsibilities for making wholesalers more effective through programs of product development, careful pricing, promotional support, technical assistance, order servicing, and training for wholesaler sales representatives and management.[58] Specifically, manufacturers employing wholesalers must do the following:[59]

1. Make certain that the functions to be performed are clearly understood and that margins fairly reflect the value of these functions to the manufacturer and the cost to the wholesaler of performing them well.
2. Train, supervise, and compensate company sales agents so that they are knowledgeable about working with wholesalers and are motivated to do so.
3. Take an active role in building up the competence of the wholesaler's organization, with particular emphasis on product knowledge, salesmanship, account management inventory level decisions, product line profitability analysis, and market area analysis.
4. Expect to take an active role in marketing, because many activities (such as direct mail promotions, the development of effective catalogs, and local advertising) may be beyond the wholesaler's capabilities.

All of these activities will result in making the wholesaler a more effective channel partner. In the long run, the manufacturer can expect to deal with a

[55] Frank Lynn & Associates, Inc., *Distributor Marketing Handbook*, Vol. 1 (Chicago: Frank Lynn & Associates, 1977), pp. 2–3.

[56] James D. Hlavacek and Tommy J. McCuistion, "Industrial Distributors: When, Who, and How?" *Harvard Business Review*, Vol. 61 (March-April 1983), p. 98.

[57] W. C. Howard, "Capitalizing on Distributor Strengths," a speech to the Conference Board Marketing Conference in New York, 1975. (Reprint obtained from the Norton Company, Worcester, Mass.)

[58] Webster, *Industrial Marketing Strategy*, p. 208.

[59] Derived from *ibid.*, pp. 208–9. Although Webster focuses here on industrial goods wholesaling, it is the authors' belief that his suggestions apply with equal, and sometimes with more, force to consumer goods wholesaling. Therefore, they are presented here as being generic to wholesaling, irrespective of the type of goods.

larger and stronger wholesaling organization, which he has helped to create. The development of mutual dependencies will produce a more cohesive channel system.

SUMMARY AND CONCLUSIONS

The significance of the wholesaler's role in a channel of distribution is defined by the efficiency of his sorting function, whereby he helps match the heterogeneous output of suppliers on the one hand with the diverse needs of retailers and industrial and business users on the other. There have been increased pressures on wholesalers to prove their economic viability in this respect.

Many suppliers use wholesalers to reach their smaller customers because they prefer to turn troublesome, supposedly lower-return distribution activities over to specialists. The benefits available to suppliers (manufacturers, growers, etc.) from wholesalers are continuity in and intimacy with local markets, local availability of stocks, coverage of small-order business, lower costs because wholesalers can spread overhead over many suppliers' products, and relief from the burden of holding inventory.

Often wholesalers' perceived interests are more directly involved with the well-being of retailers than those of manufacturers; therefore, it is logical to assume that wholesalers would develop approaches to assure the survival of retailers. Many wholesalers do, in fact, offer retailers direct selling aid, expert assistance in all aspects of retail operations, local and speedy delivery, relief from inventory burdens, quick adjustments, credit extension, and, in some cases, guaranteed sales. Business users can receive many of the same benefits, which may be especially important when it comes to production scheduling and technical assistance.

While it has been noted in this chapter that the average wholesaler appears to have some significant weaknesses as a marketing entity, it is important to reemphasize, in any discussion of wholesaling, that a wholesaling firm can be removed from a channel of distribution, but that some other institution must be capable of performing the tasks formerly done by the firm. Removal of a wholesaler is valid from a societal point of view only if the tasks performed by the wholesaler can be either partially eliminated or performed more efficiently by some other institution.

DISCUSSION QUESTIONS

1. Distinguish between a wholesale sale and a retail sale (e.g., sales at wholesale versus sales at retail).
2. Consider the following statement:
   "A wholesaling operation can be eliminated as an entity, but someone must perform the wholesaling tasks and absorb the costs formerly sustained by the wholesaler, if it is assumed that those tasks are necessary."
   Take a position on this statement, pro or con, and offer support for your reasoning.
3. Why do manufacturers appear to have a "keener desire to participate more actively in the wholesaling process," as evidenced by the existence of manufacturer sales branches and sales offices?

4. Debate the pros and cons of forward vertical integration, particularly of wholesaling functions.

5. Prescribe what a wholesaler needs to do over the next ten years in order to remain a viable entity. Should he stand pat or make changes? If the latter, what changes? (Pick specific industries, such as steel, groceries, hardware, drugs, electronics.)

6. Would you say that inventory control is a more *or* less important policy decision for wholesalers than it is for retailers? How might inventory management and control problems and approaches differ between wholesalers and retailers?

7. Wholesaling is often thought of as a less than glamorous intermediary venture when compared with other channel intermediary operations, such as retailing. In your opinion, which of these two would be the more difficult to manage—a wholesaling or a retailing operation? Which would seem to have the best chance, on the average, of achieving a high ROI (return on investment) today? Which line of trade would you say has had to face more challenges to its survival in the last 50 years?

Appendix 3A

Participation in the Marketing Flows by Different Types of Wholesalers

Wholesaling agencies, their functions, and the marketing flows are described in this appendix. *Note:* All of the agencies described are pure types; in real life we often find agencies that are composites of several of these types.

A. *Merchant wholesalers.* Merchants whose principal business is buying goods in job lots and reselling them for a profit to customers who (1) resell the goods again to someone else, or (2) consume the goods in the course of operating a profit-making enterprise. A merchant wholesaler's compensation is a *profit* made *on the sale of the goods.*

1. *Full-function or service wholesalers.* The "traditional" wholesalers who perform all or most of the marketing functions normally associated with wholesaling. Participate directly in all or most of the flows of marketing. Particularly useful in broad retail lines, such as groceries and drugs.

   a. *Physical possession flow.*
      (1) Take possession of goods.
      (2) Maintain storage facilities.
      (3) Maintain stocks of goods sufficient in both variety and quantity to supply customers on regular basis.
      (4) Deliver goods to customer.

   b. *Ownership flow.* Take legal title (ownership) from supplier, pass it on to customer when sale is made.

   c. *Promotion.* May participate in manufacturer's advertising allowances; may print catalogs for trade; may advertise to trade; maintain sales force.

Source: Department of Marketing, Wharton School, University of Pennsylvania.

d. *Negotiation.* Make contact and negotiate over prices, quality, quantity, terms of sale, etc., with *both* supplier and customer.

e. *Financing.* Extend credit to customers (thereby financing the customer's inventory). Help to finance manufacturer to extent that wholesaler relieves manufacturer of burden of carrying large stocks of finished goods.

f. *Risking.* By taking ownership, assume all risks of failure to sell goods and of changes in the prices of the goods. Risk assumption may be offset by manufacturer's willingness to accept returns and/or guarantee price.

g. *Ordering.* In effect, flow of ordering moves from retailer to manufacturer. In reality, anticipate needs of retailers and order from manufacturer in advance of actual sale to retailer (see "Risking").

h. *Payment.* Accept payment for goods from customers; pass payment minus expenses and profit to supplier. May pay supplier *before* collecting from customer (another form of risk).

2. *Limited-function wholesalers.* Wholesalers who do not perform some of the marketing functions, either eliminating them entirely or passing them on to someone else. Some limited-function wholesalers *participate* in all of the marketing flows, but their *degree* of participation in any one flow may be considerably less than that of the service wholesaler.

   a. *Drop shipper (desk jobber).* A wholesale merchant who passes on the order of his customer with instructions to the manufacturer to ship directly to a location specified by the customer. Maintains no warehouse or inventory, *does not take physical possession* of the goods. Much contact with his customers by telephone, hence may have no sales force and may be much less active in promotional flow. Particularly useful in bulky goods and where merchandise typically moves in carlot quantities. (Sometimes called a *carlot wholesaler.*)

   b. *Cash-carry wholesalers.*

      (1) *Financing.* Do not finance customers because of no-credit policy.

      (2) *Physical possession flow.* Same position in this flow as the service wholesaler, except that customer assumes burden of delivery.

      (3) *Promotion.* Operation, by its nature, is a cost-cutting one. Dealing often in small orders with small retailers, therefore less likely to have an outside sales force.

   c. *Wagon jobbing (truck jobbing).*

      (1) *Wagon jobbers* (self-employed merchants).

         (a) Little capital, often extend no credit to customers.

         (b) May own goods, but often get them on consignment from supplier.

         (c) Often maintain no warehouse, buy on hand-to-mouth basis.

      (2) *Driver–sales agents* (not really wholesalers). Take goods on consignment or salary rather than profit.

      (3) Used with perishables and semiperishables; sometimes with auto parts, cigars and cigarettes, candy, sundries.

   d. *Rack jobbers.* Important in variety and specialty lines, especially in supermarkets. Maintain racks stocked with merchandise at the retailer's location.

      (1) *Ownership and risk.* Heavy assumption of risk, since the *jobber keeps title* and the *retailer is billed only for goods sold from the rack.*

     (2) *Finance.* Assume the sole financial burden for the goods, finance customer's inventory by maintaining ownership. Retailer's only investment is in the space allotted to the rack.

     (3) *Promotion.* Deal widely in highly advertised, branded, well-known goods. Have to do little promotion of the goods, which are "self-selling" through display. (*Note:* Use of the well-known brands partially offsets the risks of ownership.)

  3. *Other types of wholesale operations, often of a special-purpose nature.*

    a. *Converters.*

      (1) *Ownership.* Purchase cloth from textile mills; process, dye, or print it on contract basis for garment manufacturers.

      (2) *Physical possession.* Cloth frequently finished in outside plants; converter may never touch it.

      (3) *Finance.* May take entire output of textile mill; may extend heavy credit to garment manufacturers.

      (4) *Risking.* Ownership risk assumed by converter heavy because of fluid changes in popularity of patterns and colors; risk also strong when financing small garment manufacturers (high bankruptcy rate).

      (5) *Ordering.* Highly anticipatory of needs of garment makers.

    b. *Franchise wholesalers.* Retailers affiliate with existing wholesaler, who gives them right (franchise) to use certain name or storefront design. Most *voluntary chains* operate under franchises from wholesalers.

      (1) *Promotion.* May furnish advertising material for affiliates; may aid retailers in display and point-of-sale promotion.

      (2) Often operate on a *cost-plus* basis.

      (3) Often use *preprinted order forms;* outside sales force may give service more of an advisory nature to retailers.

      (4) May furnish accounting service for retailers.

      (5) Participation in marketing flows very similar to that of service wholesalers, except that *more services* are often provided to affiliates.

B. *Retailer-sponsored cooperatives.* Independent *retailers* form an association, which buys or builds wholesale warehouse facilities that they own cooperatively. The *wholesale* operation is thus not a profit-making institution, but exists only as an arm of the associated retailers. *As a unit,* however, it participates in many of the marketing flows.

  1. *Ownership.* As a legal entity, the cooperative takes title to the merchandise. Legal responsibilities will depend on the form of organization.

  2. *Physical possession.* Cooperative performs all acts of possession, and physical handling of goods.

  3. *Promotion.* Cooperative advertising is executed by the staff of the organization for the membership. Sales force for *selling* purposes often eliminated; outside staff members may render aid to member stores in display, point-of-sale promotion, etc.

  4. *Negotiation.* The cooperative negotiates (on behalf of its membership) with suppliers. Cooperative organization usually set up so that members are supplied on *cost-plus* basis (landed or invoice cost plus estimated allowable expenses).

  5. *Financing.* May carry members' accounts on credit basis, but does not really finance members, since it is the *member's* capital that finances the cooperative.

6. *Risking.* The cooperative, as a unit, may lose money on inventories, but the risk (and profits or losses) are shared by the membership.

7. *Ordering.* The cooperative is, in effect, passing on the orders of the membership to suppliers. Often uses *preprinted order forms.*

8. *Flow of payment.* Normal-membership, through organization to suppliers.

C. *Other agencies involved in wholesaling. Functional middlemen,* specializing in performance of one or more specific marketing tasks, especially those concerned with *negotiation.* As a rule, participate in only a *few* of the flows. *Not merchants:* their compensation is in the form of a commission or fee for a service rendered, *not* a profit on the sale of goods.

1. *Brokers.* Agents who specialize in buying or selling goods for a principal. Usually have neither title to, nor possession of, the merchandise.

   a. *Ownership and physical possession.* Through making a sale, they *facilitate* changes in ownership and possession. They do not participate directly in these flows.

   b. *Promotion.* May advertise in trade journals, have sales agents to call on trade. Broker himself may be a salesman.

   c. *Negotiation.* Negotiate with customers on price, quantity, quality, terms of sale, etc., within limitations of authority granted by principal. Results of negotiation *binding* on principal so long as broker does not exceed authority given him.

   d. *Financing.* Brokers seldom give or receive credit. Financial arrangements between principal and customer.

   e. *Risking.* Brokers never own goods, take no risk on them, do not figure in the flow of risk *on the goods.* (Naturally, they take their own risks in choosing whom to represent, etc.)

   f. *Ordering.* Customer orders from principal, through broker.

   g. *Payment.* Payment for goods usually goes from their customers to the suppliers. They *may* (but not always) collect from customer and deduct their commission.

   h. With free-lance brokers, each sale is a separate and distinct transaction; may frequently change principals whom they represent.

2. *Manufacturers' agents.* Sell part of the output of manufacturers on an extended contract basis.

   a. Difference from brokers.

      (1) Represent limited number of principals, whom they represent regularly.

      (2) Usually represent several noncompeting lines from different manufacturers.

      (3) Territory definite and limited.

      (4) Prices, terms of sale, etc., set by principal.

   b. Involvement in marketing flows similar to broker, except:

      (1) May be more active in promotional aspects of selling (e.g., having outside sales representatives) than broker.

      (2) Will often sell in smaller lots than broker.

3. *Selling (or sales) agents.*

   a. Normally handle entire output of the principal (thus, in effect, become sales force of manufacturer).

   b. Usually given more complete authority over prices, terms of sale, territory, etc.

    c. May use manufacturers' agents or brokers in places where they maintain no office.

    d. May have quite an extensive sales force and promotional program.

4. *Commission merchants.* (Sometimes called *factors.*) Receive goods on consignment for sale on a commission basis.

    a. Maintain a warehouse, involved in physical handling of goods, thus participate in the flow of *physical possession.*

    b. *Ownership.* Receive goods on consignment basis, have no title.

    c. *Promotion.* May maintain full sales force, print catalogs, have sales offices in various cities, advertise in trade magazines.

    d. *Negotiation.* Have full power to negotiate price, terms of sale, etc., with customer.

    e. *Financing.* May extend credit to customers, often assuming the risk of making collections as *del credere* agent.

        (1) *Factoring.* Finance their principals, often by *discounting accounts receivable* from buyers.

    f. *Risking.* May assume risk of collecting accounts in factoring; may be responsible for payment to principal prior to collection of discounted account receivable.

    g. *Ordering.* May order entire output of manufacturer on consignment in anticipation of orders from customers.

    h. *Payment.* May collect from customers, forward payment to principal after deduction of expenses and commission.

CHAPTER FOUR

Physical Distribution: Structure and Strategy

In all marketing channels the product must be moved in the right quantity at the right time to a specific place in order to be delivered most efficiently to the end-user. *Physical distribution management* is the generic term widely used for the management of the flow of goods and services from the point of origin to the point of consumption. On reflection, however, it becomes apparent that in most marketing channels, individual firms must organize the physical flow of goods and services and manage the related flow of information in two separate but related phases:

The Materials Management Cycle.   Goods and services flow to the firm through a process of material acquisition (or purchasing) and must be managed as incoming material with an effective system that includes inbound transportation and inventory management. This process is typically called the *materials management cycle* in most firms. Transportation and purchasing strategies, warehousing design and operation, and inventory control methods are tailored in this cycle to the cost-effective introduction of these material resources into the firm. Methods utilized include materials requirements planning (MRP), just-in-time (JIT) systems, and co-maker purchasing. The emphasis in this inbound materials management cycle is clearly on the efficient acquisition, delivery, control, and application of raw materials, finished or semifinished goods, and services used in the internal operations of the firm. This materials management flow, which involves an interface with vendors and suppliers, is tied directly to internal firm operations. Scheduling, control, information flow, coordination, and smooth interface with both vendors and the transportation systems are paramount to ensure profitability. Demand projections for raw materials and supplies are often based on a projected production schedule or other internal usage plan and are generally deterministic in nature. Given discipline in internal planning, these demand projections provide an opportunity for a highly integrated materials management process. We will examine current approaches to integrated materials management later in this chapter.

The Physical Distribution Cycle. *Physical distribution* is a term more appropriately applied to the outgoing product flow from the firm to customers through some defined network of transportation links and storage or distribution nodes called a *distribution network*. This network may tie the firm to an individual consumer or to other firms that may either use the products produced in another stage of manufacturing, conversion, or service generation or serve as wholesalers or retailers in the distribution of the products to another set of customers. Thus, the physical distribution cycle as viewed from the producer of the product is often likely to represent the materials management cycle to the buyer of the product, and it is often repeated several times in a given marketing channel. Perhaps the key to the methods used to manage transportation, storage, and inventory control in the physical distribution cycle of a firm is the nature of the materials management process of the buyer. Where products or services are being distributed in a physical distribution network subject to stochastic customer demand, inventories are often decoupled both from production and from other inventory levels and managed under traditional reorder point systems. Some forward-looking firms have implemented so-called distribution requirements planning (DRP) systems for these inventories. However, where products or services are distributed in a physical distribution network subject to deterministic demand, production, transportation, and inventory control decisions can often be tied directly to the buyer's materials management process. We will examine these relationships and concepts later when we discuss JIT systems and DRP systems in greater detail.

Viewed together, the materials management cycle and the physical distribution cycle form the overall logistics cycle for the firm. Thus, the term *logistics management* encompasses the total flow of materials from acquisition of raw materials to the delivery of the finished product to the ultimate consumer and the counterflow of information that controls and records the material movement. Because of the common use of the term *physical distribution*, we use that term and *logistics* interchangeably in this chapter. Fig. 4–1 illustrates the components of the logistics system and Fig. 4–2 presents an operational view of the system. Although physical distribution focuses on the physical movement of material, the smooth functioning of a physical distribution system relies on the interface between physical and information flows, as shown in Fig. 4–3.

THE SIGNIFICANCE OF PHYSICAL DISTRIBUTION

Although the significance of distribution costs may vary in different sectors of the economy, as shown in Table 4–1, the importance of this aspect of marketing channels in the entire economy is intensified by the fact that the physical distri-

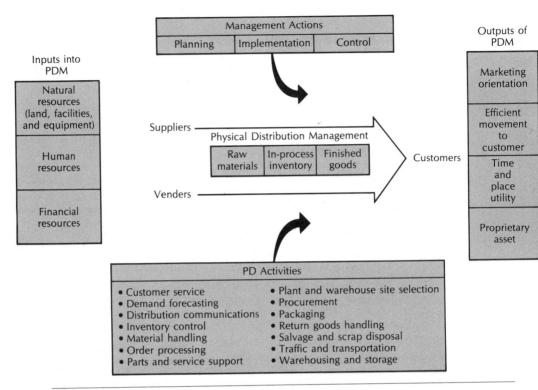

Figure 4–1 Components of physical distribution management

Source: Douglas M. Lambert and James R. Stock, *Strategic Physical Distribution Management* (Homewood, Ill.: Richard D. Irwin, © 1982), p. 10.

bution of goods from point of origin to ultimate consumers costs more than $420 billion a year, or between 20 and 25 percent of GNP.[1]

Not only has physical distribution taken on increased economic significance, it has also taken on increased management significance, for several reasons. First, many managers have realized that improving the efficiency of individual logistics operations such as production, warehousing, or transportation is useless if the efficiency of the individual function throws the total system out of balance. Second, the logistics system has become an important competitive tool and is the area where the struggle to control distribution takes place. Third, many of the technological developments over the last 20 years have been system-oriented and as such force consideration of the logistics system as a whole. Finally, logistics is no longer just a part of the business where cost can be minimized but is seen instead as an important strategic consideration.[2] These factors will be examined in greater detail throughout this chapter.

[1] Don Firth et al., *Distribution Management Handbook* (Toronto: McGraw-Hill Ryerson, 1980), p. 8.

[2] John F. Magee, Copacino, and Rosenfield, *Modern Logistics Management* (New York: John Wiley, 1985), pp. 8–9.

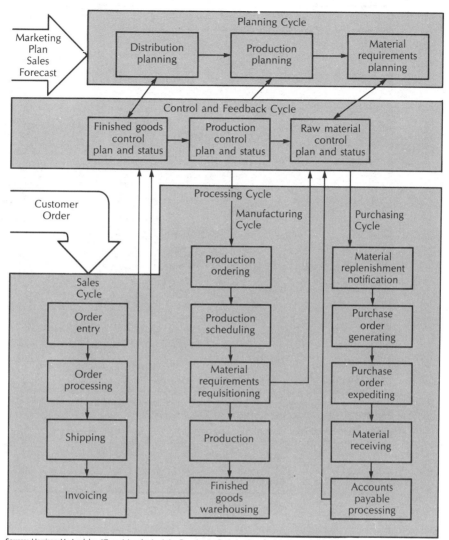

Figure 4–2 Operational elements of a physical distribution system

Source: Harrison J. Appleby, "Organizing the Logistics Function to Optimize Benefits," in *Proceedings of the Sixteenth Annual Conference of the National Council of Physical Distribution Management, October 16–18, 1978,* p. 184.

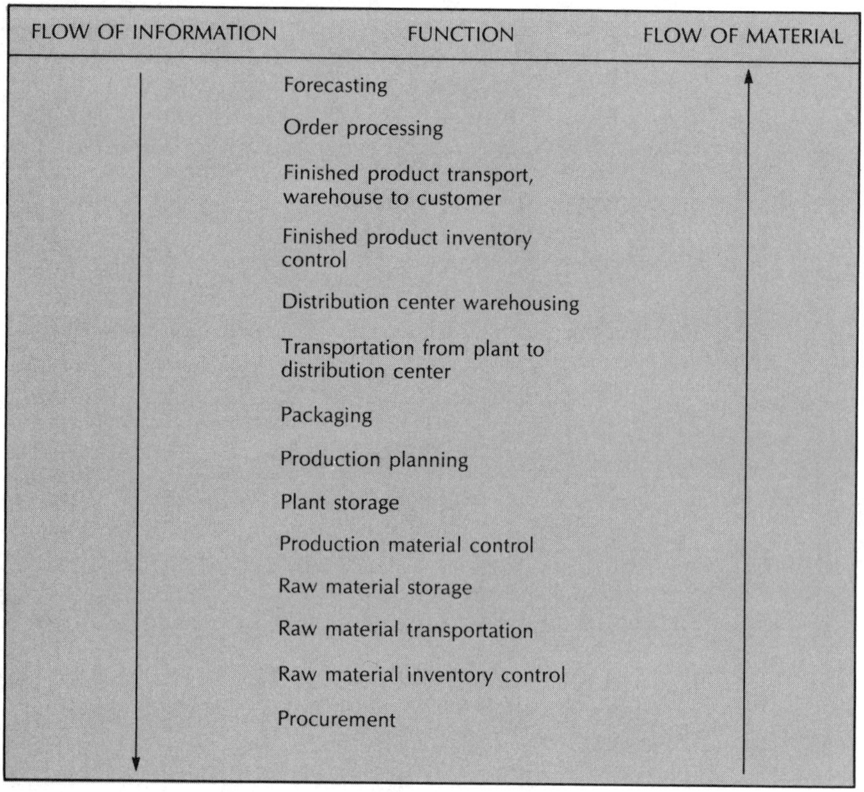

FLOW OF INFORMATION	FUNCTION	FLOW OF MATERIAL
	Forecasting	
	Order processing	
	Finished product transport, warehouse to customer	
	Finished product inventory control	
	Distribution center warehousing	
	Transportation from plant to distribution center	
	Packaging	
	Production planning	
	Plant storage	
	Production material control	
	Raw material storage	
	Raw material transportation	
	Raw material inventory control	
	Procurement	

Figure 4–3   Flows within the logistics pipeline

Source: Reprinted by permission from *Logistics Strategy: Cases and Concepts,* by Roy D. Shapiro and James L. Heskett; copyright © 1985 by West Publishing Company. All rights reserved, page 7.

Table 4–1   Physical distribution costs relative to sales

Type of Manufacturer	Annual Sales $Million	Distribution Costs $Million	Distribution Costs as a Percent of Annual Sales
Copper Refiner	100	55	55%
Plumbing & Heating Products	30	5.8	20%
Electrical Hardware	60	8.4	14%
Packaged Foods	120	34.5	28%
Brewery	45	12	27%
Bakery	45	16	36%
Pharmaceuticals	16	2.4	15%
Petroleum Products	45	13	29%

Source: Don Firth et al., *Distribution Management Handbook* (Toronto: McGraw-Hill Ryerson, 1980), p. 8.

IMPLICATIONS FOR PHYSICAL DISTRIBUTION MANAGEMENT

In an economy characterized by high energy costs, potential energy and materials shortages, and declining growth rates in productivity, maintaining acceptable levels of corporate profitability is becoming increasingly difficult. The physical distribution function offers great potential for profit improvement.[3] The fact is, in many industries, distribution costs can exceed 25 percent of each sales dollar at the manufacturing level, and the assets required by distribution can account for more than 30 percent of corporate assets.

With an integrated physical distribution system, *visible costs* such as transportation, warehousing, and inventory management can be reduced. Therefore, one of the concerns of physical distribution management is to keep these visible costs down.

In addition to controlling visible distribution costs, the physical distribution manager must also be concerned with *hidden costs*. These are the profit opportunities lost due to failure to ship the product on time and the cost of lost sales, canceled orders, and customer dissatisfaction associated with stockouts.

In theory, management cost control is very straightforward. In practice it is often very difficult to identify hidden costs, pinpoint controllable costs, and assign organizational responsibility for control of these costs. In addition, the interdependence of customer service levels and these costs makes the job of controlling costs even more difficult.[4]

Improving the service level provided by the physical distribution system increases cost; conversely, a cost reduction may lower the level of customer service. The total cost concept or physical distribution concept, as it is called here, provides guidelines for achieving the critical balance between cost and the level of service provided by the system.

THE PHYSICAL DISTRIBUTION CONCEPT

The *physical distribution concept* emerged from a renowned study completed over thirty years ago.[5] This concept can be described as a *cost-service* orientation, backed by an integrated physical distribution network, that is aimed at *minimizing the total costs of distribution at a given level of customer service*. The four main components of the PD concept are (1) a total cost perspective, (2) the understanding of relevant tradeoffs among costs, (3) the notion of zero suboptimization, and (4) the total system perspective. Each is discussed briefly here.

---

[3] Douglas Lambert and Robert Quinn, "Increase Profitability by Managing the Distribution Function," *Business Quarterly* (Spring 1981), p. 56.

[4] Magee, Copacino, and Rosenfield, *op. cit.*, p. 236.

[5] Howard T. Lewis, James W. Culliton, and Jack D. Steele, *The Role of Air Freight in Physical Distribution* (Boston: Division of Research, Harvard University Graduate School of Business Administration, 1956). See also John F. Magee, "The Logistics of Distribution," *Harvard Business Review*, Vol. 38 (July-August 1960), pp. 89–101.

The Total Cost Perspective

The key to the total cost approach is to consider *simultaneously* the cost of all physical distribution elements, visible and hidden, when trying to achieve specified levels of customer service.[6] Since all physical distribution activities are interdependent, a change in one will affect the others. Management should strive to minimize the *total costs* of physical distribution rather than attempt to minimize the cost of each element.[7]

Cost Tradeoffs

Even though certain costs may increase while others are purposively reduced, the desired result, under the PD concept, is that total distribution cost will decline. For example, setting a limit on inventory levels for a company with a seasonal demand may result in lower inventory costs, but the additional costs incurred by manufacturing in adjusting output levels to match demand (through hiring, layoffs, or some other means) may more than offset the inventory savings. A level production strategy could result in the lowest total costs.[8]

Zero Suboptimization

When one distribution function is optimized, the result will likely be an impairment of the *performance* of other distribution functions. Distribution network goals should be set with the realization that the achievement of goals in one area of distribution may affect the attainment of goals in other distribution areas. For example:

- Lowering warehousing costs by reducing inventory levels might also reduce customer service or inhibit corporate purchasing agents from making advantageous purchases.
- Reducing inventories might involve reducing assortment and thus reducing the system's ability to fill orders on time.
- Increasing the speed of delivery might increase customer service but could also involve higher transportation costs and thus a higher total cost.
- Setting a high level of customer service might involve an increase in inventory and in inventory-carrying costs.
- Attaining a goal of lower transportation costs might result in increased inventories and a reduced level of customer service.[9]

When physical distribution functions are coordinated and integrated, the focus of system management should be to minimize suboptimization or, ideally, reach zero suboptimization.

---

[6] Lewis, Culliton, and Steele, *op. cit.*, pp. 64–65. See also Stephen B. Oresman and Charles D. Scudder, "A Remedy for Maldistribution," *Business Horizons* (June 1974), p. 63.

[7] Douglas M. Lambert and James R. Stock, *Strategic Physical Distribution Management* (Homewood, Ill.: Richard D. Irwin, 1982), p. 36.

[8] Magee, Copacino, and Rosenfield, *op. cit.*, p. 7.

[9] These examples are from Daniel Cooper and Kenneth Nilsen, "Distribution Can Be Easier and Cheaper," *Management Focus*, Vol. 29, No. 2 (March/April 1982), p. 17.

The Total System Perspective

This concept is an extension of the PD concept and is the key to managing the physical distribution function.[10] It extends the PD concept to cover trading off the cost of performing different functions throughout the entire marketing channel. For example, price-ticketing of goods is normally performed at the retail level. The process is time-consuming and labor-intensive. Some large retailers have resorted to direct negotiations with suppliers of goods to shift the price-ticketing operation to the assembly line at the supplier's production facilities. Retailers provide up-to-date price lists to their suppliers, and the goods are received preticketed at the retailer's premises. Naturally, manufacturers have increased their prices to retailers to compensate for the prolonged production process resulting from the assumption of the price-ticketing function. Usually retailers are ready for these increases, because they are more than offset by the reduction of their own cost. The result is a reduction in the total distribution cost in the channel system.

In order to implement the PD concept, management must design and implement a logistics system that coordinates the components of the entire system so as to minimize its total cost at a given level of customer service,[11] as shown in Fig. 4–4. The core component of the system is customer service standards, shown in the center of the diagram. Below it are the five basic PD system components; above it are support system components.

This chapter concentrates on the six core and basic components:

1. The development of customer service standards
2. The selection of transportation modes
3. The determination of the optimal number and location of warehousing facilities
4. The design of order processing and information systems
5. The determination of production scheduling involving the quantity and kind of finished products to produce
6. The setting of inventory management and control procedures

We emphasize those six areas because they represent the most strategic, as well as the most cost-significant, components of physical distribution for most channel members.

Once system design is accomplished, attention to physical distribution system management, or the effective melding of all decision areas into a meaningful whole, is required. We discuss this in the final section of the chapter.

CUSTOMER SERVICE STANDARDS

It must be continually emphasized that channel strategy formulation begins with a determination of customer needs and requirements for service output levels. The key elements of *customer service* identified in a study sponsored by the Na-

---

[10] Lambert and Quinn, *op. cit.*, pp. 58–59.

[11] Douglas M. Lambert, *The Development of an Industry Costing Methodology: A Study of Costs Associated with Holding Inventory* (Chicago: National Council of Physical Distribution Management, 1976), p. 7.

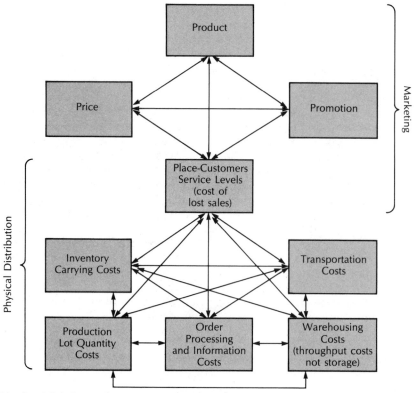

Objective: Minimize total costs

Total costs = Transportation costs + Warehousing costs
+ Order processing and information costs + Production lot quantity costs
+ Inventory carrying costs + Cost of lost sales

Figure 4–4   Cost trade-offs in a physical distribution system

Source: Adapted from Douglas M. Lambert, *The Development of an Inventory Costing Methodology: A Study of the Costs Associated with Holding Inventory* (Chicago: National Council of Physical Distribution Management, 1976), p. 7; as reported in Douglas M. Lambert and James R. Stock, *Strategic Physical Distribution Management* (Homewood, Ill.: Richard D. Irwin, 1982), p. 35.

tional Council of Logistics Management are shown in Fig. 4–5. Those elements are grouped into pretransaction, transaction, and posttransaction categories.

Pretransaction elements, though not directly involved with physical distribution, provide the opportunity to establish a climate for good customer service. As such they have a sizable impact on product sales.

Transaction elements are those activities that are directly associated with the delivery of the product to the customer. Thus, the customer is directly affected by the level of service provided here.

Posttransaction elements are those activities that support the product after it has been sold, protect customers from defective products, provide for the return

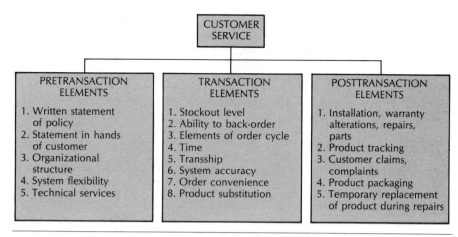

Figure 4–5   Elements of customer service

Source: Ronald H. Ballou, *Business Logistics Management: Planning and Control,* 2nd ed., © 1985, p. 55. Reprinted by permission of Prentice-Hall, Inc., Englewood Cliffs, N.J.

of packages, and handle complaints, claims, and returns. Those services can have a significant impact on the purchase decision.[12]

The first step in developing customer service standards is to determine which of the elements in Fig. 4–5 are most important to the customers. This information can be obtained through questionnaires or customer service surveys.[13] An example of the relative importance of physical distribution service elements in a study by Perreault and Russ is shown in Table 4–2. Naturally, the importance of each of these elements will vary from industry to industry and even from company to company within an industry. In addition, the distribution manager's level of control over each element varies.

The following four steps must be taken after the important elements of customer service are determined:

1. Quantitative standards of performance for each service element must be set.
2. Actual performance for each service element must be measured.
3. Variance between actual services provided and the set standard must be analyzed.
4. Corrective action must be taken as needed to reduce the variance between actual performance and the set standard.

The service standards *must* be set according to customer needs, not according to what management thinks these needs are. Any discrepancies between actual and desired performance should be reported to the appropriate level of management on a regular basis. Finally, a strategy for improving customer service performance must be determined. This strategy must be in line with the long-range profit and return-on-investment objectives of the company.

---

[12] Ronald H. Ballou, *Business Logistics Management Planning and Control,* 2nd ed. (Englewood Cliffs, N.J.: Prentice-Hall, 1985), p. 54.

[13] For examples of customer service audits, questionnaires, and surveys, see Lambert and Stock, *op. cit.,* pp. 81–97.

Table 4–2   Relative importance of various elements in the physical distribution service offering

Customer Service Element	Correlation Coefficient[a]
Average delivery time	0.76
Delivery time variability	0.72
Order status information	0.67
Rush service	0.59
Order methods	0.56
Action on complaints	0.56
Accuracy in filling orders	0.46
Returns policy	0.44
Billing procedure	0.39

[a] Correlation between the service element and customer satisfaction.

Source: William D. Perreault, Jr., and Frederick A. Russ, "Physical Distribution Service in Industrial Purchase Decisions," *Journal of Marketing*, Vol. 40 (April 1976), p. 8. Reprinted from *Journal of Marketing*, published by the American Marketing Association.

TRANSPORTATION DECISIONS

The problems of inadequate transportation service and uncertain transit times can cause a company to hold several days' more inventory than physical distribution plans call for. This problem, in turn, adds to the cost of carrying inventory and reduces the number of times that capital invested in inventory can be turned over during the year, not to mention the undesirable effects of poor customer service and missed product promotions. Consequently, the selection of appropriate transportation modes and the maintenance of a concerted effort by physical distribution management to ensure efficient and reliable transportation are prerequisites for accomplishing distribution objectives. In this section, we describe various transportation modes and the functions they can perform for various channel members in facilitating the movement of products.

In the United States there are a variety of options available to a firm that must move its goods from one point to another. The five basic modes of transportation are rail, truck, water, air, and pipeline. In addition, a variety of combinations are available, including rail–motor (piggyback), motor–water (fishyback), motor–air, and rail–water. These combinations can provide services normally not provided by a single mode. Freight movement, whether by a single mode or by a combination, is facilitated by a variety of transportation agencies, including freight forwarders, shippers' associations, parcel post, and air express. The various legal forms of transportation are discussed in more detail in Appendix 4A.

In making transportation mode selection decisions, logistics managers in the marketing channel must consider cost, speed, dependability, and possibility of loss and damage associated with the modes available to them. Table 4–3 ranks the cost and performance characteristics of each of the five basic modes of transportation according to these criteria.

Table 4–3 Relative rankings of cost and operating performance characteristics by transportation mode[a]

Mode Transportation	Cost[b] 1 = Highest	Performance Characteristics			
		Average Delivery Time[c] 1 = Fastest	Delivery Time Variability		Loss and Damage 1 = Least
			Absolute 1 = Least	Percent[d] 1 = Least	
Rail	3	3	4	3	5
Truck	2	2	3	2	4
Water	5	5	5	4	2
Pipe	4	4	2	1	1
Air	1	1	1	5	3

[a] Service is assumed to be available.
[b] Cost per ton-mile.
[c] Door-to-door speed.
[d] Ratio of absolute variation in delivery time to average delivery time.

Source: Ronald H. Ballou, *Business Logistics Management: Planning and Control,* 2nd ed., © 1985, p. 190. Reprinted by permission of Prentice-Hall, Inc., Englewood Cliffs, N.J.

Transportation Modes

The percentage of total ton-miles that each of the five basic transport modes account for has shifted dramatically. The percentage share of the total ton-mile market accounted for by motor carriers, waterways, and pipeline increased both relatively and absolutely from 1946 to 1983. The percentage accounted for by air transportation also increased during this time, but it is still less than 1 percent of the total.[14] Figure 4–6 shows projections for ton-mile percentages by mode of transport for 1985, excluding air transport because of its fractional share.

Rail. Although the railroads' share of the total declined from 66 percent in 1946 to 37 percent in 1983, there was an absolute increase in ton-miles by rail because the total ton-mile market increased from 903 billion to 2 trillion 5 billion during this period. The railroad is still considered the major long-haul mover of bulk commodities such as coal and grain and of low-value manufactured products. Furthermore, it offers important services to shippers, such as expedited handling to guarantee arrival within a certain number of hours, pickup and delivery, stop-off privileges, which permit partial loading and unloading between origin and destination points, and diversion and reconsignment, which allow circuitous routing and en-route changes in the destination of a shipment.

[14] This discussion of transportation modes is based on U.S. Department of Transportation, *National Transportation Annual Report, 1983;* Stephen Tinghitella, "Two Decades of Change and Distribution Progress," *Traffic Management* (January 1982), pp. 48–56; and Charles A. Taff, *Management of Physical Distribution and Transportation,* 7th ed. (Homewood, Ill.: Richard D. Irwin, 1984), pp. 113–30.

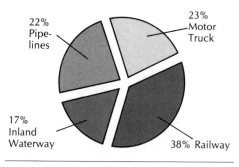

Figure 4–6 Ton-mile percentages by mode of transport for 1985

Source: Charles A. Taff, *Management of Physical Distribution and Transportation,* 7th ed. (Homewood, Ill.: Richard D. Irwin, 1984), p. 114.

These special services enhance the attractiveness of the railroad as a mover of a large number of products.

Truck. Motor carriers and rail transport compete for many of the same product shipments, even though they are different in many ways. Motor carriers have some inherent advantages over the railroad, including door-to-door service and flexibility in scheduling. In general, trucking has a service advantage in the "small" (less than 10,000 pounds) shipments, which account for the major portion of their business. Trucking is a relatively short-range transportation service that, because of highway safety restrictions on the dimensions of shipments and their weight, is less capable than rail of handling all types of freight. Motor carriers held approximately 23 percent of the market in 1985.

Water. Water transportation was the earliest domestic means for moving cargo in large volumes. It has played a vital role in the economic history of the United States. Water transportation is relatively slow, its circuitability is restricted during certain times of the year due to weather, and it is limited to bulk cargo service along waterway systems. However, it has a competitively lower cost, including lower loss and damage costs. Water transportation represented 17 percent of the market in 1985.

Air. Air transportation is being considered by an increasing number of shippers for regular service, despite its high rate charges. In 1981 air transportation costs were over three times the cost of motor carriers, the second most costly mode.[15] Despite the increased use of air transportation, it held less than 1 percent of the total ton-mileage market as of 1985. The inherent advantage of air transportation is its unmatched origin–destination speed. However, this speed is not directly comparable with that of other modes of transportation, because it

[15] Air Transport Association of America, *Air Transport 1981* (New York, 1981); and American Trucking Association, *American Trucking Trends 1979–1980* (Washington, D.C., 1981).

does not include pickup and delivery times or ground handling time. Thus, a well-managed and coordinated truck–rail operation often can match the schedules of air transport systems.[16]

Pipeline.   Pipeline carriers are basically specialized carriers that move a commodity in one direction during a specific operating period. Pipeline is used mainly to transport petroleum and petroleum products and liquid fertilizer. Pipeline transportation provides a very limited range of services and capability because of the physical limitations on the products that can be moved by pipelines. However, transportation by pipeline offers the most dependable service of any transportation mode and has lower rates of loss and damage to the product. Pipeline carriers have significantly increased their share of total ton-miles, from 9.5 percent in 1947 to 22 percent in 1985.[17] Further, the Department of Transportation estimates that this upward trend will continue through 1990.[18]

WAREHOUSING DECISIONS

There are two basic types of warehouse facilities available to channel members— *private* (company-owned) facilities and *public* facilities, in which space is leased by retailers, wholesalers, or manufacturers. In general, private warehouses offer greater flexibility in design to meet special storage and handling needs, greater control over the warehouse facility and its operations, more effective information feedback, and lower cost per unit since it does not have to recover advertising and selling costs.

In contrast, public warehouse facilities require no fixed investment by the firm; offer location flexibility and the ability to increase warehouse space to cover peak requirements; and can offer lower cost under certain circumstances, as when it is necessary to store seasonal inventories. Often public warehouse personnel will provide many other services in order to compete with their private warehouse counterparts.[19] Table 4–4 summarizes the characteristics of each type of facility.

Public Warehousing

Due to the varied needs of commodities at different stages from production to ultimate consumption, different types of warehouse facilities are needed. Public warehouses can be classified into six types of facilities, which offer a company a wide variety of options.

[16] Transportation Association of America, *Transportation Facts and Trends,* 15th ed. (Washington, D.C., 1979); and Transportation Association of America, "What's Happening in Transportation," *Transport Review for 1979* (Washington, D.C., 1980).

[17] Transportation Association of America, *Transportation Facts and Trends;* and Taff, *op. cit.,* p. 114.

[18] U.S. Department of Transportation, *National Transportation Trends and Choices to the Year 2000* (1977), p. 69.

[19] Taff, *op. cit.,* p. 166.

- *Special commodity warehouses.* These warehouses are most widely used for storing agricultural commodities. Such items as peanuts, cotton, corn, tobacco, and lumber may be stored in them.
- *Field warehouses.* These facilities warehouse products on the property of the owner under the custody of a bona fide public warehouse employee. The purpose of field warehousing is to obtain credit financing for products in inventory. Such credit financing is secured by a certain percentage of the value of the inventory held in the field warehouse.
- *Refrigerated or cold-storage warehouses.* These are controlled, low-temperature warehouses for perishable items such as eggs, fruits, and frozen foods as well as some chemicals and drugs.
- *Household good warehouses.* Storage and handling of household furnishings, furniture, and people's personal effects are provided by these warehouses. These items may be held in open storage, container storage, or private room or vault storage.
- *General merchandise warehouses.* These warehouses are used by manufacturers or shippers for storing goods until they are needed by retailers, distributors, or ultimate consumers. Merchandise that does not require special handling or special facilities is stored in these warehouses.
- *Bonded warehouses.* These warehouses store commodities or merchandise for which they bond themselves to the U.S. Treasury in order to secure payment of internal revenue taxes or import duties, which must be paid before the goods are released.

In practice, most facilities are a hybrid of these types. For example, a general merchandise warehouse handling food products may have to operate a cold-storage section to meet the needs of food grocers. According to the Ameri-

Table 4—4 Summary of factors influencing the public/private warehousing decision

	Public Warehouses	Private Warehouses
Operating costs	Higher due to inclusion of profit factor, selling, and advertising costs	10% to 25% lower if sufficient volume
Initial investment	None	Large facility, startup, equipment, train personnel
Control	Good due to incentive to perform on short-term contract	Direct responsibility over personnel and procedures
Risk	Minimal	Risk of obsolescence due to change in technology or demand
Tax advantages	Free-port states real estate taxless, no property advantage	Depreciation allowance
Economies of scale	Possible due to serving many customers	Dependent on company's volume
Consolidation of shipments	Can consolidate to warehouse and from warehouse to customer	None
Storage and handling costs	Know exact charges for decision making	Generally only estimated

Source: Douglas M. Lambert and James R. Stock, *Strategic Physical Distribution Management* (Homewood, Ill.: Richard D. Irwin, © 1982), p. 211.

can Warehousemen's Association, public warehouse facilities offer a wide variety of services, among them:[20]

- Carrying physical inventories
- Freight consolidation planning
- Packaging and assembly services
- Providing credit information
- Storing goods in transit
- Yard storage
- Handling and storage of materials in containers
- Order filling
- Dry bulk commodity handling, storage, and bagging

Private Warehousing

A major development in private warehousing is the emergence of distribution centers. *Distribution centers* are distinguished from conventional private warehousing operations in that they are major centralized warehousing operations that:

- Serve regional markets
- Process and regroup products into customized orders
- Maintain a full line of products for customer distribution
- Consolidate large shipments from different production points
- Frequently employ a computer and various materials-handling equipment and may be highly automated rather than labor-intensive
- Are large and single-story, rather than multistory[21]

Clearly, most of these criteria can be met by the more modern public warehousing facilities already mentioned. However, technologically sophisticated public operations are still few in number, and the preponderance of distribution centers in operation today are owned or leased for private corporate use.[22] Moreover, there is one other characteristic of distribution centers that clearly separates them from the vast majority of public warehousing operations: distribution centers are established primarily for the movement rather than the storage of goods.[23] As one marketing executive observed regarding his company's distribution center,

> our terminal is in constant motion. At no time is merchandise warehoused here . . . we're strictly a distribution terminal.[24]

[20] *Ibid.*, pp. 208–10.
[21] See Kenneth Marshall and John Miller, "Where Are the Distribution Centers Going?" *Handling and Shipping* (November 1965), p. 38; and Marjorie Person and Diane Mitchell, "Distribution Centers: The Fort Wayne Experience," *Business Horizons,* Vol. 19 (August 1975), pp. 89–95.
[22] In fact, a study carried out in Fort Wayne, Indiana—one of the havens for distribution centers in the United States—found that 96.2 percent of all distribution centers in the area (26) were owned or leased: 65.4 percent were company-owned and 30.8 percent were leased. See Person and Mitchell, *op. cit.,* p. 92. See also H. G. Becker and Liz Jelenic, "Where the Distribution Centers Are," *Handling and Shipping Management* (November 1980), pp. 52–56.
[23] Marshall and Miller, *op. cit.;* and Person and Mitchell, *op. cit.*
[24] Quoted in "Meeting Those Distribution Center Needs," *Handling and Shipping* (July 1975), p. 37.

Thus, the rationale underlying the development of distribution centers is to maintain the company's product in a constant and efficient flow from the moment it leaves production until the day it arrives at its destination.

Many of the world's foremost corporations now operate distribution centers as an integral part of their physical distribution systems. For example, IBM's World Trade Distribution Center (WTDC) is one of the largest and most sophisticated of its kind in the world. From its location in New York, the WTDC uses a complex communications network to control the annual movement of more than 23 million pounds of equipment, parts, and supplies.[25] Similarly, Levi Strauss operates a huge distribution center in Little Rock, Arkansas, responsible for the rapid movement of its 48,000 product line items from its ten U.S. manufacturing plants to distributors in 70 foreign lands and more than 17,000 domestic stores.[26] Further, from a single distribution center covering 28 acres and more than 1¼ million square feet, the Anchor Hocking Corporation ships 1¼ million pounds of houseware products daily, one of the highest tonnage-shipped-per-day figures in the United States.[27]

Many other firms employing private warehousing operations have also begun to rethink the economics of storage, and to search for ways to boost productivity and save time and money in their distribution pipelines. Probably the single most important development has been the widespread application of computer technology to private warehousing operations. Linked with equipment and lines for rapid transmission of data, the computer has, in fact, become the key element in virtually all distribution center operations. Computers are being used to provide extremely rapid service to customers by determining the availability of items required, issuing the proper order-filling, furnishing shipping and billing documentation, maintaining inventory control records, and in some instances providing an automated order-picking function. It seems certain that this trend toward reevaluation and redesign of private warehousing facilities will continue. In turn, the result for private warehousing is a movement toward increasing sophistication and change.

Storage in Transit

Storage in transit—the time that goods remain in transportation facilities during delivery—reduces the need for and cost of warehousing. Here is an example.

The United Processors Company harvests and processes a variety of fruits and vegetables in southern and western farming regions of the country. For certain of these products such as strawberries and watermelons there tends to be strong demand in the East and Midwest just ahead of the local growing season. Because United must harvest earlier than the northern climates allow, supply builds before demand peaks. Inventories normally build in the growing areas before truck ship-

[25] Janet Bosworth Dower, "How IBM Distributes—Worldwide," *Distribution Worldwide* (October 1973), pp. 51–54, 58–60.

[26] Jim Dixon, "Streamlining Storage and Distribution," *Distribution Worldwide* (May 1975), p. 32.

[27] *Ibid.*, pp. 28–29.

ments are made to the demand areas. By switching to rail service and the longer delivery times associated with it, the company could, in many cases, ship immediately after harvesting and have the products arrive in the marketplace just as strong demand develops. The railroad serves the warehousing function. The result is a substantial reduction in warehousing costs and transportation costs, too![28]

Therefore, transportation equipment can be viewed as moving warehouses and be utilized accordingly.

Determining the Number and Location of Warehouse Facilities

Whether a channel member chooses to use public or private warehousing operations in his physical distribution system, the questions of how many warehouses to establish and where they should be located must be answered. The determination of the number and location of warehouses is directly dependent on the customer service level set by the firm and the purpose the warehouses are intended to serve.

A channel member with high customer service requirements will often establish a series of warehouses. A warehouse will often be located close to the manufacturing plant if the material it stores needs to be processed. In contrast, if the warehouse is to be used for maintaining finished goods, it will most likely be located near the consumer market. When all variables are considered, warehouses must be positioned so that they provide the desired level of service at the least distribution cost. The least-cost solution is unique for each organization because of differences in customer service standards, inventory carrying costs, transportation costs, and other physical distribution costs, but the total cost of the logistical network can be generalized as in Fig. 4–7.

Transportation costs decline as the number of warehouses in the distribution system increases. Inventory and warehousing costs increase at a decreasing rate as the number of warehouses in the system increases. Thus, once cost tradeoffs have been accounted for, the lowest total cost of the overall logistical system is seen in Fig. 4–7 to be the point at which the two cost curves coincide.

The location of warehouse facilities will also have a significant impact on the competitive thrust of an organization and, concomitantly, of an entire marketing channel. Just as the number of warehouses established directly affects the ability of the organization and channel to serve its customers and at the same time keep logistical costs in line, so too does the location of warehouses. A number of warehousing facility location models and solution techniques have been developed to help management make better decisions.[29] Critical to each are estimates of sales lost because of customer distance from warehouses, the cost of operating warehouses, and transportation costs (both inbound and outbound).

[28] Ballou, *op. cit.*, pp. 257–58.
[29] For a summary of a number of useful models, see John T. Mentzer and Alan D. Schuster, "Computer Modeling in Logistics: Existing Models and Future Outlook," *Journal of Business Logistics,* special supplement (March 1982), pp. 1–55.

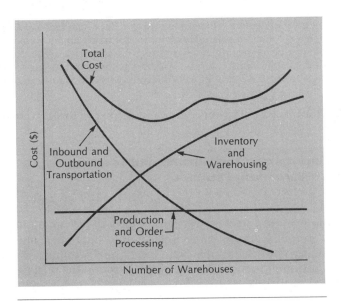

Figure 4–7 Generalized cost tradeoffs in the facility location problem

Source: Ronald H. Ballou, *Business Logistics Management: Planning and Control,* 2nd ed., © 1985, p. 335. Reprinted by permission of Prentice-Hall, Inc., Englewood Cliffs, N.J.

INVENTORY MANAGEMENT AND CONTROL

In this section we discuss the control of distribution inventories held in a distribution channel to meet anticipated customer demand. These inventories may be held at the point of production or positioned in wholesale or retail distribution centers that serve, together with outbound transportation, to define the physical distribution strategy of the firm. In a later section we will address the management of inventories held to support production or the firm's internal operations in the materials management cycle.

If it were not for the presence of and need for inventories, there would be no purpose served in discussing warehousing decisions. In fact, although the decisions involving ownership, type, and location of warehouses are obviously important, solutions to problems associated with inventory management and control are crucial to the viability of all commercial channel members, irrespective of the warehousing decisions arrived at. As can be seen in Fig. 4–8, there are significant differences in average number of days of inventory between companies with the best and the worst logistics practices. Those companies at the high end of the scale pay a significant penalty, which escalates during times of high interest. In addition, they operate at a decidedly competitive disadvantage. This observation is particularly salient when you consider that inventory represents the largest single investment in assets for most manufacturers, wholesalers, and retailers. For example, the inventory investment of manufacturers of consumer

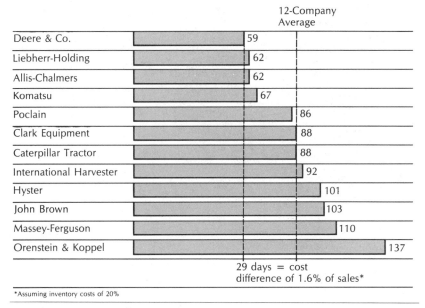

Figure 4–8 *Logistics performance: Average days of inventory in the earth-moving and farm equipment industry, 1980–1982*

Source: Reprinted by permission of the Harvard Business Review. An exhibit from "The Rediscovery of Logistics," by Graham Sherman (September–October 1984), p. 73. Copyright © 1984 by the President and Fellows of Harvard College; all rights reserved.

packaged goods can represent up to one-third of their total investment in assets. For wholesalers and retailers, inventory can represent more than 60 percent of assets.[30] This tendency to maintain such a large inventory is frequently observed in today's highly competitive markets, where companies are trying to satisfy the needs of diverse market segments. In addition, today's consumer is accustomed to and demands high levels of product availability. In order to meet these demands, firms have reacted by maintaining high levels of inventory.

In general, inventory control theory deals with the determination of optimal procedures for procuring stocks of commodities to meet future demand.[31] The decision concerning when and how much to reorder is a matter of balancing a number of conflicting cost functions. The objective is to minimize total inventory costs subject to demand and service constraints. The primary cost functions that must be balanced are those associated with holding inventory, ordering inventory, and risking stockouts. Figure 4–9 shows the tradeoffs among the relevant cost functions and their respective components. The fundamental purpose of any inventory control system is to tell a firm (1) how much to reorder, (2) when to reorder, and (3) how to control stockouts at the lowest cost. The following discussion focuses on these three key problem areas and on related issues,

[30] Douglas Lambert and Robert Quinn, "Profit Oriented Inventory Policies Require a Documented Inventory Carrying Cost," *Business Quarterly* (Autumn 1981), p. 63.

[31] This discussion of optimal procedures for procuring stocks draws on Richard J. Schonberger, "Why the Japanese Produce Just in Time," *Industry Week* (November 29, 1982); and Vivian Brownstein, "The War on Inventories Is Real This Time," *Fortune* (June 11, 1984).

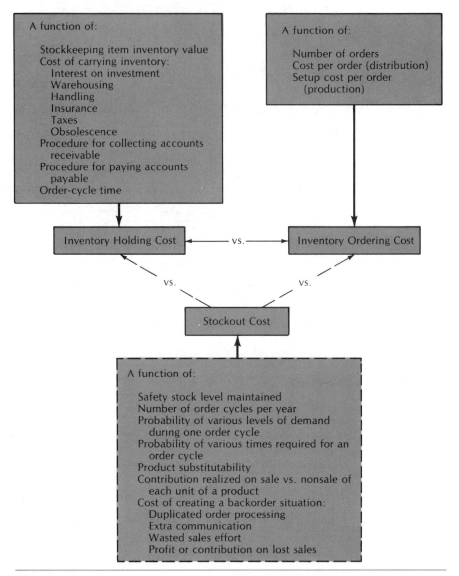

Figure 4–9 Tradeoffs typically found in managing and controlling inventory levels

Source: Business Logistics, 2nd ed., James L. Heskett, Nicholas A. Glaskowsky, Jr., and Robert M. Ivie, copyright © 1973 by The Ronald Press. Reprinted by permission of John Wiley & Sons, Inc.

including the amount of safety stock that should be kept on hand and the need for and impact of sales forecasting on inventory management.

How Much to Reorder and When to Reorder

The traditional approach to managing distribution inventories where customer demand is stochastic (random) and cannot be forecast with complete accuracy is the classic reorder point inventory model. In Appendix 4B we provide a detailed description of this model, its assumptions and limitations, and relevant applications of it. The reorder point approach uses forecast demand and forecast resupply lead time to develop inventory levels that minimize the total variable costs of investment in inventory subject to a specified maximum rate of stockouts or lost sales. In order to meet these objectives, this family of models develops three separate inventory levels, each intended to serve a separate purpose:

Order Level. This is the level of inventory intended to satisfy expected demand between reorders. It is equivalent to the order quantity and is determined through standard economic order quantity (EOQ) computations, which balance the cost to order the item against the cost to hold the item, thereby arriving at the lowest total variable cost. When a reorder is required in a reorder point system, the order level or order quantity determines how much material the firm will order.

Lead-time Level. This is the level of inventory required to meet expected customer demand during expected resupply lead time. In a world of complete certainty (or perfect forecasting), the lead-time level would be used to alert the firm to reorder and would serve as the reorder point of the system.

Safety Level. This is the level of inventory that is held to meet unexpected variation in either customer demand or in resupply lead time during the reorder cycle. Often called *buffer stocks* or *hedge stocks*, safety level assets allow the firm to manage the percentage of stockouts it is willing to experience. In combination with the lead-time level, the safety level determines the reorder point in most reorder point systems, and it is the reorder point that triggers the replenishment action in the system. Clearly, the existence of safety stocks in an inventory system reflects a recognition that customer demand for distribution inventories is often difficult to predict with a high degree of accuracy. Nevertheless, cost pressures in today's logistics environment are forcing firms to develop innovative alternatives to the classic reorder point approach. One of these alternatives, which is becoming increasingly popular in managing distribution inventories, is distribution requirements planning (DRP).

Distribution Requirements Planning Systems

DRP systems are intended to link the production process (or a wholesale level of inventory) to other inventory levels positioned further down in the distribution channel. Hence, DRP methods generally apply to several layers of inventory in a given distribution channel but would not typically be used to develop inventory requirements for the lowest retail level, which supports the ultimate customer directly. Thus, the presumption in a DRP system is that the inventories being managed are intended to resupply other inventories. Given this important assumption, DRP systems take advantage of the fact that lower-level inventories have established demand forecasts, lead times, and order quantities in order to plan for future requirements. Pioneered by Abbott Laboratories, DRP systems do more than simply develop inventory requirements. They allow for the planning, scheduling, and allocating of other key logistics resources as well, including the transportation and personnel needed to support customer requirements.

The central feature of DRP systems is their ability to continually reforecast inventory requirements as the inventory position of lower-level inventories in the distribution channel changes. Thus, DRP systems require that echelons of inventory be linked electronically and that higher-level inventory managers have visibility of demand, inventory assets, and planned reorders for all lower-level inventory customers. Given this visibility and the timely update of these parameters, an upper-level inventory manager can plan for inventories needed at a specific point to meet a specific customer reorder. Planning for inventory requirements in a time-phased manner means that the need to actually stock material in inventory at the upper level is minimized. Ideally, for example, a production facility supporting a lower-level inventory is able, through DRP systems, to actually schedule production in production-lot sizes equal to the EOQ of the lower-level inventory manager and to schedule this production to meet the anticipated reorder timing inherent in the reorder point system being used at the lower level. Transportation scheduling and personnel assignments are derived from the DRP system, and no finished goods inventory is required by the producer.

Forecasting

Whether the long-used methods of inventory control or a new innovative method such as DRP is used, an accurate sales forecast of future demand is a most critical variable in achieving effective inventory management. In fact, the short-term sales forecast is the heart of any system designed to manage inventory. For any channel member, the type of forecasting method to be used depends upon the type of demand pattern his customers exhibit.

In general, customer demand patterns can be categorized as (1) regular and highly predictable, (2) irregular but mathematically consistent, and (3) irregular and unpredictable.[32] Regular and highly predictable demand does not require a sophisticated sales forecast system. Type 2 demand (irregular but mathematically consistent) requires statistical forecasting, whereas type 3 demand requires the greatest degree of sophistication in designing an inventory control system.

For most types of customer demand patterns, a short-term forecast is the most efficient and most consistent way of obtaining future sales projections. It assumes that the historical sales patterns of a product can be used to predict its future sales, and therefore relies upon such historical data-based forecasting methods as moving averages, weighted moving averages, regression, and exponential smoothing.

Exponential smoothing, the most popular of these techniques, uses the past forecast of demand together with the most recent actual demand observation to determine the forecast of demand for the coming period. The system assumes that the past forecast represents the best estimate of demand prior to the current period and that this forecast, updated appropriately with information from the current period, will provide an accurate forecast for the coming period. In applying the exponential smoothing methodology, smoothing weights must be selected. The issue in making this determination is one of sensitivity. The man-

---

[32] Edward W. Smykay and Allan D. Dale, "Inventory Control: What Price Service? Part 1," *Handling and Shipping* (July 1966), p. 48.

ager must determine how much weight to place on the most recent observed demand value relative to the previous demand for the item. This is analytically equivalent to choosing the base period to be used in any moving average technique. Typically, alternative smoothing weight combinations should be analyzed to determine the combination that provides a balance of stability, accuracy, and sensitivity in demand forecasts. Exponential smoothing methods are quite common in mechanized inventory control systems and are particularly effective in estimating demand for type 1 and 2 patterns. Although the application of such historical data-based techniques is less reliable for type 3 demand patterns, this problem can be alleviated somewhat by considerably reducing the forecasting interval—say, to one week—which enhances the reliability of the data and, hence, improves prediction.

Lack of a sales forecast, inaccurate sales forecasting, and/or lack of sales forecast information sharing among retailers, wholesalers, and manufacturers can create inventory problems throughout the marketing channel. First, a sudden increase in sales volume at the retail level creates a ripple effect back through the channel because of time lags in order processing and in the flow of goods. For example, as shown in Fig. 4–10, the effect of a sudden 10 percent increase in retail sales causes a 16 percent increase in manufacturer warehouse orders from distributors almost three months after the retail increase takes place. When distributors' orders are placed with manufacturers, they reduce factory inventories by 13 percent. Unfilled orders to replace depleted invento-

Figure 4–10   Effect of a sudden 10 percent increase in retail sales on inventories and factory output

Source: Reprinted by permission of the *Harvard Business Review.* An exhibit from "Industrial Dynamics: A Major Breakthrough for Decision Makers," by Jay W. Forrester (July–August 1958), p. 43. Copyright © 1958 by the President and Fellows of Harvard College; all rights reserved.

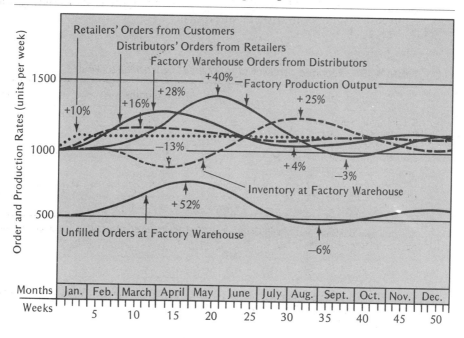

ries begin to build up and production does not peak until almost four months after the retail sales increase.

Unpredicted sales increases also result in stockouts. Frequent stockouts may result in substantial lost sales and customer ill will.

Controlling Stockouts

If sales forecasting were perfectly accurate, stockouts would never occur. If, however, it is known in advance that each forecast will have some error in it (as it almost surely will), then action must be taken to ensure that this error does not seriously weaken customer service.

Ideally, a firm would never have a stockout, but maintaining a 100-percent service level is usually prohibitively costly. The firm must balance the cost of maintaining the desired level of service with the cost associated with a stockout.

The visible cost of a stockout is the direct loss of revenue to the supplier and possibly to the store. In addition, if a store frequently encounters stockouts, its customer service is weakened, and it may begin to lose its power to attract patrons. Table 4–5 shows the reported behavior of shoppers experiencing stockouts. In order to minimize stockouts at a reasonable cost to the firm, it is necessary to understand stockout behavior by consumers and related store and product decisions, as well as retail store merchandising strategy, as illustrated in the process model for a stockout shown in Fig. 4–11. It is equally important to predict the likely forecasting error. The term used for this prediction is the *standard error of the estimate* (S.E.). The standard error is employed to determine how much extra safety stock is needed to cushion against customer demand larger than the sales forecast.[33] The application of the S.E. method in controlling stockouts is presented in Appendix 4B.

As indicated, every channel member must determine through research the customer service level best suited to it by balancing the cost of holding additional safety stock versus the costs of stockouts.

Table 4–5   Reported behavior of shoppers experiencing stockouts

Action Taken	Number	Percentage
Bought same brand, different size	21	4.8
Bought different brand	22	5.0
Bought different product	54	12.4
Postponed purchase until next visit to same store	48	11.1
Decided not to buy	81	18.7
Decided to search in other stores	208	47.9
TOTAL	434	100.0

Source: Philip B. Schary and Martin Christopher, "The Anatomy of a Stock-Out," *Journal of Retailing,* Vol. 55, No. 2 (Summer 1979), p. 66.

[33] Edward W. Smykay and Allan D. Dale, "Inventory Control: What Price Service? Part 2," *Handling and Shipping* (August 1966), pp. 60–63.

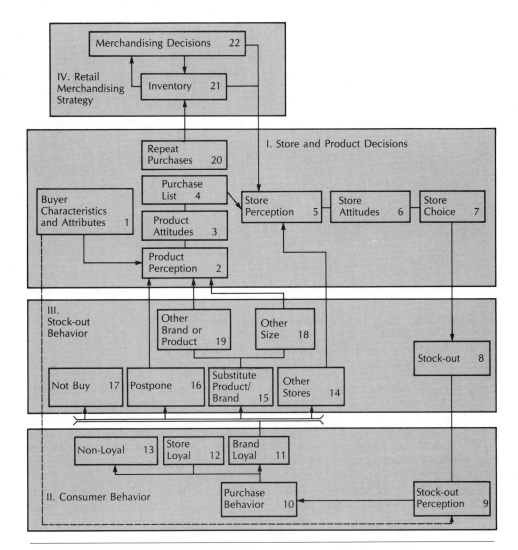

Figure 4–11 Process model of a stock out

Source: Philip B. Schary and Martin Christopher, "The Anatomy of a Stock-Out," *Journal of Retailing,* Vol. 55, No. 2 (Summer 1979), p. 62.

PRODUCTION CONTROL AND MATERIALS REQUIREMENT PLANNING

In most organizations, production control, purchasing, and raw materials handling fall under the materials management function. A few contemporary organizations include these activities as an integral part of a larger logistics organization. Naturally, there is a great deal of interface among physical distribution, materials management, manufacturing, and marketing, as shown in Fig. 4–12.

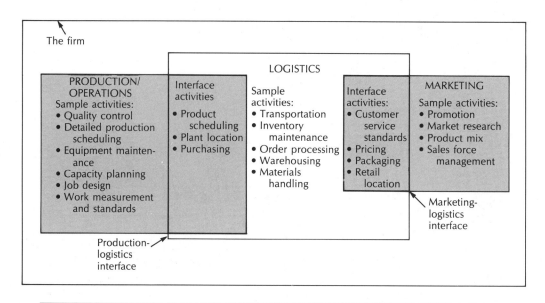

Figure 4–12   The logistics interfaces with marketing and production

Source: Ronald H. Ballou, *Business Logistics Management: Planning and Control,* 2nd ed., © 1985, p. 21. Reprinted by permission of Prentice-Hall, Inc., Englewood Cliffs, N.J.

Often the operating objectives set by management for each of those areas will not coincide. This may lead to a lack of coordination among PD activities as a whole, which in turn could lead to lower customer service levels and/or total physical distribution costs that are higher than necessary. Thus, to maintain the necessary level of customer service, *production control* must be seen as an integral element of the physical distribution network. The role of production in the physical distribution process is twofold. The production activity determines how much and what kinds of finished products are produced, which in turn influences when and how the products are distributed to the firm's customers. Also, the company's need for raw materials, subassemblies, and parts is directly affected by production.

Organizations that adopt the spirit of the physical distribution concept integrate raw materials requirement planning, purchasing, receiving, handling, inventory control, warehousing, and sometimes production scheduling under a single manager responsible for materials management. Materials management is "the single-manager organization concept embracing the planning, organizing, motivating, and controlling of all those activities and personnel principally concerned with the flow of materials into an organization."[34] In 1984 A. T. Kearny completed a study for the National Council of Physical Distribution Management (now the Council of Logistics Management) in which it surveyed a large number of U.S. firms to determine the degree to which they had integrated the materials management and physical distribution functions. Survey results indicated that most integration efforts to date have been directed at physical distri-

[34] Harold E. Fearon, "Materials Management: A Synthesis and Current View," *Journal of Purchasing,* Vol. 9, No. 1 (February 1973), p. 33.

bution. Only about 15 percent of the firms analyzed had gone further in integrating both the inbound materials management function and the outbound physical distribution function. For these firms, however, the results of the integration effort were impressive—productivity increases of 12 to 15 percent. Although materials management does not interface directly with the final consumer, its effect on the level of customer service must not be overlooked. The availability of products to the customer is determined by the degree to which raw materials, parts, and subassemblies are made available to the production process.

Typically, the materials manager is responsible for the following basic activities:[35]

1. Forecasting materials requirements
2. Developing the materials requirement plan
3. Sourcing and obtaining materials
4. Introducing materials into the organization
5. Monitoring the status of materials as a current asset

Materials requirements planning (MRP) is critical to the success of a materials management system. MRP consists of "a set of logically related procedures, decision rules, and records designed to translate a master production schedule into time-phased net requirements, and the planned coverage for such requirements for each component inventory item needed to implement this schedule."[36] Once MRP is completed, the materials manager may proceed with *sourcing decisions* and other tasks of materials management.

MRP systems provide the link between vendors and the internal production processes of the firm. The success of MRP is based on several critical factors:

- The material requirements of the firm must be based on a known production schedule that exhibits a high degree of stability over a given MRP planning horizon. Production discipline is a very important prerequisite to making MRP work effectively.
- Individual material requirements for parts, subcomponents, raw materials, etc., must be quantified relative to the planned production levels for the finished product. These relationships are typically established through a bill-of-materials file.
- Supplier lead times must be within the production planning horizon and must be reasonably accurate.

Given these factors, an MRP system allows the firm to support internal operations effectively while minimizing the investment in incoming and work-in-process inventories. A stable, disciplined master production schedule provides a deterministic demand base on which to build material requirements. Reorder levels are replaced by the time-phased generation of orders a lead time in advance of actual production requirements. Thus, orders in an MRP system are placed in a discrete pattern at the latest point possible to arrive in time to support production. With stable lead times and dependable suppliers, safety stocks are eliminated or at least minimized.

In summary, the functions materials managers are responsible for are purchasing and procurement, production control, inbound traffic and transpor-

---

[35] *Ibid.*
[36] Lambert and Stock, *op. cit.*, p. 354.

tation, warehousing and storage, management of components of the firm's information system, inventory planning and control, and salvage and scrap disposal. The activities performed in materials management are very similar to those performed in the distribution of finished goods. The materials manager is concerned with inventory control, warehousing and storage, order processing, transportation, and almost all other distribution activities. The major differences between materials management and finished goods distribution are that the items handled in materials management are all raw materials, parts, and subassemblies rather than finished goods, and the recipient of the product is the production or manufacturing group as opposed to the final consumer.

Just-in-Time Logistics Systems

Faced with increasing cost pressures, the opportunity costs of inflated inventories, and growing operational problems, many U.S. firms are embracing an innovative approach to logistics management called *just-in-time (JIT)*. The JIT philosophy is quite simple: material resources should flow through the logistics system so that they arrive at the point of intended use just in time. In theory, the system provides for the right materials in the right quantities at the right time, and does so without the need for inventories. Thus, JIT systems focus on material movement and recognize the importance of maximizing the productivity with which material assets are applied in a logistics system. Further, today's JIT systems take full advantage of the technology available to manage information and to effectively coordinate material flows. In reality, JIT systems are much more than inventory control systems, in that the implementation of JIT will substantially affect purchasing, transportation, warehousing, production, quality control, and data processing within a firm. In each of these functional areas, JIT processing requires a level of discipline and coordination that is beyond the capability of many organizations. This requirement must be recognized if JIT is to be implemented successfully. For example, consider the following requirements for the smooth implementation of JIT.

Purchasing. Purchasing must locate and cultivate a limited number of highly reliable suppliers and establish workable, mutually beneficial long-term contractual relationships with them. Suppliers must be particularly strong in lead-time dependability and quality. Moreover, suppliers must have access to the production and inventory planning data of the buyers in order to adequately plan for their own production. On-line electronic data interchange (EDI) is a necessity, and suppliers must be committed over a realistic time horizon to providing continuing material support to the buyers.

Transportation. Transportation is a critical element in any JIT system where it is called on to perform at a level of efficiency and dependability much greater than that required in traditional logistics systems, where buffers of inventory essentially decouple the transportation system from the operations of the firm. Delivery schedules and turnaround times for transportation assets are often highly disciplined in JIT systems. Shipment sizes tend to be small and shipment frequencies greater in JIT systems, and the ability to effectively monitor and control the transportation process becomes extremely important.

Warehousing. JIT systems, by their design, focus on material movement and not on material storage. Automated storage systems, therefore, are far less important than the ability to move material quickly and efficiently to the point of use within the organization. Central storage facilities are often eliminated in favor of very limited staging capabilities adjacent to the point of use.

Inventory Control. The inventory control function (including the management of incoming inventories of raw materials, semifinished goods, and components; the management of WIP inventories; and the management of finished goods or distribution inventories) is a central element in a JIT system. As safety stocks are eliminated and order quantities tied to a specific, time-phased intended use are implemented, room for error in the inventory system is significantly reduced. Traditional approaches, which assume the existence of inventories of materials in storage, give way to MRP and DRP, which assume inventory in motion. Production-lot sizes are reduced and WIP inventories decline. Ideally, the JIT concept envisions a smooth material flow from the basic raw material source, to various stages of conversion, to some ultimate level of inventory that directly supports a customer who cannot, by the nature of the customer demand, be linked directly to the flow.

Production. JIT systems rely on small production lots, short production runs, and rapid setup times in flexible manufacturing systems to stabilize the flow of materials and products through the manufacturing process. In the best case, production at each stage is geared directly to support input requirements at the following stage and WIP buffers are eliminated.

Quality Control. As inventories are eliminated throughout the logistics system, the importance of quality grows proportionally. Because each unit of inventory is moving to some intended use, there are no allowances in the system for defective units either in incoming deliveries or in the WIP pipeline. Quality problems force an interruption of the flow and are often very expensive to the firm in a JIT environment. The JIT process by its very design forces quality problems to the surface and dictates timely resolution of them.

In summary, JIT systems are intended to stress the functional linkages in the logistics flow, to force operating inefficiencies to the surface, and to reduce the costs of the logistics process. Typically, where JIT systems have proved successful the concept is implemented by each participant in a given distribution channel. In this way, the benefits of the JIT approach are shared throughout the channel. Finished goods are produced and delivered just in time to be sold, subassemblies just in time to be assembled into finished goods, fabricated parts just in time to go into subassemblies, and materials just in time to be transformed into fabricated parts.[37] The JIT concept calls for all materials to be active as work-in-process; there is never a pause to collect carrying charges. It is a hand-to-mouth operation in which the ratio of production and delivery quantities approaches 1.

The point is to make sure each person involved in the manufacturing process gets the right parts in the right quantity just in time. JIT works best in

[37] Brownstein, *op. cit.*

repetitive manufacturing situations involving at least some of the following criteria: (1) there are significant levels of inventory to begin with; (2) demand and production can be forecast accurately; and (3) suppliers are located nearby, manufacture quality parts, and are willing to cooperate.[38] The improvement seen in various Osmark Industries plants after they implemented their own version of JIT, called ZIPS, testifies to the significant benefits that can be reaped from the application of JIT:

- At the Mesabi plant, large size drill inventory was cut by 92 percent, productivity increased by 30 percent, scrap and rework (imperfect pieces that must be redone) dropped 20 percent, and lead time (the time it takes to go from order to finished product) was slashed from three weeks to three days.

- At the Oroville plant, which produces reloading equipment for firearms, inventories were reduced by 50 percent, lead time plummeted from six weeks to two days, and lot sizes (the number of parts produced during an individual run) were progressively cut from 500 to 30. In less than one year, some 200 products, more than 70 percent of the plant's entire line, were ZIPSed.

- At pilot operations in a log-loader plant in Prentice, Wis., total inventories were reduced by 45 percent and, thanks to a new layout, parts that have once traveled 2000 feet now move only 18 inches to get from one machine to another. As distances shrank, and the need for long runs disappeared, lead times fell from 30 days to a matter of minutes.[39]

ORDER PROCESSING AND RELATED INFORMATION SYSTEM FLOWS

A customer order is the message that sets the physical distribution process in motion, as clearly illustrated in Fig. 4–13. The customer order cycle includes the total time consumed by order preparation and transmittal, order receipt, order entry, order processing, warehouse picking and packing, order transportation, and delivery and unloading at the customer's dock. Therefore, the length of the customer's order cycle is determined not only by the speed of the physical movement of the goods but also by the speed and efficiency of the information and communication flows in the marketing channel. The experience of major corporations such as Eli Lilly, American Cyanamid, and E.R. Squibb and Sons demonstrates that faster order cycles achieved through the institution of an on-line computer-to-computer ordering system result in reduced order lead time, reduced ordering errors, reduced inventory, and fewer stockouts.[40] Because of the significance of channel communications and information systems for the entire channel operation and their impact on channel member and channel system performance, Chapter 10 of this text is devoted to channel communications and information systems, including computer-to-computer ordering systems, as well as to other aspects of electronic data interchange (EDI) in marketing channels.

[38] Craig R. Waters, "Why Everybody's Talking about 'JUST–IN–TIME,'" *Inc.* (March 1984), pp. 78–80.

[39] *Ibid.*, p. 78.

[40] For details see "Order Processing and Inventory Control—The On-Line Revolution: Cutting Down the Order Cycle Time," *Traffic Management*, Vol. 22, No. 5 (May 1983), pp. 33–42.

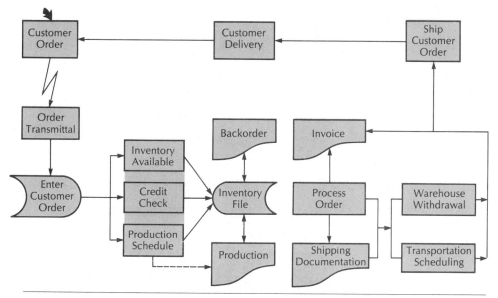

Figure 4–13 The path of a customer's order

Source: Douglas M. Lambert and James R. Stock, *Strategic Physical Distribution Management* (Homewood, Ill.: Richard D. Irwin, © 1982), p. 312.

A STRATEGIC PLANNING PROCESS FOR PHYSICAL DISTRIBUTION SYSTEM DESIGN AND MANAGEMENT

The physical distribution design is a complex task involving the integration of all system components. A strategically planned physical distribution system can provide the company with (1) a better understanding of the impact corporate strategy has on physical distribution activities, (2) increased physical distribution responsiveness, (3) increased sensitivity to the distribution environment, and (4) increased awareness and understanding of distribution cost reduction and service optimization opportunities.[41]

The strategic planning process for a physical distribution system design involves an evaluation of alternate physical distribution system configurations that meet customer service requirements at the lowest total system cost.[42] Therefore, the process begins with the determination of customer service goals and strategies, as shown in Fig. 4–14. Customer service goals and strategies in turn serve as the bases for the determination of inventory, warehousing, transportation, and order processing strategies and programs as well as for related invest-

---

[41] Michael A. McGinnis and Bernard J. LaLonde, "The Physical Distribution Manager and Strategic Planning," *Managerial Planning*, Vol. 31, No. 5 (March/April 1983), p. 41.

[42] Robert E. Murray, "Strategic Distribution Planning: Structuring a Plan," proceedings of the 18th Annual Conference of the National Council for Physical Distribution Management, Atlanta, 1980, pp. 210–11.

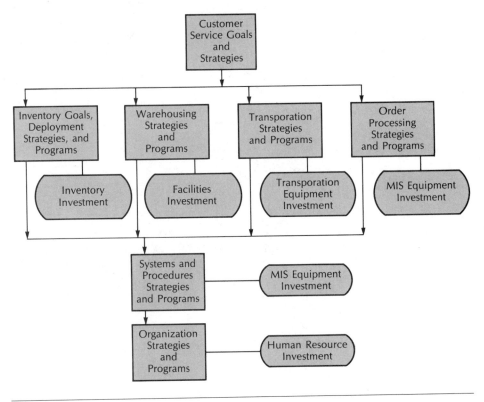

Figure 4–14   The physical distribution strategic planning process

Source: Adapted from Robert E. Murray, Booz, Allen and Hamilton, Inc., from a presentation to the 18th annual conference of the National Council of Physical Distribution Management in Atlanta, Georgia, October 13–15, 1980.

ments in inventories, warehousing and distribution center facilities, transportation equipment, and management information system hardware. The next step is to specify systems and procedures for handling physical distribution activities that are based on the physical and information flows in the system. Finally, organization strategies are developed and translated in terms of the human resources needed to implement the system.[43]

After the strategic physical distribution plan has been developed, methods for carrying out the plan and criteria for selecting individual channel members must be established.

The performance of the physical distribution system must be evaluated periodically and action taken to improve the performance if it is below set standards. The case study in Exhibit 4–1 illustrates one method of analyzing the physical distribution system.

[43] *Ibid.*, pp. 216–19.

EXHIBIT 4–1   Case study: The MIDAS approach in action

A consumer products division of a well-known U.S. electronics and communications conglomerate has used the MIDAS framework to analyze a costly and perplexing problem with its principal product line.

The division was suffering heavy losses despite chalking up a hefty $200 million in annual sales at the manufacturing level. At that time, the production cost per unit was under $1.00 and the selling price to retailers was over $4.00. Yet the division was losing $25 million a year. In other words, a 400 percent markup was failing to yield a profit.

DISTRIBUTION

A channel map of the company's distribution network was drawn up. The picture was enlightening.

Physical Distribution.   Mismanagement of the division's inventory control, warehousing, and transportation systems were tying up and siphoning off large amounts of cash.

The first step in analyzing the division's distribution problems was to age the product inventory in its warehouses. This was done by dividing monthly sales by the end-of-the-month inventory in each warehouse. The results of this analysis were startling. There was a one-year supply of inventory on hand for slightly over 50 percent of the 500 products in the line and a five-year supply for another 10 percent.

Division managers cleared out the warehouses by holding inventory sales of obsolete products, thereby reducing inventory value from $20 million to $6 million. After the inventory control system was reorganized, the inventory turnover rate increased from about 2.5 times a year to a little over 8.3 times a year.

The company did not use the investment theory of inventory, but based on a modest 20 percent annual carrying cost, the reorganization of the inventory control system saved the company about $2.8 million a year ($0.20 × $20 million − 0.20 × $6 million). After the reorganization, warehousing and operating costs also dropped by about $500,000.

Next, *warehousing operations* were analyzed. They were in total disarray. Orders were being filled as they came in, and in some cases, five separate orders were being processed, packed, and shipped to the same customer on the same day. The backorder rate was averaging over 40 percent, but this reflected the fact that a single backorder could show up as many as three times before the completed order was shipped.

In addition, products were being placed in warehouses according to their production sequence numbers. This meant that some fast-moving items were located at the back of the warehouse, thereby inflating shipping costs through long travel and repositioning time. Also, no distinction was being made between case-lot and broken-case orders.

The entire warehousing system was overhauled at a cost savings of over $2 million. Corrective actions included:

- Redesigning the order processing system so that orders from the same customer could be batched
- Rearranging warehouse space allocations to provide separate locations for full-case and broken-case lots
- Installing a stock location system based on the sales volume of each product

An ABC analysis revealed that 20 percent of the products in the line accounted for over 85 percent of the orders. Twenty items were placed near the loading dock to reduce travel time for pickers.

Before the MIDAS analysis, *transportation* costs were averaging about $8 million a year. Some products were being shipped at a cost of over $1000 per 100 pounds. These astronomical transportation costs were primarily due to the division's ship-when-received policy.

Transportation cost savings of over $1 million were achieved by redesigning customer service standards to fit market realities. Criteria were established by customer and by product so that shipping dates could be adjusted in response to variations in ordering cycles.

The second major transportation problem was that customer fulfillment responsibility and shipping patterns had not been established in a cost-effective manner. As a result, shipments to retailers were often made from the wrong warehouse.

Management responded to this problem by developing a new computer program for shipping control. In its first year of operation, the new control program reduced transportation costs by almost $1 million.

ALLOCATION

Originally a uniform price for all orders existed. In addition, the company absorbed all freight costs. A study was designed where customers were broken down by size of shipment rather than size of order because some customers requested that all orders be shipped to one location while others required as many as two hundred ship-to-locations on one order.

Order processing and filling costs, as well as transportation costs, were calculated for a range of order sizes. The analysis revealed that small shipments were extremely costly and generated large losses. Large shipments, on the other hand, generated a good profit contribution.

As a result of the analysis, a minimum order quantity was established at the break-even point plus a normal profit contribution. All orders below the minimum required that the customer pay the freight charges. In addition, a discount policy was established related to shipment size and related attendant cost savings for larger orders. Pricing zones were also established to reflect the high cost of doing business in smaller distant markets.

The net result of the analysis was a variable pricing system that more accurately reflected cost per order by size and distance.

Source: Edward W. Smykay and Mary A. Higby, "Shifting Shoals in Marketing Channels: The MIDAS Approach to Channel Analysis," *Management Review* (July 1981), pp. 20–22.

DISTRIBUTION STRATEGY REVISION

The question most often asked by management is when to revise the firm's physical distribution strategy. Existing strategies can become outdated even if they are continually undergoing improvement. Substantial changes in the following factors may indicate a need for strategy revision.

1. Demand.   Geographic dispersion and level of demand greatly determine the configuration of distribution networks. Firms may project disproportionate growth or decline in one region of the country compared with a general growth or decline overall.

The latter may require only expansion or recession at current facilities. However, shifting demand patterns may require that new warehouses be located in rapidly growing markets while facilities in slow-growth areas experience little or no expansion.

Disproportionate growth of only a few percentage points a year indicates that network replanning is economically beneficial.

2. Customer Service. This usually includes inventory availability, speed of delivery, and order filling speed and accuracy.

The costs of transportation, warehousing, inventory carrying, and order processing rise disproportionately as service levels are increased. Therefore, distribution costs will be sensitive to the level of customer service provided, especially if it is already high.

Replanning usually is needed when service levels are changed due to competitive forces, policy revisions, or arbitrary service goals different from those on which the distribution strategy originally was based.

Conversely, minor changes in service levels—when they already are low—probably will not trigger the need for replanning.

3. Product Characteristics. Distribution costs are sensitive to product weight, volume, value, and risk. In the channel, these characteristics can be altered through package design or finished state of the product during shipment and storage.

For example, shipping a product in a knocked-down form can considerably affect the weight–bulk ratio of the product and the associated transportation and storage rates.

But if altering a product characteristic substantially changes one cost element of distribution without affecting others, a new cost balance point for the distribution system is created and replanning would be needed.

4. Distribution Costs. The amount of money a firm spends on distribution often determines how often its strategy should be replanned. All other factors being equal, a firm producing high-valued goods, such as machine tools and computers, with total distribution costs of 10 percent of sales or less may give little attention to distribution strategy. On the other hand, companies producing packaged industrial chemicals or food products may have distribution costs as high as 30 percent of sales. When costs are that high, even small changes in interest rates and fuel prices can make distribution strategy reformulation worthwhile.

5. Pricing Policy. Some suppliers transfer the responsibility and cost of transportation to the buyer, thus taking decisions on important distribution cost elements out of their own hands.

Many industrial products firms do this through pricing policies such as F.O.B. factory, prepaid transportation charges, and invoice add-ons. Since these firms do not pay for transportation, there is little incentive to include it as an economic force in setting distribution strategy.

Should the price policy be changed to a delivered arrangement, the supplying firm would directly incur the transportation charges. This can result in the addition of warehouses and inventory to the distribution system.

Shifting the terms of the price policy, especially shipment routing and quantities and responsibility for the transportation decision, can signal a need for strategy reformulation.

If changes have occurred in one or more of these five areas, substantial cost-reduction opportunities are available. Firms usually start by replanning inventory policy, location, freight consolidation and scheduling, and customer service.[44]

SUMMARY AND CONCLUSIONS

Physical distribution management is a critical factor in the effective and efficient marketing of all products. However, the costs of activities associated with the flow of physical possession are surprisingly high—so high, in fact, that efforts must be expended to reduce them if distributive firms are to reach their profit goals, particularly when sales are growing at very slow rates. Underlying effective and efficient physical distribution management is the physical distribution (PD) concept. This concept takes a cost-service orientation that is aimed at minimizing the costs of distribution at a given level of customer service. The tenets of the concept can be achieved only through a coordinated systemwide physical distribution network.

Developing a PD system should begin with the determination of customer service standards. Arriving at an appropriate customer service standard involves determining the important elements of customer service from the customer's viewpoint. This information can be obtained through questionnaires or surveys. Once this is done, quantitative standards of performance must be set for each service element, actual performance for each service element should be measured and compared with the standards that have been set, and corrective action must be taken as needed if there is variance between the actual performance and the standard. Once customer service standards are developed, management can undertake a selection of the transportation, warehousing, inventory, and production policies that will assure their proper implementation.

Problems in transporting merchandise can create difficulties in maintaining proper inventory levels and can impair customer service. Therefore, selection of suitable transportation modes is an integral part of developing a sound PD system. Rail, highway, water, air, and pipeline networks each have advantages for different shippers and receivers. However, it appears that highway and air transport are becoming more important, even though rail is still the major means of freight movement in the United States. Increasingly, though, combinations of the various modes are being used. Aided by various transportation agencies, such as freight forwarders, the existing transportation system in the United States presents channel members with myriad reasonably efficient transport choices.

The two basic categories of warehouses available to channel members are private facilities, which are either owned or leased by the firm, and public facili-

---

[44] Ronald H. Ballou, "How to Tell When Distribution Strategy Needs Revision," *Marketing News* (May 1, 1981), p. 12.

ties, in which space is rented by the firm. The choice between the two often involves tradeoffs between managerial control on the one hand and capital investment on the other. Use of public warehouses appears to be growing rapidly, because the public warehousing industry is becoming more sophisticated in the scope and performance of a wide variety of distributive services. For firms having private warehouses, the development of distribution centers has emerged as a major service factor in physical distribution management. Clearly, the widespread application of data processing technology has significantly increased the ability of warehousing operations of all types to meet the needs of the firms they serve. Determining the number and location of warehouses is a problem the manager faces, irrespective of the private-versus-public decision. A total cost approach is required, because the solution demands tradeoffs among all physical distribution costs, especially those costs associated with warehouse operation, transportation, inventory, and lost sales resulting from slow service.

Inventory management and control will always play a vital role in the operation of firms directly involved in distribution; their significance is even more salient in periods of shortages, slow economic growth, and high interest rates. Inventory control encompasses decisions over how much and when to order as well as how much inventory to keep in stock. The objective of inventory control is to minimize total inventory cost subject to demand and service constraints. A new approach to inventory control is the just-in-time (JIT) concept. Ideally, a firm operating under JIT produces and delivers materials just in time to be transformed into fabricated parts, fabricated parts just in time to go into subassemblies, subassemblies just in time to be assembled into finished goods, and finished goods just in time to be sold. It is a hand-to-mouth mode of operation in which the ratio of production and delivery quantities approaches 1.

Critical to decisions on when and how much to order is an accurate sales forecast. The forecasting model used depends on whether customer demand can be categorized as regular and highly predictable, irregular but mathematically consistent, or irregular and unpredictable. Exponential smoothing models are frequently used by manufacturers and wholesalers, because the demand facing them is generally not highly volatile. Retailers, though, often face fluctuating or, at the least, highly seasonal demand. Therefore, adaptive forecasting is needed to cope with the latter's inventory problems. Furthermore, because sales forecasts are subject to error, controls must be established so that these errors do not lead to a reduction in customer service standards. In order to minimize stockouts at a reasonable cost to the firm, it is necessary to utilize a standard error of the estimate so that appropriate levels of safety stock can be established.

Production control is an important element of the PD system. It is just one function performed by the materials manager. When and how finished products are distributed to the customer are affected by how much and what kinds of products a firm produces. These are production decisions that indirectly influence the level of customer service.

PD system management is a complex task involving the integration of all system components. It is critical to the continued success of a firm that the distribution strategy not become outdated. Thus, the question most often asked by management is when to revise the firm's strategy. Substantial changes in demand, customer service, product characteristics, distribution costs, or pricing policy can indicate a need for strategy revision.

DISCUSSION QUESTIONS

1. What is systems analysis, and why is it so useful an approach to managing physical distribution activities?

2. The physical distribution manager has been called "a manager of tradeoffs." Explain what this means.

3. What is the major advantage of using JIT inventory control? What are its assumptions, and how do they compare with the EOQ assumptions in terms of applicability to retailers?

4. Compare and contrast private ownership of storage space with rented storage space, with reference to:
   a. the services that can be obtained with each
   b. the cost of storage
   c. the degree of administrative control
   d. the flexibility to meet future uncertainties

5. Assume that you are employed by a retailing firm. What are the tradeoffs involved in obtaining delivery in three to four days of a given item from a wholesaler versus delivery in three to four weeks from the manufacturer?

6. The following estimates are made about a certain inventory item:
   Demand: 100 units per week
   Inventory carrying cost: 20 percent
   Order costs: $20 per order
   Item value: $20
   Lead time: 1.5 weeks
   Determine the order quantity and reorder point. What would you need to know in order to calculate appropriate levels of safety stocks in this example? (Read Appendix 4B first.)

7. Give an example of a situation where the EOQ formula is likely to be useful, and explain why. (See Appendix 4B.)

8. Suppose you are given the following data:

Period	Demand	Forecast (stock)	Overstock/ Understock
1	520	520	0
2	500		
3	470		
4	620		

   a. Compute forecasts for periods 2, 3, and 4 using (1) a simple unweighted average; (2) exponential smoothing where weight (α) = 0.8.
   b. Compute the average overstock or understock.
   c. Explain which forecasting method is superior and why.

9. Contrast the following in terms of speed, reliability, availability, and cost of service.
   a. truck and rail
   b. rail and inland water
   c. piggyback and truck
   d. piggyback and rail
   e. company-owned trucking with common carrier trucking
   f. air and truck

10. Transportation used to be a regulated industry, but recently deregulation has occurred in trucking, the railroads, and the airlines. What are the advantages of a

firm's having experts in the fields of traffic and transportation, and how has the recent deregulation affected their jobs?

11. In what ways may the computer be applied to physical distribution?

12. Many U.S. companies are moving to distribution requirements planning systems as a way to reduce finished goods inventories and to improve customer service. Briefly discuss the forces that are motivating this shift, contrast DRP approaches with traditional reorder point models, and evaluate the potential impacts of DRP on echelon and distribution network decisions made by the firm.

13. As the new marketing director of Annapolis Aviation, you are projecting monthly sales demands for your most popular engine control. Given the following data, and assuming you are working in August:
   a. Determine the three-month moving averages.
   b. Determine the single exponentially smoothed forecasts with $\alpha = 0.2$, and determine the MAD for this model. Assume that the forecast for January is 1000.
   c. Calculate the tracking signal for the model in step b.

	Actual Demand
January	900
February	1200
March	1000
April	1100
May	1500
June	1300
July	1000

14. Tappahonic Tape produces a line of high-quality reflecting tape for industrial use. The major product line is a three-inch tape called product A. The annual demand for the finished product, A, is 25,000 units. The cost to process a manufacturing order is $200, and the inventory holding cost is $10 per unit per year. Product A is made of one unit of B and two units of C. A, B, and C have lead times of 1 week. There are 50 working weeks in a year.
   a. Determine the production run size.
   b. Draw the product structure tree.
   c. Determine the MRP schedule for the next eight weeks, assuming the first production run will be completed in the fourth week. On-hand inventory for A, B, and C is zero.

15. Given the changing makeup of the U.S. transportation system and innovations occurring in materials management, production, and physical distribution in U.S. industry, evaluate the future role of transportation in the logistics equation. Support open analysis and projections with relevant data where appropriate.

16. Dumfries Distributing carries a wide range of electrical consumer products, which are sold to area retail outlets. Demand for a particular condensor is 40,000 units per year. The cost to Dumfries Distributing to process an order is $25, and the holding cost per condensor in stock is $0.50 per unit per year. The time it normally takes to receive an order, once placed, is three months.
   a. What is the EOQ?
   b. How many orders will be placed each year?
   c. What is the annual cost of processing purchase orders for condensors?
   d. What is the annual cost of carrying the inventory of condensors?
   e. Compute the required reorder point.

Legal Forms of Transport, Transportation Agencies, and Coordinated Systems

LEGAL FORMS OF TRANSPORT

There are currently four legal forms of transport for shippers: common carriers, contract carriers, exempt carriage, and private transportation. Freight brokers are sometimes considered a fifth legal form. However, brokers merely match freight with carriers without assuming ownership or the risks of operating transport equipment.

Common Carriers.   Common carriers are the most regulated for-hire transport firms. They are required to publish and make available to the public all rates charged for their services. A common carrier is any transportation firm that makes its services available to all shippers and accepts responsibility for carrying goods anytime and any place, on a fee basis. Therefore, a basic characteristic of common carriers is that their services are offered to all potential shippers without discrimination. In 1983, the Interstate Commerce Commission (ICC) ruled that a common carrier does not violate its obligations if it declines to provide service within the scope of its operating authority in cases where such services are economically or operationally impractical at the time of the request.

Contract Carriers.   In contrast with common carriers, contract carriers make themselves available for business on a selective basis. They service a limited number of shippers and carry a restricted number of commodities, as specified by their operating permits. Although contract carriers are required to publish the actual rates they charge shippers, they may charge different rates to different customers for the same service. Operation permits issued to contract carriers are less restrictive that those issued to common carriers. They do specify routes to be utilized and commodities to be transported, however.

The Motor Carrier Act of 1980 liberalized contract carriage in a number of ways. First, it no longer restricts the number of shippers with which the carrier may enter into contracts. Second, the carrier no longer has to file its contracts with the commission. Furthermore, in 1983, the ICC permitted contract carriers to serve entire industries or classes of shippers rather than individual companies.

Exempt Carriers.   This form embraces a wide variety of transportation activities that are exempt from direct regulation; thus the name *exempt* carriers. Exemptions usually fall into one of three categories. The first is geographic exemptions, such as those defined by the ICC around the periphery of certain cities mainly because of the administrative difficulties of keeping track of the operations of the numerous small, local cartage operators and small delivery trucks. The second category is exempt commodities, under which carriage of "unprocessed" agricultural and fishing products is largely exempt from economic regulations. Exempt commodities, therefore, are moved at prices lower than those of regulated forms of transport, especially common carriers. Finally there are exempt associations, such as agricultural cooperatives and the shippers' associations described in the next section. The Motor Transportation Act of 1980 increased the percentage of nonexempt tonnage that could be transported by farm cooperatives from 15 to 25 percent.

Private Transportation. Carried on as an activity incidental to the primary purpose of a business, private transportation is defined as the "common ownership of goods transported and the lease or ownership of the equipment in which they are moved." Private transportation falls outside the regulation of the ICC. Where volume of shipment is high, private transportation may prove to be an attractive alternative for users who hope to gain better operating performance, availability, and lower cost. Even when the volume is low, some companies are forced to own or contract for transportation to meet their special transportation requirements not commonly met through the purchase of common carrier services. The Motor Carrier Act of 1980 exempts from regulation transportation performed by a member of a corporate family for members of the same corporate organization.

TRANSPORTATION AGENCIES

Transportation agencies offer transportation services to shippers by handling small shipments and consolidating them into vehicle load quantities. They do not own any line-haul equipment.

Freight Forwarders. Freight forwarders are considered to be common carriers of freight and, as such, have similar rights and obligations. However, they utilize the services of other common carriers for long-distance shipments. Their major function is the consolidation of small shipments into large ones, thereby offsetting the differential between LTL (less-than-truckload) and TL (truckload) rates and LCL (less-than-carload) and CL (carload) rates, respectively.

Parcel Post and Competitive Services. Parcel post services are offered by the United States Post Office. Directly competitive services are available through such firms as Federal Express, United Parcel Service, and Emery. They are designed for small shipments and can be used by nearly everyone. The parcel post uses all air and surface line-haul carriers except pipeline. The rates for air parcel post are usually higher than the surface rates.

Shippers' Associations. These are cooperative organizations operating on a nonprofit basis to take advantage of consolidation economies. They perform the same functions as freight forwarders.

Shippers' Agents. These are transportation brokers who provide ramp-to-ramp transportation from railroads and truckers at origin and destination using truckers as needed, under one bill of lading. They do not provide LTL transportation requiring consolidation at origin or break-bulk at destination. Shippers' agents are exempt from regulation.

Brokers. The track broker is a third party between the owner-operator of the truck or shipper who arranges for the transportation of specific loads at specific prices. The broker's fee is paid for by the owner-operator. Brokers can act as shippers, carriers, and forwarders.

COORDINATED (INTERMODAL) SYSTEMS

The idea of coordinating the services of two or more transportation modes can be traced to the early 1920s. However, interest in coordinated systems has been renewed in recent years. Coordinated systems offer point-to-point through-movement by means of two or more modes of transportation on a regularly scheduled basis. There are numerous possible combinations among the rail, water, air, and truck transportation modes. In addition, pipeline connections with other modes are commonly used among oil transportation companies. Here are some examples of coordinated service:

1. *Piggyback* services are a combination of truck and rail services. This combination is also known as *trailer-on-flatcar (TOFC)* service. It involves transporting truck trailers on railroad flatcars over longer distances than trucks normally haul. The cost is usually less than a truck trailer might incur over the road for the same distance. The result of such a coordinated system is the extension of the trucking industry's range of operation. TOFC service is offered under seven different plans to provide flexibility to shippers.
2. *Fishyback* coordinates truck movement with water movement on inland waterways as well as on coastal and intercoastal routes.
3. *Rail–water* is also called *train–ship* service.
4. *Truck–air* service is widely available throughout the United States.
5. The pipeline combinations include *truck–pipe, water–pipe,* and *rail–pipe*. Almost all of these services exist in the United States, although they may not be available for all shippers because of the special operating characteristics of pipelines.

Appendix 4B

Continuous–Review Reorder–Point Models

This family of models allows a firm to manage inventories in a world of stochastic demand where material requirements planning (MRP) or distribution requirements planning (DRP) is not appropriate and where the nature of the material being managed makes a fixed period or fixed review cycle approach undesirable. The basic information and decision flow in such a reorder point method is illustrated in Fig. 4B–1.

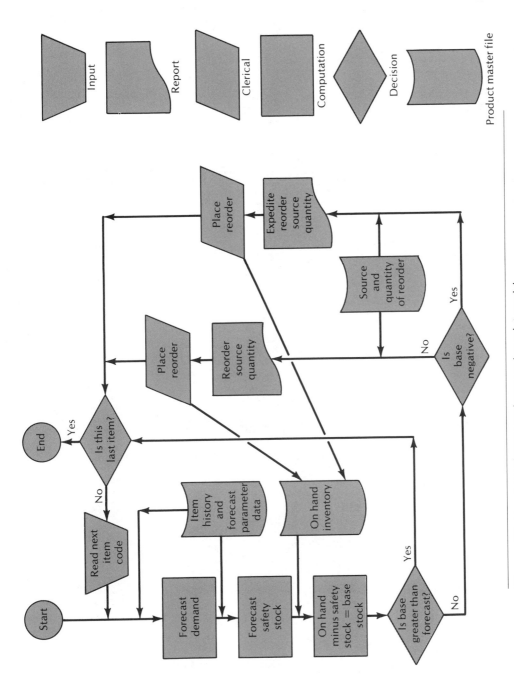

Figure 4B–1 A continuous-review reorder-point model

Input

Report

Clerical

Computation

Decision

Product master file

HOW MUCH TO REORDER

The quantity to order can be arrived at with an economic lot size formula or an economic order quantity (EOQ) formula. One of the oldest and most widely accepted economic lot size formulas is as follows:

$$Q^* = \sqrt{\frac{2DS}{IC}}$$

where

Q^* = the order quantity in units[1]
D = annual demand in units
S = the order processing cost (cost per order in dollars)
I = annual inventory carrying cost as percentage of C
C = value of a unit held in inventory (unit price in dollars)

As an illustration, consider an inventory control problem having the following specifications for a particular item:[2]

D = 50 units per week, or 50 × 52 = 2600 units per year
I = 10 percent[3]
S = $10
C = $5

The optimum order quantity according to the EOQ formula would be

$$Q^* = \sqrt{\frac{2(2600)(10)}{(0.10)(5)}}$$

$$= 322 \text{ units}$$

---

[1] The optimum Q is found by the first derivative of $TC(Q)$—i.e., the total cost equation for an annual period, setting the derivative equal to zero and solving for Q. Thus,

$$TC(Q) = \frac{D}{Q}S + IC\frac{Q}{2}$$

Taking the derivative and setting it equal to zero, we obtain

$$\frac{dTC(Q)}{dQ} = \frac{-DS}{Q^2} + \frac{IC}{2} = 0$$

Solving for Q gives

$$Q^* = \sqrt{\frac{2DS}{IC}}$$

[2] This example is drawn from Ronald H. Ballou, *Business Logistics Management*, 2nd ed. (Englewood Cliffs, N.J.: Prentice-Hall, 1985), p. 374.

[3] Interest on investment 4.0%
Obsolescence 3.0
Storage, transportation, and handling 0.8
Insurance, taxes 0.2
Depreciation 2.0
                                                                          10.0%

Although this classical EOQ formula is straightforward and widely used, its underlying assumptions must be recognized. These assumptions are listed here, along with the reasons they are not applicable to retailing operations:[4]

1. *Demand is known, constant, and continuous.* Demand in retail is usually not known. It is rarely constant and is seasonal for most types of merchandise. In fact, order quantities are used to build up or reduce inventory in anticipation of varying seasonal demand. Also, demand is not continuous, because of such merchandise as end-of-season (that is, merchandise carried only during one season, such as winter or summer jackets).
2. *The only costs significant to reordering decisions are inventory carrying and ordering costs.* Frequently, in managing the inventory of a whole department or classification factors not considered by the classical EOQ equation become very important. The problem of being out of stock is probably the most important single consideration. Furthermore, the costs for individual stockkeeping units (SKUs)[5] are not as significant for the total department as overall inventory and ordering strategies. The EOQ equation certainly does not include all the costs relevant to retail management objectives.
3. *The marginal cost of an additional order or an additional SKU is fixed, and the marginal cost of carrying an additional unit in inventory is fixed.* Marginal costs are synonymous with variable or incremental costs. In other words, marginal costs are the out-of-pocket costs of an additional order or an additional unit in inventory. These costs are different from fixed, indirect, or overhead costs incurred regardless of ordering strategy.

The most serious problem in applying the classical EOQ equation is that of determining costs. In practice, the actual ordering costs are not fixed, as required by the classical EOQ equation. Inventory carrying cost can vary, for example, with management's changing estimates of the cost of capital. Both inventory carrying cost and ordering cost, when applied to retail situations, include fixed and variable costs that would be very difficult to separate.

The determination of cost elements has been a problem since the classical EOQ equation was first developed, and many attempts have been made to solve it. Quite often the costs used are not representative of the real costs involved. Many of the cost elements in actual use are based on estimates involving management decisions, and are "correct" so long as there is full agreement on the decisions made. In many cases the cost estimates are reduced to subjective assessments because of the excessively time-consuming studies involved.

4. *The whole order quantity arrives at one time.* In retail shipments, such an assumption frequently does not hold true. For many reasons, partial shipments do occur, and serious consideration should be given to them. Retail shipments, like many other activities in a department store, are complicated by the highs and lows of volume from month to month, week to week, and day to day. The order quantities should be sufficiently flexible to permit satisfactory adjustment to partial shipments.

[4] *Retail IMPACT: Inventory Management Program and Control Techniques Application Description,* 6th ed. (White Plains, N.Y.: IBM Technical Publications Department, 1970), pp. 71–72.
[5] An SKU is the lowest level of identification of merchandise. SKUs are usually defined by department, store, vendor, style, color, size, and location.

5. *Transaction sizes are small relative to order quantity.* For two reasons, transaction sizes for some staple merchandise are actually large relative to their order quantity. The first reason is the batching of transactions (usually representing sales for one or two weeks) because of data-handling problems and the convenience that batch processing offers. The second reason involves the retail demand process as reflected in customer buying patterns for slow and medium sellers. Customers frequently buy multiple units of many types of merchandise, such as shirts, underwear, and women's hosiery.

6. *There are no overriding restrictions on order quantity.* The classical EOQ formulation does not include any restrictions on the size of the order. For a fixed review time system, the order quantity should be as large as the expected sales during a review time. The order quantity should be at least one pack size in order to be acceptable to the vendor. In many cases, it cannot be greater than a specified maximum, such as three months' supply or a year's supply. The EOQ equation does not include any of these constraints, and therefore it is frequently impractical to apply the results derived from the formula directly.

Consequently, a different order quantity technique has been developed that offers a better solution to retail inventory problems. This approach, called the *modified EOQ*,[6] attempts to remove the largest stumbling block—the problem of determining costs. The classical approach previously explained attempts to identify and quantify all the "true" costs of inventory carrying and reordering. The modified approach, however, treats the costs in the EOQ formula as control "knobs." These control knobs are made available to management and are to be used primarily for selecting management policies, such as the amount of investment in total inventory and overall ordering workload. In other words, the classical "costs," transposed now to modern control "knobs," should be viewed merely as one of the policy variables in the inventory management system. Turning the control knobs to the "left" or "right" makes it possible to vary the balance between inventory investment on the one hand and the number of orders on the other, thus allowing management to examine many alternate strategies.[7] This approach also implies that costs should not be considered fixed. Management can manipulate the modified EOQ equation in order to get results that will match goals. Furthermore, management can now view inventories as a total investment, not as an investment in an individual inventory unit.

To derive the modified EOQ, we begin by spelling out the components of the classical EOQ formula:

$$\text{Economic order quantity in units} = \sqrt{\frac{2 \times (\text{cost per order in dollars}) \times \text{Annual sales in units}}{\text{Inventory carrying rate per year (percent)} \times \text{Unit price in dollars}}}$$

This equation can be broken down into:

$$\sqrt{\frac{2 \times (\text{Cost per unit in dollars})}{\text{Inventory carrying rate per year (percent)}}} \times \sqrt{\frac{\text{Annual sales in units}}{\text{Unit price in dollars}}}$$

[6] See *Retail IMPACT, op. cit.,* p. 73.
[7] *Ibid.*

Now, let the expression under the first square root equal K, and rewrite the EOQ formula somewhat differently to obtain the modified EOQ equation:

$$\text{Modified economic order quantity in units} = K \sqrt{\frac{\text{Annual sales in units}}{\text{Unit price in dollars}}}$$

The K factor is the management control knob referred to previously. Varying K changes the order quantity and, consequently, the number of orders in a year.[8] In reorder-point models, the determination of when to reorder is provided by the established reorder point or reorder level, which is the sum of expected lead-time demand and safety level. Lead time is usually expressed as the number of days in which stock is received in available inventory after the inventory replenishment signal has been given. The main components of lead time are order processing time, order picking and handling time, transit time, and unloading and stocking time. In a steady-state environment, the size of the order quantity (Q^*) in conjunction with expected demand will determine the number of times that the reorder level is reached and hence the number of reorders over any given time horizon. If the economic order quantity is Q^*, then the number of orders that should be placed in a year's time is given by dividing projected demand for the year by Q^*. Dividing the number of orders that should be placed in a year into the number of weeks or days in a year will tell how frequently the stock level should be reviewed. Thus, using the data from the previous EOQ example, and letting N stand for the order interval, we estimate that a reorder will be placed every 6.45 weeks:

$$N = \frac{D}{Q^*} = \frac{2600}{322} = 8.07 \text{ orders per year}$$

$$\frac{52 \text{ weeks}}{8.07 \text{ orders per year}} = 6.45 \text{ weeks}$$

In retailing, the review period is often very short (e.g., a week), not because of economic order quantity considerations but rather because sales of many items sold at retail are highly seasonal and fluctuate continuously over time, thus necessitating frequent review. In wholesaling and manufacturing, the length of the review period is typically longer and frequently coincides more closely with estimates derived from EOQ considerations, although the period's length varies widely, depending on the characteristics of the product category under concern.

WHEN TO REORDER

In reorder-point models, the determination of when to reorder is provided by the established reorder point or reorder level that is the sum of expected lead-time demand and safety level. Lead time is usually expressed as the number of

---

[8] *Ibid.* Two of the many excellent sources that describe EOQ formulas for almost any application are Fred Hanssman, *Operations Research and Inventory Control* (New York: John Wiley & Sons, 1962); and John F. Magee, *Production Planning and Inventory Control* (New York: McGraw-Hill Book Co., 1958).

days to receive stock in available inventory after the inventory replenishment signal has been given. The main components of lead time are order processing time, order picking and handling time, transit time, and unloading and stocking time. Safety level inventories provide a buffer or hedge against uncertainty in either demand or lead time and are intended to minimize the potential for stockout relative to the economic costs of the investment in safety level.

To compute a reorder point, the safety level is added to the projected demand for the product during the delivery lead time. The result is then compared to the quantity of the product available in inventory (or already on order). For example, assume that a retailer has a safety level of 15 units, a lead time of ten days, and an available inventory of 110 units. Assume, also, that the daily sales forecast is 6 units. The reorder level (6 units/day × 10 days + 15 units) is therefore 75 units. When available inventory is reduced to 75 units or less, the reorder-point system will generate a reorder requirement. Figure 4-B2 illustrates the same reorder process graphically using an established order quantity (Q*) of 200 units and a specified reorder level of 100 units (a lead-time level of 60 units plus a safety level of 40 units). When available inventory on hand plus on order is equal to or less than the established reorder level of 100 units, an order for 200 units will be placed. If the order is received exactly at the end of expected lead time, on-hand units will be 40 units when the order for 200 is received. This situation is reflected in the first reorder cycle in Fig. 4B−2. In the second reorder cycle shown, demand is higher during lead time than forecast,

Figure 4B–2   Reorder-point model with variation in demand and lead time

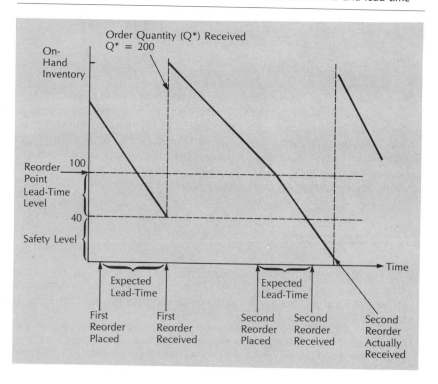

and actual lead time is longer than expected. As a result, on-hand units are well below 40 units (the safety level) when the order is received.

CONTROLLING STOCKOUTS

If it is assumed that sales forecast errors are random and normally distributed, it is possible to set average stockouts at any level desired. If forecast errors are, in fact, random and normally distributed, then adding one S.E. (standard error of the estimate) to the average inventory will reduce stockouts from 50 to 16 percent, giving an in-stock frequency of 84 percent. However, additional safety stocks yield diminishing returns in improved customer service levels. For example, adding two S.E. of safety stock to average inventory reduces average stockouts to 2.3 percent, while the third S.E. reduces stockouts to 0.3 percent. Furthermore, adding one S.E. increases inventory in-stock frequency by 34 percent, while the second S.E. brings 11 percent improvement. By adding a third S.E., an improvement of less than 2 percent is achieved. Table 4B–1 illustrates many of

Table 4B–1 Hypothetical problem dealing with the control of stockouts

Order Cycle	Forecast (stock)	Actual	(Actual-Fcst)^2
1	311	280	961
2	273	260	169
3	191	195	16
4	225	180	2,025
5	300	260	1,600
6	411	385	676
7	306	400	8,836
8	220	280	3,600
	2237	2240	17,883

$$\text{S.E.} = \sqrt{\frac{17,883}{8}} = 47.3$$

$$\text{Average inventory} \frac{2237}{8} = 279.6^a$$

[a] If this firm were willing to endure stockouts for about 50 percent of its order cycles, it could hold an average inventory of 279.6 units. To increase customer service levels to 84 percent, average inventory would have to be increased to 326.9 units (279.6 + 47.3). To increase customer service levels to 97.7 or 99.7 percent would take an increase in average inventory to 374.2 units and 421.5 units. In this example, a 17 percent increase in average inventory brought a 34 percent increase in customer service levels. The second and third 17 percent increments brought only 14 and 2 percent increase in customer service levels.

Source: Edward W. Smykay and Allan D. Dale, "Inventory Control: What Price Service? Part 2," *Handling and Shipping* (August 1966), p. 60.

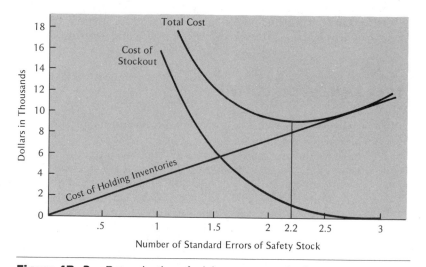

Figure 4B–3 *Determination of minimum-cost service levels*

Source: Edward W. Smykay and Allan D. Dale, "Inventory Control: What Price Service? Part 2," *Handling and Shipping* (August 1966), p. 62.

these tradeoffs by showing how a hypothetical problem concerning the control of stockouts is solved.

To compute average inventory for decision-making purposes, simply divide the established operating level by two and then add safety stocks. This is done because safety stocks are assumed to be the same at the beginning and end of a cycle.

As indicated earlier, every channel member must determine, through PDS research, the customer service level best suited to it by balancing the cost of holding additional safety stock versus the costs of stockouts. Figure 4B–3 shows one method of finding a service level that will minimize costs, if different customers' reactions to a stockout have already been determined.

In summary, the sequence of events that should be employed by a channel member in instituting an inventory control system designed to minimize stockouts is as follows:

1. Establish customer service level.
2. Gather demand history.
3. Test alternatives to determine best forecasting model.
4. Gather pertinent inventory cost information.
5. Compute EOQ.
6. Forecast demand over lead time.
7. Forecast safety stock requirement.
8. If on-hand inventory is greater than reorder point, take no action and go to next item.
9. If on-hand inventory is equal to reorder point forecast, place order using Q^*.
10. If net on-hand inventory is less than reorder point, place order using Q^* and expedite.

PART THREE

CHANNEL MANAGEMENT: PLANNING, COORDINATING, ORGANIZING, AND CONTROLLING

Management is a process involving planning, organizing, and controlling. When we discuss management in marketing channels, however, our concern is less with planning, organizing, and controlling the behavior of individuals and more with planning, organizing, and controlling the behavior of organizations. Indeed, channel management demands an *interorganizational* focus. But it is no easy matter to convince another organization, *as a whole,* to do something it would not normally have done.

In implementing objectives, plans, and programs that will generate competitive distribution systems, it is useful, from a managerial/analytical perspective, to think of marketing channels as *superorganizations.*[1] The term *superorganization* implies that

[1] See Torger Reve and Louis W. Stern, "Interorganizational Relations in Marketing Channels," *Academy of Management Review,* Vol. 4 (1979), pp. 405–516.

channels have characteristics of all complex organizations, even though channels comprise collectivities (business firms, day-care centers, welfare agencies, and the like) rather than individuals. According to organization theory, *any* complex organization can be operationally defined in terms of the following characteristics:[2]

- A cooperative relationship among its members
- Collective goal(s)
- Differentiation of function among its members
- A highly formalized unit with explicit rules and policies
- Structural complexity
- Interdependency among its members relative to task performance
- Communication among its members
- Criteria for evaluating the communication
- A stable and explicit hierarchical structure
- Integration through strictly defined subordination

Likewise, within *any* given distribution channel network, almost all of these characteristics can be found. There exists a *cooperative relationship;* otherwise, the network could not exist. There is, however, no assumption made here as to the extent or effectiveness of the cooperation; obviously, cooperation varies widely, and some channel situations are more chaotic and atomistic in this respect than others. For example, many fast-food franchise systems have engendered a high degree of cooperation between franchisor and franchisee (e.g., Kentucky Fried Chicken, McDonald's, 7-Eleven Food Stores) while others have witnessed franchisee revolts (e.g., Chicken Delight, Sambo's, Arthur Treacher's).

It is also possible to argue that *collective goals* operate within distribution channel networks, even though the goals themselves may not be explicitly noted or constantly accepted. Certainly, the desire to serve the ultimate consumer in a satisfactory manner seems to pervade distribution systems, although there are frequent occasions when one might question whether such a goal is being pursued adequately. In addition, channels represent a grandiose *division of labor* among the institutions and agencies constituting them.

There would be no channels of distribution without transactional routines among members, and for a transaction to be routinized, it must happen according to *explicit rules.*[3] Channel members must understand the rules. Performance rests on the belief that one channel member will behave as another expects him to. Although channels are often not as formalized as typical complex organizations, they approach such formalization by the adoption of rules. In fact, within any channel system, positions and duties are generally fairly well ordered and defined. Relationships are also institutionalized. Channels are not simply ad hoc assemblages, but are among the more enduring forms of socioeconomic organization in our society. Explicit rules and policies regarding delivery, billing, order size, standardization, customer care, and the like are the vehicles

---

[2] Karl E. Weick, "Laboratory Experimentation with Organizations," in James G. March (ed.), *Handbook of Organizations* (Chicago: Rand McNally, 1965), pp. 194–260.

[3] Wroe Alderson, "Factors Governing the Development of Marketing Channels," in Bruce Mallen (ed.), *The Marketing Channel* (New York: John Wiley & Sons, 1967), p. 39.

that permit routinization and the formation of what Alderson termed *organized behavior systems.*[4]

It is not necessary to document the self-evident notion that channels are *structurally complex* or that *communication* (and criteria for evaluating it) exists among their memberships. It is, however, possible to note that many channels are different from complex organizations in that they lack formal chains of command. Thus, if "a stable and explicit hierarchical structure" and "integration through strictly defined subordination" are required in the formation or identification of a superorganization, surrogates for such a structure or subordination must be located in order to implement interorganization management. Although it is reasonably clear that chains of command exist within vertically integrated systems (e.g., within General Foods' distribution center network or among the clinics making up the Kaiser health maintenance organization in California) and within some franchised systems, such authority networks are not immediately evident in the majority of extant distribution channels (e.g., within the furniture, food, and steel industries). Therefore, if the dictates or organization theory are followed, it would seem essential to build into interorganization systems an *informal* system of authority, at the very least. In order to organize the resources of distribution channels, it may be necessary to uncover or develop loci of power, or power centers, within the system.

All told, viewing a marketing channel as a superorganization, and especially as an interorganizational system, is important as you approach the next seven chapters. Combined with Chapter 1, these chapters form the core of this text. Part Three spells out, in considerable detail, what channel management (the management of interorganizational networks involved in the marketing of goods and services) is all about.

Chapter 1 focused on why marketing channel structures emerge. It introduced such concepts as sorting, accumulation, routinization, and service outputs. Using the principles discussed in Chapter 1 (e.g., postponement-speculation), one should be able to predict when and why intermediaries appear at certain points in the channel.

In Chapter 5, we focus on the strategy and design parts of channel planning. Clearly, planning is the linchpin in the process. Without it, management cannot proceed with any strong assurance of success. In channels, planning means the setting of objectives and the development of strategies—just what it means in any other context. However, the key determinants for channels are the service output levels desired by industrial, institutional, or household users. That is, assessing whether the service outputs can be adequately provided by independently owned institutions and agencies or whether vertical integration is required is a central feature of channel planning. In answering this question, which emanates from other questions concerned with market coverage and support within the channel, management must develop mechanisms for choosing among alternative channel configurations. Overlaying this entire process are the constraints management faces because, for example, middlemen think and act differently than manufacturers or because the firm's products are perishable.

Having established what is involved in strategy and design, we focus next on how to coordinate the interorganizational system called a marketing channel. Because coordination is so essential (it is the "organizing" of the planning, organizing, and

[4] Wroe Alderson, *Dynamic Marketing Behavior* (Homewood, Ill.: Richard D. Irwin, 1965), pp. 37, 43–45.

controlling trilogy), Chapter 6 is devoted entirely to how to achieve it. We turn here to the behavioral sciences for some lessons—particularly from psychology, sociology, and political science. The importance of the use of power and the significance of conflict management in the channel is explained, and something we have called the *coordinative process* is detailed. Chapter 6 provides an essential theoretical backdrop against which to position the various organizational forms of channels examined in Chapter 7.

There are all sorts of ways one can put together organizations into channel systems. For clarity of explanation, we have adopted the classification developed by Davidson and McCammon some years ago,[5] which divides channels into conventional, administered, contractual, and corporate systems. This scheme permits us to discuss every possible configuration, ranging from very loose coalitions of firms to vertically integrated operations. Almost all channels, if they are organized in a purposive fashion, require that social and economic power be used to marshal resources and coordinate efforts. The more tightly organized the channel must become, especially in response to competitive or other environmental pressures, the greater the importance of power as a coordinative mechanism.[6]

In many countries around the globe, there are no or minimal governmental restraints on the use of power in commercial transactions. In others, the opposite is true. The United States sits somewhere between. Chapter 8 is devoted to a discussion of *federal restraints* only. However, there are those who believe that state law will begin to dominate federal law in the antitrust area in the near future. It behooves channel managers to have at least a rough idea of when they might be running afoul of the law and to have more than a nodding acquaintance with a very good law firm specializing in commercial and antitrust law. We realize that the legal chapter is bound to be confusing; that's because the whole antitrust area is confusing. There are no straightforward answers, and indeed, a channel manager could easily become discouraged by it.

Chapter 9 discusses channel management by various channel participants and shows what has been and might be done to manage the channel. It isolates institutions and agencies that seem to be assuming leadership roles. It provides an amalgamation of planning notions combined with organization examples and outlooks. Chapter 10 continues along the same line, but focuses on communication within the channel. Again, emphasis is placed on examples of channel management and how communication opportunities and problems enhance or impair channel organization.

The final chapter in Part Three—Chapter 11—examines the "controlling" or auditing aspect of the management process. But, to impose management controls, one must first know about performance. That is, in the absence of performance standards, auditing mechanisms are simply academic toys. Two aspects of performance should be kept in mind by individuals interested in channels. One is the social welfare or macro aspect. Are marketing channels in fact providing the greatest good for the greatest number, or are they simply encouraging elitism at the expense of the poor and disad-

---

[5] William R. Davidson, "Changes in Distributive Institutions," *Journal of Marketing*, Vol. 34 (January 1970), pp. 7–10; Bert C. McCammon, Jr., "Perspective for Distribution Programming," in Louis P. Bucklin (ed.), *Vertical Marketing Systems* (Glenview, Ill.: Scott, Foresman and Co., 1970), pp. 32–51.

[6] Those interested in examining an extremely insightful theory of the relationships among interorganizational coordination, environmental demands, and the use of power should read Jeffrey Pfeffer and Gerald R. Salancik, *The External Control of Organizations: A Resource Dependence Perspective* (New York: Harper & Row, 1978).

vantaged? Are channels producing service outputs desired by society? Are the distributive trades efficient or basically wasteful of resources? The other aspect is the commercial or micro aspect. Are the channels employed by the firm profitable? Do the various channel members earn adequate returns on their investments, or is there a weakness in their earnings that indicates a weakness in their ability to compete?

Once these questions are addressed, it is then useful to explore auditing mechanisms, such as the strategic profit model, the channel audit, and distribution cost accounting. If these mechanisms are successfully applied, they will permit judgments of the efficacy of the firm's entire channel management process.

CHAPTER FIVE

Channel Planning: Strategy and Design

In the late 1970s, Iveco, a European truck manufacturer with an 18 percent share of Western Europe's commercial vehicle market, decided to crack the U.S. market with a line of medium-duty diesel trucks.[1] With a proven and dependable product and in the face of increasing demand for gasoline alternatives in the medium truck market, Iveco was confident of success. However, difficulties in organizing a strong dealer network greatly impeded Iveco. Because reducing downtime is one of the primary concerns of truck owners, a truck manufacturer must establish a strong system of servicing its products and maintaining adequate parts inventories. Without such a system, the manufacturer cannot achieve market acceptance—no matter how good its products may be.

A nearly identical situation exists in the construction machinery industry, where Komatsu, number one in earthmovers in its Japanese homeland and number two to Caterpillar in worldwide sales, has made a concerted effort to increase its penetration of the U.S. marketplace.[2] Komatsu prices its products very competitively (sometimes 10 to 20 percent lower than Caterpillar), offers prospective customers extensive free tryouts, and keeps sales agents–engineers ready to fly on short notice to cope with breakdowns in its machinery. However, Komatsu has a tremendous disadvantage relative to Caterpillar—the strength of Caterpillar's dealer network. Cat sells earthmovers direct only to the U.S. gov-

[1] See "A New Challenger in Trucks," *Business Week* (July 3, 1978), p. 88.

[2] This example was developed from Bernard Krisher, "Komatsu on the Track of Cat," *Fortune* (April 20, 1981), pp. 164–74; "Komatsu Digs Deeper into the U.S.," *Business Week* (October 1, 1984), p. 53; "Caterpillar: Sticking to Basics to Stay Competitive," *Business Week* (May 4, 1981), pp. 74–80; Harlan S. Byrne, "Caterpillar, Facing Japanese Competition in Earth-Movers, Tries to Regain Footing," *Wall Street Journal,* December 9, 1981, p. 48; and Bill Kelley, "Komatsu in a Cat Fight," *Sales & Marketing Management* (April 1986), pp. 50–53.

ernment, the Soviet Union, and the People's Republic of China. All other earth-mover sales are handled by over 200 independent dealers, 90 of them in the United States. Cat has developed a series of complex yet workable arrangements with its dealers that serve the dual goals of enhancing the dealers' positions as entrepreneurs and enabling them to provide exemplary service to the customer. Those arrangements include:

- Encouraging dealers to establish side businesses in rebuilding parts. This not only boosts dealer profitability but also makes Caterpillar products more economical for customers because machines can be repaired at lower cost.
- Introducing new products only after building up a two-month supply of spare parts. This lets dealers service new offerings immediately.
- Keeping tight control of parts inventory to provide 48-hour delivery of any item to any customer in the world.
- Repurchasing parts or equipment that dealers cannot sell. This makes it relatively painless for dealers to keep a full stock of items.

Caterpillar's attitude towards its dealers is articulated thus by its chairman: "We approach our dealers as partners in the enterprise, not as agents or middlemen. We worry as much about their performance as they do themselves."[3] And the dealers are generally effusive in their praise of their relations with Caterpillar. Therefore, even though Komatsu's crawler tractors are perceived as well made and carry a lower price than similar Caterpillar machines, many potential customers turn away from them because of Komatsu's relatively small parts and service capability. Furthermore, in contrast with Caterpillar, few of Komatsu's 50 U.S. dealers sell its equipment exclusively, and many are financially weaker than their local Cat opponents. Without a dealer network comparable to Cat's, Komatsu will likely remain second best.

Channel issues are equally critical for consumer goods marketers. For example, in the late 1970s Welch Foods, a producer of grape products, entered the soft drink market with a new grape-flavored soda.[4] Welch attempted to reach food retailers through its existing network of food brokers. This decision was motivated by management's expectation of making a profit without selecting a new marketing channel. The predominant and firmly established marketing channels of the competition (e.g., Coca-Cola, Pepsi, and Seven-Up) comprised franchised soft drink bottlers who primarily distribute soft drinks and who service retail shelves weekly. Welch's food brokers called on retailers only about once a month and provided service for a line of products, of which the new grape-flavored soda was only one. Welch's initial failure to penetrate the soft drink market should have been easily predictable. (Eventually, Welch's management realized the extent and source of their strategic mistake and were later able to enter the market successfully, using their own network of franchised bottlers.)

The Iveco, Komatsu, and Welch vignettes could be repeated scores of times by simply changing the names of companies. In fact, after interviewing managers from 18 consumer and industrial goods manufacturers, Lambert discovered a distinct absence of formal planning and evaluation procedures for marketing channels.[5] He found that the majority of channels he studied were not

[3] Quoted in "Caterpillar: Sticking to Basics to Stay Competitive," *op. cit.,* p. 77.
[4] See Phil Fitzell, "Distribution: How Welch Cracked the Soft Drink Market," *Product Marketing,* Vol. 6 (June 1977), p. 19.
[5] Douglas M. Lambert, *The Distribution Channel Decision* (New York: National Association of Accountants; Hamilton, Ont.: Society of Management Accountants of Canada, 1978), pp. 56–59.

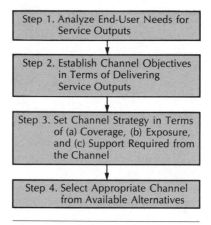

Figure 5–1 *Steps in the channel planning process*

purposively designed but simply evolved over time. Because marketing channels have such an enormous impact on market acceptance and overall economic performance, a formal planning process for designing and selecting channels is imperative. The steps in such a planning process are depicted in Fig. 5–1 and discussed throughout this chapter.

THE STARTING POINT: KNOWLEDGE OF END-USER BEHAVIOR

The starting point in planning the marketing channel is the industrial, commercial, institutional, or ultimate household end-user. Channel design and selection of channel partners cannot be meaningful unless they take place in the context of the target markets that the designer wishes to serve and the specific needs of the end-users within those markets. This axiom holds true whether one is considering the decisions of producers relative to middlemen or vice versa. Knowledge about what end-users need, where end-users buy, why they buy from certain outlets, when they buy, and how they buy is critical. Planning a marketing channel involves sellers in determining the most profitable and effective ways to reach the markets they want to serve, and such a determination is possible only from an understanding of end-user behavior.

An essential feature of studying end-user behavior relative to channel decisions is determining the service output levels desired by end-users. Recall from Chapter 1 that a commercial marketing channel is capable of producing a number of service outputs, among which are lot size, spatial convenience or market decentralization, delivery or waiting time, and product variety or assortment breadth and depth. Once it is ascertained whether the end-users in the target market desire high service output levels or whether they are willing to forego service for lower prices, it is possible to lay out a number of alternative channel designs that would satisfy demand.

IBM Corporation's decision to sell personal computers through computer dealers provides an excellent illustration of what we have been talking about.[6] One of the target markets isolated by IBM is small-business customers. IBM had been unable to serve this market successfully through its existing marketing channels (direct sales force plus company-owned distribution centers). Because small-business customers are geographically dispersed and do not require large amounts or large pieces of equipment, their needs differ from those of IBM's directly served, more sizable customers. The development of computer dealer and other third-party channels (such as value-added resellers) was an effort to provide the service outputs desired by small businesses—small lot size, market decentralization, and quick delivery. Consideration of other service outputs, such as technical advice, availability of repair facilities, provision of warranties and/or guarantees, product demonstration, and flexible financing, was equally important in this decision. The product variety service output, however, is not satisfied entirely by computer dealers. For example, while dealers such as Computerland and Businessland generally carry multiple brands of personal computers (e.g., Apple, AT&T, Compaq, and IBM), they do not carry a wide variety of the office equipment also needed by small business (e.g., typewriters, copiers, phone systems, and furniture). To some extent, the development of IBM Product Centers was a response to this need for variety. These stores were wholly owned and operated by IBM; they sold a number of pieces of IBM equipment beyond personal computers and computer peripherals. They did not, however, sell competitors' brands. Because many small businesses prefer to comparison-shop before deciding on office equipment, outlets like Sears Business Centers may be better positioned to satisfy end-user demands, because they not only stock different types of office equipment but also carry multiple brands within each line. In 1986, IBM sold its Product Centers to Nynex, in part because of its weak position on this comparison shopping dimension.

The determination of service output levels demanded by end-users plays a central role in management decision making. In fact, it is from the determination of the desired services that objectives for the channel as a whole should be formed. For example, market coverage, efficiency, and effectiveness objectives all emanate from what it is that must be provided to consumers in order to remain viable in a highly competitive environment. And, given the increased difficulty in achieving high corporate growth, it is also essential that management learn how to adapt to, combat, and challenge competitors by designing new channel systems that are more attractive to consumers or by preempting those channels that are already available.

ESTABLISHING AND SETTING OBJECTIVES AND STRATEGY

Channel strategy must follow from channel objectives. The objectives for the channel are derived from an analysis of the service output levels desired by end-users and management's overall long-run goals for the corporation (e.g., in

---

[6] For an overview of what IBM calls its *alternate channel* strategy and the internal IBM conflicts it has sparked, see Robert McCarthy, "IBM Meets the Real World," *High-Tech Marketing* (September 1985), pp. 56–64.

terms of return on investment, market share, absolute level of profits achieved, and sales growth). The reason the inclusion of global goals is important here is that the design and selection of a channel, once accomplished, are more long-term than many other marketing decisions. In other words, changing channels is a very infrequent (and often highly risky) occurrence. Clearly, a firm may make modifications once in a while, but altering the channel radically is a decision that often requires the approval of the board of directors of a corporation. Changes in a channel may affect the entire character of an enterprise and the way it is perceived.

The specific (as opposed to global) objectives for the channel must, however, be couched in terms of the service outputs needed to meet the demands of the target markets that management has isolated. As mentioned, if several different segments are isolated, then different sets of service outputs may be demanded by them. The firm will then be involved in something Robert Weigand has called *multimarketing,* or the use of multiple channels.[7] In fact, the use of a single channel is becoming rare in today's marketplace. This is true for industrial as well as consumer goods. For example, Illinois Tool Works (ITW), a manufacturer of engineered fasteners and components, electronic products and components, packaging products, and precision tools and gearing, sells directly to large original equipment manufacturers (OEMs) but reaches small customers through industrial distributors. To discourage competition between its direct and indirect channels, it prices its products in such a way that distributors cannot provide an advantage to large buyers who might wish to purchase from them rather than directly from ITW. The lower prices ITW offers to its large customers are a result of the fact that the latter are willing to order individual products in large lots, hold inventory, receive no spatial convenience, and wait for delivery. Hence, in terms of the postponement-speculation principle articulated in Chapter 1, they are willing to speculate on ITW's products in return for a favorable price. On the other hand, ITW can postpone the production of large OEM orders until they can be efficiently scheduled. The lower price offered to these customers is offset by the lessened service output levels. The type of service outputs required by small customers cannot be effectively met by ITW's direct channel. Thus, distributors are utilized to provide them with quick delivery time, small lots, spatial convenience, and product variety.

Once channel objectives have been stated in service output terms, it is possible to turn to two critical strategic issues. The first is the market coverage required and the degree of support one might expect to receive from the channel based on the adoption of different coverage strategies. For example, the more intensively a manufacturer distributes his products, the less in the way of support he can expect to receive from each channel member employed in his distribution system. The second issue is ownership. That is, does the firm need to own its entire marketing channel or parts of it in order to ensure that the required service output levels will be achieved? Is the cost of ownership prohibitive, given the extent of market coverage and support needed? The ownership question logically follows the coverage and support question.

---

[7] Robert E. Weigand, "Fit Products and Channels to Your Markets," *Harvard Business Review,* Vol. 55 (January-February 1977), pp. 95–105.

Coverage and Support

One of the key elements of channel strategy, which is evident in the Illinois Tool Works and IBM examples, is the degree of market coverage, exposure, and channel support necessary to achieve corporate objectives. In other words, it is crucial to know how many sales outlets should be established in a given geographic area and what kind of participation in the marketing flows should be required from each of the outlets so that the needs of existing, potential, and past customers may be adequately served. Three basic strategic choices appear to be available: (1) *intensive distribution,* whereby a product or brand is placed in as many outlets as possible, (2) *selective distribution,* whereby a product or brand is placed in a more limited number of outlets in a defined geographic area, and (3) *exclusive distribution,* whereby a product or brand is placed in the hands of only one outlet in a specific area. These choices are applicable to both vertically integrated and nonvertically integrated systems, although clearly the capital required to establish a wholly owned channel characterized by intensive distribution might be staggering. Generally, however, discussion of these strategies is most directly applicable to channels comprising independently owned institutions and agencies.

Intensive distribution appears to be a rational strategy for goods that people wish to purchase frequently and with minimum effort; examples are tobacco products, soap, newspapers, chewing gum, gasoline, candy bars, and aspirin among consumer goods, and maintenance, repair, and operating items (e.g., lubricants, drill bits, and light bulbs) among industrial goods. Selective distribution can be used for goods that buyers seek out and can range from almost intensive to almost exclusive; examples are certain brands of television sets (e.g., Zenith, RCA), mattresses (e.g., Simmons), cosmetics (e.g., Revlon, Estee Lauder), industrial supplies (e.g, Norton abrasives), electrical equipment (e.g., Square D circuit breakers), and clothing (e.g., Arrow shirts). Exclusive distribution is used to bring about a greater partnership between seller and reseller and is commonly found in the marketing channels for commercial air-conditioning equipment, some brands of apparel, high-priced furniture, and construction and farm machinery. In addition, channel structure tends to interact with the degree of market exposure. For example, the use of numerous wholesale intermediaries (i.e., "long" channel structures) often permits greater market decentralization and thus intensive distribution, while the opposite tends to hold for shorter, more direct channels.

Pitfalls of Intensive Distribution. It could be argued that the more intensive a product's distribution, the greater the sales that product will achieve in the short run. In fact, one could call this statement a law of marketing. Thus, if Pioneer, a producer of high-quality stereophonic components, decided to disband its present system of selective distribution in favor of a more intensive arrangement, one could predict with certainty that its sales would increase in the short run. But, as Pioneer expanded the number of its outlets to include drugstores, catalog stores, supermarkets, discount stores, and other outlets, adverse consequences would be highly likely over the long term. First, because some of the new outlets would undoubtedly begin to use the Pioneer brand as a leader item to attract traffic, retail prices on Pioneer components would begin to drop, and valued dealers such as Team Electronics might have second thoughts about selling a product on which profit margins were becoming slimmer and slimmer.[8]

Second, service would deteriorate. Drugstores, supermarkets, and discount stores might not be willing to install service facilities, and repair work under warranty arrangements with consumers would have to be assumed by those stores with such facilities or by the manufacturer. Often, warranty business is not the most lucrative element of a service department's repair work, and leading stores offering such service would become increasingly disaffected at having to handle problems with equipment sold by other concerns. When General Electric decided to adopt a more intensive distribution strategy for its small electrical appliances some years ago, it found that it could not obtain adequate service from its expanded retail network. The company had to institute a nationwide, company-owned chain of service centers in order to solve this significant marketing problem.

Third, it is likely that, because of its intensive distribution strategy, Pioneer would find itself assuming a greater participation in a number of the marketing flows. Thus, promotion by the company would probably have to be increased, because dealers who once were willing to promote the product (through advertising and especially through in-store personal selling and display) might find their margins reduced to the point where such efforts were no longer warranted, and turn instead to other brands of stereo equipment that they might have in stock. In addition, more of the burden of holding inventory would undoubtedly have to be assumed by Pioneer as smaller outlets were added. In fact, it is possible to conceive of Pioneer's having to sell stereo equipment on a consignment basis in order to secure distribution in outlets where cash flow is a considerable problem.[9]

A circumstance not unlike the Pioneer example befell Sony during the late 1970s. Sony built its overall marketing strategy on a high-quality, premium-pricing plan. When the fair trade laws were repealed, Sony found itself unable to control directly the price of its color television sets or to prevent their resale to what it considered undesirable outlets. Price-cutting at the retail level began to undermine the Sony quality image. The problem became so severe that Sony finally had to cancel all of its dealers and selectively accept them back into the channel under a new franchise agreement that provided it with the necessary control to prevent dealer resale to other outlets.[10]

Clearly, the type of distribution strategy employed interacts with the product itself (e.g, notice that the Pioneer and Sony examples involve shopping or specialty goods, not convenience items) and with other elements of the market-

---

[8] It is interesting to note that when W. T. Grant, a major retail chain, was attempting to avoid bankruptcy in 1975, it decided to drop the lines of major appliances that it was carrying because margins had been competed away on them. While this move did not save Grant's, it did at least permit the chain to concentrate on more profitable lines. Other retailers are having similar problems in selling major appliances at a profit, given the extent of discounting on these items.

[9] Although the Pioneer example was contrived for illustrative purposes, it is not far from the truth. See *U.S. Pioneer Electronics Corporation*, Harvard Business School, ICH 9-579-079 (Boston: Harvard Business School, 1978; revised 1980).

[10] See Paul Ingrassia, "In a Color-TV Market Roiled by Price Wars, Sony Takes a Pounding," *Wall Street Journal,* March 16, 1978, p. 1; and "Sony's U.S. Operation Goes in for Repairs," *Business Week* (March 13, 1978), pp. 31–32. Severe problems with distribution strategies that were too intensive have also been experienced by Michelin; see "Michelin: Spinning Its Wheels in the Competitive U.S. Market," *Business Week* (December 1, 1980), p. 121.

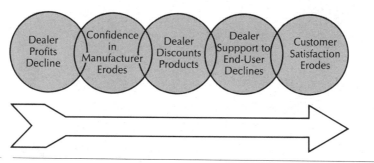

Figure 5–2 Effects of saturation

Source: Richard E. Koon, Director of Retail Sales, IBM Corporation, Presentation at the Marketing Science Institute/Duke University Conference on "Managing Marketing Channel Relationships" held at Duke University on September 13–14, 1984.

ing mix. Gaining sales volume in the short run is not an appropriate goal for numerous companies, and uncontrolled distribution is likely to bring with it some of the serious problems depicted in Fig. 5–2. These problems were experienced by both Apple and IBM personal computer dealers during the early 1980s. Dealers had been complaining for years that because of overdistribution and rampant price-cutting, they were making little profit selling products made by Apple, IBM, and some other vendors, and could not afford to spend time training and advising customers. In 1986, as a response, Apple decided to reduce by about 23 percent the number of stores authorized to carry its products in the United States, thereby eliminating 600 dealers, while IBM halted the growth of new dealerships, freezing the number at about 2500. Similar problems plague brand-name clothing manufacturers. For example, when Levi Strauss & Company decided in 1982 to sell its jeans through Sears and Penney, R. H. Macy Company retaliated by dropping the line. And Dayton's department store in Minneapolis reduced the number of its Levi's jeans promotions. A vice-president at Dayton's explained, "The product is so widely available at low prices that it isn't something we want to expand."[11] Richard Hamilton, former chairman and CEO of Hartmarx Corporation, a major clothing manufacturer and retailer, has observed that "you can take 50 years to build a brand and you can ruin it in three through careless distribution."[12]

On the other hand, intensive distribution in the context of a well-developed marketing program for meeting the needs of both distributors and end-users is a logical and appropriate approach for tens of thousands of products. And, if properly managed, it can pay handsome dividends. For example, American Greetings, Hallmark's largest competitor, has historically approached the market by making relatively inexpensive greeting cards for the masses and by wooing retailers, not card buyers, on the assumption that consumers will buy whatever is most readily available. By offering to retailers such services as free shipment and return of unsold seasonal cards (neither service is offered by Hallmark on its principal line), American Greetings garnered more and more

[11] Quoted in Steve Weiner, "Caught in a Cross Fire, Brand-Apparel Makers Design Their Defenses," *Wall Street Journal,* January 24, 1984, p. 1.

[12] Quoted in *ibid.,* p. 12.

Table 5–1 Selection of suitable distribution policy based on the relationship between type of product and type of store

Classification	Consumer Behavior	Most Likely Form of Distribution
Convenience store/ convenience good	The consumer prefers to buy the most readily available brand of product at the most accessible store.	Intensive
Convenience store/ shopping good	The consumer selects his purchase from among the assortment carried by the most accessible store.	Intensive
Convenience store/ specialty good	The consumer purchases his favorite brand from the most accessible store carrying the item in stock.	Selective/exclusive
Shopping store/ convenience good	The consumer is indifferent to the brand of product he buys but shops different stores to secure better retail service and/or retail price.	Intensive
Shopping store/ shopping good	The consumer makes comparisons among both retail-controlled factors and factors associated with the product (brand).	Selective/exclusive
Shopping store/ specialty good	The consumer has a strong preference as to product brand but shops a number of stores to secure the best retail service and/or price for this brand.	Selective/exclusive
Specialty store/ convenience good	The consumer prefers to trade at a specific store but is indifferent to the brand of product purchased.	Selective/exclusive
Specialty store/ shopping good	The consumer prefers to trade at a certain store but is uncertain as to which product he wishes to buy and examines the store's assortment for the best purchase.	Selective/exclusive
Specialty store/ specialty good	The consumer has both a preference for a particular store and for a specific brand.	Selective/exclusive

Source: Louis P. Bucklin, "Retail Strategy and the Classification of Consumer Goods," *Journal of Marketing,* Vol. 23 (January 1963), pp. 50–55. The table itself was developed by and appears in Burton Marcus et al., *Modern Marketing* (New York: Random House, 1975), p. 550.

outlets until they numbered 50,000—two and a half times the number of stores that sell Hallmark's lines. American Greetings achieved close to a 30 percent share of the greeting card market.[13]

In selecting a distribution strategy, it is best to consider the relationship between store and product types. As indicated in Chapter 2, Bucklin has combined the traditional threefold classification of consumer goods (convenience, shopping, and specialty goods) with a threefold classification of outlets according to patronage motives (convenience, shopping, and specialty stores) in order to facilitate decision making in this area.[14] As can be seen in Table 5–1, knowledge of consumer behavior is again the key to unlocking the problem of distribution strategy.

[13] See Dean Rotbart, "American Greetings Cares Enough to Try Its Very Hardest," *Wall Street Journal,* March 17, 1982, p. 1.
[14] Louis P. Bucklin, "Retail Strategy and the Classification of Consumer Goods," *Journal of Marketing,* Vol. 23 (January 1963), pp. 50–55.

Tradeoffs in Selecting a Distribution Strategy. The selection of a distribution strategy involves a consideration of relevant tradeoffs. As indicated, channel members who decide to adopt an intensive strategy generally relinquish a significant amount of control over the marketing of their products within the channel. The only way they can reestablish control in these cases is to assume greater participation in each of the marketing flows. For example, O. M. Scott & Sons Company, a prominent manufacturer of lawn products, decided to adopt a less selective distribution strategy because it wanted to obtain more exposure for its product line among the large percentage of medium- to upper-income homeowning families who according to a marketing research study were not users of lawn fertilizers.[15] In order to obtain the proper merchandising support and control throughout its expanded reseller base, Scott found it necessary to develop special detailed programs for each retail account. Monthly sales plans were formulated by Scott account executives in terms of the retailers' requirements, and promotional plans were defined for each store. Many of these programs involved more than fifty pages of plans developed for an individual account. As a result of this programmed merchandising, retail store executives rarely had to make a decision that was not covered in detail in the individual account prospectus. Scott's programs were first instituted in department stores and subsequently were developed for supermarkets and other types of mass merchandisers. Therefore, not only did Scott assume the investment burden involved in formulating marketing plans for each channel member, but it was also able, through its store-by-store programmed merchandising efforts, to retain many of the policies it had adopted when its distribution was more selective (display guidelines, advertising incentives, and the like). Scott relied heavily on its expert power base in the marketing of lawn products, as well as the promise of significant profits, to convince resellers to participate in programs they would not otherwise have adopted.[16]

On the other hand, as channel members move towards exclusive distribution, role expectations become more sharply delineated. Specific agreements are possible with respect to degrees of participation in the marketing flows. But each of these agreements demands careful bargaining over rights and obligations. For an exclusive distribution strategy, the bargaining points (and relevant tradeoffs) generally concern the following:

1. *Products covered.* The specific items in the line that are to be handled by the exclusive wholesaler or retailer must be clearly delineated. For example, there may be certain products, especially those of a highly technical nature, that a supplier will wish to sell through his own sales force directly to ultimate customers. Other products will be made available for sale through exclusive distributors. To avoid future conflict over the division of product line responsibilities, a clear understanding must be forged among the channel members as to the domains of each with regard to the items in the line. In the cases where an item has been assigned to a distributor, any sales of that item by the supplier in the distributor's territory should be credited to the distributor. Otherwise, a domain violation is obvious.

2. *Classes or types of customers.* Agreement over who is responsible for various types of customers must be arrived at to prevent future dysfunctional conflict. Thus, as in

---

[15] Ronald D. Michman and Stanley D. Sibley, *Marketing Channels and Strategies,* 2nd ed. (Columbus, Ohio: Grid Publishing, 1980), pp. 321–22.

[16] Programmed merchandising is discussed again in Chapter 7, in the section on administered vertical marketing systems.

the case of products covered, the supplier may wish to retain the right to sell directly to specific classes of customers, such as the military, or to very large commercial accounts (e.g., General Motors). Any sales to customers allocated to distributors or dealers must be credited to the latter if domains are not to be violated. The expectations of who is to serve whom must be clearly understood and/or resolved through bargaining at the outset.

3. *Territory covered.* Clearly, this is another crucial element in establishing relevant domains. In many cases, agreement on territories can prevent future jurisdictional disputes among the distributors handling the supplier's products. However, restrictions on territories and types of customers to be served can be subject to challenge under the antitrust laws, as indicated in Chapter 8.

4. *Inventories.* The questions to be resolved here are who is going to bear the burden of holding and owning inventories and how much inventory is to be held, and where. In situations of fluctuating price levels, these questions become particularly acute. Suppliers may have to enter into price guarantees or may have to consign merchandise when economic conditions are turbulent.

5. *Installation and repair services.* This bargaining issue is obviously relevant for durable goods in both the industrial and consumer goods sectors. Here, questions about handling warranties are crucial, and the rights and obligations of suppliers and distributors must be clearly specified. Distributors may be asked to commit resources to the training of service personnel, and suppliers may have to assure distributors that troubleshooters will be on call for situations that are beyond the distributors' service capabilities. Considerable conflict between middlemen and manufacturers has appeared in the automobile, home appliance, and capital equipment industries due to inadequate specification of installation and repair roles.

6. *Prices.* Under exclusive distribution policies, the supplier is likely to agree to some form of price or margin guarantee in times of declining market prices. The distributor may agree to maintain "reasonable margins" in its prices to end-users, but legal constraints prohibit any collusion on this matter between the supplier and the distributor unless entered into on a strictly unilateral (one-on-one) basis.

7. *Sales quotas.* The establishment of unrealistic sales quotas has brought about considerable friction in channel relations. In agreeing to an exclusive distribution arrangement, the parties involved should arrive at a consensus on the way in which the quotas are to be calculated. They should also agree on the rewards to be received or the punishments to be levied for performance above or below the quotas arrived at.

8. *Advertising and sales promotional obligations.* Responsibilities for the development of catalogs, sales aids, display work, local advertising and promotion, etc., must be specified in the agreement. The basis for calculating cooperative advertising allowances should be spelled out in detail so that each party realizes its obligation to the other.

9. *Exclusive dealing.* In some situations, suppliers prefer that their distributors handle no products that will compete directly with their own. If this is the case, then these suppliers will often be called upon to give added promotional support to their distributors to ensure that the latter will be able to achieve a satisfactory sales volume in the product category affected. As with territorial and customer restrictions, exclusive dealing is also circumscribed by federal law.

10. *Duration, provision for renewal, and termination.* If exclusive distribution is desired, then it is important that the specifics of each of the previous nine points be agreed upon in writing. The contract established should, however, allow the parties enough flexibility to meet extraneous events and contingencies, should they arise.

In addition, it is important for the parties to agree on the length of time that the agreement is to be in effect and on renewal provisions. Especially important, given the legal implications involved, are specifics regarding when and how the arrangement can be terminated by either of the parties.

The preceding list is not exhaustive; it serves merely to indicate the detail required in formulating distribution strategy as one moves toward the exclusive end of the spectrum. For a more complete perspective of the specifics involved in establishing such a strategy, read the distributor sales agreement and the distribution policy and practices of Rex Chainbelt, reproduced in Appendix 5A. It is very important to note, however, that the establishment of such strategies is not a one-way street. Implicit in such agreements is a tone of mutual support: each of the parties gains something from the other under each and every point. Thus, benefits and costs are, or should be, divided equitably. Appendix 5B contains a policy statement that Square D Corporation uses with its distributors.[17]

Ownership

As is discussed in the next chapter, one of the key elements of channel strategy is determining whether, and if so to what extent, a firm can divide labor with others in its attempt to assure delivery of the appropriate service output levels. A basic strategic choice involves the use of independent middlemen or suppliers versus vertical integration of manufacturing, wholesaling, or retailing functions. With a vertically integrated system, control of the channel is accomplished through internal planning and monitoring. Vertical integration or outright ownership is an effective means of securing increased coordination, integration of effort, and heightened channel commitment. However, as pointed out in Chapter 7, where corporate vertical marketing systems are discussed, vertical integration is often an extremely costly undertaking and involves a number of tradeoffs, not the least of which is bureaucratic inflexibility. Therefore, it may not be justified in a wide variety of circumstances.

On the other hand, associating with independent businessmen as channel partners is more difficult, from a managerial point of view, than owning one's own system, because of the existence of divergent goals and expectations, which bring about control and coordination problems. However, a nonvertically integrated management allows producers or middlemen to concentrate on activities within their specific areas of expertise. Thus, channel functions that can be performed more effectively and efficiently by specialized institutions are assigned to various channel members. In certain circumstances and for certain kinds of products, this division of labor may result in lower overall distribution costs than a vertically integrated system.

One of the most insightful approaches to determining whether a firm should vertically integrate marketing channel flows or deal with independent middlemen is transaction cost analysis. As developed by economist Oliver E.

[17] The authors have resisted reproducing *Coors' Distributor Policy Manual*, which runs over 50 pages and covers such items as "Unloading Beer from Railcars" and "Truck Washing."

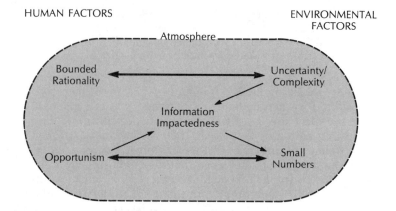

HUMAN FACTORS   ENVIRONMENTAL
                                                    FACTORS

Figure 5–3   Williamson's conception of the factors determining channel structure

Source: Reprinted with permission of The Free Press, a division of Macmillan, Inc., from *Markets and Hierarchies: Analysis and Antitrust Implications* by Oliver E. Williamson. Copyright © 1975 by The Free Press.

Williamson,[18] the approach assesses when the costs of transacting business "across a market" are too high relative to those of bringing the transaction in-house via vertical integration. Profit-maximizing firms will choose to undertake only those activities that they find cheaper to administer internally than to purchase them in the market from independently owned firms.

Transaction costs are defined as the costs of running the system. They include costs associated with bargaining, assembling information, monitoring compliance, and the like. To Williamson, the choice of channel structure is the consequence of the interaction between the set of human factors (bounded rationality and opportunism) and the set of environmental factors (uncertainty/complexity and small numbers) shown in Fig. 5–3. Borrowing from Herbert Simon,[19] Williamson assumes that people have limited cognitive capabilities—they are not able to solve highly complex problems in order to arrive at objectively rational behavior. In other words, their rationality is "bounded" by their capacities. He also assumes that people are basically opportunistic, and defines opportunism as "self-interest seeking with guile." Examples of opportunistic behavior are withholding or distorting information and shirking or failing to fulfill promises or obligations. For example, pressuring a retailer to add a new

---

[18] See Oliver E. Williamson, *Markets and Hierarchies: Analysis and Antitrust Implications* (New York: The Free Press, 1975); and Oliver E. Williamson, "Transaction-Cost Economics: The Governance of Contractual Relations," *Journal of Law and Economics,* Vol. 22 (October 1979), pp. 233–62. Our discussion of Williamson's theory also draws on Erin M. Anderson and Barton A. Weitz, "A Framework for Analyzing Vertical Integration Issues in Marketing," Marketing Science Institute Report No. 83-110 (Boston: Marketing Science Institute, 1983); Erin Anderson, "The Salesperson as Outside Agent or Employee: A Transaction Cost Analysis," Marketing Science Institute Report No. 84-107 (Boston: Marketing Science Institute, 1984); George John, "An Empirical Investigation of Some Antecedents of Opportunism in a Marketing Channel," *Journal of Marketing Research,* Vol. 21 (August 1984), pp. 278–89; and Lynn W. Phillips, "Explaining Control Losses in Corporate Marketing Channels: An Organization Analysis," *Journal of Marketing Research,* Vol. 19 (November 1982), pp. 525–49.

[19] Herbert A. Simon, *Models of Man* (New York: John Wiley & Sons, 1957).

product would be considered opportunistic behavior if such pressure violated a promise not to do so. The essense of opportunism is the deceit involved.

Market-base exchange between two channel members (e.g., a manufacturer and a distributor) who can choose partners from competitive (large-numbers) markets is safeguarded from the hazards of opportunism because either channel member could easily substitute another exchange partner if opportunistic behavior were discovered. The existence of large numbers of alternative partners effectively curbs opportunism. On the other hand, in "small numbers" situations, where alternatives are limited, opportunism can cripple the exchange by elevating transaction costs significantly. And when there is a high level of uncertainty in a channel member's environment, the information required to cope with the environment begins to exceed the individuals' capacities to process it, given their bounded rationality, thus elevating transaction costs even higher. The result, Williamson argues, is that for environments typified by small numbers and uncertainty, the hazards of opportunism and the limits of rationality can be confronted more efficiently by using more administratively coordinated (as opposed to market-coordinated) channel structures to govern long-run channel relationships. Vertical integration impedes opportunism via enhanced monitoring capabilities and the sanctions that can be applied to bureaucratic employees in contrast with independent entrepreneurs.

Two additional key concepts, among others, that should be understood in Williamson's theory are *information impactedness* (see Fig. 5–3) and *transaction-specific assets*. Information impactedness arises mainly because of uncertainty and opportunism. It exists when only one party to a transaction is knowledgeable or fully informed about a given situation and when obtaining knowledge or information about that situation is very difficult for the other party. Transaction-specific assets are tangible or intangible assets that are tailored to a particular transaction or relationship (e.g., a McDonald's restaurant sign) and cannot be freely transferred across a variety of applications. The narrower the range of alternative uses, the more transaction-specific the asset. If only a few firms are uniquely qualified to participate in a channel because they alone possess transaction-specific assets, they become very difficult to replace. Therefore, they may become opportunistic or inflexible, creating extra transaction costs. If these costs are high enough, vertical integration or, at the very least, some form of administration may be more efficient than operating across an unregulated market. In other words, it may make sense to subvert the market by imposing controls over it.

Characteristics of firms, products, and transactions also influence the vertical integration question. For example, Lilien has shown that for industrial products the following factors are significant in discriminating between vertically integrated and nonvertically integrated channels:

- *Size of firm.* As a firm grows larger, it is better able to support a company-owned distribution system.
- *Size of average order.* As average order size increases, the captive (essentially direct) option becomes more economical.
- *Technical-purchase complexity.* The more important technical service is to a product's success and the more important the buyer views the purchase, the more likely a manufacturer will be to sell it through company-owned distribution channels.
- *Stage in the product life cycle.* A new or growing product is more likely to use a captive form of distribution than one that has leveled off in sales.

- *Degree of standardization.* A product that is complex, unique, or made-to-order is more frequently sold through direct means than through independent middlemen.
- *Purchase frequency.* As a product becomes more of a common purchase item, with less personal selling necessary to secure a sale, it becomes advantageous for a manufacturer to sell through distributors or other convenient outlets.[20]

In a number of cases, marketing channels have the characteristics of vertically integrated systems without actual ownership. Chapter 7 discusses a variety of such channels. One of these channel systems is franchising, which is employed by such companies as McDonald's and Southland Corporation (7-Eleven Food Stores). Through franchising, McDonald's and Southland maintain tight control over the provision of service outputs within their channels without the enormous capital and other resource requirements of outright ownership.

CHOOSING AMONG ALTERNATIVE CHANNELS

Once channel objectives have been set and the coverage, support, and ownership issues associated with channel strategy have been isolated, the marketing manager should be ready to determine which path his organization should follow in making its product or service available to end-users. In fact, because organizations are rarely restricted to one means of reaching their markets or obtaining their supplies, the relevant question to be answered often is: How can managers efficiently arrive at a rational choice of which *channels* to employ? Kotler has laid out a number of different approaches to choosing channels.[21] His suggestions, including an example he developed to illustrate them, are summarized here.

Assume that an old line manufacturer of chemicals facing declining profits is considering marketing a product that can be used to kill germs in swimming pools. Assume further that the product is a significant departure from the company's present line—that the company has never done any previous consumer marketing and that its present channels of distribution are far from ideal for tapping the swimming pool market.

The first step in determining the type of middlemen to use in reaching this market would be to itemize alternative ways in which swimming pool owners could purchase this product. For example, the swimming pool owner might obtain the product from at least the five sources listed below:

1. Conventional retail outlets, such as hardware stores and drugstores
2. Specialized swimming pool supply and equipment retailers
3. Swimming pool service companies
4. Mass retailer outlets such as supermarkets, department stores, and discount houses
5. Direct-mail supply companies

[20] Gary L. Lilien, "ADVISOR 2: Modeling the Marketing Mix Decision for Industrial Products," *Management Science*, Vol. 25 (February 1979), pp. 198–99.
[21] Philip Kotler, *Marketing Decision Making: A Model Building Approach* (New York: Holt, Rinehart and Winston, 1971), pp. 290–98.

Management will want to assess the relative volumes of swimming pool germicides that move through each of these types of outlets, their relative rates of growth, and their relative profitability as channels. It will also want to find out from swimming pool owners the value they place on price, convenience, packaging, germicide effectiveness, etc., in order to further assess the relative standing of the various outlets in facilitating the delivery of these features. For this example, it is assumed that management has the option of using one or more of these sets of outlets.

The next step in the analysis of alternatives is to specify the primary channel paths the company might follow in reaching these various outlets or in tapping the various markets. Five radically different paths the company might take to market the new product are as follows:

1. Marketing through the present distributors of its industrial chemicals (*present distributors alternative*)
2. Marketing through new distributors already selling to the swimming pool trade (*new distributors alternative*)
3. Buying a small company already in this market and utilizing its distributors (*acquisition alternative*)
4. Selling the chemical in bulk to companies already in this market (*private brand alternative*)
5. Packaging and selling the chemical through mail campaigns directed at swimming pool owners (*direct-mail alternative*)

Each of these alternatives obviously has drawbacks as well as strengths. In order to analyze these, however, it is useful to go beyond debating their merits and demerits. Thus, the third step in the channel alternative assessment process is to attempt to quantify the relevant factors in the consideration of each.

A number of different decision techniques can be fruitfully applied to this problem. For example, all of the multi-attribute choice models specified in Appendix 2A are directly applicable to the problem of channel design. Here, we focus first on the three methods suggested by Kotler—linear averaging, sequential elimination, and simulation. Appendix 5C briefly describes some analytical approaches to channel planning that have come from the management science literature.

Linear Averaging[22]

This method calls upon management to list the major factors or attributes that the company should consider, assign weights that reflect their relative importance, rate each distribution alternative on each factor, and determine the overall global utility index for each alternative. In this way, the five distribution alternatives can at least be ranked and the lowest-ranked ones dropped.

An example of this method is shown in Table 5–2 relative to the present distributors alternative. Clearly, different factors might be selected and different weights applied to each factor. It has been assumed here that the relevant factors involve an alternative's likely effectiveness in reaching the target market, its

---

[22] Kotler calls this method the *weighted factor score method*. It is also known as the *expectancy value method*. For reasons of consistency, we have chosen to use the terminology introduced in Appendix 2A.

Table 5–2 Linear averaging applied to distribution of swimming pool germicide: present distributors alternative

Factor	(A) Factor Weight	(B) Factor Score											Rating (A × B)
		.0	.1	.2	.3	.4	.5	.6	.7	.8	.9	1.0	
1. Effectiveness in reaching swimming pool owners	.15				✔								0.045
2. Amount of profit if this alternative works well	.25						✔						0.125
3. Experience company will gain in consumer marketing	.10			✔									0.020
4. Amount of investment involved (high score for low investment)	.30									✔			0.240
5. Ability of company to cut short its losses	.20								✔				0.140
	Σ 1.00				Global Utility Index								0.570

Source: Philip Kotler, *Marketing Decision Making: A Model Building Approach* (New York: Holt, Rinehart and Winston, 1971), p. 293.

profitability, the experience that the company will gain in consumer marketing, the level of investment required to implement the alternative, and its ability to aid the company in cutting short its losses on other operations. It should be noted that the factor weights sum to 1.00; thus, they reflect the *relative* importance of each factor to management.

Although this method represents an improvement over simply listing the pros and cons of each alternative and is particularly useful in the early stage of evaluation, when little data are available, it is subject to a number of statistical limitations, the major one of which is that the method misleadingly uses an interval scale for data that are properly only ordinal. The sequential elimination method avoids this criticism.

Sequential Elimination[23]

This method calls for management to (1) rank, not rate, the five factors or attributes in order of importance, (2) set a minimum level from 0.00 to 1.00 for each factor that a distribution alternative must satisfy in order to be considered, and (3) examine all distribution alternatives against the first important factor, then the second, etc., eliminating those strategies at each stage that fail to satisfy that factor. Table 5–3 illustrates this method, again using the swimming pool germicide example. Note that the factors have been reordered according to the factor weights shown in Table 5–2. For each factor, a minimum pass level is established by management. In this example, all but one distribution alternative scored at or above the pass level. Thus, alternative 3 is eliminated from further consideration because it requires too much investment. Alternative 5 is eliminated when the second most important factor is considered, because it fails to

---

[23] Kotler calls this method the *hierarchical preference ordering method*. As with linear averaging, we have chosen, for consistency, to use the terminology introduced in Appendix 2A.

Table 5–3 Sequential elimination applied to five distribution alternatives

Factors in Order of Importance	Minimum Pass Level	Alternative 1	Alternative 2	Alternative 3	Alternative 4	Alternative 5
1. Amount of investment involved	0.3	0.8 = P	0.6 = P	0.2 = F	0.9 = P	0.9 = P
2. Amount of profit if this alternative works well	0.5	0.5 = P	0.8 = P	0.6 = —	0.5 = P	0.4 = F
3. Ability of company to cut short its losses	0.5	0.7 = P	0.6 = P	0.1 = —	0.8 = P	0.8 = —
4. Effectiveness in reaching swimming pool owners	0.3	0.3 = P	0.7 = P	0.8 = —	0.6 = P	0.3 = —
5. Experience company will gain in consumer marketing	0.4	0.2 = F	0.5 = P	0.6 = —	0.2 = F	0.4 = —
Ranking		3rd	1st	5th	2nd	4th

Note: P = Pass
　　　 F = Fail

Source: Philip Kotler, *Marketing Decision Making: A Model Building Approach* (New York: Holt, Rinehart and Winston, 1971), p. 295.

Table 5–4 Example of data input for simulation
of alternative distribution strategies

| | Distribution Strategies | | | |
| | (1) | (2) | (3) | (4) |
Variables	Present Distributors Alternative	New Distributors Alternative	Acquisition Alternative	Private Brand Alternative
Investment	$300,000	$500,000	$2,500,000	$100,000
Price per bag	$2.70	$2.50	$2.70	$2.20
Contribution margin per bag	$1.20	$1.00	$1.20	$0.70
Mean monthly advertising budget	$5,000	$50,000	$10,000	$5,000
Advertising effectiveness coefficient	1/2	1/1.8	1/1.9	1/2
Initial number of distributors	80	20	60	60
Growth rate per month in number of distributors	0.02	0.04	0.01	0.02
Maximum number of distributors permitted	150	150	150	150
Distribution effectiveness coefficient	1/2.5	1/2.0	1/2.2	1/2.2

Source: Philip Kotler, *Marketing Decision Making: A Model Building Approach* (New York: Holt, Rinehart and Winston, 1971), p. 296.

promise enough profits. The procedure is continued by bringing in successively less important factors until, as Table 5–3 indicates, only alternative 2 remains. The relative standings of the five alternatives are shown in the bottom row.

Although this method probably comes close to reflecting how many managers tend to think about choosing among alternatives, it gives no credit to how well a particular distribution alternative exceeds a minimum level required by some factor. A particular strategy may be almost perfect on the most important criterion and slightly below the minimum level on a minor criterion and as a result be eliminated. In these situations, it may be necessary for management to adopt another choice strategy, such as one of those suggested in the appendix to Chapter 2, that would more equitably discriminate among the options under consideration.

Both linear averaging and sequential elimination fail to produce an actual estimate of profit and risk for each alternative. To accomplish this, it would be desirable to create a simulation model for examining the estimated monetary consequences of each alternative under different assumptions and sets of data.

Simulation

Plausible data were developed for four of the five distribution strategies previously specified.[24] These data are shown in Table 5–4. For example, the acquisition alternative was considered to require the highest investment, and the private brand alternate the lowest. Furthermore, each distribution alternative involves a somewhat different pricing policy and contribution margin as well as different levels of advertising expenditures and effectiveness. Thus, under the new distributors alternative, the initial number of distributors would be low but

[24] Kotler, *op. cit.,* p. 296.

Table 5–5 Results of simulation of alternative distribution strategies

Criterion	(1) Present Distributors Alternative		(2) New Distributors Alternative		(3) Acquisition Alternative		(4) Private Brand Alternative	
	Value	Rank	Value	Rank	Value	Rank	Value	Rank
Pay-back period (months)	14	3	8	1	25	4	9	2
Share of potential	44%	4	100%	1	62%	2	43%	3
Accumulated discounted profit (millions)	3.25	3	6.10	1	5.60	2	1.99	4

Source: Philip Kotler, *Marketing Decision Making: A Model Building Approach* (New York: Holt, Rinehart and Winston, 1971), p. 297.

the growth rate would be high, because it is assumed that potential distributors would react favorably to the large advertising budget and the higher margin given to them.

Other inputs used by Kotler and Vialle, but not shown in Table 5–4, were (1) the rate of growth in demand expected under the different distribution alternatives, (2) a provision for substantial competitive reaction if the company's market share started to exceed a certain figure, and (3) a provision for the effect of test marketing before making a decision. The four distribution alternatives were simulated for a 48-month period; the results, in terms of three different measures of performance, are shown in Table 5–5. *Pay-back period* refers to how many months will pass before the accumulated revenue covers the accumulated cost to the company. *Share of potential* refers to the percentage of the company's potential share of the market that is realized by a particular distribution alternative. *Accumulated discounted profit* refers to the present value of the 48-month earnings stream discounted at 10 percent. Clearly, the new distributors alternative is superior on the basis of these criteria.

Qualitative Criteria

Although it should be clear that the methods described above are useful for determining the most profitable channel alternative, more qualitative considerations must enter into the analysis as well.[25] Simplistically put, the choice among channel alternatives in the discussion thus far comes down to judgments on the basis of mainly economic criteria. Thus, if it were possible to assume that two alternative channels (for example, employing one's own sales force versus using manufacturers' representatives, or developing a wholly owned system of warehouses versus renting space in public warehouses) produce the same sales, a

[25] A theoretical treatment of this subject is found in Frederick E. Balderston, "Design of Marketing Channels," in Reavis Cox, Wroe Alderson, and Stanley Shapiro (eds.), *Theory in Marketing* (Homewood, Ill.: Richard D. Irwin, 1964), pp. 176–89. See also Ronald Artle and Sture Berlund, "A Note on Manufacturers' Choice of Distribution Channels," *Management Science* (July 1959), pp. 460–71; and Helmy H. Baligh, "A Theoretical Framework for Channel Choice," in P. D. Bennett (ed.), *Economic Growth, Competition, and World Markets* (Chicago: American Marketing Association, 1965), pp. 631–54.

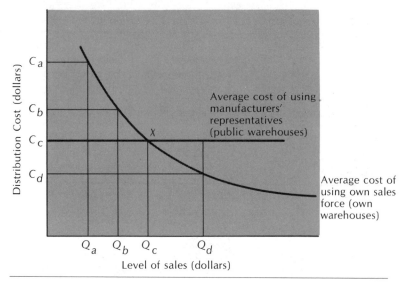

Figure 5–4 Breakeven cost chart: Manufacturers' representatives versus own sales force and public warehouses versus own warehouses

straightforward break-even analysis could be developed to aid in making the decision between the two.[26] Figure 5–4 portrays the average costs associated with these alternatives. The average cost of using manufacturers' representatives (or public warehouses) is constant over the range of sales, while the per-unit cost of employing one's own sales force (or owning one's own warehouses) declines as the level of sales increases (if it is assumed that the sales agents are paid on a straight salary basis or that the warehouses are bought outright and not leased back).

In this highly simplified example, the break-even point between the various alternatives is X. Thus, at sales levels less than Q_c, the decision maker should employ manufacturers' representatives (or use public warehouses) and at sales levels greater than Q_c, he should hire his own sales force (or purchase his own warehouses).

There is, however, a constraint in the marketplace that is not readily apparent when one is considering economic variables alone: it is likely that channel alternatives will be limited for new entrants to a market. Thus, when sales are at level Q_a, the manufacturer (or middleman, in the case of alternatives available to intermediaries) may be forced to integrate the personal selling or the warehousing function even though the break-even analysis indicates otherwise, because the volume he can generate is not sufficiently attractive to independent intermediaries. The missionary effort that the latter would have to expend on the new entrant's product or service might not, in their eyes, be justified by the returns they would receive. Therefore, the shifting of marketing flows within the channel may be restricted until the market becomes larger—when the sales level

[26] A similar approach can be found in Philip Kotler, *Marketing Management: Analysis, Planning, and Control*, 5th ed. (Englewood Cliffs, N.J.: Prentice-Hall, 1984), pp. 556–57.

reaches Q_b. The division of labor in channels may be limited by the extent of the market.[27]

Management's desire to exert sufficient control over channel members' activities to ensure adequate performance throughout the channel system frequently modifies decisions based on economic criteria alone. Management may be willing to trade off short-term economic benefits in order to gain a long-term ability to manipulate the channel. In conventional channels of distribution, the members are independent businessmen. Therefore, each is primarily interested in maximizing his own profits, which can sometimes lead to suboptimization within the system, as pointed out in Chapter 1. Suboptimization means that each channel member may make a set of decisions on the various elements of marketing strategy (e.g., price, advertising, and physical distribution) that maximizes his profits but conflicts with the ability of the entire system to perform most efficiently, effectively, or at a desired quality level. As Stasch has observed, the remedy to this problem is to seek an adjustment of the strategy decisions of each member so that total channel performance (measured in terms of profits, market share, or some other commonly shared goal) will be higher.[28] The greater the difference between present channel performance and projected channel performance under the systems approach, the greater will be the incentive of channel members to pursue joint planning.

Adaptability

Another critical noneconomic factor in choosing among alternative channels is the ability of various potential or existing channel members to adapt to changing conditions. Problems of adaptability are most evident during times of economic downturn or when a channel is being threatened by innovative import or intertype competition. Indeed, adaptability for most marketing institutions is a slow and tortuous process. Many marketing institutions are relatively rigid and conservative and therefore tend to go into "shock" and/or "defensive retreat," as described in Exhibit 5–1, when faced by radical changes in their environments rather than acknowledging them or creatively adapting. Given the volatility of the economy and the amazing advances in technology over the past decade, it is likely that (1) ability and (2) willingness to make adaptations may be among the criteria most used by managers in choosing among channel alternatives and selecting specific channel partners. Indeed, adaptability is one of the four major standards—along with efficiency (expense-to-revenue), effectiveness (market share), and quality (end-user satisfaction)—that should be applied to channel decisions.

---

[27] For a discussion of this point, see George J. Stigler, "The Division of Labor is Limited by the Extent of the Market," *Journal of Political Economy*, Vol. 59 (June 1951), pp. 185–93. The break-even analysis presented above is directly consistent with the concepts of postponement-speculation and functional spinoff introduced in Chapter 1 to show how channel structure emerges and evolves.

[28] Stanley F. Stasch, "A Method of Dynamically Analyzing the Stability of the Economic Structure of Channels of Distribution," unpublished doctoral dissertation, Northwestern University, 1964, pp. 63ff. See also V. K. Rangan, A. A. Zoltners, and R. J. Becker, "The Channel Intermediary Selection Decision: A Proposed Model and an Application," *Management Science*. Vol. 32 (1986), pp. 1114–22.

EXHIBIT 5–1   The crisis-change model

The crisis-change model isolates four distinct phases through which organizations pass as they adapt to crisis situations. According to this theory, adaptation begins with an initial period of shock and is followed by a period of defensive retreat, then by acknowledgment, and finally by adaption and change.

THE SHOCK PHASE

An organization is considered to be in crisis when any factor critical to the viability of the total system of which it is a part is threatened. The shock phase occurs when members of a channel become aware of a threat to the survival or to the objectives of the system, as when a new type of competing retailing institution emerges. At this point, individual survival is the paramount objective of each member of the total system, and this objective leads in turn to a fragmentation of intergroup (intrachannel) relations. The primary focus is therefore placed upon the threat, and day-to-day operations become irrelevant. It is during this stage that the established system loses ground to its new competitor as the individual members contemplate *noncompetitive means* of destroying the source of crisis. An example is the emergence of the chain grocery store and the threat it posed to the independent grocer. When chains first developed, independents spent their efforts predicting the former's eventual demise; their energies were absorbed in developing rationalizations for the "short-term" predicament.

THE DEFENSIVE RETREAT PHASE

This stage is marked by the established system mobilizing its forces by imposing controls designed to reduce the threat. These controls do not resolve the crisis but merely postpone a confrontation, possibly on another plane. Thus, during the emergence of the chain store, the defensive retreat phase was marked by lobbying for legislation to curtail chain store activities. The small grocer realized he could not compete in the marketplace with the chain and therefore felt he had to eliminate or weaken the chains by subjecting them to crippling controls. Collectively, the small grocers carried out this objective by seeking legislation that would restrict the activities of the newer, more progressive, and more efficient organization and thereby curtail its effectiveness. The result in the grocery trade was the passage of chain store taxes and the Robinson-Patman Act. Although the threatened system survives during this phase, such defensive actions eventually become self-defeating because they are not consistent with the objectives of long-term organizational growth.

THE ACKNOWLEDGMENT PHASE

During this phase, the individuals in the threatened system engage in self-examination and interpersonal confrontation. It is here that they search for new and better ways of communication, ways that ultimately lead to a genuine understanding and a sharing of information. Leadership and decision making now become open to a wider range of influences, which are given fair consideration. Problems are explored and are not assumed to be manageable by some simple formula. As a result, solutions become more attuned to the nature of the problems. During this acknowledgment phase, the established system comes to doubt the validity of its own traditions and begins to experiment with some new alternatives, but in a

Source: Stephen L. Fink, Joel Beak, and Kenneth Taddeo, "Organizational Crisis and Change," *Journal of Applied Behavioral Science,* Vol. 7 (January-February 1971), pp. 15–37.

rather cautious manner. As some structural changes are tried out, the system becomes less and less dependent upon its past and more in touch with current developments. It begins to discover ways of using structure to facilitate the functions it must perform, rather than attempting to fit functions into preestablished structures. In our example, the independent grocer finally realized that he would have to innovate in order to survive. The result of the crisis was the birth of the Independent Grocers Alliance (IGA) and other wholesaler- and retailer-sponsored cooperatives. Overall, then, characteristic of the acknowledgment phase is an increasing excitement about the discovery of something new and better as well as a certainty that it is undesirable, if not impossible, to return to the former patterns of operation.

THE ADAPTION AND CHANGE (GROWTH) PHASE

The processes that characterize the period of adaption and change reflect effective coping, and they sharply contrast with those that characterize the defensive retreat. The adaption and change phase represents a renewal of the growth process. In this sense it is not really a phase but a rebirth of an ongoing state of development. By the time the system has reached this phase, it has, to a large degree, disposed of dysfunctional behavior in that the subsystems are working interdependently, and each institution complements the total system. It is here that cooperatives like the IGA begin to mature and prosper, not only with respect to isolated functions, such as quantity purchases, but throughout the entire realm of the business. The result is that the new system triggers a shock phase for the system that posed the original threat.

SELECTING SPECIFIC CHANNEL PARTNERS

The choice of a specific channel partner or partners is, of course, the ultimate determinant of the success or failure of the channel relationship. All of the planning suggested up to this point means absolutely nothing if the right parties cannot be found to execute it.

A list of suggested criteria for the selection of specific channel partners by an individual supplier is presented in Exhibit 5–2. These criteria can be used as relevant attributes in the choice models described earlier. Exhibit 5–3 details the factors that retailers use in selecting suppliers.

CONSTRAINTS ON CHANNEL STRATEGY AND DESIGN

Aside from the strong stipulation that channel planning start from an understanding of consumer behavior and, in particular, consumer demand for service output levels, there are several critical factors that place constraints on and, in a number of cases, are instrumental in determining channel organization. These factors are discussed in some detail in basic marketing and marketing management texts and, therefore, will be reviewed only briefly here.[29]

[29] See, for example, Kotler, *Marketing Management*, pp. 552–53.

EXHIBIT 5–2 Criteria for selecting channel partners: The supplier's viewpoint

1. Financial strength of prospective channel partner
   a. Revenue, profit, and loss
   b. Balance sheet
2. Sales Strength
   a. Number of sales agents
   b. Sales and technical competence
3. Product lines
   a. Competitive products
   b. Compatible products
   c. Complementary products
4. Reputation
   a. Leadership
   b. Well-established
   c. Community standing
   d. Background of key executives
   e. Level of expertise
5. Market coverage
   a. Geographic coverage: outlets per market area
   b. Industry coverage
   c. Call frequency or intensity of coverage
6. Sales performance
   a. Performance of related lines
   b. General sales performance
   c. Growth prospects
   d. Ability to penetrate accounts
   e. Success in reaching target markets/individuals
   f. After-sales follow-up
7. Management strength
   a. Planning
   b. Employee relations
   c. Marketing orientation
   d. Strategic direction

8. Advertising and sales promotion programs
9. Training programs
   a. Self-administered
   b. Willingness to allow suppliers to participate
10. Sales compensation programs
11. Plant, equipment, and facilities
    a. Transportation/delivery methods and record
    b. Inventory
       (1) kind and size
       (2) inventory minimums: safety stocks
       (3) service levels
    c. Warehousing
       (1) supplied in field
       (2) ability to handle shipments efficiently
12. Ordering and payment procedures
13. Installation and repair services
    a. After-sales follow-up
    b. Warranty work
14. Quality of demonstrator programs
15. Willingness to commit resources to individual lines/brands
16. Willingness to cooperate in joint programs
17. Willingness to share data
    a. Customers
    b. Sales force
    c. Inventory
    d. Delivery
18. Willingness to accept a quota

Entry Barriers. It is important to realize at the outset that the choice of outlets, in the case of manufacturers, and of suppliers, in the case of middlemen, is frequently highly restricted. For example, in the automotive passenger tire industry, a new manufacturer would find it extremely difficult to find retail outlets for his replacement tires, because most of the suitable outlets have already been secured by the existing manufacturers (e.g., Goodyear, Firestone,

Michelin, Bridgestone, Goodrich, General, and Uniroyal). In order to generate sales volume and thus achieve scale economies in production, a new tire manufacturer would probably have to vie for private label business. The manufacturer would likely be forced into an unequal bargaining position with his prospective customers, because in such situations, middlemen can usually play suppliers off against one another and thereby establish highly favorable terms of trade in private label arrangements. On the other hand, wholesalers are obviously foreclosed from many channels in which direct distribution is practiced (e.g., automobiles, mainframe computers), and specific retailers may find themselves similarly foreclosed if the policy of the supplier is to deal only with certain types of outlets (e.g, Schwinn bicycles and Stiffel lamps are not sold through discount houses). While the problem of channel choice is particularly vexing for new, unestablished organizations, it is also worrisome for units wishing to diversify or to broaden their distribution. Certainly, the extent of financial and other sources of power held by a channel member seeking to enter or enlarge a distribution network will have a strong effect on the amount of freedom of choice available to him.

Middleman Orientation.   The pros and cons of particular distribution policies from a middleman's point of view may differ radically from those of manufacturers. Wittreich has presented examples of the brewing, appliance, and building products industries to show that small retailers speak a different language than and are not as growth-oriented as the large manufacturers whose products they sell.[30] In fact, in their perceptions and outlook it is likely that wholesalers are more congruent with retailers, and vice versa, than are manufacturers with either.

Marketing programs can fail because managers at the manufacturer's level do not tailor their programs to the capabilities and orientations of their middlemen. For example, a promotion campaign may be too complicated for middlemen to understand or implement properly. The number of calls per customer required by a manufacturer from his wholesalers may exceed the wholesalers' capacity, or the minimum orders specified by the manufacturer may be beyond the inventory handling and storage facilities of a middleman.

In general, the "independence" of independent middlemen can work at cross-purposes to the desires of manufacturers. First of all, the middleman is in business to satisfy his customers.[31] In consumer goods marketing, there are relatively few exceptions to the rule that consumers buy from retailers, not from manufacturers. Thus, retailers possess "veto power" over virtually all marketing programs.[32] (An analogous situation holds when manufacturers of industrial goods employ industrial distributors or manufacturers' representatives.) Although the manufacturer could theoretically market his products directly to consumers, consumer buying behavior and distribution economics often preclude this possibility. As Star observes:

> While retailers *can* influence brand sales significantly in most product categories, such influence is clearly a more decisive factor in some product categories than in others. Conceptually, we would expect such influence to be most important in product categories (1) where the buying process is very unimportant to the consumer (e.g., frequently purchased, low-priced staple commodities), and (2) where the buying process is extremely important to the consumer (e.g., infrequently purchased, high-priced products perceived to be differentiated along complex dimensions). In the first case, the consumer's need for information is so low that manufacturers are generally unable to create strong brand preference. As a result, retailers are free to carry any brand(s) they wish without fear of lost sales or lessened consumer goodwill. In the second case, the consumer's need for information is so great that manufacturers can directly satisfy the need only partially. Under these circumstances, the retailer must provide additional information in order to "close" a sale. In the process of providing this information, the retailer has considerable opportunity to influence the consumer's ultimate brand choice.[33]

Thus, the manufacturer is continually engaged in seeking support from middlemen, especially for the kinds of products mentioned by Star (and their analogues in the industrial market). Such support is by no means automatically available.

[30] Warren J. Wittreich, "Misunderstanding the Retailer," *Harvard Business Review,* Vol. 40 (May-June 1962), pp. 147–59. This communication problem, among others, is examined in Chapter 10.

[31] For an interesting discussion of the weaknesses inherent in assuming too much about middlemen's orientations, see Philip McVey, "Are Channels of Distribution What Textbooks Say?" *Journal of Marketing,* Vol. 24 (January 1960), pp. 61–65.

[32] Steven H. Star, *Obtaining Retailer Support for Marketing Programs,* Project Description P-82 (Cambridge, Mass.: Marketing Science Institute, 1973), p. 1.

[33] *Ibid.,* pp. 4–5.

Second, independent middlemen are in business for themselves, not for manufacturers.[34] For example, retailers resort to selling private brands to increase their independence from manufacturers of branded merchandise and to guarantee a continuous source of supply of products they desire to provide for their customers. Third, middlemen generally have existing lines of products. The manufacturer seeking to employ a specific middleman must develop a product that closely fits the line that the middleman handles. Finally, in the case of retailers, the middleman allocates display space, which is indeed a scarce resource given the number of items to be placed. Although some manufacturers have gained considerable control over the display space allocation process in the grocery trade (e.g., Kraft with certain dairy products, Campbell with soup, Nabisco with crackers and cookies, and Kellogg with breakfast cereals), and in the sale of cosmetics through department stores, the majority of manufacturers must vie for this space by granting significant concessions or by investing heavily in various consumer promotions.

In addition, a manufacturer seeking to market through middlemen must recognize and sell to three publics—the middlemen's customers, the managements of the various intermediary organizations, and the sales agents employed by the latter. Successful wooing of management does not automatically mean that market penetration will be forthcoming. A middleman's sales staff have to be convinced of the merits of the product, and thus manufacturers must themselves sell to these sales agents via sales training programs, sales contests, special promotions, and other incentives.

On the other hand, a manufacturer may have considerable power to recruit and influence channel intermediaries. Instead of trying to *push* his brand through a channel and pursuing a hard-sell policy with middlemen, he can try to *pull* his brand through the channel by using missionary selling and by advertising heavily to gain end-user preference. If the latter strategy works, middlemen may actually solicit the manufacturer to carry his brand, and reseller support is likely to be available to him. However, the alternative costs must be carefully assessed in a manner similar to that specified earlier. The different strategies require varying amounts of capital investment. The key problem is to determine whether greater channel performance can be generated by manufacturers assuming more participation in the marketing flows *or* by shifting more of the work of the channel to middlemen or end-users.

Customer Characteristics. The number, size, and geographic and industrial concentration of customers will have a direct effect on channel design. For example, in a study of factors that influence the length of channels, Jackson, Krampf, and Konopa found that channel length increases as (1) the availability of capable middlemen and (2) the number of customers increase.[35] They also found that channel length decreases as (1) the significance of the purchase, (2) the customer volume potential, (3) the geographic concentration of the market, and (4) the industrial concentration of the market increase.

Product Characteristics. Product characteristics will directly influence channel design. Perishable products require direct marketing or at least the use

[34] McVey, *op. cit.*
[35] Donald M. Jackson, Robert F. Krampf, and Leonard J. Konopa, "Factors That Influence the Length of Industrial Channels," *Industrial Marketing Management*, Vol. 11 (1982), p. 267.

of middlemen who can assure rapid turnover of merchandise. Bulky products require channels that minimize shipping distance and excessive handling. Unstandardized products that call for technical expertise in their sale may require direct selling because of the need for specialized attention. Nonperishable, nonbulky, standardized products can be handled more readily by indirect channels.

Other Characteristics. Middleman, competitive, company, and environmental characteristics also influence channel design. Thus, in certain lines of trade (e.g., furniture), manufacturers' representatives are particularly well adapted to serve producers and customers because of their ability to carry full lines of complementary products assembled from a variety of manufacturers. Comparisons as to style, price, and suitability are significant to consumers who are purchasing shopping goods, and therefore the selection of appropriate channels is dictated to a large degree by the need to provide such comparisons. Furthermore, companies obviously vary in their financial strength, the breadth of their product mix and assortments, the orientation of their marketing policies, the attitudes of management towards the use of various kinds of intermediaries, and their experience with certain types of outlets or suppliers. All of these factors constrain channel design.

Clearly, economic conditions and legal restrictions are influential in determining the amount of channel strategy discretion an organization will have. Fluctuating interest rates, periods of growth and stagnation, and increased international competition, along with currency fluctuations and energy problems, are likely to be hallmarks of the environment of the 1990s. In the face of such uncertainty, it would be foolish to attempt to generate any universal "principles." Each channel situation must be measured carefully against the altering environment. The outcome will vary in each case. Legal issues may confound the picture even more, as we will see in Chapter 8.

SUMMARY AND CONCLUSIONS

Channel strategy and design are critical elements of marketing strategy. The starting point in the channel planning process is the end-user, irrespective of the type of goods and services involved. Channel objectives must emanate from a knowledge of the service output levels desired by the end-user. Once objectives are established for the channel, managers can focus on questions of channel strategy. One such issue is the degree of market coverage, exposure, and support an organization's products require. Channel strategy involves determining, broadly, how adequate coverage, exposure, and support can be obtained (e.g., via independent middlemen or vertical integration).

Market coverage and exposure issues focus on a determination of both the number of suppliers *and* the number of intermediaries with whom to deal. As the marketing manager looks down the channel (from manufacturer to wholesaler to retailer), the three basic strategic choices seem to be intensive, selective, or exclusive distribution. It is likely that the more intensive the distribution of a product or brand, the greater its sales will be in the short run. However, there is an important tradeoff between sales and control over the channel, which must be taken into consideration by the manager. Loss of control can result in lower long-term profits.

Development of an appropriate distribution strategy for consumer goods requires consideration of the relationship between type of good and type of outlet. Again, as in choosing the relevant middlemen, knowledge of end-user purchasing behavior is critical.

If channel strategy dictates a more exclusive type of distribution policy, specific agreements are possible with regard to the allocation of marketing effort among channel members. An appropriate allocation is arrived at through bargaining over products covered, class or types of customers, territory covered, inventories, installation and repair services, prices, sales quotas, advertising and sales promotional obligations, and exclusive dealing. These agreements should be put in writing, reviewed yearly, be reasonably flexible, and contain information on their duration, renewal, and termination. The forging of such an agreement, if it is to be functional over the long term, must reflect mutual support and an equitable division of benefits and costs in carrying forward distribution. It involves the specification of the rights and obligations of each of the parties.

Once channel objectives are established and the basic parameters of channel strategy have been isolated, it is possible to begin choosing among alternative channels. Four basic steps are involved:

1. Itemize the alternative ways in which end-users can purchase the product in question and assess the relative volume of the product class moving through the purchase outlets, their relative rates of growth, and their relative profitability. Underlying this step is a thorough evaluation of end-user preferences.
2. Specify the primary channel paths that can be used in reaching these various outlets or in tapping the relevant markets for the product.
3. Quantify the relevant factors in the consideration of each channel path by employing linear averaging, sequential elimination, simulation, or some other systematic choice method.
4. Evaluate qualitative criteria relative to the amount of control and adaptability desired.

Channel choice may, however, be highly restricted. Not every wholesaling and retailing establishment is available to every supplier, and vice versa. Achieving distribution through Sears is not a foregone conclusion for manufacturers, just as obtaining clothing supplies from Ralph Lauren is not a certainty for middlemen.

Efforts by managers to organize an efficient and effective channel system are sometimes futile because they do not fully account for the differences in perspective and orientation of independent middlemen. The latter are in business to satisfy their customers and not the desires of other channel members. In addition, middlemen generally have existing product lines from which they frequently do not wish to deviate. Finally, middlemen, especially retailers, control display space and the process by which it is allocated. Therefore, gaining reseller support is often not a simple matter, to say the least.

Along with entry barriers and the orientation of middlemen, a number of additional constraints often determine exactly how a channel is (or should be) designed. They include customer, product, competitive, company, and environmental characteristics. All of these constraints clearly will influence the distribution strategy to be employed in any specific situation. They place boundaries around channel management or, as examined in the next chapter, the means available to coordinate the activities of marketing institutions and agencies.

DISCUSSION QUESTIONS

1. Explain how the characteristics of the following consumer and industrial goods affect the channels for them:

Consumer Goods	Industrial Goods
Bread	Typewriter ribbons
Breakfast cereal	Uranium (for nuclear power plants)
Women's hats	Cement
Refrigerators	Data processing equipment

2. For Oliver Williamson, the choice of channel structure is the consequence of the interaction between a set of human factors and a set of environmental factors. Explain the two major human factors of *bounded rationality* and *opportunism* and the two major environmental factors of *uncertainty/complexity* and *small numbers*. Give an example of each.

3. A prestigious designer of men's fashions (suits, pants, shirts, ties, etc.) has just decided to manufacture his own designs, but has no experience in distribution methods.
   a. Conceive of four alternative retail outlets for his line of merchandise.
   b. Conceive of four major alternative distribution strategies for his line.

4. What are the strengths and weaknesses of linear averaging, sequential elimination, and simulation as methods for choosing marketing channels?

5. What additional variables should have been included in the simulation of alternative distribution strategies shown in Table 5–4? How would you obtain relevant input data on these variables in order to use them in the simulation?

6. What are the strengths and weaknesses of analyzing channel planning in terms of management science (as described in Appendix 5C, for example)?

7. Discuss four different variables that might prohibit a manufacturer from gaining distribution through a prestige department store. Discuss four different variables that might prohibit a discount department store chain from obtaining a manufacturer's product line. Finally, discuss four different variables that might prohibit a manufacturer from gaining distribution through an industrial wholesaler.

8. Debate the pros and cons of intensive versus selective versus exclusive distribution of the following product classes: (a) panty hose; (b) drill presses; (c) tractors; (d) toasters.

9. Develop a checklist of questions for rating prospective suppliers, taking the perspective of wholesalers.

10. Develop a checklist of questions a manufacturer might use in selecting a specific outlet (store A versus store B) to market a product.

Rex Chainbelt's Distributor Sales Agreement for the Bearing Division

REX CHAINBELT INC., a Wisconsin Corporation (herein called REX CHAIN-BELT), having its principal place of business in Milwaukee, Wisconsin, is pleased to submit this Agreement to

of

(herein called DISTRIBUTOR). Under this Agreement, DISTRIBUTOR will act as an authorized stock-carrying distributor for the products listed in this Agreement for the purpose of actively soliciting and serving users of REX CHAINBELT products in DISTRIBUTOR'S territory to secure satisfactory sales of these products from each type of industry.

The purpose of this Agreement is to set forth the basis on which DISTRIBU-TOR and REX CHAINBELT INC. agree to do business together, and to insure understanding and cooperation between both parties.

Appointment and Territory

1.   REX CHAINBELT hereby appoints

its distributor in

Source: National Industrial Conference Board, *Building a Sound Distributor Organization* (New York: National Industrial Conference Board Experiences in Marketing Management, No. 6, 1964), pp. 20–31.

(a) While DISTRIBUTOR may sell outside of the above area, REX CHAIN-BELT will furnish sales promotion and field selling assistance only in the area described in this Agreement. Since this area is not exclusive, REX CHAINBELT will not pay commissions or other compensation for sales or shipments made into the DISTRIBUTOR'S area except by specific arrangements in connection with individual orders.

(b) REX CHAINBELT will follow the general policy of not appointing additional stock-carrying distributors other than such as we already have in the described area for those products listed in attached Supplement A provided the volume of business developed by DISTRIBUTOR is satisfactory and reasonable, taking into consideration prevailing business conditions. DISTRIBUTOR will be consulted whenever changes in distribution in his trading area seem necessary.

Products

2. The products covered in this Agreement are listed in attached Supplement A. Any new or different products which REX CHAINBELT may from time to time manufacture or sell are expressly excluded except by REX CHAINBELT'S specific consent.

Sales Coverage

3. The area of DISTRIBUTOR'S primary sales responsibility will be the Industrial Consumer and reselling accounts. REX CHAINBELT will sell directly to Original Equipment Manufacturers and Contract Engineers. While it will be REX CHAINBELT'S policy to direct sales from consumer accounts to the distributor best able to handle the sale, REX CHAINBELT reserves the right to make sales direct to any consumer when this seems necessary in the best interests of customer service.

Prices and Terms

4. REX CHAINBELT shall sell to DISTRIBUTOR the products listed in Supplement A at prices set forth in the schedule of published net distributor prices then prevailing, or according to discounts applicable to the prevailing REX CHAINBELT price lists. Terms and conditions of sale are set forth in the section entitled, "Conditions of Sales" for the Industrial Equipment Section in the prevailing REX CHAINBELT price lists.

Changes in Prices, or Terms, etc., of Sale

5. REX CHAINBELT will endeavor to give DISTRIBUTOR advance notice of changes in price, discounts, and terms and conditions of sale, but reserves the right to make such changes without prior notice if circumstances necessitate it.

Quality

6. The DISTRIBUTOR is authorized to extend to his customers on the resale of REX CHAINBELT products the same warranty then being made by REX CHAINBELT in prevailing price lists (see paragraph on Quality in Standard

Conditions of Sale). DISTRIBUTOR is not authorized to make any other warranty.

Stock Requirement

7.   To perform the proper distribution function, DISTRIBUTOR will carry an adequate inventory of REX CHAINBELT products as outlined in Paragraph 10 of the Statement of Policy attached.

Return of Stock

8.   DISTRIBUTOR may, during the term of this sales Agreement, return any standard REX CHAINBELT products purchased under this Agreement according to the provisions of Paragraph 11 of the Statement of Policy attached.

Sales Promotion and Sales Coverage

9.   Distributor shall at all times vigorously promote the sale of REX CHAIN-BELT products by means of:

(a) adequate number of qualified salesmen for good market coverage.
(b) an adequate stock and warehouse service.
(c) sales promotion activity including effective use of catalogs and advertising.

REX CHAINBELT will cooperate with DISTRIBUTOR in promoting the sale of REX CHAINBELT products, and will supply DISTRIBUTOR with catalogs, product bulletins, and other sales promotion aids. REX CHAINBELT District Sales Engineers and Representatives will provide the DISTRIBUTOR with field sales assistance in the promotion of REX CHAINBELT products, but will be free to contact directly all customers to demonstrate, promote and otherwise advertise REX CHAINBELT products.

Acceptance of Orders

10.   All orders placed by DISTRIBUTOR are subject to acceptance or refusal by REX CHAINBELT, at its originating plants, and delivery is F.O.B. the originating plant.

Adherence to Manufacturer's Policy

11.   Distributor agrees to follow the policies of REX CHAINBELT as announced in the Policy Statement attached herein as well as subsequent changes in such policies.

Construction of Agreement

12.   This Agreement does not constitute DISTRIBUTOR as the legal representative or agent of REX CHAINBELT for any purpose, nor authorize DISTRIBUTOR to transact business in REX CHAINBELT'S name. The rights and privileges of DISTRIBUTOR under this Agreement are personal, cannot be assigned and will not inure to the benefit of any receiver, trustee in bankruptcy

or any other legal representative, unless consented to by REX CHAINBELT INC. This Agreement supercedes all previous agreements and constitutes the entire Agreement between the parties.

Effective Date, Term and Termination

13. This Agreement shall become effective when formally signed and accepted by DISTRIBUTOR and REX CHAINBELT and shall continue until _____. Execution of orders after said date shall not constitute a renewal of this Agreement.

(a) Termination of this sales agreement can be made by either party. Notice of intent to terminate shall be made by letter by either party to the other's headquarters. The mailing date of such letter shall be considered the date of said notice. Termination shall become effective thirty (30) days after date of notice.

(b) In the event of termination by REX CHAINBELT, DISTRIBUTOR may within thirty (30) day termination period, return for credit all standard stock items. Credit will be issued at current prices for all such returned items which are current, unused and salable, less any cost of reconditioning.

(c) In the event of termination by DISTRIBUTOR, REX CHAINBELT will have the option of purchasing within thirty (30) days at current prices any or all of REX CHAINBELT products in DISTRIBUTOR'S inventory at the time of termination. Reshipment transportation charges shall be paid by the party terminating the Agreement, and shall not exceed those for transportation back to REX CHAINBELT'S originating plant.

_____

(Distributor's Corporate or Firm Name)

By _____

Date of Distributor's Signature _____ 19 _____

REX CHAINBELT INC.

By _____

(Authorized Official)

Date of Acceptance by

REX CHAINBELT INC. _____ 19 _____

REX CHAINBELT'S DISTRIBUTION POLICY AND PRACTICES FOR THE BEARING DIVISION

Objectives

1. Our primary objective in the distribution of REX CHAINBELT products is to provide:

(a) Prompt availability to all customers

(b) Assistance to distributors in carrying out their part of our marketing program

In order to

(c) Sell the largest possible share of the market at the lowest possible cost

(d) Provide a fair return to REX CHAINBELT and its Distributors

2. Our Sales Agreement covers our fundamental sales relationship. The following paragraphs are intended to explain recommended procedures and to serve as a guide in directing our mutual selling efforts.

REX CHAINBELT Indirect Sales Through Distributors

3. The purpose of our Distributor Policy is to provide the most effective sales coverage to produce the largest share of available business in each trading area and to permit distributors to obtain maximum sales volume. To accomplish this purpose, REX CHAINBELT'S Standard Industrial Products as shown in the current merchandise catalog are sold to all consumer accounts and to all resale or jobber accounts through the following Distribution channels:

(a) Industrial Supply and Power Transmission Distributors

(b) Bearing Specialist Distributors

(c) Special Industry Distributors in market not satisfactorily covered by 3-a

REX CHAINBELT Direct Sales

4. To accomplish the sales objectives previously mentioned, REX CHAINBELT sells directly as follows:

(a) Original Equipment Manufacturers and Contract Engineers

(b) Agencies and offices of the U.S. Government or subcontracts for such agencies and offices

Definition of Territory

5. The basic territory definition is given in Article 1 of our Distributor Agreement.

6. Distributors may sell REX Standard Products to all Consumer and Resale or Jobber accounts in their regularly traveled area. Any questions concerning area assignment should be cleared through the REX District Office.

7. When two or more REX Distributors in the same trading area solicit the same account, the REX District Office will provide product application assistance as required but will maintain impartiality in respect to each distributor's position with such accounts.

Selective Distribution

8. REX CHAINBELT'S objective is to appoint the minimum number of Distributors necessary to obtain satisfactory market penetration in each trading area. Generally only one Bearing Specialist distributor will be appointed in a small size trading area. Where heavy industry concentration or unusual market conditions make additions or changes in distribution seem necessary, the Distributor affected will be consulted before any action is taken.

Handling of Inquiries and Orders

9. (a) REX CHAINBELT, where practical, will refer orders and inquiries from consumer accounts to the Distributor best equipped to service the account. However, inquiries and orders received directly will be handled directly where such handling seems necessary in the best interests of customer service.

(b) When such inquiries are handled directly by REX CHAINBELT INC., whenever possible, copies of the inquiry and reply will be furnished to the Distributor, and the customer will be advised of the services available from the Distributor.

(c) In the case of orders received and shipped directly to such consumer accounts, we will advise the consumer account of the service available from the Distributor and recommend that their future orders be placed with the distributor.

(d) All orders and inquiries received from resale or jobber accounts will be referred to the local Distributor on an impartial basis.

(e) Customer preferences will be major influencing factors in all inquiry or order referrals.

Distributor's Inventory
of REX CHAINBELT Products

10. The Distributor will be required to carry an adequate stock of REX products to perform the proper distribution function in his trading area. The stock should amount to *not less* than (_____%) of the Distributor's current annual purchases. This percentage is based on the relation between a Distributor's out-

of-stock and direct sales. The out-of-stock sales should account for a minimum of (_____%) of the Distributor's volume resulting in an inventory of no less than (_____ %) of annual purchases to achieve a desirable inventory turnover of four times. In no case should the Distributor's inventory be less than ($_____) to adequately service the industries in Distributor's Marketing area.

The (_____ %) or ($_____) minimum Distributor inventory will apply to each branch warehouse location of the Distributor's operation.

Review and Return of Distributor Stock

11.   Periodically, at least every twelve (12) months, the Distributor stock should be reviewed and a list of slow moving, unaltered stock items submitted to the REX District Office or Representative. Credit for return stock will be allowed in accordance with the following provisions:

(a) Written approval has been obtained from REX CHAINBELT INC.

(b) Full credit at current prices less any original transportation allowance will be allowed on current standard catalog items in good salable condition. Credit on this basis will be issued upon receipt of an order for stock material equal to the dollar value of the credit.

(c) Where returned stock as outlined in 11-b is not to be accompanied by an order of equal dollar value, credit will be allowed as under 11-b except that a 10% handling charge will be deducted from the value of the credit.

(d) The credit on returned stock in any one year should not exceed 3% of the average of the Distributor's annual purchases for the preceding three years.

(e) If it is necessary for REX CHAINBELT to recondition any stock returned under 11-b or 11-c, all reconditioning costs will be deducted from any credit issued.

(f) The Distributor will prepay return transportation charges on all returned material.

(g) Each request for return of slow moving stock must be accompanied by a complete stock analysis sheet.

(h) In event of termination of our Agreement with a distributor, return of stock will be in accordance with Article 13 of REX CHAINBELT Distributor Agreement.

Sales Coverage

12.   The Distributor will provide sufficient qualified salesmen properly trained to sell REX BEARING Division products, covered in Supplement A of the REX CHAINBELT Distributor Sales Agreement, to consumer and reselling accounts in his trading area.

REX CHAINBELT will cooperate with the Distributor in training Distributor's organization in the sales and application of BEARING Division products.

The Distributor is expected to cooperate in reporting sales volume to selected accounts in order to help in evaluation of account coverage.

The Distributor is also expected to cooperate in reporting sales activities of Bearing Division products from each individual branch warehouse to assist in the evaluation and increased effectiveness of territory coverage.

Sales Training

13. (a) Each Distributor should hold a minimum of two sales meetings annually in cooperation with the REX District Sales Engineer or Representative. It is strongly recommended that the sales meetings be held more frequently in the more active marketing areas. The meetings will be held to instruct the Distributor personnel in the selling and application of Bearing Division products, and the meetings will be so conducted as to be closely related to each Distributor's marketing problem.

(b) The Distributor will be asked to hold sales meetings wherever necessary to tie in with REX's sales promotion plans on any product line. Meetings should be arranged at least two weeks in advance and generally will be approximately one and a half hours in length.

Field Sales Assistance

14. The REX District Sales Engineer or Representative will provide field sales assistance to the Distributor through cooperation on local sales meetings and through field sales calls with Distributor salesmen.

All field sales call schedules should be carefully planned in advance. Distributor management should cooperate with the REX District Sales Manager or BEARING Representative in setting up agendas for such calls. The agenda should show, insofar as possible, the problems and subjects which the Distributor salesman intends to cover with the customer.

REX CHAINBELT and the Distributor must recognize the continued need for application selling and the creation of brand preference, and the responsibility of the REX Field Sales organization in this regard. Therefore, our sales organization shall be free to contact all customers in a Distributor's territory to demonstrate, promote and apply REX products. Where practical, calls on the Distributor customers will be made with the Distributor salesman. In the case where such calls are made without Distributor salesmen, the Distributor involved will be informed of the results of such calls and suggestions will be made by our sales organization for follow-up action required by the Distributor to gain the maximum benefits from such REX CHAINBELT direct contacts.

Pricing

15. Individual net price schedules are furnished for each trade classification.

Occasionally, the Distributor may submit inquiries or orders for special products, repair parts, or requirements for major modifications to existing products. In such cases, the prices and discounts will be determined from manufacturing and engineering costs and current market conditions. The Distributor margin on such products may not be the same as the discount on standard products in the same product class.

Price Protection

16. REX CHAINBELT'S standard practice is to hold prices firm for orders that are on our books on the effective date of a price increase, provided shipment is requested, scheduled and made within sixty (60) days from date of price change. However, we reserve the right to make price changes without advance notice; in such cases, Distributors will be notified not later than effective date.

Resale Prices

17. REX CHAINBELT strongly recommends the maintenance of suggested resale prices. Such prices are based on providing Distributors with a gross margin adequate for maintaining a reasonable operating profit based on current average Distributor operating costs.

Advertising and Sales Promotion

18. (a) Distributors will be furnished regularly with information about REX promotion plans and lists of available literature and bulletins and necessary requisition blanks. The Distributor should maintain a stock of sales literature applicable to his marketing area. The REX District Sales Engineer or Representative will assist the Distributor wherever possible in selecting the literature to be requisitioned.

(b) REX CHAINBELT will assist the Distributor in preparing the material for use in Distributor Catalogs but will not pay any of the cost incurred for the actual publication of this Distributor Catalog. Available inserts for catalog use will be furnished at no charge.

(c) REX CHAINBELT will furnish suitable displays for Distributor Open Houses and Exhibits. REX personnel will cooperate in manning the displays wherever possible, but will not share the cost of exhibition space. The displays will be shipped by REX CHAINBELT prepaid to the Distributor and the Distributor will prepay the freight in return shipment of display.

(d) REX CHAINBELT will cooperate with the Distributor in furnishing visual aids and other program material for product clinics which the Distributor conducts before special groups such as Plant operating and engineering personnel or technical societies.

The REX World

19. The REX World is a REX CHAINBELT publication providing customers with information on the use of REX products. It includes good reference material and is also a valuable advertising piece. The use of the REX World is beneficial to the Distributor. REX World issues are available to the distributor in bulk quantities for him to distribute through his own mailing facilities.

Customer Service

20. In addition to supplying product information and carrying adequate stocks of REX BEARING Division products, the Distributor should render any other service which the customer may expect or require.

REX CHAINBELT Warehousing

21. REX District Warehouses are strategically located so that there is a warehouse stock available to practically all REX Distributors. Warehouse stock lists are printed to show the range of stocks available for any one or more of the warehouses which can be drawn on by each Distributor to serve his trading area. It is important that each Distributor Salesman be familiar with the warehouse stocks available, and that his name be placed on the warehouse stock mailing list.

REX CHAINBELT Distributor Advisory Board

22. The REX CHAINBELT Distributor Advisory Board consists of one management representative from twelve REX Distributors selected from varied geographical areas. Membership is composed of individuals from power transmission, bearing specialist, and general line houses. One third of the Board is succeeded each year by new members. The function is advisory in relation to current and contemplated REX Distributor programs and policies.

DISTRIBUTOR Personnel Mailing List

23. REX CHAINBELT will maintain a list of all Distributor personnel to insure prompt receipt of product and pricing information, stock lists, and other important releases by proper parties. The Distributor should cooperate with the Rex District Sales Engineer or Representative in periodically furnishing an up-to-date list of personnel.

Financial Responsibility

24. The Distributor will be expected to furnish REX CHAINBELT, upon request, any financial information having a direct bearing on our mutual relationship. In turn, the REX CHAINBELT Credit Department will be happy to confer with the Distributor at any time on matters of finance.

The Distributor should immediately refer any questions of policy or procedure not covered by this Statement or our Agreement to the REX District Office. A clear understanding of mutual objectives is imperative.

Appendix 5B

Square D and Its Distributors: A Discussion of Policy and Procedure

The Distributor . . . a Vital Part of the Square D Marketing Concept. The Square D Company is convinced that the bulk of its products can best be marketed through electrical wholesale distribution channels. Experience has proven that, by working with distributors, we

Source: Square D Company. Used with permission of Square D Company.

can achieve maximum sales efficiency and at the same time maintain better service to our customers.

As a result of over three-quarters of a century in this business, we have reached some definite conclusions about the proper relationship between our distributors and ourselves. This brochure records our thinking for the benefit of our distributors, our own sales organization, and those distributors who may join us in the future.

Qualifications. Because we look upon our distributors as far more than customers or resellers, we are very selective in choosing our distributors. Not just any distributor can become a Square D distributor.

A prospective Square D distributor must have an excellent local reputation as a fair and honest business house. He must have an aggressive organization and be financially able to expand to match the growth of the electrical industry. Only wholesale houses handling electrical supplies are eligible for selection as distributors of our complete line of equipment. In a very few instances (e.g., the coverage of a highly specialized market), specialty wholesale houses may qualify as distributors of certain highly specialized products.

Both Square D and the distributor assume certain obligations and become responsible for certain functions. The following pages discuss what we believe to be the logical and equitable division of these responsibilities.

Certain Responsibilities Are Exclusively Square D's . . . Square D Company carries the sole responsibility of designing, manufacturing and packaging the products to be sold. We manufacture a complete line of distribution equipment and industrial control, as well as related products. Our equipment has been designed with the distributor in mind—for flexible merchandising. Even special products are often reduced to standard components which can be merchandised like standard products.

Modern laboratory research facilities, plus highly developed engineering and technical skills, enable us to maintain our position as leader in product innovation, a position we have enjoyed for over three-quarters of a century.

Packaging is tailored to our distributors' needs and convenience. We feature informative labeling, convenient cartoning, functional sacks for small parts and packaged parts kits for conversion and maintenance.

SQUARE D AND ITS DISTRIBUTORS SHARE CERTAIN RESPONSIBILITIES

Square D Will . . . Provide its own offices in the country's major trading areas and staff these offices with competent engineers and other technically qualified sales personnel. Before receiving an initial assignment, new personnel undergo intensive company training that thoroughly encompasses all aspects of the application and sale of Square D products.

Use its field organization to help create and develop markets for Square D products through regular contact with customers and potential customers.

Use its field organization to help train distributor personnel in the operation and sale of Square D products. Such training enables them to do a better job for both the distributor and Square D.

Use its demonstration equipment, displays and specialized talents to help distributors plan promotional programs, displays, catalogs, direct mail advertising and other sales stimulating activities.

Provide back-up, specialized engineering help at Square D headquarters locations to assist in the solution of any application problem which cannot be handled in the field.

Our Distributor Is Expected to . . . Promote the Square D line as a primary line.

Employ trained, courteous, inside personnel who have a genuine interest in helping the customer with all his needs and problems.

Provide supplementary sales coverage through informed, trained professional sales personnel.

Become a Blue Chip distributor to utilize Square D's program of inventory control in accordance with Blue Chip II Policy.

Participate in our Product Educational Programs. Trained personnel who know our products can give the best customer service and produce more sales for both of us.

STOCKING PRODUCTS IS ALSO A MUTUAL RESPONSIBILITY

Square D Will . . . Provide a system of strategically located regional service centers, adequately stocked with products, to provide prompt delivery to meet the requirements of the marketing area.

Inventory the distributor's stock at regular intervals, in accordance with Blue Chip II policy, and recommend items and quantities of our products to be stocked. Our field organization is familiar with general market requirements and can make such recommendations as well as share any knowledge they have of current and future market trends and new product plans. A detailed knowledge of the distributor's stock enables the field representative to refer specific customer requests to the distributor.

Keep the distributor informed, insofar as practical, of future design changes that may tend to obsolete items in his stock and also work with him in liquidating his stock of old style items prior to the introduction of the newer designs.

Maintain various "Quick Ship" programs in order to meet urgent customer needs.

Our Distributor Is Expected to . . . Carry adequate stocks to service the demands of the area. Our field organization will help maintain an adequate stock by making recommendations based on their knowledge of current market requirements.

Permit our field organization to physically inventory Square D stocks at regular intervals and recommend items and quantities that should be ordered. Blue Chip II distributors shall cooperate with Square D personnel to determine target quantities based on inventory objectives mutually agreed upon.

Order stock from us periodically in large amounts and standard quantities, giving us the "lead time" characteristic of our normal delivery schedules. Blue Chip II distributors will enter orders as outlined in the Blue Chip II policy manual.

Cooperate with our field organization and establish a plan to liquidate stocks of old style equipment upon being informed of the introduction of new product designs.

SALES PROMOTION . . . ANOTHER TWO-WAY RESPONSIBILITY

Square D Will . . . Provide sales tools to produce maximum results. One of the major tools is the consistent, strong, national advertising program conducted by Square D. Because Square D ads appear in a wide selection of industrial publications, they are seen each month by millions of people. Among the audiences reached are industrial users, contractors, utilities, architects, purchasing agents, original equipment manufacturers, inspectors and consulting engineers. Many of these ads emphasize our authorized Square D distributors as logical marketing channels. The following additional sales promotion tools are available:

Catalogs and publications on all product lines for every important customer in the distributor's area.

Product bulletins, envelope stuffers and direct mail pieces. Most of these can be furnished with a distributor's imprint, at no cost.

Local promotion pieces, specifically designed for use by individual distributors, are produced as self-mailers, envelope stuffers or handouts; and many of them can be imprinted at no cost to the distributor.

Assistance in copy, artwork and general planning of promotional programs.

Repair parts manuals and bulletins to help the distributor provide the best customer service.

Competitive cross-reference sheets to enable the distributor to identify the proper equivalent to competitive items.

Displays, posters, plaques, wall charts, calculators, and specialty promotional items to help the distributor's selling efforts.

Our Distributor Is Expected to . . . Pay for his local advertising in newspapers and other local publications.

Display Square D products prominently and attractively to create interest and stimulate sales.

Cooperate with Square D on promotional programs. The best national promotional program is of little value if it is not backed by strong promotion at the local level.

Provide his own catalog for local distribution when, in his opinion, he can justify this sales expense. We will furnish standard illustrations and related material, without charge, for illustrating local catalogs and sales promotion pieces. On request, our staff will help with copy and layout. Typesetting, printing and other direct production costs involved in a distributor's local advertising and sales promotion programs are the distributor's responsibility and are not underwritten by Square D.

Provide his prospective customers with the literature which the distributor receives periodically from Square D.

BEING COMPETITIVE IS A TEAM JOB!

Square D Is Expected to . . . Give the distributor what he wants, when he wants it, where he wants it, at a price that should enable him to be competitive in the marketplace.

Sell to all authorized Square D distributors on the same basis in accordance with our published price schedule.

Provide field or headquarters assistance to the distributor when necessary to combat customer preference for competitive apparatus.

Sponsor programs on specific products or lines to assist the distributor to be competitive.

Our Distributor Is Expected to . . . Be competitive at the secondary market level whenever economically possible.

Inform us of current local market conditions. Knowledge of market fluctuations and competitive prices is primarily our responsibility. However, the distributor can be of great help by promptly keeping us informed of local changes.

Advise us of any customer resistance encountered in the sale of our products so we may initiate corrective action.

Call upon us for field assistance when necessary to combat competitive situations beyond the sales capabilities of the distributor's organization.

Sell Square D by promoting features and qualities that distinguish Square D products from other products. Distributors who act as unofficial "purchasing agents" and sell on the basis of price alone do a disservice to their customers.

Participate in the Blue Chip II Program to help maintain an adequate inventory to meet local market needs.

GENERAL POLICY

Situations frequently arise which tax any business relationship unless a previous understanding has been reached. Some of the situations which might be considered controversial in nature are covered in the following questions and answers:

Questions and Answers

What is our attitude toward price protection?

When market conditions force a drop in price levels, we immediately apply the lower levels to any unshipped portions of distributor orders. We delay establishing new recommended selling prices as long as practical to provide inventory relief. When prices must go up, we are forced to apply the higher levels to unshipped portions of distributor stock orders. Over a period of time there is an inventory "pick-up" or "write-off," depending on price trends and sound purchasing. Any plan which eliminates this normal business risk depreciates good management as a basic business element. This policy is a two-way street which divides responsibility on an equitable basis.

How do we feel about our authorized distributors selling Square D products to competitive distributors on a cost plus basis?

Our policy of selective distribution was created to ensure the most effective market coverage. We have selected our distributors on the basis of their operating policies, business reputation, integrity and ability to service our customers. Although we encourage our distributors to sell our products to a broad base of customers within their approved territory, we request that "courtesy exchanges" or other deals between our distributors and competitive wholesalers not be made. When our distributors make it possible for competitive distributors to obtain our merchandise, they are defeating the purpose of selective distribution and are narrowing their, and our, competitive position.

Why do we have a policy of minimum billing?

Our policy of minimum billing was established to help pay the cost of the invoicing and clerical work associated with processing each individual order. We encourage our distributors to place orders of economical size to help us give them better service.

Do we sell all our products through our distributors?

The vast majority of our product sales are made through authorized distributors. We appoint only enough distributors to assure complete coverage of the market with our broad product line. This assures sufficient potential to merit all-out effort by all Square D distributors. We prefer this marketing channel for the many reasons previously mentioned. However, some industrial and institutional users, original equipment manufacturers, and utilities have special product requirements which demand highly technical counsel and "custom-made" equipment. If they can best be served by dealing directly with us, we reserve the right to do so. Also, in cases of acquisitions made by the Square D Company, products manufactured by the acquired companies may continue to be handled by wholesale outlets that are not authorized to sell the entire Square D line, or may be appointed to sell those specialized products.

Why do we stress our complete line of products?

A complete line of products is an electrical distributor's major asset. The ability to bid on a complete job and assume unit responsibility for a complete package places a powerful tool in his hands. Because we provide such an unusually complete line, we often find it advantageous to advertise and promote related items of equipment together. We believe this presents a convincing story to the ultimate user, emphasizing the way Square D products team up to do a better job. However, distributors of acquired companies who are not Square D distributors may be retained and some definite purpose distributors may be appointed to serve specialty markets.

Why are there different profit margins on different products?

A distributor's profit margins on our products are usually consistent with the function performed by the distributor in selling these products. We have pioneered in a pricing policy which distinguishes between standard products and special items not normally stocked by a distributor. This policy provides an additional margin on those standard products that require greater handling and stocking expense on his part.

What is our position with respect to distributors who handle competing lines of equipment?

A distributor's performance can be measured by sales volume, market penetration, cooperation in the business relationship, promotional efforts, and other factors. We firmly believe that few distributors can serve adequately the manufacturers they represent when they carry a multiplicity of competing product lines. To do so dilutes the efforts of the manufacturer as well as those of the distributors. We expect our distributors to use their best efforts in the promotion and sale of Square D products. To this end, we believe that Square D products must be a primary line. We do not prohibit our distributors from handling competing lines of equipment. However, we will not appoint a distributor whose attention to competitive equipment seems likely to result in poor representation of Square D. We endeavor, through our marketing and advertising programs, to create such a demand for Square D products that our distributors find it more profitable to stock, sell and service Square D products than competitive lines.

Do we believe in consigned stocks?

No! We believe that consigned stocks have no place in the distribution of equipment such as ours. When a supplier consigns stock, he may try to assume other distributor functions as well. Isn't it equally true that, following this line of reasoning, he could eliminate the distributor altogether? There is a growing tendency to bypass distributors, a trend with which we do not agree. We suggest that distributors can best combat this trend by insisting on performing all functions which logically are their responsibilities.

How do we feel about contractor/distributor affiliations?

We will not appoint as an authorized Square D distributor any organization known by us to engage in electrical contracting or electrical equipment installation work. We have found that to do otherwise creates the opportunity for an improper price advantage for the contractor and thereby alienates other independent contractors from doing business with that distributor. Likewise, where an existing Square D distributor becomes so engaged we will terminate our business relationship with that distributor.

How do we feel about manufacturers' local stock?

A supplier who maintains local stocks tends to negate one of the principal reasons for selling through distributors. Local manufacturers' stocks also provide product availability to distributors with insufficient working capital to maintain adequate inventories. These distributors remain competitive without assuming their normal business responsibility. Competitive conditions and decentralized manufacturing dictate maintaining stocks in certain strategic locations to provide ready availability in areas remote from our manufacturing facilities. This also permits consolidated shipments to distributors' warehouses from one location. These stocks are administered in such a way as to not eliminate or replace distributor inventories but to replenish distributor inventories promptly and economically.

What conditions of sale apply?

All sales by the Square D Company to its distributors are governed by the published Square D "Conditions of Sale" in effect at the time of order acceptance. Each distributor indicates his acceptance of these Conditions at the time of his appointment as an authorized Square D distributor.

In this regard, we wish to emphasize that we will not be responsible for any warranties which a distributor gives to his customers that exceed the warranties contained in the Conditions of Sale which govern the purchase from us. We urge distributors to explain to their customers the exact nature and limitations of warranties of the Square D Company.

Our terms of payment vary with the product line. Our cut-off date for accounts receivable is the 25th of each month or the previous Friday should the 25th fall on a weekend.

Payments should be mailed to the address which appears on invoices and statements. If there is a dispute on an invoice, the distributor should deduct only the amount in dispute from his remittance and support the deduction with a debit memo which shows purchase order number, invoice number, amount of dispute and an explanation of the dispute.

Occasionally the Square D Company may request a financial statement from a distributor. Failure to furnish this information could result in orders being held until financial condition can be determined.

How may distributors use our trademarks?

Square D encourages the use of its trademarks and logotypes on distributor invoices, quotations, purchase orders, catalogs, advertising and other sales material, but only in connection with the promotion or sale of Square D products. Standard drawings and other reproducible artwork will be made available upon request. Also available are Square D decals and trademark signs for display on windows, trucks and in counter areas. All trademarks and logos must conform exactly to Square D specifications; the usage must be proper under the trademark laws and may be used only with reference to our products. All use thereof must be discontinued immediately upon termination of the distributor relationship.

To whom do we send distributor cost information?

Only to personnel authorized to receive it by the distributor's top management.

Why do we often have more than one distributor in a marketing area?

Experience has shown that several distributors are sometimes necessary to adequately service the requirements of a marketing area. Although an exclusive or limited distribution policy appeals to some distributors, we feel that the advantages of a multiple distribution policy outweigh those of an exclusive arrangement. First of all, multiple distribution permits distributor specialization without impairing penetration of the overall market. Also, by having several distributors promote a product in an area, a larger market can be developed. This can result in an increase of the individual distributor's share of any given market. Square D will not add distributors to the extent that the market is oversaturated and individual incentive reduced.

When one branch of a multi-house distributorship is authorized as a Square D distributor, are all branches authorized?

No. Each branch is considered a separate operation and must qualify independently from the main house or other branches. Local conditions dictate the need for additional distribution.

In addition, our policy prohibits the trans-shipment of Square D material to non-authorized locations.

What is our policy as to "drop shipment" outside of a distributor's normal marketing area?

Good customer service and prompt attention by the distributor to the customer's problems are a vital part of the distributor's function. It is through the maintenance of such desirable customer relationships that the distributor ensures maximum sales of Square D products. Consequently, we believe that overall sales of Square D products would be severely impeded if we were to accept orders from distributors calling for shipment to locations outside the area in which they can and do provide effective customer service. While we do not tell our distributors where they can sell, we reserve the right to refuse a distributor order calling for shipment to a location outside the area he normally serves in accordance with our policy of providing optimum customer service. However, exceptions do exist such as U.S. Government agencies, etc.

What is the Blue Chip II Program?

Realizing the profitable movement of merchandise depends upon its availability and that it is costly to store merchandise for which there is little or no demand, Square D established the Blue Chip II Program as an integral part of its distributor policy. Designed to be mutually beneficial, the main objectives of the program are to increase sales and develop a closer working relationship between Square D and its distributors. Briefly stated, a Blue Chip Distributor is an authorized Square D distributor in good standing who:

Considers the complete Square D line of major importance to which he devotes primary marketing effort.

Permits us to take, and assists us in taking, inventory audits at regular intervals.

Provides and maintains adequate storage and shelf space and promptly places incoming stock in its assigned space.

Agrees to the program of inventory control provided under the Blue Chip II Program.

Agrees to the entering of his stock orders on our preprinted order forms or by other acceptable means as outlined in the Blue Chip II policy manual.

What do we do about local advertising help?

Any request for direct financial support of a distributor's local advertising and sales promotion program is a problem to a manufacturer. The manufacturer's advertising budget is fixed and he must decide where his effort is best spent. Square D's well defined policy is based on the following considerations:

Support given one distributor must be available to all. The law prohibits discrimination. The spirit of fair play also dictates such a policy.

National advertising and sales promotion programs are a necessary background for successful local effort. We invest substantially in such national activities in meeting this important obligation.

As previously mentioned, we will furnish product bulletins, direct mail pieces, catalogs, display material, plaques, posters, and related material as part of our obligation.

Standard illustrations and reproducible art are furnished without charge for illustrating local catalogs and sales promotion pieces. In addition, our staff can help in the preparation of copy and layout. We will, however, not underwrite any typesetting, printing or other direct production costs involved in local advertising and sales promotion programs.

Appendix 5C

Insights into Channel Planning from Management Science

Management science consists of a set of analytical approaches that use logically consistent mathematical tools to address problems. It includes such disciplines and techniques as economics, game theory, decision theory, operations research, and mathematical programming. Some insights from a few of these perspectives are discussed in this appendix and in Appendix 6A. The goal is to provide an introduction to some paradigms for thinking in this area rather than to present an exhaustive survey of this literature. Citations provided in the footnotes should permit the interested reader a more in-depth study.

Management scientists attempt to develop a mathematical formulation of a complex social situation in a manner that allows an analytical solution by conventional means. This inevitably leads to a tradeoff. Some of the complexity and richness of the social situation being modeled must be sacrificed in order to gain analytical tractability. Management scientists use abstraction as their intellectual device; by choosing elements of the problem that are the "most important," they hope to capture enough of it to represent it adequately. Solutions suggested by the model are then applied to the problem at large. Of course, the validity of these conclusions clearly depends on how adequate the original representation of the problem was.

The management science approach to channel planning problems has a relatively long history. The specialists in this area have sought answers to a variety of questions, such as whether a company's channel should be owned (i.e.,

The authors gratefully acknowledge the significant contribution of Shumeet Banerji to the development of this appendix.

integrated versus decentralized),[1] which channel(s) among a set of alternatives a company should use,[2] how many levels a channel should have,[3] and, within a level, how many intermediaries the company should have.[4] Two separate emphases—theoretical and prescriptive—have been employed. For example, using a theoretical emphasis, analysts have attempted to characterize the structure that might be observed given a set of conditions. In these models, the goal is to describe, explain, and, hopefully, predict some critical features of channel systems. On the other hand, models employing a prescriptive (or normative) emphasis are intended to serve as decision aids to managers. This appendix focuses on models concerned with channel planning.

THE MCGUIRE-STAELIN MODEL

Several management scientists have investigated the vertical integration question—whether to distribute through an integrated (i.e., fully owned) channel or a decentralized channel with one or more levels of independently owned intermediaries. For example, Jeuland and Shugan have suggested that integration (or any arrangement that approximates it) is superior to decentralization, because it minimizes the inefficiencies induced by the divergent objectives of different channel members.[5] On the other hand, a standard argument for a decentralized channel structure is that intermediaries may perform certain necessary channel tasks more efficiently than the manufacturer.[6]

McGuire and Staelin have proposed an explanation for why a manufacturer may opt to use a decentralized channel even when he can perform distribu-

---

[1] See, for example, Anne T. Coughlan, "Competition and Cooperation in Marketing Channel Choice: Theory and Application," *Marketing Science*, Vol. 4 (Spring 1985), pp. 110–29; Michael Etgar, "The Effects of Forward Vertical Integration on Service Performance of a Distributive Industry," *Journal of Industrial Economics*, Vol. 26 (March 1978), pp. 249–55; Abel P. Jeuland and Steven M. Shugan, "Managing Channel Profits," *Marketing Science*, Vol. 2 (Summer 1983), pp. 239–72; and two papers by Timothy W. McGuire and Richard Staelin, "An Industry Equilibrium Analysis of Downstream Vertical Integration," *Marketing Science*, Vol. 2 (Spring 1983), pp. 161–92, and "The Effect of Channel Member Efficiency on Channel Structure," in David Gautschi (ed.), *Productivity and Efficiency in Distribution Systems* (New York: Elsevier Science Publishing Co., 1983), pp. 3–15.

[2] See footnote 1 and Marcel Corstjens and Peter Doyle, "Channel Optimization in Complex Marketing Systems," *Management Science*, Vol. 25 (October 1979), pp. 1014–25.

[3] See Helmy H. Baligh and Leon E. Richartz, *Vertical Market Structures* (Boston: Allyn and Bacon, 1967); and Leon E. Richartz, "A Game Theoretic Formulation of Vertical Market Structures," in Louis P. Bucklin (ed.), *Vertical Marketing Systems* (Glenview, Ill.: Scott, Foresman and Co., 1970), pp. 180–213.

[4] See Corstjens and Doyle, *op. cit.;* Michael Etgar and Pinhas Zusman, "The Marketing Intermediary as an Information Seller: A New Approach," *Journal of Business*, Vol. 55 (1982), pp. 505–15; B. P. Pashigian, *The Distribution of Automobiles: An Economic Analysis of the Franchise System* (Englewood Cliffs, N.J.: Prentice-Hall, 1961); and L. J. White, *The Automobile Industry Since 1945* (Cambridge, Mass.: Harvard University Press, 1971).

[5] Jeuland and Shugan, *op. cit.*, prove this result for a monopoly, a situation where one manufacturer sells one product through one reseller with no competition at either level. Because they focus on the problem of coordinating the efforts of the manufacturer and retailer, their paper is discussed in Appendix 6A.

[6] See, for example, Philip Kotler, *Marketing Management: Analysis, Planning and Control*, 5th ed. (Englewood Cliffs, N.J.: Prentice-Hall, 1984), p. 540.

tion tasks as efficiently as distributors.[7] Their findings, based on economic and game theory, suggest that when manufacturers compete in markets where their products are highly substitutable, an incentive to use a decentralized channel may exist because the presence of a profit-maximizing entity between the manufacturer and the market shields the manufacturer from the competition in the marketplace.

The McGuire-Staelin model is framed in a highly stylized setting. Two manufacturers produce one product each, which they sell through two retailers. The retailers are constrained to carry the product of, at most, one manufacturer. The manufacturers compete with each other, although their products are differentiated. The aim of the model is to investigate the influence of product substitutability on the choice of channel structure.

With two manufacturers and two retailers, three types of industry structure are possible. In the first (called *fully decentralized*), both manufacturers sell through independently owned retail stores. In the second (*vertically integrated*), each manufacturer sells through his own retail store. In the third (*mixed*), one manufacturer is decentralized and the other integrated.

The approach adopted by McGuire and Staelin in analyzing this problem is that of noncooperative game theory,[8] which seeks to predict the outcomes of competitive situations in which intelligent and rational players are engaged.[9] Two essential notions in game theory are *strategies* and *payoffs*. All players have a set of alternative strategies, some of which have certain outcomes that in turn have specific payoffs associated with them. One way of predicting the outcome of such a "game" is to seek a Nash equilibrium—a set of strategies, one for each player, from which no player has an incentive to deviate because it does not pay to play any other strategy.[10]

Two levels of games, played in sequence, are used by McGuire and Staelin to answer the question of the influence of substitutability on channel choice. The players are the two manufacturers and the two retailers. In the first-level games, Nash equilibrium prices and associated profits are sought under each of the three industry structures discussed. In these games, given an industry structure, the players' strategies are the prices they set, and the payoffs are the profits associated with any combination of chosen prices. In the second-level game, given that the maximum attainable profits under each industry structure are known from the first-level games, the manufacturers choose the optimal (Nash equilibrium) structure for themselves. Here, strategies are structure choices, and payoffs are the associated profits from the first-level games. When the solutions to the two levels of games are expressed in terms of the substitutability of the products, a particular level of substitutability leads to a particular prediction of the equilibrium channel structure. Therefore, the effect of substitutability on structure can be studied by systematically varying the level of substitutability.

[7] McGuire and Staelin, "Industry Equilibrium Analysis."

[8] For an excellent introduction to noncooperative game theory and its application to marketing problems, see K. Sridhar Moorthy, "Using Game Theory to Model Competition," *Journal of Marketing Research,* Vol. 22 (August 1985), pp. 262–82.

[9] Players are regarded as *intelligent* in the sense that they understand everything about the structure of the situation that is understood by theorists, including the fact that all players are intelligent, rational decision makers. *Rationality* means that the players are maximizers of their utilities given the decision rules of the other players.

[10] Note that nothing about the definition of Nash equilibrium precludes the existence of multiple equilibriums in a game.

The First-Level Games

An important first step in determining a Nash equilibrium is to characterize the sets of players and their strategic variables under the various industry structures. In the fully decentralized structure, there are four players; in the fully integrated structure, two players; and in the mixed structure, three players.[11] The decision variables (or strategies) for the players are the prices charged by them to the next level in the channel. In the fully decentralized structure, the manufacturers set the wholesale prices (w_1, w_2) and the retailers set the retail prices (p_1, p_2). In contrast, the manufacturers set the retail prices (p_1, p_2) in the fully integrated structure. In the mixed structure, assuming that the ith channel is decentralized, manufacturer i sets w_i, retailer i sets p_i, and the integrated manufacturer j sets p_j.

Next, the assumptions under which the games are to be played are stipulated. McGuire and Staelin specify three basic assumptions:

1. Manufacturers are "first movers" with respect to their corresponding retailers. (In the jargon of game theory, they are *Stackelberg leaders*.) This means that retailers set their prices *in response to* the wholesale price decisions of the manufacturers, and manufacturers set their prices (w_1, w_2) knowing this response function of retailers.
2. Each manufacturer makes decisions accounting for the *reaction* of the other manufacturer. Operationally, this means that manufacturers take each other's actions as given when making their optimal decisions. If each player chooses optimal actions as a reaction to the other's optimal actions, this simultaneous determination leads to a pair of strategies from which neither player has an incentive to deviate—i.e., a Nash equilibrium.
3. Retailers behave in much the same way: each reacts to the actions of the other.

Keeping these three basic assumptions in mind, one can detail the specific behavioral rules of the players in the three industry structures (see Table 5C–1).

Illustrative Analysis. McGuire and Staelin assume that the retail level demand functions, $q_i = f_i(p_1, p_2)$, are linear in prices. It is possible to express them as a relatively simple demand structure depending on prices and a single parameter, θ, which captures the substitutability of the two products. The parameter θ takes on values between zero and one.[12] Lower values of θ imply that the two products are poor substitutes, whereas higher values imply greater substitutability.

The demand structure is given by

$$q_i = 1 - p_i + \theta p_j, \qquad i = 1, 2, \qquad j = 3 - i. \qquad (1)$$

[11] The number of players in any structure is the number of independent decision-making entities in it. So, for example, in the fully decentralized structure, both manufacturers and both retailers are independent decision makers; hence there are four players in this structure.

[12] θ is defined as the ratio of the rate of change of quantity with respect to the competitor's price to the rate of change of quantity with respect to own price:

$$\theta = \frac{\partial q_i / \partial p_j}{\partial q_i / \partial p_i}, \quad i = 1, 2, \qquad j = 3 - i.$$

θ is assumed to be identical for both manufacturers' products. Additionally, if $\partial q_i / \partial p_j \leq \partial q_i / \partial p_i$, $i = 1, 2, j = 3 - i$, then the value of θ is bounded and always lies in the interval $[0, 1]$.

Table 5C–1 Behavioral rules for the manufacturers and retailers under various industry structures

Industry Structure	Behavioral Rules			
	Manufacturer 1	Manufacturer 2	Retailer 1	Retailer 2
Pure Decentralized Structure (DD)	Set w_1 to maximize π_1^M, taking w_2 as given and accounting for the retailers' price response functions.[a]	Set w_2 to maximize π_2^M, taking w_1 as given and accounting for the retailers' price response functions.	Set p_1 to maximize π_1^R, taking w_1, w_2, and p_2 as given.	Set p_2 to maximize π_2^R, taking w_1, w_2, and P_1 as given.
Pure Integrated Structure (II)	Set p_1 to maximize π_1^M, taking p_2 as given.	Set p_2 to maximize π_2^M, taking p_1 as given.		
Mixed Structure[b]	Set p_1 to maximize π_1^M, taking p_2 as given, conditioned on w_2.	Set w_2 to maximize π_2^M, accounting for the retailers' price response functions.		Set p_2 to maximize π_2^R, taking w_2 and p_1 as given.

[a] π_1^M is the profit of the first manufacturer, π_2^R is the profit of the second retailer, etc.

[b] We assume without loss of generality that channel 1 is the integrated channel in the mixed structure.

In order to demonstrate how the analysis proceeds, we will focus here on the purely decentralized structure. If we now assume that variable manufacturing and selling costs are zero, so that the wholesale prices w_1 and retail prices p_i are pure margin, then the profits of the retailer and the manufacturer in the decentralized structure can be written as

$$\pi_i^R = (p_i - w_i)\, q_i, \qquad i = 1, 2, \tag{2}$$

$$\pi_i^M = w_i q_i, \qquad i = 1, 2, \tag{3}$$

where π_i^R is the ith retailer's profit and π_i^M is the ith manufacturer's profit.

Given all of this, it is now possible to derive the Nash equilibrium prices in the purely decentralized structure. The sequence of decisions is as follows.

The retailers set their prices (p_1, p_2) to maximize profits, assuming that the other retailer's price and the wholesale prices remain fixed, or

$$\underset{p_i}{\text{Maximize}}\ \pi_i^R = (1 - p_i + \theta p_j)(p_i - w_i), \qquad i = 1, 2, \qquad j = 3 - i. \tag{4}$$

This is accomplished by differentiating π_i^R partially with respect to p_i, holding w_i and p_i constant and setting the derivative equal to zero:[13]

$$\left. \frac{\partial \pi_i^R}{\partial p_i} \right|_{w_i, p_j} = 1 - 2p_i + \theta p_j + w_i = 0, \qquad i = 1, 2, \qquad j = 3 - i. \tag{5}$$

[13] This will be recognized from the rules of calculus as the first-order necessary condition for a maximum.

Solving for p_i yields conditional Nash equilibrium price functions in terms of the w_i, $i = 1, 2$, or

$$p_i = \frac{1}{2 - \theta} + \frac{2}{(2 + \theta)(2 - \theta)} w_i$$
$$+ \frac{\theta}{(2 + \theta)(2 - \theta)} w_j, \quad i = 1, 2, \quad j = 3 - i. \tag{6}$$

The manufacturers can now substitute these price functions into the demand functions in (1) and obtain their *derived demand functions*, given by

$$q_i = \frac{1}{2 - \theta} - \frac{2 - \theta^2}{(2 + \theta)(2 - \theta)} w_i$$
$$+ \frac{\theta}{(2 + \theta)(2 - \theta)} w_j, \quad i = 1, 2, \quad j = 3 - i. \tag{7}$$

Substituting these functions into the profit functions in (3), differentiating partially with respect to w_i, setting the derivatives equal to zero, and solving for w_i yield the Nash equilibrium wholesale prices (w_1, w_2), given by

$$w_1 = w_2 = \frac{2 + \theta}{4 - \theta - 2\theta^2}. \tag{8}$$

Substituting (8) into (6) and (7) yields the Nash equilibrium values of prices (p_1, p_2) and the quantities sold (q_1, q_2) in equilibrium:

$$p_1 = p_2 = \frac{2(3 - \theta^2)}{(2 - \theta)(4 - \theta - 2\theta^2)}, \text{ and} \tag{9}$$

$$q_1 = q_2 = \frac{2 - \theta^2}{(2 - \theta)(4 - \theta - 2\theta^2)}. \tag{10}$$

Multiplying (8) and (10) gives the manufacturers' profits in the purely decentralized structure in terms of θ:

$$\pi_1^M = \pi_2^M = \frac{(2 + \theta)(2 - \theta^2)}{(2 - \theta)(4 - \theta - 2\theta^2)^2}. \tag{11}$$

Note that the manufacturers' profits are expressed in terms of the single parameter θ, which implies that profits can be computed for all values of θ from zero to one.

McGuire and Staelin repeat this type of analysis for the purely integrated structure and the mixed case, obtaining similar characterizations of profits in terms of θ.[14] These profit functions are mapped in Fig. 5C–1 for all values of θ.

[14] See McGuire and Staelin, "Industry Equilibrium Analysis," pp. 176–77 for a summary of these analytical results.

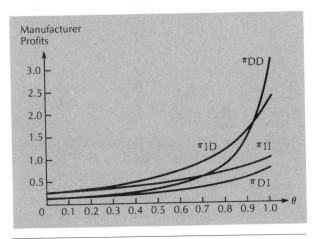

Figure 5C–1 Manufacturer's profits as a function of θ under pure and mixed channel structures

Source: Adapted from Timothy W. McGuire and Richard Staelin, "An Industry Equilibrium Analysis of Downstream Vertical Integration," *Marketing Science*, Vol. 2 (Spring 1983), p. 178.

π_{DD} and π_{II} are the profits under the purely decentralized and integrated structures; π_{ID} and π_{DI} are the first manufacturer's profits when he is integrated and decentralized, respectively, in a mixed industry structure.

The Second-Level Game

We can see from Fig. 5C–1 that for low values of θ ($\theta \leq 0.708$), profits are higher in the purely integrated structure than under the purely decentralized structure, and vice versa for higher values of θ. This means that at lower levels of θ (i.e., when the products are poor substitutes), the manufacturers have an incentive to integrate forward, whereas when θ is high (i.e., when the products are highly substitutable), the manufacturers have an incentive to shield themselves from competition by using a decentralized channel. Although the behavior of profits at levels of θ above and below $\theta = 0.708$ seems to suggest that particular structures should be preferred by the manufacturers, it is not known whether these are the Nash equilibrium structures.

In the second-level game, the players are the two manufacturers and their strategic options are to integrate or to use the decentralized channel structure. The payoffs are the profit pairs for the two manufacturers resulting from the structure choices by both at any given level of θ. There are only three ranges of θ that need to be considered, given Fig. 5C–1. Within these ranges, the relative magnitudes of profits retain a particular ordering so that characterizing the Nash equilibria in each leads to a complete characterization for all θ. These ranges, with corresponding orderings of profits and Nash equilibrium structures, are summarized in Table 5C–2.

Several conclusions can be drawn from the results shown in Table 5C–2. First, mixed structures are never Nash equilibria. This implies that if we observe

Table 5C–2 Orderings of profits under different industry structures for three ranges of θ with equilibrium industry structures

Range of θ	Ordering of Profits	Nash Equilibrium Structure(s)
$0 \le \theta \le 0.708$	$\pi_{ID} \ge \pi_{II} \ge \pi_{DD} \ge \pi_{DI}$	II
$0.708 \le \theta \le 0.931$	$\pi_{ID} \ge \pi_{DD} \ge \pi_{II} \ge \pi_{DI}$	II
$0.931 \le \theta \le 1$	$\pi_{DD} \ge \pi_{ID} \ge \pi_{II} \ge \pi_{DI}$	II and DD

a market having a mixed industry structure, it is likely to be in transition to one or the other of the pure structures. Second, the purely integrated structure is a Nash equilibrium for all values of θ. Third, at higher levels of θ, *both* decentralized and integrated structures are Nash equilibria. This oddity follows from the definition of Nash equilibrium, which does not rule out multiple equilibria in a game. The practical implication of this is that in markets where products are more highly substitutable, there is some probability of observing a decentralized structure.

Clearly, these results are highly restrictive in that they apply to markets with very few competitors where retailers are constrained to sell the product of one manufacturer. Given this, McGuire and Staelin argue that in markets where products are highly substitutable, manufacturers should use independent marketing intermediaries even if they themselves are as efficient as the intermediaries,[15] because the use of intermediaries shields them from price competition in the marketplace.[16]

THE CORSTJENS-DOYLE MODEL

An important issue in channel planning is channel choice: given a set of channel alternatives, which one(s) should a manufacturer select so that his objectives might be best fulfilled? Corstjens and Doyle have attempted to answer this question by focusing on an example drawn from the confectionery industry.[17] Specifically, in order to assist a confectionery manufacturer in determining which channels to concentrate on, how many outlets to develop within any given channel, and what margins to seek in each channel, Corstjens and Doyle developed a channel optimization model employing general (or signomial) geometric programming. The manufacturer owned some of his own retail outlets but also sold through other channels. In all, there were five different channel alternatives—

[15] McGuire and Staelin, "Channel Member Efficiency," discuss the case where the manufacturer is less efficient than the retailer in performing the retailing task. The effect of this is to expand the range of values of θ over which the fully decentralized structure is a Nash equilibrium.

[16] Coughlan, *op. cit.*, derives a set of results that corroborate and extend the conclusions of the McGuire-Staelin model. In addition, she reports results from an empirical study of the international semiconductor industry that support these conclusions.

[17] Corstjens and Doyle, *op. cit.*

large wholly owned stores, small wholly owned stores, franchising, export, and private label.

The problem formulation starts with the conventional normative assertion that the manager seeks to select a distribution policy that maximizes profits, subject to constraints on the relevant decision variables. The objective function—the focal organization's total profit— is composed of the following set of demand and cost functions:

TOTAL DEMAND STRUCTURE

$$Q = \sum_{i=1}^{K} \alpha_i(p_i)^{\beta_i} \prod_{\substack{j=1 \\ j \neq i}}^{K} (p_j)^{\delta_{ij}} (N_i)^{\varepsilon_i}, \tag{1}$$

where Q represents the sales of the focal organization; K is the number of channels available to the organization; β_i represents the direct elasticity with respect to price (p_i) for an average outlet in channel i; δ_{ij} refers to the cross-price elasticity between channels i and j; and ε_i represents economies ($\varepsilon_i > 1$) or diseconomies ($\varepsilon_i < 1$) from increasing the number of outlets (N_i) within channel i.

TOTAL COST STRUCTURE

$$TC = \sum_{i=1}^{K} \omega_i(q_i)^{\nu_i}(N_i)^{\tau_i}, \tag{2}$$

where q_i is the sales per outlet in channel i and ν_i represents economies of scale in the cost function. If $\nu_i < 1$, the average cost curve is decreasing. Parameter τ_i is the possible economy resulting from increasing the number of outlets in channel i—for example, unit savings in buying, transportation, and production costs.

The constraints on the relevant decision variables include a capacity constraint, a control constraint, a system inflexibility constraint, and a nonnegativity constraint:

CAPACITY CONSTRAINT

$$\sum_{i=1}^{K} q_i(N_i) \leq Q^*, \tag{3}$$

where Q^* is the corporate production capacity constraint.

CONTROL CONSTRAINT

$$q_i N_i \leq zQ^*, \text{ for all } i, \tag{4}$$

where z is percentage of production capacity.

SYSTEM INFLEXIBILITY CONSTRAINT

$$N_i^L \leq N_i \leq N_i^U \quad \text{and} \quad p_i^L \leq p_i \leq p_i^U, \text{ for all } i, \tag{5}$$

where superscripts L and U refer to the lower and upper bounds of the decision variables.

NONNEGATIVITY CONSTRAINT

$$q_i \geq 0, \, p_i \geq 0, \quad \text{and} \quad N_i \geq 0, \text{ for all } i. \tag{6}$$

The reason for the capacity constraint is that in the short run, there is likely to be some upper bound on potential output. The control constraint ensures that sales through any single channel are limited to some discretionary percentage (set by management) of production capacity. For example, a supplier may wish to avoid being dependent on any single channel for more than a given fraction of sales. The system inflexibility constraint limits the number of outlets opened in a channel and the price charged to that channel to within feasible ranges. In other words, it limits the amount of discretion a manager has to change the parameters of any channel system. Some channels will be closed to him, as will be pointed out, and others will have output restrictions. The nonnegativity constraint simply ensures reasonable solution values. The constraints can be modified to model other issues of importance, such as channel power and conflict.[18] For example, the control constraint can be formulated so as to permit investigation of optimal levels of dependency among channel members.

The various elements of this model can be combined to present the overall decision problem facing the manufacturer. This is done by writing out the profit function (prices times demands minus costs) and substituting the full demand function for quantities q_i wherever they appear.[19]

THE MANUFACTURER'S DECISION PROBLEM

$$\text{Max} \sum_{i=1}^{K} \left\{ \alpha_i (p_i)^{\beta_i + 1} \prod_{\substack{j=1 \\ j \neq i}}^{K} (p_j)^{\delta_{ij}} (N_i)^{\varepsilon_i} \right\}$$

$$- \sum_{i=1}^{K} \left\{ \omega_i \left[\alpha_i (p_i)^{\beta_i} \prod_{\substack{j=1 \\ j \neq i}}^{K} (p_j)^{\delta_{ij}} \right]^{\nu_i} (N_i)^{\tau_i} \right\} \tag{7}$$

[18] For an excellent start at developing an optimization model incorporating relevant behavioral factors, see Leigh McAlister, "Distribution Channels: A Decision Theoretic Model with Efficiency Considerations," in David Gautschi (ed.), *Productivity and Efficiency in Distribution Systems* (New York: Elsevier Science Publishing Co., 1983), pp. 47–56.

[19] Note, however, that there may be some serious problems with the demand function in Cortsjens and Doyle's model. Zoltners and Becker have pointed out that

when the distribution strategy decision is incorporated into the model, solutions for which $N_i = 0$ become admissible. As would be expected, the i-th channel's sales contribution to the manufacturer will drop completely out of the demand equation when $N_i = 0$. However, the price cross-elasticities δ_{ij} are not a function of N_i and N_j. Hence, if $N_i = 0$ the sales volumes in other channels are still affected by the price charged in channel i. This is due to the fact that $p_i^{\delta_{ij}}$ does not drop out of the equation, since $p_i > 0$ and $\delta_{ij} \neq 0$. Consequently, total demand is a function of the prices charged in channels that are not being used. This undermines the demand equation. The cost and capacity equations are also questionable since they, likewise, employ price cross-elasticities.

See Andris A. Zoltners and Robert J. Becker, "A Decision Framework and Model for Distribution Channel Design," working paper, Northwestern University Department of Marketing, 1980, p. 24.

$$\text{subject to } \sum_{i=1}^{K} \alpha_i(p_i)^{\beta_i} \prod_{\substack{j=1 \\ j \neq i}}^{K} (p_j)^{\delta_{ij}}(N_i)^{\varepsilon_i} \leq Q^*,$$

$$\alpha_i(p_i)^{\beta_i} \prod_{\substack{j=1 \\ j \neq i}}^{K} (p_j)^{\delta_{ij}}(N_i)^{\varepsilon_i} \leq zQ^*, \text{ for all } i,$$

$$N_i^L \leq N_i \leq N_i^U, \text{ for all } i,$$

$$p_i^L \leq p_i \leq p_i^U, \text{ for all } i,$$

$$q_i \geq 0, p_i \geq 0, \text{ and } N_i \geq 0, \text{ for all } i.$$

Because of the nonconvex, nonlinear, and polynomial structure of their model, Corstjens and Doyle could not employ traditional optimization techniques such as linear programming, nonlinear programming, or prototypical (posynomial) geometric programming to obtain a solution. Therefore, they used general or signomial geometric programming, because it places no constraints on the structure of the objective function or on the type of constraints.[20]

Before the model can be optimized, it is necessary to estimate the parameters of the demand and cost functions. Theoretically, various sources of data exist to carry out such a parameterization. Statistical estimates based on objective data would be the most desirable, but unfortunately, satisfactory data are rarely available for the solution of channel problems.[21] Hence, Corstjens and Doyle had to rely heavily on the subjective judgment of managers, using objective data whenever they were available.

CONCLUSION

In this appendix two models from management science that address the channel planning problem have been described in some detail. The first, by McGuire and Staelin, is an attempt to *understand* why and how manufacturers choose to use vertically integrated or decentralized channels to perform the distribution task. In particular, the model assesses the effect of the extent of product substitutability on the choice of channel structure. The second model, by Corstjens and Doyle, is geared towards *helping managers decide* certain channels issues—which

---

[20] See Corstjens and Doyle, *op. cit.*, pp. 1019–20, 1023–24, for an explanation of the rationale for using signomial geometric programming and for a discussion of the solution procedure.

[21] Corstjens and Doyle list four reasons for the unavailability of satisfactory data: (1) few companies have seen the value of systematically recording over time information on all the relevant variables; (2) use of conventional budgeting methods and rules of thumb mean that there is commonly a lack of variability across and within channels in the key marketing instruments with which to statistically estimate their effects; (3) generating the data by experimental methods is usually viewed by managements as too costly, time-consuming, and problematical; and (4) the marketing environment since the mid 1970s may have been subject to such significant shifts that past observations are seen as of questionable relevance to the future business environment. *Ibid.*, p. 1020.

(of a set of) channels to use, what prices to charge in the channels, and the number of outlets to use in each channel. The models have different aims, one descriptive and the other normative.

Both models share drawbacks common to most models in management science. These result largely from the greatly simplified world created in order to ensure that the models can be formulated mathematically and are tractable.

CHAPTER SIX

Mechanisms for Achieving Channel Coordination

In order to improve or maintain the competitive viability of any marketing channel, it is essential that the activities and flows within it be coordinated and controlled in an effective and efficient manner. It is only through purposive *interorganizational* coordination that channels can obtain their full potential in producing satisfactory outputs for ultimate, business, and industrial consumers.[1] In this chapter, a process for achieving effective coordination is presented. Emphasis is placed on understanding the relevant behavioral dimensions of interorganizational relations, because it is through such an understanding that the manager can learn how to organize, manipulate, and exploit the resources available to him in the commercial channel system of which his firm is a part. (Appendix 6A outlines some suggestions from management science for achieving channel coordination.) The approach taken is prescriptive rather than descriptive; the focus is on how the economic, social, and political relationships within channels *should* be managed so as to assure their long-term competitive success.

---

[1] It should be noted that the coordinative approach advocated here and in later chapters is heresy when viewed from a classical economics perspective. This is because the classical model implicitly denounces collective action and concentration of resources. However, in the United States and around the world, it has been shown, consistently and over time, that those entities capable of organizing collective and consistent approaches to their respective markets have been most successful in garnering the rewards of "free" enterprise. On the other hand, those units that have permitted themselves to be buffeted by the whims of the marketplace without trying to satisfy those whims through coordinated activities with other channel members or through vertical integration of one form or another have been left at the starting gate. See Johan Arndt, "Toward a Concept of Domesticated Markets," *Journal of Marketing*, Vol. 43 (Fall 1979), pp. 69–75.

THE COORDINATIVE PROCESS

The long-run objective of channel management is to achieve, at a reasonable cost, the greatest possible impact at the end-user level so that the individual members of the channel can obtain satisfactory returns (profits, market share, or other rewards) for their specific contributions. Channel performance is determined by channel structure and by individual channel member behavior. The specific channel designs available to marketing managers have been discussed in previous chapters, especially Chapters 1 and 5. We can now turn to the process required for organizing the relationships within channels—that is, for ensuring that within any given structural arrangement, channel member behavior is conducive to achieving high-yield performance.

Once the marketing management of an organization isolates the market targets that the organization should attack and the products and services it must supply to satisfy needs and wants in those various segments, it can turn to the question of how best to make the products and services available for consumption by the various end-users constituting the targeted segments. As indicated in Chapter 5, the *first* step in answering this question is determining the level of the service outputs demanded by end-users of the commercial channel system.[2] The *second* step is specifying which marketing tasks must be undertaken in order to generate the requisite service outputs and which of the wide variety of channel members potentially available to be employed in forming a delivery system are equipped to perform the tasks. Sometimes such an assessment concludes that existing institutions and agencies are inadequately performing the required tasks. It is then the job of management to determine whether, through the use of appropriate influence or channel control strategies, it will be able to adjust the behavior of potential or present channel partners or whether it will be compelled to vertically integrate channel functions and flows so that the desired service outputs are provided to end-users. Even if functions and flows are vertically integrated, there is no guarantee that plans to provide the outputs will be successful. Therefore, the *third* step in the coordinative process is to determine exactly which influence strategies should be used to accomplish the hoped-for results, whether management decides to invest in integrating functions or whether it decides to deal with independently owned companies. The *fourth* and final step of the coordinative process is setting up mechanisms to deal with the conflict issues that inevitably arise in channels, so that the channel will continue to provide the desired service outputs even in the face of disagreements among channel members.

The following sections of this chapter detail each step of this coordinative process, depicted in Exhibit 6–1.

---

[2] The commercial channel is the subset of the entire channel that excludes the consumer. Institutions and agencies within the commercial channel can be organized in such a way as to enhance competitive abilities—that is, to satisfy consumer needs and wants in a more complete way than less organized systems might. The focus is on end-user needs, not on channel member needs. To some extent, the U.S. automobile industry got into its major difficulties in the early 1980s because manufacturers were more concerned with their dealers' desires than their consumers' during the 1970s. See Jack Honomichl, "Consumer Signals: Why U.S. Auto Makers Ignored Them," *Advertising Age* (August 4, 1980), pp. 43, 44.

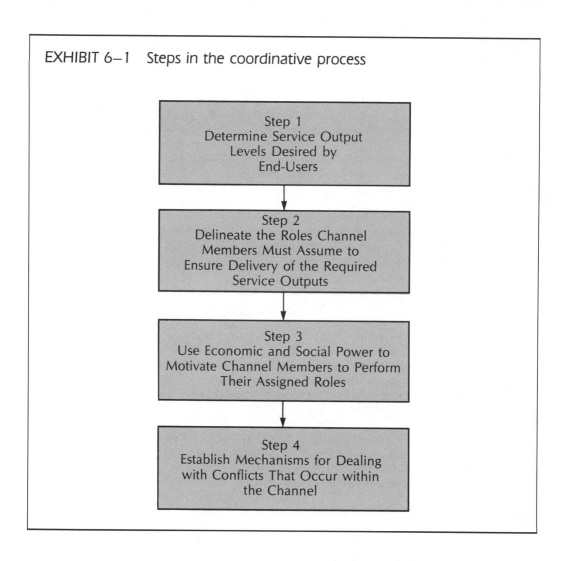

EXHIBIT 6–1 Steps in the coordinative process

Step 1
Determine Service Output
Levels Desired by
End-Users

Step 2
Delineate the Roles Channel
Members Must Assume to
Ensure Delivery of the Required
Service Outputs

Step 3
Use Economic and Social Power to
Motivate Channel Members to Perform
Their Assigned Roles

Step 4
Establish Mechanisms for Dealing
with Conflicts That Occur within
the Channel

STEP 1.
DETERMINING SERVICE OUTPUT LEVELS

As emphasized in Chapter 5, a primary consideration in designing a marketing channel is an estimation of the service output levels required by end-users. The service outputs that are among the most significant in distribution are (1) lot size, (2) delivery or waiting time, (3) market decentralization or spatial convenience, and (4) breadth and depth of product or service assortment. The relevant list of service outputs to consider depends, of course, on the buying situation. For complex products, technical assistance, demonstration, and flexible financing may be called for, while for more simple products, emphasis may be placed on availability and delivery.

Example 1: Cigarettes. In order to estimate the appropriate output levels that should be built into any channel system, it is imperative to perform an in-depth study of consumer demand with respect to the outputs. For example, consumers wish to purchase cigarettes in very small lot sizes (one pack per purchase, generally), desire immediate delivery of the product once requested, prefer as many outlets as possible from which to purchase, and want the broadest and deepest possible assortment from which to choose. Therefore, channels that provide these outputs have been designed to meet these needs. Individual packs of cigarettes are available for purchase from widely placed outlets that offer almost every conceivable type (filtered, nonfiltered, etc.) and brand. Delivery time is instantaneous. However, in order to provide these outputs, the channel is generally long and complex. It includes distribution centers of manufacturers that ship to tobacco and grocery wholesalers or chain warehouses that, in turn, ship to individual retail outlets (e.g., stores, vending machines, and restaurants). In addition, because of high turnover, the supplies at the retail level have to be continuously replenished, making the labor costs of maintaining point-of-purchase stocks very high. The result is that retail cigarette prices are extremely high relative to the cost of manufacturing cigarettes.

Example 2: Automotive Replacement Parts. A similar situation is found in the marketing of automotive replacement parts. When a consumer takes his car to a service station to have a worn-out gasket replaced, the price for the gasket is, even exclusive of labor charges for its installation, several times greater than the cost of manufacturing it. The reason for the high price of automotive parts can be traced to the service output levels demanded by consumers. The consumer wants to have the gasket replaced as quickly as possible, but the service station does not generally maintain an inventory of gaskets. In this circumstance, the mechanic will call a local automotive parts jobber, who will deliver the part in a very short time (usually within an hour) to the service station. Furthermore, consumers demand such parts in small lot sizes (one gasket at a time) but do not want to travel long distances to obtain them. The channel system must therefore maintain an enormous, widely decentralized inventory of parts to support the anticipated demands of consumers. It is thus no mystery why such parts cost what they do. And it is also clear why consumers, in increasing numbers, have begun to purchase automotive parts from discount stores and perform their own service. The do-it-yourselfers are willing to forego some of the service outputs available from the traditional automotive repair channel in order to achieve a lower cost of car maintenance. (Clearly, if the consumer were to place a higher value on his time, the cost savings might not be as great.)

Example 3: Groceries. What appears to be happening in distribution is that alternative channel systems have been erected that provide varying levels of service outputs within any given line of trade. This is because markets have become more and more segmented. For example, some consumers of groceries still demand "full service" and shop at local butcher shops or specialized produce stores. However, most consumers prefer to forego such service in order to obtain the lower prices available at supermarkets, even though they must travel by car to reach them and must generally purchase in larger lot sizes during any one transaction period. And there are other consumers who are willing to provide even more of their own labor (by bagging their own groceries, for example).

These latter consumers prefer to shop at warehouse outlets, where prices are discounted because service outputs are significantly curtailed (e.g., stores are not as conveniently located as supermarkets, assortments are narrower and not as deep, and other services, such as check cashing, are eliminated).

Example 4: Stainless Steel.   The analogy can be carried to industrial goods marketing as well. If the purchaser of stainless steel sheet prefers to purchase in large lots, is not concerned about speed of delivery, desires only one or a limited number of grades of sheet, and is willing to transact business over long distances as opposed to dealing with someone located around the corner, he is likely to find much better prices in a direct channel of distribution (buying from the steel mill, for example) than in an indirect channel (a local wholesale steel service center).

As pointed out in Chapter 5, there are numerous factors that influence channel design beyond the determination of service output levels demanded by end-users. However, in the process of managing channel relationships, knowledge of end-user demand for service outputs is critical. Once this is known, the channel manager can ferret out the specific institutions and agencies capable of providing the desired outputs.

STEP 2.
DELINEATING ROLES IN THE CHANNEL

Service outputs are provided by organizing the marketing functions and flows—physical possession, ownership, promotion, negotiation, financing, risking, ordering, and payment—in a wide variety of ways. Each channel member participates in at least one flow; otherwise, it would have no reason for its existence. Most channel members participate in several flows, and some participate in all of them. In the cigarette example mentioned earlier, many channel members must participate in the flow of physical possession in order to provide the lot sizes, spatial convenience, and delivery times demanded by consumers. Therefore, almost every channel member will have to maintain an inventory. On the other hand, not all cigarette channel members have to invest heavily in the flow of promotion. In fact, the normal procedure in the purchase of cigarettes is self-selection. The media advertising aspect of the promotion flow has been assumed almost totally by the manufacturers. This is not the case in the marketing of consumer durables, where retailers are expected to play a much more significant role in promotion via local advertising, personal selling, and providing large display areas.

Therefore, a major issue in channel management is where and to what extent marketing flow participation should be assumed in order to generate the requisite service outputs. If automobile buyers need financing, for example, the manufacturer (e.g., General Motors Acceptance Corporation), the retailer, or some outside intermediary (e.g., Chase Manhattan Bank or Beneficial Finance) can provide it. But the output (in this case, variety in lending services) must be readily available if the consumer is to feel comfortable in considering a specific purchase requiring financing. Where no channel intermediary is willing to accept the risk of financing, the initial supplier may have to assume the flow. But in many instances, the supplier would prefer to allocate tasks in the channel. That is, he would prefer to specialize in those flows he can perform best and rely on others to invest their capital in flows they can perform at a comparative advantage. To a large extent, this is why it is possible to think of a marketing channel as a mechanism for dividing labor on a macro scale.

The Demand for Specialization

In the marketing of many goods and services, there is a network formed of specialized institutions and agencies. Indeed, channel members choose positions in the channel (e.g., manufacturer, wholesaler, retailer) based on their capabilities, interests, goals, expectations, values, and frames of reference. This is particularly true for independent entrepreneurs. For example, one such individual markets an orange drink nationally. He holds a patent right on the drink formula and contracts its manufacturing to a contract packer. He has engaged five brokers to call on dairies, which he franchises to sell his product via their home delivery routes. In explaining his rationale for selecting this system, he said,

> I simply do not like to be involved with that mess of manufacturing. It involves lots of detailed work. You've got to worry about the darn machines breaking down and stuff like that. I once owned a soft drink bottling plant, and it was all dirty detail work. We got bogged down all the time in operations and maintenance. It is a mess. You know what I like? I love to fool around with product development, and promotion is my bag.[3]

Given the desire to specialize, it is clear that in order to deliver the service outputs required, channel members must be highly interdependent in performing marketing tasks. Therefore, in a system in which parties must cooperate in order to achieve an end, the effective functioning of that system dictates that the role each party will assume in the marketing flows be understood and clearly defined.

The Significance of Role Prescriptions

When role relationships among channel members are specified, prescriptions for role behavior evolve. Basically, role prescriptions are determined by the norms or behavioral standards (values and commonly shared ideals) of channel members for each other. Role prescriptions define certain levels of cooperation and coordination in the performance of marketing tasks. For example, a wholesaler has a set of role prescriptions for his position as well as for the positions of his suppliers and customers. The wholesaler may expect the manufacturers who supply him to stimulate ultimate consumer demand, to provide consistent levels of product quality, to consider the impact that major product additions and deletions would have upon his business, and to furnish up-to-date information about inventory conditions. By the same token, the wholesaler may expect the retailers to whom he sells to forecast their needs adequately, to cooperate with manufacturer-sponsored cooperative advertising programs, and to participate in wholesaler-sponsored training programs. In actuality, role prescriptions indi-

---

[3] Quoted in Robert A. Robicheaux and Adel I. El-Ansary, "A General Model for Understanding Channel Member Behavior," *Journal of Retailing*, Vol. 52 (Winter 1975–76), p. 18.

cate what each member desires from all channel members, including himself, in the various marketing flows.[4]

The Relationship between Roles and Compensation

From a channel management perspective, the extent to which any given institution or agency within the channel participates in the various flows should determine the compensation received by that unit for its role in the total channel system. It would seem obvious that channel members should be paid only for what they actually do within the system. However, such is not always the case. In many lines of trade, standard trade discounts have been established based on the position (e.g., wholesaler, retailer, carrier) that an institution occupies within the system. Although these discounts are frequently called "functional" discounts, they are often based not on what flows a specific institution is performing and its coverage of these flows but rather on trade tradition. For example, one manufacturer has been known to grant large discounts to his distributors on the basis of the warehousing (physical possession) functions they perform. An analysis of these distributors' financial positions found that they were earning returns on their investments of 50 to 100 percent. Middlemen are entitled to earn satisfactory returns, but the amounts generated by these distributors were inordinate and indicated that they were coasting on the high level of market demand for the product of the channel. Upon further investigation, it was found that undue compensation was being granted for the warehousing operations of the distributors because the manufacturer was, in actuality, consigning much of the component inventory needed for the installation of the product to public warehouses located near the distributors. The manufacturer was also assuming a large portion of the expense associated with the leasing of the space in the warehouses. The conclusion was apparent: the manufacturer had been overcompensating the distributors for their rather minimal participation in the flows of physical possession, ownership, and financing.

Role behavior within the channel is the most critical variable in determining whether appropriate service output levels will be generated, whether high-yield performance will be achieved, and whether individual channel members are being adequately compensated for their contributions to the delivery of the requisite service outputs to end-users. Therefore, a central task for channel management is to *specify* the appropriate roles for each of the various system members so that performance goals will be attained. To achieve this end, channel managers must employ economic and social power.

STEP 3.
USING POWER TO SPECIFY ROLES

Simply put, *power* is the ability of one channel member to get another channel member to do what the latter would not otherwise have done. More rigorously stated, one channel member's (A's) power over another (B) can be defined as the

---

[4] For a discussion of role theory as applied to marketing channels, see Lynn E. Gill and Louis W. Stern, "Roles and Role Theory in Distribution Channel Systems," in L. W. Stern (ed.), *Distribution Channels: Behavioral Dimensions* (Boston: Houghton Mifflin Co., 1969), pp. 22–47.

net increase in the probability of B's enacting a behavior after A has made an intervention, compared with the probability of B's enacting the behavior in the absence of A's intervention.[5] Several implications of this formal definition should be noted:

1. In stating a power relationship, it is not sufficient to say, "A is powerful"; rather, A must be powerful over someone else (e.g., B). Think of Sears relative to Tinkertoy versus Sears relative to Goodyear.)

2. The definition makes no distinction as to the means of getting B to do what he would not otherwise have done. The range of available means—rewards, coercion, expertise, reference, and legitimacy—are discussed later in this section.

3. The definition does not require each application of power by A to result in overt reactions by B in order to be considered successful. Power attempts may only increase the probability of desired overt action by B. Additional efforts may be required to achieve the actual movement of B.[6]

This formal statement of power can be put into the language of marketing as follows:

> The power of a channel member is his ability to control the decision variables in the marketing strategy of another member in a given channel at a different level of distribution. For this control to qualify as power, it should be different from the influenced member's original level of control over his own marketing strategy.[7]

In addition, power can be viewed in terms of the extent to which one channel member depends upon another. The more highly dependent B is on A, the more power A has over B. For example, a small neighborhood retail druggist may be much more dependent upon his wholesaler than the wholesaler is on the druggist. According to Emerson, the dependence of B on A is (1) directly proportional to B's motivational investment in goals mediated by A, and (2) inversely proportional to the availability of those goals to B outside of the A–B relation.[8] That is, the more A can directly affect B's goal attainment and the fewer the number of alternatives open to B to obtain what he needs in order to function properly, the greater the power A has over B.

The importance of the dependency concept is nowhere more evident than in the automobile industry. In the past, automobile manufacturers kept most of their parts suppliers in the dark about new-product plans and forced their suppliers to operate on very low margins by requiring them to engage in competitive bidding for contracts each year. But now General Motors, Ford, and Chrysler are all openly courting their suppliers with purchasing contracts that

[5] John Schopler, "Social Power," in Leonard Berkowitz (ed.), *Advances in Experimental Social Psychology*, Vol. 2 (New York: Academic Press, 1965), p. 187. See also Robert A. Dahl, *Modern Political Analysis* (Englewood Cliffs, N.J.: Prentice-Hall, 1964), p. 40; and Kjell Grønhaug, "Power in Organizational Buying," *Human Relations*, Vol. 32 (1979), pp. 159–80.

[6] J. L. Heskett, Louis W. Stern, and Frederick J. Beier, "Bases and Uses of Power in Interorganization Relations," in Louis P. Bucklin (ed.), *Vertical Marketing Systems* (Glenview, Ill.: Scott, Foresman and Co., 1970), p. 76. See also Ian Wilkinson and David Kipnis, "Interfirm Use of Power," *Journal of Applied Psychology*, Vol. 63 (1978), pp. 315–20.

[7] Adel I. El-Ansary and Louis W. Stern, "Power Measurement in the Distribution Channel," *Journal of Marketing Research*, Vol. 9 (February 1972), p. 47.

[8] Richard M. Emerson, "Power–Dependence Relations," *American Sociological Review*, Vol. 27 (February 1962), pp. 32–33.

run for two to three years, with negotiated arrangements, and with communications about product plans. The reason for this change is that the manufacturers will have to spend over $100 billion to make their cars and trucks safer, cleaner, and more efficient as the result of government-mandated guidelines and foreign competition, and they need the expertise of the suppliers to help them reach their goals. However, the suppliers have become less dependent on the manufacturers over time by diversifying away from heavy reliance on the passenger-car original equipment business. As one industry executive stated, "You won't have a lot of suppliers scrambling for the auto business any more. I think the car people will be seeking suppliers for a change." And another executive observed, "We're moving into the realm of partnership, rather than arm's length dealings, as it was in the days of competitive bids in the auto-supply business."[9]

It is important to understand that all channel members are *inter*dependent. This means that each channel member has at least *some* power. When the dependencies of channel members are not equal, those who are the *most* dependent have the least amount of power *relative* to the others.[10] The ability of channel member A to get channel member B to do what he otherwise would not have done is based on the dependence of B on A for desired outcomes that cannot be obtained from other sources.[11] The causes of the dependency are the bases of power explained below. In other words, dependency and sources of power are inseparable.[12] To the extent that channel member A controls the resources that channel member B desires and cannot obtain elsewhere, or to the extent that A copes with or reduces uncertainties that are critical to B, then B is said to be dependent on A, and A is said to have power over B.[13]

Another way to look at the dependency issue in channels is to apply social exchange theory.[14] This theory rests on two major constructs: *comparison level*

[9] The quotations are from "Detroit's New Face toward Its Suppliers," *Business Week* (September 24, 1979), p. 140. See also "Detroit Raises the Ante for Parts Suppliers," *Business Week* (October 14, 1985), pp. 94–97; Amal Nag, "Auto Companies Push Parts Makers to Raise Efficiency, Cut Prices," *Wall Street Journal,* July 31, 1984, p. 1; and "EM-Supplier Accords Yield Productivity Improvements," *Marketing News* (October 25, 1985), p. 20.

[10] See Peter R. Dickson, "Distributor Portfolio Analysis and the Channel Dependence Matrix: New Techniques for Understanding and Managing the Channel," *Journal of Marketing,* Vol. 47 (Summer 1983), p. 41.

[11] For example, in a major study of wholesaler-manufacturer relationships, Bagozzi and Phillips found that supplier (manufacturer) control is a function of supplier substitutability, control of critical resources by the supplier, and the magnitude of the resources exchanged. Richard P. Bagozzi and Lynn W. Phillips, "Representing and Testing Organizational Theories: A Holistic Construal," *Administrative Science Quarterly,* Vol. 27 (September 1982), p. 484.

[12] See John F. Gaski, "The Theory of Power and Conflict in Channels of Distribution," *Journal of Marketing,* Vol. 48 (Summer 1984), p. 23. See also James R. Brown, Robert F. Lusch, and Darrel D. Muehling, "Conflict and Power-Dependence Relations in Retailer-Supplier Channels," *Journal of Retailing,* Vol. 59 (Winter 1983), p. 72.

[13] These concepts are central to strategic contingency theory and resource dependence theory. For the former, see D. J. Hickson et al., "A Strategic Contingencies Theory of Intraorganizational Power," *Administrative Science Quarterly,* Vol. 16 (June 1971), pp. 216–29, and for the latter, see Jeffrey Pfeffer and Gerald R. Salancik, *The External Control of Organizations: A Resource Dependence Perspective* (New York: Harper & Row, 1978). An excellent summary may be found in Robert J. House, "Power in Organizations: A Social Psychological Perspective," working paper, University of Toronto, 1984, pp. 1–30.

[14] See John W. Thibaut and Harrold Kelley, *The Social Psychology of Groups* (New York: John Wiley & Sons, 1959); and Harrold Kelley and John W. Thibaut, *Interpersonal Relations: A Theory of Interdependence* (New York: John Wiley & Sons, 1978). For an excellent discussion of social exchange

(CL) and *comparison level for alternatives* (CL_{alt}). Basically, the comparison level is the quality of outcomes an individual channel member (say, a manufacturer) has come to expect from its relationships with channel members of a specific kind (say, distributors) on the basis of its past and present experience and its knowledge of the experience of firms similar to itself. Assuming that the manufacturer is linked with a particular distributor, the comparison level of alternatives, by contrast, is the average quality of outcomes that the manufacturer can expect from the best alternative to its present relationship. Thus, a firm will assess what it expects from a relationship (CL) and what it can get by going elsewhere (CL_{alt}). But the same is true for the other channel members with which the firm interacts: they will assess their relationship with the firm in the same way. Therefore, the members of the channel have some dependence on one another, especially if the alternatives available to them are mediocre. Given this dependency, each channel member, by varying its actions, can affect the quality of the others' outcomes. The ability to affect the quality of others' outcomes is how power is defined in social exchange theory.

A dramatic example of the significance of dependency relationships in marketing channels is provided by just-in-time production/delivery methods. As discussed in Chapter 4, just-in-time is an exacting discipline. Parts and material should arrive at the factory just as they are needed in the manufacturing process. This lets the manufacturer eliminate inventories and the costs of carrying them.

> Too often the dream turns into a nightmare for suppliers. They must ensure not only that materials get there at the right moment, but also, in some cases, that different parts, sizes, and colors arrive in precisely the right sequence for the assembly line. Even more taxing, suppliers have to deliver materials of uniformly high quality; with just-in-time, there is no backup inventory to reach into if a newly arrived part is defective. . . .
>
> Just-in-time suppliers need a lot of handholding from their customers. Suppliers must have plenty of advance notice of what and how much to make, and the customers must stick to the schedules. A few smart companies are even bringing suppliers in on the early stages of designing new products. This helps ensure that the supplier can fulfill the contract at a profit, and that the customer gets the quality needed. And when customers help suppliers get on a just-in-time footing with *their* suppliers, inventories dissolve throughout the [marketing channel], along with the carrying costs. If inventory just gets pushed down onto someone else in the [channel], the cost of carrying it eventually gets pushed back onto the customer.[15]

Bases of Power

The use of power by individual channel members to affect the decision making or the behavior of others is the mechanism by which congruent and effective roles become specified, roles become realigned when necessary, and appropriate role performance is enforced. As indicated, a number of bases of

---

theory in a channels context, see James C. Anderson and James A. Narus, "A Model of the Distributor's Perspective of Distributor-Manufacturer Working Relationships," *Journal of Marketing*, Vol. 48 (Fall 1984), pp. 62–74. Our discussion of this theory is based on page 63 of Anderson and Narus's article.

[15] Dexter Hutchins, "Having a Hard Time with Just-in-Time," FORTUNE (June 9, 1986), p. 64. © 1986 Time Inc. All rights reserved.

power may be available to a channel member. These include rewards, coercion, expertness, reference, and legitimacy.[16]

Rewards.   Reward power is based on the belief by B that A has the ability to mediate rewards for him. The effective use of reward power rests on A's possession of some resource that B values and believes he can obtain by conforming to A's request. Specific rewards that may be used by individual channel members may include the granting of wider margins, the allocation of various promotional allowances, and the assignment of exclusive territories. For example, if a group of hospitals is willing to link itself to American Hospital Supply's order entry system and purchase a fixed minimum volume of its products per year (say, $2500), AHS will guarantee that future price increases will not rise above a preset ceiling.[17] Thus, reward power employed by AHS enables hospital groups to fight inflationary pressures and contain costs. Similar results are hoped for in the automotive industry as the major auto companies shift to long-term supplier agreements in which productivity improvements are mandated. From a supplier point of view, the reward (long-term agreements for substantial volumes of business) will ensure business stability, which makes investing in new equipment far more financially attractive. It also results in better utilization of human resources and a more experienced work force. In fact, some auto manufacturers, such as Ford, are strongly considering going all the way to *single sourcing*—concentrating the bulk of their business with better-performing suppliers—in order to gain lower costs (via purchasing economies and longer production runs) and less variability in the finished product from their suppliers.

Coercion.   Coercive power stems from B's expectation that he will be punished by A if he fails to conform to A's influence attempt. Coercion involves any negative sanction or punishment that a firm is perceived to be capable of. Examples would be reductions in margins, the withdrawal of rewards previously granted (e.g., an exclusive territorial right), and the slowing down of shipments. In fact, coercive power can be viewed as the other side of reward power. It should be noted, however, that the threat and use of negative sanctions can often be viewed as "pathological" and may be less functional over the long run than other power bases that may produce more positive side effects.[18] Therefore, coercion should be employed only when all other avenues to evoke change have been traveled.

Coercive power is often used in situations where there is an extreme imbalance of power within the channel—for example, where very large and well-financed retailers face small, highly dependent manufacturers, and vice versa. Thus, despite the enlightened self-interest implicit in the previously mentioned changing purchasing patterns of automakers, suppliers still feel enormous coer-

[16] Our discussion of the bases of power draws on John R. P. French and Bertram Raven, "The Bases of Social Power," in Dorwin Cartwright (ed.), *Studies in Social Power* (Ann Arbor, Mich.: University of Michigan Press, 1959), pp. 150–67.

[17] "American Hospital Supply's Pricing Promise," *Sales & Marketing Management* (January 14, 1980), p. 24.

[18] David A. Baldwin, "The Power of Positive Sanctions," *World Politics*, Vol. 24 (October 1971), pp. 19–38; Robert F. Lusch, "Channel Conflict: Its Impact on Retailer Operating Performance," *Journal of Retailing*, Vol. 52 (Summer 1976), pp. 3–12; and Robert F. Lusch, "Sources of Power: Their Impact on Interchannel Conflict," *Journal of Marketing Research*, Vol. 13 (November 1976), pp. 382–90.

cive pressure in their dealings with the industry. Wielding their considerable clout, automakers force suppliers to modernize operations, share the cost of research and development, and assume the burden of carrying inventories (especially for just-in-time systems).[19]

A blatant example of the use of coercive power is found in the marketing channels for apparel. Here, retailers have the upper hand. Some of department stores' buying practices have upset suppliers for a long time. These practices include arbitrary deductions from the agreed-to price ("charge-backs") for minor and sometimes falsified reasons, late payments, required contributions to retail advertising expenses, and unauthorized returns of merchandise.[20] Some retailers have decided to boycott the brand-name apparel manufacturers who supply off-price retailers.[21] Relationships within these channels are often strained, to say the least.[22] Apparently, the adversarial behavior patterns in the apparel industry have become so ingrained that alumni carry them along when they enter new industries. For example, Michael Shane, founder and chairman of Leading Edge, previously sold wigs and blue jeans. When he entered the personal computer industry, he gambled that he could succeed by applying to computers the aggressive tactics of the garment industry. He squeezes dealers and suppliers to reduce costs. During the mid 1980s, Leading Edge was sued for nonpayment of bills by a computer-disk supplier, a public relations agency, an employment agency, a photographic company, and two printing companies.[23]

When coercive power is continuously applied, countervailing power will eventually develop in the channel. Thus, Florida citrus growers have formed associations to counteract the coercive activities of processors and grocery chains. Franchisees in the fast-food, petroleum, and automotive industries have formed very strong and cohesive dealer associations. The increasing power of major appliance dealers, many of whom are members of groups that order hundreds of millions of dollars in merchandise a year, has sparked a merger movement among suppliers. In 1986, mergers put 80 percent of that $11 billion industry in the hands of just four companies—Whirlpool, General Electric, White Consolidated Industries, and Maytag.[24] And countervailing forces in grocery channels are bringing about radical changes, as described in Exhibit 6–2.

This does not mean, however, that there are never any situations where coercive power might be productively employed. For example, so-called gray marketers (unauthorized outlets) sell IBM personal computers for 20 percent or more below list price.[25] Gray marketers buy the machines from authorized dealers, corporations, universities, and other large purchasers, who get them at discounts of about 30 percent to more than 40 percent, depending on volume.

---

[19] Nag, *op. cit.*, p. 1.

[20] Jeffrey H. Birnbaum, "Suppliers Accuse Big Department Stores of Fudging on Bills Due and Paying Late," *Wall Street Journal*, February 11, 1981, p. 48; Jeffrey N. Birnbaum, "Major Department Stores Are the Focus of an FTC Probe over Buying Practices," *Wall Street Journal*, November 20, 1980, p. 4; and Hank Gilman, "Wholesalers Caught in a Squeeze by Retailers," *Wall Street Journal*, May 29, 1986, p. 6.

[21] Claudia Ricci, "Retailer Gets Tough in Off-Price Battle in Apparel Business," *Wall Street Journal*, June 22, 1983, p. 52.

[22] Some of Sears's actions with its suppliers have been particularly notorious. See, for example, Carol J. Loomis, "The Leaning Tower of Sears," *Fortune* (July 2, 1979), pp. 78–85.

[23] Bob Davis, "To Sell PCs on Price, Leading Edge Presses Suppliers and Dealers," *Wall Street Journal*, April 10, 1986, p. 1.

[24] "Turning Up the Heat in the Kitchen," *Business Week* (August 4, 1986), p. 76.

[25] "Blue vs. Gray: IBM Tries to Stop the Discounters," *Fortune* (May 27, 1985), p. 79.

EXHIBIT 6–2   Countervailing power in the marketing channels for groceries: The case of Procter & Gamble

Procter & Gamble once viewed the middlemen who sell its products as interlopers standing between them and the customer. Not long ago, wholesalers and retailers had to put up with the shabby treatment they got from P&G because the company's products were in such high demand. P&G restricted the quantity supermarkets could buy when it offered special discounts. Salesmen also insisted that they routinely load up on all sizes of a product. If a retailer refused to carry a size all the time, he reportedly couldn't get it when P&G discounted it.

The day of the imperious P&G may be ending as the company adapts to some radical changes in consumer retailing. The food industry is consolidating at both the retail and wholesale levels, concentrating more sales in the hands of fewer companies. Their control over enormous shelf space gives the big retailers and wholesalers a powerful influence over how a product fares. The retailers have also found new muscle in the advent of computerized checkout scanners. With instantaneous data from scanners, they can assess product needs neighborhood by neighborhood. They can also predict the consumer reaction to local newspaper advertising and coupons. A General Foods executive has observed that "Retailers no longer shudder when a manufacturer tells them, 'We're going to drop two million coupons on Philly.' Before, they feared having too little or too much product during a special promotion and felt compelled to buy whatever the manufacturer suggested."

Another source of strength for middlemen is a new product evaluation technique called direct product profitability, or DPP. Using DPP, retailers can measure the handling costs of a product from the time it reaches the warehouse until a customer takes it out the front door. DPP has revealed that some high-volume products have such high handling costs that they are less appealing—and deserve less shelf space—than retailers once thought.

Along with competitors, P&G has responded to the new might of the distributors by redesigning products and building larger profit margins for the retailer into wholesale prices. The chief executive for Supermarkets General has been quoted as saying: "It's been a quantum change. There's certainly a greater willingness to pay attention to what we want and need."

Source: Bill Saporito, "Procter & Gamble's Comeback Plan," *Fortune* (February 4, 1985), p. 30. © 1985 Time Inc. All rights reserved.

The large buyers can resell the computers profitably for less than what a small buyer would pay IBM. In many cases, they can make money simply by ordering huge quantities to earn the biggest discount and then selling the excess at cost. (There are similar problems with imported cameras, where gray marketers rely on arbitrage. For instance, when a strong dollar cheapens the French franc against the Japanese yen, importers sometimes can acquire and bring to the United States Japanese cameras from France at a much lower dollar cost than they could from Japan.[26])

The troublesome thing about these practices is that the "illegitimate" dealers do not provide advice and service, and sometimes they make unauthorized

[26] Ann Hughey, " 'Gray Market' in Camera Imports Starts to Undercut Official Dealers," *Wall Street Journal,* April 1, 1982, p. 23.

alterations in the equipment. Most important, these dealers undermine the efforts of legitimate dealers. The former get a free ride from the latter's attempts to cultivate and educate potential customers. IBM has exercised its coercive power by cutting off or threatening to cut off supplies to unauthorized dealers. Because gray markets are virtually impossible to police and eliminate, IBM's coercive actions are largely symbolic. Even so, they reinforce in the minds of its legitimate dealers the company's interest in building a channel system that will deliver the appropriate service outputs to end-users, and that in support of this goal it is willing to flex its muscles.

From a channel management perspective, it would appear that the use of reward power should generally produce better results in helping forge long-term working relationships than would the use of coercive power. After all, the prospect of receiving a reward is a lot more pleasant than the prospect of receiving a punishment. There are, however, some very close ties between reward power and coercive power that make rewards suspect if one is concerned with building a system of distribution. First, reward power and coercive power are both *contingent* types of influence: their effects are contingent on factors external to the party being influenced.[27] In other words, the rewards and punishments are controlled and mediated by an influence agent. Motivation to act is impelled by "outside" forces, not by internal (intrinsic) ones, as is the case with expert, referent, and legitimate power. Second, reward and coercive power are also different from the other bases of power in that they rely on *direct* outcome control to achieve effects whereas the others depend on *indirect* outcome control.[28] While their "directness" may make them more efficient bases of power (e.g., outcomes may come quicker), the potential for unfavorable reactions to their use is greater.[29] Third, withdrawing a reward is perceived as a coercive act. Fourth, rewards are also subject to diminishing returns. To keep rewards salient, it is necessary to increase their size over time. Fifth, both coercive and reward power demand that the influence agent monitor the actions of the party whose behavior is supposed to change, so that the appropriate rewards or punishments can be administered in case of compliance or noncompliance. In sum, reward power has many of the attributes of coercive power, and therefore it is a double-edged base of power. Rather than focusing on reward and coercion, one should pay more attention to the remaining three power bases, even though there may be no effective way to avoid using the first two.

Expertness.   Expert power is based on B's perception that A has special knowledge. Examples of channel members assuming expert roles are wide-

[27] George John, "An Empirical Investigation of Some Antecedents of Opportunism in a Marketing Channel," *Journal of Marketing Research*, Vol. 21 (August 1984), p. 281.

[28] Jack Kasulis, Robert Spekman, and Richard Bagozzi, "A Taxonomy of Channel Influence: A Theoretical-Operational Framework," in George Fisk et al. (eds.), *Future Directions in Marketing* (Cambridge, Mass.: Marketing Science Institute, 1978), pp. 165–84. See also Anderson and Narus, *op. cit.*

[29] For example, Etgar shows that reward power and coercive power (what he calls *economic power sources*) contribute more to the accumulation of power by a channel leader than expertise, legitimacy, and reference (*noneconomic power sources*). Michael Etgar, "Selection of an Effective Channel Control Mix," *Journal of Marketing*, Vol. 42 (July 1978), pp. 55–57. On the other hand, John shows that reward power and coercive power are correlated *positively* with opportunism and *negatively* with three attitudinal scales. See John, *op. cit.*, pp. 284–86. For further discussion of this issue, see Robert F. Lusch and James R. Brown, "A Modified Model of Power in the Marketing Channel," *Journal of Marketing Research*, Vol. 19 (August 1982), pp. 318–20.

spread. It has become very common, for example, for small retailers to rely heavily on their wholesale suppliers for expert advice. For example, in the drug, grocery, automotive parts, and hardware trades, merchant wholesalers, such as McKesson, Super Valu, Genuine Parts, and Cotter, generally provide retailers with sales promotion counsel and aids, sales training for store employees, information about other retailers' promotions, advice on getting special displays, advice on store layout and arrangement, information on sources of items not stocked by the wholesaler, and managerial counseling. Such services may also be provided by manufacturers in the form of management training for marketing intermediaries.

In American Hospital Supply's order-entry system for hospital groups, referred to in our discussion of reward power, teams of experts arrive to analyze a hospital's inventory needs, brand-name preferences, and materials flow once it joins AHS's plan. Then an order transmitter linked to a central computer at the company's headquarters is installed. Benefits to the hospital include reduced inventory requirements, improved cash flow, less paperwork, and 24-hour delivery on the great majority of orders.[30]

Another example of the use of expert power in marketing channels is provided by Sweda International, the cash register subsidiary of Litton Industries. Sweda uses 200 independent dealers to sell its high-technology products. Such a policy is often frowned upon, because customers sometimes question the sophistication and responsiveness of independent dealers. Sweda has overcome this concern by intensive dealer training. The strategy appears to have paid off. For example, an executive of McCrory Corporation, which purchased 2000 Sweda electronic cash registers for 750 department stores, was quoted as saying, "We have found in some locations that Sweda's dealers are better than the company's employees."[31]

Another outstanding example of the use of expert power comes from an industry we have characterized as cutthroat—apparel. Proving that there can be enlightenment in even the darkest of places, companies such as Burlington Industries, Haggar International Company, and Levi Strauss & Company are laying the groundwork for a new strategy aimed at winning back market share from foreign competitors.[32] They are betting that they can reduce to a matter of weeks the year or more it now takes to turn a retailer's order into garments on the shelf. This effort recognizes the importance of close cooperation between the apparel makers and their textile suppliers. It also puts the apparel and textile makers in a new alliance with retailers—a sharp change from the antagonism that prevailed in the past. By sharing strategic information, interactive control systems, and investments in new equipment, such as computer-controlled design, cutting, and sewing machines, domestic textile and apparel makers may be able to cut 45 weeks out of the estimated 66 weeks it usually takes to make and deliver a garment to a retailer's shelf. For retailers, such a reduction would mean

[30] "American Hospital Supply's Pricing Promise," p. 24.

[31] "Sweda: Aggressive Marketing Produces a Spirited Turnaround," *Business Week* (March 31, 1980), p. 101.

[32] Douglas R. Sease, "Move to Fight Apparel Imports Is Set," *Wall Street Journal*, December 17, 1985, p. 6. For additional examples of expert power at work, see Ronald Alsop, "Retailers Exert More Influence in Selling of Packaged Goods," *Wall Street Journal*, April 25, 1985, p. 33; Dan Baum, "Polaroid Corp. Is Selling Its Techniques for Limiting Supplier Price Increases," *Wall Street Journal*, February 13, 1985, p. 36; and Joel Dreyfuss, "Networking: Japan's Latest Computer Craze," *Fortune* (July 7, 1986), pp. 94–96.

much lower inventory costs and much more accurate predictions about what items will sell and how many of each to order. The major hurdle in implementing this "quick response" strategy is the degree of coordination necessary among all the participants in the manufacturing and retailing processes. The key will be the massive use of expert power in organizing the system.

The durability of expert power presents a problem in channel management, however. If expert advice, once given, provides the recipient with the ability to operate without such assistance in the future, then the expertise has been transferred and the power of the original expert in the relationship is reduced considerably. The student's dependence on his tutor is lessened or eliminated. A firm that wishes to retain expert power in its relationships with other firms in a given channel over the long run has three options. First, it can dole out its expertise in small portions, always retaining enough vital data so that other channel members will remain dependent on it. But this would mean it would have to keep other channel members in the dark about some critical aspect of channel performance. Such a strategy would be self-defeating, because it is important that all channel members work up to their capacities if the channel as a whole is to function successfully. They cannot do so if they are kept "stupid." Second, the firm can continually invest in learning, and thereby always have new and important information to offer its channel partners. This means the firm would have to try to accumulate knowledge about market trends, threats, and opportunities that other channel members would find difficult to generate on their own. The cost of this option is not trivial, but the benefits, in terms of achieving channel goals, are likely to be high.

A third option is to encourage channel partners to invest in transaction-specific expertise that would be so specialized that they could not easily transfer it to other products or services.[33] In other words, the specific nature of the expertise, along with the costs involved in acquiring it, would impede exit from the channel. In cases where expertise can be readily tranferred to "outsiders," marketers have sometimes taken rather drastic action to protect it. Burger King Corporation filed a suit against Horn & Hardart Company, one of its largest franchisees. At issue was Horn & Hardart's plan to become the Manhattan franchisee for Arby's, a roast-beef chain owned by Royal Crown Company of Atlanta. Burger King informed Horn & Hardart, which at the time operated 20 Burger Kings in the New York City area, that it was terminating several of its franchises, claiming that Horn & Hardart's plan to open the Arby's units violated its franchise agreement and would be a conflict of interest. Similarly, McDonald's contract with its franchisees specifies that McDonald's may take over a restaurant without advance notice for cause if a franchisee discloses confidential McDonald's documents. The contract also forbids franchisees from investing in another restaurant business. Both Burger King and McDonald's guard with considerable fervor the expertise they have developed, and have no desire to share it with others.[34]

Crucial to the retention of expert power is the ability of a channel member to position himself well in the flow of communication and information within a

---

[33] See Erin Anderson, "The Salesperson as Outside Agent or Employee: A Transaction Cost Analysis," *Marketing Science,* Vol. 4 (Summer 1985), p. 238.

[34] See "Burger King Sues Firm Controlled by President of Horn & Hardart Co.," *Wall Street Journal,* November 9, 1979, p. 17; and Paul Merrion, "Tougher Pact Riles Big Mac Owners," *Crain's Chicago Business,* Vol. 2 (September 17, 1979), p. 33.

channel system. For example, manufacturers may be highly dependent on the other channel members for information on consumer demand. Retailers and industrial distributors occupy preferred positions in this regard because of their close contacts with consumers of the manufacturers' products. By gathering, interpreting, and transmitting valuable market information, a channel member can absorb uncertainty for other channel members. Through this process of *uncertainty absorption*,[35] the latter become more dependent upon the former for inferences about market developments. For example, General Foods performed a massive study of materials handling in distribution warehouses and then made its results and recommendations available to wholesalers through a group of specialists carefully trained to help implement the recommendations. The company also undertook a major study of retail space profitability and then offered supermarket owners the opportunity to learn a new approach to space-productivity accounting called *direct product profit*, discussed in Chapter 11.

Reference Identification. According to French and Raven identification power and referent power are linked in a cause-and-effect sense.

> The referent power of A over B has its basis in the identification of B with A. By identification, we mean a feeling of oneness of B to A, or a desire for such an identity. . . . If A is an attractive group, B will have a feeling of membership or a desire to join. If B is already closely associated with A, he will want to maintain this relationship.[36]

Consider, for example, an individual who is simultaneously offered a Mercedes Benz dealership and a Renault dealership. If he discovers, through careful analysis, that both dealerships will yield him the same rate of return on his investment and that the management of both companies will give him comparable support in promotion, training servicemen, finding a location, and the like, the individual might choose the Mercedes Benz dealership because of the greater desire to be *identified* as a Mercedes dealer. In turn, the Mercedes Benz organization would be able to exercise referent power over its new dealership. The existence of referent power within many channels is undeniable, especially in situations where wholesalers or retailers pride themselves on carrying certain brands (e.g., Schwinn bicycles, IBM's personal computers, Estee Lauder's perfumes) and where manufacturers pride themselves on having their brands carried in certain outlets (e.g., Neiman-Marcus and Saks Fifth Avenue). And in certain industrial selling situations, it has been found that industrial purchasing agents' and chemists' responses to sales presentations are strongly influenced by

---

[35] See James G. March and Herbert A. Simon, *Organizations* (New York: John Wiley & Sons, 1958), p. 165. The implementation of uncertainty-absorbing techniques could also be viewed more broadly as the use of *information power* rather than the enhancement of *expert power*. Informational influence or persuasion is involved when A provides information not previously available to B or when A points out contingencies of which B had not been aware. B may do what he might not otherwise have done, because with the new information he may view the specific action suggested by A to be in his own best interest, aside from any consideration for A or possible rewards and punishments that A might mete out. Thus, information power is based on the acceptance by B of the logic of A's arguments rather than on A's perceived expertise. See Bertram H. Raven and Arie W. Kruglanski, "Conflict and Power," in Paul Swingle (ed.), *The Structure of Conflict* (New York: Academic Press, 1970), p. 73.

[36] French and Raven, *op. cit.*, p. 161.

the reputation of the company the sales agent represents. In general, the agent of the company with the better reputation obtains a more favorable response.[37]

Legitimacy.   Legitimate power stems from values internalized by B that give him a feeling that A "should" or "has a right" to exert influence and that he, B, has an obligation to accept it. The appearance of legitimate power is most obvious in *intra*organizational relations. That is, when a supervisor gives a directive to a subordinate, the latter feels that the former has a right to direct in a certain manner and therefore will generally conform to the superior's desires. Such legitimized power is synonymous with authority.

Within a nonintegrated marketing channel, there is no formal hierarchy of authority. However, individual firms may perceive that such a hierarchy exists. For example, the largest firm could be considered the leader by other channel members. If this is the case, then legitimate power may be available to that firm. It is also likely that retailers and industrial distributors will believe that they have a right to tell their suppliers what to do simply because they are positioned next to markets and their suppliers aren't. This *position power* is explored in more detail in Chapter 9. However, the scope of legitimate power may be limited; that is, the number of marketing flows over which a firm may be thought to have a right to exert influence may be quite small (e.g., wholesalers may have legitimate power relative to physical possession, and retailers relative to the flow of local promotion and pricing).

Obviously, the law allows firms to maintain agreements, such as franchises and other contracts, that confer legitimate power. In addition, patent and trademark laws give owners a certain amount of freedom and justification in supervising the distribution of their products. Another example of this type of legitimate power is the protection afforded a manufacturer and his dealers when the former adopts an exclusive distribution policy.

Combining the Power Bases

The preceding discussion of power bases has treated each separately. In reality, however, the power bases are used in combination. For example, Digital Equipment Corporation, one of the largest computer manufacturers in the world, has instituted a Commercial Distributor Program which incorporates a variety of influence strategies using mainly reward, referent, and expert power bases. Its program includes the following features, among others:

- A Trade Show Program, which supports distributors' participation in trade shows
- An Open House Program, which provides assistance in attracting prospects and creating new sales leads for distributors
- A *Product Guide,* which contains the latest information on Digital products, prices, configurations, and environmental requirements
- Executive Seminars for distributor personnel
- A Demonstrator Program, which allows distributors to purchase a Digital computer for demonstration and development purposes at a premium discount

[37] Theodore Levitt, *Industrial Purchasing Behavior: A Study of Communications Effects* (Boston: Division of Research, Graduate School of Business Administration, Harvard University, 1965), pp. 31–32.

- A Warehouse Program, which assures shipment of certain standard small business systems and computer peripherals within seven working days
- A *Commercial Operations Guide,* which contains recommended guidelines for handling customer surveys, detailed specifications, proposals, contracts, acceptance criteria, warranties, and user documentation
- An Authorized Digital Computer Distributor Logo, which authorized distributors may use on all sales, stationery, sign, collateral, and advertising materials
- A Cooperative Advertising Program, under which Digital will reimburse to authorized distributors 40 percent of their approved advertising expenditures

Certain synergistic effects may be operative when power bases are used in combination; e.g., legitimacy may enhance expertise and vice versa, identification may increase with the use of rewards, and coercion may sometimes be necessary to reinforce legitimacy. On the other hand, there may be conflict between certain bases. For example, the use of coercion by a channel member may destroy any referent power that member might have been able to accumulate. It may have a similar effect on expert power, for which trust is a prerequisite.

In addition, there are economic, social, and political costs associated with the use of the various power bases, and these must be taken into account prior to the implementation of programs in which they are incorporated. Influence attempts are also constrained by norms that exist within channel systems. These norms, which are, in fact, "rules" of the competitive "game," aid in defining appropriate industrial behavior and can be even more restrictive than public laws in certain situations. For example, during periods of short supply in the steel industry, many buyers are willing to pay above-"normal" prices for steel. This alternative is less expensive than shutting down production. Because of short supply, steel distributors in the established marketing channels can command higher prices; however, they frequently refrain from doing so, because they feel that their customers expect certain restraints from them, even though some of their customers go outside the established channel structure and purchase higher-priced steel from gray market sources.[38] The established distributors also refrain from using coercive power, such as boycotts, against the latter customers, because the norms of market behavior among them do not sanction such actions.

Scope and Significance of the Use of Power

The bases of power can be used to shift the marketing flows among institutions and agencies within the channel, thereby creating a more efficient and effective allocation of resources. The control achieved by some firms over selected decision variables or marketing efforts of others is a major factor in the level of performance obtained by the channel as a whole and by each of its members. It should, however, be noted that the scope of control does not have to be broad in order for success to be achieved. In fact, within most channels, because of the degree of specialization referred to earlier, the scope of any channel member's power over others may be limited to only a few of the marketing flows. For example, transportation agencies are likely to have little desire to

[38] Louis Kriesberg, "Occupational Controls among Steel Distributors," in Stern (ed.), *op. cit.,* pp. 48–62.

influence promotional activities in the channel, and many manufacturers do not wish to concern themselves greatly with problems associated with financing ultimate consumers' purchases.

The main factors involved in the use of power are summarized in Fig. 6–1 in terms of the relationship between two firms, A (the power holder) and B (the power subject).[39] The general power of A over B (box 1 in the middle of the diagram), which is related to the power A has over B in specific policy areas (box 2), is shown to stem from the dependence of B on A (box 3). In turn, this dependence derives from a combination of factors: the resources controlled by A (box 4); B's perceptions of A, the "bases of power" (box 5); the efficiency with which A controls its power resources (box 6); and the demand and supply conditions pertaining to each resource (box 7). A's use of power (box 8), which relates in part to the amount of power A has over B (box 1), leads to certain results (box 9). The results of A's use of power—the specification of roles in the channel and, ultimately, the success (sales volume, profitability, market share, etc.) of the relationship—produce certain feedback. As a consequence of this feedback, the various sources of power may be changed. They may, for example, be enhanced or depleted by the use of rewards, punishments, expertise, and the like. Finally, the nature of the environment surrounding the relationship is likely to affect a number of elements in the model. For example, the demand for and supply of the resources in A's power base will be affected by the availability of substitutes from other firms. Furthermore, the cultural setting in which the relationship exists, including the history of interactions in the channel, will affect the way in which power is used and the way the firms perceive each other. The environment comprises many elements—B's power over A, relationships the firms have with other firms, other channels for competing or complementary goods, and the general social, political, and economic environment.

Having the sources of power to evoke changes in marketing channels does not mean that a firm necessarily must use them in order to achieve its ends. In fact, the use of certain power bases is sometimes destructive, yet the nonuse of others is viewed negatively. Gaski and Nevin have found support for their observation that

> if sources of power are present but application is withheld, the consequences may be much different from, perhaps opposite, what they would be if the sources were actively exercised. For instance, the imposition of harsh sanctions on channel members (exercised coercive sources of power) seems certain to cause dissatisfaction and conflict, but the dormant presence of the potential to invoke such sanctions (unexercised coercive sources) could conceivably be regarded by franchisees or dealers as benevolent restraint. Likewise, the granting of beneficial assistance (exercised noncoercive sources) should be favorably received, but withholding of such benefits (unexercised noncoercive sources) may not be.[40]

The fact that a channel member has power sources simply indicates that it has the potential for influence.[41] When it wants to change the behavior of an-

---

[39] Our discussion of Fig. 6–1 draws on Ian Wilkinson, *Power in Distribution Channels*, Cranfield Research Papers in Marketing and Logistics, Session 1973–1974 (Bedfordshire, England, 1974), pp. 16–18.

[40] John F. Gaski and John R. Nevin, "The Differential Effects of Exercised and Unexercised Power Sources in a Marketing Channel," *Journal of Marketing Research*, Vol. 22 (May 1985), p. 132.

[41] Gary L. Frazier, "Interorganizational Exchange Behavior in Marketing Channels: A Broadened Perspective," *Journal of Marketing*, Vol. 47 (Fall 1983), p. 71.

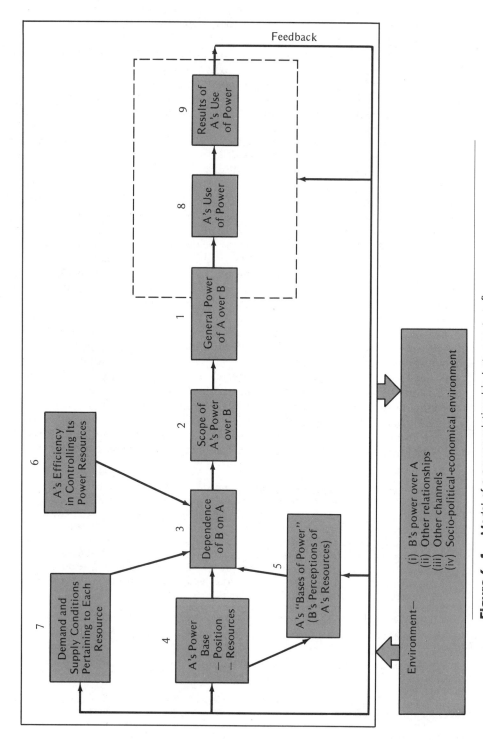

Figure 6–1 Model of a power relationship between two firms

Source: Ian Wilkinson, *Power in Distribution Channels, Cranfield Research Papers in Marketing and Logistics,* Session 1973–1974, (Bedfordshire, England, 1974), p. 17.

other channel member, it will employ a variety of *influence strategies*—the means of communication used in the application of a firm's power. Frazier and Summers suggest, for example, that when channel members have common or compatible goals, the use of information exchange and/or recommendations as influence strategies is likely to bring positive results.[42] In other situations, channel members tend to rely on promises, threats, legalistic strategies, and requests, frequently with mixed results.[43] The degree of success that a channel member has in influencing others will be strongly linked to its leadership behavior. Schul, Pride, and Little have found, for instance, that participative, supportive, and directive leadership styles are associated with lower levels of conflict in the franchised real estate brokerage industry.[44] They define these styles as follows:

- *Participative leadership* consults with other channel members, solicits their suggestions, and considers these suggestions when designing and introducing channelwide policies and procedures.
- *Supportive leadership* considers other channel members' needs, displays concern for other channel members' well-being, creates a pleasant atmosphere for interaction, and accentuates other channel members' accomplishments.
- *Directive leadership* communicates what is expected of other channel members, gives special guidance in operations, and establishes standard rules and regulations.[45]

Channel leadership and influence strategies are discussed more fully in Chapter 9.

STEP 4.
DEALING WITH CHANNEL CONFLICT

As indicated, channel members tend to specialize in certain functions; their roles are unique, at least in part. Thus, manufacturers specialize in production and national promotions while retailers specialize in merchandising, distribution, and promotions on the local level. This specialization results in a significant amount of operational interdependence among channel members. Each channel member becomes dependent on the other members to realize his organizational objectives. For example, both the manufacturer and the retailer are dependent on each other to reach the final consumer. Members are "pushed" into such interdependencies because of their need for resources—not only money, but specialized skills, access to particular kinds of markets, and the like. Thus, functional interdependence requires a minimum level of cooperation in order to accomplish the channel task. Without this minimum cooperation, the channel ceases to exist. Such cooperation allows channel members to find means to coordinate their planning, information, and decision making and to arrange the payoff structure so that each member can justify joint goals on independent criteria.

[42] Gary L. Frazier and John O. Summers, "Interfirm Influence Strategies and Their Application within Distribution Channels," *Journal of Marketing*, Vol. 48 (Summer 1984), p. 45.
[43] *Ibid.*, pp. 46–47.
[44] Patrick L. Schul, William M. Pride, and Taylor L. Little, "The Impact of Channel Leadership Behavior on Intrachannel Conflict," *Journal of Marketing*, Vol. 47 (Summer 1983), pp. 21–34.
[45] *Ibid.*, pp. 23, 30, 31.

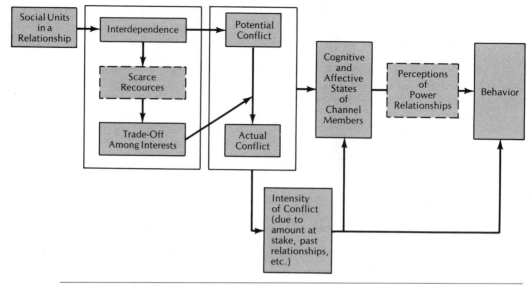

Figure 6–2 *The conflict field*

Source: Reprinted from Fuat A. Firat, Alice M. Tybout, and Louis W. Stern, "A Perspective on Conflict and Power in Distribution," in Ronald C. Curhan (ed.), *1974 Combined Proceedings of the AMA Fall and Spring Conferences* (Chicago: American Marketing Association, 1975), p. 436.

However, organizations strain to maximize their autonomy; therefore, the establishment of interdependencies creates conflicts of interest. In channels comprising independently owned institutions and agencies, this strain toward autonomy will be juxtaposed with the desire to cooperate; a mixture of motives will be present. It is, therefore, possible to predict with certainty that distribution channels will exhibit conflict following a process similar to that shown in Fig. 6–2. The greater the interdependence, the greater the opportunity for interference with goal attainment, and hence the greater the potential for conflict among organizations. However, cognitive and affective states generally precede overt opponent-centered actions by either party to a conflict situation. That is, the parties must usually first become aware of the conflict as well as personalize the conflict so that hostile feelings develop.

A notorious example of channel conflict occurred in 1984 when Porsche AG, the maker of expensive sports cars, attempted to revamp its distribution channel, which at the time comprised 323 dealers under agreement with Volkswagen of America.[46] From a strategic perspective, what Porsche planned to do made abundant sense. The company wanted to establish a three-tier distribution structure to gain increased flexibility to meet changing market conditions,

[46] See David B. Tinnin, "Porsche's Civil War with Its Dealers," *Fortune* (April 16, 1984), pp. 63–68; Matt DeLorenzo, "Porsche Casts a Pall on Franchise System," *Automotive News* (February 20, 1984), p. 1; "Porsche Retailers Start War Chest to Fight New System," *Automotive News* (February 27, 1984), p. 3; "Porsche, Volkswagen Sued by Distributor on Shift in U.S. Sales," *Wall Street Journal,* March 7, 1984, p. 4; "Porsche Pulls Back Plan to Eliminate Franchised Dealers," *Wall Street Journal,* March 15, 1984, p. 58.

improved customer satisfaction, and increased profit opportunities. The three tiers were as follows:

- *Tier I.* Two centralized inventory facilities located in Nevada and New Jersey and owned by Porsche.
- *Tier II.* Forty "Porsche Centers" (owned by Porsche of America) dispersed across the country in nonprime real estate locations such as industrial parks. These centers would have been responsible for:
    New car preparation and delivery
    Processing customer orders from agents
    Display and demonstration vehicles
    Retail sales (at manufacturer's suggested resale prices)
    Major service, body, and paint repairs
    Computerized customer service files
    Limited used-vehicle reconditioning
    Limited parts inventory
    Processing wholesale parts orders
- *Tier III.* "Porsche Agencies" run by private capital operators (primarily existing Porsche dealers) under 90-day renewable contracts (not franchise contracts). Essentially, the operators would have been sales agents with no responsibility for specific trade areas, no sales quotas, and no allocation requirements. In addition, the agents would have carried no inventory except for a few demonstration vehicles. (Additional vehicles could have been provided on consignment.) For each sale, the agent would have received an 8 percent commission, including any referrals to a Porsche Center. The agent would have also been responsible for providing service and selling wholesale parts businesses, accepting trades, and selling used vehicles.

From Porsche's point of view, the new system was going to streamline and improve the distribution of its cars to its end-users. (Recall that the product is a very expensive high-quality, luxury automobile.) It was going to give Porsche more flexibility to react to geographical customer preferences and market changes. It was also going to:

- Eliminate Porsche's sales/service field staff
- Provide manufacturer-coordinated advertising/merchandising programs over a large geographic area
- Upgrade Porsche's retail image to reflect product/buyer characteristics
- Provide upgraded and consistent preparation and delivery practices
- Improve customer satisfaction and service
- Allow market representation actions to be taken expeditiously
- Increase Porsche's power and control over the distribution system

In other words, given its knowledge of the extreme demands of its end-users for quality in sales and service, Porsche's plan was basically to assure these consumers the delivery of relevant service outputs.

So, what happened? The plan backfired. In fact, it blew up in Porsche's face. Why? Because Porsche underestimated the tenacity with which its existing dealers would hold onto the franchised system. Porsche publicly announced the distribution plan in mid February. Within a week, the major dealer trade associations had conferred with their legal counsels and warned dealers against signing applications for agency status. By the end of February, the National Automobile Dealers Association (NADA) had outlined a course of action beginning at the state level using laws that would be used to stop terminations of current franchises and/or forbid factory stores and brokers (i.e., agents). In addition, Porsche dealers on both coasts initiated their own actions aimed at pursuing litigation:

- The 14 Porsche dealers in New Jersey formed a Porsche Dealer Alliance and set up a legal defense fund.
- In California, about 40 Porsche dealers agreed to start a legal war chest (with pledges of more than $1 million) to protect their interests.

By the middle of March, lawsuits on behalf of Porsche dealers and distributors had reached more than $3 *billion*. Porsche announced the withdrawal of its plan and reverted to the current franchise system. It is estimated that Porsche would probably have been tied up in court for six years and would have had to expend millions of dollars in legal fees, plus suffer ongoing negative publicity.

Porsche's plan represents a case history of a thoughtful channel strategy scuttled by channel conflict. To put it mildly, Porsche's understanding of the interdependencies in the existing system was shallow, and therefore the groundwork it had laid prior to implementing its strategy was woefully inadequate. All it succeeded in doing was arousing the "cognitive and affective states of channel members" (see Exhibit 6–2) to a fever pitch. The lesson of the Porsche example should not be lost on anyone dealing with marketing channels comprising independent middlemen: the potential for dysfunctional conflict is high, and unless changes are carefully orchestrated and implemented, they may never see the light of day.

Conflict over Role Performance

Obviously, role performance frequently deviates from the prescriptions established by various channel members. This deviation occurs for many reasons, the most likely being specific situational factors (e.g., a price war in a retailer's trading area), incompatible organizational objectives, lack of clear and open communication flows between channel members, and differences between the deviating channel member's personal expectations and other members' expectations. Furthermore, it is extremely important to understand that these problems are not confined to relationships in channels comprised of independently owned institutions and agencies. In fact, it is possible that they can be as sharply experienced in vertically integrated systems as they are in nonvertically integrated ones. For example, many of Sears's problems in the 1970s were created because of significant differences in objectives and expectations between its retail stores, its vertically integrated distribution centers, and its merchandising and buying offices in its Chicago headquarters. Each of the units of the organization operated semiautonomously. Centralized planning was minimal, and conflict was enormous, both within the organization and between the organization and its suppliers.

Causes of Channel Conflict

Channel conflict is a situation in which one channel member perceives another channel member(s) to be engaged in behavior that is preventing or impeding it from achieving its goals. It is, in essence, a state of frustration brought about by a restriction of role performance.[47] The amount of conflict is, to a large extent, a function of goal incompatibility, domain dissensus, and differing perceptions of reality among channel members.[48] Furthermore, as channel member interdependence increases, it is likely that even relatively minor incompatibilities in goals, domain definitions, and perceptions can create intense conflict.

Goal Incompatibility.   Each channel member has a set of goals and objectives that are very often incompatible with those of other channel members. For example, among the most common conflict issues that arise between manufacturers and industrial distributors are (1) how to handle large accounts, (2) required inventory stocking levels for the distributor, (3) the quality of distributor management, (4) overlapping distributor territories, (5) size of distributor margins, and (6) whether the distributor's primary obligations and loyalty are to the customer or the supplier.[49] Clearly underlying many of these issues are differences in goals, aims, or values. Furthermore, in consumer goods marketing, there are literally tens of thousands of small retailers served by large manufacturers. Large manufacturers tend to be growth-oriented, whereas small retailers are more interested in maintaining the status quo. The likelihood of conflict is high in such situations because, in their pursuit of "dynamic" goals (e.g., increased market share and higher investment returns), the former will probably adopt innovative programs that contradict the more static orientation of the latter. For example, the interests of an independent bottler and those of Coca-Cola Company (known as "Big Coke" in the trade) do not always coincide. Big Coke thrives on selling syrup—the more the better—but volume is not always the bottler's top priority. A bottler can increase profitability by cutting investment in plant and equipment and raising prices. Some Coke bottlers, especially those that have been family-owned for generations, have tended to milk their operations.[50] During the early 1980s, the conflict set off by this incompatibility caused Coke to reevaluate and readjust its entire bottler strategy.

[47] Louis W. Stern and Ronald H. Gorman, "Conflict in Distribution Channels: An Exploration," in Stern (ed.), *op. cit.,* p. 156.

[48] See Louis W. Stern and J. L. Heskett, "Conflict Management in Interorganization Relations: A Conceptual Framework," in Stern (ed.), *op. cit.,* pp. 293–94; Larry J. Rosenberg and Louis W. Stern, "Conflict Measurement in the Distribution Channel," *Journal of Marketing Research,* Vol. 8 (November 1971), pp. 437–42; Michael Etgar, "Sources and Types of Intrachannel Conflict," *Journal of Retailing,* Vol. 55 (Spring 1979), pp. 61–78; Ernest R. Cadotte and Louis W. Stern, "A Process Model of Dyadic Interorganizational Relations in Marketing Channels," in Jagdish N. Sheth (ed.), *Research in Marketing,* Vol. 2 (Greenwich, Conn.: Jai Press, 1979); and Torger Reve and Louis W. Stern, "Interorganizational Relations in Marketing Channels," *Academy of Management Review,* Vol. 4 (July 1979), pp. 405–16.

[49] Frederick E. Webster, Jr., "The Role of the Industrial Distributor in Marketing Strategy," *Journal of Marketing,* Vol. 40 (July 1976), p. 11.

[50] See Peter W. Bernstein, "Coke Strikes Back," *Fortune* (June 1, 1981), p. 30.

EXHIBIT 6–3   Franchise/franchisor goal sets

FRANCHISEES' OPERATIVE BUSINESS GOALS SET	FRANCHISOR'S STATED SET OF GOALS
Maintain market share	Achieve profitability
Maximize return on capital invested	Capture target market share in key trading areas
Minimize cost of operating business	Meet local market conditions
Maintain reputation	Identify and seize attractive market opportunities
Maximize sales volume	Obtain efficient cost of product
Increase profitability	Achieve uniqueness in product design and performance
	Achieve ability to expand or contract resources in response to economic swings
	Achieve reliable and prompt product delivery
	Maintain pricing and cost effectiveness
	Maintain competent and motivated employees with an effective organizational structure
	Maintain effective communication with the customers and employees

Source: Reprinted from Jehoshua Eliashberg and Donald A. Michie, "Multiply Business Goals Sets as Determinants of Marketing Channel Conflict: An Empirical Study," *Journal of Marketing Research,* Vol. 21 (February 1984), p. 80, published by the American Marketing Association.

In their study of the franchised distribution network of a large industrial installations manufacturer, Eliashberg and Michie point out that

> a distribution channel in general, and a franchise system in particular, is . . . a multilevel hierarchical system designed to achieve a set of *system goals* through functional differentiation (specialization) and interdependence among its members. As in any organization, a channel member also may have a distinct set of *operative goals* which typically consists of a few goals arranged, like system goals, in a hierarchy. This hierarchy can be captured explicitly by the member's preference structure. For a channel system to function effectively, a certain degree of preference congruity with respect to each set of goals must be present between the members. However, total congruity is unlikely because each party has its own business philosophy and interests.[51]

Their research turned up different sets of goals for the franchisees and for the franchisor, as shown in Exhibit 6–3. Eliashberg and Michie found differences in preference orderings between franchisees and the franchisor; they also felt their data suggested that "determinants other than business goals (e.g., domain dissensus) may better 'explain' the franchisees' perceived conflict issues."[52]

---

[51] Jehoshua Eliashberg and Donald A. Michie, "Multiple Business Goals Sets as Determinants of Marketing Channel Conflict: An Empirical Study," *Journal of Marketing Research,* Vol. 21 (February 1984), pp. 75–76.

[52] *Ibid.,* p. 84.

Domain Dissensus. Conflict in marketing channels can be caused by differences in domain definitions among channel members. A channel domain comprises four critical elements:

1. *Population to be served.* For example, are all large accounts supposed to be handled by the direct sales force and all small accounts by distributors or dealers?
2. *Territory to be covered.* For example, what is distributor A's area of primary responsibility, and are there any overlaps with distributors B or C?
3. *Functions or duties to be performed.* What exactly is the role of each channel member in each of the eight marketing flows?
4. *Technology to be employed in marketing.* For example, how are prospects to be approached? What level of training is required for the sales force? What should be the role of telemarketing? Are computer linkups required for order placement? Hard-sell or soft-sell?

Domain dissensus is often present in so-called dual distribution situations, such as these:

> Independent businessmen who fabricate finished products made from steel, copper, aluminum, and other metals widely report that they must compete with outlets that are owned by their suppliers. These fabricator middlemen must purchase much of their supplies from those with whom they compete, but must also meet the prices established by their suppliers' outlets.[53]

> Automobile manufacturers market the bulk of their output through franchised retailers, but they sell directly to major leasing and rental companies. Hertz buys from the factory and regularly resells part of its slightly used fleet through more than 100 retail outlets throughout the country. Some of the Hertz outlets are located near franchised new car dealers.[54]

> In some instances Sears asks its suppliers to procure their raw materials through Sears; for example, Sears might buy corduroy in bulk from textile mills and then resell it to companies that make clothing for it. Sears' traditional justification of this practice is that it helps to ensure quality, supply, and the rock-bottom prices available to a volume buyer. "I've never believed that," one apparel supplier has stated. "I've always thought they were just trying to make a markup on the goods."[55]

> Several years ago, Honeywell had established two separate sales organizations: a traditional, end-user direct sales force, and a reseller organization made up of value-added resellers (VARS) and manufacturer's reps who combined their applications with Honeywell hardware and software and sold to smaller system-users. In the words of Honeywell's director of indirect sales: "Theoretically, these two organizations were chartered to do quite different things. But what would happen was that anytime a department, say, within a large Honeywell account wanted a new mini-level system, the direct sales group considered that their territory, regardless of whether or not they even had the correct applications. At the same time, the local VAR wanted to, and often did, pursue this same business because he had the

---

[53] Robert E. Weigand, "Fit Products and Channels to Your Markets," *Harvard Business Review,* Vol. 55 (January-February 1977), pp. 95–105.

[54] *Ibid.,* p. 97. The fleet sales problem is a heated one generally. See Amal Nag and William Celis III, "Auto Dealers Seeking Legislative Support to End Detroit's Discounts to Fleet Buyers," *Wall Street Journal,* May 16, 1984, p. 31.

[55] Loomis, *op. cit.,* p. 81.

application and was thus a better fit for the customer's needs. The result was confusion and conflict."[56]

To resolve domain dissensus with its travel agents caused by its direct marketing and telemarketing efforts, Royal Viking Line, a pleasure cruise company, assigns the customers it wins via its direct efforts to "appropriate" travel agents—either those who have handled travel arrangements for the customers before or those located in the customers' localities. To ensure that Royal Viking and its agents stay friends, the company pays the standard 10 percent commission to agents on sales its own people actually make.[57]

Conflict may also occur when a channel member is assigned a role that he does not have the capacity to fulfill, when demands are made upon the channel member that are more than can be expected from the position within the channel that he holds, and when a channel member feels he must relate to two reference groups and cannot decide which role is dominant. There is also a strong likelihood that a channel member will define his own domain in a way that is, at least in part, incongruent with the definition held by those with whom he deals. For example, in the outdoor power equipment industry (e.g., lawn mowers, garden tractors, rotary tillers, and snow blowers), there is considerable conflict among manufacturers, wholesalers, and retailers over such issues as (1) overlapping territories, (2) where inventory will be held in the channel, (3) who will provide service facilities and handle warranty claims, (4) inadequate levels of spare parts at different levels in the channel, (5) inadequate inventory control, especially at the retail and wholesale levels, and (6) inadequate financing throughout the channel.

Differing Perceptions of Reality.   Differing perceptions of reality are also important sources of conflict, because they indicate that there will be differing bases of action in response to the same situation. As a result, behaviors stemming from these perceptions are likely to produce frustration and conflict. Among the perceptions that have traditionally led to poor supplier-retailer relations are retailer perceptions that:

- Supplier salespeople oversell without regard to production and delivery capability.
- Supplier salespeople lack an understanding of the retailer's goals and merchandising philosophy.
- Supplier salespeople do not provide adequate in-store service.
- Suppliers do not offer a planned approach to promoting and merchandising products.

and supplier perceptions that:

- Retail buyers are preoccupied with "chiseling" the best prices out of suppliers.
- Retail buyers lack decision-making autonomy.
- Retail buyers ignore or move too slowly in accepting promotional deals and other allowances.

[56] Robert McCarthy, "How to Handle Channel Conflict," *High-Tech Marketing* (June 1985), p. 30.
[57] Arthur Bragg, "When Your Sales Team Yells 'Foul,'" *Sales and Marketing Management* (July 1, 1985), p. 66.

- Retail buyers handle too many product lines to be effective product managers and ignore merchandise once an order is placed.
- Retailers refuse to cooperate for fear of being "locked in" to a supplier.[58]

Differing perceptions are also a major cause of a number of conflict issues between manufacturers and industrial distributors.[59] Incongruent perceptions of reality can be attributed to technical problems of communication as well as to differences in goals and orientations.

In an attempt to develop a comprehensive measure of channel conflict, Etgar formulated a series of questionnaire items (reproduced in Appendix 6B).[60] A reading of them provides an extremely useful picture of the depth and breadth of the conflict that potentially exists in all marketing channels. For purposes of effective questionnaire construction, some of the questionnaire items were worded positively so as to prevent leading the respondents to express negative reactions about their channel partners. Etgar found that disagreements about channel roles, expectations, perceptions, and channel communications were the most important ones in the conflict situations he investigated.[61]

The Required Inducements–Contributions Balance

A commercial channel system continues to function as long as the subsystems are willing to remain in the system. Each unit is induced to participate in a channel of distribution by the offering of certain rewards for its supposedly unique potential contributions. The basic problem, then, is to achieve an inducements–contributions balance for each of the channel members—that is, a condition where the rewards offered by the channel to a member are commensurate with the efforts expended by that member. Theoretically, this is accomplished when a channel member is successfully utilizing the distribution system of which he is a part for the achievement of his own organizational objectives, while the distribution system is effectively employing this member to attain its objectives. If either of these conditions is not fulfilled, a satisfactory inducement–contributions balance cannot be effected, since dissatisfaction will flow from such a disparate relationship. Thus, conflict is inevitable when there is an imbalance between inducements and contributions.

Pathological Conflict

Without *any* conflict, channel members will tend to become passive and noninnovative. Eventually, the system of which they are a part will become nonviable. Conflict motivates channel members to adapt, grow, and seize new opportunities. In fact, conflict is one of the most useful social forces available.

[58] Ronald L. Ernst, "Distribution Channel Detente Benefits Suppliers, Retailers, and Consumers," *Marketing News* (March 7, 1980), p. 19.

[59] Frederick E. Webster, Jr., *Industrial Marketing Strategy*, 2nd ed. (New York: John Wiley & Sons, 1984), pp. 199–201.

[60] Etgar, *op. cit.*

[61] Data for Etgar's study were collected in 1976 from 138 furniture, stereo equipment, life insurance, shoe, liquor, and automobile dealers operating in large northeastern metropolitan areas. *Ibid.*, pp. 68, 69. For a typology of channel sentiments, see Louis W. Stern and Torger Reve, "Distribution Channels as Political Economies: A Framework for Comparative Analysis," *Journal of Marketing*, Vol. 44 (Summer 1980), pp. 52–64.

Conflict should impel better channel performance, especially if (1) moderate levels of conflict are not considered too costly by channel members, (2) divergent views produce better ideas, and (3) aggression is not irrational or destructive.[62]

However, because conflict is opponent-centered behavior,[63] it can degenerate into actions calculated to destroy, injure, or thwart another party in an interdependent relationship. What one must seek to avoid is *pathological conflict*—moves that are malign for the parties involved and for the entire system itself.[64] For example, John has found that certain channel management practices can induce opportunistic behavior, or "self-interest seeking with guile."[65] These practices stimulate channel members to make attributions of influence to reward power and coercive power and to perceive the channel system as subject to continuous rule enforcement and surveillance.

In international relations, wars may be viewed as pathological conflict: in engaging in behavior designed to thwart another country, the aggressor also kills off its own young men and women. In distribution channel relations, pathological moves are less vivid but nonetheless easily defined. For example, when Sears's suppliers complained in 1978 about the great pressure they were under as Sears abruptly changed strategies, began to reduce inventories, and sharply cut back its promotional efforts, they were advised publicly and testily by Sears's chairman that the company had its own business to run and did not owe them a living.[66] Similar examples are a supplier slowing up deliveries if a reseller is slow with his payments and a retailer boycotting brands that customers expect to find in their stores. All of these actions are evidence that conflict management mechanisms are either nonexistent or inadequate.

Effective Conflict Management

A central task in channel management is to manage conflict. In other words, ways must be found to keep conflict from becoming dysfunctional and to harness the energies in conflict situations to produce innovative resolutions. If conflict within marketing channels is to be managed, the members involved must eventually come to grips with its underlying causes. The specific strategy employed will depend not only on the cause of the conflict but also on the weight of power of the channel member seeking to manage the conflict.[67] Therefore, the effective use of power is required not only in specifying roles within the channel

---

[62] K. W. Thomas and W. H. Schmidt, "A Survey of Managerial Interests with Respect to Conflict," *Academy of Management Journal*, Vol. 19 (June 1976), pp. 315–18.

[63] Whereas conflict can be viewed as opponent-centered behavior, competition is behavior that is object-centered, and cooperation involves joint striving. For a discussion of each type of behavior, see Louis W. Stern, "Antitrust Implications of a Sociological Interpretation of Competition, Conflict, and Cooperation in the Marketplace," *Antitrust Bulletin*, Vol. 16 (Fall 1971), pp. 509–30.

[64] Kenneth E. Boulding, "The Economics of Human Conflict," in Elton B. McNeil (ed.), *The Nature of Human Conflict* (Englewood Cliffs, N.J.: Prentice-Hall, 1965), pp. 174–75. See also William P. Dommermuth, "Profiting from Distribution Conflicts," *Business Horizons* (December 1976), pp. 4–13; and Lewis A. Coser, *The Functions of Social Conflict* (Glencoe, Ill.: Free Press, 1956). For contrary evidence, see Lusch, "Channel Conflict," *op. cit.*, pp. 3–12, 89.

[65] John, *op. cit.*, p. 287. The definition of opportunism is that of Oliver E. Williamson, *Markets and Hierarchies: Analysis and Antitrust Implications* (New York: Free Press, 1975), p. 6.

[66] Loomis, *op. cit.*, p. 79.

[67] The *weight* of power is a specification of how much A influences B. When the weight of A's power over B is at its maximum, it may be referred to as *control*. At this point, A can predict with certainty that B will respond in the desired manner.

but also in dealing with the conflicts that inevitably arise among channel members.

Several strategies for use in channel relations are briefly described in the remainder of this section. Each can be modified depending upon the variables and structure of the channel.

Diplomacy. In an analogy from international relations, channel *diplomacy* is the method by which interorganizational relations are conducted, adjusted, and managed by "ambassadors," "envoys," or other persons operating at the boundaries of member organizations. Channel members engage in, cultivate, and rely upon diplomatic procedures, especially in nonintegrated systems. In the widest interpretation, the functions of a channel "diplomat" should be to help shape the policies he is to follow, to conduct negotiations with channel members to whom he is assigned, to observe and report on everything that may be of interest to the firm employing him, and to provide information about his firm to the operatives in counterpart channel organizations.

The presence of individual diplomats or of diplomatic committees is common in distribution channels (e.g., the use of business management specialists in the automobile industry and of factory specialists in the U.S. electrical equipment industry). In the early 1980s, when Coca-Cola Company was trying to work more effectively with its bottler network so that it could blunt Pepsi's inroads into its markets, the president of Coke's domestic soft drink division reorganized and expanded the duties of the bottler liaison office and ordered field personnel to pay more attention to bottlers' complaints or risk dismissal.[68] A major cause of discontent among bottlers was the way Coke tried to force national promotions (e.g., requiring bottlers to purchase racks to be put in retail outlets). In line with its new conflict management program, Coke dropped national promotions. Instead, the company's 160 field representatives now meet with bottlers to devise ways to improve market share by zeroing in on local market conditions.

Because of some well-documented strains on boundary personnel,[69] it would probably be best to place the diplomat position at a management level within organizations. It is essential that the status of diplomats be high enough so that their power is at least relatively obvious to the parties with whom they interact. This caveat would probably exclude sales or purchasing agents in most companies as candidates.

Joint Membership in Trade Associations. There are numerous instances where membership in the trade associations of channel counterparts has proved extremely beneficial in managing conflict. Perhaps the best example is the close relationship between the Grocery Manufacturers of America (GMA) and the Food Marketing Institute, composed mainly of food chains. Besides making certain that channelwide problems are addressed at the annual conventions of both organizations via joint presentations, the two associations formed a committee of manufacturers and retailers that was responsible for developing the Universal Product Code. The code is now found on almost all packaged goods sold

[68] Anthony Ramirez, "Coke Adopts a Style That Blunts Rivalry of Pepsi and Makes Peace with Bottlers," *Wall Street Journal*, December 22, 1980, p. 7; and "Coke's New Program to Placate Bottlers," *Business Week* (October 12, 1981), p. 48.

[69] Robert L. Kahn, Donald M. Wolfe, Robert P. Quinn, and J. Diedrick Snoek, *Organizational Stress: Studies in Role Conflict and Ambiguity* (New York: John Wiley & Sons, 1964), pp. 123–24.

through supermarkets and represents one of the major innovations in the food industry in the past 50 years.[70] Other programs are under way that combine the talents of various channel members from both associations in resolving conflict issues in distribution, such as those associated with ordering and billing.[71]

Interaction among the various representatives in trade association–sponsored events is, however, infrequent. More desirable would be the creation of a network of primary relations among channel members. But even infrequent interorganizational collaboration on a task jointly accepted as worthwhile and involving individuals as operating equals should result in more effective coordination and lessened hostility among organizations. Perhaps one of the most meaningful conflict management mechanisms in this respect might be an "exchange of persons" program among channel members, similar to those implemented in international relations.

Exchange of Persons. This conflict management strategy involves a bilateral trade of personnel for a specified period. The technique involved is essentially the same as role reversal, a procedure where one or both of the participants in a discussion present the viewpoint of the other. Conflict theorists have long suggested that role reversal would create an understanding of the other party's position greater than that obtained from merely presenting one's own side of the issue.[72]

In distribution channels, an exchange of persons could take place at several different levels of an organization or at all levels. Thus, as part of the initial executive training program, the marketing recruit (perhaps fresh from college) could spend a prescribed period working in the organization of suppliers, middlemen, and/or customers. Gallo has worked out just such a program with the independently owned wine wholesalers it employs in its marketing channels. In like fashion, sales, purchasing, traffic, and inventory personnel could be exchanged, as well as other line and staff personnel. It has also been possible to work out a sabbatical system similar to that at universities so that certain types of employees can assume temporary positions either closer to or farther from the ultimate market in which the product of their channel is sold. For example, Illinois Central Gulf Railroad conducts employee exchanges with DuPont, U.S. Gypsum, Exxon, and Shell Oil. Similarly, Weyerhaeuser Company has an exchange program with General Electric Company.[73]

While such exchanges require clear guidelines because of the possible disclosure of proprietary information, the participants take back to their home organizations a view of their job in an interorganizational context and a personal and professional involvement in the channel network, as well as added training. In addition to learning something of the complexities of another channel member's organization and mission, participants in such programs have the opportu-

---

[70] The functions and potential impact of the Universal Product Code are addressed in some detail in Chapter 10.

[71] See Louis W. Stern and Patrick J. Kaufmann, "Electronic Data Interchange in Selected Consumer Goods Industries," in Robert D. Buzzell (ed.), *Marketing in an Electronic Age* (Boston: Harvard Business School Press, 1985), pp. 52–73.

[72] For relevant citations, see Louis W. Stern, C. Samuel Craig, and Brian Sternthal, "Conflict Management in Interorganizational Relations," *Journal of Applied Psychology*, Vol. 60 (August 1975).

[73] "Executive Swapping: Experiments Pay Off at Some Major Firms," *Wall Street Journal*, April 24, 1973, p. 1. For a discussion of some of the possible pitfalls in exchange programs, see "When Bureaucrats and Executives Swap Jobs," *Business Week* (February 18, 1980), pp. 99, 103.

nity of meeting with channel counterparts who have the same specific tasks, professions, and interests. These shared tasks form the basis of continuing relationships that are extraorganizational in content and interorganizational in commitment. It is highly likely that positive changes in attitudes toward other channel members will occur as a result. For example, when Levi Strauss broadened its distribution of jeans beyond specialty and department stores to include Sears and Penney, it caused considerable resentment among its former channel partners (for example, Macy's discontinued Levi jeans and Gap Stores narrowed its Levi product line severely[74]). Around the same time, the company also instituted a cooperative advertising program that was perceived by retailers as overly demanding.[75] These policies, among others, threatened to tear apart the distribution network Levi had worked so long and effectively to cultivate. To manage the conflicts, Levi began to provide its major clients with "one-stop-shop" service. Major executives worked on the shop floors of more than 35 major customers to gain an understanding of their operations and problems. Back at headquarters in San Francisco, these executives began serving as "account sponsors," fielding questions and mediating among various divisions.

An exchange-of-persons program in a distribution channel would be of little significance, however, if the only individuals with whom the "exchangee" came into contact were no potential threat to channel cooperation or were already "converted" to an interorganizational view of channel relations. Furthermore, the best type of exchange might involve a transfer not merely of persons but of common enterprises, jointly initiated and carried out on a relatively large scale. That is, optimally, the individuals in the exchange should participate in major projects concerned with policy making within the channel.

Co-optation.   Co-optation is the process of absorbing new elements into the leadership or policy-determining structure of an organization as a means of averting threats to its stability or existence. For example, some members of the Independent Grocers Alliance (IGA) have long used co-optation successfully. A number of wholesalers within the IGA have formed retailer advisory councils. Although the composition and functions of the councils vary from region to region, depending on the desires of the wholesalers serving the retailers in each region, the councils generally meet four times a year with the wholesaler and comprise elected representatives of the retailers in the region. At each meeting, the council members discuss a wide variety of merchandising and logistics subjects and raise questions that concern the retailers they represent. When council members return to their stores, they inform their "constituency" of what happened at the meeting. If a new program was presented, they tell their retailers about it and recommend whether it should be accepted or rejected.[76]

The advantages of co-optation as a conflict resolution strategy are many. Co-optation may bring about ready accessibility among channel members in that it requires the establishment of routine and reliable channels through which information, aid, and requests may be brought. Administration of the channel may become more centralized so that the execution of a broad policy is adapted

[74] Marilyn Chase, "Levi Emerges from Recession with Plan That Helps Boost Profit and Stock Price," *Wall Street Journal*, September 23, 1983.

[75] "Levi Strauss: A Touch of Fashion—and a Dash of Humility," *Business Week* (October 24, 1983), p. 88.

[76] "The Retail Senate," *IGA Grocergram*, Vol. 51 (October 1977), p. 31.

to local market conditions through utilization of the special knowledge of individuals attached to distributive organizations located in diverse markets. Co-optation also permits the sharing of responsibility so that a variety of channel members may become identified with and committed to the programs developed for a particular product or service.

There are, however, some dangers in implementing this device, especially for the co-opting organization. Co-optation makes inroads into the process of deciding goals and means. Not only must the final choice be acceptable to the co-opted channel member(s), but to the extent that co-optation is effective, it places an "outsider" in a position to determine the occasion for a goal decision, to participate in analyzing the existing situation, to suggest alternatives, and to take part in the deliberation of consequences. When in 1979 Chrysler Corporation decided to nominate the president of the United Auto Workers for a seat on its board of directors during its financial crisis, a New Jersey–based automobile dealer organization immediately requested that a Chrysler dealer be added to the board as well.[77] If both labor and dealers are represented on a board, the decision-making powers of a company's management will likely be severely circumscribed. Furthermore, co-optation may be used to create a semblance of communication from others to those in control without effective communications really existing. Manipulated or fictitious co-optation only conceals the need for real communication and influence. Establishing dealer and distributor advisory councils, for example, is merely patronizing if the firms convening such councils pay only lip service to what the participants say. It can also raise legal issues, as pointed out in Exhibit 6–4. In many cases, however, especially for such firms as Prudential Insurance and Belden, these councils or advisory boards have used co-optation in its most effective sense.[78]

Mediation. Mediation is the process whereby a third party attempts to secure settlement of a dispute by persuading the parties either to continue their negotiations or to consider procedural or substantive recommendations that the mediator may make. Mediation essentially involves operating on the field of the conflicting parties in such a way that opportunities or trading moves are perceived that otherwise might not have been perceived. Solutions might be given acceptability simply by being suggested by the mediator. Effective mediation succeeds in clarifying facts and issues, in keeping parties in contact with each other, in exploring possible bases of agreement, in encouraging parties to agree to specific proposals, and in supervising the implementation of agreements. Perhaps one of the most significant roles of a mediator might be to encourage conflicting channel members to disclose their utility functions to each other, since these functions represent risk attitudes and preferences for various outcomes. In fact, it is possible for a mediator to combine channel members' often conflicting utility functions to arrive at an appropriate group (or channel) utility function. This function, which also can take into account the power of the

---

[77] "Chrysler May Face Rush of Candidates for Seats on Board," *Wall Street Journal*, October 29, 1979, p. 14. Apparently, the appointment of the labor leader worked out very well for Chrysler. See Robert L. Simison, "Chrysler Lauds Strong Performance of UAW's Fraser as Board Member," *Wall Street Journal*, March 12, 1981, p. 29.

[78] Industrial distributors have had very positive reactions to advisory councils. See "Why Join an Advisory Council," *Industrial Distribution* (March 1982), pp. 63–65.

individual channel members, can be used to predict outcomes in bargaining situations.[79] Eliashberg and his colleagues have argued,

> the measurement and sharing of information on utilities relative to projected outcomes of . . . negotiations . . . might provide channel members with an input they need to predict the likely negotiation outcome and evaluate its fairness. This should make the bargaining process more efficient and perhaps more effective as well.[80]

A worthwhile investment in industries with a record of distribution conflicts might be to place on retainer respected individuals (e.g., retired judges, professors, and consultants) to mediate with the consent of the parties. Many trade associations attempt to play the role of mediator, but their usually slanted interest makes them inappropriate for the task (not to mention the possible antitrust implications of their actions).

[79] Jehoshua Eliashberg, Stephen A. LaTour, Arvind Rangaswamy, and Louis W. Stern, "Assessing the Predictive Accuracy of Two Utility-Based Theories in a Marketing Channel Negotiation Context," *Journal of Marketing Research*, Vol. 23 (May 1986), p. 102.
[80] *Ibid.*, pp. 108–9.

Arbitration.   Arbitration can be compulsory or voluntary. Compulsory arbitration is a process wherein the parties are required by law to submit their dispute to a third party whose decision is final and binding. In a channel context, the government (or the courts) has arbitrated disputes, as when automobile dealers and manufacturers clash publicly over certain distribution policies. Voluntary arbitration is a process wherein parties voluntarily submit their dispute to a third party whose decision will be final and binding.

An important development regarding this conflict management strategy was enacted under a 1979 Federal Trade Commission order. Airco, a producer of industrial gases, settled FTC antitrust charges by agreeing to permit its distributors to take disputes over purchases of certain Airco products to private arbitration.[81] Under the order, Airco agreed that, among other things, if it refused to sell any gas or welding product to a distributor, the distributor could demand arbitration to determine if Airco's action was in reprisal for the distributor's election to purchase from a supplier other than Airco. The order states that arbitration must be held in accordance with the Commercial Arbitration Rules of the American Arbitration Association unless otherwise agreed by the parties, and that the decision of the arbitrators will be final and binding on both parties. The FTC's directive is far from unique: more and more companies are seeking dispute resolution in private courts because the public courts are jammed with a huge backlog of cases.[82]

It should be noted, though, that the whole question of relying on law and law enforcement to manage conflicts in distribution is suspect, because it is doubtful that permanently legislated solutions can be equitably applied to future conflicts in different channel contexts. As Assael has found, "internal" (intra-channel) conflict resolution has proved, historically, to be more satisfactory, from both a micro and a macro viewpoint, than "external" (legally imposed) resolution.[83]

Adopting Superordinate Goals.   Superordinate goals are those ends that are greatly desired by all those caught in dispute or conflict, that cannot be attained by the resources and energies of each of the parties separately, but that require the concerted efforts of all parties involved.[84] Conflict resolution of a relatively permanent nature requires an integration of the needs of both sides to the dispute so that they find a common goal without sacrificing their basic economic

[81] "Airco Agrees to Settle Disputes with Distributors through Arbitration," *FTC News Summary* (April 13, 1979), p. 3.

[82] See "Center Helps Firms Avoid Litigating Circumstances," *Chicago Tribune*, January 12, 1986, section 7, p. 7; Richard Koenig, "More Firms Turn to Private Courts to Avoid Expensive Legal Fights," *Wall Street Journal*, January 4, 1984, p. 23; and G. Christian Hill, "California Is Allowing Its Wealthy Litigants to Hire Private Jurists," *Wall Street Journal*, August 6, 1980, p. 1. For more details about the use of arbitration in business relationships, including marketing channels, see *Business Law*, Vol. 28 (1973), especially pp. 595, 623.

[83] Henry Assael, "The Political Role of Trade Associations in Distributive Conflict Resolution," *Journal of Marketing*, Vol. 32 (April 1968), pp. 21–28. See also S. Macaulay, "Non-Contractual Relations in Business," *American Sociological Review*, Vol. 28 (1963), pp. 55–70.

[84] Muzafer Sherif, *Social Interaction* (Chicago: Aldine Publishing Company, 1967), p. 457. See also Muzafer Sherif, O. J. Harvey, B. Jack White, William R. Hood, and Carolyn W. Sherif, *Intergroup Conflict and Cooperation: The Robbers Cave Experiment* (Norman, Okla.: University of Oklahoma, 1961), p. 202.

and ethical principles. The difficult task is, obviously, to articulate a goal or common interest on which all parties can agree.

A superordinate goal could be the explicitly agreed-upon resistance by channel members to some outside threat (e.g., competitive, legal) to the channel's survival or growth. In such situations, the channel members may set aside their differences for the sake of defense. Meeting an external threat to the system will serve to displace or transfer hostility among channel members to the "common enemy." However, a major question remains: When the outside threat is removed, will the internal conflicts return? In other words, is the cohesion ephemeral and is the prior conflict among channel members merely postponed?

The unified reaction of channel members to an outside threat can be viewed as a behavior change, and as behavior changes, attitudes are usually altered to become more consistent with the new behavior. These new attitudes may remain once the threat is removed. In addition, during the countering of the threat, information will be exchanged, some of which may have a bearing on sources of conflict beyond that posed by the threat. Because of the information exchanged and because of the monetary and psychological costs jointly borne by the parties while they combat the threat, future relationships between the parties may be significantly different from those during previous interactions. Channel members may gain empathy by seeing, perhaps for the first time, other channel members' points of view, even though these viewpoints are presented in a context different from "normal" circumstances. Finally, the original conflict issues—those present prior to the threat—may decay as energies are directed at the outside threat.

On the other hand, there is a strong possibility that the prior conflict will reemerge unaffected by the temporary unity of the parties. Thus, establishing superordinate goals on the basis of threats from the outside, whether conjured or real, can be a double-edged sword. Extended periods of integrated effort can be achieved only when the institutions and agencies within the channel come to grips with the causes of their conflict and attempt to resolve them. The strategies previously discussed, if employed wisely, could lead channel members to the eventual adoption of *positive* superordinate goals, such as increased efficiency in moving a product through the channel, with the result that greater sales volume is obtained at lower, or at least stable, distribution costs. This goal motivated channel members in the grocery industry to develop electronic data interchange systems in order to reduce lead times (and therefore inventory levels) throughout the channel.

Conflict Management Programs.   Just as no base of power will likely be used in isolation, conflict management strategies must be combined into effective programs. For example, in their explanation of how manufacturers can forge excellent working relationships with industrial distributors, Narus and Anderson suggest several action steps and cite manufacturers who do particularly well in implementing them:[85]

---

[85] James A. Narus and James C. Anderson, "Forging Working Partnerships with Industrial Distributors," Northwestern University Department of Marketing Working Paper, February 1985, pp. 5–8. See also James A. Narus and James C. Anderson, "Turn Your Industrial Distributors into Partners," *Harvard Business Review* (March-April 1986), pp. 66–71.

Action Step	Representative Companies
1. Get out into the field and listen	Timken
	Square D
2. Learn from companywide experience	DuPont
3. Conduct market research studies	Parker Hannifin
4. Establish a distributor council	Dayco
5. Train distributors carefully at the outset of the relationship	DuPont
6. Train own people on how to work well with distributors	Timken
7. Develop sound, multi-level communication systems with distributors	Cherry Electrical
	Dayco
8. Refer customers to distributors	Timken
	DuPont
9. Respond quickly to problems	Cherry Electrical
10. Use selective distribution	Square D
	Parker Hannifin

The best working relationships will take into account almost all of these steps, not simply a few and certainly not just one. For instance, 3M, a company noted for its marketing skills, uses eleven different ways of staying in close contact with and managing conflict in its office products distribution system: (1) association involvement, (2) a dealer advisory council, (3) a program called Business Planning Partners, (4) fieldwork, (5) personal letters, (6) a Market Needs Conference, (7) a Branch Coordinators' Conference, (8) a national office study, (9) market needs research, (10) individual distributor conferences, and (11) informal mini-councils.[86]

THE NEED FOR CHANNEL LEADERSHIP

The most significant output of effective implementation of the four steps of the channel management process is improved performance of the channel system. Indeed, a concomitant result is likely to be increased satisfaction of the members of the system with their roles within it. In their study of retailers' and wholesalers' perceptions of a manufacturer of consumer batteries and ancillary products, Ruekert and Churchill uncovered four dimensions of channel members' satisfaction:

1. A *product* dimension, which reflects the demand for, awareness of, and quality of the manufacturer's products
2. A *financial* dimension, which captures the attractiveness of the arrangement with respect to such matters as intermediary margins and return on investment
3. An *assistance* dimension, which assesses how well the manufacturer supports the intermediary with such aids as cooperative advertising programs and point-of-purchase displays

[86] Presentation by J. P. Wilkins, Marketing Director, Office Products, 3M Company, St. Paul, Minn., 1984.

4. A *social interaction* dimension, which reflects how satisfactorily the interactions between intermediary and manufacturer are handled, primarily through the sales representative servicing the account[87]

Studies of distribution channels have found owner-manager satisfaction to be highly correlated with high levels of organizational performance.[88] Although it is difficult to specify causal relationships between performance and satisfaction (it is not known whether high satisfaction causes high performance, or vice versa), it is possible to assert that effective channel management strategies should produce benefits relative to both variables and thus, in the long run, constitute a key determinant in ensuring the survival and growth of any given channel system.[89]

In order to achieve effective channel management and thus improved coordination and performance within a channel system, it will be necessary to locate an institution or agency within the system that is willing to assume a leadership role—that is, an organization that will use its power bases to aid in overcoming the spontaneous variability of individual channel member behavior and to allocate the resources within the system so as to enhance the system's viability. Thus, channel leadership can be viewed as the use of power to intentionally affect the behavior of other channel members in order to cause them to act in a manner that contributes to the maintenance or achievement of a desired level of channel performance.[90] In fact, control may be required to assure performance.

Channel control is the ability of a channel member to predict events and achieve desired outcomes in his relations with other channel members.[91] Channel control can result from channel leadership. Furthermore, like channel power, the level of channel control achieved by one firm over others in a channel may be issue-specific. For example, while the manufacturer may have control over pricing, retailers may have control over inventory levels in the channel. Whether or not control can be exerted depends, of course, on the power at the command of the channel leader, on the drive for autonomy of the members over whom control is being exerted, and on the latter's tolerance for control. Channel members exhibit different levels of willingness to exert power and to tolerate power exerted by others. Therefore, effective channel management requires that the deployment of power resources to influence other channel members be

[87] Robert W. Ruekert and Gilbert A. Churchill, Jr., "Reliability and Validity of Alternative Measures of Channel Member Satisfaction," *Journal of Marketing Research*, Vol. 21 (May 1984), p. 227.

[88] Hal B. Pickle and Brian S. Rungeling, "Empirical Investigation of Entrepreneurial Goals and Customer Satisfaction," *Journal of Business*, Vol. 46 (April 1973), pp. 268–73. See also Ian F. Wilkinson, "Power and Satisfaction in Channels of Distribution," *Journal of Retailing*, Vol. 55 (Summer 1979), pp. 79–94.

[89] The importance of channel member satisfaction has been particularly stressed by F. Robert Dwyer, "Channel Member Satisfaction: Laboratory Insights," *Journal of Retailing*, Vol. 56 (Summer 1980), pp. 45–65; Shelby D. Hunt and John R. Nevin, "Power in a Channel of Distribution: Sources and Consequences," *Journal of Marketing Research*, Vol. 11 (May 1974), pp. 186–93; Robert F. Lusch, "Franchisee Satisfaction: Causes and Consequences," *International Journal of Physical Distribution*, Vol. 7 (1976), pp. 128–40; and James C. Anderson and James A. Narus, "A Model of the Distributor's Perspective of Distributor-Manufacturer Working Relationships," *Journal of Marketing*, Vol. 48 (Fall 1984), pp. 62–74.

[90] Channel leadership is examined more fully in Chapter 9.

[91] Adel I. El-Ansary and Robert A. Robicheaux, "A Theory of Channel Control: Revisited," *Journal of Marketing*, Vol. 38 (January 1974), pp. 2–7.

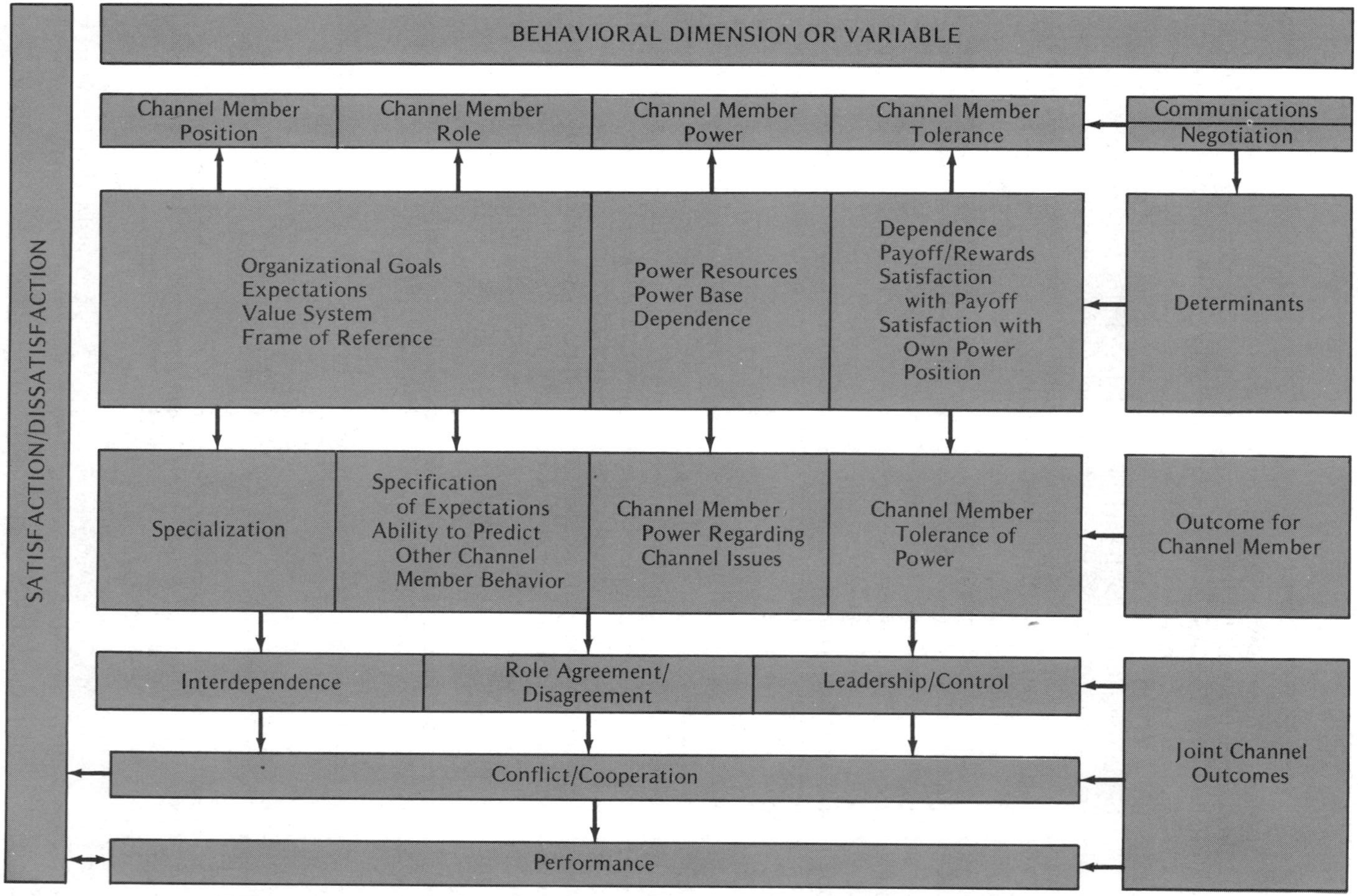

Figure 6–3 A behavioral framework for channel system performance

Source: Adel I. El-Ansary, "Perspectives on Channel System Performance," In R. F. Lusch and P. H. Zinszer (eds.), *Contemporary Issues in Marketing Channels* (Norman, Okla.: The University of Oklahoma Printing Services, 1979), p. 50.

undertaken in magnitudes that are tolerable to them. Channel members are especially likely to relinquish control to another channel member if they attribute their past success to the ability or the effort of that member to make marketing decisions that they perceive to have positively affected their performance.[92]

Certainly, numerous intra- and extrachannel factors will determine how successful leadership attempts can be. Some of these factors include the demand and supply conditions pertaining to each source of power held by the potential channel leader, his efficiency in controlling his resources, the attractiveness of alternatives, the activities of other competitive channels, and developments in the social, political, and economic environment of which the channel in question is a part.

Clearly, the proof of the pudding for channel leadership is whether or not the performance of the channel is strong or weak. Strong channel performance depends on the purposive specification of roles throughout the channel. Thus, channel performance is a result of (1) the effectiveness of channel control and, possibly, (2) the satisfaction or dissatisfaction of channel members with the channel relationship. Channel control is a function of a channel member's power base and resources, the dependency in the system, the actual use of power, the tolerance for control among channel members, the desire on the part of a channel member to influence others, and leadership effectiveness. All of these factors can be combined in a behavioral framework for channel system performance such as the one in Fig. 6–3.

SUMMARY AND CONCLUSIONS

The central theme of this chapter is that a high degree of interorganizational coordination is required within a marketing channel if that channel is to have a long-run impact on the markets it serves.[93] The basic coordinative process involves four key steps:

1. Determining service output levels
2. Delineating roles in the channel
3. Using power to specify roles
4. Dealing with channel conflict

Each is briefly summarized here.

All marketing efforts should begin with assessment of the needs and wants of end-users. It is the responsibility of marketing management to encourage the development of goods and services that will satisfy defined market segments. Once relevant markets have been isolated and appropriate products have been developed and tested, it then becomes critical to ask how the products will be

---

[92] See Punam Anand and Louis W. Stern, "A Sociopsychological Explanation for Why Marketing Channel Members Relinquish Control," *Journal of Marketing Research*, Vol. 22 (November 1985), pp. 365–76.

[93] For an application of the concepts introduced in this chapter to a specific industrial setting (property and casualty insurance) by an industry executive, see F. Dean Hildebrandt, Jr., "The American Agency System: It's More Than a Partnership," *Best's Review*, Vol. 81 (December 1980), pp. 12ff.

made available to potential end-users. To answer this question, it is essential to know the service output levels demanded of the commercial channel by the end-user. Then a channel can be constructed that will deliver these outputs. Important service outputs are lot size, delivery or waiting time, market decentralization, and product variety, among others.

Once the marketing manager knows the service outputs that must be delivered, he can begin to search the firm's environment for potential channel partners capable of generating the outputs. Because the services can be generated only by organizing the marketing flows and functions, the manager must delineate which roles various channel members should perform in the flows. In the specifying of role relationships, a series of prescriptions for role behavior evolves. Role prescriptions indicate the degree of participation each member desires from all channel members in the various marketing flows.

Power generally must be used in a marketing channel to specify appropriate roles, assure role congruence, gain cooperation, and induce satisfactory role performance.[94] Power is the ability of one channel member to get another channel member to do what the latter would not otherwise have done. Power is the inverse of dependence: the more highly dependent one channel member is on another, the more power the latter has relative to the former. Available to channel members are several power bases they may use to evoke change or gain continued cooperation; these include rewards, coercion, expertness, reference, and legitimacy. They are almost invariably used in combination. There is a cost associated with their use, however, which must be an integral part of the analysis in the development of interorganization management programs.

There is a strong likelihood that role performance will deviate, at least occasionally, from prescriptions because of situational factors, differing objectives, communication problems, and differing personal expectations among channel members. More generally, conflict is brought about because of the operational interdependence of channel members. The need to cooperate is juxtaposed with the desire to retain autonomy, and thus channels can be characterized as systems encompassing mixed motives. Channel conflict can be defined as a state in which one channel member perceives another channel member to be engaged in behavior that is impeding or preventing him from achieving his goals. Conflict is caused by incompatibility, domain dissensus, and differences in perceptions of reality as well as by the level of interdependence in the system. It results when there is an imbalance between the rewards a member receives from and the contribution he makes to the channel. Although conflict is a positive social force that breeds adaptation and innovation, it must be managed, because it can prevent a system from achieving effectiveness and efficiency in providing service outputs.

Perhaps one of the most significant functions of channel management is the generation of conflict management strategies, given that conflict is inherent in interorganizational systems. Therefore, employing channel diplomacy, joint membership in trade associations, exchange-of-persons programs, co-optation, mediation, and arbitration, and establishing superordinate goals should prove

---

[94] For empirical results showing the connection between role performance and power, see Gary L. Frazier, "On the Measurement of Interfirm Power in Channels of Distribution," *Journal of Marketing Research*, Vol. 20 (May 1983), pp. 158–66.

highly beneficial. The implementation of these strategies is likely to bring forth more rational and functional collective decision making within the channel.

Channel leadership will likely be a prerequisite to effective interorganization management. It is even possible that control will need to be exercised within the system. The only means remaining for achieving control in certain situations will be vertical integration. There are, however, a number of interorganizational programs that can be enacted prior to actually acquiring a variety of channel institutions and agencies. Such programs (such as franchising and programmed merchandising) are discussed in the next chapter.

DISCUSSION QUESTIONS

1. What is the value of a prescriptive model for the interorganization management of distribution channel systems?
2. Distinguish among the terms *position, role, role behavior, role prescription, role conflict,* and *role consensus.* Develop a diagram of a wholesaler–retailer relationship that highlights the interrelationships of these terms. What other variables must be included in such a diagram to make it a complete description of the relationship?
3. Generate a list of potential sources of conflict in distribution channel relations. Give examples of each of these potential sources by relating them to any channel situation with which you are familiar.
4. "All conflict in channel relations is undesirable." Critically evaluate this statement.
5. Why is the use of power double-edged? Does conflict provoke the use of power, or does the use of power provoke conflict? Of the various bases of power, which would tend to produce less (more) conflict? Why?
6. Describe what you believe should be the executive background requirements and task obligations for the hypothetical corporate position of vice-president—interorganizational relations. For what types of industries, as well as for what types of channel organization, would such a position seem necessary? How might the position's requirements and obligations change as channel structure changes?
7. Develop a list of likely role conflicts within channels of distribution. Discuss how such conflicts are or might be resolved.
8. How is the process of uncertainty absorption related to the amassing of power? When can the process of uncertainty absorption lead to less rather than more power for the absorber?
9. Describe the manufacturer–dealer system in automobiles in terms of power and role relationships. What are the dominant bases of power that are likely to be employed by either party in this channel system?
10. More and more buyers are emphasizing product warranties and product service in their purchasing decisions. However, warranty programs have long been a source of conflict in marketing channels for consumer durables, especially in the appliance, automobile, and television industries, with the ultimate result often being poor warranty program performance. Typically, conflict arises from dealer dissatisfaction with the warranty programs, stemming from such issues as increased dealer parts-inventory costs, the overloading of dealer-service capabilities, and the attendant substandard service levels these problems cause at the consumer level.

    Select any of the industries just mentioned and develop at least *five* specific and realistic manufacturer–dealer conflict issues involving a warranty service program. Then describe what you believe to be the most effective conflict management strategies that might be applied to each issue. Justify your selection.

Appendix 6A

Insights into Channel Coordination from Management Science

The methods outlined in Chapter 6 for achieving channel coordination were drawn mainly from sociology, political science, social psychology, and anthropology—the behavioral sciences. Management scientists, drawing primarily on the fields of economics and game theory, have also begun to study the channel coordination problem. Some of the insights available from this approach are described in this appendix.

Management scientists have tended to focus on bilateral monopoly as the setting in which they address channel coordination problems. In a bilateral monopoly, end-users are supplied by a vertical alignment of two channel members, each a monopolist at its own level. Each member is also assumed to be an independently owned, profit-maximizing organization. The bilateral monopoly setting (or structure) can readily be extended to a channel with three members— a manufacturer, a wholesaler, and a retailer. Assuming that channel members deal only with their successive levels, this three-member case involves two pairs of bilateral monopolists aligned vertically.

Within channels described as a bilateral monopoly, members are independent of each other in the sense that each makes its own decisions on the marketing mix elements, such as the prices to be charged to the subsequent level in the channel. But these choices are obviously interdependent in that one channel member's decision affects the other member's. Because these choices and actions can conflict, they must somehow be coordinated in order to achieve a desirable outcome for the channel as a whole. The problem of how to achieve channel coordination is attacked by the authors of two models to be discussed in this appendix. Both models present economic mechanisms to achieve channel coordination, but under different scenarios, even though both use bilateral monopoly settings.

Clearly, bilateral monopoly settings are vast oversimplifications of the real world. However, the purpose of the models discussed or referenced in this appendix is to examine coordination problems, abstracting away the effects of competition and other environmental factors.

THE JEULAND-SHUGAN MODEL

Jeuland and Shugan have proposed a model of channel coordination in a bilateral monopoly context.[1] In this model, a retailer sells a manufacturer's single

The authors gratefully acknowledge the significant contribution of Shumeet Banerji to the development of this appendix.

[1] Abel P. Jeuland and Steven M. Shugan, "Managing Channel Profits," *Marketing Science*, Vol. 2 (Summer 1983), pp. 239–72.

product. Both channel members are regarded as mutually and equally dependent. It is assumed that both have equal and full information on all factors relevant to their decisions and that there is no uncertainty about these factors. This implies that each firm's costs and revenues as well as the consumer's demand function for the product are common knowledge. The demand function facing the channel is assumed to be downward-sloping, which implies monopoly power, because the retailer, given the absence of competition, has discretion over what price he will charge (and correspondingly what quantity he will sell). The decision variables for the manufacturer and the retailer are the markups (margins) that they will add to their costs.

Some Basic Definitions and Model Formulation

In the notation of Jeuland and Shugan, capital letters are associated with the manufacturer and small letters with the retailer. For the manufacturer and the retailer, let F and f be their total fixed costs, C and c their constant variable costs per unit for the product under study, Π^M and Π^R their profit functions, and G and g their margins. Finally, let $D(p)$ be the consumer demand as a function of retail price p with the condition that $dD/dp < 0$. In other words, the demand curve is downward-sloping.

Manufacturer profits are given by $\Pi^M = GD - F$, and the retailer's profits by $\Pi^R = gD - f$, so that total channel profits are $\Pi^M + \Pi^R = (G + g)D - F - f$. The decision problem for the manufacturer and the retailer is to set their margins, G and g. The channel margins are linked to retail price by the relation $p = G + g + C + c$. In other words, the price to consumers is determined by the margins and the variable costs per unit of both channel members. Fixed costs are not included in price determination, because, by standard economic theory, fixed costs are regarded as sunk.[2]

The Importance of Coordination

If the channel were owned by a single individual, his objective would be to maximize the sum of the manufacturer and retailer profits. The manufacturer and retailer would be directed to set margins, G^* and g^*, consistent with achieving this objective. Their activities would be said to be perfectly coordinated, because they would be consistent with achieving maximum total channel profits. At the joint maximum, $\Pi^M + \Pi^R$ is maximized, and channel members would have the most profits to divide up among themselves.

However, Jeuland and Shugan show that without single ownership or some other form of coordination mechanism, independent channel members are not able to achieve this joint maximum.[3] Essentially, the reason for this is that each party feels it stands to gain some revenue in the short run by raising its margins to higher levels (G^{**} and g^{**}) as long as the other member does not raise its

---

[2] While the basic model presented here uses only margins as channel decision variables, immediate extensions are available by incorporating other decision variables that affect the demand for the product, such as advertising, product quality, or point-of-sale effort. Jeuland and Shugan, *op. cit.*, provide these extensions for quality as a manufacturer decision variable and point-of-sale effort as a retailer decision variable. However, these results are not different in any way, in terms of their implications, from those with only margin setting. Hence, we will discuss only the basic model here.

[3] See *ibid.*, pp. 245–48, for a proof of this proposition.

margin. But each member realizes that it stands to lose a great deal if it holds at the jointly optimal level while the other raises. Hence, the only equilibrium situation is the individually rational choice G^{**} and g^{**}, which leads to joint profits well below that possible with the choices G^* and g^*. If the margin-setting decisions of the channel members are viewed in the context of a noncooperative game, this is the Nash equilibrium of the game. Jeuland and Shugan focus on deriving a coordination mechanism that will tie both channel members to jointly optimal margins.[4]

Mechanisms for Coordination

Jeuland and Shugan discuss several mechanisms by which channel coordination might be achieved. One option is vertical integration. If the channel were owned by either of the channel members, the owner would presumably dictate the optimal levels of the decision variables. But for a variety of reasons, vertical integration may not be feasible.[5] Another alternative is for channel members to enter into contracts that bind them to the jointly optimal levels of the decision variables. In practice, though, such contracts can probably never include all relevant decision variables, and even if they can, they may be impossible to monitor. It is possible, however, that rigid interventions such as vertical integration and contracts may not be necessary. If, in the course of everyday interaction in business, channel members learn something about the decision rules used by their partners and if they incorporate this learning into their decision making so that implicit understandings are formed between them, then some of the benefits of coordination may accrue as part of the process.[6]

One way to make the objectives of individual channel members consistent with that of joint profit maximization would be to compensate them on the basis of joint profits rather than via individual profit maximization. Jeuland and Shugan argue that this can be accomplished by instituting a system of profit sharing. Each channel member receives a share of overall channel profits and therefore decides to maximize that amount. The share to be received would have to be negotiated and fixed in advance.

Expressed differently, profit sharing would imply profit functions for the manufacturer and retailer of the following form:

$$\Pi^M = k_1((G + g)D) + k_2 - F \quad \text{and}$$
$$\Pi^R = (1 - k_1)((G + g)D) - k_2 - f \tag{1}$$

Recall that $(G + g)D$ are overall or joint channel revenues. k_1 is the fraction, $0 < k_1 < 1$, of joint revenues that is received by the manufacturer. In addition,

---

[4] Coordination problems of this nature arise even in channels with multiple levels or when retailers carry several products. See *ibid.*, pp. 248–49.

[5] Jeuland and Shugan suggest three reasons vertical integration may be infeasible: (1) if vertical integration means the retailer carries the product(s) of one manufacturer alone, the reduction in the assortment of products available at the store may make it undesirable to consumers; (2) there may be legal constraints to vertical integration; (3) the owner-manager of the channel may not be able to manage all aspects of channel operations with the same efficiency as decentralized and specialized channel members. See *ibid.*, p. 250.

[6] In fact, it can be shown that when channel members form implicit understandings, profits and margins are closer to the jointly optimal levels than they are in the Nash equilibrium. See *ibid.*, pp. 251–53. For a complete development of this issue, see Steven M. Shugan, "Implicit Understandings in Channels of Distribution," *Management Science*, Vol. 31 (April 1985), pp. 435–60.

the manufacturer receives k_2, a constant payment (such as a franchise fee) if k_2 is positive, or incurs a constant cost (such as a continuous rebate to the retailer) if k_2 is negative. The retailer keeps a fraction $(1 - k_1)$ of channel revenues and pays (receives) the fixed amount k_2 if $k_2 > 0$ ($k_2 < 0$). k_1 and k_2 are direct outcomes of negotiations between the channel members.

Π^M, Π^R, and $\Pi^M + \Pi^R = (G + g)D - F - f$ are linearly related through the constants k_1 and k_2. This ensures that the conditions for their maximization will be compatible. Put differently, decisions that maximize Π^M or Π^R in (1) are in complete conformity with the maximization of $\Pi^M + \Pi^R$, which is the goal of coordination. However, while profit sharing is a theoretically appealing mechanism, the question arises of whether, and how, it can be implemented. Jeuland and Shugan show that quantity discount schedules, where manufacturers offer a lower per-unit price for larger quantities purchased by the retailer, represent such a mechanism.

To see how quantity discounts work to achieve profit sharing, consider the case where a manufacturer offers no discounts and receives a constant margin G on each unit sold by the retailer. If the retailer is to sell additional units, he can do so only by reducing the retail price—his own margin. Because the retailer bears the brunt of reducing the retail price, additional units up to the joint profit maximizing volume are not sold, and thus, additional profits are foregone. Now, if the manufacturer shares these additional profits with the retailer by reducing the cost of additional units to him, the retailer has an incentive to sell the additional units. In effect, starting at the inoptimal individually rational margins G^{**} and g^{**}, if both channel members reduce their margins to the points G^* and g^*, the joint profit-maximizing volume is sold, and joint profits are maximized and shared between them. At these margins, it does not pay to reduce G or g any further, because the volume gained by doing so is insufficient to justify the revenue lost.

It can be seen that as the volume sold is increased above that corresponding to G^{**} and g^{**}, the per-unit price to the retailer is reduced (until G^*). This is, in actuality, a quantity discount schedule, and the use of such a schedule results in the sharing of the "additional" profit. Of course, not every quantity discount schedule will do; the schedule must be such that it results in profit sharing of the kind specified in (1), linking individual profits to total channel profits. Jeuland and Shugan show that the schedule must take the form

$$t(D) = [k_1(p(D) - c - C) + (k_2/D)] + C \qquad (2)$$

where $t(D)$ is the per-unit price paid by the retailer to the manufacturer as a function of quantity sold; D, k_1, and k_2 are as defined earlier; and $p(D)$ is the inverse function of $D(p)$. Recall that the price paid by the retailer to the manufacturer is $G + C$, so that $t(D) - C = G = [k_1(p(D) - c - C) + (k_2/D)]$. The component of this price that varies with quantity sold is the margin, G. And, by the definition of retail price, $p = (G + C + g + c) = (t + g + c)$. The schedule $t(D)$ is derived from the expressions in (1). Hence, by substitution, it can be shown that the use of this schedule leads to manufacturer, retailer, and total profits being related in the manner required by (1).

In order to interpret the schedule in (2) clearly as a sharing rule, let us rewrite it by collecting terms in the form

$$t(D) = k_1 p(D) + (1 - k_1)C - k_1 c + (k_2/D) \qquad (3)$$

The schedule $t(D)$ simultaneously operationalizes revenue and cost sharing. First, note that a proportion k_1 of the final per-unit price, $p(D)$, is paid to the manufacturer. Second, note that per-unit costs C and c are also shared between the two parties. The retailer absorbs a proportion $(1 - k_1)$ of the manufacturer's cost, C, while the manufacturer absorbs a proportion k_1 of the retailer's cost, c. In addition, the manufacturer receives (pays) the fixed amount k_2 if $k_2 > 0$ ($k_2 < 0$). k_2 is indeed a fixed payment independent of D, because $t(D)$ is a per-unit price that must be multiplied by D to yield revenues.[7]

THE ZUSMAN-ETGAR MODEL

Zusman and Etgar present a model of a three-level (manufacturer-wholesaler-retailer) channel where the actions of the parties are coordinated by contractual means.[8] In their model, one party, say the wholesaler, is responsible for making decisions on behalf of another party, say the manufacturer, in return for some kind of payment. Very generally, such an arrangement is called a *contract*. In economics, this class of problems is referred to as the *theory of the principal and agent*.[9] The focus is on finding the payment scheme that makes an agent perform in the best interests of a principal under certain conditions. The authors derive the contracts between successive pairs in the channel that provide the optimal incentives for action.

The conditions on which the contracts in this model depend are related primarily to the issues of whether—and if so, when and by whom—the demand conditions facing the channel are known. Thus, the Zusman-Etgar model incorporates two major issues in modern economics—*uncertainty* and *information*.

It is assumed that when contracts are being formed (i.e., when the optimal payment scheme is being negotiated between parties), demand conditions, θ, are not known with certainty. At best, the players share a common probabilistic assessment of the conditions likely to prevail. If there is uncertainty in the model, it becomes necessary to account for the risk attitudes of the players, because chance plays a part in the realization of planned outcomes.

The informational problem is as follows. Subsequent to contract formation, it is assumed that the final agent, the retailer, always knows what demand conditions prevail at the time of sales decisions. The wholesaler and, further up the channel, the manufacturer can observe the quantity sold by the retailer. But depending on whether demand conditions, θ, can or cannot be observed by the

---

[7] K. Sridhar Moorthy points out, however, that a quantity discount schedule is not the *only* mechanism by which channel coordination can be achieved. Essentially, any mechanism that sets the retailer's effective marginal cost at the level of the channel's marginal cost, $C + c$, will do, because by setting marginal revenue equal to this cost, the retailer will pick the optimal price and quantity. For example, the manufacturer could set a price equal to his constant marginal cost, C, and negotiate with the retailer over the (fixed) amount to be paid in addition by way of profit sharing. See K. Sridhar Moorthy, "Managing Channel Profits: Comment," *Marketing Science*, in press.

[8] Pinhas Zusman and Michael Etgar, "The Marketing Channel as an Equilibrium Set of Contracts," *Management Science*, Vol. 27 (March 1981), pp. 284–302.

[9] For an excellent nontechnical introduction to this subject, see Kenneth J. Arrow, "The Economics of the Agency," in John W. Pratt and Richard J. Zeckhauser (eds.), *Principals and Agents: The Structure of Business* (Boston: Harvard Business School Press, 1985). This essay also has a bibliography on the subject.

principal, different types of contracts will result.[10] It is important to pay close attention to these contracts (or payment schedules). They are the sole means by which coordination can be achieved such that the sales decisions of the retailer are in the best interests of the wholesaler (and the decisions of the wholesaler are in the best interests of the manufacturer). If the retailer's interests are divergent from those of the wholesaler, but θ can be observed, a contract can be devised that provides the retailer with the appropriate incentives, permits rewards for risk bearing, and yields optimal actions for the principal. But if θ is not observable, even the best contract possible yields outcomes that are worse than those under full information.

Model Formulation and Results

Zusman and Etgar derive the optimal contracts between successive pairs in the three-level channel. This treatment amounts to a representation of the channel as a pair of vertically aligned bilateral monopolies.[11] Contracts between any two channel members are viewed as the outcome of negotiations in the framework of a two-person cooperative game. Nash bargaining theory is used to derive the contract. Nash bargaining is a cooperative game-theoretic method of predicting the outcome of a negotiation between self-interested individuals.[12]

A contract here has a very narrow and strict interpretation. The sole contractual problem is to derive a payment schedule from one channel member to another that solves the Nash bargaining game. Such a schedule must address two problems. One is to find the *incentives* that make the agent in a principal-agent relationship act in the best interests of the principal. The other is the problem of finding the best way to compensate the agent for *risk bearing*. Hence, the twin objectives are to find optimal incentives and a mechanism to ensure that the riskiness implied by the uncertain environment is shared optimally between the

[10] When one party in a negotiation has complete information on a parameter of interest and another does not, a situation called *asymmetric information* obtains.

[11] Zusman and Etgar, *op. cit.*, actually account for multiple wholesalers and retailers. But in their basic model the demand facing a given retailer is assumed to be independent of the other retailers, making each retailer a virtual monopolist. For a treatment of the case where retailers have interdependent demand, see *ibid.*, pp. 300–302.

[12] The concept of Nash bargaining should not be confused with the concept of Nash equilibrium used in the McGuire-Staelin model in Appendix 5C and the Jeuland-Shugan model just described. The Nash equilibrium is a noncooperative solution concept for games where players make decisions knowing that the decisions of other players affect them, so that they are interdependent. Nash bargaining is a model of cooperative game theory that aims to predict the outcomes of negotiations between players or the solution to a bargaining game. John Nash showed that the only solution that meets a particular set of requirements is the point on the *agreement frontier* (a collection of the possible points of agreement) that maximizes the product of the differences between each party's utilities from agreement and disagreement. So if two players, A and B, are bargaining over their payoff, X_a and X_b, and their payoffs if they fail to agree are D_a and D_b, the determinate solution to the game are the values that

$$\text{maximize } (X_a - D_a)(X_b - D_b)$$
$$X_a, X_b$$

For a lucid nontechnical discussion of Nash bargaining, see Samuel B. Bacharach and Edward J. Lawler, *Bargaining: Power, Tactics, and Outcomes* (San Francisco: Jossey-Bass Publishers, 1981), pp. 6–17. For details, see John F. Nash, Jr., "The Bargaining Problem," *Econometrica*, Vol. 18 (1950), pp. 155–62.

principal and the agent. The contract must be based on some parameters related to the productive activity of the agent that can be observed by both the principal and the agent. These parameters (called *monitors*) are sales and the demand conditions revealed at the time of the sales decisions.

The manufacturer-wholesaler contract has a form very similar to that of the wholesaler-retailer contract; hence, we will only examine the latter relation here. Consider the case where both monitors, the retailer's sales, q, and the demand conditions, θ, are observable by the wholesaler. The retailer's profits are:

$$\Pi^R = R(q,\theta) - v(q,\theta) \tag{1}$$

where R(q, θ) is the net revenue function—the gross revenue net of the retailer handling cost—and $v(q, \theta)$ is the retailer payment schedule. The retailer's utility is assumed to depend solely on his profits; i.e., $V = V(\Pi^R)$. As long as the utility function, V, is well behaved, the utility-maximizing choice of quantity sold is the same as the profit-maximizing choice. Given $v(q,\theta)$ and demand conditions, θ, the retailer will equate marginal revenue to marginal cost, or,

$$\frac{\partial R}{\partial q} = \frac{\partial v}{\partial q} \tag{2}$$

The wholesaler's profits are given by:

$$\Pi^W = v(q, \theta) - Cq - Wq \tag{3}$$

where C and W are the per-unit handling and procurement costs of the wholesaler. The wholesaler's utility is assumed to depend on his profits alone; i.e., $U = U(\Pi^W)$.

If the retailer and wholesaler fail to reach an agreement, their (disagreement) payoffs are assumed to be t^R and t^W, respectively. As pointed out earlier, the retailer payment schedule is the outcome of bargaining between the parties. According to Nash, the solution to the bargaining game is obtained by finding the function $v(q, \theta)$ that maximizes the expression

$$\Gamma(v) = [E_\theta(V) - t^R][E_\theta(U) - t^W] \tag{4}$$

subject to the condition in (2), where $E_\theta(V)$ and $E_\theta(U)$ are the expected utility of the retailer and wholesaler. Zusman and Etgar show that the optimal retailer payment schedule $v(q, \theta)$ that solves (4) is given by

$$v(q, \theta) = (C + W)q + \beta(\theta) \tag{5}$$

$\beta(\theta)$ is a function related to demand conditions and the risk attitudes of the wholesaler and retailer. It is a mechanism by which income variation due to fluctuations in demand is absorbed by the channel members in some proportion depending on their risk attitudes. The retailer payment schedule has the important property of combining marginal cost pricing via the first term with optimal risk sharing via the second term. Marginal cost pricing (by the standard arguments of microeconomics) induces the retailer to sell optimal quantities for the system. But the additional risk-sharing term provides the incentives necessary for the retailer to perform the selling function in an uncertain environment.

The risk-sharing term in (5) depends upon demand conditions θ being observable by the wholesaler. Under asymmetric information, when the wholesaler cannot observe θ, he must depend on the observable monitor q to improve the contract. Zusman and Etgar show that under these circumstances employing the retailer payment schedule,

$$\hat{v}(q) = (C + W)q + \beta + \alpha(q - \bar{q}) \tag{6}$$

leads to an increase in the value of the maximand in (4), thereby improving the contract. Notice that in (6), the payment to the retailer is a function only of q because θ is not observable. α is a positive coefficient, and $\bar{q}$ is the mean level of sales. The $\alpha(q - \bar{q})$ term in (6) is necessary in order to improve the risk-sharing properties of the contract.

In the absence of information on θ, the wholesaler must depend on the variation of q about its mean level $\bar{q}$ to compensate the retailer for risk bearing. But the result is a distortion of incentives; now, the retailer not only pays some per-unit price $(C + W)$ but also pays (or is paid) $\alpha(q - \bar{q})$. Marginal cost pricing, represented by $(C + W)$, yields an efficient level of sales, but in order to improve risk sharing it becomes necessary to distort those prices via the term $\alpha(q - \bar{q})$.

This tradeoff between the incentive mechanism and the risk-sharing mechanism is a direct result of incomplete information and yields a so-called second-best contract. Under full information, the contract relies on q for optimal incentives and on θ for optimal risk sharing. When θ is not observable, the contract must rely on q for both, and hence the loss. As a result, overall profits and sales are lower while final prices are in general higher under second-best.

CONCLUSION

Two economic models employing bilateral monopoly settings and addressing the issue of coordinating the actions of channel members are presented in this appendix. The Jeuland-Shugan model presents the case that without a coordination mechanism, individually rational actions by channel members fail to achieve a situation that is jointly optimal for the channel. The model shows that cost and revenue-sharing mechanisms are an important way to attain the joint optimum, and a particular form of quantity discount schedule is found to be a workable profit-sharing mechanism.

Zusman and Etgar incorporate the phenomena of uncertainty and incomplete information in their model. They derive the nature of pricing schemes that induce actions by agents in channel dyads that are in the best interests of principals. Like Jeuland and Shugan, they find that sharing rules are beneficial to channel performance.

Questionnaire Items Used to Measure Channel Conflict

GOALS DIVERGENCE

1. The leading manufacturer often wants to prod dealers to buy more products than are good for the dealers.
2. The manufacturer often complains that dealers prefer maintaining their professional status over improving their modes of operation.
3. The manufacturers often demand that dealers concentrate fully on their brands, while it is to the dealer's advantage to add major sidelines to his business.
4. A major function of a dealer is to advise and counsel its customers as to which products they should choose while manufacturers consider dealer's major function to be developing contacts with buyers and sellers.
5. Manufacturers are often too concerned with market shares to ensure proper profitability for their products.
6. Manufacturers often do not recognize that there is an optimal size for retailers' operations and that expanding beyond that brings the retailer losses and not profits.

DRIVE FOR AUTONOMY

1. My leading manufacturer influences strongly my choice of other suppliers.
2. In this industry, through couponing, discounting, and advertising, etc., manufacturers practically dictate to dealers the type of promotion the latter will use in their stores.
3. Most of the dealers selling in this channel are forced to adjust their inventories according to the decision of the manufacturers.
4. In this industry retailers have little choice on pricing but to follow manufacturer's suggested retail price.

COMPETITION OVER CHANNEL RESOURCES

1. The manufacturer restricts considerably dealers' use of cooperative advertising monies.
2. The manufacturer often allocates insufficient share of choice items to a dealer.

Source: Michael Etgar, "Sources and Types of Intrachannel Conflict," *Journal of Retailing*, Vol. 55 (Spring 1979), pp. 76–78.

3. The manufacturer often ties-in less desirable items with orders for choice items.
4. The manufacturer and his dealers often disagree about the size of territories allocated to the dealers.
5. Allocation of shelf space/showroom space is a major issue of negotiations between the manufacturer and his dealers.
6. The manufacturer often attempts to sell directly to large accounts and in this way to circumvent the dealers.
7. The manufacturer does not allow too many dealers to operate in one territory.

ROLE CLARITY

1. In this industry, the duties of the manufacturers and dealers are well defined; only rarely is it not known who should perform a specific function.[a]
2. In this industry there is no agreement as to who should pay for merchandise damaged on the way to the retailer.
3. My leading manufacturer has clear-cut rules about returning unsold merchandise.[a]
4. With some bargaining, dealers get better credit terms from their suppliers.

NONFULFILLMENT OF ROLES BY MANUFACTURERS

1. In this industry, manufacturers often attempt to take over activities which rightfully belong to the dealers.
2. Production innovation by the manufacturer is relatively poor.
3. My leading manufacturer provides enough sales assistance (advertising, salesmen training, etc.) to his dealers.[a]
4. The product line provided by the manufacturer is broad enough to allow his dealers to compete effectively in the market.[a]
5. The manufacturer often prices his products too high and reduces the competitive advantage of the dealers.
6. The delivery scheduling of the products by the manufacturer leaves much to be desired.

NONFULFILLMENT OF ROLES BY DEALERS

1. The manufacturer often complains that dealers do not stock enough of his items.
2. The manufacturer has few complaints about the aggressiveness of the dealers' sales people.[a]
3. The manufacturer is highly satisfied with the servicing provided by his dealers to the customers.[a]
4. The manufacturer often complains that the dealers do not promote his products sufficiently.

[a] Ratings were reversed.

5. The manufacturer is in general very satisfied with the quality of dealer's sales force.[a]

PERCEPTIONS DIVERGENCE

1. In my opinion, the leading manufacturer treats his dealers very fairly.[a]
2. Dealers are often more knowledgeable about their market than manufacturers expect.
3. A manufacturer and dealer often view each other as rivals where one can only gain at the expense of another.
4. The manufacturers in this industry erroneously think that they are irreplaceable.
5. Manufacturer and dealers often have different opinions about the real nature of competition in this industry.
6. The manufacturer rarely helps the dealer when competition in his area is getting rough.

EXPECTATIONS DIVERGENCE

1. Manufacturers usually expect their products to perform better than they actually do.
2. The manufacturer and dealers often have different opinions about the future of this industry.
3. The manufacturer often relies too much on planned operations and is not ready to adjust rapidly to changing market conditions.
4. The manufacturers rely too much on their own promotional campaigns.

INTRACHANNEL COMMUNICATIONS NOISE

1. My leading manufacturer often does not bother to inform his dealers early enough about out of stock items or discontinuation of models.
2. Manufacturer's salesmen and detail men are well equipped to serve dealers promptly.[a]
3. The manufacturer is often late in informing dealers about the introduction of new products.
4. In this industry, dealers often aggravate manufacturers by cancelling early orders.
5. Dealer's complaints are well taken care of by the manufacturer.[a]
6. Orders forwarded to the manufacturer often get mislaid or misdirected.

[a] Ratings were reversed.

CHAPTER SEVEN

Organizational Patterns in Marketing Channels

A traditional or conventional marketing channel can frequently be described as a piecemeal coalition of independently owned and managed institutions, each of which is prompted by the profit motive but little concerned about what goes on before or after it in the distributive sequence. As McCammon notes:

> Goods and services in the American economy have historically been distributed through highly fragmented networks in which *loosely* aligned manufacturers, wholesalers, and retailers have bargained with each other at arm's length, negotiated aggressively over terms of sale, and otherwise behaved autonomously. For the most part, the firms participating in these provisional coalitions have traditionally operated on a relatively small scale and performed a conventionally defined set of marketing functions.[1]

From an interorganization management perspective, such coalitions have no inclusive goals. The locus of decision making and authority is exclusively at the unit or individual channel member level. There is no formally structured division of labor, and commitment is only to one's own organization. In fact, there is little or no prescribed systemwide orientation of the members.[2] The members are almost totally self-oriented as they pursue their goals.

[1] Bert C. McCammon, Jr., "Perspectives for Distribution Programming," in Louis P. Bucklin (ed.), *Vertical Marketing Systems* (Glenview, Ill.: Scott, Foresman and Co., 1970), p. 43.
[2] The basis for this perspective can be found in Roland L. Warren, "The Interorganizational Field as a Focus for Investigation," in M. B. Brinkerhoff and P. R. Kunz, *Complex Organizations and Their Environments* (Dubuque, Iowa: Wm. C. Brown Co., 1972), p. 316.

In contrast with the conventional channel, vertical marketing systems can be described as

> professionally managed and centrally programmed networks [that are] preengineered to achieve operating economies and maximum market impact. Stated alternatively . . . vertical marketing systems are rationalized and capital intensive networks designed to achieve technological, managerial, and promotional economies through the integration, coordination, and synchronization of marketing flows from points of production to points of ultimate use.[3]

Thus, the emergence of vertical marketing systems implies the existence of a power locus in the system that provides for channel leadership, role specification, coordination, conflict management, and control.

In this chapter, the organization and design of such systems are explained in some detail. Comparisons and contrasts between conventional marketing channels and the various types of vertical systems (administered, contractual, and corporate) are enumerated. To provide a basis for comparison, it is first necessary to briefly elaborate on the organization of conventional channels.

CONVENTIONAL MARKETING CHANNELS

As mentioned, conventional marketing channel networks generally comprise isolated and autonomous units, each of which performs a traditionally defined set of marketing functions. Coordination among channel members is achieved primarily through bargaining and negotiation. The operating units within such channels are frequently unable to achieve systemic economies. Furthermore, there is usually a low index of member loyalty and relatively easy entry to the channel. The network, then, tends to be relatively unstable. As Etgar points out,

> firms at each level only concern themselves with the distribution of a product to the next adjacent level. [Conventional channels] are coordinated through the operation of prices and the related modes of market mechanisms; the types and variety of products to be handled, levels of promotion, and location of retail outlets are determined by the interaction of manufacturers and distributors as buyers and sellers in intermediary markets.[4]

Within conventional channels, there are a large number of decision makers who tend to be preoccupied with cost, volume, and investment relationships at a *single* stage of the marketing process. Decisions are often tradition-oriented, and decision makers are frequently emotionally committed to established patterns of operation and interaction.

The distribution channel for motion pictures provides an excellent example of the dysfunctional consequences of conventional channel organization.[5]

[3] McCammon, *op. cit.*, p. 43.

[4] Michael Etgar, "Effects of Administrative Control on Efficiency of Vertical Marketing Systems," *Journal of Marketing Research*, Vol. 13 (February 1976), p. 12.

[5] Gene Siskel, "Five Powerful Pieces Set into Place," *Chicago Tribune*, February 23, 1975, section 6, pp. 2, 3, 8. Copyrighted 1975, Chicago Tribune Company, all rights reserved, used with permission. See also Paul Hirsch, "Processing Fads and Fashions: An Organization-Set Analysis of Cultural Industry Systems," *American Journal of Sociology*, Vol. 77 (January 1972), pp. 639–59.

The commercial channel for movies comprises companies that make movies (producers), distributors, and theater owners. Prior to 1948, the channel was almost totally integrated: the companies that made the movies also owned the theaters that played them. In 1948, the United States Supreme Court ordered the five major film production-distribution companies to divest themselves of their movie theaters.[6] Since 1948, the locus of power in the channel has shifted from the distributor to the theater owner and back to the distributor:

> At first, the new, independent theater chains were able to bully producers and distributors suddenly bedeviled by television. In recent years, however, the distributors have gained the upper hand. With fewer and fewer pictures being made, the movie world has become a seller's market. The distributors have a limited number of films to rent, and the theater owners are competing furiously with each other to land the few prize attractions.[7]

"There has never been any love lost between the major distributors (companies like Universal, Twentieth Century–Fox, and United Artists) and theater owners," Siskel reports. "For example, one Chicago representative of a distribution company has been quoted as telling a theater owner, 'If you make any money on this deal, I'm not doing my job right.'"[8]

While the remark by the representative is obviously facetious, the actions taken by distributors show that there is considerable truth behind it. Apparently, the drive for a good cash-flow position stimulates distributors to ask theater owners to give them advances or guaranteed money *before* a picture even opens. As a consequence, the public suffers, because only the large downtown movie houses and a few shopping center theaters are able to afford the large, first-run, advance-guarantee costs. Smaller theaters are squeezed. Particularly disadvantaged are people who live near the small theaters typically located between downtown and the suburbs.

Furthermore, the major distributors are much less active as producers than they were some years ago. They still produce some pictures on their own (Twentieth Century-Fox Film Corporation and *Star Wars*), but they also frequently participate with independents under various percentage-of-profit arrangements. In many cases, the "majors" rent their lots and equipment to, and distribute pictures produced by, independent companies. Often the stars and directors form their own companies to produce one or more pictures, with distribution through a major company. Clearly, though, this places the majors in an even more powerful position. When producers Michael Douglas and Saul Zaentz took the script of *One Flew Over the Cuckoo's Nest* to the major studios for backing, they were turned down by every one of them. Only when United Artists acquired the *finished* film from Douglas and Zaentz was it assured any distribution at all.[9]

Suboptimization within the marketing channel for movies has severely impaired the output of the channel from the consumer's perspective. Certainly, distributors could use their power in more constructive ways to provide for more effective competition vis-à-vis television, but rather than practice interorganiza-

[6] *United States v. Paramount Pictures, Inc.*, 334 U.S. 131 (1948). Also see *Theatre Enterprises, Inc. v. Paramount Film Distributing Corp.*, 346 U.S. 537 (1954).

[7] Siskel, *op. cit.*, p. 2.

[8] *Ibid.*

[9] Tom Shales, "The Selling of 'Cuckoo's Nest,'" *Morning Advocate* (Baton Rouge, La.), April 19, 1976, p. 6-C. (Copyrighted story by *The Washington Post*, 1976.)

tion management, distributors are obviously maximizing their own interests and thereby engendering a high degree of conflict within the channel. In his excellent article, Siskel describes additional evidence of myopic behavior by distributors, the existence of which has placed both the consuming public and the theater owners in somewhat untenable positions.[10] As a reaction, a countervailing force has emerged within the channel in the form of the Association of Specialized Film Exhibitors. The association comprises 34 members who run art theaters all over the United States. One of the major goals of the association is to improve the availability of films for its membership.

The efforts of the Association of Specialized Film Exhibitors aside, the behavior of the theater owners has been as questionable, from the consumers' perspective, as that of the producer-distributors. After the 1948 Supreme Court decision, when the major Hollywood studios settled antitrust suits by agreeing to sell their movie houses, theater owners ended up controlling the only picture shows in town. As the easy profits eventually rolled in, many owners lost touch with their customers, milking the business and letting their theaters deteriorate. The success of videocassettes and pay TV in converting moviegoers to stay-at-homes is forcing the theater owners to recognize their negligence. No longer the only shows in town, the theaters suffered a 12 percent drop in attendance in 1985.

It would seem that the distributors and the theater owners would combine forces to combat their "common enemies" (e.g., network television, pay TV, videocassettes, and cable TV), but instead they have spent most of their energies fighting each other over the division of box office revenues. The major producers (with the obvious approval of the distributors who control them) have tried to reduce their dependence on theaters by investing in the videocassette and pay TV markets. In fact, they increased production so much in order to chase those markets that they created a glut. Like wolves, the theater owners seized on the oversupply to negotiate a larger share of the box office receipts. Rather than cooperating to make the most of the business they share, the members of the marketing channels for motion pictures have been at each other's throats, and moviegoers have suffered the consequences.[11] In fact, the only route to channel management being traveled is a throwback to the pre-1948 days—vertical integration.[12] Encouraged by freely available capital and a relaxed regulatory environment, Hollywood's studios have taken increasingly daring steps to gain control of movie and television distribution. Television stations have been acquired by Fox, MCA, and Lorimar-Telepictures Corporation, and studios, such as Columbia and Paramount as well as MCA, have bought theaters—and a few have seriously considered buying a television network.

[10] Siskel, op. cit.

[11] See Stratford P. Sherman, "Movie Theatres Head Back to the Future," *Fortune* (January 20, 1986), pp. 90–94. The chaos faced in the motion picture business has spread to videocassettes, cable TV, network television, and almost all facets of film distribution. For excellent examples of the failure of conventional channels to organize distribution properly, see Laura Landro, "Movie Studios Put More Emphasis on Home-Video, Pay-TV Markets," *Wall Street Journal*, May 1, 1984, p. 37; "The Networks Produce Some Panic in Hollywood," *Business Week* (August 6, 1984), pp. 90–92; "Pay-TV: Even HBO's Growth Is Slowing," *Business Week* (July 9, 1984), pp. 40–42; "How TV Is Revolutionizing Hollywood," *Business Week* (February 21, 1983), pp. 78–89; and Stratford P. Sherman, "Coming Soon: Hollywood's Epic Shakeout," *Fortune* (April 30, 1984), pp. 204–16.

[12] Michael Cieply and Peter W. Barnes, "Movie and TV Mergers Point to Concentration of Power to Entertain," *Wall Street Journal*, August 21, 1986, p. 1.

Conventional marketing channels rely heavily on unrestricted open-market forces, especially via the price mechanism, to bring about a division of labor among channel members. Such channels are, in terms of numbers, among the most common forms of distribution in capitalist societies. However, these channels may run into severe problems, particularly when human failings, such as opportunistic tendencies and bounded rationality, are combined with technological and environmental complexities and uncertainties. As we saw in Chapter 5, Williamson argues that the economic and sociopolitical costs of transacting business across unrestricted markets become very high when there is a high degree of uncertainty facing the members of conventional channels due to environmental changes (e.g., new regulations, shortages, slow growth, competition from other channels, and technological breakthroughs) coupled with opportunistic modes of exchange among the members. In such cases, conventional channels begin to lose their viability.[13]

Several significant modes of channel organization have emerged as ways to eliminate or penalize the suboptimization that frequently exists in conventional channels and thus to improve channel effectiveness and efficiency. Each limits open-market activities so that transaction costs—defined very broadly to include the costs associated with the allocation of marketing activities and the establishment of the terms of trade among channel members—are held to reasonable levels. The modes of channel organization are, in Williamson's terms, *governance structures*.[14] The type of governance structure employed depends, to a significant extent, on three variables: (1) the frequency of interaction among channel members, (2) the degree of uncertainty facing each of the members and the channel as a whole,[15] and (3) the extent to which channel members have incurred transaction-specific (nonmarketable) expenses in order to do business with one another. Thus, the more frequent the interaction, the more uncertain the environment, and the more the investments required are idiosyncratic to the specific exchange relationship, the more rapidly channels will move towards tighter and more comprehensive forms of governance. We shall discuss each of the channel organization modes in turn, starting with the least integrated (in a formal, ownership sense) and moving by steps to the most highly integrated form. It should be noted at the outset, however, that as one moves closer to formal vertical integration, there are powerful tradeoffs between the control achieved *and* the investment and bureaucracy required to maintain the system.

ADMINISTERED SYSTEMS

Administered vertical marketing systems are one step removed, in an analytical sense, from conventional marketing channels. In an administered system, coor-

[13] Oliver E. Williamson, *Markets and Hierarchies: Analysis and Antitrust Implications* (New York: The Free Press, 1975). See also Louis W. Stern and Torger Reve, "Distribution Channels as Political Economies: A Framework for Comparative Analysis," *Journal of Marketing*, Vol. 44 (July 1980), pp. 52–64; and Etgar, *op. cit.*, pp. 12–24.

[14] See Oliver E. Williamson, "Transaction-Cost Economics: The Governance of Contractual Relations," *Journal of Law and Economics*, Vol. 22 (October 1979), pp. 233–61.

[15] For an excellent study supporting the relationship between environmental uncertainty and channel organization, see F. Robert Dwyer and M. Ann Welsh, "Environmental Relationships of the Internal Political Economy of Marketing Channels," *Journal of Marketing Research*, Vol. 22 (November 1985), pp. 397–414.

dination of marketing activities is achieved through programs developed by one or a limited number of firms. In such systems, administrative strategies combined with the exercise of power are relied on to obtain systemic economies. Successful administered systems are conventional channels in which the principles of effective interorganization management have been correctly applied.

In administered systems, units can exist with disparate goals, but a mechanism exists for informal collaboration on inclusive goals. Decision making takes place by virtue of the effective interaction of channel members in the absence of a formal inclusive structure. The locus of authority remains with the individual channel members. The latter are structured autonomously but are willing to agree to an *ad hoc* division of labor without restructuring. As in conventional channels, commitment is self-oriented, but there is at least a minimum amount of systemwide orientation among the members.[16]

Marketing channels can be fully administered (i.e., all aspects of the system can be "programmed") or they may be partially administered (i.e., only a few of the marketing flows are purposively managed). In either case, the channel qualifies as an administered system. Here are some prominent examples:

- Grocery wholesalers, such as Fleming Companies, Super Valu, Malone & Hyde, and Wetterau, provide independent retail grocers with a variety of services, such as shelf management programs, retail accounting programs, and pricing assistance. They help their retailers to plan, buy, and maintain scanning equipment. They have private label programs, store development programs, and store location and construction programs. Their sales service representatives counsel retailers on promotion and advertising, merchandise display, store layout, space management, and the like.

- Inland Steel offers a computer system that customers can use to order steel and to check their order as its shipping date nears. The immense complexity of steelmaking makes it hard to predict when a made-to-order batch of steel will emerge from the mill. To reduce the uncertainty—and the amount of costly inventory that Inland and its customers maintain as a cushion—Inland spent ten years constructing a $20 million production scheduling and monitoring system that is the most advanced in the industry. Inland's prompt, reliable steel deliveries supposedly produce inventory savings large enough to offset the average 10 percent cost advantage held by Japanese suppliers, who are slower to deliver made-to-order steel because it spends at least a month in transit.

- Frito-Lay's 9500-member store–door delivery sales force enables the company to go to individual retail outlets, clear out unsold merchandise, and restock shelves with fresh merchandise as often as 55 times a year in some stores.

- In 1980, State Farm unveiled a system that its agents could use to automate their businesses. Besides keeping the books, the system provides agents with a few simple but powerful marketing tools. For example, it can sort through the records of customers for those holding automobile but not homeowner's insurance and automatically print out letters offering to expand their coverage.

- Sears administers its relationships with almost all of its suppliers. In fact, very few suppliers would have the power to administer Sears. (An exception was Levi Strauss, when Levis were first made available to Sears in the early 1980s.) For example, in white goods (washing machines, refrigerators, etc.), Sears accounts for almost one in every three machines sold. Sears sells an appliance to over half of the

---

[16] See Warren, *op. cit.*, p. 316.

customers who step through its doors to shop there.[17] It's not surprising that it dominates its relationships with its white-goods suppliers.

- American Airlines' Sabre system, introduced in 1976, enables travel agents to summon information about American and other airlines' flights, make reservations, and print tickets and itineraries. The system also automates the agencies' bookkeeping. Since Sabre's introduction, travel agents have doubled their share of total bookings, from 35 percent to 70 percent, and in agencies equipped with Sabre, American has gained 12 to 20 percentage points in market share.[18]

- Kraft has developed facilities management programs to administer the allocation of space in supermarket dairy cases. Kraft's power stems the company's 60 percent share of dairy case volume, exclusive of milk, eggs, and butter.

- Building Marts of America (BMA), primarily a wholesaler, offers a choice of five computer systems designed by BMA specifically for retailers who sell and inventory lumber and building materials; profit planning, asset and credit management, gross margin control, and inventory control systems; property, casualty, and group medical insurance coverage; and business perpetuation counseling via employee stock-ownership programs.

- Wrigley has become a "front-end merchandising expert." In 1980, it adopted a five-point strategy: (1) ensure that checkout merchandising continues to flourish; (2) be an objective source of data on all products merchandised at the checkout, even though they compete with Wrigley for space; (3) stress return on inventory investment as the fairest and most objective way to compare the performance of items merchandised at the checkout; (4) provide superior display fixtures for retailers to better merchandise their checkout area; and (5) do continuing research at the retail store level in order to constantly increase its knowledge of the area. Between 1981 and 1986, Wrigley has had considerable influence, as a result of this and other marketing programs, over the checkout merchandising programs in virtually every major food, drug, convenience, and mass merchandiser chain in the country. Its market share increased over 12 points and its volume over 16 percent during this period.[19]

The list could go on and on, to include such activities as General Foods' Scanlab, which takes information from scanners and develops profiles of individual retail stores by adding to it demographic and economic data; American Hospital Supply's order-entry system, referred to numerous times in this text; Genuine Parts' organization of the NAPA auto parts system; General Electric Credit Corporation's financing plans for wholesalers and retailers; McDonald's purchasing arrangements with its suppliers (forged primarily on the basis of gentlemen's agreements, not by contracts); Fisher-Price's shelf management planograms for discount stores; O. M. Scott's merchandising programs for the sale of lawn-care products; Milliken's (a textile manufacturer) customized computer graphics system for interior designers to use in inventing their own carpet patterns; and Gallo's joint selling programs with wine distributors.

[17] William L. Wilkie and Peter R. Dickson, "Shopping for Appliances: Consumers' Strategies and Patterns of Information Search," Marketing Science Institute Working Paper Series, Report No. 85-108 (Cambridge, Mass.: Marketing Science Institute, 1985), pp. 26–27.

[18] Peter Petre, "How to Keep Customers Happy Captives," *Fortune* (September 2, 1985), pp. 43–44.

[19] Presentation by Ronald O. Cox, group vice president of marketing, Wm. Wrigley Jr. Company, at J. L. Kellogg Graduate School of Management, Northwestern University, February 18, 1986.

In developing an administered system, one must usually couple expert power with reward power. The channel members to be influenced must first be convinced that the "administrator" (1) is trustworthy and (2) knows more about the situation than they do. They must then be given incentives to do what the administrator would like. Appendix 7A lists some concessions available to consumer goods suppliers who are seeking to gain support for their marketing programs. Appendix 7B lists some of the requirements of industrial distributors who consider entering into administered arrangements with their suppliers. And Appendix 7C lists the elements that IBM believes marketing channels add to their products and that it attempts to administer in its relationships with its dealers, value-added resellers (VARs), and other third parties that sell its products.

A major mechanism used to motivate channel members to enact specific programs or activities in administered systems is the *functional discount system.* These systems set up payment schedules for levels of participation in the marketing flows. For example, a manufacturer of medical equipment and supplies, in an attempt to encourage the performance of specific activities that would generate appropriate service outputs for end-users, adopted the following strategy to administer the dealer channel through which its products sold. The manufacturer changed its policy from one where it simply gave its dealers 40 percent off of the list price to one where it paid directly for services rendered. In a letter sent to all dealers, the manufacturer explained that the concept it was instituting (a functional discount system) "uses a value added principle that rewards dealers for services which we feel are essential to improving market penetration and preserving end-user satisfaction of our exclusive range of brand name products." Exhibit 7–1 details the "value-added principle" outlined by the manufacturer.

One of the most innovative approaches to developing administered systems has been the programmed merchandising agreement. Under this arrangement, manufacturers formulate specialized merchandising plans for each type of outlet they serve.

> Programmed merchandising is a "joint venture" in which a specific retail account and a supplier develop a comprehensive merchandising plan to market the supplier's product line. These plans normally cover a six-month period but some are of longer duration.[20]

Such programming generally involves the activities listed in Exhibit 7–2 for each brand and for each store included in the agreement. Manufacturing organizations currently engaged in programmed merchandising activities include General Electric (on major appliances), Baumritter (on its Ethan Allen furniture line in nonfranchised outlets), Sealy (on its Posturepedic line of mattresses), Villager (on its dress and sportswear lines), Scott (on its lawn-care products), and Haines (on its L'eggs pantyhose).

If the supplier and distributor are to develop effective merchandising programs, their relationship must be characterized by a high degree of cooperation. Planning, communication of intentions, and coordination of effort are impera-

---

[20] McCammon, *op. cit.,* p. 48.

EXHIBIT 7–1 Example of a functional discount system

All dealers will receive a *20%* discount from published suggested retail price lists. Value added incremental discounts will be awarded upon field and written verification for services as follows:

	VALUE ADDED DISCOUNT
*1. Dealers with salespeople who routinely and personally visit, call on, and promote our products to at least fifteen percent (15%) of the end-users in the dealer's trading area	10%
*2. Provide a catalog that is distributed to at least 80% of your customer base in which all our major products are featured.	02%
3. Maintain an inventory of our products that represents no less than sixty (60) days of estimated or historical annual sales and at least one item of equipment for demonstration or display.	05%
4. Offer open account privileges to all responsible customers and provide financing or leasing alternatives for large purchases.	02%
5. Dealers who annually schedule at least one (1) week of detailing with us and organize not less than two (2) clinics per year where at least twelve (12) end-users are present at each clinic (held either in the store or at a location convenient to the attending end-users), the cost for which to be paid by the dealer.	02%
6. Provide a reasonable parts inventory and employee capability to handle routine returns, exchanges and warranty replacement and repair.	01%

Note: Only one can be considered for value added additional discount.

---

tives.[21] This places an administered or programmed system in sharp contrast with a conventional marketing channel, as pointed out in Table 7–1. As Ernst has observed,[22] the key benefits to various channel members from engaging in programmed merchandising are:

TO THE SUPPLIER

- The development of maximum sales and profit potential without competing for it on a day-to-day basis
- Continuity of promotion and sales for more economic scheduling of production and distribution activities

[21] Ronald L. Ernst, "Distribution Channel Detente Benefits Suppliers, Retailers, and Consumers," *Marketing News* (March 7, 1980), p. 19.
[22] *Ibid.*

**EXHIBIT 7–2 Plans and activities covered
in programmed merchandising agreements**

1. Merchandising Goals
   a. Planned sales
   b. Planned initial markup percentage
   c. Planned reductions, including planned markdowns, shortages, and discounts
   d. Planned gross margin
   e. Planned expense ratio (optional)
   f. Planned profit margin (optional)

2. Inventory Plan
   a. Planned rate of inventory turnover
   b. Planned merchandise assortments, including basic or model stock plans
   c. Formalized "never out" lists
   d. Desired mix of promotional versus regular merchandise

3. Merchandise Presentation Plan
   a. Recommended store fixtures
   b. Space allocation plan
   c. Visual merchandising plan
   d. Needed promotional materials, including point-of-purchase displays, consumer literature, and price signs

4. Personal Selling Plan
   a. Recommended sales presentations
   b. Sales training plan
   c. Special incentive arrangements, including "spiffs," salesmen's contests, and related activities

5. Advertising and Sales Promotion Plan
   a. Advertising and sales promotion budget
   b. Media schedule
   c. Copy themes for major campaigns and promotions
   d. Special sales events

6. Responsibilities and Due Dates
   a. Supplier's responsibilities in connection with the plan
   b. Retailer's responsibilities in connection with the plan

Source: Bert C. McCammon, Jr., "Perspectives for Distribution Programming," in Louis P. Bucklin (ed.), *Vertical Marketing Systems* (Glenview, Ill.: Scott, Foresman and Company, 1970), pp. 48–49.

- Improved sales forecasting ability for manufacturing and distribution planning
- Achievement of maximum product exposure by middlemen
- Achievement of a totally coordinated, planned, and controlled marketing approach to reach the end-user
- Clearly specified middleman inventory requirements, thus allowing inventory management and control efficiencies

Table 7–1 Comparison of characteristics of supplier-distributor relationships in a conventional channel versus a programmed system

Characteristics	Conventional Channel	Programmed System
Nature of contacts	Negotiation on an individual order basis	Advanced joint planning for an extended time period
Information considered	Supplier sales presentation data	Distributor's merchandising data
Supplier participants	Supplier's territorial salesperson	Salesperson and major regional or headquarters executive
Distributor participants	Buyer	Various executives, perhaps top management
Distributor's goals	Sales gain and percent markup	Programmed total profitability
Supplier's goal	Big order on each call	Continuing profitable relationship
Nature of performance evaluation	Event centered; primarily related to sales volume and other short-term performance criteria	Specific performance criteria written into the program

Source: Ronald L. Ernst, "Distribution Channel Detente Benefits Suppliers, Retailers, and Consumers," *Marketing News* (March 7, 1980), p. 19. Published by the American Marketing Association.

TO THE DISTRIBUTOR (WHOLESALER OR RETAILER OR BOTH)
- Adequate and timely availability of merchandise
- Preferential consideration from key resources
- Assortment planning and merchandise control assistance
- Clearly specified inventory investment requirements
- The security of merchandising on a price maintained basis
- High levels of vendor service with regard to product quality and general account maintenance
- Economy and efficiency through shifting functions, such as ordering, to the supplier

An example provided by Ernst in his discussion of programmed merchandising is the Norwalk (Ohio) Furniture Corporation.[23] Norwalk is one of the few upholstery-furniture manufacturers that can guarantee 30-day delivery on all special orders, due to a unique type of manufacturing facility. The company instituted a total-effort dealer program containing the following key elements:

1. Total-effort dealers agree to display Norwalk furniture in nine out of ten upholstered-furniture room settings.
2. Total-effort dealers agree to operate on a special-order basis and not sell floor samples that would jeopardize future sales.

In turn, Norwalk:

1. Guaranteed 30-day delivery
2. Provided customized ad materials, catalogs, and extra-large fabric swatches
3. Conducted an annual factory-authorized sale

[23] *Ibid.*

4. Provided floor plan financing
5. Provided an advertising allowance
6. Conducted sales meetings for floor sales personnel
7. Provided in-store merchandising assistance

Because all dealer sales are made on a custom-order basis with 30-day guaranteed delivery, the only inventory the dealer needs to carry is in floor samples. Also, because all sales under the program are special orders, the dealer typically experiences higher gross margins as a result of the reduced risk of carrying poor-selling items. Markdowns are minimized, and lower warehousing and handling costs are achieved.

The concept of administering channels by implementing systemic programs is also being applied in the logistics field. For example, Ryder System has instituted a program that eliminates several intermediate warehousing operations for its truck-leasing customers. Ryder offers its trucks as rolling warehouses. Newly manufactured goods usually go first into the manufacturer's warehouse, next are shipped to a retailer's warehouse, and then are shipped once again either to the store or to the retailer's customer. This process often leads to a minimum of six loadings and unloadings into warehouses before the goods get to their final destination. By using trucks as warehouses, and thereby minimizing loadings and unloadings while speeding up the shipment cycle, Ryder claims it can reduce a customer's trucking needs by 20 percent.[24]

CONTRACTUAL SYSTEMS

Often organizations desire to formalize role obligations within their channels by employing legitimate power as a means of achieving control. In these situations, vertical coordination is frequently accomplished through the use of contractual agreements. According to Thompson:

> Independent firms at different levels can integrate their programs on a contractual basis to achieve systemic economies and an increased market impact. . . . Contractual integration occurs where the various stages of production and distribution are independently owned, but the relationships between vertically adjacent firms are covered in a contractual arrangement.[25]

Whereas virtually every transaction among businesses and between businesses and individuals is covered by some form of contract, either explicit or implied, the primary function of the contracts in these vertical marketing systems is that they specify, in writing, the marketing roles to be assumed by each party to the contract.[26]

[24] "Marketing When the Growth Slows," *Business Week* (April 14, 1975), p. 50. Another logistics company that has administered its channels in a unique and profitable way is CAST, a Canadian shipping company. See James O'Shea, "Rival Calls U.S. Shippers Lazy," *Chicago Tribune*, April 20, 1980, section 5, pp. 1, 2.

[25] Donald N. Thompson, "Contractual Marketing Systems: An Overview," in D. N. Thompson (ed.), *Contractual Marketing Systems* (Lexington, Mass.: D. C. Heath, Lexington Books, 1971), p. 5.

[26] For an excellent example, see Rex Chainbelt's Distributor Sales Agreement for the Bearing Division, reproduced in Appendix 5A.

Contractual integration takes a variety of forms, as shown in Exhibit 7–3. However, the three principal forms are wholesaler-sponsored voluntary groups, retailer-sponsored cooperative groups, and franchise systems. The focus here is primarily on these three forms.

From an interorganization management perspective, contractual vertical marketing systems can be viewed as networks in which the members have disparate goals but where there exists some formal organization for inclusive goals. Decision making is generally made at the top of the inclusive structure but is subject to the ratification of the members. The locus of authority in such networks resides primarily (but not exclusively) with the individual members. The latter are structured autonomously, but will generally agree to a division of labor that may in turn affect the basic structure of the channel. In such networks, norms of moderate commitment to the channel system exist, and there is at least a moderate amount of systemwide orientation among the members.[27] Clearly, along each of these dimensions, contractual systems are more tightly knit than administered systems. To a significant extent, channel members are willing to trade some degree of autonomy to gain scale economies and market impact.

Voluntary and Cooperative Groups

A wholesaler, by banding together a number of independently owned retailers in a voluntary group, can provide goods and support services far more economically than these same retailers could secure solely as individuals. Perhaps the most well known wholesaler-sponsored voluntary is the Independent Grocers Alliance (IGA). In the hardware field, Pro, Liberty, and Sentry are examples of wholesalers who provide retail establishments with services similar

[27] Warren, *op. cit.*, p. 316.

to those found in the IGA system. Other examples of voluntary groups are found in the automobile accessory market (Western Auto) and in the notions and general merchandise market (Ben Franklin). The principal services provided by seven major hardware voluntaries and buying groups are shown in Table 7–2.

Automatic Service, Genuine Parts, Super Valu, Malone & Hyde, and Canadian Tire are other leading proponents of the voluntary group concept. Automatic Service sponsors a voluntary group program for vending machine operators. Genuine Parts is the largest member of the NAPA (auto parts) network, and Super Valu and Malone & Hyde are leading voluntary group wholesalers in the food field. Canadian Tire is a large voluntary group wholesaler that supplies affiliated stores with a variety of lines, including automotive parts and accessories, hardware, housewares, small appliances, and sporting goods. A typical Canadian Tire outlet contains approximately 25,000 square feet of space and carries over 20,000 items in inventory.

Table 7–2 Principal services provided by seven major hardware wholesaler-sponsored voluntary groups and wholesaler buying groups

	Sentry	Trustworthy	Pro	Gamble-Skogmo	Coast To Coast	Stratton & Terstegge	American Wholesale Hardware Company
Store Identification	yes	yes	yes	yes	yes	yes	yes
Telephone Ordering	yes	yes	*	yes	yes	yes	yes
Microfiche	yes	yes	yes	yes	no	yes	yes
Catalog Service	yes	yes	yes	yes	yes	yes	yes
Circular Programs	yes	yes	yes	yes	yes	yes	yes
Private Label Merch.	yes	yes	*	yes	yes	yes	no
Merchandising Aid	yes	yes	yes	yes	yes	yes	yes
Basic Stock Lists	*	yes	yes	yes	yes	yes	yes
Direct/Drop Ship Programs	yes	yes	yes	yes	yes	yes	yes
Pool Orders	yes	yes	yes	yes	yes	yes	yes
Consumer Advertising	yes	yes	yes	yes	yes	yes	yes
Co-Op Advertising Programs	yes	yes	yes	yes	yes	yes	yes
Advertising Planning, Aid	yes	yes	yes	yes	yes	yes	yes
Reprinted Order Forms	yes	yes	yes	yes	yes	yes	yes
Data Processing Programs	yes	yes	yes	yes	yes	yes	yes
Inventory Control Systems	yes	yes	yes	yes	yes	yes	yes
Accounting Services	*	yes	no	yes	yes	yes	*
Mgmt. Consultation Services	yes	yes	yes	yes	yes	yes	*
Employee Training	*	*	yes	yes	yes	yes	yes
Dealer Meetings	yes	yes	yes	yes	yes	yes	yes
Volume Rebates/Dividends	yes	yes	yes	no	yes	yes	yes
Store Planning, Layout	yes	yes	yes	yes	yes	yes	yes
Financing	*	yes	*	yes	yes	no	yes
Insurance Programs	no	yes	yes	yes	yes	yes	yes
Field Supervisors/Slsmen	yes	yes	yes	yes	yes	yes	yes
Dealer Shows	yes	yes	yes	yes	yes	yes	yes

* Limited service, or offered by some member wholesalers.

Source: Hardware Age Survey of Hardware Wholesalers, Hardware Age Verified Directory of Hardlines Distributors, *Hardware Age* (October 1979), p. 79.

The retailer-sponsored cooperative is also a voluntary association, but the impetus for the cooperative comes from the retailers rather than from a wholesaler. The retailers organize and democratically operate their own wholesale company, which then performs services for member retailers. The members receive rebates at the end of the year based on their cumulative purchases from the cooperative. Historically, retailer-sponsored cooperatives have been important in the marketing of foods (e.g., Topco Associates, Associated Grocers, and Certified Grocers). For example, Topco Associates is owned cooperatively by a group of supermarket chains and grocery wholesalers located in various markets throughout the country. Topco's central function is to serve its owner-member companies in the purchasing, product development, quality control, packaging, and promotion of a wide variety of private-label (controlled-brand) food and nonfood products. Its brands include Top Frost, Gaylord, and Food Club, among others. Its owner-members represent over $3 billion in retail sales volume, and include such firms as Big Bear Stores in Columbus, Ohio; Dillon Stores in Hutchinson, Kansas; and Fred Meyer in Portland, Oregon.

Retailer-sponsored cooperatives have also become prominent in the hardware business, where they now account for approximately 35 percent of total wholesale sales. Thumbnail sketches of the two largest, Cotter and Ace, are given in Exhibit 7–4.

Except for ownership differences, wholesaler- and retailer-sponsored contractual systems operate in much the same ways. Members join with the understanding that they will purchase a substantial portion of their merchandise from the group and will standardize retail advertising, identification, and operating procedures as necessary to conform with those of the group to obtain economies and better impact. Members usually contribute to a common advertising fund and operate stores under a common name.

These contractual systems are not new forms of channel organization. Voluntary and cooperative groups emerged in the 1930s as a response to the appearance of chain stores. However, the scope of the cooperative effort has expanded from concentrated buying power to the development of a vast number of programs involving centralized consumer advertising and promotion, store location and layout, training, financing, accounting, and in some cases a total package of support services. For example, Malone & Hyde serves 1600 stores in 15 southern states and is the nation's fifth largest food wholesaler, outranked by two voluntaries, Super Valu Stores and Fleming Companies, and by two retailer-sponsored cooperatives, Certified of California and Wakefern Foods. It has achieved its strong position by instituting efficient, innovative procedures that enable it to serve its customers better. Some of these procedures are as follows:

- When Malone & Hyde's customers place an order, it is accompanied by a signed blank check, virtually eliminating the wholesaler's collection problems and giving it the use of cash for several extra days. This procedure allows Malone & Hyde to pay cash for whatever it buys.

- Using electronic inventory devices, supermarket operators can place an entire week's order directly with the Malone & Hyde computer in minutes by telephone instead of waiting for a salesman to visit. Groceries in all but one of the firm's nine warehouses are stacked according to family groups, just like the groceries in supermarket aisles. This means that orders can be filled without backtracking by warehouse workers.

COTTER & COMPANY, CHICAGO

Cotter has 11 distribution centers that serve as the axis of a sprawling operation that includes its own manufacturing facilities, 22 retail stores owned outright, a finance company, a real estate agency, and a wholesale subsidiary operating on a cash-and-carry basis. With over 6000 member-dealers buying at least something every week from one of its warehouses, Cotter has put its famous True Value sign up over roughly one out of every five hardware stores in the country. Its sales are over $1.5 billion. Cotter prides itself on keeping its distribution costs low and on its national advertising program. To join, a retailer must operate a hardware store or know of an investment opportunity in a market without a True Value member, purchase ten shares of Class A voting stock at $100 each, and agree to order a minimum quantity of goods on a weekly basis. Cotter has full lines of private-label goods in hand tools (Master Mechanic), paint (Tru-Test), plumbing (Master Plumber), electrical (Master Electrician), outdoor power equipment (Lawn Chief), and lawn and garden supplies (Green Thumb). Cotter manufactures lawn-mowers, paint, lawn and garden wheel goods, and electric heaters in its own factories.

ACE HARDWARE CORPORATION, OAK BROOK, ILL.

Ace has grown into the second largest dealer-owned distributor in the hardware industry, covering all 50 states and delivering goods to over 4000 retailers. 1983 sales were $733 million. With roughly 38,000 SKUs available out of warehouse, Ace probably offers about the broadest product selection of any dealer-owned hardware distributor. Like other dealer-owned distributors, Ace is governed by a board of directors consisting of Ace retailers elected regionally. Ace members order via electronic order entry. Ace offers semiannual dealer shows, ongoing dealer education programs, and regular weekly delivery of merchandise. Warehoused items are available to members at distributor cost plus 10 percent. Seasonal and promotional items are available at cost plus 6 percent. Ace dealers can also buy from manufacturers on a drop-ship basis at handling charges ranging between 0 and 2 percent. Because it uses a cost-plus pricing method, the rebate it gives its members is smaller than other dealer-owned wholesalers not using an identical system. Ace offers its dealers purchase analysis reports, preprinted price tickets, bin tags, and other services designed to enable dealers to control costs. Ace requires dealers to invest $5000 in corporate stock on a pay-as-you-go basis.

Source: Adapted from *Hardware Age* (October 1983), pp. 52, 58.

- The company has developed a labor-saving system whereby cases in the warehouse are stacked on a cart that can be rolled directly onto a truck, into the supermarket, and down the aisles.
- In addition to distributing food and other items to the retailer, the company provides the retailer with such services as store design, site location, insurance, inventory and accounting controls, and group advertising.

- The company will lease a site location and turn it over to an independent operator. It will also sell the operator equipment and initial inventory on credit and may also inject a sizable amount of operating cash into the store. In return, the new owner-operator completely commits to the store whatever assets he has.[28]

Contractual systems have experienced phenomenal growth. For example, IGA now operates more stores than A&P, and Super Valu outlets' annual sales are higher than Kroger's. In fact, nationally, the share of grocery store sales enjoyed by voluntary and cooperative groups combined is equal to that held by corporate chains. One of the reasons for this successful growth is the "clarity of total offer" made possible by the implementation of systemwide programs. Once customers sees the store sign, they clearly understand the outlet's marketing orientation, including the product, service, and atmosphere.[29]

Generally, wholesaler-sponsored voluntary groups have been more effective competitors than retailer-sponsored cooperatives, primarily because of the difference in channel organization between the two. In the former, a wholesaler can provide strong leadership, because he represents the locus of power within the system. In a retailer-sponsored cooperative, power is diffused throughout the membership, and therefore role specification and concomitant allocation of resources are more difficult to accomplish. In the voluntary groups, the retail members have relinquished some of their autonomy by making themselves highly dependent on specific wholesalers for expertise. (Recall from Chapter 6 that the more one party depends upon another, the more power the latter has relative to the former.) In retailer cooperatives, individual members tend to retain more autonomy and thus tend to depend much less strongly on the supply unit for assistance and direction.

Before we turn to perhaps the most popular form of contractual vertical marketing system—franchising—we should note that one other type of cooperative has played a major role in distribution in the United States—the farm cooperative.[30] While the subject of the emergence and growth of farm cooperatives could fill an entire textbook, suffice it to say here that organizations such as Farmland Industries, Associated Milk Producers, Agway, and Land O'Lakes have become extremely powerful forces in behalf of their memberships in organizing both the farm equipment and supply market as well as the markets into which farmers sell their produce. By the late 1970s, dairy co-ops commanded an 80 percent share of the wholesale dairy market and agricultural co-ops were marketing 37 percent of the nation's cotton crop. On the supply side, co-ops had a 42 percent share of the retail fertilizer market, a 40 percent share of the farm petroleum market, and a 40 percent share of the retail market for agricultural chemicals. While some farm coops have vertically integrated both backward and forward within their marketing channels, they are primarily wholesalers of

[28] Richard A. Shaffer, "Why Farm-Price Dips Don't Help You Much at the Grocery Store," *Wall Street Journal*, May 8, 1975, pp. 1, 17. Reprinted by permission of The Wall Street Journal, © 1975 Dow Jones & Company, Inc. 1975. All rights reserved.

[29] For an excellent description of Super Valu's operation, see Bill Saporito, "Super Valu Does Two Things Well," *Fortune* (April 18, 1983), pp. 114–18.

[30] For an excellent discussion of the power of farm cooperatives, see "The Billion-Dollar Farm Co-ops Nobody Knows," *Business Week* (February 7, 1977), pp. 54ff. On the other hand, consumer cooperatives have never achieved significant power in U.S. distribution. See "Consumer Co-ops Win Some Aid," *Business Week* (July 31, 1978), p. 105.

goods and services, and they administer the channels that they control with the approval of the farmers who own them.

During the 1980s, however, farm cooperatives fell on hard times. Declining revenues and soaring interest expenses brought huge operating losses for even the largest and healthiest co-ops. The downturn led to major efforts at slashing overhead costs, selling off manufacturing assets, and merging operations.[31] These poor results can partly be explained by the mission of the farm cooperatives. Because these co-ops place primary emphasis on expanding markets for their farmer-members, they probably do not do as good a job as independent organizations at looking for return on their investments. As an executive of Land O'Lakes, the largest dairy cooperative, put it, "a cooperative doesn't diversify just to make money. We are restricted to doing those things that favorably affect the farmer-owners."[32]

Franchise Systems

Franchise systems constitute a major component of the distribution structure of the United States. In 1985, sales of goods and services by all franchising companies exceeded $529 billion. Approximately 33 percent of all U.S. retail sales flow through franchisees or company-owned units in franchise chains. There are roughly half a million establishments in franchise-related businesses. Including part-time workers and working proprietors, over 5.6 million people are employed in these businesses.[33] Franchise arrangements take many forms, as shown in Exhibit 7–5. The number and sales of franchised outlets by type of franchised system for 1983 are presented in Table 7–3.

Perhaps one of the most confusing problems in understanding contractual vertical marketing systems is the term *franchise* itself. *Franchising* generally refers to a specific way of getting into business and ensuring a revenue stream once outlets are established. It involves such things as royalty payments, fees, and initial charges that *franchisees* pay to *franchisors*. There are, however, lots of franchise arrangements that do not involve such cumbersome transactions. In these cases, someone (a manufacturer or a wholesaler, usually) *franchises* (authorizes) retailers or dealers to be part of his system of selective or exclusive distribution. Payment to the organizer of the system is generally through the gross margins received on the sale of merchandise to the "authorized franchise outlets." Businessland stores are authorized franchise outlets for IBM personal computers; in contrast, the local McDonald's restaurant is most likely a franchisee of McDonald's Corporation. In both cases the retailers are independent businessmen, and in both cases a contract exists that specifies roles. But the systems are very different in terms of the financial and managerial arrangements that bind the parties. In the former instance, the relationship between Businessland and IBM is forged with respect to specific products trademarked by IBM that it sells outright to Businessland. In the latter case, McDonald's relationship with its franchisees involves an entire business format that McDonald's instructs its franchisees to use. On the other hand, over 45 percent of franchise

---

[31] "The Golden Years Are Gone for Farm Co-ops," *Business Week* (July 23, 1984), pp. 156–59.

[32] Quoted in *ibid.*, p. 157.

[33] Data on franchising were obtained from U.S. Department of Commerce, International Trade Administration, *Franchising in the Economy 1983–85* (Washington, D.C.: U.S. Government Printing Office, 1985), pp. 1, 14.

EXHIBIT 7–5 Types of franchise systems

TYPE	EXPLANATION
Territorial franchise	The franchise granted encompasses several counties or states. The holder of the franchise assumes the responsibility for setting up and training individual franchisees within his territory and obtains an "override" on all sales in his territory.
Operating franchise	The individual independent franchisee who runs his own franchise. He deals either directly with the parent organization or with the territorial franchise holder.
Mobile franchise	A franchise that dispenses its product from a moving vehicle, which is either owned by the franchisee or leased from the franchisor. Examples include Country Store on Wheels and Snap-On Tools.
Distributorship	The franchisee takes title to various goods and further distributes them to subfranchisees. The distributor has exclusive coverage of a wide geographical area and acts as a supply house for the franchisees who carry the product.
Co-ownership	The franchisor and franchisee share the investment and profits. Examples include Denny's Restaurants.
Comanagement	The franchisor controls the major part of the investment. The partner-manager shares profits proportionately. Examples include TraveLodge and Holiday Inn in the hotel and motel business.
Leasing	The franchisor leases the land, buildings, and equipment to franchisees. Leasing is used in conjunction with other provisions.
Licensing	The franchisor licenses the franchisee to use his trademarks and business techniques. The franchisor either supplies the product or provides franchisees with a list of approved suppliers.
Manufacturing	The franchisor grants a franchise to manufacture its product through the use of specified materials and techniques. The franchisee distributes the product, utilizing the franchisor's techniques. This method enables a national manufacturer to distribute regionally when distribution costs from central manufacturing facilities are prohibitive. One example is Sealy.
Service	The franchisor describes patterns by which a franchisee supplies a professional service, as exemplified by employment agencies.

Source: Based on Gerald Pintel and Jay Diamond, *Retailing*, 4th ed. (Englewood Cliffs, N.J.: Prentice-Hall, 1987), pp. 73–76.

system sales are made by automobile and truck dealers (see Table 7–3), yet these types of franchises possess only a few of the characteristics of a full-fledged, business-format franchisor/franchisee program. White and Bates argue that auto and truck dealers

> are really highly elaborate forms of authorized dealerships and should be excluded when developing a true understanding of the franchising phenomenon.[34]

As pointed out in detail in Chapter 8, all sorts of legislation affect distribution channel strategy. The franchising area has been subject to a great deal of scrutiny over time. Later in this section we mention franchise disclosure rules. The Federal Trade Commission's trade-regulation rule on franchising and busi-

[34] Phillip D. White and Albert D. Bates, "Franchising Will Remain Retailing Fixture, but Its Salad Days Have Long Since Gone," *Marketing News* (February 17, 1984), p. 14.

Table 7–3 Number and sales of franchised outlets by type of franchised system, 1983

	Number of Establishments (Thousands)	Percentage of Total	Sales (billions)	Percentage of Total
Manufacturer-Retailer	163.4	37.0	296.1	70.0
Automobile and truck dealers	26.8	6.1	193	45.7
Gasoline service stations	136.6	31.0	103.1	24.4
Manufacturer-Wholesaler	1.6	0.4	16.2	3.8
Soft drink bottlers	1.6	0.4	16.2	3.8
Wholesaler-Retailer	74.7	16.9	21.9	5.2
Automotive products and services	36.5	8.3	8.7	2.1
Retailing (nonfood)	38.2	8.7	13.2	3.1
Service-Sponsor Retailing	201.4	45.7	88.5	20.9
Business aids and services	46.4	10.5	8.6	2.0
Construction, home improvement Maintenance and cleaning services	17.5	4.0	2.7	0.6
Convenience grocery stores	14.7	3.3	10.1	2.4
Educational products and services	6.5	1.5	0.6	0.1
Restaurants (all types)	67.5	15.3	38.7	9.2
Food retailing (other than restaurants and convenience stores)	15.2	3.4	8.6	2.0
Hotels, motels, and campgrounds	6.8	1.5	12.4	2.9
Laundry and dry cleaning services	2.9	0.7	0.3	0.1
Recreation, entertainment, and travel	6.5	1.5	1	0.2
Rental services (including auto-truck and equipment)	12.9	2.9	4.8	1.1
Miscellaneous	4.5	1.0	0.7	0.2
TOTAL, ALL FRANCHISING	441.1	100.0%	$422.7	100.0%

Source: Adapted from U.S. Department of Commerce, International Trade Administration, *Franchising in the Economy 1983–85* (Washington, D.C.: U.S. Government Printing Office, 1985), p. 25.

ness-opportunity ventures, for example, is designed to protect relatively unsophisticated and inexperienced investors by requiring franchisors to disclose to prospective franchise *purchasers* information needed to make informed *investment* decisions. Note that the words *purchasers* and *investment* are emphasized here, because the FTC's rule is basically aimed at franchisor/franchisee relationships, not at authorized franchise dealers. This is why it was logical for the FTC to issue the following statement about wholesaler-sponsored voluntary chains (such as IGA) that "franchise" retail outlets:

> Grocery chains organized by wholesale grocers who supply independent retailers have been exempted from the Federal Trade Commission's franchise rule. . . . The exemption means the presale disclosure requirements of the franchise rule do not apply when a wholesale grocer offers grocery retailers the chance to join the wholesaler's chain. . . . Unlike franchisors, wholesale grocers offer a chain affiliation on a voluntary basis with or without the other optional services they provide, have no economic incentive to engage in unfair or deceptive practices, and no prior record of such practices.[35]

[35] "Franchise Rule Exemption for Wholesale Grocers Announced by Federal Trade Commission," *FTC News Note*, Vol. 25–83 (March 18, 1983), p. 3.

It is because of this confusion that the remainder of this section is divided into two parts, the first dealing with authorized franchise systems and the other with franchisee/franchisor systems.

Authorized Franchise Systems. To maintain some semblance of control over the marketing of their products, suppliers will *authorize* wholesale or retail outlets. Simply put, this means that they are trying to limit the distribution of their products to those outlets that meet some minimum criteria they have established regarding the outlets' degree of participation in one or more of the marketing flows. Examples are authorized tire, auto, computer, major appliance, television, and household furniture dealers whose suppliers have established strong brand names. Such authorization can also be granted at the wholesale level—for example, to soft drink bottlers and to wholesalers by manufacturers of electrical and electronics equipment (Square D, Allen Bradley, Gould), office furniture (Steelcase), machine tools (DoAll), and semiconductors (Texas Instruments, Motorola). Cotter authorizes True Value hardware stores, as we saw in Exhibit 7–4, and Wetterau (a major grocery wholesaler) authorizes IGA, Foodland, and Red & White stores in the markets it serves.

A case history may be helpful in understanding the motivation behind establishing an authorized franchise system. Some years ago, Goodyear decided to expand its distribution by introducing a new channel, the Franchised Tire Center.

> [Goodyear] felt that this type of channel would accomplish five things: (1) expand its presence in the marketplace, particularly in the emerging suburban markets, (2) build a mutual dependence and loyalty between the franchisee and the company, (3) reduce vulnerability to competitive takeover, (4) reduce dependence on the company's outlets, and (5) reduce investment, at least as compared to a company outlet. In other words, Goodyear hoped to use the new channel to gain the stability that its independent dealer channel lacked without the investment and effort involved with its company-owned stores.
>
> Goodyear's franchises are designed somewhat differently from those of other companies who have become franchisers. Rather than trying to earn money from franchising per se, Goodyear simply wants to use the channel to move tires, and its fee structures are set up to facilitate this objective. Goodyear requires no franchise fee and has only two requirements of the prospective franchisee: (1) an unincumbered $50,000 for working capital and (2) a good track record in business (it does not want these outlets to fail). As for continuing fees, there is only a small fee on sales, to cover the cost to Goodyear of the data processing, accounting, and counseling services for the franchisees.[36]

It is also important to understand that suppliers can include, as part of their authorized franchise network, outlets that are already part of an ongoing "independent" franchisor/franchisee relationship. Thus, Entre is the name of a franchisee/franchisor system of computer stores. IBM has authorized Entre to sell its personal computers. Therefore, IBM has a dual channel management problem: it must work closely with each Entre store to make certain that the appropriate service outputs are being delivered to end-users *and* it must work

---

[36] William T. Ross, "Managing Marketing Channel Relationships," Marketing Science Institute Working Paper Series, Report No. 85-105 (Cambridge, Mass.: Marketing Science Institute, 1985), p. 8.

with the franchisor, who plays a critical role in the performance of the franchisees via the various programs the franchisor administers and the incentives it establishes. To make certain it can control its own destiny, however, IBM has developed contracts specifying role relationships with the *individual* stores in franchising systems such as Entre's and Computerland's. It has also retained the

---

EXHIBIT 7–6 Business classification of franchise organizations, with representative examples

Accounting and Tax Services
  H&R Block, Inc.
  Tax Offices of America
Advertising Services
  ASI Sign Systems, Inc.
  Graphics One, Inc.
Art Galleries
  Diversified Arts
  Famous French Galleries, Inc.
Automobile Rentals
  Avis Rent A Car System, Inc.
  Budget Rent-A-Car Corp. of
    America
  Rent-A-Wreck
Automotive Products and
  Services
  AAMCO Transmissions, Inc.
  Midas International Corp.
Beauty Salons, Services &
  Cosmetics
  Command Performance
  Redken Beauty Salon & Retail
    Center
Building Services & Products
  Eureka Log Homes, Inc.
  Independent Home
    Builders of America, Inc.
Business Services
  Best Resume Service
  Computer Servicenters, Inc.
Candy Stores
  Jo-Ann's Nut House, Inc.
  Karmelkorn Shoppes, Inc.
Carpet & Upholstery Cleaning
  Duraclean International
  Servpro Industries, Inc.
Car Wash
  Hanna Car Wash
  MacClean's Car Wash
Cleaning Services
  General Server Service
  Comet International Inc.

Credit and Collection Services
  Audit Controls, Inc.
  Fidelis Commercial Credit
    Corp.
Donut Shops
  Dunkin' Donuts of America,
    Inc.
  Tastee Donut, Inc.
Employment Agencies and
  Personnel
  Dr. Personnel, Inc.
  Manpower, Inc.
Entertainment
  Fun Services, Inc.
  TV Focus, Inc.
Fast Food
  Arby's Systems, Inc.
  Brown's Chicken
  Dairy King Distributors
  International House of
    Pancakes
  Mr. Pizza
  Taco Tico, Inc.
Fire and Theft Prevention
  Beltway Alarm Company
  Video Guard, Inc.
Food Stores—Retail
  Atlantic Richfield Co.
  White Hen Pantry Div.
    Jewel Companies, Inc.
Health Aids and Services
  Health Clubs of America
  Jazzercise, Inc.
  Nutri-System Weight Loss
    Medical Centers
Ice Cream Stores
  Baskin-Robbins Ice Cream
    Co.
  Mister Softee, Inc.
Industrial Products and
  Equipment
  Chem-Mark International
  Snap-on-Tools Corp.

Laundry and Dry Cleaning
  Stores
  The Maids International
  The Maytag Company
    (Commercial Laundry Div.)
Lawn Care Services
  Lawn King, Inc.
  Superlawns, Inc.
Men's and Women's Clothing
  and Specialty Shops
  Gingiss International, Inc.
  Just Pants
Motels and Hotels
  Holiday Inns, Inc.
  Ramada Inns, Inc.
  Travelodge International, Inc.
Pet Stores and Services
  Docktor Pet Centers, Inc.
  Petland, Inc.
Printing Services
  Insty-Prints, Inc.
  Sir Speedy, Inc.
Rental Services
  A to Z Rental Center, Inc.
  Taylor Rental Corp.
Retail Stores
  American Phone Centers
  Computerland Corp.
Schools
  Barbizon School of Modeling
    & Fashion
  Mind Power, Inc.
Sports & Recreation
  The Athletic Attic, Inc.
  Kampgrounds of America
Travel
  Empress Travel Franchise
    Corp.
Vending Machines
  Canteen Corp.
  Mechanical Servants, Inc.

Source: 1984 Directory of Franchising Organizations (Babylon, N.Y.: Pilot Industries, 1984), pp. 5–76.

Table 7–4 Top franchise industries: Projected growth

Business Category	Sales (in millions) 1985	1990*	Annual Growth (%)
Restaurants (all types)	$ 48,926	$ 86,109	12.0
Retailing (nonfood)	18,790	33,560	12.3
Hotels/motels/campgrounds	14,631	22,511	9.0
Convenience stores	12,309	19,377	9.5
Business services	12,076	21,282	12.0
Automotive products and services	10,604	15,944	8.5
Food retailing (other than convenience stores)	10,370	14,544	7.0
Rental services (auto/truck)	5,282	8,900	11.0
Construction and home services	3,720	9,255	20.0
Recreation/entertainment/travel	1,840	6,573	29.0
TOTAL	$138,548	$238,055	11.5%

* Forecasted by The Naisbitt Group.

Source: Meg Whittemore, "Franchising's Future: More Than $1.3 Trillion Sold," *Daily Market Digest,* April 28, 1986, p. 22. (Originally published in *Nation's Business,* February 1986.)

right *not* to authorize individual stores within a franchising system if the stores do not meet its criteria for admission to its authorized dealer network.

Franchisor/Franchisee Systems. A franchisee/franchisor system is defined here as an *entire* business format where one firm (the franchisor) licenses a number of outlets (franchisees) to market a product or service and engage in a business developed by the franchisor using the latter's trade names, trademarks, service marks, know-how, and methods of doing business. While heavily circumscribed by law, as pointed out in Chapter 8, the franchisor may sell the products, sell or lease the equipment, and/or sell or lease the premises necessary to the operation.[37] For example, McDonald's insists that all of its units purchase from approved suppliers, provides building and design specifications, provides or helps locate financing for its franchisees, and issues quality standards that each unit must abide by in order to hold its franchise.

Franchisee/franchisor systems are present in almost all business fields, as indicated in Exhibit 7–6. It can be readily seen that the franchise system covers a wide variety of goods and services—accounting services, auto accessories, auto rentals, campgrounds, child care, computer services, dance studios, dry cleaning, employment agencies, fast foods, convenience food markets, sewer cleaning, home care, movie theaters, book stores, construction, industrial and commercial chemical products, and vending machine operations. It has also become a highly significant form of organization in the real estate industry.[38] The projected growth of the top franchise industries is shown in Table 7–4.

[37] In addition to reading Chapter 8, the reader interested in the extent of restrictions on tying agreements should see Shelby D. Hunt and John R. Nevin, "Tying Agreements in Franchising," *Journal of Marketing,* Vol. 39 (July 1975), pp. 20–26.

[38] See "Franchising the Local Realty Broker," *Business Week* (September 13, 1976), p. 13; and Gary Washburn, "Forget Big Mac and the Colonel, Real Estate Gets the Franchise Prize," *Chicago Tribune,* October 9, 1977, section 12, p. 1.

Table 7–5   Initial services to franchisees, as reported by franchisors

	Franchisors Reporting				
Type of Service Provided	Total, All Companies	Fast-food & Beverage	Nonfood Retailing	Personal Services	Business Products & Services
Operating manuals	100.0%	100.0%	100.0%	100.0%	100.0%
Management training	100.0	100.0	100.0	100.0	100.0
Franchisee employee training	88.3	83.9	83.7	90.9	100.0
Market surveys and site selection	84.4	98.2	93.0	83.6	42.3
Facility design and layout	80.0	100.0	83.7	81.8	26.9
Lease negotiation	62.7	78.5	72.0	58.1	23.0
Franchisee fee financing	37.7	25.0	37.2	47.2	46.1
All other services	21.1	21.4	25.5	20.0	15.3

Note: Based on information reported by 180 franchise companies. Includes 56 franchisors of fast-foods and beverages, 43 of nonfood consumer products, 55 of personal services, and 26 of business (or industrial) products and services.

Source: National Industrial Conference Board, *Franchised Distribution* (New York: National Industrial Conference Board, 1971), p. 23.

Modes of Operation.[39]   All franchisees are expected to provide a continuing market for a franchisor's product or service. The product or service offering is, in theory, differentiated from those offered by conventional outlets by its *consistent* quantity and quality and strong promotion. Through his market- and image-building promotional strategy, which is instituted at an early stage of a franchise system's development, a franchisor hopes to gain automatic and immediate acceptance from prospective franchisees and the public.

Franchisors provide both *initial* and *continuous* services to their franchisees. *Initial services* include:

- Market survey and site selection
- Facility design and layout
- Lease negotiation advice
- Financing advice
- Operating manuals
- Management training programs
- Franchisee employee training

The extent to which these initial services are provided is shown in Table 7–5. While the amount of involvement with franchisees is clearly high in many cases, it should be noted that a franchisor's provision of an initial service indicates nothing about the depth of his involvement. For example, over 95 percent of all franchised outlets are built from the ground up. That is, similar and ongoing businesses did not previously exist on the current franchisee's location.

[39] This section is based largely on National Industrial Conference Board, *Franchised Distribution* (New York: National Industrial Conference Board, 1971).

However, the degree of involvement a franchisor exercises in site location and development varies widely. On the one hand, McDonald's does all site analysis and most land acquisition and development; on the other hand, Budget Rent-A-Car merely assigns a territory and allows the franchisee to build where he pleases, subject to franchisor review and advice. Also, franchisee employee training varies in length based on the complexity of the operation and the degree to which the franchisor uses this service to enhance the stability of a franchise. For instance, training by Hilton Hotels is a major selling point of its franchise program. In fact, Hilton provides such a host of training services that it never fully escapes the personnel difficulties inherent in company-owned, service-related outlets.[40] As an example of the comprehensiveness of some initial services, information from Southland Corporation, the franchisor of 7-Eleven Convenience Food Stores, is reproduced in Appendix 7D.

Continuous services include:

- Field supervision
- Merchandising and promotional materials
- Management and employee retraining
- Quality inspection
- National advertising
- Centralized purchasing
- Market data and guidance
- Auditing and record keeping
- Management reports
- Group insurance plans

Table 7–6 presents data on the extent to which continuing services are provided by franchisors.[41] Almost all franchisors have a continuous program of field services. Field representatives visit the franchise outlet to aid the franchisee in everyday operation, check the quality of product and service, and monitor performance.

All franchisees are usually required to report monthly or semimonthly on key elements of their operations—weekly sales, local advertising, employee turnover, profits, and other financial and marketing information. This regular reporting is intended to facilitate the various financial, operating, and marketing control procedures.

As might be expected, the reaction of franchisees to field services and operating controls is not always positive. Franchisees are independent businessmen, even though they have signed contractual agreements with franchisors. When conflict over supervision exists within their systems, franchisors have tended to rely on their field representatives to act as channel diplomats. However, these representatives not only are responsible for field service and liaison with franchisees but also must recruit additional franchisees. Complaints are often heard that the franchisor is providing too little attention to franchisees'

---

[40] Examples provided by Henry Bullock. The authors gratefully acknowledge the data he gathered in interviews with executives of some major franchise companies.

[41] See also Michael Etgar, "Differences in the Use of Manufacturer Power in Conventional and Contractual Channels," *Journal of Retailing*, Vol. 54 (Winter 1978), pp. 49–62.

Table 7–6 Continuing services to franchisees, as reported by franchisors

	Franchisors Reporting				
Type of Service Provided	Total, All Companies	Fast-food & Beverage	Nonfood Retailing	Personal Services	Business Products & Services
Field supervision	96.1%	92.8%	100.0%	100.0%	89.6%
Merchandising and promotion materials	94.5	94.6	100.0	96.3	79.3
Franchisee employee retraining	85.1	78.5	83.3	94.5	82.7
Quality inspections	79.6	98.2	80.9	69.0	62.0
Advertising	66.4	62.5	61.9	83.6	48.2
Centralized purchasing	65.3	64.2	73.8	61.8	62.0
Market data and guidance	62.6	48.2	69.0	67.2	72.4
Auditing and recordkeeping	51.0	48.2	57.1	52.7	44.8
Group insurance plans	48.9	50.0	47.6	58.1	31.0
All other continuing services	13.1	8.9	21.4	12.7	10.3

Note: Based on information reported by 182 franchise companies. Includes 56 franchisors of fast-foods and beverages, 42 of nonfood consumer products, 55 of personal services, and 29 of business (or industrial) products and services.

Source: National Industrial Conference Board, *Franchised Distribution* (New York: National Industrial Conference Board, 1971), p. 24.

management problems, especially when the field representatives have too many conflicting responsibilities.[42]

Another source of conflict is the fact that many franchisors own a number of their outlets and some of these outlets compete with those owned by franchisees. Managers of franchise systems, however, try to avoid the problems generally associated with dual distribution. Besides the necessity of owning certain outlets because of bankruptcy of the franchisee (the franchisors may be the only available source of funds for ownership in these cases), there are a number of other reasons a franchisor might wish to vertically integrate. First, franchisor-owned and -operated units serve as models for the rest of the system and can be used for research and training purposes. Second, such units may accelerate network growth, especially during the initial development period. Third, wholly owned units may be profitable. They will also permit the franchisor firsthand insight into day-to-day operating problems. Finally, court decisions and legislation may force franchisors to own more and more of their outlets if they wish to maintain strong control over the operations of the system as a whole. Although

[42] For documentation of conflict issues in franchising, see Shelby D. Hunt and John R. Nevin, "Power in a Channel of Distribution: Sources and Consequences," *Journal of Marketing Research*, Vol. 11 (May 1974), pp. 186–93. For an interesting case example, the conflicts that have arisen in soft drink bottling, see Bill Abrams and John Koten, "New York Coke Agrees to Amend Franchise Accord," *Wall Street Journal*, April 17, 1979, p. 13; and John Koten, "Some Coca-Cola Bottlers Seek to Make Their Own Syrup for Sale to Restaurants," *Wall Street Journal*, February 27, 1979, p. 14. See also "Fotomat Agrees to Pay $10 Million to Settle Franchise Holder Suits," *Wall Street Journal*, May 3, 1982, p. 12. Franchisees charged, among other things, that Fotomat placed new stores too close to existing stores and that the prices Fotomat charged franchisees for photo processing and other services were excessive.

there is some feeling that the number of company-owned outlets is increasing,[43] the move to company-owned operations is *highly* significant only in the fast-food-restaurant field, where the percentage of company-owned outlets rose from 19.4 in 1972 to 32.3 in 1983, and in the nonfood retailing area, where the percentages for 1972 and 1983 were 14.5 and 32.3, respectively.[44] However, the percentage of company-owned stores for *all* franchising was 19.4 in 1983, compared with 17.4 in 1972—certainly not a dramatic increase.[45]

To illustrate some of the significant conflict issues that exist between franchisors and franchisees, Exhibit 7-7 details a small bit of the history of Burger King, a subsidiary of Pillsbury Company.

Sources of Franchisor Revenue. Sources of franchisor revenue and their relative importance are illustrated in Fig. 7-1. The various sources include:

1. *Initial franchise fees.* Many franchisors charge an initial fee to new franchisees. The fee ranges from $1000 to $150,000, with the mode falling between $10,000 and $25,000. The fee is charged to cover the franchisor's expenses for site location, training, setting of operating controls, and other initial services as well as developmental costs in building the system. Initial fees tend to rise as a franchise becomes more successful.

2. *Royalty fees.* Many franchisors charge a royalty fee or commission based on the gross value of a franchisee's sales volume. Five percent of gross sales is the most common royalty agreement in franchising. Some franchisors require a minimum payment of $150 to $200 per month. In certain cases the royalty rate decreases as sales volume increases, while in others the royalty fee is a flat rate regardless of the sales volume. Some franchisors collect a royalty on a unit-of-sale basis. For example, motel franchisors charge a fee per room; soft ice cream franchisors charge a fee for each gallon of mix sold to the franchisee; car wash equipment franchisors charge a fee per car washed. Figure 7-2 presents survey results regarding franchise royalty practices.

3. *Sales of products.* Some franchisors function as wholesalers in that they supply franchisees with raw materials and finished products. Other franchisors manufacture their products; for example, a significant amount of Coca-Cola's revenue is derived from the sale of its soft drink syrups to its franchised bottlers. In some cases, the franchise company sells the equipment needed by the franchisee.

4. *Rental and lease fees.* The franchise company often leases the building, equipment, and fixtures used in its outlets. Some franchise contracts involve an escalator clause that requires the franchisee to increase his lease payment as sales volume increases.

5. *License fees.* The franchisee sometimes is required to pay for the use and display of the franchisor's trademark. The license fee is used more in conjunction with industrial franchises, where a local manufacturer is licensed to use a particular patent or process.

6. *Management fees.* In a few cases, franchisees are charged fees for consulting services received from the franchisor, such as management reports and training.

---

[43] See Donald W. Hackett, *Franchising: The State of the Art*, American Marketing Association Monograph Series No. 9 (Chicago, 1977), p. 41; and Charles L. Vaughn, *Franchising*, 2nd ed. (Lexington, Mass.: D. C. Heath, Lexington Books, 1979), pp. 9, 61–70.

[44] U.S. Department of Commerce, *op. cit.*, pp. 25, 34. Nonfood retailing franchise systems include general merchandise, wearing apparel, hardware, paints and floor covering, drugs, electronics, and cosmetic items, among others.

[45] *Ibid.* For an example of a fast-food franchise chain that has moved to company-owned outlets, see "Denny's: A Brisk Turnaround," *Business Week* (December 15, 1980), p. 101.

EXHIBIT 7–7 Conflicts in franchising: A case example— Burger King

- 1489 [2729] Burger King restaurants out of a total of 2726 [3278] are operated by franchisees who own the land and buildings themselves, or rent them from someone other than Pillsbury. In contrast, McDonald's owns or leases nearly all of the land and buildings used by its 5747 restaurants. The advantages of ownership to the franchisor are compelling. The land is an appreciating asset and the building a source of depreciation writeoffs. Equally important, however, is the fact that, as the franchisee's landlord, the franchisor has power. McDonald's franchisees, for example, are not allowed to own any other fast-food restaurants, and they have no territorial rights or protection. On the other hand, until relatively recently, Burger King granted exclusive rights to large territories and allowed franchisees to buy land and build as many stores as they liked. A franchisee was free to sell sections of his territory to others if he wanted; he could even diversify into other fast-food businesses.

- The consequence of Burger King's early policies has been that some of its franchisees have grown so large that they are very difficult for the franchisor to control. Two of its franchisees—Chart House, Inc. and Horn & Hardart Co.—have engaged in all-out battles with Pillsbury over such issues as expansion and diversification into other restaurant businesses. (Chart House owns Cork 'N Cleaver, the Chart House group in California, and over 350 Burger King restaurants. Horn and Hardart operates its famous Automats as well as a number of Arby's restaurants in addition to over 20 Burger King restaurants.

- Burger King has established a far more demanding contract with its franchisees. Franchisees must now agree not to own any other fast-food business and to live within an hour's drive of their Burger King restaurants, which makes it difficult for a franchisee to own more than a dozen restaurants.

- Burger King franchisees are interested in their restaurants' profits and losses. Pillsbury is more interested in their sales. (Apart from a one-time franchise fee of $40,000, Pillsbury obtains most of its revenue from the franchisee's sales—3½ percent of sales as royalty; 4 percent for the marketing fund; and, if Pillsbury owns the land and building, an additional 8½ percent as rent. McDonald's levies a franchise fee of $12,500, a royalty of 3 percent, a marketing fee of 4 percent and rent of 8½ percent.) There is a potential incompatibility of goals in almost all franchise arrangements, including Burger King's, especially when increasing sales push costs so high that the franchisee's profit goes down. For example, many Burger King franchisees originally strongly resisted Pillsbury's desire that they shift to multiple lines, such as McDonald's was using, in existing restaurants. The franchisees believed that the additional cash registers and extra help would cost more than the increased sales would justify.

Source: Lee Smith, "Burger King Puts Down Its Dukes," *Fortune* (June 16, 1980), pp. 90–98. Figures for 1984 added in brackets. As an epilogue, see "Horn & Hardart Co., Burger King Settle Franchise Dispute," *Wall Street Journal,* November 5, 1980, p. 12.

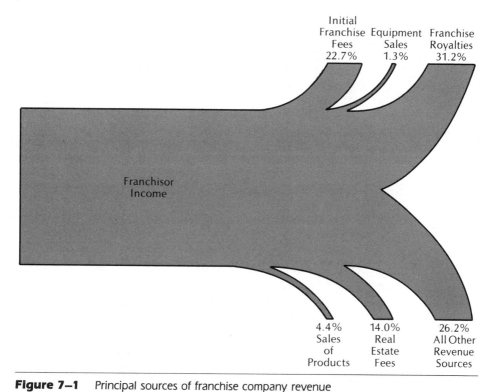

Figure 7–1   Principal sources of franchise company revenue

Source: E. Patrick McGuire, *Franchised Distribution* (New York: The Conference Board, 1971), p. 20.

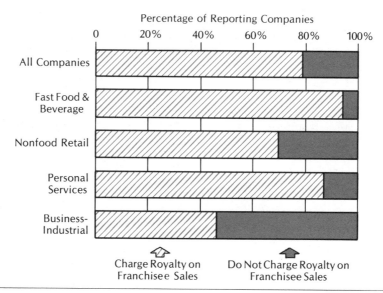

Figure 7–2   Franchise company royalty practices

Note: Survey of 185 franchise companies, including 56 fast-foods and beverages, 45 nonfood retail, 56 personal services, and 28 business/industrial franchisors.
Source: E. Patrick McGuire, *Franchised Distribution* (New York: The Conference Board, 1971), p. 21.

EXHIBIT 7–8   Elements of an ideal franchise program

- *High gross margin*—In order for the franchisee to be able to afford a high franchise fee (which the franchisor needs), it is necessary to operate on a high gross margin percentage. This explains the widespread application of franchising in the food and service industries.

- *In-store value added*—Franchising works best in those product categories where the product is at least partially processed in the store. Such environments require constant on-site supervision—a chronic problem for company-owned stores using a hired manager. Owners simply are willing to work harder over longer hours.

- *Secret processes*—Concepts, formulas, or products which the franchisee can't duplicate without joining the franchise program.

- *Real estate profits*—The franchisor uses income from ownership of property as a significant revenue source.

- *Simplicity*—The most successful franchises have been those which operate on automatic pilot: all the key decisions have been thought through, and the owner merely implements the decisions.

Source: Reprinted from Phillip D. White and Albert D. Bates, "Franchising Will Remain Retailing Fixture, but its Salad Days Have Long Since Gone," *Marketing News* (February 17, 1984), p. 14, published by the American Management Association.

Consider the case of Gymboree exercise centers for children, which started operating in the mid 1970s. Once or twice a week, for 45 minutes, children three months to four years, accompanied by their mothers, limber up tiny muscles by doing light exercises. About 300 Gymboree centers were operating by 1986. A franchise costs $12,000 for a single site, but less if the franchisee buys more than one, down to $10,000 apiece for four or more. For this fee, the franchisee gets the right to use the company name and methods, exclusive territory, and nine days of training. In addition, the franchisee pays a royalty of 6 percent of revenues. Gymboree's income from fees and royalties came to $980,000 in 1985.[46]

Despite the fee and royalty structures in franchisee/franchisor systems, many new franchisors grossly underestimate the amount of money it takes to build a network.

> They believe the franchise fee will be a windfall. They also rely on royalty income too early in the game. The franchise fee, they soon learn, is needed to cover the costs of backup systems for franchisees—particularly marketing materials and advisory services. And in general royalties do not cover the franchisor's operating and selling expenses until he has built up a large network of units with good sales.[47]

New franchisors might also keep in mind the elements of an ideal franchise program suggested by White and Bates in Exhibit 7–8.

[46] See Faye Rice, "How to Succeed at Cloning a Small Business," *Fortune* (October 28, 1985), pp. 60–61.

[47] *Ibid.*, p. 61.

Table 7–7 Buying in

Average amount required by a franchiser to start a new franchise, excluding real estate costs

Franchiser	Type of Business	Investment Cost
Aamco Transmissions Inc.	Car transmission service shops	$101,000
Athlete's Foot Marketing Associates Inc.	Athletic shoe and clothing stores	$107,500 to $157,500
Baskin Robbins Inc.	Ice cream stores	$50,000
Command Performance	Haircutting and styling salons	$75,000 to $105,000
Dunkin' Donuts of America Inc.	Donut shops	$45,000 to $58,000
Entre Computer Centers Inc.	Computer stores	$125,000
Godfather's Pizza	Pizza parlors	$200,000 to $285,000
Gymboree Corp.	Play centers for pre-schoolers	$21,000 to $27,000
Jani-King Inc.	Commercial janitorial services	$6,500
Mail Boxes Etc. USA	Postal and business service centers	$46,000
McDonald's Corp.	Hamburger restaurants	$300,000 to $360,000
Moto Photo Inc.	One-hour film processing labs	$160,000
Pier 1 Imports Inc.	Gift and home furnishings stores	$100,000 to $130,000
Southland Corp.	7-Eleven convenience stores	$37,075
Video Biz Inc.	Videotape movie rental shops	$55,000

Source: Brenton R. Schlender, "Working on the Chain Gang," *Wall Street Journal,* May 19, 1986, p. 14D. Reprinted by permission of *The Wall Street Journal,* © Dow Jones & Company, Inc. 1986. All rights reserved. Schlender utilized 1986 Commerce Department figures.

The average amount required by selected franchisors to start a new franchise in 1986 is shown in Table 7–7. As can easily be imagined, there are lots of potential points of conflict between franchisors and franchisees over money matters. In fact, there is often a built-in adversarial relationship. The franchisor wants royalties, and the franchisee hates paying them. For example, in 1986, Computerland's franchisees revolted over what they perceived to be overly high royalty fees, and a group of 350 franchisees threatened to take the founder and former chairman, William H. Millard, to court if he did not reduce them. And as time goes on, the franchisor wants more outlets, but the franchisee doesn't want to compete with new franchisees.

The Social View of Franchising. A number of arguments have been raised, pro and con, about the socioeconomic and legal consequences of franchising.[48] On the pro side, for example, it has been contended that franchising greatly increases the opportunity for individuals to become independent businessmen, even though it is becoming more difficult to qualify for a franchise.[49] Hunt

[48] See Shelby D. Hunt, "The Socioeconomic Consequences of the Franchised System of Distribution," *Journal of Marketing,* Vol. 36 (July 1972), pp. 32–38. Also see Charles G. Burck, "Franchising's Troubled Dream World," *Fortune* (March 1970), pp. 116ff.

[49] See Gary Washburn, "Franchising Good but Hard to Enter," *Chicago Tribune,* September 21, 1975, section 2, p. 13. See also Sanford L. Jacobs, "Operating a Franchise Often Pays but Demands on Buyer Are Great," *Wall Street Journal,* November 3, 1980, p. 27.

estimates that if franchising did not exist, approximately 52 percent of the owner-managers he surveyed would not be self-employed.[50] It has also been argued, that franchised businesses have lower failure rates than other businesses.[51] Furthermore, to various observers, franchising seems to decrease economic concentration by providing a viable alternative to completely integrated corporate vertical marketing systems.

On the con side, some claim that (1) franchise agreements are one-sided in favor of the franchisor; (2) franchisors employ unethical techniques in selling franchises, including "pyramid" distribution schemes,[52] celebrity promotion of franchises, and misrepresentation of the potential profitability of the franchise; and (3) franchising is an anticompetitive system of distribution. Most of these contentions, especially the last one, involve legal as well as socioeconomic factors.[53]

The bulk of evidence seems to support the contention that franchise agreements favor the franchisor. Franchise contracts involve termination clauses, provisions on operating-manual changes at the prerogative of the franchisor, and "covenants not to compete" clauses that prohibit a franchisee from practicing his trade for a specified period within a specific geographic area after franchise termination. Sixty percent of sample contracts examined by Hunt included such clauses.[54] Also observed in these contracts were clauses requiring the franchisee to buy supplies and equipment from the franchisor, clauses restricting the franchisee's right to sell, and clauses prohibiting the franchisee from joining any union of franchisees. Lack of arbitration clauses was evident in 77 percent of the contracts Hunt examined. It is interesting to note, however, that 40 percent of the sample of franchisees responding to Hunt's survey did not consult a lawyer prior to signing a contract.[55]

Partly as a result of some of these practices of franchisors, the Federal Trade Commission approved in 1979 a trade regulation rule titled "Disclosure Requirement and Prohibitions Concerning Franchising and Business Opportunity Ventures," which requires sellers of franchises to disclose a wide variety of information to franchise buyers. The rule bars misrepresentations of actual or potential sales, income, or profits. It requires the disclosure of information about the franchise seller, such as its business experience, the business experience of its

[50] Hunt, *op. cit.*, p. 33.

[51] The failure and/or discontinuance rate of all franchises in the U.S. is only 4 percent. See Teri Agins, "Owning Franchises Has Pluses, but Wealth Isn't Guaranteed," *Wall Street Journal*, October 22, 1984, p. 33.

[52] A pyramid distribution scheme is one in which a parent company sells the right to a territory to an individual, who in turn has the right ("franchise") to sell the right to operate under him or her. The procedure may be repeated at several descending levels and has been used to amass fortunes in the cosmetics field, especially by Glenn W. Turner with firms he named Koscot Interplanetary and Dare-to-Be-Great. Vaughn, *op. cit.*, p. 23.

[53] For a discussion of socioeconomic factors, see Bruce Mallen, "Channel Power: A Form of Economic Exploitation," *European Journal of Marketing*, Vol. 12, No. 2 (1978), p. 198; and Robert F. Lusch, "Franchisee Satisfaction: Causes and Consequences," *International Journal of Physical Distribution*, Vol. 7 (1977), pp. 128–40.

[54] Hunt, *op. cit.*, p. 37. See also Paul Merrion, "Tougher Pact Riles Big Mac Owners," *Crain's Chicago Business*, Vol. 2 (September 17, 1979), p. 1; and Stanley Penn, "Franchisees Form Militant Trade Groups to Meet Fears about Power of Licensers," *Wall Street Journal*, August 8, 1979, p. 8.

[55] Hunt, *op. cit.*, p. 37. For corroborating evidence, see William Renforth, "Legal Hassles of Franchising Are Commensurate with Business and Marketing Sophistication of Franchisees," *Marketing News* (February 17, 1984), p. 8.

key management personnel, its bankruptcy and litigation history, and its certified balance sheet for the most recent year. In addition, the seller is mandated to disclose:

- Costs, both initial and recurring, that will be required to be paid by the franchisee
- Restrictions placed on the franchisee's conduct of business
- Termination, cancellation, and renewal provisions of the franchise agreement
- Statistical information about the number of franchises and their rates of termination
- Training programs for the franchisee[56]

The trade regulation rule, which went into effect on October 21, 1979, does not preempt state laws governing franchises. In fact, there is a multiplicity of regulatory rules and statutes at both state and local levels that govern the actions of franchisors and their franchisees.[57] But the existence of all these regulations has by no means ended the problems.[58]

The Rationale for Franchising   Why is it that franchise systems evolve, if they are so loaded down with controversy? Tightly controlled franchise systems represent the extreme form of limiting the market, short of outright ownership. That is, through the stipulations in the contract they sign, the parties purposively subvert and circumscribe the marketplace existing between them.[59] Schedules are set, programs are constructed, and commitments are made so that the end-user can receive the product of the synergistic (it is to be hoped) efforts of the franchisor and franchisee. Thus, in theory at least, the franchise system provides substantial franchisee training, sales, service, promotional, and capital assistance so that overall system performance will be enhanced.

In addition, franchise systems facilitate the flow of critical market information between franchisors and franchisees so that consumer preferences, complaints, and purchasing intentions can more quickly be reflected in marketing and production planning. Routinizing information flows is also important when it is necessary to monitor compensation claims, such as those for warranty work. The long-run mutual interest fostered by such routinization reduces incentives for exaggerated compensation claims, while the uniform accounting and report-

[56] "FTC Gives Details on Requirements and Coverage of Franchise Rule," *FTC News Summary* (August 3, 1979), p. 2. See also "FTC Will Require Sellers of Franchises to Disclose Variety of Data to Buyers," *Wall Street Journal,* December 21, 1978, p. 2; "Oil and Auto Concerns Receive FTC Franchise-Rule Exemptions," *FTC News Summary* (August 1, 1980), pp. 2, 3; and "FTC Seeks Comment on Request from Wholesale Grocers for Franchise-Rule Exemption," *FTC News Summary* (February 20, 1981), p. 3.

[57] For example, only a very few states have a so-called fractional franchise exemption from state disclosure laws, even though such an exemption is available in the federal rule. The federal exemption has two requirements. First, the parties must reasonably anticipate that the sales that will arise from the relationship they are about to begin will not exceed 20 percent of the total dollar sales of the reseller in the coming year. Second, the reseller must have been in the same type of business represented by the franchise relationship for at least two years. For further discussion of federal and state disclosure laws, see Shelby D. Hunt and John R. Nevin, "Full Disclosure Laws in Franchising: An Empirical Evaluation," *Journal of Marketing,* Vol. 40 (April 1976), pp. 53–62.

[58] See David Diamond, "The Dark Side of Franchising," *New York Times,* January 12, 1986, Business Section, p. 4.

[59] See Victor P. Goldberg, "The Law and Economics of Vertical Restrictions: A Relational Perspective," *Texas Law Review,* Vol. 58 (1979), pp. 91–129.

ing procedures and greater access to information permit effective monitoring of the entire franchise system.[60]

Finally, the franchise system provides needed investment incentives by making substantial sales, service, and management assistance readily available to potential franchisees; by harmonizing interdependent investment decision making through realignments of business risks; and by mitigating opportunities for the exploitation of invested capital by free-rider franchisees.[61]

According to a 1986 study by The Naisbitt Group commissioned by the International Franchise Association, sales by business-format franchises will likely reach $1.3 trillion in the year 2010.[62] The startling growth of franchising will take place as a result of five emerging trends:

- The transition from a manufacturing-based to a service economy. Franchising has long been at the forefront of the service sector.
- Consumer preference for convenience and consistent quality—two of the principal strengths of franchising
- A rise in consumer demand for specialty items
- The increasing numbers of women and minorities in franchising. This trend will usher into the franchising arena new markets, new products, and a largely untapped management pool.
- Franchising abroad. Franchising is quickly becoming an export business.

Given the clear desire of a wide variety of manufacturers, wholesalers, and service-oriented organizations to control their marketing channels by establishing franchises or some other form of contractual marketing system, the next logical question would seem to be: Why don't they go all the way and vertically integrate the relevant marketing flows? We will pursue the answer to this question while we examine corporate systems.

CORPORATE SYSTEMS

Corporate vertical marketing systems exist when channel members on different levels of distribution for a particular product are owned and operated by one organization. Corporate forward integration occurs frequently when a manufacturing firm decides to establish its own sales branches, distribution centers, and/or wholesale outlets, as when Evans Products Company (a manufacturer of plywood) purchased wholesale lumber distributors in order to more aggressively promote its products through retail lumber establishments and when Espirit de Corp. (a designer and manufacturer of apparel) began opening its own retail stores. Evidence of extensive forward vertical integration is found in such di-

---

[60] For an outstanding example of routinization of information flows, see Craig Zarley, "Captains of Video," *PC Week* (September 10, 1985), pp. 53–56, which describes National Video's franchise-linking PC network.

[61] A discussion of externalities, economies of scale in information processing, and investment incentives as applied to franchise systems in the automobile, tire, and petroleum industries can be found in Thomas G. Marx, "Distribution Efficiency in Franchising," *Business Topics*, Vol. 28 (Winter 1980), pp. 5–13. The free-rider problem is also addressed in Chapter 8 of this text.

[62] Meg Whittemore, "Franchising's Future: More Than $1.3 Trillion Sold," *Daily Market Digest*, April 28, 1986, p. 22.

verse companies as Singer, Sherwin-Williams, Hartmarx, J. I. Case, Goodyear, and Sohio.

Corporate backward integration occurs in distribution when retailers or wholesalers assume ownership of institutions that normally precede them in the marketing flow of goods and services. To many, corporate systems are regarded as roughly synonymous with integrated chain store systems. While all chain store organizations have integrated wholesaling functions, many food chains, like Safeway, Kroger, and Giant Food, obtain 15 to 20 percent of their requirements from company-owned processing facilities.

Sears has a financial interest in 31 of its 12,000 suppliers.[63] The companies range from small companies with less than 100 employees to large corporations listed on the New York Stock Exchange, including Armstrong Rubber Company, Whirlpool Corporation, and DeSoto, The 31 "affiliated manufacturing sources," as Sears refers to them, supply about 28 percent of Sears' purchases.[64] Examples of its affiliated manufacturing sources are shown in Fig. 7–3. In most cases, Sears has a minority interest in terms of common stock ownership, but may account for a large percentage of their sales, as indicated in Table 7–8. According to company executives, Sears' interest in maintaining factory ownership, a practice that dates back to 1906, is to provide its retail and catalog outlets with "a reliable and continuous supply of merchandise, built to our specifications, delivered in the right quantities at the right time and at the lowest possible cost."[65] However, Sears will become interested in a manufacturing investment only when it "insures continuity of sound management, quality, service, price and design obtainable in no other way."[66] In fact, Sears uses nine criteria to determine whether to establish an investor relationship with a supplier:

> a competent management, adequate facilities, an accurate cost accounting system that permits both management and Sears buyers to know the actual cost of each product, effective production and budget controls, enlightened personnel policies, a sound sales policy, creative research and development programs, profitable factory operations, and "acceptance by the merchandising departments of their full merchandising responsibility."[67]

Some major wholesalers are engaged in successful backward vertical integration as well. For example, W.W. Grainger, an electrical distributor, operates seven manufacturing facilities and has an aggressive private brand program. American Hospital Supply Corporation is both a major distributor and a manufacturer of health care products and services. In addition, a number of steel wholesalers (e.g., Joseph T. Ryerson & Son, A. M. Castle & Company, and Earle M. Jorgenson Company) have become metal service centers, offering a wide variety of preprocessing services, including slitting, welding, and forming. These service centers now dominate the wholesale segment of the steel market.

[63] William Gruber, "Sears' Success Affects Many," *Chicago Tribune*, September 2, 1975, section 2, p. 7. See also Carol J. Loomis, "The Leaning Tower of Sears," *Fortune* (July 2, 1979), pp. 78–85.
[64] Gruber, *op. cit.*, p. 7.
[65] Quoted in *ibid.*
[66] *Ibid.*
[67] *Ibid.*

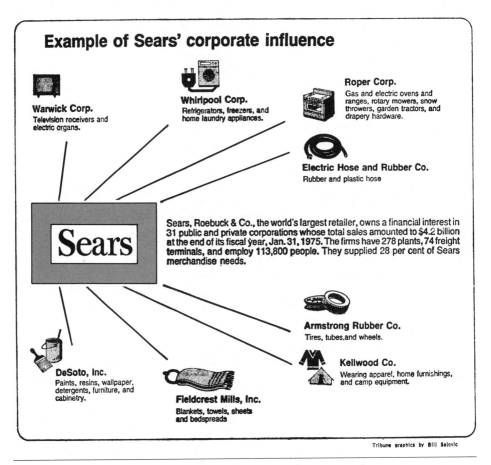

Figure 7–3 Examples of Sears' manufacturing sources

Source: William Gruber, "Sears' Success Affects Many," *Chicago Tribune*, Section 2, September 7, 1975, p. 7. Reprinted, courtesy of the Chicago Tribune.

Comparing Corporate to Other Systems

By virtue of ownership, a channel member can achieve operating economies and *absolute* control over the marketing activities of other channel members. From the perspective of organization behavior, corporate systems are those in which units are organized for the achievement of inclusive goals and in which the locus of both inclusive decision making and authority is clearly delineated within the structure. Thus, decision making is *not* subject to unit ratification, as it is in contractual systems. Wholly owned channel members are structured for a division of labor within the organization. Norms of commitment are high. Most important, perhaps, the systemwide orientation of the members is greater than in other vertical marketing systems.[68]

[68] Warren, *op. cit.*, p. 316.

Table 7–8 Sears' ownership of and extent of purchases from selected affiliated manufacturing sources, 1974

Affiliated Manufacturing Source	Sears' Ownership of Stock (percent)	Total Sales of Source (millions)	Sears' Share of Total Sales (percent)
DeSoto, Inc.	32.0%	$271	64%
Roper Corp.	41.4	366	71
Whirlpool Corp.[a]			
Parent company	4.7 ⎫		
Heil-Quaker subsidiary	20.0 ⎬	1260	62
Warwick Electronics subsidiary	25.5 ⎭		
Kellwood Co.	23.0	400	79
Armstrong Rubber Co.	10.0	259	36
Globe-Union Co.[b]	2.6	276	33
Fieldcrest Mills	4.2	NA[c]	NA
Electric House and Rubber Co.	5.6	NA	NA

[a] Includes trash compactors, vacuum cleaners, home heating equipment, and home entertainment units, in addition to the products listed in Fig. 7–3.
[b] Globe-Union supplies Sears with automobile batteries and other electronic components.
[c] NA = not available.

Source: William Gruber, "Sears' Success Affects Many," *Chicago Tribune,* September 7, 1975, section 2, p. 7. (In 1986, Roper purchased all of Sears' equity interest.)

As indicated earlier in this chapter, administered and contractual systems are the result of joint efforts by channel members to limit, subvert, and/or circumscribe the market that lies between them. As a result, their costs of transacting business are likely to be lower and the effectiveness of their marketing is likely to be higher than they would be if the functioning of a perfectly free market were the resource-allocating mechanism between them. However, it should be noted that although the market has been "tampered" with, it still exists for parties in administered and contractual systems. In corporate systems, markets do *not* exist, unless they are simulated. (Some divisions of vertically integrated companies set transfer prices, for example, on the basis of the existing market price levels between nonintegrated buyers and sellers with whom they compete.) In fact, the mere existence of a corporate system means that, for the corporation involved, the market has "failed." That is, from the perspective of management, the channel cannot aid the corporation in attaining its goals unless it is fully integrated into the corporation.

As discussed in Chapter 5, markets fail when the costs of completing transactions become unbearable.[69] Markets are at this level when transactions are surrounded by a high degree of uncertainty because of environmental factors *and* when channel members do not trust one another because generally deceptive behavior has become commonplace among them. Under these conditions, exchange occurs between channel members only with the protection of ironclad contracts, lengthy specifications of obligations accounting for all possible contingencies in an uncertain future, and extensive auditing of performance. When this happens, vertical integration will be preferred to the relatively greater costs of market transactions. For example, Dwyer and Welsh have shown that vertical

[69] Williamson, *Markets and Hierarchies,* pp. 20–40.

integration is the likely response of a marketing channel facing intense competition, resource scarcity, and variable demand.[70] Williamson believes that a wholly integrated operation is more capable of suppressing opportunistic tendencies, resolving conflicts, and monitoring performance than is one that relies on market transactions. In fact, it could be argued that the only reason for the existence of a corporate vertical marketing system is its ability to achieve transactional efficiency. Thus, the formation of a corporate system will tend to reduce the suboptimization that often prevails in more fragmented and decentralized systems. Such a system will usually have better opportunities to exploit economies of scale through increased programming of distribution activities. Also, it is likely that corporate systems will allow more free and rapid communication among the various distributive levels.

A corporate system assures a channel member strong and long-term contact with customers and/or suppliers. Through this form of channel organization, the member may secure adequate representation in a market, reduce the cost of goods purchased, secure relatively scarce supplies, reduce production costs, gain greater inventory control and more pertinent market information, and employ excess funds that have been generated in effective ways.[71] Vertical integration may permit a manufacturer, for example, to set and maintain the price at which his goods are sold at wholesale or retail. In addition, the vertically integrated firm may find it easier to control the quality of the product, engage in selective store promotions, or sell to its various retail outlets at different prices for the purpose of achieving greater market penetration in selected geographic areas. During 1979 and 1980, interest rates skyrocketed to over 20 percent. Many firms restricted retail lending because they could not charge enough to make money. In durable goods marketing, this lack of financing was particularly disastrous. In the automobile industry, the manufacturers' vertically integrated finance companies, such as Ford Motor Credit Company and General Motors Acceptance Corporation (GMAC), were called upon to fill the gap. General Motors gave its finance company a $500 million interest-free loan to help the unit operate smoothly.[72] The other automobile companies made similar arrangements with their finance companies. Although the latter are supposed to operate as profit centers, they are mandated to make certain that automobile sales do not dry up because of lack of available financing.

The integrated firm may also find it easier to protect its good will and trademarks than if it were to depend on a large number of independently owned middlemen who simply use its name. For example, one of the major reasons Church's Fried Chicken, an 830-store chain based in San Antonio and concentrated mostly in the South and Southwest, has become one of the most profitable companies in the fast-food industry is the control it maintains over its primarily company-owned outlets. The company has, for the most part, avoided franchising in order to maintain meal quality by directly owning and managing the operations side of the business.[73] In the soft drink industry, both Coca-Cola and

[70] Dwyer and Welsh, *op. cit.*

[71] Frederick D. Sturdivant et al., *Managerial Analysis in Marketing* (Glenview, Ill.: Scott, Foresman and Co., 1970), pp. 649–53.

[72] Amanda Bennett, "Auto Makers' Finance Units Squeezed between Fund Costs, Duty to Aid Sales," *Wall Street Journal*, May 12, 1980, p. 16.

[73] "Church's: A Fast-Food Recipe That Is Light on Marketing," *Business Week* (February 20, 1978), pp. 110, 112.

Pepsi are increasing control of their bottling networks via vertical integration. About one-third of their sales come from bottlers they have acquired. The driving force behind the trend is the number of new products that both companies have introduced over the past decade. By increasing control, Coke and Pepsi have improved their ability to get new products onto store shelves quickly. Most product introductions can be expensive headaches for bottlers, who must invest in new packages and labels, make room for the new drinks in production runs, and organize distribution and promotions. Analysts believe that bottlers are keys to the future. As one analyst has stated, "No longer is it possible to have a bottler who may or may not do your wishes, and who may or may not have the financial flexibility to carry them out. There's only one way around it. Buy the bottler."[74]

Advantages and Disadvantages of Corporate Systems

The advantages and disadvantages of corporate marketing systems have been explored by many economists and marketing scholars.[75] Exhibit 7–9 lists some of the benefits and costs of vertical integration that have been isolated by a few representative investigations. Most of the studies on the subject place their major emphasis on the ability of such systems to achieve economies of scale through standardization, automation, and streamlining of channel operations. For example, Cargill owns a vast galaxy of milling, transportation, processing, and storage networks. It is therefore well equipped to buy commodities in areas of surplus and sell them in areas of scarcity, or store them until surpluses disappear. It can also choose the most profitable way to sell a commodity, as processed or raw foodstuffs, depending on the current demand. Such marketing advantages are critical in unbranded products, which can't be promoted through advertising and which leave merchants and processors at the mercy of commodity-market cycles. Cargill buys, sells, stores, processes, transports, or produces almost every commodity, from grain and cotton to meat and sugar.[76]

It has been argued, though, that in order to achieve scale economies, there must also be a concomitant reduction in the level of services provided to end-users. Etgar's conclusions from research on property and casualty insurance are not altogether consistent with this assumption. He found that, compared with

[74] Timothy K. Smith, "Coke, Pepsi Seek Control over Bottling," *Wall Street Journal*, July 3, 1986, p. 8.

[75] See, for example, R. H. Coase, "The Nature of the Firm," in G. J. Stigler and K. Boulding (eds.), *Readings in Price Theory* (Homewood, Ill.: Richard D. Irwin, 1952), p. 331; Arthur R. Burns, *The Decline of Competition* (New York: McGraw-Hill Book Company, 1936); Melvin G. de Chazeau and Alfred Kahn, *Integration and Competition in the Petroleum Industry* (New Haven: Yale University Press, 1959); Nugent Wedding, *Vertical Integration in Marketing* (Urbana, Ill.: University of Illinois Bureau of Economic and Business Research, 1952); Oliver E. Williamson, "The Vertical Integration of Production: Market Failure Considerations," *American Economic Review*, Vol. 61 (May 1971), pp. 112–23; Lars Mattson, *Integration and Efficiency in Marketing Systems* (Stockholm, Sweden: Stockholm School of Economics, 1969); Louis P. Bucklin, "The Economic Base of Franchising," in Thompson (ed.), *op. cit.*, pp. 33–62; Samuel H. Logan, "A Conceptual Framework for Analyzing Economies of Vertical Integration," *American Journal of Agricultural Economics*, Vol. 51 (November 1969), pp. 836–48; and Michael Etgar, "Determinants of Structural Changes in Vertical Marketing Systems," Working Paper No. 201, School of Management, State University of New York at Buffalo, 1974.

[76] See Sue Shellenbarger, "Bigness Counts in Agribusiness, and Cargill Inc. Is Fast Becoming a Commodities Conglomerate," *Wall Street Journal*, May 7, 1982, p. 40.

the independent agency system, the direct writing (vertically integrated) system will tend to have:

1. Less intrasystem duplication in claim handling, underwriting, and billing
2. A higher degree of similarity between insurers' and dealers' record-keeping procedures

---

EXHIBIT 7–9 Benefits and costs of vertical integration

	PORTER[1]	WILLIAMSON[2]	BUZZELL[3]	BHASIN AND STERN[4]

Benefits	1. Secure economies of
	  a. combined operations
	  b. internal control and coordination
	  c. information
	  d. avoiding the market
	  e. stable relationships
	2. Tap into technology (esp. via tapered integration)
	3. Ensure supply and/or demand
	4. Offset bargaining
	5. Enhance ability to differentiate (value added)
	6. Elevate entry and mobility barriers
	7. Enter a higher-return business
	8. Defend against foreclosure
		1. Facilitate adaptive sequential decision making (economize on bounded rationality)
		2. Attenuate opportunism
		3. Promote convergent expectations (reduce uncertainty)
		4. Overcome conditions of information impactedness
		5. Obtain a more satisfying trading atmosphere
			1. Reduce transaction costs
			2. Ensure supply
			3. Improve coordination
			4. Enhance technological capabilities
			5. Elevate entry barriers
				1. Secure supply
				2. Rationalize inventory levels
				3. Utilize managerial slack
				4. Secure operating economies via:
				  a. technological interdependencies
				  b. eliminating risk premiums
				  c. reduced transaction costs
				  d. economies of scale
				  e. reducing the risk buffer
				  f. stable relationships
				  g. obtaining capital resources
				5. Gain managerial information
				6. Achieve product differentiation
				7. Achieve price differentiation
				8. Adaptability
				9. Coordinate demand and supply
				10. Erect entry barriers
				11. Achieve diversification

Sources:
[1] Michael E. Porter, *Competitive Strategy* (New York: The Free Press, 1980).
[2] Oliver E. Williamson, *Markets and Hierarchies: Analysis and Antitrust Implications* (New York: The Free Press, 1975).
[3] Robert D. Buzzell, "Is Vertical Integration Profitable?" *Harvard Business Review,* Vol. 61 (January–February 1983), pp. 92–102.
[4] Ajay Bhasin and Louis W. Stern, "Vertical Integration: Considerations of Efficiency, Risk, and Strategy," in M. G. Harvey and R. F. Lusch (eds.), *Marketing Channels: Domestic and International Perspectives* (Norman Okla.: University of Oklahoma Printing Services, 1982).

| Costs | 1. Cost of overcoming mobility barriers
2. Increased operating leverage
3. Reduced flexibility to change partners
4. Higher overall exit barriers
5. Capital investment requirements
6. Foreclosure of access to supplier or consumer research or know-how
7. Maintaining balance
8. Dulled incentives
9. Differing managerial requirements | 1. Biases favoring the maintenance or extension of internal operations
2. Communication distortion
3. Internal opportunism
4. Bounded rationality (spans of control)
5. Bureaucratic insularity
6. Loss of moral involvement
7. Dulled incentives | 1. Capital requirement
2. Unbalanced throughput
3. Reduced flexibility
4. Loss of specialization | 1. Diseconomies of:
a. imbalanced stages of integrated operations
b. management
c. lower returns
d. transactional distortions
2. Increased operating leverage
3. Barriers to mobility |

3. Faster intrasystem movements of new homeowner policies and endorsements of automobile and homeowner policies
4. Higher quality of intrasystem communication
5. Lower risk of operation
6. Greater use of management training, salesman training, and financial planning
7. Greater use of electronic data processing
8. Higher productivity at the distributive level[77]

There are, however, numerous disadvantages to vertical integration in distribution, many of which are listed in Exhibit 7–9. Phillips puts the arguments against vertical integration neatly:

> Shifting a transaction from the market to the firm does not . . . ensure greater efficiency. A decision to integrate vertically into the wholesale or retail stage of an industry necessarily entails expanding the size and complexity of the enterprise. As firms grow larger and more complex, various inefficiencies can emerge. Diseconomies of scale may be associated with the internalization of marketing tasks, resulting in management's inability to control efficiently such aspects of distribution operations as inventory costs and salesforce expenditures. Also, because the vertically integrated unit has a captive source of supply instead of having to compete for business, incentives to perform efficiently may be dulled. In turn, managers and employees of the integrated units may pursue goals incongruent with corporate objectives, such as the use of corporate expense accounts for personal consumption purposes or investment in unproductive overhead. . . . The cumulative result of

[77] Etgar, "Effects of Administrative Control," *op. cit.,* p. 72, See also Michael Etgar, "The Effects of Forward Vertical Integration on Service Performance of a Distributive Industry," *Journal of Industrial Economics,* Vol. 26 (March 1978), pp. 249–55.

these and other inefficiencies is termed *control loss*—that is, the failure of a vertically integrated firm to achieve goal pursuit and cost behavior on the part of employees consistent with profit-maximization objectives.[78]

If a channel member finds that it must make what is often a massive investment in order to own and, thus, control its distribution system, then, as Sturdivant and colleagues point out,

> the hoped-for advantages . . . [may] prove illusory. The product mix and the marketing style of firms on different levels of the channel are, of necessity, quite different. To alter strategy in one level to meet the needs of another level may result in disaster simply because survival on the annexed level cannot be maintained in this manner.[79]

Indeed, distribution is typically a multi-product activity, with the product mix of distributors substantially different from that of any one manufacturer and, for that matter, often from that of other channel members engaged primarily in distribution. Vertical integration under these circumstances involves a substantial broadening of the corporation's product responsibility as well as its functional role. Picture, if you will, the changes in orientation that would have to ensue if, in order to secure greater control over the marketing of its products at point of sale, General Foods were to purchase Safeway Corporation, or if Marshall Field & Company were to purchase Brown Shoe Corporation to ensure adequate supplies. In addition, the local managerial problems and personal service content of wholesaling and retailing often discourage manufacturers from integrating forward, just as mechanical production problems discourage distribution firms from acquiring manufacturing concerns.

Also, a host of organizational behavior problems are encountered when corporate systems are formed. As Ouchi has observed, organizations must permit subunits to adapt to local ecological demands in order to cope with environmental uncertainty.[80] However, as they do, the subunits (i.e., the vertically integrated channel members, such as distribution centers, sales branches, and retail outlets) develop differentiated objectives, standards of performance, and underlying values. According to Ouchi,

> this leads to heterogeneity of interests, which undermines trust and thus gives rise to opportunistic behavior. In extreme circumstances, the option of close performance auditing is also lost because the parties cannot agree even on what constitutes acceptable performance. Under this condition, organizations fail. . . .[81]

Furthermore, humanistic social psychologists have long argued that formal organizations, such as corporate systems, will "fail" when (1) workers are placed in a dependent state, which denies them the possibility of psychological success, (2) lack of trust among employees distorts cooperation and communication, (3) jobs

---

[78] Lynn W. Phillips, "Explaining Control Losses in Corporate Marketing Channels: An Organizational Analysis," *Journal of Marketing Research*, Vol. 19 (November 1982), pp. 525–26.

[79] Sturdivant et al., *op. cit.*, p. 653.

[80] William G. Ouchi, "An Organizational Failures Framework," Graduate School of Business, Stanford University, 1978, p. 16. This paper, in significantly different form and content, was published in the *Administrative Science Quarterly*, Vol. 25 (1980), pp. 129ff.

[81] *Ibid.*, 16–17.

are specialized to the point of dehumanization, and (4) control is based exclusively on following a set of rules.[82]

Some of these reasons explain why automobile and tire manufacturers, for example, have not integrated more extensively down to the retail level. Marx points out that forward integration in these industries was limited by "the superior market incentives for entrepreneurial performance and the mechanisms for decentralized decision making at the retail level."[83] The large firm has developed refined incentive instruments of a long-run employment nature, but, as Williamson notes, "such incentives are poorly suited to satisfy the entrepreneurial appetites of individuals who are prepared to risk their personal savings and careers in pursuit of big stakes."[84] Also, a large number of complex on-the-spot decisions must be made at the retail level in these industries. Again, as Marx observes,

> the information and communications systems necessary to coordinate the millions of complex transactions, evaluate the multitude of possibilities, and provide the pricing flexibility needed to meet each transaction would have placed a heavy burden on an integrated firm.[85]

Dealings with customers may require a measure of flexibility or discretion in negotiating individual transactions that is relatively high to entrust to a salaried employee—as in bargaining on the price of an automobile or a set of steel-belted radial tires.[86]

Other managerial problems that may attend the formation of corporate vertical marketing systems include the likelihood that more employees may be needed to serve the various levels of distribution, and this can mean higher payroll, more insurance, and perhaps involvement with different unions. The firm must also consider the possible diseconomies of inventory control and, in the case of manufacturers, whether the product is marketed more efficiently by more diversified wholesale and retail outlets. Integration may also require increased warehousing and storage capacities and showrooms with adequate floor and shelf space to achieve reasonable product exposure. Finally, as is pointed out in the next chapter, there are certain legal restrictions on corporate integration, particularly when such integration is accomplished via merger or acquisition.

As a conclusion to his enlightening analysis of the profitability of vertical integration, Buzzell issues the following warnings, among others, to those considering forming corporate systems:

1. *Beware heightened investment.* Rising investment requirements offset the higher profit margins associated with intensified vertical integration. If integration can somehow be achieved without the penalty of a proportionately higher investment base, then increasing vertical integration should be extremely beneficial.

2. *Consider alternatives to ownership.* Long-term contracts and long-term relationships with suppliers or distributors can produce benefits comparable to vertical integration.

---

[82] *Ibid.*, p. 8.

[83] Thomas G. Marx, "Distribution Efficiency in Franchising," *MSU Business Topics*, Vol. 28 (Winter 1980), p. 10.

[84] Williamson, *Markets and Hierarchies*, p. 201.

[85] Marx, *op. cit.*, p. 12.

[86] Richard E. Caves and William F. Murphy II, "Franchising: Firms, Markets, and Intangible Assets," *Southern Economic Journal*, Vol. 42 (April 1976), p. 575.

3. *Carefully analyze scale requirements.* A significant risk in many vertical integration strategies is that a production or distribution stage has too small a scope to be run competitively against independent suppliers or customers.[87]

And, in support of Buzzell's point 2, Harrigan's research has shown that if channel members can use their power creatively, they can administer their channels and achieve performance levels equal to or better than those in channels that are more formally integrated via ownership.[88]

ADVANTAGES OF VERTICAL MARKETING SYSTEMS

As contrasted with conventional channels, vertical marketing systems are networks of interconnected units, each of which, in theory, participates in an optimum combination of the marketing flows. Coordination is achieved through the use of detailed plans and comprehensive programs; channel members are, in fact, programmed to achieve systemwide economies. Entry is rigorously controlled by the system's requirements and by market conditions. In the case of contractual and corporate systems, membership loyalty is assured through the use of specific agreements or ownership. As a result, the network tends to be relatively stable. The limited number of strategies in such systems are preoccupied with cost, volume, and investment relationships at *all stages* of the marketing process. There is likely to be a heavy reliance on relatively "scientific" decisions, and the decision makers are generally committed, in a philosophical and analytical sense, to sophisticated marketing concepts and the formation of viable systems rather than emotionally committed to established business methods and traditional approaches.[89]

Unlike the tasks of many conventional channels, those of vertical marketing systems are routinized. As Bucklin has observed:

> Of the many dimensions that form the relationship between agencies on different levels of a distribution channel, perhaps the most important is the extent of the role of day-to-day market pressure. Day-to-day market forces comprise the panoply of shifting prices, deals, allowances, promotions, and minor competitive crises that constitute the most visible strains of a market agency's work. Their presence in the interfirm relationship is manifested by detailed negotiations for each contract for the sale of goods to provide continuous adjustment to these prices. They disappear when goods are transferred as part of long-range plans where the issue is not optimal profit on each sale, but the means of better exploiting the market for the mutual advantage of both parties.
>
> If the importance of day-to-day forces is defined as a continuum ranging from one pole, where each transaction is negotiated separately in the light of market conditions, to the other, where the movement of goods is an automatic

---

[87] Robert D. Buzzell, "Is Vertical Integration Profitable?" *Harvard Business Review*, Vol. 61 (January-February 1983), pp. 96, 100.

[88] Kathryn Rudie Harrigan, "A Framework for Looking at Vertical Integration," *Journal of Business Strategy*, Vol. 3 (Winter 1983), p. 34.

[89] This paragraph is based on McCammon, "Perspectives for Distribution Programming," p. 44.

element part of a long-range marketing plan, then franchising as a mode of distribution may be said to occupy the middle ground. At the planned end of the continuum is to be found the integrated [corporate vertical] system; at the day-to-day pole is the independent [conventional] system.[90]

Vertical marketing systems seem to capitalize on programmed organization, economies of scale, and economies of standardization that exist within activities at the various levels of distribution. On the other hand, although the absence of long-term planning in independent channels results in higher distribution costs, it must be recognized that the independent retailer is free to tap supplies from a number of manufacturers and wholesalers in order to better adapt to his market. Thus, for example, corporate chain store managers are heavily circumscribed in adapting to their markets. The franchise operator seems to occupy the middle ground on both the cost and adaptation fronts. While cost advantages often work in favor of vertical marketing systems, independent operators seem to have an advantage in adapting to a heterogeneous market opportunity.[91] The standardized level of performance achieved within vertical marketing systems is, though, rarely attained in conventional channels. Both industrial and household consumers prefer uniformity in the quality of the goods and services they purchase, which gives systems capable of delivering such uniformity a strong advantage.

From a managerial perspective, vertical marketing systems are developed in order to achieve a degree of control over the cost and quality of the functions performed by various channel members. The strength of such systems lies in their capitalization on role specification through shifting and allocating the marketing flows. In theory, the performance of a vertical marketing system can approximate the performance of Bucklin's "normative channel"[92] in that institutions can be grouped and organized in such a way that no other type of grouping could create greater profits or more consumer satisfaction per dollar of product cost.

In conventional channels, power is often diffused among channel members.[93] In corporate systems, power is concentrated at one channel level through ownership. At least a moderate degree of expert and reward power must exist at the administrator's level in administered systems, whereas legitimate power obviously resides with the initiator of the legal agreements in contractual systems.[94] All in all, unlike many conventional marketing channels, vertical marketing systems contain a locus of power, and, as was pointed out in earlier chapters, such a locus is a prerequisite for channel leadership.[95] Because power is central-

---

[90] Louis P. Bucklin, "The Economic Base of Franchising," in Thompson (ed.), *op. cit.*, p. 33.

[91] *Ibid.*, pp. 33–62.

[92] Louis P. Bucklin, *A Theory of Distribution Channel Structure* (Berkeley, Calif.: Institute of Business and Economic Research, University of California, 1966), p. 5; Louis P. Bucklin, "A Normative Approach to the Economies of Channel Structure," in Louis P. Bucklin (ed.), *Vertical Marketing Systems*, pp. 164–73; and discussions of Bucklin's theory earlier in this book.

[93] For an example, see Adel I. El-Ansary and Louis W. Stern, "Power Measurement in the Distribution Channel," *Journal of Marketing Research*, Vol. 9 (February 1972), pp. 47–52.

[94] Other bases of power are also in evidence in contractual systems, as shown in Hunt and Nevin, "Power in a Channel of Distribution," *op. cit.*

[95] See also Louis W. Stern, "The Interorganizational Management of Distribution Channels: Prerequisites and Prescriptions," in George Fisk (ed.), *New Essays in Marketing Theory* (Boston: Allyn and Bacon, 1971), pp. 301–14.

ized, role specification and conflict management are more likely to be accomplished, and thus better channel performance can be expected.

Implicit within the concept of a vertical marketing system is management recognition that the entire channel is the relevant unit of competition. In conventional channels, independent members tend to believe that competitive viability is the result solely of actions taken on their specific levels of distribution.

SUMMARY AND CONCLUSIONS

Conventional marketing channels composed of independently owned institutions and agencies frequently suffer from several weaknesses, the foremost among them being the absence of a systemwide orientation and inclusive goals. If a locus of power is also absent, the specification of roles and the management of conflict in conventional channels are likely to be difficult, at best. Even when a locus of power is present (as in the marketing channel for motion pictures), there is no guarantee that the performance of the channel will be any better than when power is diffused.

Vertical marketing systems have emerged as significant forms of channel organization. They represent, for the most part, sophisticated attempts by management to overcome the inherent weaknesses of conventional channels. Administered vertical marketing systems are those in which marketing activities are coordinated through the use of programs developed by one or a limited number of firms. Administrative strategies combined with the exercise of power are relied on to obtain systemic economies. Such strategies have been most frequently adopted by suppliers and by carriers. They have involved the use of facilities management, modular merchandising, coordinated display, and automatic replenishment programs as well as programmed merchandising agreements.

Contractual vertical marketing systems are those in which independent firms at different channel levels integrate their programs on a contractual basis to achieve systemic economies and increased market impact. They include, among other forms of organization, wholesaler-sponsored voluntary groups, retailer-sponsored cooperative groups, and franchise systems. By virtue of the use of legitimate power in their formulation, contractual systems tend to be more tightly knit than administered systems.

Corporate vertical marketing systems are those in which channel members on different levels of distribution are owned and operated by one organization. In fact, such systems are synonymous with both forward and backward vertical integration. Forward integration is on the increase, even within franchise systems. Backward integration has long been typified by corporate chain store systems. The key tradeofís in instituting any corporate vertical marketing system are the investment required plus the flexibility lost, on the one hand, versus the control secured over marketing activities of channel members plus the operating economies gained, on the other.

The organizational dimensions of conventional and vertical marketing systems are summarized in Exhibit 7–10. From a managerial perspective, vertical marketing systems appear to offer a series of advantages over conventional channels. The former employ a systemic approach and are committed to scien-

Organizational dimensions of conventional and vertical marketing systems

DIMENSION	CONVENTIONAL	ADMINISTERED	CONTRACTUAL	CORPORATE
Relation of units to an inclusive goal	No inclusive goals	Units with disparate goals, but informal collaboration for inclusive goals	Units with disparate goals but some organization for inclusive goals	Units organized for achievement of inclusive goals
Locus of inclusive decision making	Within units	In interaction of units without a formal inclusive structure	At top of inclusive structure, subject to unit ratification	At top of inclusive structure
Locus of authority	Exclusively at unit level	Exclusively at unit level	Primarily at unit level	At top of hierarchy of inclusive structure
Structural provision for division of labor	No formally structured division of labor within an inclusive context	Units structured autonomously, may agree to *ad hoc* division of labor, without restructuring	Units structured autonomously, may agree to a division of labor, which may affect their structure	Units structured for division of labor within inclusive organization
Commitment to a leadership subsystem	Commitment only to unit leaders	Commitment only to unit leaders	Norms of moderate commitment	Norms of high commitment
Prescribed collectivity-orientation of units	Little or none	Low to moderate	Moderate to high	High

Source: Adapted from "The Interorganizational Field as a Focus for Investigation," by Roland L. Warren, published in *Administrative Science Quarterly*, Vol. 12 (1967), by permission of *Administrative Science Quarterly*. Copyright © 1967.

tific decision making while engendering channel member loyalty and network stability. Tasks are routinized, and economies of standardization are likely. Because a locus of power is available and utilized in a positive manner, it is possible to gain at least some control over the cost and quality of the functions performed by various channel members. Furthermore, inherent within systems management is the notion that the channel itself is the relevant unit of competition.

DISCUSSION QUESTIONS

1. According to Bucklin, the issue of channel performance focuses on the major conflict that exists between two major dimensions of channel performance. On the one hand, consumers and users are concerned primarily with lowering the costs of the goods and services sold and therefore with reducing the costs of distribution. On the other hand, consumers want to benefit from and receive some marketing services in conjunction with the good or service they purchase. However, provision of these services increases the cost of distribution.

Evaluate conventional, administered, contractual, and corporate systems relative to the performance dimensions mentioned by Bucklin. Which, if any, would tend to be superior overall?

2. It has been argued that the price mechanism is the formal means through which vertical coordination is achieved in conventional or fragmented channels. What does this mean, and what are its consequences for channel performance, both from a macro and a micro perspective?

3. Suggest three ways in which the marketing channel for motion pictures might be improved.

4. What are the advantages of administered systems versus contractual systems? What are the disadvantages of administered systems that might be overcome through the formation of contractual systems?

5. A number of concessions are available to suppliers who are seeking to gain reseller support of their marketing programs (see Appendix 7A). Classify the concessions listed below by the various bases of power (coercive, reward, expert, referent, and legitimate).

Price Concessions

A. Discount Structure:
    Trade (functional) discounts
    Quantity discounts
    Cash discounts
    Anticipation allowances
    Free goods
    Prepaid freight
    Seasonal discounts
    Mixed carload privilege
    Drop shipping privilege
    Trade deals

B. Discount Substitutes:
    Display materials
    Premarked merchandise
    Inventory control programs
    Sales promotion literature
    Training programs
    Shelf stocking programs
    Management consulting services
    Merchandising programs
    Sales "spiffs"
    Technical assistance

Financial Assistance

A. Conventional Lending Arrangements:
    Term loans
    Inventory floor plans
    Notes payable financing
    Installment financing of fixtures and equipment
    Lease and note guarantee programs

B. Extended Dating:
    E.O.M. dating
    Seasonal dating
    R.O.G. dating
    "Extra" dating
    Post dating

Protective Provisions

A. Price Protection:
    Premarked merchandise
    "Franchise" pricing
    Agency agreements

B. Territorial Protection:
    Selective distribution
    Exclusive distribution

C. Inventory Protection:
    Consignment selling
    Memorandum selling
    Liberal returns allowances
    Rebate programs
    Reorder guarantees
    Guaranteed support of sale events
    Fast delivery

6. Which of the various concessions listed in question 5 are likely to be useful in marketing through supermarkets? Through department stores? Through catalog showrooms? Through warehouse showrooms? Through industrial (full-function) distributions?

7. Which type of cooperative—wholesaler-sponsored, retailer-sponsored, or consumer-sponsored—would you expect to be most successful? Why have consumer cooperatives never enjoyed widespread popularity in the United States?

8. Write a plan for starting your own franchising operation. What would be the essential ingredients of the plan? What specific points would you include in the contractual arrangement you establish with your franchisees?

9. Assume you are the manufacturer of a broad line of moderately priced furniture. When would you seriously consider forming a corporate vertical marketing system for your line? What factors would you take into account in making your decision?

10. Montgomery Ward describes its supplier investments as "very minimal" and says it will consider such relationships "only as a last resort in order to meet the company's requirements for satisfying its customer needs." According to a Ward's executive, the firm's only major supplier investment is in the Standard T Chemical Company, which manufactures paint.

   Compare and contrast Ward's philosophy with that of Sears. Which would you endorse as an overall corporate policy if you were running a comparable retailing organization (e.g., Penney)?

Appendix 7A

Selected Concessions Available to Suppliers Seeking to Gain Reseller Support of Their Marketing Programs

I. *"Price" Concessions*
   A. Discount Structure:
      Trade (functional) discounts
      Quantity discounts
      Cash discounts
      Anticipation allowances
      Free goods
      Prepaid freight
      New product, display, and advertising allowances (without performance requirements)
      Seasonal discounts
      Mixed carload privilege
      Drop shipping privilege
      Trade deals
   B. Discount Substitutes:
      Display materials
      Premarked merchandise

Source: Bert C. McCammon, Jr., "Perspectives for Distribution Programming," in Louis P. Bucklin (ed.), *Vertical Marketing Systems* (Glenview, Ill.: Scott, Foresman and Co., 1970), pp. 36–37.

Inventory control programs
Catalogs and sales promotion literature
Training programs
Shelf-stocking programs
Advertising matrices
Management consulting services
Merchandising programs
Sales "spiffs"
Technical assistance
Payment of sales personnel and demonstrator salaries
Promotional and advertising allowances (with performance require-
ments)

II. *Financial Assistance*
    A. Conventional Lending Arrangements:
        Term loans
        Inventory floor plans
        Notes payable financing
        Accounts payable financing
        Installment financing of fixtures and equipment
        Lease and note guarantee programs
        Accounts receivable financing
    B. Extended Dating:
        E.O.M. dating
        Seasonal dating
        R.O.G. dating
        "Extra" dating
        Post dating

III. *Protective Provisions*
    A. Price Protection:
        Premarked merchandise
        "Franchise" pricing
        Agency agreements
    B. Inventory Protection:
        Consignment selling
        Memorandum selling
        Liberal returns allowances
        Rebate programs
        Reorder guarantees
        Guaranteed support of sales events
        Maintenance of "spot" stocks and fast delivery
    C. Territorial Protection:
        Selective distribution
        Exclusive distribution

Common Industrial Channel Offerings, Categorized by Distributor Requirements

Distributor Requirements	Channel Offerings
Ease of Marketing	High value products for customer
	Complementary product lines
	New products to satisfy customer needs
	Discounts to meet competition
	Price promotions
	Promotional allowances
	National advertising and publicity
	Joint sales calls
	Missionary sales calls
	Sales training
	Telemarketing training
	Sales aids and product literature
	Spiffs
	Sales leads and market research
	Factory schools
	Catalogues and merchandising assistance
	Manufacturer's reputation for quality and service
	Direct order entry systems
	Expedited delivery for critical customers
	Drop shipping
Financial Returns	Functional discounts
	Delivery terms (esp. freight absorption)
	Financial management training
	Management succession training
	Computer usage courses
	Inventory control, working capital management, and receivables management training
	Software packages
	Logistic and materials handling consulting
	Information on government regulation
	Product standardization
Minimized Risk	Liberal return policies on defectives, discontinued lines and annual returns
	Product and service warranties
	Products on consignment
	Liberal credit policies
	Ample warning of price changes and product deletion
	Reasonable number of competing distributors franchised per trade area
	Technical assistance by phone or visit
	Product repair service
Continuity in Business Relationship	Continual communication
	Distributor councils
	Participation in planning process
	Written sales agreements or contracts

Source: James A. Narus and James C. Anderson, "Gaining a Competitive Edge through Positioning to Industrial Distributors," Northwestern University Department of Marketing Working Paper, 1984, pp. 16, 17.

IBM's View of Channel Value-Added Elements

Marketing	Opportunity identification
	Marketing strategy
	Advertising/promotion
	Product positioning
	Product requirements
	Demand creation
Sales	Prospecting
	Account planning
	Education/briefing
	Configure design
	Propose/justify
	Demonstration
	Financing
	Contract negotiation
Order/Administration	Order entry
	Customer verification
	Backlog management
	Contract administration
	Billing
	A/R
	Sold to records
Distribution	Logistics support
	Inventory management
	Delivery
Support/Service	Education
	Installation planning
	Install/set-up
	Pilot test
	Software
	Problem determination
	Warranty
	Technical support
	Service
Integration/Customization	Hardware
	Software
	Connectivity
Coverage/Access/Capacity	Geography
	Enterprise
	Industry
	End user

Source: IBM Corporate Marketing, 1985.

The 7-ELEVEN® Store Franchise

7-ELEVEN . . . A Way of Life

7-ELEVEN is, to busy people of all ages, the friendly little store that's "just around the corner." It's the convenient place to stop for a loaf of bread, quart of milk, package of cigarettes, groceries, beverages, picnic supplies, candy, "Hot to Go" foods, or everyone's favorite ice drink . . . Slurpee. 7-ELEVEN Stores are small, compact, easily accessible, and usually open for business 24 hours a day, 7 days a week. Their convenient locations, fast service, and friendly image have combined to make 7-ELEVEN shopping a familiar part of the American lifestyle.

7-ELEVEN is a division of The Southland Corporation, pioneer of the convenience store and a recognized leader in the food and dairy industries. Approximately 7,200 7-ELEVEN Stores are located virtually throughout the nation and, in some areas, stores are available for franchise to qualified applicants.

7-ELEVEN offers a business system for a ready-to-operate store. It includes training, counselling, bookkeeping, financing, and merchandising assistance. This brochure, which briefly introduces the 7-ELEVEN System, is your invitation to discuss in detail how you and your family can become a part of 7-ELEVEN.

Real Estate

7-ELEVEN's real estate representatives research and select sites based upon population, traffic flow, convenience to homes, and competition. After 7-ELEVEN buys or leases a site, the completed 7-ELEVEN store is leased to the franchisee.

Equipment

All equipment in the store, including heating and air conditioning, vaults, shelving, cash registers, and refrigerated cases, are included in the lease to the franchisee, who is responsible for equipment maintenance.

Merchandise

7-ELEVEN arranges for the initial inventory of merchandise in the store. Thereafter, the franchisee orders and stocks all the merchandise. 7-ELEVEN prepares for the franchisee lists of recommended merchandise and retail selling prices. These lists are based on the Company's many years of experience in convenience store merchandising. 7-ELEVEN also recommends vendors who, it is believed, offer the best service and the highest quality merchandise at the lowest cost. Some recommended vendors may be affiliated with 7-ELEVEN, and some recommended merchandise may be produced by divisions of The Southland Corporation. A franchisee is free to purchase merchandise from any ven-

Source: The Southland Corporation, *The 7-ELEVEN Franchise*, promotional brochure. Reprinted with the permission of The Southland Corporation.

dor and to establish the retail prices. The franchisee receives credit for all discounts and allowances on merchandise purchased.

Advertising

Advertising plays a significant role in assisting a franchisee in building sales and profits. For many years, 7-ELEVEN advertising has received widespread recognition.

"AMERICA LIKES THE FREEDOM"
"IT'S ABOUT TIME"
"IF IT'S NOT AROUND THE HOUSE,
IT'S JUST AROUND THE CORNER"

A franchisee is, of course, free to place additional advertising.

Training

Prior to final acceptance by 7-ELEVEN franchise applicants are required to successfully complete the 7-ELEVEN Store Operations Training Program, including actual in-store experience in a Training Store, which is an operating 7-ELEVEN Store. The Training Store experience is followed by one week of classroom training at the Regional Training Center, where the prospective franchisee learns a variety of management skills, techniques, and procedures essential to successful operation of a 7-ELEVEN store. The cost of training is included in the initial Franchise Fee.

Employees

Although most franchised 7-ELEVEN Stores are family operated, it is usually necessary for the franchisee to employ additional part-time and full-time help.

The franchisee is responsible for the hiring and training of employees and for all payroll expenses, including employee taxes. Based on the franchisee's authorization and employees' time cards, 7-ELEVEN prepares the payroll checks for the franchisee's employees.

Personal Insurance

A 7-ELEVEN franchisee, family, and employees are eligible to participate in the 7-ELEVEN Franchisee Group Insurance program which provides insurance for dental, sickness, disability (franchisees only), or death. An H.R. 10 Retirement Plan is also available in most areas at the option of the franchisee.

Bookkeeping

7-ELEVEN keeps bookkeeping records on the franchisee's operation of the 7-ELEVEN Store. A franchisee makes daily cash deposits of sales receipts. From these, 7-ELEVEN pays for all operating expenses and merchandising purchases approved by the franchisee in connection with operations of the store.

Investment

The investment requirements for a 7-ELEVEN Store franchise include the cost of the inventory, the cash register fund and all necessary operating expenses. The exact amount varies depending upon the location of the store and the inventory requirements. On December 31, 1985 the average total investment in the inventory for a 7-ELEVEN Store was $38,806, the average cash register fund was $773, and the approximate cost for licenses and permits was $500. 7-ELEVEN will finance a portion of the investment for qualified applicants.

Franchise Fee

The initial franchise fee for a 7-ELEVEN Store may vary for each store, however, the fee is computed for each store as follows: for stores which have been continuously operated for the preceding 12 months, the fee is 15% of the total GROSS PROFIT of the store for such period of time (excluding gross profit from gasoline); for all other stores, the fee is 15% of the annualized average per store month gross profit for all stores within the District in which the store is located (excluding gross profit from gasoline).

A Franchisee Can Most Affect Profits by:

- General management aptitude
- Ability to hire and train competent employees
- Control of employee and customer pilferage
- Creative salesmanship
- Sincere customer relations
- Ability to create a friendly store atmosphere
- Maintenance of a clean and orderly store

Profits

A local 7-ELEVEN representative will discuss the financial history of the store being considered.

The GROSS PROFIT of the store is shared by the franchisee and 7-ELEVEN.

The percentage of GROSS PROFIT paid by the franchisee to 7-ELEVEN is a continuing charge for the rental of the store building and equipment, utilities, advertising, bookkeeping, and merchandising and general advisory assistance.

From the franchisee's share of the GROSS PROFIT, the franchisee pays all other operating expenses, such as:

• Payroll	• Cash Variation	• Equipment Repair
• Store supplies	• Advertising	• General Maintenance
• Telephone	• Employees' Group Ins.	• Janitorial Service
• Laundry	• Security Expense	• Interest Expense
• Payroll Taxes	• Bad Merchandise	• Taxes and License
• Bad Checks	• Inventory Variation	• Miscellaneous Expense

The amount remaining, if any, after payment of the operating expenses is the franchisee's net income.

CHAPTER EIGHT

Legal Constraints on the Interorganization Management of Marketing Channels

Instituting effective interorganization management requires the use of power, as pointed out in the preceding chapters. There are, however, significant legal constraints on how power may be employed in the marketing channel. Prior to developing and implementing interorganizational strategies and programs, marketing managers at all levels of distribution must comprehend the intention and the scope of these constraints so that any strategy or program that is promulgated will not run afoul of the various antitrust enforcement agencies.[1]

The focus in this chapter is on federal legislation, even though there are myriad international, state, and local laws that directly affect distribution practices. In addition, attention is given only to legislation directly affecting relations among commercial channel members. Excluded from the discussion is consumer-oriented legislation, even though such legislation obviously tempers certain activities among commercial channel members.[2]

---

[1] Some of the material in this chapter comes directly from Louis W. Stern and Thomas L. Eovaldi, *Legal Aspects of Marketing Strategy: Antitrust and Consumer Protection Issues* (Englewood Cliffs, N.J.: Prentice-Hall, 1984). For elaboration of many of the topics covered in this chapter, the reader is encouraged to see that book.

[2] The Federal Trade Commission has attacked thousands of devious schemes in distribution that directly affect the consumer. The largest categories have been fictitious pricing, wherein goods are falsely advertised as bargains; "bait and switch" advertising, by which customers, lured into a store by a spectacular bargain not intended to be sold, are "switched" to other, more expensive purchases; exaggerated claims for the efficacy of drugs and cosmetics; the selling of used products as new; failure to disclose the limitations of guarantees; and misrepresentations of the quality of products. In addition, the FTC polices the labeling of furs and textiles, so that a buyer can be sure the product is made of the material claimed on the label; the Flammable Fabrics Act, to protect consumers from dangerously flammable clothing; the Fair Packaging and Labeling Act, to inform the consumer of the net contents of a package; the Truth in Lending Act, which enables consumers to

Table 8-1 Principal laws affecting the interorganization management of marketing channels

Act	Key Provisions
Sherman Antitrust Act, 1890	1. Prohibits contracts or combinations in restraint of interstate and foreign commerce. 2. Makes monopoly or attempt at monopoly a crime in interstate or foreign commerce.
Clayton Antitrust Act, 1914	Where competition is substantially lessened it prohibits: 1. Price discrimination in sales or leasing 2. Exclusive dealing 3. Tying contracts 4. Interlocking directorates among competitors 5. Intercorporate stockholding
Celler-Kefauver Act, 1950	Prohibits purchase of assets of another firm if competition is lessened.
FTC Act, 1914	1. Prohibits unfair trade practices injurious to competition or a competitor. 2. Sets up FTC to determine unfairness.
Robinson-Patman Act, 1936	1. Discriminatory prices are prohibited if they reduce competition at any point in the channel. 2. Discriminatory prices can be given in good faith to meet competition. 3. Brokerage allowances are allowed only if earned by an independent broker. 4. Sellers must give all services and promotional allowances to all buyers equally if the buyers are in competition. Alternatives must be offered. 5. Buyers are prohibited from knowingly inducing price discrimination. 6. Price discrimination can be legal if it results from real cost differences in serving different customers. 7. Prohibits agreement with competitors to charge unreasonably low prices to destroy competition.
State Sales Below Cost	Prohibits selling below cost or without minimum markup.
FTC Trade Practice Rules	1. Enforced by FTC. Define unfair competition for individual industries. These practices are prohibited by FTC. 2. Define rules of sound practice. These rules are not enforced by the FTC, but are recommended.

Although all legislation may be said to affect the legitimate power of channel members, the legal constraints examined in this chapter basically confine the use of coercive power and reward power in channel management. There are additional laws that inhibit the means by which vertical integration can be employed to achieve the goals of a given distribution system. Therefore, the following discussion centers on legal limitations to the use of coercive power, reward power, *and* vertical integration. The principal laws constraining interorganization management in marketing are listed in Table 8–1.

There are a large number of marketing policies that suppliers can implement to control or create incentives for their distribution systems. And there are

shop for credit by comparing the finance charges and the annual percentage rates of creditors; the Fair Credit Reporting Act, which seeks to protect consumers from the reporting of erroneous personal information by credit bureaus; and the Consumer Product Safety Act, which attempts to minimize the number of physical injuries to consumers caused by dangerous or defective products. Major federal consumer legislation is reviewed in Laurence P. Feldman, *Consumer Protection: Problems and Prospects* (St. Paul: West Publishing Co., 1976); Joe L. Welch, *Marketing Law* (Tulsa: PPC Books, 1980); and Stern and Eovaldi, *op. cit.*

numerous antitrust precedents that deal with these policies, because some of them represent blatant restraints of trade. A critical issue that has evolved in antitrust cases, especially in the late 1970s, is whether certain of these policies, while severely restricting *intrabrand* competition, are actually promoting, or at least not substantially lessening, *interbrand* competition. Intrabrand competition is defined as competition among wholesalers or retailers of the same brand (e.g., Coca-Cola, Chevrolet, or Apple). Interbrand competition is defined as competition among all the suppliers of different brands of the same generic product (e.g., brands of soft drinks, automobiles, or personal computers). By restricting intrabrand competition via stipulations regarding resellers' activities, a supplier can supposedly motivate its wholesalers and retailers to give appropriate attention to the supplier's brand. This "appropriate attention," in turn, generates interbrand competition as the resellers of brand X attempt to win out over the resellers of brand Y in the sales and servicing of product Z.

As appealing as this argument must sound to marketing strategists who would like to implement a variety of distribution policies, the issues are frequently more complex than this. Control over distribution is sought for many reasons, some of which are highly opportunistic and self-serving. Furthermore, not all distribution policies deal with intrabrand competition; several involve restricting interbrand competition directly by foreclosing competitors from resellers' outlets. Therefore, despite the increasingly sophisticated rationale being employed to defend vertical restrictions in distribution, there are scores of reasons why marketing executives should remain alert to potential antitrust problems. While control over distribution practices may make abundant sense from a marketing perspective in a variety of different situations, there is no mandate from the Congress, the courts, or the enforcement agencies that indicates that executives are free to exert such control without considerable scrutiny.

LEGAL LIMITATIONS ON THE USE OF COERCIVE POWER

If a firm desires intensive distribution for its product, it will try to put it into as many channels as possible. This leads to relatively few legal problems in the area of customer selection, since *intrabrand* competition is usually unrestricted under these conditions. If, however, a firm wishes to limit the distribution of its product to certain outlets or to limit the freedom of its outlets in their methods of doing business, legal problems are more likely to arise. In such situations, a firm's refusal to sell or its adherence to distribution control policies may ultimately restrict intrabrand or interbrand competition and lead to conflict with the antitrust laws. Each of the distribution policies and practices discussed in the following pages involves the use of coercive power in its implementation and enforcement, and each is circumscribed by law.

Exclusive Dealing

Exclusive dealing is the requirement by a seller or lessor that its customers sell or lease only its products, or at least no products in direct competition with the seller's products. If the buyer does not comply, the seller may invoke negative sanctions by refusing to deal with the buyer. Such arrangements clearly reduce the freedom of choice of the buyer. In establishing exclusive dealing provisions, suppliers ensure that their products will be merchandised with maximum energy and enthusiasm. As Scherer points out, "the dealer confined to a single manufacturer's line can scarcely be indifferent as to whose brand consumers purchase."[3] Buyers, however, will generally receive some benefits from the arrangements, such as promotional support. They also avoid the added inventory costs that go with carrying multiple brands.

Requirements contracts, a variant of exclusive dealing, are subject to the same legal constraints. Under a requirements contract, a buyer agrees to purchase all or a part of his requirements of a product from one seller, usually for a specified period. Such arrangements clearly reduce the freedom of choice of the buyer. They also have the possibly undesirable effect of foreclosing a potential customer to alternate sellers, and vice versa, during the period stipulated in the agreement.

The use of exclusive dealing or requirements contracts is not illegal per se. These arrangements are generally viewed under a modified rule of reason, which has meant that they are subject to a measure of the effect of foreclosure on competing sellers.[4] Such marketing policies in distribution channels are circumscribed mainly by Section 3 of the Clayton Act, which stipulates that

> it shall be unlawful for any person . . . to lease or make a sale or contract for sale of goods, wares, merchandise, machinery, supplies or other commodities, whether patented or unpatented, . . . on the condition, agreement, or understanding that the lessee or purchaser thereof shall not use or deal in the goods, . . . of a competitor or competitors of the lessor or seller, where the effect of such lease, sale, or contract for sale or such condition, agreement or understanding may be to substantially lessen competition or tend to create a monopoly in any line of commerce.

However, these policies may also violate Section 1 of the Sherman Act and Section 5 of the Federal Trade Commission Act. Under the Sherman Act, various types of exclusive contracts may be deemed unlawful restraints of trade when a dominant firm is involved and when the contracts go so far beyond reasonable business needs as to have the necessary effect, or disclose a clear intention, of suppressing competition.[5] Under the FTC Act, the Federal Trade Commission has the power to stop such trade restraints in their incipiency without proof that they amount to an outright violation of Section 3 of the Clayton Act or other provisions of the antitrust laws. In other words, the FTC, using Section 5, has broad powers to declare "unfair" those practices that conflict with the basic policies of the Sherman Act and the Clayton Act, even though such practices may not constitute a violation of those laws.

Exclusive dealerships do tend to lessen competition and create monopoly, since other sellers are excluded from the outlet. Whether this is considered substantial by the courts depends on two major factors:

1. Whether the volume of the product in question is a substantial part of the total volume for the product type

---

[3] F. M. Scherer, *Industrial Market Structure and Economic Performance*, 2nd ed. (Chicago: Rand McNally College Publishing Co., 1980), p. 586.

[4] Ernest Gellhorn, *Antitrust Law and Economics in a Nutshell* (St. Paul: West Publishing Co., 1976), p. 291.

[5] A. D. Neale and D. G. Goyder, *The Antitrust Laws of the U.S.A.*, 3rd ed. (New York: Cambridge University Press, 1980), p. 266.

2. Whether the exclusive dealership excludes competitive products from a substantial share of the market

When either of these conditions obtains, the agreement is subject to attack as a restraint of competition. Both of these conditions depend on the relative size of the firms in their respective markets.

In the *Brown Shoe* case,[6] the Supreme Court decided that Brown Shoe Company, one of the world's largest shoe manufacturers, could be prohibited by the FTC from using exclusive dealerships as an unfair trade practice under the FTC Act. According to the Court, the contracts were in conflict with the spirit of the Sherman and Clayton acts; therefore, the FTC was not required to prove actual or potential injury to competition, as required by either of these acts. This finding means that exclusive dealerships or franchises are more vulnerable to prosecution under Section 5 of the FTC Act than under provisions of the other antitrust laws.

In the *Standard Oil of California* case (referred to as *Standard Stations*), exclusive dealership arrangements between the company and its independent stations were declared illegal by the Supreme Court under Section 3 of the Clayton Act on grounds that competitors had been foreclosed from a substantial share of the line of commerce affected.[7] At the time, these exclusive dealerships accounted for only 7 percent of the total sales of petroleum products in the area. The use of exclusive dealing contracts by Standard and other companies had, however, foreclosed over 50 percent of the market to independent oil refiners and wholesalers. The court declared "that exclusive dealing contracts as such are not illegal and that they might be a useful competitive device when employed by smaller firms, particularly when entering the market, but that their use by large, established firms might constitute an unwarranted restriction with consequent 'substantial lessening of competition.'" Therefore, it becomes apparent that the use of exclusive dealerships by several firms in a market may be relevant to the legality of their use by one firm.

However, in a case decided in 1961, the Court's economic impact analysis was considerably more intensive, both as to markets likely to be affected and as to the probable effect of the particular foreclosure, than that given in *Standard Stations*. The decision did not expressly overrule *Standard Stations*, but it significantly modified some of the more restrictive interpretations of the circumstances in which exclusive dealing arrangements would be allowed. The case, *Tampa Electric Co.* v. *Nashville Coal Co. et al.*,[8] involved a contract between Nashville Coal and Tampa Electric, a Florida public utility producing electricity, covering Tampa's expected requirements of coal (i.e., not less than 500,000 tons per year) for a period of 20 years. Before any coal was delivered, Nashville declined to perform the contract on the ground that it was illegal under the antitrust laws. (In actuality, the price of coal had jumped, making the arrangement less profitable for the coal company.) Tampa brought suit, arguing that the contract was both valid and enforceable.

Quantitatively, the commerce over the 20-year period of the contract would have amounted to $128 million, and on this basis the district court and the court of appeals found a violation. But the Supreme Court, in a surprising move,

---

[6] *Brown Shoe Co., Inc.* v. *Federal Trade Commission*, 384 U.S. 316 (1966).
[7] *Standard Oil Company of California and Standard Stations Inc.* v. *U.S.*, 337 U.S. 293 (1949).
[8] 365 U.S. 320 (1961).

held flatly that "the dollar volume, by itself, is not the test," thereby rejecting "quantitative substantiality" as the standard to be used in these situations. To be illegal, the Court explained, such arrangements must have a tendency to work a substantial, not merely remote, lessening of competition in the relevant competitive market. Mr. Justice Clark, speaking for the majority, indicated that "substantiality" was to be determined by taking into account the following factors:

- The relative strength of the parties involved
- The proportionate volume of commerce involved in relation to the total volume of commerce in the relevant market area
- The probable immediate and future effects that preemption of that share of the market might have on effective competition within it

The district court and the court of appeals had accepted the argument that the contract foreclosed a substantial share of the market, because Tampa's requirements equaled the total volume of coal purchased in the state of Florida before the contract's inception. The Supreme Court, in an interesting piece of economic reasoning, defined the relevant market as the *supply* market in an eight-state area, noting that mines in that coal-producing region were eager to sell more coal in Florida. When the market was defined as the entire multistate Appalachian coal region, the foreclosure amounted to less than 1 percent of the tonnage produced each year. The Court concluded that given the nature of the market (i.e., the needs of a utility for a stable supply at reasonable prices over a long period as well as the level of concentration), the small percentage of foreclosure did not actually or potentially cause a substantial reduction of competition, nor did it tend toward a monopoly.

In their summary of the *Tampa Electric* case, Neale and Goyder point out that

> the Court, finding for Tampa, distinguished earlier cases on a number of grounds. In this case, there was no seller with a dominant position in the market, as in *Standard Fashion,* nor were there myriad outlets with substantial sales volume coupled with an industry-wide practice of relying upon exclusive contracts, as in *Standard Stations.*[9]

The decision in this case indicates that the type of goods or merchandise, the geographic area of effective competition, and the substantiality of the competition foreclosed must all be assessed in determining illegality or legality. It also indicates that exclusive dealing arrangements or requirements contracts that are negotiated by sellers possessing a very small share of the relevant market have a good chance of standing up in court.[10] The critical issue may involve the definition of the relevant market; firms with large shares may still be circumscribed.

The Justice Department, in its controversial *Vertical Restraints Guidelines* issued in 1985, recognized the potential dangers of exclusive dealing but also indicated that conditions in which the policy is likely to substantially lessen competition are probably rare.

> It is . . . possible that . . . exclusive dealing . . . may have the effect of excluding rivals by prohibitively raising either their cost of a vital input or their cost of

[9] Neale and Goyder, *op. cit.,* p. 273.
[10] Scherer, *op. cit.,* pp. 585–86.

distribution. For example, . . . a supplier . . . may require that its dealers not deal in the goods of competing suppliers. This would force rival suppliers either to secure alternative independent dealer outlets or to integrate vertically into distribution. If these two alternatives are much more costly than dealing with the "foreclosed" dealers would have been, rivals of that supplier may be prevented from entering the market or from expanding output, or may be forced to exit the market.

Alternatively, a firm . . . at any stage of the manufacturing or distribution chain may enter into long-term exclusive contracts for the supply of a vital input, leaving little or no present production of the input for new entrants or fringe firms. . . .

An exclusive dealing arrangement is unlikely to be used to exclude rivals unless it has two characteristics: (a) it must significantly raise rivals' costs of gaining access to an input or to distribution facilities, and (b) if the restraint raises a firm's own costs, the firm . . . employing this restraint must be able to collect a sufficiently large return from the practice to offset the increase in its . . . costs caused by the restraint.

In turn, for exclusive dealing to facilitate anticompetitive exclusion, the following market conditions normally must be met:

(1) The "nonforeclosed market" is concentrated and leading firms in the market use the restraint
(2) The firms subject to the restraint control a large share of the "foreclosed market"
(3) Entry into the "foreclosed market" is difficult[11]

In fact, the Justice Department has argued that exclusive dealing arrangements may be procompetitive because they may prevent dealers or distributors from using the training, advertising, displays, or other transaction-specific investments in services a manufacturer has provided to sell rival manufacturers' brands. In other words, exclusive dealing can prohibit competitors from getting a "free ride" from a manufacturer's efforts to make its dealers or distributors effective in serving their customers.

Tying Contracts

Tying contracts exist when a seller, having a product or service that buyers want (the *tying product*), refuses to sell it unless a second (*tied*) product or service is also purchased, or at least is not purchased from anyone other than the seller of the tying product. Thus, a manufacturer of motion picture projectors (the tying product) might insist that only his film (the tied product) be used with the projectors, or a manufacturer of shoe machinery (the tying product) might insist that lessees of the machinery purchase service contracts (tied service) from him for the proper maintenance of the machinery. A tying agreement in effect forecloses competing sellers from the opportunity of selling the tied commodity or service to the purchaser. Indeed, like exclusive dealing arrangements, the critical issue in the condemnation of tying contracts is the foreclosing of competi-

---

[11] U.S. Department of Justice, *Vertical Restraints Guidelines,* January 23, 1985, pp. 18–20. The *Guidelines* generated considerable debate in Congress because they do not reflect legislative or judicial history. Instead, they reflect the perspective of the Antitrust Division of the Justice Department during the Reagan administration.

tion from a marketplace. But tying contracts are viewed much more negatively by the courts than exclusive dealing arrangements or requirements contracts. For example, in distinguishing between a requirements contract and a tying contract in the *Standard Stations* case mentioned previously, Justice Frankfurter stated that tying arrangements "serve hardly any purpose beyond the suppression of competition. . . ."[12] The courts have often viewed tie-ins with concern because, as they have reasoned, such arrangements force buyers into giving up the purchase of substitutes for the tied product, and they may destroy the free access of competing suppliers of the tied product to the consuming market. Thus, tying agreements are seen to have the anticompetitive effect of limiting competition in the market for the tied product.

Like exclusive dealing, tying is circumscribed by the Sherman Act, the Clayton Act, and the FTC Act. Given the overwhelmingly negative attitude of the courts toward tying, it is little wonder that its use would rarely be approved. Indeed, as Sullivan points out, "a black letter statement of the current law" would probably assert three propositions:

1. That a tie violates Section 1 of the Sherman Act whenever the seller possesses any discernible degree of market power in the tying product and the tie effects more than a *de minimus* amount of commerce
2. That a tie also violates Section 3 of the Clayton Act when it meets that test, so long as there is a "sale or lease" of a commodity or a contract therefore[13]
3. That any tie violating Section 1 alone or Sections 1 and 3 also violates Section 5 of the FTC Act[14]

But, as Sullivan also points out, "statements of this kind, useful as they can be at times, are terribly simplistic and for that reason dangerous."[15]

Certain types of tying contracts are legal. The courts have ruled that if two products are made to be used jointly and one will not function properly without the other, a tying agreement is within the law. In other cases, if a company's goodwill depends on proper operation of equipment, a service contract may be tied to the sale or lease of the machine. The practicality of alternatives to the tying arrangement appears to be crucial. If a firm will suffer injury unless it can protect its product, and there is no feasible alternative, the courts go along with tying agreements. Despite these exceptions, the general rule is that tying agreements are inherently anticompetitive and thus illegal per se.

Serious legal questions regarding tying agreements have been raised in recent years relative to the franchising of restaurants and other eating places, motels, and movie theaters, among others. As detailed in Chapter 7, an individual or group of individuals (the franchisee) is usually permitted to set up an outlet of a national chain in return for a capital investment and a periodic fee to the parent company (the franchisor). In some cases, the parent company also requires the franchise holders to buy various supplies, such as meat, baked goods, and paper cups in the case of restaurants, either from the corporation or

---

[12] *Standard Oil Company of California* v. *U.S.*, 337 U.S. 293 (1949) at 305.

[13] Section 3 of the Clayton Act is inapplicable to tying contracts for the sales of land, or when the tying item is the provision of services rather than of "goods, wares, merchandise, machinery, supplies or other commodities . . . ," whereas the Sherman Act applies to every kind of contract.

[14] Lawrence A. Sullivan, *Handbook of the Law of Antitrust* (St. Paul, Minn.: West Publishing Co., 1977), p. 434.

[15] *Ibid.*

an approved supplier. In franchising, the tying product is the franchise itself and the tied products are the supplies that the franchisee must purchase to operate his business. Companies with such requirements have argued that they are necessary in order to maintain the quality of their services and reputation. However, critics of such agreements assert that franchisors often require franchisees to purchase supplies and raw materials at prices far above those of the competitive market. The potential for a conflict of interest on the part of the franchisors is high.

In franchising, the primary tying "product" is the trademark itself (e.g., "McDonald's," "Budget" Rent-A-Car, "Sheraton" Hotels). Therefore, tying agreements that link the trademark to supplies have been sustained by the courts only when franchisors have been able to prove that their trademarks are inseparable from their supplies and that the tied products (the supplies) are, in fact, essential to the maintenance of quality control. For example, in a lawsuit involving Baskin-Robbins, a franchised chain of ice cream stores, certain franchisees contended that Baskin-Robbins ice cream products were unlawfully tied to the sale of the Baskin-Robbins trademark.[16] However, the tie-in claim was disallowed because the franchisees did not establish that the trademark was a product separate from the ice cream; in tying cases, two distinct products must be involved in order for tying to be present.

In its decision, the 8th Circuit Court of Appeals distinguished between two kinds of franchising systems: (1) the business format system and (2) the distribution system. It stated that a business format system is usually created merely to conduct business under a common trade name. The franchise outlet itself is generally responsible for the production and preparation of the system's end product; the franchisor merely provides the trademark and, in some cases, the supplies used in operating the franchised outlet and producing the system's product (e.g., Budget Rent-A-Car, Sir Speedy Instant Printing). Under a distribution system, the franchised outlets, according to the court, serve merely as conduits through which the trademarked goods of the franchisor flow to the ultimate consumer. These goods are generally manufactured by the franchisor or by its licensees according to detailed specifications. In this context, instead of identifying a business format, the trademark serves merely as a representation of the product marketed by the system (e.g., Chevrolet automobile dealerships, Texaco gas stations). Consequently, sales of substandard products under the trademark would dissipate goodwill and reduce the value of the trademark. The court felt that the Baskin-Robbins Ice Cream Company is representative of a distribution system.

The decision in the *Baskin-Robbins* case is similar to that in a lawsuit against Carvel (a soft ice cream franchise), where the court concluded that Carvel's ingredient supply restrictions were justified by the need for quality control connected with the problem of ingredient secrecy.[17] In addition, in a lawsuit involving Dunkin' Donuts, the court stated that such tying agreements may be justified not only when the franchisor is attempting to maintain product quality, but also when it is attempting to enter a new market or industry *or* to preserve its market identity.[18]

[16] *Norman E. Krehl, et al. v. Baskin-Robbins Ice Cream Company, et al.*, 42 F.2d 115 (8th Cir. 1982).
[17] *Susser v. Carvel Corp.*, 332 F.2d 505 (2nd Cir. 1964).
[18] *Ungar v. Dunkin' Donuts of America, Inc.*, 531 F.2d 1211 (3d. Cir. 1976).

In a decision involving the Chock Full O'Nuts Corporation, it was held that the franchisor "successfully proved its affirmative defense (to tying charges) of maintaining quality control with regard to its coffee and baked goods."[19] On the other hand, Chock Full O'Nuts was unsuccessful in defending its tying practices with respect to a number of other products (e.g., french fries, soft drink syrups, napkins, and glasses). The latter finding paralleled that in an antitrust case involving Chicken Delight.[20] The parent company's contract requiring Chicken Delight franchisees to purchase paper items, cookers, fryers, and mix preparations from the franchisor was declared to be a tying contract in violation of Section 1 of the Sherman Act. Chicken Delight failed to convince the court that its system should be considered a single product. The paper products were viewed as illegally tied to the franchise because they were easily reproducible. The issue of the cookers, fryers, and spice items was less clear-cut, and the court left it to a jury to decide whether they were justifiably tied on the basis of quality control of the finished product. The jury eventually determined that quality control could have been effected by means other than a tie-in and thus rejected the franchisor's claims.

Tying agreements were also involved in the *Brown Shoe* case, referred to earlier. Under Brown's franchise plan, held to be unfair and illegal by the Federal Trade Commission, independent dealers were given what was admittedly a valuable package of services—architectural plans, merchandising records, the help of a Brown field representative, and an option to participate in inexpensive group insurance in return for a simple promise of the dealer-franchisee to concentrate on the Brown Shoe line and not to handle "conflicting" lines. Justice Hugo Black, in writing the Supreme Court's decision, stated that the records showed "beyond doubt" that Brown's program required shoe retailers "unless faithless to their contractual obligations with Brown, substantially to limit their trade with Brown's competitors." The conclusion in this case was that franchising poses a restraint to trade if the parent company places unreasonable limitations on the right of the franchisee to make his own business decisions.

Related Policies Subject to Scrutiny.   Policies similar to or having the effect of tying agreements have also been challenged. For example, tires, batteries, and accessories have been sold in service stations of major oil companies in two different ways:

1. *Purchase–resale agreements.* Under this plan, the products are purchased from the manufacturer by the oil company and resold to gasoline wholesalers and retailers.
2. *Sales commission plans.* Under these plans, the products are sold directly to gasoline wholesalers and retailers by the manufacturer. The oil company receives a commission on all sales, and in return it assists with promotion.

In three cases ending in 1968, the courts held that the sales commission plan is inherently coercive because of the control the oil company has over its dealers.[21] Market exclusion of other brands will result, and thus the plans are an unfair

---

[19] *In re Chock Full O'Nuts Corp. Inc.,* 3 Trade Reg. Rep. 20, 441 (Oct. 1973).
[20] *Siegel v. Chicken Delight, Inc.,* 448 F.2d 43 (9th Cir. 1971), *cert. denied,* 405 U.S. 95 (1972).
[21] Donald F. Dixon, "Market Exclusion and Dealer Coercion in Sponsored TBA Sales," *Journal of Marketing,* Vol. 35 (January 1971), pp. 62–63.

practice whether illegal intent is shown or not. In the *Atlantic Refining* case the Supreme Court confirmed this view.[22] The merits of purchase–resale agreements were not ruled upon by the courts.

In addition, the Federal Trade Commission has used Section 5 of the FTC Act to challenge retailers to stop making, carrying out, or enforcing anticompetitive leasing agreements. These agreements or boycotts, which are also similar to tying contracts, have given a retailer the right to be the only retailer of its kind (e.g., drugstore) in a shopping center, the right to reject or accept the opportunity to operate an additional outlet in a shopping center where it already has one (*rights of first refusal*), the right to prohibit or control the entrance of tenants into shopping centers, and the right to restrict the business operations of other tenants in shopping centers.[23] For example, FTC consent orders in 1976 and 1979 prohibited Sears, Roebuck[24] and Federated Department Stores,[25] respectively, from making or forcing any agreement with shopping center developers that

- Prohibits entry into centers of particular tenants or classes of tenants (e.g., discount stores) or allows Sears or Federated to approve tenant entry
- Grants Sears or Federated the right to approve floor space to others or their use of it
- Specifies that tenants shall sell their merchandise at any particular price or within any range of prices, fashions, or quality (when the latter terms connote price)
- Limits discount advertising, pricing, or selling
- Limits the types of merchandise or services that tenants may sell
- Prescribes minimum hours of operation
- Grants Sears or Federated the right to approve tenant location
- Provides for radius restrictions upon tenants

These prohibitions apply to all shopping centers, including those developed and built by a Sears wholly owned subsidiary, Homart Development Company.

Another form of tying arrangement is called *full-line forcing*. Here a seller's leverage with a tying product is used to force a buyer to purchase his whole line of goods. This policy is not illegal unless the buyer is prevented from handling competitors' products. In the case of a farm machinery manufacturer, a court held that the practice was within the law, but implied that full-line forcing that caused the exclusion of competitors from this part of the market might be illegal if a substantial share of business were affected.[26] Block booking imposed by motion picture distributors and producers on independent theater owners can

[22] *Atlantic Refining Co.* v. *FTC*, 381 U.S. 357 (1965).

[23] "Order against Drug Chain Bans Shopping Center Lease Restrictions," *FTC News Summary* (October 10, 1975), p. 1. See also "Antitrust Action in Shopping Malls," *Business Week* (December 8, 1975), p. 51. In survey results released by the FTC on March 13, 1981, it was pointed out that "larger stores in shopping centers have generally abandoned the practice of exercising excessive power over smaller stores and discounters in lease arrangements." See "Shopping Centers Complying with an FTC Decision on Leasing Practices," *FTC News Summary* (March 20, 1981), p. 2.

[24] "Order against Sears, Roebuck Bans Anticompetitive Shopping Center Conduct," *FTC News Summary* (October 29, 1976), p. 1.

[25] "FTC Shopping Center Order Would Ban Control by Department Stores," *FTC News Summary* (January 19, 1979), p. 1.

[26] *U.S.* v. *J. I. Case Co.*, 101 F. Supp. 856 (1951).

also be viewed as full-line forcing. This practice compels theaters to take many pictures they do not want in order to obtain the ones they do. Independent producers have consequently been unable to rent their films to theaters whose programs were thus crowded with the products of the major firms. Such practices have typically been held to be illegal, especially when copyrighted films have been used as tying mechanisms.[27]

Other instances of prohibition of full-line forcing have occurred. For example, in 1976, E&J Gallo Winery, the largest seller of wine in the United States, consented to a Federal Trade Commission order prohibiting it from, among other things, requiring its wholesalers to distribute any Gallo wines in order to obtain other kinds.[28] And in 1977, Union Carbide Corporation agreed to a consent order prohibiting the company from requiring its dealers to purchase from it their total requirements of six industrial gases (acetylene, argon, helium, hydrogen, nitrogen, and oxygen) and from making the purchase of six gases a prerequisite for dealers buying other gases or welding products.[29]

The Per Se Issue.   In spite of references to the per se illegality of tying contracts in a number of cases, it is still necessary to determine when conditions of economic power exist. In theory, where no leverage exists in a product, there can be no tying arrangement by coercion; the buyer can always go elsewhere to purchase. Thus, plaintiffs must prove more than the existence of a tie. As Sullivan points out, they must also show that the tying product is successfully differentiated and that the commerce affected by the tie is not *de minimus*.[30] The presumption against tying arrangements is not quite as strong as the per se rule against price-fixing conspiracies.

Evidence of this comes from a 1984 Supreme Court case involving hospital services.[31] In *Jefferson Parish Hospital,* anesthesiologist Edwin G. Hyde, who had been denied admission to the staff of East Jefferson Hospital, sued the governance board of the hospital because the hospital had an exclusive contract with a firm of anesthesiologists requiring that all anesthesiological services for the hospital's patients be performed by that firm. The Supreme Court agreed with the district court that the relevant geographic market was Jefferson Parish (i.e., metropolitan New Orleans) and not the neighborhood immediately surrounding East Jefferson Hospital. The Court reasoned that "Seventy percent of the patients residing in Jefferson Parish enter hospitals other than East Jefferson. . . . Thus, East Jefferson's 'dominance' over persons residing in Jefferson Parish is far from overwhelming." The Court further explained that "the fact that the exclusive contract requires purchase of two services that would otherwise be purchased separately does not make the contract illegal. Only if patients are forced to purchase the contracting firm's services as a result of the hospital's market power would the arrangement have anticompetitive conse-

[27] *U.S.* v. *Paramount Pictures,* 334 U.S. 131 (1948); *U.S.* v. *Loew's Inc.,* 371 U.S. 45 (1962).

[28] "Consent Agreement Cites E&J Gallo Winery," *FTC News Summary* (May 21, 1976), p. 1. See also "Gallo Winery Consents to FTC Rule Covering Wholesaler Dealings," *Wall Street Journal,* May 20, 1976, p. 15.

[29] "Union Carbide Settles Complaint by FTC on Industrial-Gas Sales; Airco to Fight," *Wall Street Journal,* May 20, 1977, p. 8.

[30] Sullivan, *op. cit.,* p. 439.

[31] *Jefferson Parish Hospital District No. 2* v. *Hyde,* 104 U.S. 1551 (1984). See also Robert E. Taylor and Stephen Wermiel, "High Court Eases Antitrust Restrictions on Accords Linking Sale of Goods, Services," *Wall Street Journal,* March 28, 1984, p. 6.

quences." East Jefferson's market power was not significant enough to make the contract illegal.

Customer Restrictions

A supplier may wish to impose restrictions on to whom a wholesaler or retailer may resell his goods and services. These arrangements may be very desirable for manufacturers or distributors in the marketing of some goods, since they can reserve certain large customers to themselves for direct sales and can also control the reselling of their goods through the channel. Posner has pointed out the economic rationale underlying the use of such restrictions:

> There may be a class of customers who, because of size, sophistication, or special needs, do not require dealer services. The manufacturer may be in a better position than any dealer to provide these customers with whatever presale services they do require. If so, the manufacturer who allows his dealers to compete with him for such an account is inviting them to take a free ride on his services. He provides the services at a cost that he hopes to recoup in the price charged these customers; the dealers then offer the customers a lower price, which they can do since they do not incur any services expense with respect to these customers. In such a case, forbidding dealers to compete for these accounts is just like limiting competition among dealers in order to prevent some of them from taking a free ride on presale services provided by others.[32]

Contracts of this type become illegal when it can be shown that their effects tend to reduce competition. At present, however, there are no clear guidelines that determine just how far a supplier may go in dictating to wholesalers or retailers the classes and kinds of customers to whom they may resell his product or brand. The reason for this confusion is due primarily to the fact that the Supreme Court in its decision in the *Sylvania* case[33] did not distinguish between customer (resale) restrictions and territorial restrictions. The former are basically exercises of coercive power (e.g., prohibitions on selling to discount houses) whereas the latter are basically exercises of reward power (e.g., the granting of a monopoly on the sale of a brand within a defined territory). Discussion of the *Sylvania* decision is reserved for the section on restrictions on reward power, because the issue in the *Sylvania* case related directly to location agreements and not to customer restrictions. Suffice it to say here that resale restrictions are viewed as a restraint of trade and therefore are directly challengeable under the Sherman Act. But, given the *Sylvania* decision, their legality is to be judged under a rule-of-reason approach. That is, they will be considered *legal* if they have not substantially lessened competition.

Some of the legal limits to resale restrictions were defined in the *General Motors* case,[34] which preceded *Sylvania* but was not overturned by it. General Motors used location restrictions to prevent dealers in the Los Angeles area from selling new cars through discount houses. The Chevrolet franchise agreement provided that dealers could not change the location of their businesses or open at new locations without permission from the company. When several dealers

---

[32] Richard A. Posner, *Antitrust Law: An Economic Perspective* (Chicago: University of Chicago Press, 1976), p. 162.

[33] *Continental T.V., Inc.* v. *GTE Sylvania, Inc.*, 433 U.S. 36 (1977).

[34] *U.S.* v. *General Motors Corp., et al.*, 384 U.S. 127 (1966).

started to sell spare parts through discount houses, the company found them in violation of the location clause and forced them to suspend the practice. A key element in the case was that other Chevrolet dealers in the area helped GM to police the ban, and, indeed, complaints from them had been a primary motive of General Motors' enforcement actions. The Supreme Court ruled that the cooperation between GM and the other dealers was a conspiracy to eliminate a class of competitors and was therefore illegal. This decision indicates that enforcement of resale restrictions must be absolutely unilateral if the restrictions are to be legal.

Reciprocity

Reciprocity is the practice of making purchasing decisions at least partly on the basis of whether the vendor is also a customer. In some cases the relationship may be more complex, involving three or more customer-vendors in a circular arrangement. Reciprocity amounts to doing business with your friends. Business reciprocity has come under antitrust scrutiny, especially if there is an inequality of bargaining power in the relationship. This may arise from differences in the relative sizes of the firms. The antitrust laws regulate reciprocity, because sellers influence their customers to buy not only on the basis of marketing competition but also because the buyer wishes to sell his own products to the seller.

There is a body of cases that determines the division between illegal and legal reciprocity. In general, reciprocity is illegal under two circumstances:[35]

1. Coercive reciprocity involving the use of pressure may be illegal as an unfair trade practice.
2. A merger that may cause a reciprocity program to be formed will violate Section 7 of the Clayton Act if the reciprocity may reduce competition.[36]

This latter circumstance can come about when a firm that operates a reciprocity program merges with another firm and one of the two has a customer that sells to the other. In some cases a corporate policy against reciprocity will shield a merger from Section 7.[37] We will return later in this chapter to the issue of reciprocity stemming from mergers when we discuss vertical integration.

Noncoercive reciprocity is legal so long as the policy is not aggressive, is outside of a merger context, and is not supported with elaborate records of purchases and sales from and to other firms. The Federal Trade Commission has held that where reciprocity is prevalent and systematized and where a substantial amount of commerce is involved, there is a violation of Section 5 of the Federal Trade Commission Act.[38] A 1971 case in which a major tire manufacturer and its three subsidiaries were barred from any reciprocity purchases from their suppliers confirmed this view.[39] In many respects, reciprocity is analogous to tying agreements. However, it is very difficult to draw a line between "coer-

[35] R. Moyer, "Reciprocity: Retrospect and Prospect," *Journal of Marketing*, Vol. 34 (October 1970), p. 48.

[36] See *FTC v. Consolidated Foods Corp.*, 380 U.S. 592.

[37] Moyer, *loc. cit.*

[38] "Federal Trade Commission Statement on Reciprocity," *Journal of Marketing*, Vol. 35 (April 1971), pp. 76–77.

[39] "United States v. General Tire and Rubber Co., Aerojet-General Corp., A. M. Byers Co., and RKO General Inc.," *Journal of Marketing*, Vol. 35 (April 1971), p. 71.

cive" reciprocity and the situation where two firms do business "voluntarily" with each other because it is to their mutual advantage.

Indicative of the Reagan administration's relatively relaxed stance toward the potential dangers of vertical restraints, the Justice Department in 1981 dropped a reciprocity case against General Electric Company, which had been filed by a previous administration in 1972.[40] The lawsuit charged GE with making reciprocal purchasing arrangements with customers and suppliers since 1965. The government had originally alleged that these arrangements prevented GE competitors from selling to GE customers and that they limited the number of suppliers that could sell to GE. The rationale used for dropping the case was that "the passage of time had reduced the significance of the case and the value of injunctive relief."[41] Likewise, the FTC has brought very few cases involving reciprocal dealing over the past decade. In fact, in 1983 it actually freed Southland Corp., the Dallas-based owner of the 7-Eleven convenience store chain, from a 1974 order barring it from reciprocal dealing.

Price Maintenance

Resale price maintenance is the specification by a supplier, typically a manufacturer, of the prices below or above which resellers, typically wholesalers and retailers, may not sell its products. It represents one of the few channel policy areas where the use of coercive power was sanctioned, in a positive manner, by federal laws. Originally, resale price maintenance (so-called fair trade) laws were passed by states (starting with California in 1931) enabling manufacturers to fix resale prices for their goods if they chose to do so. The U.S. Congress passed the Miller-Tydings Act in 1937 and the McGuire Act in 1952 exempting retail price fixing by manufacturers from the federal antitrust laws in states that permitted such vertical pricing arrangements. However, by the end of 1975, the repeal of state fair trade laws had proceeded to the point where resale price maintenance was enforceable against contracting parties in only 22 states. And, as a final blow, Congress passed the Consumer Goods Pricing Act late in 1975, repealing the Miller-Tydings and McGuire acts. This meant that the fair trade agreements that were previously exempted from the Sherman Act's prohibitions against vertical price restraints became per se unlawful.[42]

Ostensibly, resale price maintenance (fair trade) laws were supposed to facilitate a manufacturer's desire to influence prices at the retail level. However, their initial development was instigated through the collective efforts of coalitions of small, independent retailers who wished to be protected from the direct price competition of mass merchandisers and discounters.[43] In more recent history, though, there have been some logical economic arguments explaining the potential significance of resale price maintenance by manufacturers as a

[40] "GE Antitrust Suit Filed 9 Years Ago Is Dropped by U.S.," *Wall Street Journal*, October 15, 1981, p. 20.

[41] *Ibid.*

[42] The history of resale price maintenance legislation is fascinating. For colorful accounts, see Scherer, op. cit., pp. 590–94; and Joseph C. Palamountain, Jr., *The Politics of Distribution* (Cambridge, Mass.: Harvard University Press, 1955), pp. 235–53. For a complete outline of the legal status of resale price maintenance, see John W. Clark, Oliver F. Green, Jr., and Paul E. Slater, "Resale Price Maintenance: Outline of Relevant Law," *Antitrust Law Journal*, Vol. 49, Issue 2 (1981), pp. 839–43.

[43] See Palamountain, op. cit., pp. 235–53.

mechanism for inducing service competition among resellers.[44] In fact, as Scherer points out, resale price maintenance is in some respects "analogous in motivation and effect to vertical territorial restrictions."[45] If there is merit to the contention that impeding intrabrand competition may further interbrand competition, then perhaps resale price maintenance ought to be treated in the same manner as customer and territorial restrictions (i.e., as a rule-of-reason offense) rather than as per se illegal, its current status. Posner puts the argument neatly:

> Resale price maintenance is more flexible than exclusive territories as a method of limiting price competition among dealers, and it may be the only feasible method where effective retail distribution requires that dealers be located close to one another; any free-rider or other arguments that are available to justify exclusive territories are equally available to justify resale price maintenance.[46]

He has also argued that the distinction between price and nonprice restriction is "indefensible."

> To forbid a dealer or distributor to sell outside of its territory, when it is the only distributor or dealer of the manufacturer's brand in the territory, has if anything a greater adverse effect on intrabrand competition than fixing the price at which it may resell the product. The territorial restriction affects both price and service competition; the price restriction affects only price competition.[47]

Despite Posner's opinion, price-fixing in any form is still per se illegal, and it makes no difference whether maximum[48] or minimum prices are set. However, it appears that evidence of collective action will be a critical indicator of illegality. This point was emphasized in 1984 in *Monsanto Company v. Spray-Rite Service Corporation*.[49] Spray-Rite (now defunct) sued Monsanto after Monsanto cut off Spray-Rite's distributorship of herbicides in northern Illinois in 1968. Spray-Rite claimed that Monsanto did this because Spray-Rite would not join in an effort to fix prices at which herbicides were sold. Spray-Rite alleged a conspiracy between Monsanto and some of its distributors to fix resale prices. The Court found in Spray-Rite's favor, but made it clear that the presence of concerted action between Monsanto and its distributors was critical to its per se ruling. In fact, the Court explicitly stated that "a manufacturer . . . generally has a right to deal, or refuse to deal, with whomever it likes, as long as it does so independently." Citing the *Colgate* doctrine (discussed later in this chapter), the Court went on to say that "the manufacturer can announce its resale prices in advance and refuse to deal with those who fail to comply." In other words, manufacturers may stipulate resale prices to their distributors as long as the stipulations are made on a one-to-one (unilateral) basis. Where concerted, conspiratorial action is found, a per se illegal ruling can be expected.

---

[44] See Posner, op. cit., pp. 147–67. See also Richard A. Posner, "The Next Step in the Antitrust Treatment of Restricted Distribution: Per Se Legality," *University of Chicago Law Review*, Vol. 48 (Winter 1981), pp. 6–26.

[45] Scherer, op. cit., p. 590.

[46] Posner, "The Next Step," p. 9.

[47] *Ibid.*

[48] For a court ruling on the setting of maximum prices, see *Albrecht* v. *Herald Co.*, 390 U.S. 145 (1968).

[49] *Monsanto Co.* v. *Spray-Rite Service Corp.*, 104 U.S. 1464 (1984).

Reliance on the *Colgate* doctrine was the main reason why in 1981 Russell Stover, a major manufacturer of boxed chocolates, was not found guilty of unlawfully fixing retail candy prices. Russell Stover had announced in advance that it would refuse to deal with retailers who resold below the prices designated on lists, invoices, and order forms and the boxed candy itself. Stover wouldn't sell initially to stores that it believed would sell its products at less than designated prices, and it stopped dealing with established retailers who actually did so.[50]

Nevertheless, the *Colgate* doctrine has not always received uniform interpretation by the courts, as we will see. Therefore, this issue is not resolved. Indeed, resale price maintenance became one of the most hotly debated antitrust topics throughout industry, Congress, and the executive branch of the government during the Reagan administration.

It is also important to realize that unfair practices acts are still in effect in a number of states. These laws regulate the right of sellers to sell below costs or below specified markups on some or all products. These laws are designed to prevent deep and predatory price cuts or "loss leader" selling. Marketing managers whose firms operate in states having such laws must be familiar with the provisions of the laws of each state, since they vary. Sales made for charitable purposes, sales to relief agencies, sales for clearance, closeout, or liquidation of business, and sales of goods whose marketability is declining are usually exempted from these laws.[51]

Price Discrimination by Buyers

When a seller discriminates in his pricing between two customers, such an action can be viewed as an attempt to exercise reward power over the customer receiving the lower price. However, when one of the customers uses his power to force a discriminatory price from the seller, then such an action may be viewed as coercion by the customer. The latter situation is addressed here; the former is left to our upcoming discussion of limitations on the use of reward power.

Section 2(f) of the Robinson-Patman Act makes it unlawful for a person in commerce knowingly to induce or receive a discrimination in price. To violate this section, a buyer must be reasonably aware of the illegality of the price he has received. This section prevents large, powerful buyers from compelling sellers to give them discriminatory lower prices. It is often enforced by means of Section 5 of the Federal Trade Commission Act on the grounds that this use of coercive power is an unfair method of competition. Likewise, it is illegal for buyers to coerce favors from suppliers in the form of special promotional allowances and services.[52]

---

[50] "FTC Judge Rejects Charges That Russell Stover Unlawfully Fixed Retail Candy Prices," *FTC News Summary* (April 3, 1981), p. 1.

[51] M. C. Howard, *Legal Aspects of Marketing* (New York: McGraw-Hill Book Company, 1964), p. 45.

[52] See "Order against Retail Chain Bans Inducement of Preferential Treatment," *FTC News Summary* (February 6, 1976), p. 9; "Fred Meyer Inc. Pays $200,000 Fine to Settle an FTC Complaint," *Wall Street Journal*, January 30, 1976, p. 2; "FTC Law Judge Bars Gibson Retailers from Boycotting Suppliers Who Rebuff Gibson Trade Shows," *FTC News Summary* (March 30, 1979), p. 3; "FTC Says Foremost-McKesson Disobeyed '73 Antitrust Order, Asks for Penalties," *Wall Street Journal*, January 12, 1979, p. 8; "Zayre Consents to Ban on Coercing Suppliers to Be in Trade Shows," *Wall Street Journal*, September 11, 1978, p. 12; and "FTC Finds A&P Violated Robinson-Patman Act," *FTC News Summary* (May 28, 1976), p. 2.

In addition, large buyers (such as A&P) have been known to set up dummy brokerage firms as part of their businesses in order to obtain a brokerage allowance from sellers, which in effect permits them to receive lower prices than their competitors. This form of coercive power is deemed illegal under Section 2(c) of the Robinson-Patman Act, which makes it unlawful to pay brokerage fees or discounts or to accept them except for services rendered in connection with sales or purchases. It also prohibits brokerage fees or discounts paid to any broker who is not independent of both buyer and seller.

Refusals to Deal

A seller can select his own dealers according to his own criteria and judgment. He may also announce in advance the circumstances under which he would refuse to sell to dealers. These two commercial "freedoms" were granted in *U.S. v. Colgate & Co.* in 1919 and referred to as the *Colgate doctrine*.[53] The doctrine was formally recognized by Congress in Section 2(a) of the Robinson-Patman Act, which reads that "nothing herein contained shall prevent persons engaged in selling goods, wares, or merchandise in commerce from selecting their own customers in *bona fide* transactions and not in restraint of trade."

Clearly, refusal to deal is a major "punishment" underlying a channel member's coercive power. After a number of court decisions dealing with the right of refusal to deal, the "right" has been narrowly confined. Suppliers may formally cut off dealers for valid business reasons, such as failure to pay or poor performance in sales or service, but where the suppliers have set up restrictive, regulated, or programmed distribution systems and there are complaints that the dealers who are being cut off have somehow stepped out of line with the edicts of the programmed system, the right to refuse to deal may be a severely constrained defense in treble-damage actions brought against the suppliers by the dealers.

There continue to be generated under Sections 1 and 2 of the Sherman Act a large number of litigated cases involving decisions by suppliers or franchisors to modify their distribution systems by terminating an existing dealer, and substituting a new dealer on an exclusive or nonexclusive basis or as part of a conversion from representation by independent middlemen to a vertically integrated system. While it appears the original selection of distributors or dealers for a new product poses no legal problems, it is increasingly clear that the termination of existing distributors and dealers does pose such problems, even in the absence of group boycotts or conspiracies. As Neale and Goyder observe,

> once a manufacturer has selected a dealer he will be unable subsequently, without risking a treble-damage action, to drop him merely because he refuses to comply with the manufacturer's policy in any particular respect, unless that policy is one which in all circumstances does not constitute a violation of the antitrust laws.[54]

Thus, when exclusive dealing, customer or territorial restrictions, or other types of vertical restraints have been applied by a supplier within its distribution network and when a dealer is cut off from that network, the dealer may take the supplier to court, charging that the refusal to deal was based on the supplier's

---

[53] *U.S. v. Colgate & Co.*, 250 U.S. 300 (1919).
[54] Neale and Goyder, *op. cit.*, p. 282.

desire to maintain an unlawful practice. The orientation toward litigation in these cases has been furthered by particularistic legislation, such as the Automobile Dealers Franchise Act of 1956, which entitles a car dealer to sue any car manufacturer who fails to act in good faith in connection with the termination, cancellation, or nonrenewal of the dealer's franchise. It is open to the manufacturer, however, to produce evidence that the dealer has himself not acted in good faith and that its own action was thereby justified. In nearly all the cases to date, this defense has been successful.[55]

It should be emphasized that despite these numerous limitations on the use of coercive power in channel relations, it is still feasible for both sellers and buyers to employ negative sanctions in interorganizational management. The use of such sanctions has not been outlawed except in highly extreme forms. For example, exclusive dealing is illegal only if it can be shown that competition is substantially lessened because of its implementation, and proving *substantial* lessening is a difficult task indeed. As pointed out in Chapter 6, however, it is generally more functional, from a long-run interorganization management perspective, to mediate rewards rather than punishments in attempting to influence a channel member to do something he will not otherwise do. Whereas fear, anxiety, and resistance are typical responses to negative sanctions, the typical responses to positive sanctions are hope, reassurance, and attraction.[56] Furthermore, if a channel member uses negative sanctions in the present, it is likely that the member being influenced will be less willing to cooperate in the future, whereas the opposite is true when positive sanctions are employed.[57]

LEGAL LIMITATIONS ON THE USE OF REWARD POWER

In this section, we consider those situations in which the use of reward power is limited by law. As was the case with coercive power, the laws do not prevent a channel member from employing rewards as a central component of his interorganizational strategy; rather, they restrict how certain enticements or incentives might be used.

Territorial Allocations

In contrast to exclusive dealing arrangements, requirements contracts, and tying agreements, territorial restrictions are often designed to reduce *intra*brand competition—competition among wholesalers or retailers of the same brand. A territorial restriction either prevents or discourages a middleman from selling outside a particular area, whereas a customer restriction prohibits a middleman from selling to specific customers or classes of customers regardless of their location.

The rationale behind restricting intrabrand competition is that by protecting resellers of its brand from competition among themselves a supplier will improve their effectiveness against resellers of other brands. Specifically, a sup-

---

[55] *Ibid.*

[56] David A. Baldwin, "The Power of Positive Sanctions," *World Politics,* Vol. 24 (October 1971), p. 32.

[57] *Ibid.,* p. 33.

plier establishes territorial or customer restrictions in order to provide an incentive for distributors to make necessary investments in plant, equipment, or inventory; to generate important support activities (e.g., point-of-sale promotion, repairs, customer service); and/or to achieve the widest and deepest possible coverage of a geographical area or market segment. Distributors might be unwilling to perform these activities in the absence of such incentives because of the possibility of "free riders." For example, a retailer that provides advertising and showrooms may discover that consumers take advantage of his services and then make their purchases from another retailer—a free rider—who does not provide any services but offers the product at a lower price. Confronted with such consumer behavior, retailers may all decide to lower their service levels, despite their supplier's insistence that such amenities are necessary because of competition from other suppliers' brands. From an interorganization management perspective, the attempt to dampen *intra*brand competition in order to strengthen *inter*brand competition makes a lot of sense. A manufacturer would often rather have the middlemen handling his brand compete with those of other brands than to slug it out among themselves.

Territorial allocations or restrictions range from absolute confinement of reseller sales, which is intended to completely foreclose intrabrand competition, to "lesser" territorial allocations, designed to inhibit such competition. These lesser allocations include areas of primary responsibility, profit pass-over arrangements, and location clauses.[58]

Absolute confinement involves a promise by a reseller that he will not sell outside his assigned territory. Often combined with such a promise is a pledge by the supplier not to sell to anyone else in that territory. Such a pledge is known as the granting of an *exclusive* distributorship or franchise. When absolute confinement is combined with an exclusive distributorship, the territory can be considered "airtight."[59] On the other hand, an *area of primary responsibility* requires the reseller to use his best efforts to maintain effective distribution of the supplier's goods in the territory specifically assigned to him. Failure to meet performance targets may result in termination, but the reseller is free to sell outside his area, and other wholesalers or retailers may sell in his territory.

Profit pass-over arrangements require that a reseller who sells to a customer located outside his assigned territory compensate the reseller in whose territory the customer is located. Such compensation is ostensibly to reimburse the second reseller for his efforts to stimulate demand in his territory and for the cost of providing services upon which the first reseller might have capitalized. Finally, a *location clause* specifies the site of a reseller's place of business. Such clauses are used to "space" resellers in a given territory so that each has a "natural" market comprising those customers who are closest to the reseller's location. However, the reseller may sell to any customer walking through his door. Furthermore, the customers located closest to him may decide to purchase at locations more distant than his.

Any attempts to confine wholesalers' or retailers' selling activities to one area may be viewed as either restraints of trade or as unfair methods of competi-

---

[58] For a complete discussion of these restrictions and the legal issues surrounding their use, see American Bar Association Antitrust Section, *Vertical Restrictions Limiting Intrabrand Competition* (Chicago: American Bar Association, 1977).

[59] See Robert Pitofsky, "The *Sylvania* Case: Antitrust Analysis of Non-Price Vertical Restrictions," *Columbia Law Review*, Vol. 78 (January 1978), pp. 3–4.

tion and therefore may be challenged under the Sherman Act or Section 5 of the FTC Act. For example, in 1958, the Justice Department brought suit against the White Motor Company, charging, among other things, that its franchises, which limited the area in which its dealers could sell or solicit customers, constituted an agreement to restrain trade. The decision by the lower courts concurred with the Justice Department's argument and held that such exclusive territorial arrangements were illegal per se, regardless of their competitive effects.[60] The Supreme Court demurred and suggested a retrial.[61] Before a retrial could be held in the lower courts, White accepted a consent decree to drop the exclusive territorial provisions in its franchise agreements.

Another court case involving this issue concerned Sealy, a company that licensed other firms to manufacture and sell its products (mattresses) under the Sealy trademark at uniform prices and in specified areas.[62] However, the Sealy licensees were in reality the owners of Sealy. The courts held that the exclusive territorial restraints were simply collusive means of horizontal price-fixing and policing, in per se violation of Section 1 of the Sherman Act.

In the *Schwinn* case,[63] both customer and territorial restrictions were found to be per se violations of the Sherman Act unless Schwinn was willing to retain title, risk, and dominion over its product—that is, to sell bicycles on a consignment basis or vertically integrate.[64] It should be noted, however, that when the actual remedy was imposed by the district court, Schwinn was not prohibited from designating areas of prime responsibility for its distributors or from designating the location of the place of business in its franchise agreements. Schwinn also retained the right to select its distributors and franchised dealers and to terminate dealerships for cause so long as such arrangements did not involve exclusive dealing clauses.[65]

The decision in the *Schwinn* case proved to be immensely unpopular among businessmen, legal scholars, and even judges. Therefore, when on June 23, 1977, the Supreme Court handed down a decision in the *Sylvania* case that overturned the *Schwinn* decision, there was cause for celebration.[66] The Schwinn decision had established a rule of per se illegality for customer (resale) and territorial restrictions; the Sylvania decision held that such restraints should be judged by the rule of reason on a case-by-case basis. Because of the significance of the *Sylvania* case to the establishing of distribution policies, it is important to devote some time to understanding it.

Prior to 1962, Sylvania, a manufacturer of television sets, sold its sets through both independent and company-owned distributors to a large number of independent retailers. RCA dominated the market at the time, with 60 to 70 percent of national sales, with Zenith and Magnavox as major rivals. Sylvania had only 1 to 2 percent of the market. In 1962, Sylvania decided to abandon efforts at saturation distribution and chose instead to phase out its wholesalers and sell directly to a smaller group of franchised retailers. Sylvania retained sole

[60] *White Motor Co.* v. *U.S.*, 194 F. Supp. 562 (1961).

[61] *White Motor Co.* v. *U.S.*, 372 U.S. 253 (1963).

[62] *U.S.* v. *Sealy, Inc.*, 388 U.S. 350 (1967).

[63] *U.S.* v. *Arnold Schwinn and Co., et al.*, 388 U.S. 365 (1967).

[64] See Betty Bock, *Antitrust Issues in Restricting Sales Territories and Outlets* (New York: Conference Board, 1967), for a complete discussion of the case.

[65] "U.S. v. Arnold Schwinn and Co., et al.," *Journal of Marketing*, Vol. 33 (January 1969), p. 107.

[66] *Continental T.V., Inc.* v. *GTE Sylvania Inc.*, 433 U.S. 36 (1977).

discretion to determine how many retailers would operate in any geographic area, and, in fact, at least two retailers were franchised in every metropolitan center of more than 100,000 people. Dealers were free to sell anywhere and to any class of customers, but agreed to operate only from locations approved by Sylvania.

Continental TV was one of Sylvania's most successful retailers in northern California. After a series of disagreements arising from Sylvania's authorizing a new outlet near one of Continental's best locations, Continental opened a new outlet in Sacramento, although its earlier request for approval for that location had been denied. Sylvania then terminated Continental's franchise. Continental brought a lawsuit against Sylvania, citing the precedent established in the *Schwinn* decision regarding the per se illegality of territorial restrictions. The Court sided with Sylvania, which had argued that the use of its territorial allocation policy permitted its marketing channels to compete more successfully against those established by its large competitors.

While the situation in the *Sylvania* case did not involve customer restrictions, the Supreme Court found that the intent and competitive impact of the retail customer restriction in the Schwinn franchise agreement wherein Schwinn prohibited its franchised retailers from selling its products to nonfranchised retailers (e.g., discount stores) were indistinguishable from the territorial restriction (i.e., the location clause) in the Sylvania franchise agreement. Furthermore, in its decision, the Court favored the promotion of *inter*brand competition even if *intra*brand competition were restricted. It indicated that customer and territorial restrictions encourage interbrand competition by allowing the manufacturer to achieve certain efficiencies in the distribution of his products. And, in a footnote, the Court recognized that marketing efficiency is not the only legitimate reason for a manufacturer's desire to control the manner in which his products are sold and serviced, because society increasingly demands that the manufacturer directly assume responsibility for the safety and quality of his products.

Thus, the upshot of the *Sylvania* decision is that the customer and territorial restraints will not be found to be per se illegal if they do not have a "pernicious effect on competition without redeeming value." Increased interbrand competition appears to be of sufficient "redeeming value." Of course, such restraints may still be attacked as unreasonable restraints in violation of Section 1 of the Sherman Act or Section 5 of the Federal Trade Commission Act, but the burden will be on the plaintiff to prove that they are unreasonable. It appears, however, that the status of such restraints imposed by successful marketers with substantial market power will remain clouded pending further court decisions.[67] Also, court decisions challenging such restraints will likely be more complex and costly due to the requisite economic evidence that will be required to prove certain restraints unreasonable. The effect of this should be to reduce the amount of private litigation involving such restraints.[68]

[67] For a suggested approach in vertical restraint cases, see E. F. Zelek, Jr., L. W. Stern, and T. W. Dunfee, "A Rule of Reason Model After *Sylvania*," *California Law Review*, Vol. 68 (1980), pp. 801–36.

[68] Many of these conclusions have been drawn from James G. Hiering and Richard L. Reinish, "Vertical Restraints on Distribution: Continental TV, Inc. v. GTE Sylvania, Inc.," office memorandum of Keck, Cushman, Mahin & Cate, Chicago, July 1, 1977. See also Robert E. Weigand, "Policing the Marketing Channel: It May Get Easier," in R. F. Lusch and P. H. Zinszer (eds.), *Contemporary Issues in Marketing Channels* (Norman, Okla.: University of Oklahoma, 1979), pp. 105–11.

Incentives for Resellers' Employees

The Federal Trade Commission originally took the position that one firm could not reward (via the use of push money[69] or similar incentives) the employees of its commercial customers for reselling its product. The commission considered these incentives a violation of Section 5 of the FTC Act, alleging that competing products suffered a disadvantage under such schemes. In 1921, the courts declared that the practice was legal if the employer consented to it, because, it was curiously reasoned, if a seller sold his goods outright to a reseller, the relevant competitive market was now the reseller's. Thus, the original seller was no longer part of the competition under consideration once title passed to the reseller.[70]

The Federal Trade Commission has issued trade practice rules that forbid push money if the employer does not consent, if the payment involves a lottery, where competitive products are affected severely, where competition is lessened, or where the inducements are not available to sales agents of all competing resellers. Push money payments transferred to employers are subject to restrictions under the price discrimination articles of the Robinson-Patman Act, to be discussed shortly.

Commercial Bribery

Commercial bribery, or *kickbacks,* is the practice of paying the employees of customers to purchase from the payer. After it was discovered in 1975 that several major U.S. corporations had been involved in making illegal or questionable payoffs to foreign nationals in order to obtain business abroad, there has been an intensified drive, especially by the Securities and Exchange Commission (SEC) and the Internal Revenue Service (IRS), to uncover kickbacks and other questionable or illegal payments both domestically and internationally.[71] The SEC's interest is in the possibility that publicly owned companies engaged in illegal activities may be violating the securities laws by spending shareholders' money in this manner. The IRS's interest is founded on the fact that bribery is not a legitimate business expense and that bribery payments may be buried in income tax statements under such seemingly innocuous items as "cooperative advertising allowances." It is to be hoped that the problem is becoming less acute as the result of the SEC and IRS efforts and because of the Foreign Corrupt Practices Act of 1978, which stiffened prohibitions against secret bank accounts and instituted criminal penalties for bribing foreign-government officials.

---

[69] *Push money* is extra monetary payment from a manufacturer to a customer's salesman for "pushing" the manufacturer's brand.

[70] Howard, *op. cit.,* pp. 135–36.

[71] Burt Schorr, "Questionable-Payments Drive Stimulates Competition, Tougher Internal Controls," *Wall Street Journal,* June 23, 1978, p. 30; and Carol H. Falk, "SEC May Uncover More Domestic Bribes using Foreign-Payoff Detection Methods," *Wall Street Journal,* March 10, 1976, p. 4. For examples of domestic bribery in marketing channels, see "SEC Accuses Jacquin, 2 Aides of Making Payoffs to Retailers to Sell Its Liquors," *Wall Street Journal,* October 18, 1977, p. 11; "Schlitz Brewing, as Expected, Is Indicted for Illegal Practices in Marketing Beer," *Wall Street Journal,* March 16, 1978, p. 12; "National Distiller Says That Liquor Unit Paid Kickbacks of $4 Million to Retailers," *Wall Street Journal,* January 31, 1977, p. 5; Frederick C. Klein, "Beer Firms Are Target as Agencies Extend Bribery Probes to U.S.," *Wall Street Journal,* June 10, 1976, p. 1; "Two Gum-Rack Firms Plead Guilty in Case Linked to Kickbacks," *Wall Street Journal,* April 14, 1978, p. 10; and "Restaurant Firm Discloses Payoffs by Its Suppliers," *Wall Street Journal,* March 23, 1977, p. 16.

The Federal Trade Commission is also getting involved in bribery issues by applying Section 5 of the FTC Act (which prohibits unfair methods of competition) to situations involving questionable payments both domestically and abroad.[72] Its first attempt to apply Section 5 in such situations was in 1976. Previously, the FTC had succeeded in barring payola to disc jockeys as an unfair trade practice unless the listening public is informed of the payment. The FTC will likely become more active in policing bribes, because its staff lawyers believe that the federal securities and tax laws leave loopholes for continued payoffs that can be closed only by the antitrust laws.[73]

Price Discrimination by Sellers

Section 2(a) of the Robinson-Patman Act states,

It shall be unlawful for any person engaged in commerce, . . . either directly or indirectly, to discriminate in price between different purchasers of commodities of like grade and quality, where either or any of the purchases involved in such discrimination are in commerce, where such commodities are sold for use, consumption, or resale within [any area] under the jurisdiction of the United States, and where the effect of such discrimination may be to substantially lessen competition or tend to create a monopoly in any line of commerce, or to injure, destroy or prevent competition with any person who either grants or knowingly receives the benefit of such discrimination, or with customers of either of them.

The act allows price differentials due to differences in the cost of serving different customers, up to the amounts justified by the cost savings. However, cost-justified quantity discounts can be limited by the Federal Trade Commission. The Robinson-Patman Act also provides that sellers can select their own customers unless in restraint of trade, and that price changes due to market value, marketability of goods, distress sales, or discontinuance of business are allowed. Let's look more closely at some of these provisions of the act.

1. *Like Grade and Quality.* Where products are of different materials or workmanship level, they are not ordinarily considered to be of "like grade and quality," but where differences are small and do not affect the basic use of the goods, then selling at price differentials has been attacked.

In cases involving competition between two buyers from a single seller, products of the same composition have been declared of like grade and quality even if the brand preference enjoyed by one of them in the market is significant. In the *Borden* case,[74] the Supreme Court held that evaporated milk sold under the Borden label and evaporated milk manufactured by Borden and sold under "private" labels were of like grade and quality, illustrating the point that perceived product differentiation fails to constitute an actual difference in grade and quality under the law's interpretation.

In cases where two sellers are competing for the same buyer, the Federal Trade Commission has held that brand identification by the public constitutes a

---

[72] Burt Schorr, "FTC Staff Action against Aircraft Firms May Set Precedent for Fighting Payoffs," *Wall Street Journal*, October 18, 1977, p. 2.

[73] *Ibid.*, p. 2; John S. Estey and David W. Marston, "Pitfalls (and Loopholes) in the Foreign Bribery Law," *Fortune* (October 9, 1978), pp. 182–88.

[74] *U.S. v. Borden Co.*, 383 U.S. 637 (1966).

difference in grade and quality, so that cutting the price of a product labeled "premium" to the same level that others charge for a standard (nonpremium) product is actually to undercut the competitor's price. Price discrimination undertaken for this purpose is not protected by the "meeting competition" or "good faith" defense, soon to be discussed.

2. To Substantially Lessen Competition.

There is an important difference between injury to competitors and injury to competition. A loss of sales by one firm and their gain by another is the essence of competition, and the object of each competitor is to outsell rivals. Evidence of intent to destroy a competitor, however, may indicate an injury to competition. Other factors to consider are the number of firms in the market and the market share of the discriminating seller.[75]

In the *Anheuser-Busch* case, a court of appeals ruled that injury to competition and not injury to competitors was a critical factor in determining the legality or illegality of price discrimination.[76] The injury to competition need not be actual to be unlawful, but a remote possibility of injury is not sufficient for illegality.[77]

Because of the requirement of injury to competition, a time-and-space dimension must be applied in price discrimination cases. In one case, for example, a sulphur producer had a ten-year contract with a fertilizer manufacturer to supply a fixed quantity of sulphur every year at a specified price, or at the price charged to the fertilizer firm's competitors, whichever was lower. In times of high prices, the stipulated price was lower than that charged to other customers. Therefore, the sulphur firm attempted to have the contract declared illegal as unlawful price discrimination. The court ruled that the lower price was legal so long as the other firms were offered the same prices and terms at the time the contract was made.[78]

Price discrimination among customers who are not competing is not illegal. The Federal Trade Commission has issued an advisory opinion that an apparel manufacturer may grant extended credit terms to new stores in ghetto areas, even though other classes of customers would be excluded from the plan. The FTC justified its decision on the grounds that there should be little competition between favored and nonfavored stores in this case.[79]

Price discrimination that injures any of three levels of competition may end up being prohibited by the Robinson-Patman Act.

1. *Primary level.* Competition between two sellers may be injured when one of them gives discriminatory prices to some customers. This was the situation in the *Utah Pie* case.[80] The Utah Pie Company was a local concern that sold its frozen pies in the Salt Lake City market at low prices due to its low costs. It had 66 percent of the market. Several national concerns competed with Utah Pie in that market. They cut

---

[75] Howard, *op. cit.*, pp. 54–55.

[76] *Anheuser-Busch, Inc.* v. *Federal Trade Commission*, 265 F.2d 677 (7th Cir. 1959), 363 U.S. 536 (1960), 289 F.2d 835 (7th Cir. 1961).

[77] Howard, *op. cit.*, p. 55.

[78] "Texas Gulf Sulphur Co. v. J. R. Simplot Co.," *Journal of Marketing*, Vol. 34 (April 1970), p. 82.

[79] "Federal Trade Commission Advisory Opinion No. 253," *Journal of Marketing*, Vol. 33 (January 1969), p. 105.

[80] *Utah Pie Co.* v. *Continental Baking Co., et al.*, 386 U.S. 685 (1967).

their prices in Salt Lake City below those that they charged in other markets. In some cases these prices were below full cost. The Supreme Court ruled that the evidence in the case was sufficient for a jury to decide whether the defendants had engaged in predatory tactics and whether competition had been lessened, even though Utah's market share had declined only to 45 percent and its sales had expanded. In this case the dominant local firm was protected from discriminatory price-cutting by national firms.

2. *Secondary level.* Competition between two customers of a seller may be affected if the seller differentiates between them in price. In effect the seller is aiding one customer and harming the other in their mutual competition, and this is sufficient to cause substantial lessening of competition.[81]

3. *Tertiary level.* If a manufacturer discriminates in prices between two wholesalers such that the customers of one wholesaler are favored over those of the other, the competition is being injured by the price discrimination.[82]

3. In Commerce.   Price discrimination is illegal only if the discriminatory sales are "in commerce." In one case, a court held that National Food Stores could advertise and sell certain items at one store at lower prices than they charged at others. The court ruled that the sales were not in commerce since they were to anyone who came in and were completed on the premises.[83] Furthermore, discrimination in pricing can be lawful when the products involved are not identical, when a product is sold for different uses, when separate markets are involved, when sales of the product(s) take place at different times, and when sales are made to government agencies,[84] as well as in situations where the cost justification defense or the good faith defense can be applied, as described next.

4. Cost Justification Defense.   Different prices to different customers are permitted if they can be justified by differences in the costs of sale or delivery. The burden of proof of cost differences is on the seller. However, the courts have been reluctant to accept the cost figures as valid.[85] As one author puts it, "The record shows that few firms have been able, in litigation, to justify price differences on the basis of cost."[86] The difficulties lie in ascertaining exactly what costs are to be included in the calculation and how overhead and joint costs are to be allocated.

5. Quantity Discounts.   Quantity discounts are permitted under Section 2(a) to the extent that they are justified by cost savings. The Supreme Court has ruled that quantity discounts must reflect cost savings in deliveries made to one place at one time. This places limitations on the use of cumulative quantity discounts. Furthermore, quantity limits may be placed on discounts on some commodities by the Federal Trade Commission, if it can be determined that only

[81] Howard, *op. cit.,* pp. 53–54.

[82] *Ibid.*

[83] "Plotken's West Inc. *v.* National Food Stores, Inc.," *Journal of Marketing,* Vol. 35 (January 1971), pp. 79–80.

[84] Donald V. Harper, *Price Policy and Procedure* (New York: Harcourt, Brace & World, 1966), pp. 105–6.

[85] L. W. Stern and J. R. Grabner, Jr., *Competition in the Marketplace* (Glenview, Ill.: Scott, Foresman and Co., 1970), p. 114.

[86] Howard, *op. cit.,* p. 62.

a few very large buyers can qualify for the largest discount category in a seller's pricing schedule.[87]

6. Good Faith Defense.   Section 2(b) of the Robinson-Patman Act allows a firm to charge lower prices to some of its customers than to others if it does so "in good faith to meet an equally low price of a competitor." This defense is valid even if there is substantial injury to competition, but the burden of proving good faith falls on the defendant.[88]

   a. The price being met must be lawful and not a price produced by collusion. A seller does not have to prove the price that he is meeting is lawful, but he must make some effort to find out if it is.[89]

   b. The price being met must really exist,[90] and the price must be met and not undercut.[91] As mentioned previously, price reductions on a "premium" product to the level of "standard" products can be a form of illegal price discrimination. If the public is willing to pay a higher price for the "premium" product, the equal prices may be considered beating and not meeting competition.[92]

   c. The competition being met must be at the primary level. Granting a discriminatory price to some customers to enable them to meet their own competition is not protected.[93]

The question of whether the good faith defense is applicable to gaining new customers as well as to retaining old ones is basically unsettled. The Federal Trade Commission has argued that a company is allowed to grant price discriminations "in good faith" only to retain old customers.[94] However, the 7th Circuit Court overruled this view in holding that the law does not distinguish old and new customers.[95]

Because of the difficulty encountered by companies in trying to apply the cost justification and good faith defenses and the likelihood that in certain instances the Robinson-Patman Act merely protects competitors from competition, there is considerable question about the act's ultimate value and equity. In fact, there have been efforts to repeal the act.[96]

Promotional Allowances and Services

Sections 2(d) and 2(e) of the Robinson-Patman Act prohibit a seller from granting advertising allowances, offering other types of promotional assistance,

---

[87] *Federal Trade Commission* v. *Morton Salt Company*, 334 U.S. 37 (1948). Although the FTC may establish maximum discounts or quantity limits, its only attempt to use this power was unsuccessful because of a basic discrepancy between the FTC's order and the evidence on which it was based. See *Federal Trade Commission* v. *B. F. Goodrich et al.*, 242 F.2d 31 (1957).

[88] Howard, *op. cit.*, p. 56. See *Fall City Industries, Inc.* v. *Vanco Beverage, Inc.*, 460 U.S. 428 (1983).

[89] Howard, *op. cit.*, pp. 60–61.

[90] *Standard Oil Co.* v. *FTC*, 340 U.S. 231 (1951).

[91] Howard, *op. cit.*, pp. 56–59.

[92] Stern and Grabner, *op. cit.*, p. 116.

[93] *Federal Trade Commission* v. *Sun Oil Co.*, 371 U.S. 505 (1963).

[94] Stern and Grabner, *op. cit.*, p. 115.

[95] Howard, *op. cit.*, p. 57.

[96] Stanley Cohen, "Bigger 'n' Better Doesn't Always Mean Cheaper," *Advertising Age* (July 28, 1975), p. 54; and "Justice Department Urges an Overhaul of Key Trust Law," *Wall Street Journal*, January 18, 1977, p. 8.

or providing services, display facilities, or equipment to any buyer unless similar allowances and assistance are made available to all purchasers. Section 2(d) applies to *payments* by a seller to a buyer for the performance of promotional services; Section 2(e) applies to the actual *provision* of such services (e.g., display racks or signs). Because buyers differ in size of physical establishment and volume of sales, allowances obviously cannot be made available to all customers on the same absolute basis. Therefore, the law stipulates that the allowances be made available to buyers on "proportionately equal terms."

The prohibitions of these sections of the Robinson-Patman Act are absolute and are not dependent on injury to competition. Cost justification of the discrimination is not a defense. In other words, if it can be shown that discriminatory allowances exist and that the firms being discriminated against are in competition with each other, the violation is deemed to be illegal per se. However, for firms to be "in competition," they must be in sufficient geographical proximity to compete for the same customer groups. If, for example, retailers are involved, only those retailers in a limited market territory need be included when granting allowances. On the other hand, the market might be construed as national if mail-order companies are involved. In the latter situation, a manufacturer (or wholesaler) would have to grant allowances or services to all mail-order companies if he were to grant them to one. In addition, a time dimension is important in defining the domain of the allowance. For example, if advertising allowances are granted one month, they do not have to be granted to another buyer five months later. Otherwise, the initial allowance would determine all future allowances.[97]

Certain stipulations have been made regarding adherence to Sections 2(d) and 2(e).[98] Among them are the following:

1. Allowances may be made only for services actually rendered, and they must not substantially exceed the cost of these services to the buyer or their value to the seller.
2. The seller must design a promotional program in such a way that all competing buyers can realistically implement it.
3. The seller should take action designed to inform all competing customers of the existence and essential features of the promotional program in ample time for them to take full advantage of it.
4. If a program is not functionally available to (i.e., suitable for and usable by) some of the seller's competing customers, the seller must make certain that suitable alternatives are offered to such customers.
5. The seller should provide its customers with sufficient information to permit a clear understanding of the exact terms of the offer, including all alternatives, and the conditions upon which payment will be made or services furnished.

The FTC has stipulated that when promotional allowances or merchandising services are provided, they should be furnished in accordance with a written plan that meets the listed requirements.[99] And, in the case of sellers who market their products directly to retailers as well as sell through wholesalers, it has been

---

[97] Howard, *op. cit.*, p. 71. See *Atlantic Trading Corp.* v. *FTC*, 258 F.2d 375 (2d Cir. 1958).
[98] Federal Trade Commission, *Guides for Advertising Allowances and Other Merchandising Payments and Services*, 16 C.F.R. part 240 (1983).
[99] *Ibid.*, §240.6.

mandated that any promotional allowance offered to the retailers must also be offered, on a proportionately equal basis, to the wholesalers. The wholesalers would then be expected to pass along the allowance to their retail customers, who are in competition with the direct-buying retailers.[100]

Promotional allowances and services must be made available to all competing customers on proportionately equal terms. No single way to proportionalize is prescribed by law; any method that treats competing customers on proportionately equal terms may be used. Generally, this can be done by basing payments made or services furnished on the dollar volume or on the quantity of goods purchased during a specified period. Furthermore, unlike brokerage allowances, a company that grants a discriminatory promotional allowance may argue that the allowance was given in "good faith" to meet the promotional program of a competitor.[101]

Functional Discounts

Each level in the marketing channel performs certain specific tasks and takes certain risks as labor is divided among the various institutions and agencies responsible for making goods and services available to end-users. Historically, when there was little vertical integration and when independent wholesalers sold to numerous, relatively small retail outlets, each level in the channel was rewarded differently (e.g., the wholesaler got a larger price discount from the manufacturer than the retailer). In addition, each level in the channel dealt with a specific class of customer (i.e., the wholesaler sold only to retailers, and retailers only to consumers). Therefore, the discounts given to wholesalers and retailers, called *functional discounts* because they are payments for unique functions performed,[102] could differ without being an antitrust violation, because wholesalers and retailers normally performed different functions in different markets and thus did not compete against each other. However, in more recent years the distinctions in distribution systems have blurred as wholesalers have formed voluntary chains and as retailers have integrated wholesaling functions; therefore, the antitrust questions are much more difficult.

Functional or trade discounts are not specifically referred to in the Robinson-Patman Act or elsewhere, and yet there are clearly instances where price discrimination is being practiced due to confusing classifications of middlemen. For example, K-Mart, a major discount store chain, performs many of its own wholesaling functions. It receives in large lots from manufacturers, breaks bulk, assorts merchandise, and reships merchandise from its warehouses to its retail stores. However, it is generally classified as a "retailer" and therefore is supposedly entitled only to the *functional* discounts given to retailers. (It can, of course, avail itself of whatever *quantity* discounts are offered by its suppliers.) If K-Mart cannot receive a wholesaler's functional discount as well (assuming that such discounts are granted by its suppliers), then it is being discriminated against.

The problem here is obviously one of classification. And if K-Mart were to be given both trade discounts (a wholesaler's and a retailer's), then independent

[100] *FTC* v. *Fred Meyer Company, Inc.,* 390 U.S. 341 (1968).
[101] *FTC* v. *Simplicity Pattern Co.,* 360 U.S. 55 (1959); and *Exquisite Form Brassiere, Inc.* v. *FTC,* 301 F.2d 499 (D.C. Cir. 1961).
[102] Wholesalers and retailers can receive *both* functional discounts *and* quantity discounts. Functional discounts are granted by functions performed, whereas quantity discounts are given on the basis of amount purchased.

wholesalers who resell to independent retailers would argue that their customers (small retailers) are not able to compete with the major chains, such as K-Mart, on an equal footing because the wholesalers would be entitled to receive only the wholesaler discount.

The problem is horribly complex, and no easy solution is in hand. (Some companies have dropped their functional discount structures entirely in order to avoid the problem; they simply offer quantity discounts.) In attempting to cope with this issue, the Federal Trade Commission has been forced to pass upon the methods by which middlemen are classified. When it challenges functional discounts, it relies on the provision of the Robinson-Patman Act that condemns substantial lessening of or injury to competition. However, sellers have been permitted to use the cost savings and good faith defenses to defend their discriminatory functional discount structures. Putting it another way, functional discounts are lawful under the Robinson-Patman Act as long as they are offered on the same terms to all competing buyers of the same class or as long as the discounts granted do not exceed the cost savings of the seller.

The most significant case in recent years involving functional discounts was decided in 1986, when the Federal Trade Commission ruled that Boise Cascade Corp., the largest distributor of office products in the United States, knowingly received unlawful discounts from office-products suppliers in violation of the Robinson-Patman Act.[103] Boise Cascade purchases office supplies from manufacturers and resells them to both retail dealers and large commercial users. In selling to commercial users, Boise competes against retail stationers and other office-products dealers who buy from the same manufacturers. The commission ruled that Boise violated the Robinson-Patman Act by knowingly receiving wholesaler discounts on goods it sold at retail in competition with other dealers. (It did *not* violate the act by receiving wholesaler discounts on goods it resold to other retailers.)

The *Boise Cascade* case dealt with an instance of dual distribution: Boise was in direct competition with some of its customers. There was no dispute about the fact that Boise performs wholesaler functions, such as warehousing inventory, handling credit and bookkeeping, publishing product catalogs, and providing sales assistance to dealers in promotional activities. Discounts to compensate Boise for its performance of these functions were not at issue. The problem revolved around the fact that many retailers perform distribution functions similar to Boise's, but cannot obtain the discounts Boise receives to compensate for them, and thus cannot price competitively at retail.

In dealing with this case, the Federal Trade Commission explicitly considered two competing precedents—the so-called *Mueller* rule[104] and the so-called *Doubleday* rule.[105] The Mueller Company sold products for water and gas distribution systems to wholesalers, some of whom inventoried certain items and some of whom did not. Mueller gave the first set of wholesalers an additional 10 percent discount on the inventoried items. The Federal Trade Commission found this action to be a violation of the Robinson-Patman Act because, it reasoned, Mueller had given these wholesalers a business advantage (i.e., having the high-volume items on hand for immediate delivery to customers) by subsidizing

---

[103] *In the matter of Boise Cascade Corporation*, Federal Trade Commission, Docket No. 9133, February 11, 1986.
[104] *In the matter of Mueller Co.*, 60 F.T.C. 120 (1962).
[105] *In the matter of Doubleday and Co.*, 52 F.T.C. 169 (1955).

them. But the FTC also found that the opportunity to be an inventory-carrying wholesaler was open not to all wholesalers but only to those selected by Mueller. If the opportunity were available to all, then the functional discount might not have been viewed as blatantly discriminatory.

The *Doubleday* rule, which was overturned by the *Mueller* decision, held that discriminatory discounts no greater than the costs borne in providing services could not cause competitive injury. The justifications offered for the doctrine were distributional efficiency and promotion and toleration of diverse distribution methods. However, under the rule, a functional discount would have to be justified not by the supplier's costs savings but by the customer's. This made the rule very difficult (if not impossible) to apply. The costs of a supplier's customers in performing certain functions will surely vary, depending on differences in customer operations, efficiency, location, and product mix. Hence, the discounts allowable under *Doubleday* could vary from customer to customer. Furthermore, a manufacturer could not know in detail each customer's costs to perform certain functions. If, however, the rule had permitted discounts based on cost savings to the supplier as a result of transferring functions to the buyer (e.g., a wholesaler or retailer), the rule would have made more sense. Indeed, the concept inherent in the *Doubleday* rule, with the exception of the focus on customer's cost savings, is very congenial with the channel management notions put forward throughout this text.

The decision in the *Boise Cascade* case boiled down to the fact that the functions Boise performed as a wholesaler and those performed by retailers were virtually identical. Therefore, the FTC concluded, Boise's being given a wholesaler's functional discount and then competing with retailers who could not obtain the discount, even though they performed similar functions, put the retailers at an unfair competitive disadvantage.

A highly significant feature of the case is the FTC's reasoning regarding the *Mueller* and *Doubleday* rules. In its decision, it stated,

> Both *Mueller* and Doubleday address the conflict between the law's requirement of non-discriminatory prices and the seller's desire to compensate for shifting selling functions to distributors. Criticisms of the two doctrines stress their different "preferences." *Mueller*, favoring the legal goal of non-discriminatory prices, is alleged to prohibit compensation for valuable marketing functions, thereby penalizing efficiency. *Doubleday*, favoring the goal of distributional efficiency, is alleged to produce prices that differ widely from competitor to competitor, with discriminatory impact contradicting the Robinson-Patman amendments.
>
> But neither *Mueller* nor *Doubleday* prohibits compensation for marketing functions performed to encourage efficiencies. There are at least three specific circumstances where a seller could offer compensation consistent with the requirements of the Act and with *Mueller* and *Doubleday*. First, functional discounts may usually be granted to customers who operate at different levels of trade, and thus do not compete with each other, without risk of secondary line competitive injury under the Act. Second, even a customer that operates at more than one level of trade may still receive some functional discounts. There will ordinarily be no violation of the Act if the dual distributor receives the wholesaler discount only on the goods it resells to other dealers and receives a retailer discount on the goods it sells in competition with other retailers. . . . Finally, a customer that operates at more than one functional level might even receive a uniform discount on all of its purchases, if such a discount is practically available to this dual distributor's competitors. A supplier is free to "purchase" wholesale and inventory services for goods

that actually receive the benefit of those services, as long as such payment or consideration is available on proportionately equal terms to all other customers competing in distribution.[106]

This last point validates the use of functional discounts. From this, one can assume that as long as a functional discount plan is open to all (i.e., if an intermediary is willing to perform a specific function, he can receive a specific discount as long as the discounts can be cost-justified), then the plan should be able to withstand legal challenges. Nevertheless, the legal status of functional discounts will likely remain cloudy, because the functions of marketing channel members are scrambled and classes of trade (i.e., manufacturers, wholesalers, and retailers) will continue to overlap considerably as intertype competition intensifies and as vertical marketing systems develop.

LEGAL LIMITATIONS REGARDING VERTICAL INTEGRATION

The marketing manager is faced with another set of legal constraints when considering vertical integration. Vertical integration in the channel may come about through forward integration by a producer, backward integration by a retailer, or integration in either direction by a wholesaler or intermediate level of distribution. Integration may be brought about by the creation of a new business function by existing firms (internal expansion) or by acquisition of the stock or the assets of other firms (mergers).

The two methods of creating integration are fundamentally different in their relationship to the law. Internal expansion is regulated by Section 2 of the Sherman Act, which prohibits monopoly or attempts to monopolize any part of the interstate or foreign commerce of the United States. External expansion is regulated by Section 7 of the Clayton Act and its amendment, the Celler-Kefauver Act, which prohibits the purchase of stock or assets of other firms, if the effects may be to substantially lessen competition or tend to create a monopoly in any line of commerce in any part of the country.[107] Internal expansion is given favored treatment under the law. The theory seems to be that internal expansion expands investment and production, and thus increases competition, whereas growth by merger removes an entity from the market.[108]

Integration, whether by merger or internal expansion, may result in the lowering of costs and make possible more effective interorganizational management of the channel. It may also be a means of avoiding many of the legal problems previously discussed, because an integrated firm is free to control

---

[106] *In the matter of Boise Cascade Corporation*, Federal Trade Commission, pp. 30–31.

[107] Under the wording of Section 7 of the Clayton Act, it is necessary to prove that the restraint involved has actually restrained competition. It is enough that it "may" tend to substantially lessen competition.

[108] E. T. Grether, *Marketing and Public Policy* (Englewood Cliffs, N.J.: Prentice-Hall, 1966), p. 104. To show their goodwill toward preserving competition, some companies relinquish their voting privileges on the stock they acquire in merger. For a discussion of merger theory, see T. W. Dunfee and L. W. Stern, "Potential Competition Theory as an Antimerger Tool under Section 7 of the Clayton Act: A Decision Model," *Northwestern Law Review*, Vol. 69 (January-February 1975), pp. 821–71.

prices and allocate products to its integrated outlets without conflict with the laws governing restrictive distribution policies.

Vertical Integration by Merger

The major legal consideration in a vertical merger is the effect the merger will have on competition among firms at the various distributive levels involved in the merger. That is to say, if the merger will tend to foreclose a source of supply to independent firms at the buyer's level or to foreclose a market to other firms at the seller's level, the merger can be questioned. This kind of situation comes about when either level contains only a few firms, so that a merger involving one in each level can make it difficult for third parties to obtain suppliers or outlets that are not competitors as well. The merger of the Brown Shoe Company and the G. R. Kinney Company, the largest independent chain of shoe stores, was declared illegal by the Supreme Court because it was believed that the merger would foreclose other manufacturers from selling through Kinney.[109]

Determining whether a merger will reduce competition involves two critical variables—the definition of the line of commerce and the market involved. If either is defined narrowly enough, almost any merger can be questioned. For example, the critical nature of the definition of the relevant market is apparent in vertical merger cases in the cement industry. The Federal Trade Commission has long been interested in the trend of such mergers and has required firms to give notice to the commission before consummating any merger involving a ready-mixed concrete producer. The commission will attempt to block the merger if it feels that it has anticompetitive features. This happened when the OKG Corporation acquired 88 percent of Jahnke Service. Jahnke produces building materials, including ready-mixed cement; OKG is a producer of cement and other products. At the time of the merger, Jahnke's purchases of cement were about 27 percent of the total in the New Orleans metropolitan area and about 4 percent of the total in the southern Louisiana, Mississippi, and Pensacola areas combined. The Federal Trade Commission decided, first, that the relevant market was the smaller one, and second, that even if it had accepted the larger market as the relevant one, the extent of market foreclosure would violate the Clayton Act. It then ordered OKG to divest itself of Jahnke.[110]

Over time, it appears that the courts have adopted a rule-of-reason analysis in the vertical merger area, balancing efficiency claims against anticompetitive claims. What it amounts to is that a defendant must argue many issues, attempting to show that anticompetitive effects are not unreasonable. Among the relevant issues are market shares, the amount of business involved, the efficiencies involved, the trend to concentration in the industry, whether or not the defendant would have entered the market without a merger, the possibility of price or supply squeezes, the barriers to entry into the industry, and the existing level of concentration in the industry. Thus, Ford Motor Company's merger with Autolite was found to be unlawful because (1) the merger foreclosed 10 percent of the spark plug market to other sellers (i.e., Ford's purchases represented 10 percent of the market for spark plugs); (2) Ford was going to start its own manufacture of spark plugs, but bought Autolite instead; (3) the automotive after-market normally replaced the same type of spark plug put in the original equipment;

---

[109] *Brown Shoe Co.* v. *U.S.*, 370 U.S. 294, Vertical Aspects, 370 U.S. 323 (1962).
[110] "In re OKG Corporation, et al.," *Journal of Marketing*, Vol. 35 (April 1971), pp. 69–70.

therefore, the acquisition of Autolite by Ford would mean that the spark plug market would become exactly like the concentrated car market; and (4) the barriers to entry for new spark plug firms would be extremely high after the acquisition.[111]

As indicated earlier, vertical mergers creating the opportunity for forcing reciprocal buying agreements upon suppliers or buyers are also subject to attack under the Clayton Act. For example, Consolidated Foods, a large processor and distributor of food products, purchased Gentry, a processor of dehydrated onion and garlic, putting Consolidated in a position to require its suppliers to obtain onion and garlic from Gentry as a condition of doing business with Consolidated. The FTC objected to such uses of reciprocity, and filed suit to force Consolidated to divest itself of Gentry. The Supreme Court found that the particular practice in this situation was moving in the direction of coercion and "foreclosure" as well as possible "price squeezing," and stated that "the establishment of the power to exert pressure on customers because those customers are also suppliers, when such power was acquired by merger, is in violation of Section 7 of the Clayton Act."[112]

Vertical Integration by Internal Expansion

This form of integration is limited only by the laws preventing monopoly or attempts to monopolize. A firm is ordinarily free to set up its own distribution and retailing system unless this would overconcentrate the market for its product.[113] Section 7 of the Clayton Act specifically permits a firm to set up subsidiary corporations to carry on business or extensions thereof if competition is not substantially reduced.

Problems Created by Dual Distribution

The term *dual distribution* describes a wide variety of marketing arrangements by which a manufacturer or a wholesaler reaches its final markets by employing two or more different types of channels for the same basic product. However, the dual arrangement whereby manufacturers market their products through competing vertically integrated *and* independently owned outlets on either the wholesale or the retail level often creates controversy. This practice is customary in some lines of trade, such as the automotive passenger tire, paint, and petroleum industries. Dual distribution also takes place when a manufacturer sells similar products under different brand names for distribution through different channels. This latter kind of dual distribution comes about because of market segmentation, or because of sales to distributors under "private" labels.

In all dual distribution situations, conflict among channel members is likely to be relatively high. But serious legal questions arise mainly in two situations: (1) when price "squeezing" is suspected or (2) when horizontal combinations or conspiracies are possible between competitors. The first situation brings about issues comparable to those found when examining the legality of and difficulties

---

[111] *Ford Motor Co.* v. *U.S.*, 405 U.S. 562 (USSC, 1972).
[112] *Federal Trade Commission* v. *Consolidated Foods Corp.*, 380 U.S. 592 (1965).
[113] "Industrial Building Materials v. Interchemical Corp.," *Journal of Marketing*, Vol. 35 (July 1971), p. 76.

associated with the use of functional discounts. The second relates to potential restraints of trade arrived at in concert by vertically integrated firms and their customers. It should be noted at the outset, though, that the Supreme Court has yet to rule squarely on whether dual distribution systems fall within the rule of per se illegality. While dual distribution is not itself a violation of the Sherman Act, any action taken by a supplier engaged in full distribution that affects the prices at which its customers resell its products or that inhibits the ability of those customers to compete with the supplier has the potential of being found in violation of Section 1 of the Sherman Act, unless the supplier can convince the court that this decision was motivated solely by legitimate business reasons and not by a desire to restrain competition.

Price Squeezes. A seller operating at only one market level in competition with a powerful vertically integrated firm might be subject to a price squeeze at his particular level. For example, a manufacturer of fabricated aluminum might be under pressure from price increases by his raw material (ingot) supplier. If the supplier were also a fabricator, it could take its gain from the price increase (which represents higher costs to the customer-competitor) and use all or a portion of the increased returns for marketing activities at the fabricating level. This was exactly the scenario in the *Alcoa* case.[114] A number of lower court decisions have declared unlawful an integrated supplier's attempt to eliminate a customer as a competitor by undercutting the customer's prices and placing the customer in a price squeeze.[115]

In 1982, the Federal Trade Commission dismissed a 1976 case brought against General Motors regarding a possible price squeeze in the distribution of GM crash parts (e.g., fenders, doors, bumpers, and hoods).[116] General Motors sells its crash parts exclusively to its franchised automobile dealers. Independent body shops purchase the parts from the GM dealers. The GM dealers generally charge the independents, their competitors in the collision repair business, more for the parts than what the dealers initially paid GM. For this reason, and because the dealers are the sole source of these parts, the 1976 complaint said that GM's distribution system disadvantaged and discriminated against those other commercial repairers. In its 1982 decision, the FTC acknowledged that the independent body shops are competitively harmed by GM's distribution system but found that the injury "barely" met the required legal showing of substantial injury to competition. The commission concluded that the injury was offset by a showing of substantial business justification for the system. It may be a gross understatement to say that independent body shops did not find the FTC's decision very consoling, especially since the FTC also found that a major cause for independent body shop failure rates "is the fact that they pay, on the average, 17.7% more for GM crash parts than their competitors, the dealer-installers."[117]

---

[114] *U.S. v. Aluminum Co. of America*, 148 F. 2d 416 (2nd Cir. 1945).

[115] See, for example, *Columbia Metal Culvert Co., Inc. v. Kaiser Aluminum & Chemical Corp.*, 579 F. 2d 20 (3rd Cir. 1978); *Coleman Motor Co. v. Chrysler Corp.*, 525 F. 2d 1338 (3d Cir. 1975); and *Industrial Building Materials, Inc. v. Inter-Chemical Corp.* 437 F. 2d 1336 (9th Cir. 1970).

[116] *In re General Motors Corp.*, Federal Trade Commission docket no. 9077, July 1, 1982. See also "FTC Finds General Motors Has Business Justification to Continue Its Crash Parts Distribution System; Overturns Administrative Law Judge's Decision," *FTC News Summary* (July 16, 1982), p. 2.

[117] "FTC Finds General Motors Has Business Justification," p. 2.

The same kind of competitive inequality arises from the granting of functional discounts when different functional categories may be represented by buyers who, at least in part of their trade, are in competition with each other. Oil jobbers, for example, sometimes sell at retail, and they may use their functional discount received as jobbers to advantage in competition with retailers. Such pricing raises the possibility of Robinson-Patman Act as well as Sherman Act violations.

When a supplier to an independent retailer also competes with the retailer by owning its own outlets, the possibility of a price squeeze exists if the integrated supplier is more aggressive in setting retail prices at his own outlets than it is in setting wholesale prices to the independent. Such a possibility was no doubt behind the passage of a law in Maryland (upheld by the U.S. Supreme Court in 1978) that prohibits oil producers or refiners from directly operating gasoline outlets.[118] The law, which permits oil companies to own retail stations as long as they do not use their own employees or agents to run them, also forbids discrimination among dealers in the supply and price of gasoline. It is analogous to legislation proposed in numerous other states designed to halt the trend of oil companies opening their own cut-rate, gasoline-only stations in competition with dealer-operated stations. The specific impetus for the law was dealer complaints that oil companies gave their own stations preferential treatment when gasoline was in short supply during the 1973 Arab oil boycott.

Horizontal Combinations or Conspiracies. In dual distribution situations, the distinction between purely vertical restraints and horizontal restraints may be critical in determining the legality of a marketing activity. Section 1 of the Sherman Act is not violated by the purely unilateral action of a supplier; there must be at least one additional party present whom the court may find combined or conspired with the supplier. As Bondurant has documented, the courts have not found it difficult to identify a host of potential conspirators.[119] Indeed, Bondurant has carefully cataloged a number of lower court decisions in this area, showing that when a supplier or a franchisor has integrated forward to the level of some of its customers, the following activities may be challenged and prohibited or circumscribed, depending on the specific situation:

1. Establishing territorial boundaries between the supplier and its customer/competitors
2. Publishing lists of suggested resale prices
3. Preventing or impeding price competition on the part of customer/competitors via such actions as raising prices to or withdrawing discounts from them
4. Reserving certain national accounts and/or preventing customer/competitors from competing for such accounts[120]

And in one case, the court of appeals reversed a district court and held that where a manufacturer has dominant or monopoly power over a given product, it

[118] See Carol H. Falk, "Justices Uphold Bar to Oil Firms' Retail Outlets," *Wall Street Journal,* June 15, 1978, p. 3; and "The Oil Majors Retreat from the Gasoline Pump," *Business Week* (August 7, 1978), pp. 50–51.

[119] Emmet J. Bondurant, "Antitrust Considerations in the Selection and Modification of Distribution Systems," *Antitrust Law Journal,* Vol. 49, Issue 2 (1981), p. 778n.

[120] *Ibid.,* pp. 779–83.

must *preserve* the independent distributor of its products.[121] According to the court of appeals, the public benefits by being able to buy from a distributor who may handle competing products. A dominant manufacturer may replace a distributor, but he may not enter into competition with him and destroy him.

In sum, dual distribution is not unlawful per se, and each case must be appraised in terms of its special circumstance. However, as Bondurant warns,

> the existence of direct competition between the supplier and its customers inevitably requires that the supplier's business decisions that affect the ability of its customers to compete be subjected to close antitrust scrutiny to determine the real motivation for the supplier's action.[122]

The question of intent will be crucial. The decision may rest on the issues raised in the *Sylvania* case discussed earlier in this chapter. There, a balancing of the effects of a marketing policy on *intra*brand and *inter*brand competition was mandated by the Supreme Court in situations involving vertical restraints.

SUMMARY AND CONCLUSIONS

In setting marketing channel policy, there seems to be a host of ways in which marketing executives can run afoul of the antitrust laws. However, because of the *Sylvania* decision, many of these potential offenses will be analyzed by the courts under a rule-of-reason approach rather than viewed as per se illegal. And even where decisions have tended toward a per se approach, there are still opportunities for a firm to show that it does not meet the standards set for illegality. In other words, with the exception of vertical price fixing, there is no policy area in distribution that can be called an outright per se illegal offense. And there are even ways in which the vertical price-fixing prohibition is being circumvented. For example, manufacturers are permitted, under a 1982 ruling by the Federal Trade Commission involving U.S. Pioneer Electronics Corporation,[123] to set "minimum standards" for dealers, a de facto means for instituting resale restrictions and for cutting off supplies to discounters.[124]

This does not mean that marketing executives can now relax about the law. On the contrary, almost every aspect of their vertical relationships is covered, in one form or another, by the antitrust umbrella. Consider, once again, the long list of policies discussed in this chapter:

1. *Exclusive dealing.* The requirement by a seller or lessor that its customer sell or lease only its products or at least no products in direct competition with the seller's products. Such a policy is illegal if the requirement may substantially lessen competition and is circumscribed by all three of the major antitrust acts—Sherman, Clayton, and FTC. The dominant statute here is, however, Section 3 of the Clayton Act.

---

[121] *Industrial Building Materials* v. *Inter-chemical Corp.*, 437 F.2d 1136 (9th Cir. 1970).
[122] Bondurant, *op. cit.*, p. 783.
[123] *In the Matter of U.S. Pioneer Electronics Corp.*, Federal Trade Commission docket No. C-2755, November 5, 1982.
[124] See Claudia Ricci, "Discounters, Alleging Price-Fixing, Are Fighting Cuts in Their Supplies," *Wall Street Journal,* June 21, 1983, p. 35.

2. *Tying contracts.* The requirement by a sellor or lessor that its customers take other products in order to obtain a product that they desire. Such a requirement seems to be per se illegal, although there are notable exceptions.

3. *Territorial restrictions,* particularly the granting of exclusive territories. The granting by a seller of a geographical monopoly to a buyer for the resale of its product or brand. Such a policy is circumscribed by the Sherman Act and the FTC Act. The major emphasis in the analysis of such cases is on the potential effect of *intrabrand* restrictions on *interbrand* competition.

4. *Customer (resale) restrictions.* The requirement by a seller that its customers resell its products only to specified clientele. (The seller frequently agrees not to compete for those clientele reserved for the customers.) This policy area is treated similarly to territorial restrictions under the antitrust laws.

5. *Resale price maintenance.* The requirement by a seller that a buyer can resell its products only above or below a specified price or at a stipulated price. Price maintenance (fair trade) laws have been nullified by the repeal of the Miller-Tydings and McGuire acts. Price maintenance is per se illegal and is mainly circumscribed by the Sherman Act.

6. *Reciprocity.* The requirement by a buyer that those from whom it purchases must also be buyers of its products. Such a policy, which has frequently been compared to tying arrangements, is prohibited by Section 5 of the FTC Act when a substantial amount of commerce is involved and where reciprocity is prevalent and systematized. It is particularly circumscribed when it is established by coercion.

7. *Refusals to deal.* The right of the seller to choose its own customers or to stop serving a given customer. This threat obviously underlies the commercial enforcement of the policies just mentioned. Although its use is permitted under Section 2(a) of the Robinson-Patman Act, it is forbidden if it fosters restraint of trade or is employed so as to substantially lessen competition.

8. *Functional discounts.* The granting by a seller of price reductions to resellers on the basis of their positions in the marketing channel and the nature and scope of their marketing functions. Although no law directly deals with such discounts, they are circumscribed indirectly by the Robinson-Patman Act and the FTC Act in circumstances where they are allocated unfairly in such a way as to substantially lessen competition.

9. *Price discrimination by buyers.* The requirement by a buyer that a seller offer him a price lower than that offered or available to its competitors. Such a policy is covered under the Robinson-Patman Act if it substantially lessens competition and under the FTC Act as an unfair method of competition.

10. *Price discrimination.* The offering of different prices by a seller to two competing resellers on merchandise of like grade and quality. Such a policy is illegal when it substantially lessens competition, but is legal when it can be justified on the basis of cost differentials or as being adopted in "good faith" to meet competition. It is directly circumscribed by the Robinson-Patman Act.

11. *Promotional allowances and services.* The granting by a seller of payments to resellers for services rendered in connection with processing, handling, selling, or the offering for sale of any of its products sold by them. To be legal, such payments must be offered on proportionately equal terms to all resellers and must be used for the purpose for which they were intended (e.g., advertising allowances must be used for advertising). Again, the Robinson-Patman Act directly limits the way in which such allowances may be employed.

12. *Incentives for resellers' employees.* The offering of special incentives (e.g., push money) by a seller to buyers' employees. While generally permitted, the providing of such incentives is limited by Federal Trade Commission Trade Practice Rules and by the Robinson-Patman Act if they can be shown to injure competition substantially.

13. *Commercial bribery.* The offering of bribes by a seller to a buyer in order to induce the buyer to purchase its products. Although such bribery is viewed as an unfair trade practice under the FTC Act, it is difficult to enforce because of the liberal use of gratuities and entertainment to promote sales. Bribery has historically been policed by the SEC and the IRS.

Vertical integration via internal expansion seems to be positively sanctioned by the antitrust enforcement agencies so long as it does not lead to monopolization in restraint of trade, a Sherman Act offense. On the other hand, vertical integration by merger is much more heavily scrutinized and may be viewed rather negatively by the agencies and the courts. In the case of such mergers, Section 7 (the Celler-Kefauver Amendment) of the Clayton Act can be brought into play if the agencies believe that there may be a tendency for the merger, once consummated, to substantially lessen competition. Thus, the agencies can challenge such mergers in their incipiency.

The policy of vertical integrating often leads to dual distribution conflicts in which sellers become competitors of some of their independently owned resellers. Although there are no additional laws beyond those mentioned earlier circumscribing dual distribution, this practice has undergone considerable scrutiny in Congress, and it is not at all unlikely that legislation may be forthcoming to limit its practice, especially if it can be shown that small independent middlemen are being severely hurt by it.

It should be noted once again that this chapter has focused only on federal law. The states have become much more active in the antitrust arena, and thus marketing executives would make a serious mistake to ignore the vast outpouring of legislation regulating distribution practices in each of the states in which the products of their companies are sold. Unfortunately, no comprehensive compendium of state laws regulating distribution is available. Marketing executives must therefore rely on state-by-state analyses in order to uncover relevant guidelines.

DISCUSSION QUESTIONS

1. What laws affecting distribution are more likely to be protecting competitors rather than competition? Is the distinction important? Why?

2. Which is preferable—intrabrand or interbrand competition? Can there be one without the other? Where do you stand on the issue of intrabrand competition: is it necessary in order for there to be viable general competition from a macro perspective? Discuss these questions in the context of resale restrictions and the granting of exclusive territories.

3. Explain the relationship between vertical "arrangements" and horizontal competition.

4. Do you believe that the Robinson-Patman Act should be stricken from the laws of this country? Debate the pros and cons of this question and come out with a position on it.

5. The president of an automobile accessory manufacturing business wants to purchase a chain of automotive retail stores. What legal issues might this raise?

6. Discuss the similarities and differences between a tying contract and the business practice of reciprocity. Do the practices, on balance, appear to be significantly different?

7. Name five uses of coercive power that would be legal in interorganization management. Name five uses of reward power that would be legal.

8. Can you think of any instances where the use of expert or referent power in interorganization management might be illegal?

9. Which conflict management strategies suggested in Chapter 6 might be questionable from a legal perspective? Why?

CHAPTER NINE

Channel Management by Channel Participants

At this point in this text, it should be clear that some form of interorganization management is necessary and desirable if a channel is to maintain or achieve satisfactory performance as a competitive entity. Thus, the discussion in this chapter focuses not only on the need for management but rather on delineating the variables that affect channel control and the institutions that are capable of assuming managerial roles within commercial channel systems. To set the stage for this discussion we present a summary in Fig. 9–1 of channel management in the context of channel strategy development and implementation.

In the remainder of this chapter, we present a framework for channel leadership and control and consider the leadership potential of manufacturers, wholesalers, retailers, and physical distribution agencies. Clearly, the question of leadership hinges to a large degree on the locus of power within various channel systems, and therefore considerable attention is devoted to this subject. Be fore-warned, however, that attempts to generalize are often misleading, since the system will in reality vary widely in composition and orientation. Only through an in-depth empirical analysis is one likely to discover the best answer to the question "Who should lead the channel?"

A FRAMEWORK FOR CHANNEL LEADERSHIP AND CONTROL

The extent to which the channel of distribution is managed by a leader(s) who can stipulate marketing policies to other channel members and therefore control their marketing decisions hinges upon a number of interrelated factors, as shown in Fig. 9–2. A discussion of these factors, their interrelationships, and related research findings follows.

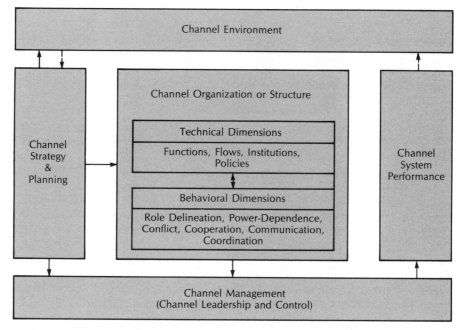

Explanation
- Channel strategy and planning processes represent the means by which the channel organization adapts to and attempts to influence its task and ultimate environments.
- Channel strategy and planning and channel organization or structure define the foundations on which channel management processes (i.e., leadership and control attempts) are based.
- Channel system performance is a function of channel management.
- Channel system performance sends feedback into the environment; therefore, it triggers mechanisms for channel strategy adjustments and evaluation processes.

Figure 9–1   *Channel management in context*

Channel Environment and Channel Leadership

The ability of a channel member to exercise control stems from his access to power resources. According to Etgar, the accrual of such power-generating resources to a channel leader may be the result of the specific characteristics, experience, or history of the firm and its management. Alternatively, power sources (or their absence) may reflect particular characteristics of the environmental forces impinging upon the channel (demand, technology, competition, legal constraints, etc.) and the channel member's ability to capitalize on these forces. Therefore, the power of a channel leader may reflect both the characteristics of his environment and his own characteristics.[1]

[1] Michael Etgar, "Channel Environment and Channel Leadership," *Journal of Marketing Research*, Vol. 14 (February 1977), p. 70.

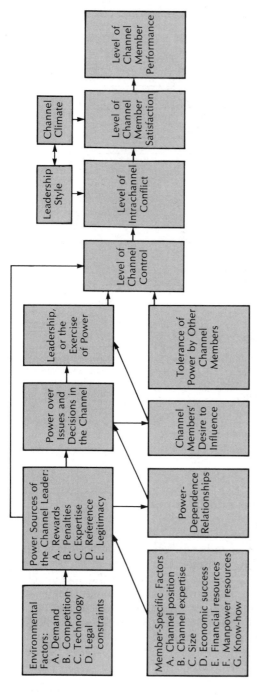

Explanation

• Power sources accrue to channel members as a result of environmental factors and/or the specific characteristics of the channel member.

• Power is issue-oriented. Power over issues and decisions is a function of sources of power accumulated by a channel member and his power-dependence relationships vis-à-vis other channel members.

• Not only do dependence and sources of power directly affect power, but bases of power have an indirect effect on power over issues via their impact on dependence.

• Leadership, or the exercise of power, can materialize only when a channel member has power over issue(s) and desires to exercise his power.

• The level and effectiveness of channel control achieved is a function of the quality of leadership, nature, and magnitude of power resources deployed, and the tolerance of power by other channel members.

• Effectiveness of channel control can be judged in terms of desirable channel control outcomes, including the following in sequence:
 (a) reduction of dysfunctional intrachannel conflict and increase in channel member coordinates and cooperation;
 (b) increase in channel member satisfaction; and
 (c) improvement of channel member performance.

• Leadership style (e.g., participative, supportive, or directive) affects the level of intrachannel conflict.

The relationships between the various environmental variables and the degree of control exercised by a channel leader over other members of a distribution channel were the focuses of a cross-sectional study conducted by Etgar.[2] Four environmental variables were chosen for empirical analysis: stage in a product's life cycle, demand uncertainty, extent of use of personal services in marketing, and intensity of interchannel competition. The results of the study indicated that the control of a channel leader is greater:

1. Under conditions of declining rather than growing demand
2. If demand is more unstable than stable
3. In situations where the importance of personal selling and of postsales servicing is high
4. When interchannel competition is strong

Jointly, these results imply that channel leaders tend to emerge in distributive channels when the environment is threatening. However, it should be noted that the environmental variables *as a group* explained only a relatively small amount of variance in the control variables. Other factors, especially those reflecting the specific characteristics of the channel leader and his channel position, apparently are more important in explaining the variance.

A recent study by Dwyer and Welsh examining the relationship between environmental homogeneity/stability or heterogeneity/instability and channel member control sheds more light on Etgar's findings. Dwyer and Welsh found some support for the hypothesis that "compared with homogeneous environments, heterogeneous channel environments are associated with more retailer control over marketing decisions."[3] In the same study, the hypothesis that "compared with counterparts in stable settings, channels facing variability in the output sector are associated with less retailer control over marketing decisions"

---

[2] *Ibid.*, pp. 74–75. It should be noted that most of the channels studies reported in this chapter suffer from some methodological deficiencies. For a thorough critique, see Lynn W. Phillips, "The Study of Collective Behavior in Marketing: Methodological Issues in the Use of Key Informants," unpublished Ph.D. dissertation, Northwestern University, 1980; and John F. Gaski, "The Theory of Power and Conflict in Channels of Distribution," *Journal of Marketing*, Vol. 47 (Summer 1984), pp. 9–29.

[3] F. Robert Dwyer and M. Ann Welsh, "Environmental Relationships of the Internal Political Economy of Marketing Channels," *Journal of Marketing Research*, Vol. 22 (November 1985), p. 409.

Figure 9–2   A framework for channel leadership and control

Sources: Based on Michael Etgar, "Channel Environment and Channel Leadership," *Journal of Marketing Research,* Vol. 14 (February 1977), p. 70; James R. Brown, Robert F. Lusch, and Darrel D. Muehling, "Conflict and Power-Dependence Relations in Retail-Supplier Channels," *Journal of Retailing,* Vol. 59 (Winter 1983), pp. 53–80; Gary L. Frazier, "Interorganizational Exchange Behavior in Marketing Channels: A Broadened Perspective," *Journal of Marketing,* Vol. 46 (Fall 1983), pp. 68–78; John F. Gaski, "The Theory of Power and Conflict in Channels of Distribution," *Journal of Marketing,* Vol. 47 (Summer 1984), pp. 9–29; James C. Anderson and James A. Narus, "A Model of the Distributor's Perspective of Distributor-Manufacturer Working Relationships," *Journal of Marketing,* Vol. 47 (Fall 1984), pp. 62–74; John F. Gaski and John R. Nevin, "The Differential Effects of Exercised and Unexercised Power Sources in a Marketing Channel," *Journal of Marketing Research,* Vol. 22 (May 1985), pp. 130–34; Patrick L. Schul, William M. Pride, and Taylor E. Little, "The Impact of Channel Leadership Behavior on Intrachannel Conflict," *Journal of Marketing,* Vol. 46 (Summer 1983), pp. 21–34; and Patrick L. Schul, Taylor E. Little, Jr., and William M. Pride, "Channel Climate: Its Impact on Channel Members' Satisfaction," *Journal of Retailing,* Vol. 61 (Summer 1985), pp. 9–37.

was statistically supported.[4] In essence, manufacturer dominance is more likely in channel environments characterized by homogeneity and stability, and retailer dominance is evident in channel environments characterized by heterogeneity and instability of demand.

The Use of Coercive and Noncoercive Power

A channel member has to command sources of power (reward, coercion, expertise, reference, or legitimacy) before he can effectively attempt to control other channel members. Gaski suggests that each power source may affect power, conflict, satisfaction, etc., not only directly but also through the intermediating effect of *qualitative power sources*—that is, the effect of the various power sources *on each other:*

> for example, though the direct impact of the reward power source on power may be positive, if it acts to decrease other power sources (perhaps by reducing the perception of expertness or legitimacy) its net effect may be weakened or even negative. As an illustration, a manufacturer that grants rewards beyond a reasonable level may appear foolish to dealers and hence less expert. Similarly, the use of coercion clearly could reduce one's likability, or referent power source.[5]

The results of Gaski's study indicate that supplier's application of reward or punishment does affect the strength of its other three power sources. Because reward enhances these sources of power and punishment detracts from them, the net effect of reward on power and satisfaction is positive and that of coercion is negative. This finding of a compound effect of the use of certain power sources may lead to a better understanding of some of the weak and incongruent results seen in studies examining the outcome of the use of different power sources.[6]

There are indications in the literature that, as pointed out in Chapter 6, under different circumstances the deployment of certain sources of power can be more effective than that of others. For example, on the basis of his research, Etgar suggests that in conventional channels involving highly independent dealers who also hold countervailing powers, control over these dealers can best be accomplished through an exchange process whereby agents agree to give up a certain degree of independence in return for services offered by the suppliers. Power tradeoffs were shown to be more effective in achieving control than reliance on the use of coercion and threats.[7]

Similarly, Lusch found on the basis of research on the effects of the use of coercive and noncoercive power that coercive power is directly related to the frequency of intrachannel conflict. The study suggested that coercive sources may increase the frequency of intrachannel conflict and decrease dealer satisfaction,[8] although no causal relationship of direction was established.

---

[4] *Ibid.*

[5] John F. Gaski, "Interrelations among a Channel Entity's Power Sources: Impact of the Exercise of Reward and Coercion on Expert, Referent, and Legitimate Power Sources," *Journal of Marketing Research,* Vol. 23 (February 1986), p. 63.

[6] *Ibid.,* p. 75.

[7] Michael Etgar, "Channel Domination and Countervailing Power in Distributive Channels," *Journal of Marketing Research,* Vol. 13 (August 1976), p. 260.

[8] Robert F. Lusch, "Sources of Power: Their Impact on Intrachannel Conflict," *Journal of Marketing Research,* Vol. 13 (November 1976), p. 388.

Further evidence of the effects of different sources of power is presented by Sibley and Michie in an exploratory investigation of cooperation in a franchise channel. Their results indicate a strong relationship between channel cooperation and the use of noncoercive power by the franchisor and no relationship between channel cooperation and the franchisor's use of coercive power.[9]

Gaski and Nevin examined the differential effects of exercised and unexercised coercive and noncoercive power on channel member power, conflict, satisfaction, and performance. This study is very significant in that it uses the coercive-noncoercive power dichotomy to investigate a number of the relationships specified in the framework for channel leadership and control presented in Fig. 9–2. Gaski and Nevin first looked at the relationship between the power of the channel leader and his exercise of power over issues and decisions in the channel. Second, previously published research had not distinguished between exercised and existing nonexercised rewards and punishments in marketing channels. Gaski and Nevin therefore tested for the possibility that the mere *presence* of sources of power and their potential use may be as effective as the actual exercise of power in achieving channel control outcomes. That is, they attempted to answer the question "Does the exercise of power make any difference?" Finally, they examined the differential effects of exercised and unexercised power in terms of desired channel control outcomes—reduction of conflict, increase in channel member satisfaction, and improvement of channel member performance. Gaski and Nevin's findings can be summarized as follows:

- *Relationship between the presence of power sources and their exercise.* The exercise of power, coercive and noncoercive, is related positively to the existence of sources of power. However, as more of a power source is held by a supplier, proportionately less of that power will actually be used to control his dealers.[10]

- *Effects of power exercise on power.* The exercise of noncoercive or reward power has a stronger positive relationship with power than does the presence of a reward power source. However, the exercise of coercive sources of power by suppliers produces stronger positive effects on supplier power than the unexercised presence of this power source.[11]

- *Effects of power exercise on conflict.* The exercise of coercive sources of power (e.g., the application of punishment by a supplier) causes intrachannel conflict to a significantly greater degree than does merely the dealer's perception of the supplier's ability to impose punishment. The same does *not* hold true for reward power sources. The potential or promise of reward was found to be practically as potent in reducing intrachannel conflict as the actualization of reward.[12]

- *Effect of power exercise on satisfaction.* The exercise of coercive sources of power by suppliers has a stronger negative effect on dealer satisfaction than the mere presence of coercive sources. However, the exercise of *noncoercive* reward sources of power by suppliers has practically the same positive effect on dealer satisfaction as the presence of noncoercive sources of power, or the potential for reward.[13]

- *Effects of power exercise on performance.* Unlike previous findings, no significant relationships were found between power sources, coercive or noncoercive, and perfor-

[9] Stanley D. Sibley and Donald A. Michie, "An Exploratory Investigation of Cooperation in a Franchise Channel," *Journal of Retailing*, Vol. 58 (Winter 1982), pp. 23–45.

[10] John F. Gaski and John R. Nevin, "The Differential Effects of Exercised and Unexercised Power Sources in a Marketing Channel," *Journal of Marketing Research*, Vol. 22 (May 1985), pp. 138–39.

[11] *Ibid.*

[12] *Ibid.*, pp. 132, 138.

[13] *Ibid.*, pp. 132, 133, 137.

mance. The researchers speculated that the relationship between power sources and performance could be suppressed by a number of intervening variables.[14]

In summary, Gaski and Nevin's results support the proposition that

> the exercise of coercive power source by a supplier has a stronger effect on dealer satisfaction and channel conflict than the mere presence of that power. In contrast, exercise of reward power source seems to have only a marginal impact on these dependent variables (i.e., satisfaction and conflict).[15]

The Use of Economic and Noneconomic Power

There is a growing body of evidence that the possession and use of economic power bases are directly related to perceptions of power, while the possession and use of noneconomic sources of power are not.[16] Etgar evaluated the relative effectiveness of the deployment of the economic and noneconomic power sources in Table 9–1 in achieving control over different channel decisions. The results of his study indicate that

> out of the array of power-generating vehicles, economic rewards and penalties have an important advantage over noneconomic ones like legitimacy, expertise, and identification. The former were found to be positively linked to channel leaders' power and therefore useful for control generation; the latter were found to be inversely related to power.[17]

The different nature of these sources of power has been advanced as a plausible explanation for these findings.[18] For example, the channel member exercising economic power directly mediates the consequences. When using noneconomic sources of power, the channel member indirectly mediates outcomes of influence through norms and values. Furthermore, the impact of economic and noneconomic sources of power upon the influenced channel member's beliefs and opinions differs. When economic power is used to influence a channel member, it may structure that member's beliefs against the wishes of the channel member exercising such power. Oppositely, the use of noneconomic power more likely will result in bending the influenced member's own beliefs in conformity with the influence attempt.[19]

In the final analysis, the use of economic and noneconomic power by a channel member must be guided by the effectiveness of a power source in achieving desired control outcomes. The effectiveness of a power source is ultimately determined by (1) the extent to which it can be applied to specific channel

---

[14] *Ibid.*, pp. 133, 138–39.

[15] *Ibid.*, p. 139.

[16] In addition to the studies examined in this section, see Shelby D. Hunt and John R. Nevin, "Power in the Channel of Distribution," *Journal of Marketing Research*, Vol. 11 (May 1974), pp. 186–93; and Ian F. Wilkinson, "Power, Conflict and Satisfaction in Distribution Channels: An Empirical Study," *International Journal of Physical Distribution and Materials Management*, Vol. 11 (1981), pp. 20–30.

[17] Michael Etgar, "Selection of an Effective Channel Control Mix," *Journal of Marketing*, Vol. 41 (July 1978), p. 57.

[18] Robert F. Lusch and James R. Brown, "A Modified Model of Power in the Marketing Channel," *Journal of Marketing Research*, Vol. 18 (August 1982), pp. 312–23.

[19] James R. Brown, Robert F. Lusch, and Darrel D. Muehling, "Conflict and Power-Dependence Relations in Retailer-Supplier Channels," *Journal of Retailing*, Vol. 59 (Winter 1983), p. 74.

Table 9–1   Measures of power and sources of power

Measures of Power	Measures of Power Sources	
Insure Control over	Economic	Noneconomic
1. Retail pricing 2. Choice of retail location 3. Minimum order size 4. Mix of units ordered 5. Retail advertising 6. Provision of credit to customers 7. Ability to buy from other suppliers 8. Salesmen training 9. Salesmen hiring 10. Physical layout of the store 11. Participation in professional & trade associations 12. Selling policies—territorial & customer restrictions	1. Financial assistance at start 2. Financial assistance on a current basis 3. Help in retail advertising 4. Assistance in store management 5. Provision of market information 6. Provision of sales leads 7. Promptness of delivery 8. Frequency of delivery	1. Selection of products 2. Assistance in training 3. Rate of development of new products 4. Backup by advertising 5. Level of expertise 6. Team association

Source: Reprinted from Michael Etgar, "Selection of an Effective Channel Control Mix," *Journal of Marketing,* Vol. 41 (July 1978), p. 56, published by the American Management Association.

members (selectivity), and (2) the extent to which it can be related to specific performance by channel members (directedness). Expert, referent, and legitimate power may be less flexible and can often be viewed as being unrelated to specific performance by channel members. For example, legal constraints may not allow channel leaders to discriminate among similar channel members and may require them to offer identical or equal rewards to all. Meanwhile, economic power can be applied individually and can be related to specific performance.[20] Above all, the reader is reminded that serious side effects attend the use of reward and coercive power, such as law violations and conflict. These factors were discussed in Chapters 6 and 8.

Leadership Style and Control of Intrachannel Conflict

As discussed in Chapter 6, one of the key desirable outcomes of channel control is the reduction of the level of intrachannel conflict. Achieving this outcome has been strongly linked to the effectiveness of the *leadership style* of the channel leader and his creation of a positive *channel climate*. In a study conducted by Schul, Pride, and Little, three leadership styles, participative, supportive, and directive, were each hypothesized to lower the level of intrachannel conflict associated with different types of policies and administrative issues affecting channel relationships.[21]

[20] Etgar, "Selection of an Effective Channel Control Mix," pp. 54–55.
[21] Patrick L. Schul, William M. Pride, and Taylor E. Little, "The Impact of Channel Leadership Behavior on Intrachannel Conflict," *Journal of Marketing,* Vol. 46 (Summer 1983), p. 21.

A *participative leader* consults with subordinates, solicits their suggestions, and considers them before making a decision.[22] These traits suggest collaboration among channel members, which is conducive to cooperation and thus could reduce intrachannel conflict. *Supportive leaders* consider subordinates' needs, display concern for their well-being, and create a friendly and pleasant task environment.[23] Supportive activities provide a more pleasant climate, which directly influences the level of conflict. *Directive leadership* is characterized by organizing and defining the task environment, assigning the necessary functions to be performed, estimating communication networks, and evaluating work group performance.[24] These traits involve planning, organizing, coordinating, and controlling channel-related activities so that channel members will be provided with consistent channelwide objectives, policies, and operating procedures, resulting in lower intrachannel conflict.

The results of the study indicate that conflict arising from both administrative and product/service issues diminishes when the leadership style emphasizes participation, support, and direction in carving out channel activities.[25] Specifically, each leadership style variously affects different conflict issues. While participative leadership reduces conflict over both administrative and product/service issues, channel members' particular sensitivity to administrative concerns such as advertising fees, service, accounting information requirements, and contract terms leads channel members to prefer participation in policy making. Therefore, for these issues, the deployment of a participative leadership style results in channel members experiencing less conflict. Supportive leadership also tends to be more associated with reduced conflict over administrative issues.[26] Directive leadership, on the other hand, tends to be related more closely to the level of product-source conflict than to the level of conflict over administrative issues.[27] However, the effect of directive leadership depends on the nature of the task. When there is a high degree of task specificity, directive leadership does not have a strong impact on conflict, but when the task is ambiguous, directive leadership can reduce ambiguity and consequently the level of intrachannel conflict.

Power over Issues and Channel Member Satisfaction

The degree of success that a channel member has in influencing others is judged, in part, on his success in increasing channel member satisfaction with the channel relationship. Channel member satisfaction refers to members' attitudes and feelings toward the internal environment of the channel organization and the relationships between that environment and other institutions in the channel.[28] Four dimensions of channel member satisfaction have been identified: (1) a *product dimension,* which reflects the demand for, awareness of, and quality expectations of the manufacturer's products; (2) a *financial dimension,* which

[22] *Ibid.,* p. 23.
[23] *Ibid.*
[24] *Ibid.*
[25] *Ibid.,* p. 30.
[26] *Ibid.*
[27] *Ibid.,* p. 31.
[28] Patrick L. Schul, Taylor E. Little, Jr., and William M. Pride, "Channel Climate: Its Impact on Channel Members' Satisfaction," *Journal of Retailing,* Vol. 61 (Summer 1985), p. 13.

captures the attractiveness of the arrangement with respect to such matters as intermediary margins and return on investment; (3) an *assistance dimension,* which assesses how well the manufacturer supports the intermediary; and (4) a *social interaction dimension,* reflecting how satisfactorily interactions between intermediaries and manufacturers are handled.[29] Studies on satisfaction have found that at higher levels of satisfaction, participants experience increased morale, greater cooperation, fewer terminations of relationships, reduced litigation, and fewer efforts to pursue protective legislation.[30] Thus, it is in the best interests of the channel leader to enhance channel member satisfaction when attempting to control the decision making of other channel firms.[31]

Channel Climate and Channel Member Performance

Channel leaders attempting to realize the benefits of channel coordination and cooperation should focus on identifying and directing attention to the *climate* of the channel.[32] The channel climate is "that set of attributes of the channel organization reflected in the evaluative description channel members make of the policies, practices, and conditions which exist in the internal channel environment."[33] Four dimensions of channel climate have been identified:

1. *Channel leader initiating structure:* the degree to which the leader organizes and defines the task environment, assigns the necessary functions to be performed, establishes communication networks, and evaluates work group performance[34]
2. *Channel leader consideration:* behavior that involves trust, mutual respect, friendship, support, and a concern for the welfare of subordinates[35]
3. *Autonomy:* the amount of perceived independence that members feel they have in performing tasks[36]
4. *Reward orientation:* the relationship between performance and extrinsic and intrinsic reward[37]

These various components of channel climate have been hypothesized to independently affect channel member satisfaction. The hypothesized relationships are as follows:

- The higher the perceived level of initiating structure provided by the channel leader, the higher the level of channel member satisfaction.
- The higher the level of consideration exhibited by the channel leader toward channel members, the higher the level of satisfaction.
- The greater the level of perceived autonomy, the higher the level of channel member satisfaction.
- The stronger the perceived performance-reward relationship provided by the channel leader, the higher the level of channel member satisfaction.[38]

[29] Robert W. Ruekert and Gilbert A. Churchill, Jr., "Reliability and Validity of Alternative Measures of Channel Member Satisfaction," *Journal of Marketing Research,* Vol. 20 (May 1984), p. 227.
[30] *Ibid.,* p. 226.
[31] *Ibid.*
[32] Schul, Little, and Pride, *op. cit.,* p. 9.
[33] *Ibid.,* p. 14.
[34] *Ibid.,* p. 15.
[35] *Ibid.,* p. 16.
[36] *Ibid.*
[37] *Ibid.,* p. 17.
[38] *Ibid.*

It is at once apparent from the results of the study that channel climate and channel member satisfaction are significantly related. In particular, initiating structure increased satisfaction by reducing channel members' role ambiguity, and increasing their understanding of channelwide policies and procedures.[39] Also, perception of a higher level of consideration appears to affect channel satisfaction. When members feel they are part of a supportive channel arrangement in which they are allowed to provide inputs, they will understand and more fully accept policies and procedures, thereby increasing their satisfaction with the arrangement. Autonomy has a significant positive effect on channel member satisfaction in the form of a perceived increase in power, which increases member commitment to attaining channel-related goals.[40] Last, members who perceive that channel-related rewards are based on channel performance expressed higher satisfaction.[41]

The results of this study indicate to channel managers several means of improving satisfaction. Channel managers can then analyze their relationships with channel members and introduce policies and procedures high on initiating structure, consideration, autonomy, or reward orientation in order to produce a climate consistent with channel members' needs and expectations.[42]

Channel Member Perceptions and the Channel Control Process

The effectiveness of channel leadership in achieving channel coordination and control hinges to a large extent on:

1. Whether the channel members perceive themselves as a channel of a distribution system or are concerned merely with their immediate suppliers and customers. If channel members do not perceive themselves as members of a total system, suboptimization is more likely to be the rule and channel coordination gets more difficult.

2. How the members perceive the control process within the channel. Differences in perceptions indicate a strong potential that channel members will have differing bases of action in responding to similar situations.

3. Which marketing strategy variables are perceived as controlled by each channel member. Control is not exercised over a range of issues as some type of total control. Rather, channel member power governs specific marketing decision variables. Unless channel members share perceptions of who is controlling what, attempts to control may result in chaos and further misunderstanding instead of the desired coordination and control.[43]

In a study designed to explore these issues, Speh and Bonfield reported the following findings:

1. Retail personnel do not firmly grasp the concept of a total channel system.

2. There are differences in the way owner/managers and sales personnel perceive the pattern of overall channel control. Both tend to look toward the member directly adjacent to themselves in the channel as the most important influencer.

[39] *Ibid.*, pp. 28–29.
[40] *Ibid.*, pp. 29–30.
[41] *Ibid.*, p. 30.
[42] *Ibid.*
[43] Thomas W. Speh and E. H. Bonfield, "The Control Process in Marketing Channels: An Exploratory Investigation," *Journal of Retailing*, Vol. 54 (Spring 1978), pp. 14–16.

3. There are differences in the way owner/managers and sales personnel perceive control over specific marketing variables. Additionally, within each group of respondents, different channel members were seen to have different amounts of influence over the marketing variables.

4. There is no overall retail firm viewpoint on control. Owner/managers and sales personnel differ in how they perceive influence patterns in the channel.[44]

These findings underscore the difficulties involved in channel management and the necessity of a channelwide communication and information system to broaden the base of common understanding and promote commonality of perception among channel members. Without such efforts, attempts to control the channel can be mere shots in the dark. Research by Frazier and Summers[45] and Frazier and Sheth[46] suggests that the success of interfirm influence attempts relies heavily on the appropriateness of the communication strategies they employ. A more detailed analysis of channel communication and information systems is found in Chapter 10.

The discussion thus far has focused on variables that influence channel members' leadership and control potential. A better understanding of these variables can be achieved through an examination of channel management by key channel members.

CHANNEL MANAGEMENT BY MANUFACTURERS

Too often it is automatically assumed that the manufacturer or producer will be the channel leader and that middlemen will be the followers. But as Mallen points out, manufacturers have not always been the channel leaders:

> The growth of mass retailers is increasingly challenging the manufacturer for channel leadership, as the manufacturer challenged the wholesaler in the early part of this century.[47]

Underlying Mallen's statement, however, is the assumption (or belief) that either manufacturers or mass retailers will manage the interorganizational relations within channels. Although this assumption has a great deal of appeal, as will be shown, it is not necessarily valid in all cases and need not be valid in the future.

Large manufacturers can always be considered potential leaders of channels because, by definition, they have amassed a significant amount of reward and coercive power, given their size and dominance in the markets in which they compete. Their power emanates from their considerable financial resources, which enable them to maintain superior product research and development, cultivate consumer franchises through promotion, maintain continuous flows of market information, offer high margins and support to middlemen, and retain

[44] *Ibid.,* p. 25.

[45] Gary L. Frazier and John O. Summers, "Interfirm Influence Strategies and Their Application within Distribution Channels," *Journal of Marketing,* Vol. 47 (Summer 1984), pp. 43–55.

[46] Gary L. Frazier and Jagdish N. Sheth, "An Attitude-Behavior Framework for Distribution Channel Management," *Journal of Marketing,* Vol. 48 (Summer 1985), pp. 38–48.

[47] Bruce Mallen, "Conflict and Cooperation in Marketing Channels," in Bruce Mallen (ed.), *The Marketing Channel: A Conceptual Viewpoint* (New York: John Wiley & Sons, 1967), p. 127.

control over their products until they reach the point in the channel where ultimate consumers or industrial buyers can purchase them.

However, small manufacturers may, as Little observes, also serve as potential sources of control and direction in an interorganizational channel network.[48] Limited economic resources hamper their opportunities, but a good product offers control possibilities.[49] Such possibilities are manifestations of their legitimate, referent, and, to some extent, expert power. The manufacturer with an outstanding product may have, from the perspective of those purchasing it, a "right" to dictate how it should be sold and consumed, an image with which others seek to identify, and probably a greater knowledge about the market for his product than anyone else. Furthermore, whether they are large or small, those controlling a new product desired by many consumers can elect to offer or withhold their product from various middlemen and therefore exercise reward or coercive power. For example, there are more than 20,000 automotive parts manufacturers in the U.S. Only 4 percent of these companies are larger than 500 employees. The small companies have small technical staffs and limited capital. At the same time, there are over 540,000 aftermarket outlets for automotive parts, including service stations, tire, battery, and accessory stores, jobbers, and mass merchandisers. These manufacturers and distributors are organized in 22 different channels of distribution, which must pursue different strategies. The majority of these distribution outlets cannot carry much inventory because of the large number of parts and part applications as well as the high cost of carrying inventory. While a large manufacturer such as Champion, the worldwide leading producer of spark plugs, capitalizes on its vast mass-production and mass-marketing expertise, small manufacturers are uniquely positioned to control parts distribution, as they do in the aftermarket for limited-edition automobiles.[50]

In general, the traditional viewpoint of manufacturer dominance in marketing channels emanates from an emphasis on production economies that can be achieved only by increases in sales. As sales grow, a manufacturer realizes the benefits of large-scale operations and can spread his overhead costs over a large number of units. In fact, Mallen argues, the manufacturer must control the channel in order to assure himself of adequate sales volume and thereby justify the investment risk he alone must take relative to development and production.[51] It has also been asserted that as long as a manufacturer has the legal right to select the middlemen with whom he will deal, he should be able to specify roles and allocate resources within the system that he selects for the marketing of his product.[52] Thus, the concept of the manufacturer-directed channel is based primarily on the belief that because the manufacturer creates and produces the product and designs the network through which it passes on to consumers, he is entitled, on the basis of legitimacy if nothing else, to impose his marketing policies on other channel members and to direct the activities of the channel.

[48] Robert W. Little, "The Marketing Channel: Who Should Lead This Extracorporate Organization?" *Journal of Marketing*, Vol. 34 (January 1970), p. 34.
[49] Neil H. Borden, *Acceptance of New Products by Supermarkets* (Boston: Division of Research, Graduate School of Business Administration, Harvard University, 1968), p. 13.
[50] "Automotive Aftermarket Is Confronted with Turbulent Times," *Marketing News* (February 18, 1983), p. 24.
[51] Mallen, *op. cit.*, p. 129.
[52] Eli P. Cox, "Federal Quantity Discount Limitations and Their Possible Effects on Distribution Channel Dynamics," unpublished doctoral dissertation, University of Texas, 1956, p. 12.

Another justification for manufacturers as channel leaders is the market power they derive from large advertising budgets. A number of studies have demonstrated that advertising decreases factory price sensitivity and increases retail price sensitivity.[53] As Albion and Farris concluded, on the basis of two studies of food and nonfood products,

> Because manufacturer advertising can stimulate retail price competition and lower retail gross margins, . . . advertising can decrease price sensitivity for the manufacturer, while increasing price sensitivity for the consumer.[54]

To retailers, gross margins are perhaps the single most important economic reward mediated by manufacturers. If manufacturers have the potential to influence retail margins by regulating advertising budgets, one cannot escape concluding that manufacturers can be the channel managers.

Although a number of channels are manufacturer-dominated for just these reasons (especially when the manufacturers in question have considerable economic power), the question of channel leadership is not as easy to answer as the discussion thus far would imply. There are many other factors that must be considered before manufacturers are deemed the logical channel managers. First, manufacturers are not always eager to concern themselves with channel management. Their sole concern may simply be the firms above and below them in the channel. After all, manufacturers usually deal with their immediate suppliers and customers and not with any of the other resellers of their products. Manufacturers may not care at all about the problems of other channel members as long as their own needs are satisfied. Similar assertions could be applied to middlemen as well. Manufacturers, it must be noted, are not unique in this respect. Furthermore, manufacturers may prefer to concentrate on product research and development because of limited marketing management capacity or capability. As was shown in Chapter 3, this latter factor accounts for the heavy reliance on wholesalers in a number of industrial goods industries.

Second, as pointed out later in this chapter, manufacturers may simply not be powerful enough to impose their marketing policies on other channel members. This is particularly true if the manufacturer is interested in employing large wholesaling and retailing institutions. In general, middlemen have as much freedom of choice as the manufacturer, if not more. They do not have to handle the manufacturer's product if they do not desire to, especially if substitutes are readily available. Given limited display and warehouse space as well as the need for immediate cash flow by many resellers, manufacturers must often curry the favor of middlemen to ensure that adequate inventories of their products are maintained, not to say promoted. In addition, middlemen frequently can develop a great deal of local strength in their markets so that customers become more loyal to them than to the various brands they carry.

In summary, manufacturer dominance of the marketing channel is not an absolute certainty, for several reasons. Among these are the manufacturer's own reluctance to lead and the relative strength of middlemen in the channel. On the

---

[53] For an extended discussion of the impact of advertising on the price of consumer products, see Paul W. Farris and Mark S. Albion, "The Impact of Advertising on the Price of Consumer Products," *Journal of Marketing*, Vol. 43 (Summer 1980), pp. 17–35.

[54] Mark S. Albion and Paul W. Farris, "The Effect of Manufacturer Advertising on Retail Pricing," Marketing Science Institute, Report No. 81-105 (Cambridge, Mass.: Marketing Science Institute, 1981).

other hand, *if* the manufacturer possesses a relatively unique product with strong end-user demand (or can provide unique services that enhance the use of his products) and *if* middlemen are relatively weak (e.g., if they have limited options and limited resources), then the manufacturer could likely assume the channel management role quite easily.

Methods of Manufacturer Dominance

Of the many methods that the manufacturer can use to dominate the channel, perhaps the most common is, as just indicated, the development of strong end-user attraction or loyalty to his products. This factor is particularly important in the case of products sold through convenience retail outlets, where little or no sales assistance is provided and where outlets are many and conveniently located. Porter has explained how manufacturers amass power in this situation:

> For products sold through convenience outlets, low unit price and frequent purchase of the product reduce the desire of the consumer to expend effort on search. The consumer demands a nearby retail outlet, is unwilling to shop around, and needs no sales help, thus the consumer considers the purchase relatively unimportant. Since the purchase is not perceived to be important, the consumer is willing to rely on less objective criteria (attributes) accordingly. . . .
>
> In view of these characteristics, the manufacturer's prime strategy for differentiating his product is to develop a strong brand image through advertising. If the manufacturer can develop a brand image, the retailer has very little power because (1) the retailer is little able to influence the buying decision of the consumer in the store; (2) a strong manufacturer's brand image creates consumer demand for the product, which assures profits to the retailer from stocking the product and at the same time denies him the credible bargaining counter of refusing to deal in the manufacturer's goods.[55]

A manufacturer may also use coercive methods or policies, such as refusing to deal with particular middlemen or limiting sales to them unless they conform to his desires. He can also employ resale restrictions, exclusive dealing, and tying contracts. When legal, these latter methods work only when middlemen strongly desire to carry a manufacturer's product line, and therefore they must generally be coupled with significant brand identification, the availability of few comparable product sources, and the opportunity for sizable rewards. Other methods of manufacturer dominance are forward vertical integration and contractual agreements.

If a manufacturer can amass sufficient expert, referent, and/or legitimate power, he may be able to assume channel leadership. In such cases, he must have made a long-term commitment to gathering and disseminating crucial market information (i.e., to absorb uncertainty for other channel members) as well as to ensuring continual innovation in products and managerial practices so that other channel members will seek to identify with him and come to believe that he has a right to direct their activities. It should be obvious, though, that such efforts, with the exception of new-product development, are not necessarily

---

[55] Michael E. Porter, "Consumer Behavior, Retailer Power and Market Performance in Consumer Goods Industries," *Review of Economics and Statistics,* Vol. 56 (November 1974), p. 423.

unique to manufacturers. If channel members at other levels choose to undertake them, the mantle of leadership (or the rights of dominance) may fall to them. Thus, it should not be surprising that, in at least some industries, channel management is practiced by wholesalers and retailers and not by manufacturers, because the former have done a more effective job of accumulating a significant amount of power within their channels than have the manufacturers supplying them.

CHANNEL MANAGEMENT BY WHOLESALERS

The wholesaler's management role in the modern marketing channel is greatly reduced from what it once was. During the early stages of economic development in the United States (prior to the mid 1800s), the merchant wholesaler was in a natural position to assume leadership because he was generally flanked by small manufacturers and small retailers who had little interest in delineating the various actors in their channels, let alone engaging in interorganization management. However, by the late 1800s the country was caught up in rapid industrial growth, and large manufacturers and retailers were beginning to develop. Increased pressure was placed on wholesalers. Manufacturers often felt that, given their increased production capacities, they could more effectively market their own goods without using wholesalers. And retailers, as their size increased, were more capable of buying direct from manufacturers, obtaining discounts and allowances that normally went to wholesalers.

From a historical and comparative perspective, the wholesaler has been able to remain in a dominant channel position only in those industries where the buyers and producers are small in size, large in number, and relatively scattered geographically, and where manufacturers are financially weak and lack marketing expertise.[56] Except in a limited number of fields, these conditions no longer exist in the United States. That wholesalers are still a significant factor in distribution, as was shown in detail in Chapter 3, attests to their success in readjusting to their changing environment, at least to some degree.

Despite this rather gloomy description of the wholesaler's opportunity for channel leadership, there are certain circumstances in which wholesalers do, in fact, engage in strong and effective interorganization management. For example, liquor wholesalers in Oklahoma have capitalized on state laws to develop a powerful position in a channel of distribution normally dominated by the franchised distributors of the distillers. Oklahoma laws require distillers to sell to independent wholesalers at the lowest prices in the country and permit wholesalers to sell to out-of-state buyers. A group of wholesalers, known as the Oklahoma Connection, buys national-brand liquors from the distillers and then ships them out of Oklahoma to out-of-state independent wholesalers who, in turn, undersell distributors franchised by the distillers.[57] In addition to these special circumstances, there are other opportunities for wholesaler dominance of marketing channels.

[56] Edwin H. Lewis, "Channel Management by Wholesalers," in Robert L. King (ed.), *Marketing and the New Science of Planning* (Chicago: American Marketing Association, 1968), p. 138.

[57] " 'Oklahoma Connection' Cut-Rate Spirits from Bible Belt Delight California's Drinkers, Irk Liquor Giants," *Wall Street Journal,* September 11, 1981, p. 54.

Methods of Wholesaler Dominance

One form of channel organization that has been particularly successful in strengthening the position of wholesalers has been the voluntary chain, especially in the marketing of grocery products. As noted in Chapter 7, wholesalers are clearly the leaders of these contractual vertical marketing systems. Retailers obtain the benefits of centralized buying, private brands, the identity of the group, large-scale promotion, and other management aids, while the wholesalers allocate the resources of their voluntary systems in such a way as to enhance their overall performance as competitive systems.[58]

Besides voluntary groups, wholesalers have also been active in franchising. The wholesaler-franchisor clearly dominates his channel by exercising strict control over and surveillance of operations at the retail level. Also, because a wholesaler-franchisor is rarely tied to brand names, his purchasing power combined with the maintenance of alternative sources of supply enable him to influence the marketing activities of his suppliers and thus to specify roles throughout the entire franchise system.

Another method used by wholesalers to achieve dominance has been the development of private brands.[59] The promotion of private brands by wholesalers appears to be successful mainly in fields where the products are relatively undifferentiated and frequently purchased and where demand for them has already been established. However, the fact that the products are relatively undifferentiated forces the wholesaler to use price as the primary appeal in order to sell his brand. In addition, unless the wholesaler can develop a private brand in each of his key lines, the control he may enjoy will be slight. The development of private brands also requires considerable capital and substantial promotion as well as products of relatively high quality. Therefore, the use of private brands to secure dominance is obviously far from easy. Perhaps the most successful wholesalers in this respect have been those who have established multi-unit operations, such as Foremost-McKesson in the drug field and W. W. Grainger in industrial distribution. Multi-unit wholesaling operations, like retailing chains, can secure buying leverage both for manufacturer's brands and for private labels. When the convenience and quick delivery attributes of multiple locations are combined with a strong private label program, it is likely that wholesalers can plan a leadership role in their channels.

It is important to note, however, that the majority of wholesalers do not actually attempt to gain significant control in their channels but instead seek merely to maintain the foothold they already have. Significant means of maintaining their present positions have included selective distribution, reduction of competing product lines, reduction of some services, the development of new and improved services, and improved operating procedures.[60]

The development of computerized interorganizational data systems (IDS) is seen by some as a means that wholesalers could use to recapture positions of dominance in specific channels. For example:

> in a channel characterized by a loose coalition of independent retailers and wholesalers, where no middleman is particularly dominant, one of the wholesalers may

[58] Lewis, *op. cit.*, p. 139.
[59] *Ibid.*, p. 140.
[60] *Ibid.*

take the lead in developing IDS, thereby "tying" a number of the retailers to him. As a consequence, it is likely that the market will sustain a "shakeout" with a few large wholesalers emerging and displacing the smaller ones. Those wholesalers who do not establish a clientele large enough to support an IDS will probably fail. In a channel situation similar to that posed above, the member(s) best able to establish strong dependency bonds and limit alternatives for those with whom they deal will dominate, and IDS is seen as a means to this end.

Positionally, wholesalers are probably best able to assume leadership in the development of IDS in such channels. It would not be feasible, from an economic perspective, to maintain a great number of parallel (communication) flows, since each data link represents a cost. In any channel with more than two retailers and more than two manufacturers, the number of links can be minimized by employing a wholesaler. With a large number of possible links, the savings can be substantial. The emergence of wholesalers as power loci is an example of technological determinism. Ipso facto their position in distribution channels bestows power on them in this regard.

Interorganizational data systems portend great promise for wholesalers in another area—computer services. A wholesaler is in an ideal position to help smaller retailers with inventory management, accounts receivable, payroll, and other applications beyond the capabilities of the latter's own equipment. . . . Moreover, with the wholesaler-retailer links established, the wholesaler can readily build on the wholesaler-manufacturer links. With a large exclusive domain of retailers, a wholesaler will be able to exert power over manufacturers. By controlling inventories, maintaining receivables, and helping to prepare the payroll, the wholesaler will further entrench himself in the retailer's operation.[61]

As indicated in Chapter 3, Foremost-McKesson, the largest U.S. ethical drugs wholesale distributor, has moved onto the center stage of its industry through a strategic combination of harnessing computer power and redefining the function of the wholesaler.[62] This strategy involves:

- Acting as middleman between drugstores and insurance offices by processing medical insurance claims
- Creating a massive "rack jobbing" service by providing crews to set up racks of goods inside retail stores, offering what amounts to a temporary labor force that brings both marketing know-how and Foremost merchandise along with it
- Designing, as well as supplying, drugstores
- Researching new uses for products it receives from manufacturers. Foremost found new customers, for example, for a Monsanto Company food preservative, from among its contacts in the cosmetics industry[63]

In summary, although it would seem that wholesalers are not qualified to lead channels in many of today's highly developed markets, their potential cannot be underestimated if they realize that their knowledge of the products they handle and of their suppliers' and customers' businesses can be parlayed into something more than a delivery service. The methods they use have enabled them to influence channels in only a few industries (e.g., hardware, drugs, groceries, motion pictures, liquor, auto accessories and parts, and industrial sup-

[61] Louis W. Stern and C. Samuel Craig, "Interorganizational Data Systems: The Computer and Distribution," *Journal of Retailing*, Vol. 47 (Summer 1971), pp. 83–85.
[62] "Foremost-McKesson: The Computer Moves Distribution to Center Stage," *Business Week* (December 7, 1981), pp. 115–22.
[63]*Ibid.,* p. 115.

plies). It seems that the strength of wholesalers lies in their role as builders of assortments, integrators of product lines, and reliable sources of merchandise for their customers. In order simply to hold their present positions, they must maintain their differential advantage in performing this role. Otherwise, they will become increasingly vulnerable.

CHANNEL MANAGEMENT BY RETAILERS

A significant number of retailers have grown to rival or even dwarf many large manufacturers. It is likely, therefore, that these retailers may want to exert some control over the channels in which they are members.

Large retailers are in reality multi-level merchandisers (MLMs).[64] That is, they have integrated the wholesaling functions within their channels, and, as was pointed out in Chapter 7, a number of them have integrated backward to the manufacturing level.[65] Like large manufacturers, MLMs have considerable coercive reward and expert power that they can employ in an effort to control channels.[66]

Large retailers have unique overlapping attributes that may give them an edge in the struggle (if there is one) for channel control. First, by virtue of their proximity to local markets, they have an opportunity to accumulate expert power by continually assessing the needs of consumers within their communities. While other members of the channel could perform the same information-generating and uncertainty-absorbing tasks, they would undoubtedly have to expend more effort in data collection, simply because of the retailers' locational advantage. Second, retail-directed MLMs have ready access to large markets that manufacturers wish to reach. In effect, they are gatekeepers. The larger the markets they serve, the more important they become to manufacturers, and thus the stronger their potential leadership becomes. Third, so long as MLMs can maintain alternative sources of supply, manufacturers will tend to be more dependent on them, especially where a generic demand for a given product class has been established. Dickinson has observed that under most conditions, the supplier has more to gain by selling to the retailer than the retailer has to gain by buying from the supplier.

> The manufacturers usually have (or think they will have) excess capacity. . . , and when they operate at full capacity it is only for a small part of the year. This is even truer of wholesalers. For manufacturers and wholesalers, then, no sale nearly always means no profit. Retailers, on the other hand, are sitting on a scarce resource whether they make a particular purchase or not. That resource is shelf space, the battle for which is so fierce that some suppliers even pay to have space reserved for them. Moreover, if a particular supplier does not sell to a particular retailer, the loss to the retailer is only relative, since there is always another supplier with other goods for a particular unit of space. In fact, it may be no loss at all, since in retailing most products can be replaced without great loss of profit by the retailer.[67]

[64] See Little, *op. cit.*, p. 33.

[65] Wholesalers can also be characterized as multi-level merchandisers when they sponsor voluntary groups.

[66] Little, *op. cit.*, p. 34.

[67] Roger A. Dickinson, *Retail Management: A Channels Approach* (Belmont, Calif.: Wadsworth Publishing Company, 1974), p. 37.

Interestingly, channel management is not always practiced by large retailers, even though they often have the power to do so. Instead, they frequently seem more concerned with obtaining specific types of concessions than they do in exerting a strong influence over new product development, promotional and inventory policies of the entire channel, and the like.[68] As a result of their self-selected task of serving wide markets, the managers of MLMs concentrate the majority of their efforts on selecting and maintaining stocks and providing and merchandising the services that accompany them.[69] Therefore, two very important functions that might be considered within the domain of channel leaders—product development and demand stimulation—are to a large extent left unattended by large retailers. Even though the latter are, by dint of their closeness to and contact with ultimate consumers, in the best position of any channel member to discover exactly what the preferences of consumers are, they are much too engrossed with the details of their own operations to consider performing these functions on a channelwide basis. Thus, by default, they frequently leave channel leadership to manufacturers. Notable exceptions exist, as in the packaged-food industry. For example, as pointed out in Chapter 2, some supermarket chains are assuming more responsibility for marketing functions in the channel and are pressuring suppliers to improve credit terms, distribution methods, and trade promotions.[70]

Methods of Retailer Dominance

The large retailers or MLMs have at their disposal a variety of means by which they could secure dominance in their channels. As with manufacturers, the most prominent means is the building of a consumer franchise through advertising, sales promotion, and branding.[71] The strong patronage motives for shopping at stores like Hudson's, Filene's, Bullock's, Sears, Target, I. Magnin, and Safeway have been established as the result of the assembling of an assortment of merchandise appropriate to each store's target market, the adequate promotion of that assortment, and the provision of ancillary services. In other words, the successful retail operations have achieved positions of power within their market through effective programming of the retailing mix elements, just as manufacturers have achieved success by combining the various elements of the marketing mix in unique ways.

In addition, many MLMs have generated private-label programs that reinforce or further the establishment of store patronage motives. Although some MLMs have probably overemphasized their private-label programs,[72] there can

[68] Roger A. Dickinson, "Channel Management by Large Retailers," in King (ed.), *op. cit.*, p. 128.

[69] Little, *op. cit.*, p. 35.

[70] "Food Chains Pressure Suppliers, Altering Industry Power Balance," *Wall Street Journal*, August 21, 1980, p. 25.

[71] Mallen, *op. cit.*, p. 131.

[72] A&P distributes no fewer than 1500 varieties of private label grocery, dairy, bakery, and fish products that account for 15 percent of the chain's total sales. Its overemphasis on private labels has been one of the factors responsible for its decline over the past 25 years. See "Can Jonathan Scott Save A&P?" *Business Week* (May 19, 1975), p. 133. Both Sears and Montgomery Ward are now carrying more manufacturers' brands in order to increase the potency of their assortments and provide consumers with on-the-spot price comparisons between these brands and their privately branded products.

be little doubt that such programs can be a means for securing channel control.[73] However, as with wholesalers' brands, retailers' brands are economically feasible only after widespread market acceptance of the product has been established.[74] On the other hand, if generic product acceptance exists, then the MLM not only can decide to enter the market with its own brand, but can decide which of the leading brands it will stock and thus be able to play off one supplier against another in order to achieve various concessions.[75]

Generics provide the best evidence of the supermarkets' new marketing power. Historically, private-label products copied national brands but sold for 15 percent less. With generics, stores created new products that are acceptable in quality but priced 30 percent lower than national brands.

> The real rub is that many leading branded manufacturers now feel compelled to produce lower-margin generics, too, because either the market has grown too big to ignore or the inroads of generics have left them with idle capacity. As a result, Borden, the No. 2 maker of coffee creamers (Cremora); Scott Paper, which markets the No. 2 paper towel (Viva); and Union Carbide, which owns the leading household-bag brand (Glad), are all making lower-margin generics that compete against their own brands.[76]

In the absence of the development by manufacturers of a strong consumer franchise for their brands, power is clearly weighted in favor of large-scale retailers in many of the channels where they are strong participants. As pointed out, however, these retailers are not always willing to assume leadership roles, and therefore the task of marshaling the resources of the various channel systems falls to other parties. Given the prerequisites of interorganization management specified earlier in this book, channelwide organization may be very difficult under these circumstances, because the units with the most power are often simply not willing to take an active part in specifying roles and managing conflict. It is likely, though, because of the power they hold, that they retain veto power over attempts to reallocate resources throughout the channel.

Small Retailers as Channel Leaders

Even though individual small retailers generally lack sufficient power to assume leadership roles within their channels, dominance may accrue to them, as well as to larger retailers, because of the nature of the buying process itself. For example, the retailer becomes very powerful when a manufacturer selling through convenience outlets is unable to develop a brand image through advertising. In such situations, the manufacturer's ability to achieve product differentiation in the eyes of the consumer is severely limited. The manufacturer becomes highly dependent on retailers, because many outlets must stock the

[73] See Louis W. Stern, "The New World of Private Brands," *California Management Review*, Vol. 8 (Spring 1966), pp. 43–50; Victor J. Cook and Thomas F. Schutte, *Brand Policy Determination* (Boston: Allyn and Bacon, 1967); Ray A. Goldberg, *Agribusiness Coordination* (Boston: Division of Research, Graduate School of Business Administration, Harvard University, 1968), pp. 181–84; and Victor J. Cook, "Private Brand Mismanagement by Misconception," *Business Horizons*, Vol. 11 (December 1968), pp. 63–74.

[74] Little, *op. cit.*, p. 35.

[75] *Ibid.*, p. 36.

[76] "No Frills Food: New Power for the Supermarket," *Business Week* (March 23, 1981), pp. 73, 76.

product in order for him to achieve an efficient density of market coverage.[77] Furthermore, where retail outlets provide significant sales assistance and the outlets are selectively rather than densely located, it is also possible to hypothesize that retailers, irrespective of size, will dominate. As Porter points out,

> for products sold through nonconvenience outlets, the consumer considers the purchase relatively important and is willing to expend effort in shopping and comparing products. For products sold through nonconvenience outlets, the retailer is influential in the consumer's purchase decision. Although advertising can lead the consumer to consider a particular brand, it will not prevent him from considering other brands and shopping several outlets. The retailer can negate the effect of advertising by changing the consumer's mind in the store.[78]

Thus, in the case of shopping goods, the retailer exerts considerable influence on the purchase decision of the consumer in several ways. First, the retailer controls or is a proxy for some of the attributes the consumer may desire. The reputation, image, physical amenities, and attendant services (e.g., credit, billing, delivery, warranty, repair) of a retail store can sway consumer purchase decisions. Second, the retailer can influence the sale of products sold through nonconvenience outlets through the provision of information via a selling presentation, advice solicited by the consumer, the perceived expertise of the salesperson with respect to the product, or any combination of these.[79] In fact, as the retailer's influence on product differentiation increases, the bargaining power of the retail stage vis-à-vis the manufacturer or the wholesale supplier increases.

Collectively, small retailers have been known to exert considerable pressure on channel activities. They have been instrumental in gaining particularistic legislation on the local, state, and national levels that has had the effect of restraining competition or impeding change.[80] They have colluded primarily through their trade associations to prevent marketing activities that they have perceived to be threatening to their survival. Through these legislative and collusive actions, they have sometimes been able to influence marketing strategy throughout the channel. Thus, there exist state and local restrictions on entry, licensing requirements, antipeddler and anti–itinerant vendor ordinances, chain store taxes, evening and Sunday closing laws, advertising restrictions (particularly price-posting regulations), and a host of other small retailer–inspired and –promoted laws designed to soften or curb competitive impacts.[81] Clearly, this form of negative leadership is not laudatory. It is fortunate that the effect of these impediments has been short-lived in many situations, and that they have been unable to effectively restrain many innovations in distribution.

On the other hand, small retailers have attempted to exert positive channel leadership by developing retailer-sponsored cooperatives. The retailer cooperative is an obvious effort to overcome the size and thus the buying disadvantages faced by individual small retailers. However, as indicated in Chapter 7, retailer-sponsored cooperatives face some very serious problems. Power is diffused

[77] Porter, *op. cit.*, p. 423.

[78] *Ibid.*, p. 424.

[79] *Ibid.*, pp. 420–21

[80] Stanley C. Hollander, *Restraints upon Retail Competition* (East Lansing: Bureau of Business and Economic Research, Michigan State University); and Stanley C. Hollander, "Channel Management by Small Retailers," in King (ed.), *op. cit.*, pp. 132–34.

[81] Hollander, "Channel Management by Small Retailers," p. 133.

within them, and therefore there is considerable doubt that they can provide the tightly knit control needed to compete successfully with corporate and voluntary chains. As Hollander points out,

> membership turnover can be high. Coordination is difficult. Investment in manufacturing or processing facilities may be hazardous and inadvisable, since acceptance of the output may not be assured. Financing problems may inhibit growth, since the members may have little interest in financing newcomers, and particularly in helping potential competitors. Risk allocation difficulties tend to deter experimentation. Personality conflicts can exacerbate many of the cooperative's problems. None of these difficulties is entirely absent from the corporate chain sector, but quite obviously, their impact is substantially reduced when ownership, risk, and control are centralized.[82]

CHANNEL MANAGEMENT
BY PHYSICAL DISTRIBUTION AGENCIES

Although not normally considered as potential managers of channel relations, common carriers could possibly assume such roles if they were to utilize more effectively the power bases at their disposal. In fact, logistical institutions of all types occupy unique positions in this respect, because they have the advantage of being *neutral* relative to many of the channel policies and activities of major concern to manufacturers, wholesalers, and retailers.[83] While the latter channel members may have difficulty in looking beyond their immediate suppliers and customers, logistical institutions can take a broader perspective of channel problems.

Consideration of common carriers as channel leaders serves to focus attention on a salient characteristic of all channel relations. That is, leadership is possible with regard to each of the marketing flows taken separately or to all of the flows. Thus, it is clear that common carriers can assume an interorganizational management stance relative to the flow of physical possession, but their influence on the remaining flows is likely to be minimal. In other words, the scope of a common carrier's power is limited to those activities with which it is directly concerned.

Figure 9–3 illustrates the position occupied by common carriers within a generalized channel arrangement and some of the power bases available to them.[84] Specific examples of the reward and expert power bases sometimes used by common carriers have been enumerated by Beier.[85] These include:

- Reducing the rates charged to shippers. (However, because of competitive reaction, such reductions are likely to have limited impact over the long run.)[86]

[82] *Ibid.*, p. 135.

[83] J. L. Heskett, "Costing and Coordinating External and Internal Logistics Activities," in Donald J. Bowersox, Bernard J. LaLonde, and Edward W. Smykay (eds.), *Readings in Physical Distribution Management* (New York: Macmillan Company, 1969), pp. 81–83.

[84] For an extended example, see J. L. Heskett, "Interorganizational Problem Solving in a Channel of Distribution," in Matthew Tuite, Roger Chisholm, and Michael Radnor (eds.), *Interorganizational Decision Making* (Chicago: Aldine Publishing Co., 1972), pp. 152–61.

[85] Frederick J. Beier, "The Role of the Common Carrier in the Channel of Distribution," *Transportation Journal*, Vol. 9 (Winter 1969), pp. 12–21.

[86] The Motor Carrier Act of 1980 allows carriers to set rates for individual customers based on

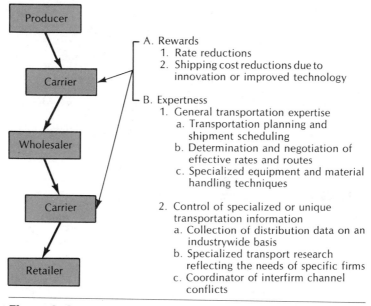

Figure 9–3   Range of common carrier contributions to other channel members

Source: Frederick J. Beier, "The Role of the Common Carrier in the Channel of Distribution," *Transportation Journal,* Vol. 9 (Winter 1969), p. 19.

- Reducing the overall cost of transportation through elimination of loss and damage claims, special schedules, and/or minimum weight requirements

- Providing special arrangements such as rent-a-train services whereby carriers rent specialized equipment designed to serve particular clients. The provision of specialized equipment increases the dependence of shippers on carriers.

- Providing consulting services to shippers, whereby staff specialists assigned to a particular industry advise shippers in that industry about rates, routing, and LTL and LCL loading-in-transit privileges. Traditionally, carriers have acted as advisers about plant locations in their operating areas.

- Making available part of a carrier's large computing facilities in order to institute a channelwide system of information about shipments. (Carriers are in a position to draw sample data on product movements from a broader population than is generally available to individual shippers. Thus, they could operate as uncertainty absorbers within the channel.)

- Providing information about the transportation and material-handling requirements of other channel members. (Carriers can thereby suggest compatible handling systems that would lead to more efficient coordination of the physical and information interfaces between channel members.)

---

actual cost. For an assessment of the impact of the act, see "Shippers Are in the Driver's Seat," *Business Week* (October 18, 1982), pp. 182–86; and "Freight Transportation Is Being Transformed in an Era of Deregulation," *Wall Street Journal,* October 20, 1983, pp. 1, 18.

Similarly, it has been suggested that the distribution center may plan an important role in channel management if it deploys its expertise and informational resource bases.

> The distribution center manager . . . is familiar with marketing-related objectives and patterns of distribution not only of his customers, but also of his customers' customers and of the carriers and other institutions in the distribution chain. He knows their needs, wants, aspirations, and operations. As he fulfills these services, the user becomes more dependent upon him and he becomes more powerful.[87]

WHO SHOULD LEAD THE CHANNEL?

At this juncture it should be noted that channel control is a dynamic process. The following anecdote illustrates power dynamics in the grocery industry:

> Manufacturers once held the upper hand because of the tremendous advertising and promotion budgets they deployed to "pull" consumers into stores. Supermarkets deferred to suppliers' merchandising suggestions and relied on their data to determine what products to stock. "There was a job that needed to be done and manufacturers stepped into the breach," says Willard Bishop, a grocery consultant.
>
> But retailers aren't willing to continue as silent conduits between manufacturers and consumers. "Just spending an enormous amount of money on TV doesn't cut the ice anymore," says David Nichol, president of Loblaw's Canadian supermarkets. Adds Lenn Daykin, director of merchandising for the Foote, Cone & Belding advertising agency, "In a battle between giants like Procter & Gamble and Safeway, five years ago, P&G would have prevailed. Now Safeway can call the tune."
>
> Even small retailers are more assertive. Genuardi's, a Pennsylvania chain of 14 stores, recently warned its suppliers that their products would be dropped if they didn't bear clear universal product code symbols.
>
> Retailers are also resisting the glut of products competing for scarce shelf space. Sloan's supermarkets in New York says it has a choice of 22 laundry soaps, each in six sizes ranging from seven ounces to 211 ounces. Of that field of 132, Sloan's carries 51. When recently offered four sizes of Pert, a new Procter & Gamble shampoo, the chain took two.[88]

Therefore, there are no guarantees that those who control the marketing channel today will continue in command tomorrow. There is no substitute for analyzing the dynamics of power and its structure in an industry to reach plausible conclusions as to who controls the marketing channel.

[87] James A. Constantin, Jack J. Kasulis, and Robert F. Lusch, "The Distribution Center: A Potential Locus of Power," in Robert J. House and James F. Robeson (eds.), *Interfaces: Logistics, Marketing and Production*, proceedings of the Sixth Annual Transportation and Logistics Educators Conference (Columbus, Ohio: Transportation and Logistics Research Fund, Ohio State University, and NCDPM, 1976), p. 42.

[88] "Food Chains Pressure Suppliers, Altering Industry Power Balance," *Wall Street Journal*, August 21, 1980, p. 25. Reprinted by permission of The Wall Street Journal, © Dow Jones & Company, Inc. 1980. All rights reserved.

Although the question of which institution or agency should lead the channel has been debated in the literature for many years by a variety of scholars,[89] there is no single satisfactory answer. The fact is that the answer demands empirical evidence from *specific* settings. The case study of the furniture industry presented in Exhibit 9–1 is an example of the need to look closely at the issues involved in each industrial setting and to define the scope of power of each commercial channel member in each of the marketing flows. It may even be necessary to break the flows down into parts in order to perform an adequate analysis. For example, the flow of physical possession incorporates both transportation and storage of merchandise. One channel member may be able to exert more influence on the first component, while another may have more power over the second. Clearly, the analysis—based on empirical findings— must account for the tolerance levels in the channel for control by each of the members as well as for the payoffs that accrue to each as a result of control.[90]

Anecdotal evidence can be accumulated that leads an individual to suspect that one particular institution is the most logical leader in a particular situation, but such evidence rarely permits the generation of counterintuitive findings. In such an important area as this—where the concern is allocation of resources throughout an entire distributive system—opinions and hearsay are not satisfactory grounds for making the appropriate selection. Furthermore, allowance must be made for the influence of a commercial channel's task environment (e.g., consumers and government) on the leadership question. It should be clear from this chapter, however, that each commercial channel member has at least the potential for leadership in one or more of the marketing flows, because each has amassed or is capable of amassing power of one form or another over other channel members. The ultimate answer as to who should lead must, however, be left to an empirical, case-by-case analysis of power and the relevant payoffs from its use.

SUMMARY AND CONCLUSIONS

This chapter has focused on factors influencing leadership and control in marketing channels and the potential of manufacturers, wholesalers, retailers, and physical distribution agencies to assume the role of channel managers or leaders. In coming to grips with this issue, one must consider the amount and kinds of power available to each institution.

[89] For a variety of different arguments and perspectives, see David Craig and Werner Gabler, "The Competitive Struggle for Market Control," *Annals of the American Academy of Political and Social Science* (May 1940), pp. 84ff. (reprinted in Howard J. Westing [ed.], *Readings in Marketing* [Englewood Cliffs, N.J.: Prentice-Hall, 1953], pp. 84–107); John K. Galbraith, *American Capitalism*, rev. ed. (Boston: Houghton Mifflin Co., 1956), pp. 110–14, 117–23; Mallen, *op. cit.*, pp. 127–34; Little, *op. cit.*, pp. 31–38; Richard B. Heflebower, "Mass Distribution: A Phase of Bilateral Oligopoly or of Competition?" *American Economic Review*, Vol. 47 (May 1957), pp. 274–85; Valentine F. Ridgway, "Administration of Manufacturer-Dealer Systems," *Administrative Science Quarterly*, Vol. 1 (March 1957), pp. 464–83; and Louis P. Bucklin, "A Theory of Channel Control," *Journal of Marketing*, Vol. 37 (January 1973), pp. 39–47. These authors present various anecdotal evidence and/or analytical models for arriving at particular choices.

[90] Adel I. El-Ansary and Robert A. Robincheaux, "A Theory of Channel Control: Revisited," *Journal of Marketing*, Vol. 38 (January 1974), pp. 4–7.

EXHIBIT 9–1   Who should lead the channel?
A case study in the office furniture industry

From points of manufacturing to point of consumption, the dominant channel in terms of dollar volume is the manufacturer-dealer channel, which accounts for 73 percent of the $4 billion in sales. The second most important channel is direct sales from the manufacturers to the end-users accounting for 23 percent of total sales. The remaining 4 percent of sales is accounted for by resellers, wholesalers, mass merchandisers, and other nontraditional distribution channels. A recent decline in the dealer channel share of the market and changes in patterns of distribution are the cause of friction between manufacturers and dealers. This trend is a result of an increase in large buyers dealing directly with manufacturers as well as the emergence of new types of distributive alternatives including catalog sellers, limited-function dealers, and architects/designers. As more manufacturers deal directly with end-users and nontraditional distribution channels grow, the risk of higher levels of intrachannel conflict increases. Competition between the dealer and the manufacturer over sales to the same segments is certain to cause unavoidable conflict.

A Delphi survey of manufacturers and dealers was conducted in order to assess the level of conflict within the industry and recommend channel management strategies. Results of the Delphi survey indicate minimal to moderate levels of conflict in the channel with a minority of those surveyed feeling that channel conflict was substantial. The survey also uncovered the major sources of conflict. These conflict sources include: (1) direct selling activities by manufacturers, (2) manufacturer enfranchisement of nondealer resellers, (3) the nature of the functional and compensatory split between dealers and manufacturers in negotiated contract sales, i.e., manufacturers do not adequately compensate dealers for the portion of the marketing job they do.

The cause and effect reasons for the change in the patterns of distribution can be assessed from the manufacturers' and dealers' points of view. The motivating force behind manufacturers' increased use of direct sale and nondealer franchisement is to gain access to the market. One response by the dealers to this move has been to reduce the number of lines they are willing to carry. Dealers are also reacting to a squeeze on margins by shifting functions such as financing back to the manufacturers. The effect of the dealer's actions on the manufacturer has been to erode the value of the dealer to the point where the manufacturer would prefer to do the job alone. When dealers become involved in negotiating manufacturer–end-user sales, the potential for conflict has arisen not from the dealer's need to share the sale with the manufacturers but because dealers feel they are inadequately compensated. The dealers' response has been to suggest that the extent and quality of their functional performance rather than their positions in the channel should be the basis for compensation.

Where the manufacturer is the channel captain because his economic power is much greater than that of the individual dealer, the responsibility for policy reevaluation and possible change is mainly his. When wholesalers or dealers dominate a channel, the responsibility for appraisal and adaptation is more widely shared. Policy areas especially amenable to change by the manufacturer or other channel captains include those associated with product, distribution, inventory, service, promotion, pricing, and communication.

PRODUCT POLICIES

The product policies of manufacturers should be guided by the needs of the marketplace. But, how can product line policy be used to reduce channel conflict?

One such policy worthy of consideration as a means of reducing or heading off channel conflict is the development of differentiated lines, each of which are carried by a single channel of distribution. For example, one line could be carried by dealers and another by architects/designers.

DISTRIBUTION POLICIES

Manufacturer's decisions regarding distribution policies affect the levels of inter- and intra-channel competition and the willingness and ability of resellers to support the manufacturer's line.

Dealer Involvement.   One constructive policy might be for a manufacturer to sell directly to large users only with dealer involvement in the sale. This policy would reduce interchannel friction of the most damaging type.

Market Delineation.   Another policy deserving consideration is splitting the market between manufacturers and dealers by the use of criteria such as type of customer served or size of sale. For example, manufacturers could adopt a policy to reserve for direct sale sales to government or to national accounts that place orders in excess of a present dollar figure. In return, manufacturers would agree to turn over to dealers all contracts for non-government sales below the cutoff figures with the dealer deciding whether or not manufacturer involvement is desirable.

A related gain from such a policy would be the early involvement of the dealer in a manufacturer-dealer negotiated sale with the increased probability that dealers will be satisfied with the functional and margin split.

The recommendation to restructure channels of dual distribution so that one channel is direct and the other is the dealer channel is equally valid for wholesalers. Here the criterion of a volume cutoff is especially useful. Customers who buy in quantities below the cutoff level, for example, would be referred to dealers. On the other hand, those who buy in quantities above the cutoff point would have the option of specifying whether they wanted to do business directly with the wholesaler or through a dealer.

Another option might be to allow customers who have grown large after years of dealer support and cultivation to buy at wholesale prices through the dealer but to have the goods drop-shipped from the wholesaler. Dealer margins on this business need only reflect the costs of selling and buying plus a modest profit. Such an arrangement will reward the dealer for past activities in building customers and will raise his morale.

The problem of conflict between dealers and nontraditional resellers such as limited-function dealers, architects/designers, and independent specifiers is extremely difficult to resolve. Given that buyers are increasingly using these sources, the manufacturer is faced with the choice of not covering a growing segment of the market or of protecting relationships with the existing dealer organizations. Each manufacturer should evaluate the trade-offs involved on the basis of the nature of the specific environment in which he operates.

Dealer Response.   The most effective course of action for a dealer faced with competition from nontraditional channels is to redouble his efforts to become a more effective partner in the selling process. The dealer must exploit his differential advantage over competition by stressing knowledge of local conditions, ability to provide a well-trained sales force, possession of design resources, breadth of line, inventory holding and staging facilities, installation capabilities and so forth. The dealers that can perform a wide array of functions well will have less to fear from interchannel competition than do those who are ineffective performers or who have reduced their service capabilities.

Intrachannel Competition. With respect to rivalry among dealers in a given market area, manufacturers must periodically reevaluate the number of dealers franchised. If market coverage is too limited, sales opportunities will be lost. In contrast, if too many dealers are franchised in relation to market potential, price competition will be so intense that the value of the line to each individual dealer will be diminished. Given the nature of the buying process in which a great deal of input is required of the dealer, the manufacturer is wise to err on the side of restricted distribution to minimize intrachannel rivalry and to gain maximum dealer support for his line.

INVENTORY, SERVICE POLICIES

Closely associated with distributive policies are those manufacturer policies that determine the amount of inventory to be held in the channels and the service levels provided resellers and thus end-users. Holding inventories of office furniture is very expensive because of the space required.

Any policy alteration that can reduce this burden will increase the profitability of the line to resellers and thus should gain added cooperation from them. Quick ship programs, shipments in knock-down form, and the like are examples of worthy efforts. Any changes which can reduce the time required between receipt of order and delivery at the customer's place of business must also be considered in terms of total costs of holding inventory at all levels in the channel. If it appears that reductions in delivery times are not feasible, then attempts must be made to reduce variability in delivery times.

Uncertainty about when shipments will arrive from the factory is more damaging to manufacturer-dealer relationships than is the length of the delivery time. Whether the answer lies in better sales forecasting, production scheduling, or in using more reliable modes of transport, the evidence points clearly to the conclusion that reliable delivery dates will reduce frictions in the channel.

Promotion and Communication Policies. Although interview data indicate that all channel members do engage in sales training, the general consensus is that more and better training must be continuous. Although manufacturers and wholesalers appear to be bearing most of the cost of current training activities, dealer contributions in terms of employee time and associated travel expenses are considerable.

PRICING POLICIES

Manufacturer pricing policies have a large impact on channel conflict. The margins paid resellers, for example, not only pay for their functional performance but also reflect the competitive pressures which they face. In other words, when a dealer complains to a manufacturer that the margin payment is too small, he may mean that it does not allow him to compete on a price basis.

Before the manufacturer (or wholesaler, if such is the case) can address the problem of margin adequacy, the following questions should be answered:

- Do manufacturer (or wholesaler) direct selling activities put pressures on the prices dealers can receive from their customers?
- Does manufacturer franchising policy put so many dealers in a territory that intrachannel competition is affecting price levels?
- Does a manufacturer division of task and margin payment in negotiated sales allow the dealer to recover costs and make a profit?

- Does manufacturer delivery service level or inventory policy require dealers to incur heavy holding costs?
- Does manufacturer variability in delivery times place unreasonable cost burdens on dealers or their customers?
- Does manufacturer pricing policy reflect reseller position in the channel rather than the extent and quality of functional performance?

It can be seen from the above questions that many manufacturer (or wholesaler) policies can influence the "effective" margin received by dealers. Perhaps alteration in these policies, either to reduce competitive pressures or cost burdens or both, may be a cheaper and more effective way of resolving the dealers' complaint of margin inadequacy than would be a direct increase in the margin payment.

With reference to those frictions that arise from price competition between dealer and nondealer channels, it might be useful to set prices based upon extent of functional performance rather than upon position in the trade channel. For example, the trade discount could be subdivided into payments for each element of functional performance such as selling activity, design activity, inventory holding and installation. If such an approach were costed out it would meet the test of legality and be a more equitable way of reflecting the fact that different resellers perform different functional mixes.

Regardless of the nature of manufacturer policies, many dealers believe that they are not well communicated either in writing or by manufacturer sales personnel or reps. Lack of knowledge of policy can be a source of friction in channel relationships. Improvements in policy development, clarification and communication should go a long way toward reducing misunderstandings and resultant channel frictions.

Source: Reprinted with permission from the March 1985 issue of *Business Marketing;* Copyright Crain Communications Inc.

The potential channel management role of manufacturers appears to hinge on the strength of their products, brands, and services as viewed by ultimate consumers, both at the household and industrial levels. In other words, manufacturers' power relative to other channel members is derived primarily from the marketplace. The traditional concept of the manufacturer-directed channel is based on the belief that because the manufacturer creates and produces the product and designs the network through which it passes to consumers, he is entitled to impose his marketing policies on other channel members and to direct the activities of the channel.

From a historical perspective, wholesalers have been able to remain in dominant positions only in those industries where the buyers and producers are small in size, large in number, and relatively scattered geographically, and where manufacturers are financially weak and lack marketing expertise. Wholesalers have, however, been particularly successful in strengthening their positions by organizing voluntary groups and franchising systems as well as by developing private-label programs and interorganizational data systems.

The potential of large (multi-level) retailers as channel leaders appears to stem from their close proximity to consumers, their roles as gatekeepers to market access, and their maintenance of alternative sources of supply. Their continuous control over display space within their outlets, their development of strong patronage motives, and their use of private-label programs have enhanced their power considerably.

Small retailers have, collectively, been able to assume leadership in the channel—but primarily from a negative perspective. Through collusion, they have been able to secure particularistic legislation that has restrained competition and impeded change. The most positive step they have taken has been to form cooperatives.

Common carriers and distribution centers might be able to assume a greater role in channel leadership if they were to utilize more effectively the reward, expert, and informational power at their disposal. Their influence would, however, generally be limited to the flow of physical possession, even if they were to become more aggressive within the channels in which they participate.

The question of who should lead the channel cannot be answered without an in-depth empirical analysis of channels on a case-by-case basis. Because each institution has at least some power over the various marketing flows, leadership may take the form of control over or management of only one or a few of the flows, depending, of course, on the scope of power enjoyed by the various institutions in a given system.

If channel management is to be instituted, it will be necessary for appropriate information and communication systems to be established. Such systems are particularly crucial if a variety of institutions take a role in channel leadership. The dovetailing of decision making must form an essential part of overall channel management. Otherwise, suboptimization of the marketing flows can be expected. The marketing flows, taken as a whole, constitute a system; they must be combined in such a way as to permit the channel to have a strong impact on its environment. This combination can be achieved only through the sharing of relevant data among channel members. Therefore, the next chapter is concerned with the development of effective communication within channels.

DISCUSSION QUESTIONS

1. How do you account for the persistence of distribution channels lacking a channel leader, captain, or manager? Does a channel have to have a leader to survive over the long term?

2. What are the consequences of increased "scrambled merchandising" for power and leadership in the channel? How will such product line diversification on the retail level affect the potential for channel leadership of manufacturers, wholesalers, and retailers?

3. If a major department store chain is the most powerful member of the channel in which it participates, what might the chain do to gain increased coordination and cooperation throughout each of the channels serving it?

4. It has been stated, "The more a retailer can concentrate his purchasing, the more dominating he can become; the more he spreads his purchasing, the more dominated he becomes." Do you agree? Explain.

5. Do private brands come into being as a result of a conflict between manufacturers and middlemen? Describe the issues and factors surrounding a decision to market private brands from the perspective of both manufacturers and middlemen.

6. It has been argued that where the number of retail buyers for a manufacturing industry's product is small and the size of these retailers is large, retailer power

flows conventionally from buyer concentration. Explain this statement from the perspective of power, dependence, and sources of power.

7. An important structural characteristic of retailing is the presence or absence of multiple forms of retailers selling a given industry's product (e.g., drugstores and supermarkets). Explain the consequences of this structural characteristic for channel management.

8. It has been stated that "as the retail outlet (establishment) becomes more specialized and carries fewer product categories, its power to influence the sale will generally increase." Give examples that support this statement. Then give examples that would support the reverse of this statement.

9. In general, which type of institution—manufacturer, wholesaler, or retailer—should lead the channel of distribution for the following products?
   a. Toys
   b. Automobiles
   c. Stainless steel
   d. Health and beauty aids

   What assumptions did you have to make in order to arrive at an answer for each product? What were the relevant variables you considered in each case?

10. In view of the current emphasis in our society on consumerism issues, do you think that the consumer will eventually be the channel leader in many consumer goods industries? If so, which industries? How will the leadership be manifested?

Appendix 9A

Selected Literature on Channel Management

ANGELMAR, REINHARD and LOUIS W. STERN (1978), "Development of a Content Analytic System for Analysis of Bargaining Communication in Marketing," *Journal of Marketing Research*, 15 (February), 93–102.

ASSAEL, HENRY (1968), "The Political Role of Trade Associations in Distributive Conflict Resolution," *Journal of Marketing*, 32 (April), 21–28.

———(1969), "Constructive Role of Interorganizational Conflict," *Administrative Science Quarterly*, 14 (December), 573–582.

BACHARACH, SAMUEL B. and EDWARD J. LAWLER (1976), "The Perception of Power," *Social Forces*, 55 (September), 123–134.

BACHRACH, PETER and MORTON S. BARATZ (1969), "Decisions and Non-Decisions: An Analytical Framework," in *Political Power: A Reader in Theory and Research*, Roderick Bell, David V. Edwards, and R. Harrison Wagner, eds., New York: Free Press.

BAGOZZI, RICHARD P. (1980), *Causal Models in Marketing*, New York: Wiley.

BALDWIN, DAVID A. (1971), "The Power of Positive Sanctions," *World Politics*, 24 (October), 19–38.

This reference list appeared in a review article by John F. Gaski, "The Theory of Power and Conflict in Channels of Distribution," *Journal of Marketing*, Vol. 47 (Summer 1984), pp. 27–29.

BEIER, FREDERICK J. and LOUIS W. STERN (1969), "Power in the Channel of Distribution," in *Distribution Channels: Behavorial Dimensions,* Louis W. Stern, ed., Boston: Houghton Mifflin, 92–116.

BETTMAN, J. R., H. H. KASSARJIAN, and R. J. LUTZ (1978), "Consumer Behavior," in *Review of Marketing 1978,* G. Zaltman and T. Bonoma, eds., Chicago: American Marketing, 194–195.

BROWN, JAMES R. (1977), "Toward Improved Measures of Distribution Channel Conflict," in *Contemporary Marketing Thought,* Barnett A. Greenberg and Danny N. Bellenger, eds., Chicago: American Marketing, 385–389.

—— and GARY L. FRAZIER (1978), "The Application of Channel Power: Its Effects and Connotations," in *Research Frontiers in Marketing: Dialogues and Directions,* Subhash C. Jain, ed., Chicago: American Marketing, 266–270.

CADOTTE, ERNEST R. and LOUIS W. STERN (1979), "A Process Model of Interorganizational Relations in Marketing Channels," *Research in Marketing,* 2, 127–158.

CAMPBELL, DONALD T. (1955), "The Informant in Quantitative Research," *American Journal of Sociology,* 60 (January), 339–342.

CARTWRIGHT, DORWIN (1959), "A Field Theoretical Conception of Power," in *Studies in Social Power,* Dorwin Cartwright, ed., Ann Arbor: University of Michigan Press.

—— (1965), "Influence, Leadership, Control," in *Handbook of Organizations,* James G. March, ed., Chicago: Rand McNally, 1–47.

DAHL, ROBERT A. (1957), "The Concept of Power," *Behavorial Science,* 2 (July), 201–218.

—— (1963), *Modern Political Analysis,* Englewood Cliffs, NJ: Prentice-Hall.

DEUTSCH, M. (1969), "Conflicts: Productive and Destructive," *Journal of Social Issues,* 25 (January), 7–42.

DWYER, F. ROBERT (1980), "Channel-Member Satisfaction: Laboratory Insights," *Journal of Retailing,* 56 (Summer), 45–65.

EL-ANSARY, ADEL I. (1975), "Determinants of Power-Dependence in the Distribution Channel," *Journal of Retailing,* 51 (Summer), 59–74, 94.

—— and LOUIS W. STERN (1972), "Power Measurement in the Distribution Channel," *Journal of Marketing Research,* 9 (February), 47–52.

EMERSON, RICHARD M. (1962), "Power-Dependence Relations," *American Sociological Review,* 27 (February), 31–41.

ETGAR, MICHAEL (1976a), "Effects of Administrative Control on Efficiency of Vertical Marketing Systems," *Journal of Marketing Research,* 13 (February), 12–24.

—— (1976b), "Channel Domination and Countervailing Power in Distributive Channels," *Journal of Marketing Research,* 13 (August), 254–262.

—— (1977), "Channel Environment and Channel Leadership," *Journal of Marketing Research,* 14 (February), 69–76.

—— (1978a), "Intrachannel Conflict and Use of Power," *Journal of Marketing Research,* 15 (May), 273–274.

—— (1978b), "Selection of an Effective Channel Control Mix," *Journal of Marketing,* 42 (July), 53–58.

—— (1979), "Sources and Types of Intrachannel Conflict," *Journal of Retailing,* 55 (Spring), 61–78.

FIRAT, FUAT A., ALICE M. TYBOUT, and LOUIS W. STERN (1975), "A Perspective on Conflict and Power in Distribution," in *1974 Combined Proceedings,* Ronald C. Curhan, ed., Chicago: American Marketing, 435–439.

FRAZIER, GARY L. (1980), "Vertical Power Relationships in Channels of Distribution: An Integrated and Extended Conceptual Framework," faculty working paper #686, College of Commerce and Business Administration, University of Illinois at Urbana-Champaign.

FRENCH, JOHN R. P. and BERTRAM RAVEN (1959), "The Bases of Social Power," in *Studies in Social Power,* Dorwin Cartwright, ed., Ann Arbor: University of Michigan Press.

GALBRAITH, JOHN K. (1956), *American Capitalism,* Boston: Houghton Mifflin.

GUILTINAN, JOSEPH P., ISMAIL B. REJAB, and WILLIAM C. RODGERS (1980), "Factors Influencing Coordination in a Franchise Channel," *Journal of Retailing,* 56 (Fall), 41–58.

HUNGER, J. DAVID and LOUIS W. STERN (1976), "An Assessment of the Functionality of the Superordinate Goal in Reducing Conflict," *Academy of Management Journal,* 19 (December), 591–605.

HUNT, SHELBY D. and JOHN R. NEVIN (1974), "Power in a Channel of Distribution: Sources and Consequences," *Journal of Marketing Research,* 11 (May), 186–193.

KELLY, J. STEVEN and J. IRWIN PETERS (1977), "Vertical Conflict: A Comparative Analysis of Franchisees and Distributors," in *Contemporary Marketing Thought,* Barnett A. Greenberg and Danny N. Bellenger, ed., Chicago: American Marketing, 380–384.

LUSCH, ROBERT F. (1976a), "Sources of Power: Their Impact on Intrachannel Conflict," *Journal of Marketing Research,* 13 (November), 382–390.

—— (1976b), "Channel Conflict: Its Impact on Retailer Operating Performance," *Journal of Retailing,* 52 (Summer), 3–12, 89–90.

—— (1977), "Franchisee Satisfaction: Causes and Consequences," *International Journal of Physical Distribution,* 7 (February), 128–140.

—— (1978), "Intrachannel Conflict and Use of Power: A Reply," *Journal of Marketing Research,* 15 (May), 275–276.

—— and JAMES R. BROWN (1982), "A Modified Model of Power in the Marketing Channel," *Journal of Marketing Research,* 19 (August), 312–323.

MACK, RAYMOND W. and RICHARD C. SNYDER (1957), "The Analysis of Social Conflict—Toward an Overview and Synthesis," *Journal of Conflict Resolution,* 1 (June), 212–248.

MALLEN, BRUCE (1963), "A Theory of Retailer-Supplier Conflict, Control, and Cooperation," *Journal of Retailing,* 39 (Summer), 24–32, 51.

Marketing News (1981), "*JMR* Seeks Causal Modeling Papers for '82 Special Issue," 15 (May 15), sect. 2, 18.

MICHIE, DONALD A. (1978), "Managerial Tactics: An Alternative Explanation of Warranty Satisfaction in a Channel of Distribution," in *Research Frontiers in Marketing*: *Dialogues and Directions,* Subhash C. Jain, ed., Chicago: American Marketing, 260–265.

MORGENTHAU, H. (1960), *Politics Among Nations,* New York: Knopf.

NAGEL, JACK H. (1975), *The Descriptive Analysis of Power,* New Haven: Yale University Press.

PEARSON, MICHAEL M. (1973), "The Conflict–Performance Assumption," *Journal of Purchasing,* 9 (February), 57–69.

PHILLIPS, LYNN W. (1981), "Assessing Measurement Error in Key Informant Reports: A Methodological Note on Organizational Analysis in Marketing," *Journal of Marketing Research,* 18 (November), 395–415.

PONDY, LOUIS R. (1967), "Organizational Conflict: Concepts and Models," *Administrative Science Quarterly,* 12 (September), 296–320.

PORTER, MICHAEL E. (1974), "Consumer Behavior, Retailer Power, and Market Performance in Consumer Goods Industries," *The Review of Economics and Statistics,* 56 (November), 419–436.

RAVEN, BERTRAM H. (1965), "Social Influence and Power," in *Current Studies in Social Psychology,* Ivan D. Steiner and Martin Fishbein, eds., New York: Holt, 371–382.

—— and ARIE W. KRUGLANSKI (1970), "Conflict and Power," in *The Structure of Conflict,* Paul Swingle, ed., New York: Academic Press, 69–109.

REVE, TORGER and LOUIS W. STERN (1979), "Interorganizational Relations in Marketing Channels," *Academy of Management Review*, 4 (no. 3), 405–416.

ROERING, KENNETH J. (1977), "Bargaining in Distribution Channels," *Journal of Business Research*, 5 (March), 15–26.

ROSENBERG, LARRY J. (1974), "A New Approach to Distribution Conflict Management," *Business Horizons*, 17 (October), 67–74.

—— and LOUIS W. STERN (1971), "Conflict Measurement in the Distribution Channel," *Journal of Marketing Research*, 8 (November), 437–442.

SEIDLER, JOHN (1974), "On Using Informants: A Technique for Collecting Quantitative Data and Controlling Measurement Error in Organization Analysis," *American Sociological Review*, 39 (December), 816–831.

SIMON, HERBERT (1953), "Notes on the Observation and Measurement of Political Power," *Journal of Politics*, 15 (November), 500–516.

STERN, LOUIS W. and ADEL I. EL-ANSARY (1977), *Marketing Channels*, Englewood Cliffs, NJ: Prentice-Hall, Inc.

—— and RONALD H. GORMAN (1969), "Conflict in Distribution Channels: An Exploration," in *Distribution Channels: Behavioral Dimensions*, Louis W. Stern, ed., Boston: Houghton Mifflin, 156–175.

——, ROBERT A. SCHULZ, JR., and JOHN R. GRABNER, JR. (1973), "The Power Base–Conflict Relationship: Preliminary Findings," *Social Science Quarterly*, 54 (September), 412–419.

——, BRIAN STERNTHAL, and C. SAMUEL CRAIG (1973), "Managing Conflict in Distribution Channels: A Laboratory Study," *Journal of Marketing Research*, 10 (May), 169–179.

——, ——, and —— (1975), "Strategies for Managing Interorganizational Conflict: A Laboratory Paradigm," *Journal of Applied Psychology*, 60 (August), 472–482.

TEDESCHI, JAMES T. and THOMAS V. BONOMA (1972), "Power and Influence: An Introduction," in *The Social Influence Process*, James T. Tedeschi, ed., Chicago: Aldine-Atherton, Inc., 1–49.

THIBAUT, J. W. and H. H. KELLEY (1959), *The Social Psychology of Groups*, New York: Wiley.

THOMAS, KENNETH (1976), "Conflict and Conflict Management," in *Handbook of Industrial and Organizational Psychology*, Marvin D. Dunnette, ed., Chicago: Rand McNally, 889–935.

WALKER, O. C., JR. (1972), "The Effects of Learning on Bargaining Behavior," in *1971 Combined Proceedings*, F. C. Allvine, ed., Chicago: American Marketing, 194–199.

WILEMON, DAVID L. (1972), "Power and Negotiation Strategies in Marketing Channels," *The Southern Journal of Business*, 7 (February), 12–32.

WILKINSON, I. F. (1974), "Researching the Distribution Channels for Consumer and Industrial Goods: The Power Dimension," *Journal of the Market Research Society*, 16 (no. 1), 12–32.

—— (1979), "Power and Satisfaction in Channels of Distribution," *Journal of Retailing*, 55 (Summer), 79–94.

—— (1981), "Power, Conflict, and Satisfaction in Distribution Channels—An Empirical Study," *International Journal of Physical Distribution and Materials Management*, 11 (no. 7), 20–30.

—— and DAVID KIPNIS (1978), "Interfirm Use of Power," *Journal of Applied Psychology*, 63 (no. 3), 315–320.

WRONG, DENNIS H. (1968), "Some Problems in Defining Social Power," *The American Journal of Sociology*, 73 (May), 673–681.

CHAPTER TEN

Channel Communications and Information Systems

Whether particular institutions or agencies assume leadership roles in specific marketing flows within distribution channels, communication in one form or another provides the means by which the work of channels is coordinated. Poor or ineffective communications can prove to be a major roadblock to coordinative efforts. As such, vigilance should be exercised to ensure that problems of this nature do not develop. Nevertheless, omission and distortion of messages are, in reality, frequent within channels. In fact, inadequate communication or miscommunication is often not only a major stimulator but also an outcome of deep-rooted and dysfunctional channel conflict.

This chapter focuses directly on the development of effective communication within channels. The difficulty in securing adequate communication in channels involves a wide variety of behavioral and structural/technical issues. Therefore, we shall deal first with the behavioral aspects of channel communications and then examine the structural/technical aspects. No such discussion is complete without an examination of related technologies such as optical scanning and computerized information systems and their applications in channel communications and information systems. Moreover, throughout the chapter we explore *intraorganizational* management perspectives of communications and information systems development, which should permit a significant start toward the development of sound *interorganizational* communications. The steps in designing a marketing channel information system are shown in Exhibit 10–1.

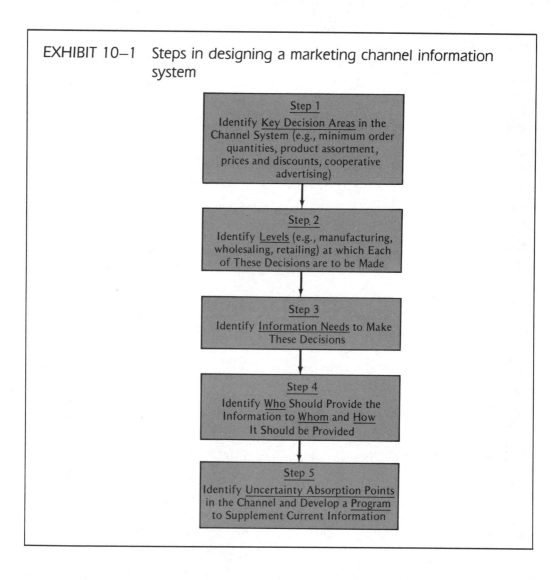

EXHIBIT 10-1   Steps in designing a marketing channel information system

Step 1
Identify <u>Key Decision Areas</u> in the Channel System (e.g., minimum order quantities, product assortment, prices and discounts, cooperative advertising)

Step 2
Identify <u>Levels</u> (e.g., manufacturing, wholesaling, retailing) at which Each of These Decisions are to be Made

Step 3
Identify <u>Information Needs</u> to Make These Decisions

Step 4
Identify <u>Who</u> Should Provide the Information to <u>Whom</u> and <u>How</u> It Should be Provided

Step 5
Identify <u>Uncertainty Absorption Points</u> in the Channel and Develop a <u>Program</u> to Supplement Current Information

RUDIMENTS OF CHANNEL COMMUNICATIONS

A communication system is a means of coordinating the activities and functions of an organization with the environment in which it operates. Effective communication increases the efficiency of a channel system's performance. Ineffective communication, such as misunderstood and delayed messages, creates mutual frustrations among channel members as it affects their ability to perform efficiently. This, in turn, is the root of conflict within a channel.

A channel of distribution resembles a pyramid. In a commercial channel for goods, for example, a manufacturer forms the apex of the pyramid. Manufacturers, wholesalers, and retailers each constitute a separate level in that channel structure. Communication travels vertically through the "pyramid" as well as horizontally among firms at the same level. Information is exchanged both among members on each level as well as between levels. Channel communication must be timely if vertical and horizontal coordination of channel flows and activities is to be achieved.[1]

Timing

The timing of communication within a channel system has a direct impact on the coordination and interpretation of a message. Information received very early may simply be ignored if the recipient cannot see its relevance. Delays in communication create dysfunctional consequences for an entire channel, such as unbalanced inventories and an uncoordinated promotional campaign.

The timing of communication can be either serial or simultaneous. In serial flows, a message is received by one or a few channel members, who then relay the information to other members. In contrast, simultaneous communication occurs when all the members who would be affected by a given message receive the message at the same time.[2]

Simultaneous is often the better of the two communication flows to be employed within a channel, as it will alleviate the dysfunctional conflict associated with message delays throughout the system. For example, the effective coordination of a promotional campaign for a new product is a critical determinant of the product's success. The promotion and inventory flows must be coordinated to avoid wasting manufacturer's advertising dollars when a product is not available on the retailer's shelf. Coordination would be difficult, if not impossible, to achieve if communication flows to channel members were improperly sequenced. Thus, coordination in a channel of distribution hinges on the timeliness of its communication system.

The growth of computerized information systems and electronic communications media has influenced channel communications by speeding up the flow of information among channel members while improving its accuracy. Channel members can have direct links with those members who receive, process, and place orders. Timely information about market conditions and rates of sales can trigger faster pricing and promotional adjustment to specific market conditions than was once possible. The crucial role that timing plays in channel communications has resulted in more attention being given to this dimension.[3] Likewise, there is a greater awareness of the critical role of *perception* in the development of effective channel communications.

Perceptions

The frequent interactions of channel members in the various communication flows enable them to identify each other's behavior and thereby each other's role and to predict future behavior. Conflicts arise when a channel member perceives that the behavior of another member is interfering with his perfor-

[1] John Grabner, Paul Ziszner, and Larry Rosenberg, "Communication in the Distribution Channel," in Arch G. Woodside, J. Taylor Simms, Dale M. Dewison, and Ian Fulkman (eds.), *Foundations of Marketing Channels* (Austin, Tex.: Lone Star Publishers, 1978), p. 218.
[2] *Ibid.*, p. 222.
[3] *Ibid.*, p. 223.

mance, autonomy, or goal attainment. Such conflict is inevitable in a vertical marketing organization, where members are functionally interdependent.

As discussed in Chapter 6, channel members go through various stages of conflict, each of which is shaped by the results of previous events. Members first experience a cognitive/affective stage, which is followed by a behavioral/manifest stage. The former conflict is primarily attitudinal and is reflected in feelings of frustration. When conflict reaches the manifest stage, members engage in behavior ranging from lack of cooperation to the extreme of leaving or forcing others to leave a channel.[4]

The sources of intrachannel conflict can be divided into two main categories: attitudinal and structural. The former stems from ways channel members absorb and process information about the channel and its environment. The latter reflects a clash of interests between members, including goal divergence, drives for autonomy, and fights over resources.[5]

A variety of communication-related factors contribute to attitudinal sources of conflict. These include different perceptions of roles, the desire for secrecy, and communication interference. Channel conflict over roles may arise because members tend to perceive their position in a communication chain to be parallel to that of their position in the channel hierarchy.[6] The role a channel member may perceive itself as occupying may conflict with other members' expectations of the one it should fulfill. Therefore, conflicts arise when a member does not recognize another's position in the communication chain, hides information, and ignores or rejects others' messages.

Secrecy

Channel members quite often withhold valuable information from each other. Before transmitting such information, a member may alter the message to avoid leaking competitive information. Therefore, tradeoffs exist between the need for efficient coordination and the need to withhold competitive information from certain channel members.

Channel members may also withhold information to prevent another member from attaining countervailing power. For example, intermediaries will retain information to prevent a manufacturer from gaining control over them. Retailers have deliberately withheld information on rates of product movement from suppliers to gain bargaining leverage. A manufacturer needs secrecy if he decides to go direct to end-users or consumers.[7] Thus, control over information through secrecy is a major determinant of a channel member's power and status. But whereas some channels suffer from little information, others suffer from information overloads and noise.

Noise

A major factor in the miscomprehension of a message is *noise*. An overload of detailed information is likely to be misunderstood because it will exceed the

---

[4] Michael Etgar, "Sources and Types of Intrachannel Conflict," *Journal of Retailing*, Vol. 55 (Spring 1979), p. 62.
[5] *Ibid.*, p. 65.
[6] Grabner, Ziszner, and Rosenberg, *op. cit.*, p. 226.
[7] *Ibid.*, p. 230.

processing capacity of the recipient. The recipient is faced with the burdensome and confusing task of having to decipher the information he needs from a large volume of data. A channel member's failure to understand information prevents other members from learning the intended message, too. Thus, an overloaded communication system is a detriment to channel coordination.

To avoid information overloads in a communication system, one should limit information exchange to exactly what the receiver needs. This can be facilitated by the steps in designing a marketing channel information system shown in Exhibit 10–1. This orderly procedure should result in limiting information volume in the entire communication system, and thus the amount of potential noise.

One efficient means of reducing noise, secrecy, and miscomprehension in messages is to use a specialized language.[8] The Universal Product Code (UPC) is an example of a specialized language designed to reduce the amount of "noise" in a message. The code enables retailers to secure sales information at exactly the time a transaction occurs. This information benefits other channel members as explained in Exhibit 10–2.

The Universal Product Code is a helpful tool in uncertainty absorption in that it provides a means of reducing detail throughout the communication system.[9] Channel members' uncertainty over which information should be deciphered is absorbed by the computerized system. For example, supermarket sales are summarized in terms of transaction totals on cash register tapes. Such details as purchasers' names and their individual purchases are not recorded. When a supermarket places an order with a wholesaler, it is based on a summary of several days' transactions. Similarly, wholesalers summarize results of transactions over a certain period when placing an order with a manufacturer. Thus, the manufacturer ends up with a summary of transactions without knowing where, when, or what amounts of his product are actually sold to the final user.[10]

Manufacturers, wholesalers, and retailers can get more detailed information if the UPC is combined with other specialized languages. For example, Information Resources, Inc. (IRI) provides manufacturers and retailers with valuable test-market information through the company's BehaviorScan test-marketing program. Weis Markets, a BehaviorScan subscriber, provides its shoppers with the Shopper's Hotline Card. By showing the card at the checkout, shoppers get a chance at a variety of prizes. The card is linked to IRI's BehaviorScan test-marketing program. The program makes it possible to monitor purchases by consumers and correlate them with information collected via gadgets installed on TV sets that monitor the commercials they watch.[11]

Although uncertainty absorption helps alleviate noise within a communication system, it can be disadvantageous as well. Inferences will be made from the summarized transactions that may be hard to verify. Therefore, someone who doubts or disbelieves the information is "forced" into accepting the data. When a

[8] *Ibid.*, p. 233.

[9] *Ibid.*

[10] *Ibid.*, p. 234.

[11] "Wired Consumers: Market Researchers Go High-Tech to Hone Ads, Weed Out Flops," *Wall Street Journal,* January 23, 1986, p. 31. Also see Fitzhugh L. Corr, "Scanners in Marketing Research: Paradise (Almost)," *Marketing News* (January 4, 1985), pp. 2, 15.

EXHIBIT 10-2   The universal product code (UPC)

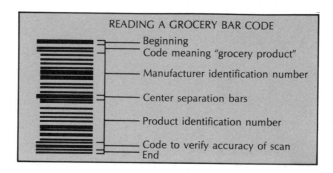

READING A GROCERY BAR CODE

- Beginning
- Code meaning "grocery product"
- Manufacturer identification number
- Center separation bars
- Product identification number
- Code to verify accuracy of scan
- End

Bar codes will soon be appearing on everything from hospital patients to hand grenades.

Grocery shoppers have been growing familiar with the codes since 1973, when the supermarket industry introduced its Universal Product Code. The black and white stripes, when passed over a laser beam, help speed checkouts. In fact the system was developed earlier, in the 1930s, and in 1967 the railroad industry adopted it to trace the movement of rail cars.

Today the codes are going almost everywhere. "Bar coding can go on any product, whether it's an automobile or a shipment of caviar," says John Hill, former president of the Materials Handling Institute.

In a bar code, a string of numbers or letters is represented by thin and wide lines on a label. These characters have access to information about the product through a computer memory system. A scanning device shines a ray of light across the bars to record or confirm the bar code. Such information as the product's maker or its country of origin is encoded in the lines.

The coding systems, also popular in Europe, Japan and Britain, are favored for their speed in tracking the movement of goods and accuracy in identifying products, which saves companies money.

In 1967, for example, General Motors installed the system at its Oldsmobile plant in Flint, Mich. The system cost $25,000 to install but it replaced a manual record keeping system that cost $75,000 in salaries, says Edmund Anderson, president of Automatic Identification Manufacturers Inc.

Workers at Ford Motor Co. plants scan bar codes on auto parts to send information about damaged items to repair shops. Workers at Southeast Paper Co., in Dublin, Ga., use the codes to keep track of containers they handle. The hospital industry is poised to put bar codes on patient-identification bracelets to better record their medical histories. And Nicholas Turkey Farms in Santa Rosa, Calif., uses the system to trace its best turkey stock, burying a bar code in each hen's tail so that it can be scanned when the bird produces an egg with a healthy chick inside.

The registration form for runners in last year's New York Marathon used a bar code to record a name, identification number, average scoring time, and predicted finishing time.

Last March, the health industry adopted a standard to track cartons entering and leaving hospitals. At American Medical International Hospital in Beverly Hills, Calif., employees will soon use badges with bar codes on them, enabling scanners to record their check-in and check-out times.

channel member has access to information unavailable to others he is in a strong position to influence them, for they rely on his interpretations of reality.[12]

Attempts to verify the accuracy of communication through feedback increase the load on a communication system. The effect of feedback on channel member behavior depends on the quality and quantity of information generated. Some studies have shown that information used for feedback is subject to the noise it attempts to overcome. Furthermore, the amount of feedback may overburden the initial sender's receiving capabilities so that he is forced to respond selectively to the feedback. As more channel members use computerized data processing, the volume of available information on the results of marketing efforts may so overcome decision makers within a channel that it becomes difficult for them to sort relevant from irrelevant data.[13]

Bargaining

Attitudinally and structurally based intrachannel conflicts not only arise from different causes but require different means of conflict resolution.[14] A major contributor to the communication problems associated with attitudinal sources of conflict is the different perceptions channel members have of each other's roles. This can be alleviated by a routinized communication program that would specify the tasks and performance expected of each member.

In contrast, to resolve structural sources of conflict, such as goal divergence, drives for autonomy, and fights over resources, channel members will have to bargain. That is, a member must be willing to give up some resources or control, and/or readjust goals.[15]

Bargaining is constantly occurring within a channel of distribution, for it enables a channel member to cope with another member's power and control attempts. A channel member's power affects his position in the negotiation process as well as the feasible behaviors he may engage in. Furthermore, a major factor in a member's bargaining position is the extent of his dependency upon another member in performing efficiently and attaining goals.

If a channel system contains an asymmetrical distribution of power, this in turn will produce asymmetrical negotiations, with the powerful member dominating the bargaining. Specifically, the member holding more power than his

---

[12] Grabner, Ziszner, and Rosenberg, *op. cit.,* p. 237.
[13] *Ibid.*
[14] James Brown and Ralph Day, "Measures of Manifest Conflict in Distribution Channels," *Journal of Marketing Research* (August 1981), p. 73.
[15] *Ibid.*

partners will be motivated by immediate self-gain. Therefore, he will be more likely to submit an extreme initial bid, yield less profit from his initial position, and send a larger portion of threatening messages than when power within a channel system is balanced.[16]

The negotiation process is an integral part of the communication process in the channel. Its efficiency has a direct impact on selling and purchasing costs, the organizational structure of these functional units, and the expertise of the personnel involved. Thus, negotiation is necessary within a channel to achieve efficient coordination.[17]

INFORMATION SOURCES
IN MARKETING CHANNELS

The variety of direct and indirect media listed in Fig. 10–1 are available to merchandise sources (factories and/or wholesalers) and resellers (wholesalers and/or retailers) to facilitate the development of information on all marketing flows. Grabner, Ziszner, and Rosenberg, referring to Guetzkow's research, caution that "the use of one type of network (e.g., task-expertise) to carry other types of messages (e.g., relating to friendship or status) may result in one type of message being submerged by others."[18] Therefore, the appropriate choice of information media is of great importance.

As shown in Fig. 10–1, salespeople top the list of direct-information media between the merchandise source and the merchandise reseller. Grace and Pointon, in a study of the use of the sales force for marketing research, report a number of advantages and disadvantages in using sales personnel (1) as respondents providing factual information, (2) as respondents providing subjective data, and (3) as interviewers of their own customers.[19] Although one can readily see how information gathered through the sales force could be used for sales forecasting, pricing, and strategic purposes, and although this method of information gathering has numerous advantages, including low cost, confidentiality, and quick implementation, Grace and Pointon conclude that sales agents are poor respondents and worse interviewers.[20]

Grace and Pointon's research implies that the use of the sales force to gather information in a channel could result in a disastrous "whisper-down-the-lane" syndrome among channel members. If manufacturers rely on their sales forces for factual information, subjective data, and especially interview responses about the retail level, the distorted information could, among other eventualities, lead to a grossly inaccurate sales forecast and subsequent poor channel planning. Thus, while the sales force may be helpful in turning up

[16] Robert Dwyer and Orville Walker, "Bargaining in an Asymmetrical Power Structure," *Journal of Marketing* (Winter 1981), p. 106.

[17] *Ibid.;* and George Huber, "Organizational Information Systems: Determinants of Their Performance and Behavior," *Management Science* (February 1982), p. 139. Huber advances a number of interesting propositions regarding message routing, summarizing, delay, and modification and their impact on the performance of organizations.

[18] Grabner, Ziszner, and Rosenberg, *op. cit.*, p. 228.

[19] David Grace and Tom Pointon, "Marketing Research through the Salesforce," *Industrial Marketing Management* (February 1980), pp. 53–58.

[20] *Ibid.*, pp. 57–58.

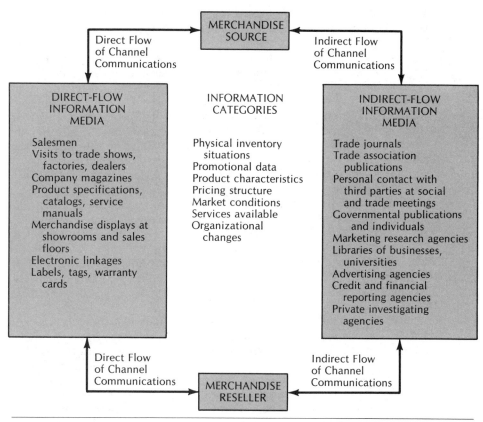

Figure 10–1 Direct and indirect communications media available to merchandise sources and resellers

Source: Walter Gross, "Profitable Listening for Manufacturers and Dealers: How to Use a Communication System," in *Marketing Channels: A Systems Viewpoint,* eds. William G. Moller, Jr. and David L. Wilemon (Homewood, Ill.: Richard D. Irwin, Inc., 1971), p. 346.

useful bits of information—albeit haphazardly—that cannot be obtained in any other way, it is ill suited as the sole source of a channel communication system.

A second disadvantage of using the sales force as a research organization in a channel system is that coordination among several levels of salespeople appears to be an insurmountable problem. For example, a survey question asked by salespeople at one level of the channel might be phrased differently at another level; the subjective elements are too great to ignore.

A disadvantage of using a salesperson to interview customers, according to Grace and Pointon, is that "the salesperson may see only the buyer when, in fact, there are others of more commercial importance in the organizational buying process."[21] In the field of marketing research, such utilization of a key informant has come under close scrutiny in a study by Phillips.[22] The study explores the

[21] *Ibid.,* p. 56.
[22] Lynn W. Phillips, "Assessing Measurement Error in Key Information Reports: A Methodological Note on Organizational Analysis in Marketing," *Journal of Marketing Research* (November 1981), pp. 395–415.

methodological problem of assessing measurement error in key informant reports. Looking at recent research on the distribution channel as the "relevant unit of analysis," Phillips notes that "these paradigms are distinguished from previous frameworks in that they attempt to explain and predict the behavior of organizations or organizational subunits rather than individuals."[23]

Phillips maintains that since organizations have characteristics distinct from individuals, measurement of "organizational characteristics requires research methods different from those used to measure individuals" and that despite their growing use in the study of distribution channels and other marketing areas, "the degree to which informant reports are valid indicators of the organizational characteristics they are intended to measure is an unresolved issue."[24] Phillips assessed the reliability and validity of reports from multiple informants in 506 wholesale distribution companies and compared the results with those obtained by the key informant method.[25] Phillips concludes, "The findings indicate that [key] informant reports on organizational characteristics often fail to serve as highly valid indicators of the concepts they intend to represent."[26] For future research, Phillips recommends (1) using several informants at different levels in the organization, (2) constructing questions in a way that requires less demanding social judgments of the informant, and (3) using questions that are less prone to distortion when informants report on relatively objective phenomena.[27]

Phillips's study holds implications for channel managers on at least two levels. First, it sets a higher standard for academic research on channel management when informant methods are to be used. Second, it underscores the problems associated with the ad hoc surveys, "ballpark" statistics, and similar "quick and dirty" analyses so frequently generated by in-house market researchers and, all too often, outside agencies. The study indicates that where it is cost-prohibitive to statistically show the validity and reliability of responses, at the very least, clear, objective research questions and multiple informants per unit are needed.

Given Phillips's analysis, the use of a sales force to obtain valid, reliable market research appears unlikely at best. Therefore, it behooves channel members to rely on a variety of information sources.[28] For example, in a study of contemporary communications devices used in franchise channels, respondents were asked, "What tools do you use to promote franchisor/franchisee relations?"[29] The results, shown in Table 10–1, indicate that the majority of the respondents rely on a multitude of sources.

---

[23] *Ibid.*, p. 395.
[24] *Ibid.*, p. 396.
[25] *Ibid.*, p. 397.
[26] *Ibid.*, p. 408.
[27] *Ibid.*, p. 411.
[28] In recent years, trade shows have received more attention as an important source of information for channel members. See, for example, Thomas V. Bonoma, "Get More Out of Your Trade Shows," *Harvard Business Review*, Vol. 61 (January-February 1983), pp. 75–83; Mike Major, "New Marketing Opportunities Come to Those with Specific Trade Show Goals," *Marketing News* (March 2, 1984), pp. 2, 19; and Fred Kitzing, "Trade Show Exhibitors Getting Down to Business with Effective Programs," *Marketing News* (March 2, 1984), pp. 1, 11.
[29] International Franchise Association, *Franchisor/Franchisee Communications Survey Report* (Washington, D.C.: 1985).

Table 10–1   Franchisors' means of regular communication with franchisees

Means of Communication	Percentage of Responding Franchisors
Phone contact	96%
Field calls	91
Meetings	89
Newsletters	87
Surveys/Questionnaires	49
Other publications	42
Other methods	30

Source: International Franchise Association, *Franchisor/Franchisee Communications Survey Report* (Washington, D.C.: 1985), p. 5.

CHANNEL STRUCTURE AND CHANNEL COMMUNICATIONS

A comprehensive treatment of channel communication system development is more meaningful when undertaken in the context of the structure of the channel and the type of communication problems with which the system is designed to deal. These variables include the length of the channel, electronic data interchange, inventory management, promotional programs, transportation and storage flows, product assortments, and pricing practices.

Channel Length

Clearly, the longer a channel—the more middlemen involved in the distribution of a given product, brand, or service—the more likely that omission and distortion of message contents will take place, all other things being equal. The number of links in a communication network is inversely related to accurate reception.[30] Perceptual and secrecy problems are compounded as more and more channel members become involved in the uncertainty absorption process. Consider, for example, the case of a pharmacist for a large public hospital who complained to the president of a drug wholesaling firm that manufacturers did not keep him well informed about their new products. He wanted to know why he was not detailed promptly on new ethicals (prescription drugs) as they were developed and why the manufacturers did not provide him with printed materials. As explained by Cox, Schutte, and Few,

> The wholesaler agreed that the manufacturers were "falling down on their job," but when he interviewed detail men for several manufacturers, he found that they, too, were frustrated. They had more than adequate information to give out—written and oral. To them, the pharmacist himself was the villain. They were fed up

[30] See, for example, Alex Bavelas, "Communication Patterns in Task-oriented Groups," *Journal of the Acoustical Society of America,* Vol. 22 (1950), pp. 725–30; and Harold Guetzkow and Herbert Simon, "The Impact of Certain Communication Nets upon Organization and Performance in Task-oriented Groups," *Management Science,* Vol. 1 (April-July 1955), pp. 233–50.

with waiting as much as four hours to conduct a detail call. "That pharmacist thinks he is God," one salesman said. "He couldn't care less about how long he makes the salesman wait." The wholesaler took the initiative, told the pharmacist what the real problem was, and made appointments for him to see the detail men at given hours.

But note that it is the manufacturer's communication line that has broken down, not the wholesaler's. The manufacturer has depended upon detail men to tell the potential pharmacist buyer about his products, which could then be sold and delivered by wholesalers to the buyer. The wholesaler's responsibility in communication was only to tell prospective buyers that they had the manufacturer's products available. Obviously, the manufacturer's feedback was inadequate in that it took a wholesaler to straighten out the manufacturer's communication problem.[31]

Thus, as Cox, Schutte, and Few imply, the longer the channel, the more highly developed the feedback system available to each channel member, and especially the channel leader, must be. Furthermore, in long channels, there is obviously a need for a mechanism permitting the bypassing of messages. That is, the information system should permit the conflicting parties to avoid one or more links in the normal communication network so that bottlenecks can be eliminated, especially during periods of crisis within the system.[32]

Reliance on indirect communication links frequently multiplies the chances for distortion.[33] This problem is exemplified by the case of a leading manufacturer of electronic products who had received indirect complaints about his order-filling service. From these complaints, certain key executives concluded that most of the customers were dissatisfied because of the length of time between the sending of an order and the receipt of goods. The executives laid detailed plans to remedy this perceived problem, among them a plan to establish an elaborate system of regional warehouses. Shortly before instituting these plans, the president of the company suggested gathering some additional information directly from customers. The results of a preliminary field survey conducted at his request indicated that the original information was completely erroneous—that most of the company's customers were highly satisfied with the service they were receiving. While the customers indicated that shorter turn-around time would be welcomed, they were impressed with the consistency of the manufacturer's service. That is, they said they could count on the receipt of

[31] Reavis Cox, Thomas F. Schutte, and Kendrick S. Few, "Towards the Measurement of Trade Channel Perception," in Fred C. Allvine (ed.), *Combined Proceedings 1971 Spring and Fall Conferences* (Chicago: American Marketing Association, 1972), pp. 190–91.

[32] The discussion of noise-reduction mechanisms in this chapter is based largely on John R. Grabner, Jr., and L. J. Rosenberg, "Communication in Distribution Channel Systems," in Louis W. Stern (ed.), *Distribution Channels: Behavioral Dimensions* (Boston: Houghton Mifflin Co., 1969), pp. 238–49.

[33] Technological advances are significant in reducing the need for indirect communication. The development of electronic funds transfer systems (EFTS) in the banking industry is an example of the substitution of direct for indirect communication links. Banks and savings and loan associations are placing electronic terminals in supermarkets, making it possible for customers to pay for their groceries via a transfer of funds from their accounts to that of the store. In these situations, the supermarket becomes the financial and operational medium between the customer and the bank. The supermarket does not, however, become a financial institution, according to some, because the terminal is only a means of communication; the actual transfer of funds takes place inside the bank's computer, which is, of course, located inside the bank and not the supermarket. The consequences of such a development could be profound, especially for the banking industry. See "Bank Cards Take Over the Country," *Business Week* (August 4, 1975), pp. 44–54. See also Robert M. Lilienfeld and Diane Wolgemuth, *Consumer Reactions toward an Electronic Funds Transfer System in Supermarkets* (Chicago: Super Market Institute, Inc., 1975).

goods from the company a specified number of days after orders had been placed and that such consistency was extremely important to them.[34]

In this example, the company was saved a considerable investment in time and money. Future problems of this sort, however, can be eliminated or mitigated only by ensuring adequate feedback from the field, instituting bypass mechanisms, and ensuring repetition of messages that bear such heavy consequences for the firm's operations. Before efforts to develop an *interorganizational* information system take place, it is necessary that individual channel members develop smooth-functioning *intraorganizational* systems. For most firms this means connecting several internal systems, such as a merchandise (inventory) information system and a system for financial management, credit management, and other management functions. Emphasis is placed on the inventory information system because it is the component over which most channel interaction takes place.

Inventory Management

As was clearly witnessed during the recessions of 1974 and 1980, problems with inventory can pose tremendous difficulties for all members of a marketing channel. In fact, the poor profit performance of both Sears and Penney's during the earlier recession can be traced directly to problems of inventory management and control, which led to the steep markdowns used by both firms to reduce excessive stocks of merchandise.[35]

Inventory management is a channelwide problem and demands channelwide communication. As Gross has observed,

> manufacturers, wholesalers, and retailers can control physical stock problems better when each knows about changes in the quantity and the location of the others' inventory. To be complete, . . . physical inventory should cover more than the number of units located at premises owned by manufacturers or resellers. It is equally important to know how much merchandise is stored in public warehouses, how much is in transit, and what is on display in wholesale showrooms and on retail sales floors.[36]

Not only will such information aid the manufacturer's production scheduling, but it will also have a direct impact on a retailer's or wholesaler's buying plans, because the latter will be able to anticipate the length of order lead times. For example, a furniture manufacturer's study revealed that his shipments were uncoordinated with dealers' needs: some merchandise was shipped too late to prevent stockouts, and other items were delivered before the dealers expected them, causing unanticipated handling problems. Finally, one retailer dropped the manufacturer's line after concluding that these inventory and warehousing problems generated costs that more than offset the advantages of the line.[37]

[34] This example was drawn from Cox, Schutte, and Few, *op. cit.,* p. 191.

[35] The consequences of Sears' and Penney's 1974 inventory problems are documented in Alvin Nagelberg, "Retailers Eye Very Merry Christmas," *Chicago Tribune,* May 25, 1975, section 2, p. 11; and in "Why Sears' Profit Tumbled," *Business Week* (April 21, 1975), pp. 32–33.

[36] Walter Gross, "Profitable Listening for Manufacturers and Dealers: How to Use a Communication System," in William G. Moller, Jr., and David L. Wilemon (eds.), *Marketing Channels: A Systems Viewpoint* (Homewood, Ill.: Richard D. Irwin, 1971), p. 344.

[37] This example was drawn from *ibid.,* p. 341.

As this example indicates, inventory problems are intimately tied to ordering, shipping, and delivery difficulties. The first step in eradicating the problems causing inventory mismanagement is the development of an intraorganizational information system. Computerized inventory information systems can lead to greater inventory turnover, reduction in freight costs, better buying decisions, rapid assessment of physical inventory, availability of disaggregated sales data, and reduced clerical costs.

One of the most sophisticated inventory control systems is that of Motorola's Fossil Creek assembly plant in Fort Worth, Texas. The plant is unique in that the building specifications were drawn around a proposed materials control system. As shown in Exhibit 10–3, by combining the use of computers and conveyers, the system provides for completely automated parts movement from receipt to production and efficiently integrates production and physical distribution.

> Materials are tracked from dock to stock to shipping with scheduled and random human checks along the way to verify the computer's inventory tallies.[38]

The system also provides absolute real-time inventory tracking, and a materials requirements planning system enables management to know not only what is in storage but also what is the work in process. On that basis and on the basis of forecasted demand, the system generates materials requirements. Implementation of the system has been so successful that Motorola is now shipping ahead of its delivery schedule and delinquent customer orders have been eliminated.[39]

Without doubt, the greatest aid to the management of inventories has been the introduction and adaptation of programs using high-speed electronic data-processing equipment. By utilizing such programs, manufacturers can systematize their production, shipping, and delivery operations and middlemen can maintain up-to-date inventory records. Implementation of *electronic data interchange (EDI)* to allow channel hookups via communication about transportation and storage problems can provide optimum automatic ordering systems.

Interorganizational Data Systems

The recent explosion in computer and information transmission technology is rapidly modifying our marketing environment and is providing marketing channel members with new opportunities and challenges. As mentioned, complex information transmission and transactions associated with marketing and distribution channels, which took days in the past, are now completed instantaneously. These technological improvements not only reflect improvements in the speed and accuracy of channel communications but also introduce complexities and external factors that may lead to a restructuring of channel organizations.

While computer systems have existed in the marketplace for over twenty years, they typically were large and expensive, required specialists to operate them and enter data, and were available only to large concerns for the purposes of collecting, storing, and evaluating data. The miniaturization of computer

---

[38] Patrick Gallagher, "An Unbeatable System," *Handling and Shipping Management* (October 1979), p. 55.

[39] *Ibid.*, p. 54.

EXHIBIT 10–3 Layout of Motorola's Fossil Creek plant

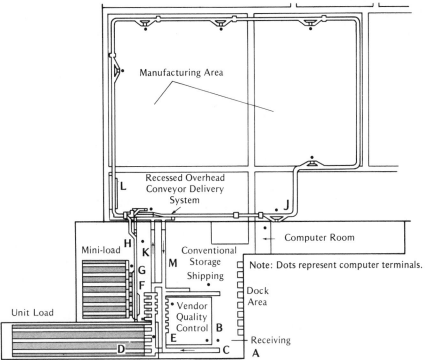

All vendor supplied parts and components from other Motorola plants arrive at receiving dock A.

Necessary information on incoming material is Input to minicomputer terminal B and a code ticket is printed and applied to the item.

The material is placed on a slave pallet and immediately sent via conveyor C to Unit Load storage D. The computer assigns a storage location for the pallet, sends it to the proper aisle, and commands the Unit Load machine to pick the pallet off the conveyor spur and store it.

When the Vendor Quality Control (VQC) department is ready to inspect the material, the computer is notified and it directs the load out of storage onto a VQC input spur E. After inspection the pallet load is returned to storage, removed from VQC quarantine status and made available for manufacturing use.

Unit Load pallets are called out to replenish the Mini-Load storage system which originates the parts kits for manufacturing. Pallets are broken down for input to Mini-Load storage at the picking spurs F.

Parts are put into tubs and set in front of the Mini-Load aisles G. The Mini-Load storage machines bring forward bins with empty storage space for the parts. The computer notifies operators where to place the parts in the bins and then has the S/R machines return the bins to storage.

A reverse sequence is performed when parts kits are to be made up for manufacturing. Under computer direction, the Mini-Load operators set an escort memory code on the kit tubs and place them on an output delivery conveyor H.

The tubs move through the overhead conveyor delivery system and are automatically diverted down elevators J at the proper "drop zones." Drop zone operators notify the computer of kit receipt.

Some bulk items on slave pallets may be commanded by the computer to be delivered to manufacturing directly out of Unit Load storage via conveyor K. Finished products are packaged at station L and returned on slave pallets to conventional storage for shipping on conveyor M. The slave pallets are then returned to the Unit Load system.

Source: Patrick Gallagher, "An Unbeatable System." Reprinted with permission from the October 1979 issue of *Handling and Shipping Management,* p. 55. © 1987, Praeger Publishing.

functions has reduced the cost of computers and greatly increased computer availability and access. Satellites, software, and telecommunications have provided the link between computers used by different channel members. Although computer networks will never fully replace the personal and behavioral aspects of marketing channel relationships and communications, the new communication technologies are the catalyst for improved channel communications.

The use of advanced computer and communications technology saw only limited marketing application during the 1960s and 1970s and was characterized by several disappointments and false starts.[40] During this period, computer technology received only limited acceptance by channel members and consumers, and prototype computer systems were involved piecemeal in marketing channel information flows. Integrated communications among the multiple networks involved in the many marketing channel flows are now possible and will become the norm during the late 1980s and beyond. Retailers, distributors, and manufacturers, as well as other channel members, are finding it necessary to evaluate and integrate their communications and information flows to meet the challenge of a changing environment, as illustrated by the following examples.

American Hospital Supply Corporation, which distributes products from 8500 manufacturers to more than 100,000 health-care providers, saw its market share soar in the 1970s after it set up computer links to its customers and suppliers. Hospitals could enter orders themselves via AHS terminals. The technology let the company cut inventories, improve customer service, and get better terms from suppliers for higher volumes. Even more important, it often locked out rival distributors that didn't have direct pipelines to hospitals. AHS stays ahead of competitors by analyzing the industry data it collects to spot order trends and customer needs more quickly.

American Airlines has used computer and communications technology to build an entirely new business with sky-high profit margins. American provides its Sabre reservation system, which lists the flight schedules of every major airline in the world, to 48 percent of the approximately 24,000 automated travel agents in the U.S. They pay American $1.75 for every reservation made via Sabre for other carriers. "We are now in the data processing as well as the airline business," says President Robert L. Crandall, a data processing expert who conceived Sabre when he was American's marketing chief.

Red Lion. When a computer flagged persistently high vacancy rates at four vacation-resort inns in Arizona, Washington State, and Oregon, the Red Lion Inns chain of 52 hotels took quick action. The company sent a computer message to all its hotels and to American Airlines' Sabre reservations network offering seasonal discounts of as much as 50 percent at the four hotels. The result: fewer vacancies. Red Lion uses a minicomputer at its Vancouver (Wash.) headquarters as a kind of inventory-control system to make sure its 11,000 rooms in eight Western states are filled. Phones in the lobbies of all Red Lion hotels are linked to its system, enabling guests to make reservations. And a 200-member marketing staff uses the computer in its promotional efforts. "This gives us much more flexibility with rates structures," says Michael McLeod, executive vice-president for operations. Red Lion claims to be an industry leader in setting discount rates for tour brokers and travel wholesalers and in offering a "guaranteed rate" for frequent travelers from top corporate accounts, who are assured a room at a stated price for six months.[41]

[40] J. Barry Mason and Morris L. Mayer, "Retail Merchandise Information Systems for the 1980's," *Journal of Retailing*, Vol. 56, No. 1 (Spring 1980), p. 57.
[41] These examples are taken from "Informational Power: How Companies Are Using New Technologies to Gain Competitive Edge," *Business Week* (October 14, 1985) pp. 109, 112.

A significant factor in determining the success of an integrated channel or channel member's communication and information system is its ability to accurately process the large volume of information needed to make decisions. The capabilities of computers and data links are virtually unlimited in this regard. In fact, careful steps must be made in planning modern channel communications so as to avoid overloading decision makers with information, which could serve to introduce as much irrelevant data and noise as it eliminates. This, in fact, is one of the most common complaints of business managers, many of whom receive information in such bulk or in such inappropriate formats as to make the information unusable or distracting.[42]

Improved information flows made possible by the advancing information technology can solve many problems traditionally observed in marketing interactions. For example, uncertainty can be reduced when information on pricing, shipping, inventory, demand forecast, and other elements of marketing flows become simultaneously available to channel members. The new computer and telecommunications nets will also provide the user with the ability to question and to obtain prompt feedback and feel confident that the information is accurate.

The flexibility of computer software and hardware has improved to meet the precise information needs of individual channel members. Naturally, these needs relate to the functions they perform and the decisions they have to make. For this reason, the capabilities and effects of computer and communications development are discussed in the following pages in the context of the flows they support within the marketing channel.

Material Management

Manufacturers and wholesalers have found substantial improvements in their ability to receive and process information regarding purchasing and order processing. One reason is electronic order entry systems. Utilizing electronic links between supplier and customer can eliminate considerable time from information search and order processing. Potential customers can be linked with the supplier either by telephone or by video computer terminal. At the supplier end, order processing staff can access stock records on a real-time basis and immediately determine availability of the desired material. Pricing information, including special promotions or data on the next quantity price break, can be provided as well.[43] Supplier marketing staff can automatically back-order out-of-stock material at a satellite distribution system or automatically direct a shipment from any other warehouse or distribution center to the customer. If the buyer decides to make the purchase, the supplier's computer can automatically modify stock inventory records, direct shipment, verify the transaction with the buyer, and print invoices and shipping labels. All this is performed without manual entry or keypunching, allowing substantial savings of time and money in order-processing costs.[44]

The flexibility of computer software is such that it makes an automated order system fit a particular channel or member's needs precisely. For example, a General Electric Supply Company system will allow detailed product informa-

---

[42] Grabner, Zinszer, and Rosenberg, *op. cit.*, p. 237.
[43] "Squibb's New Order Entry System," *Distribution* (March 1980), p. 70.
[44] "Paperless Buying: A Sales Tool," *Industrial Distribution* (June 1981), p. 53.

tion to be displayed as it might be in a catalog. If a part cannot be supplied immediately from a particular warehouse or others connected with the computer net, the computer can cross-reference the desired component to competitor substitutes that might be available.[45] Because of its speed and convenience, manufacturers and distributors who install such a system are finding that they develop a team approach with their customers and that their sales actually increase. Because sales and marketing staffs are spending less time on administrative paperwork associated with the sales, more sales time is spent actually responding to the technical needs of the customer.[46]

An additional effort to improve customer service is represented by a computerized priority system that resolves distribution problems. AVCO, a manufacturer of farm machinery, routinely factors user needs into its order-processing program. For example, a part needed by a farmer to complete his harvest is assigned high priority and is expedited by the computer.[47] The speed of automated ordering systems further improves customer service by increasing the percentage of same-day shipment and/or delivery.[48]

Suppliers are finding that installing a terminal at a major customer's business, though expensive at the front end, can yield substantial benefits. For one thing, it gives the supplier a preferred status. The supplier's competitors find it more difficult to penetrate if an on-site order system is already in place. Only a few distributors now have on-site order entry, but it will be a common marketing tool in the 1990s.[49]

Wholesalers and distributors are finding that computer-aided communications, inventory management, forecasting, transportation rating and routing, product sorting, and even equipment maintenance improve the efficiency of their operations. Consideration of the many possible computer applications is increasingly being included in channel planning.

In summary, materials management is greatly enhanced by recent developments in information technology. Depending on the channel structure and customer needs, managers can control and continuously monitor inventories of the entire distribution system through a central corporate computer. Individual distributors, linked in line to a central computer or through a distributed (decentralized) computer network connected by telephone lines, can know current inventory status at each location in the system. Incoming material is automatically entered into the network and assigned a storage location. Since several channel members can have access to the information, material that is out of stock or not carried at one location can be promptly found at another. Channel members have found that because of the immediate availability of accurate and current inventory information, customer service can be increased without changes in inventory levels.[50]

[45] "GE Computer Speeds Up Customer Communications," *Purchasing* (August 1980), p. 19.
[46] "Paperless Buying," p. 54.
[47] "Avco Distributes Its Data," *Distribution* (January 1980), p. 44.
[48] Ibid.
[49] "Squibb's New Order Entry System," p. 67.
[50] "Avco Distributes Its Data," p. 45. For more examples of computer applications and the benefits derived from them, see "Beall's Automated System Adds to Center's Lifespan," *Chain Store Age—Executive Edition* (March 1984), pp. 98–100; "Computer Update: '84," *Industrial Distribution* (February 1984), pp. 57–58; "Chain Expects Annual Savings of $500,000 via T1 Circuitry," *Chain Store Age—Executive Edition* (March 1984), pp. 97–98; "States of Art and Mind," *Handling and Ship-*

Electronic Data Interchange and Transportation Management

In addition to cutting the time spent processing orders and checking and maintaining inventories, computers have helped provide faster and less expensive transportation for products within the distribution channel. Interactive terminals in shipping offices can gain access through comparative programs and data bases to shipping schedules, routes, and rates for product delivery. Firms are finding that this capability allows a dynamic decision-making analysis prior to product distribution rather than an after-the-fact comparison. Such systems are generally expensive to develop, but subscription service and time-sharing arrangements result in considerable net savings in transportation costs to large users of shipping and freight services. One commercially available system, TRACTS (Transportation Rating Accounting Controls and Tracking System), will compare times, costs, and availability of various shipping modes. For example, if air shipment is required, the program will check competing airline rates and schedules from the official airline guide and rank the various alternatives in terms of cost or shipment times.[51]

Transportation information systems should concentrate on appropriate queuing and sequencing of messages. To a large extent, specialized languages facilitating advanced technology such as Electronic Data Interchange (EDI) are the major means by which communication noise can be reduced and coordinative mechanisms can be established between shippers and their respective transport modes. Intercompany information transactions utilizing EDI consist of electronic transmissions in which information in certain prescribed formats is either requested from or given to another company. These transactions are related to operational requirements and are initiated in the participant's internal electronic data processing (EDP) system. By means of such a system, the computer of a manufacturer, having received an order for goods from the computer of a wholesaler, would prepare the necessary documents—order form, pickup form, shipping label, etc.—and establish contact with the computer of an outside shipper, making arrangements for transportation of the goods. Once the order is shipped, the manufacturer's computer relays the information to the wholesaler's computer. Both systems, then, through communications with the shipper's computer, keep track of the shipment until it reaches its destination. Thus, the entire transaction is performed with little need for human interference, with a significant reduction (or elimination) of duplicative activities within the channel, and with extremely fast and accurate interorganizational communication.

Some transportation companies already have applied EDI to certain aspects of the distribution process. For example, the Missouri Pacific Railroad has

ping Management (December 1984), pp. 15–16; "Landing on Plymouth Rock," *Handling and Shipping Management* (February 1984), pp. 13–14; Milt Ellenbogen, "New Opportunities for Distributors Seen in Advanced Software Packages," *Industrial Distribution* (February 1984), pp. 49–51; "1984 Guide to Computer Software, Systems, Services and Vendors," *Distribution* (February 1983), pp. 63–66; James H. Huguet, "Computer-to-Computer Ordering: The Sales/Marketing Implications," *Marketing News* (September 14, 1984), pp. 1, 31; Michael Friedman, "Waldenbooks' System Runs Distribution Cycle," *Chain Store Age—Executive Edition* (March 1984), pp. 94–95; "Rite Aid In-Store System Ready," *Chain Store Age—Executive Edition* (March 1984), pp. 100–102; and "Ending the Supplier Paper Chase," *Computer Decisions* (July 30, 1985), pp. 66–72.

[51] "Computers Turn On to Rating and Routing," *Distribution* (March 1981), p. 56.

developed a railcar management program known as ComPubill, an automated system for preparing bills of lading. Under this system,

> the shipper who has a railcar ready for pickup enters a so-called instruction message into his own computer, which has a data link with the rail carrier's computer. This message is received by the rail computer, and it automatically prepares a bill of lading and any other necessary documents.[52]

Although EDI offers significant improvements in channel productivity, widespread adoption by shippers, carriers, and receivers is yet to be realized due to the incompatibility of the internal data systems and formats currently being utilized. To remedy this problem, the Transportation Data Coordination Committee (TDCC) has been given responsibility for developing a standardized format by which different organizations can communicate data. It would seem that the successful completion of this task will eliminate a major barrier to industrial adoption of EDI.

In the meantime, the continued use of specialized languages in EDP has helped various companies solve shipping problems. For example, General Mills developed a Shipment Status System (called S-3 by the company) to eliminate certain problems it was having in moving its products by its major transport mode, the railroad.[53] Specifically, to ensure on-time delivery from the railroad, General Mills, in consultation with railroad management, established standard times along every route in terms of the number of days or hours required for a shipment from a company plant or distribution center to reach various checkpoints. Under S-3, General Mills' computer communicates daily with railroad computer terminals to determine if particular freight cars have arrived at designated checkpoints. Electronic scanners positioned at railroad stations examine reflective identification tape on the cars and report the status and location of the cars to the railroad computer terminal, which in turn reports to General Mills' computer. If a car fails to arrive at a designated checkpoint within a one-day grace period, General Mills reports this fact on computer "exception" sheets to railroad management personnel, who then track down the car and correct the situation. As a result of the S-3 system, General Mills achieved the highest rate of on-time delivery service (76 percent) in the company's history.

Similar coordinative communication systems have been established with motor carriers. For example, General Electric's Insulating Materials Product Section has developed a Ship-by-Number system.[54] Under this system, each GE shipment container is marked with a large, highly visible bill-of-lading number (as opposed to plain tab-on stenciled addresses with no bill of lading). This "specialized language" enables truckers to better match freight with the proper bill-of-lading form, thus minimizing confusion on shipping docks and in carrier terminals. The result for General Electric has been improved customer service in the form of fewer misdirected shipments and speedier receipt of merchandise.

Transportation companies themselves are instituting communication-enhancing systems, which frequently involve shared services. Such efforts are ex-

[52] "Computer Interface: The Giant Step from EDP to EDI," *Distribution Worldwide* (February 1978), p. 57.

[53] Information concerning S-3 was received from James C. Johnson, associate professor of transportation and traffic at the University of Tulsa, via personal correspondence.

[54] See Jim Dixon, "Streamlining Distribution and Storage," *Distribution Worldwide* (May 1975), pp. 30–31.

emplified by the National Association of Freight Payment Banks, whose service simplifies the clerical and accounting tasks associated with freight payment. In addition, TransporData Corporation initiated a nonprofit shipper-oriented freight-bill payment service in the Northwest that not only aids in solving payment problems but performs data collection as well.[55]

Merchandising Management

The expanded use of computers in retail information processing and communications management is changing merchandising philosophies and capabilities. The new capabilities are (1) facilitating merchandise planning and decision making as related to the evaluation of retail strategies, (2) aiding in identifying profit opportunities, and (3) managing precisely all activities associated with the ordering, receiving, handling, and distribution of merchandise.[56] Additionally, through point-of-sale (POS) computerized terminals, retailers are now capable of instantaneously completing paperless financial transactions associated with retail purchases through an Electronic Funds Transfer System (EFTS), which links banking and credit institutions with retail establishments.

Retail information systems can help managers make key merchandising decisions and plans by providing sales operations data from past performance as well as by projecting future sales. This in turn can help improve managers' ability to develop inventories and individual store or department plans that allow the attainment of merchandising and sales goals.[57]

The merchandise processing and reporting capabilities of computerized retail information systems help provide the control needed for the efficient ordering, handling, receiving, distributing, and reporting of sales and material at multiple sales locations. Electronic point-of-sales terminals or computerized cash registers provide corporate managers with real-time data that allow them to plan material shipment or transfer store inventories from one location to another, reacting instantly to match consumer demand and product availability. In addition to providing more control, the improvements in distribution efficiency reduce costs and boost profits as evidenced by the Giant Food's electronically linked distribution system explained in Exhibit 10–4.

Computer applications contribute significantly to back-room retail operations in addition to their point-of-sale functions. These operations include receiving and marking of goods, and product order processing. Detailed product information can be translated to computer codes carrying price, size, quantity, and color information. This product marking function can utilize a company-specific code or one of the standard codes, the Universal Product Code (generally for food items) and Universal Vendor Marking (nonfood merchandise), which can be read by scanners or optical character readers. With the advent of standardized codes, vendors and manufacturers are able to code in price and product data, relieving the retailer of the labor-intensive price-marketing task and providing channel members with effective communication on pricing policy matters.

[55] Walter F. Friedman, "Physical Distribution: The Concept of Shared Services," *Harvard Business Review*, Vol. 53 (March-April 1975), p. 26.
[56] Mason and Mayer, *op. cit.*, p. 62.
[57] *Ibid.*

EXHIBIT 10–4 Electronic links

HOW GIANT FOOD HARNESSES HIGH TECH TO FATTEN SUPERMARKET PROFITS

By adopting high-tech solutions to the grocery industry's age-old problems of low margins and profit-draining labor costs, Giant, based in Landover, Md., has boosted its 34% market share of two years ago to its current 41%. The 130-unit regional chain is now the leader in the Washington-Baltimore area, ahead of such national chains as Safeway Stores Inc. and Grand Union Co. . . .

This month the company will unveil its latest high-tech retailing ploy: It is installing minicomputers at pharmacies in 49 of its stores. The new computers will not only summon up a customer's prescription history and cross-check drugs for potentially dangerous interactive effects but also provide updated on-line product and price information. Moreover, the computers will print prescription labels and perform bookkeeping chores, thereby freeing pharmacists to spend more time counseling shoppers.

Giant has targeted the drug business because margins there run as high as 40%, while profits from its traditional food business are usually less than one-tenth of that figure. Israel Cohen, Giant's chairman, says the pharmacy system will be even more important than scanners as a tool to increase overall store volume: "It will bring in more pharmacy customers, who are going to bring more food dollars with them."

The pharmacy computer is only the latest step in Giant's strategy of utilizing electronic wizardry in its operations. Its huge 16.5-acre warehouse complex in Jessup, Md., uses state-of-the-art automation and computers to pare costs and keep Giant's shelves fully stocked. Admits an East Coast competitor: "Computerized warehouses are a few years down the road for most other chains." . . .

The result of these programs has been an impressive bottom line. Giant claims the scanners saved it $15 million in the fiscal year ended February, 1983. Sales for that period were $1.8 billion, and earnings of $37 million netted a return on sales more than double the industry's average of less than 1%. Its 25% return on average equity ranked it second among food chains last year, behind only American Stores Co. and far ahead of the industry median of 18.9%. For the six-month period ended in August, sales and profits increased by 7% and 3%, respectively, topping last year's strong first half. . . .

But Giant believes it is more high-tech food marketing that will keep it ahead of competitors. Over the next three years, the company expects to automate such functions as employee clock-ins, inventory checking, and monitoring of freezer case temperatures. And it plans to develop computerized controls of its meat cutting and deli operations to increase productivity. The company is aLso looking at a computerized videotext service that could provide information on menu planning and nutrition. Says Buchanan: "Any company that is not getting into technologies . . . is going to disappear. It is that simple."

Source: Reprinted from the December 5, 1983 issue of *Business Week* by special permission, © 1983 by McGraw-Hill, Inc.

Effective communication between channel members on pricing policy matters is of vital importance in merchandising management by retailers and wholesalers. Typically, a manufacturer's price list is an inaccurate and misleading communication medium. The net price available to middlemen includes a host of additional factors, some of which are only vaguely transmitted to existing and potential buyers. As Gross points out,[58] allowances may be made to defray advertising and/or to cover shipping, warehousing, internal chain-unit distributing, merchandise defects, and other middlemen costs. Special pricing may be available for quantity purchases, for preferred shelf and floor positions, and for trade show market specials. Dating plans, price adjustment guarantees, and other incentives to early ordering are frequently available, but are often not explicitly included in sales presentations or, if presented, are cumbersome and confusing in many cases. In actuality, pricing traditions have given rise to specialized languages (e.g., credit terms, chain discounts), which may lead to more efficient communication but are sometimes subject to considerable interpretation.[59]

Wholesalers and retailers need such information to plan their buying effectively. For example, middlemen may decide to place preseason orders, thereby financing manufacturing operations, if they can be convinced that the discount savings available are greater than inventory carrying costs and if manufacturers are willing to guarantee price levels, especially in times of unstable economic conditions. Conversely, manufacturers need information about the price structure at retail and wholesale levels in order to be assured that their pricing is in line with competition, that they are receiving their fair share of price specials at local levels, and that realistic margins are being maintained on their lines so as to avoid price "footballing" situations and thus the possible disaffection of valued distributors and dealers.

Evidence of ineffectiveness in pricing communication and execution is found in the thousands of *trade deals* (temporary price reductions) offered to retailers by manufacturers. Manufacturers, especially in the food industry, employ various short-term inducements to encourage increased purchases and/or promotional support by retailers. The most common trade deals in the food industry are *off-invoice* and *bill-back* allowances. The former are applied directly to reduce billed costs; the latter are paid retroactively for all purchases within a specified period. The hope of the manufacturers granting these allowances is that retailers will pass along at least part of their savings to consumers and/or that they will erect special displays for and advertise the brands on which prices have been reduced. On the other hand, retailers who participate in trade deals hope to increase total direct profit through higher unit sales of the products being promoted. It is suggested that in many cases neither party receives the most mileage from these deals; often they serve merely to engender or increase the potential for conflict within the channel.[60]

Standardized labeling combined with computer reporting systems offer new possibilities in consumer and retail research. Information derived from

[58] Gross, *op. cit.*, p. 349.

[59] Frederick E. Balderston, "Communication Networks in Intermediate Markets," *Management Science*, Vol. 4 (January 1958), pp. 167–68.

[60] For a detailed study of trade deals, see Michel Chevalier and Ronald C. Curhan, *Temporary Promotions as a Function of Trade Deals: A Descriptive Analysis*, Marketing Science Institute Report No. 75-109 (Cambridge, Mass.: Marketing Science Institute, 1975), p. 13.

point-of-sale scanning can be used for tracking, modeling, and experimentation. For example, supermarket chains can obtain feedback on various promotions, display effectiveness, and stocking policies as well as determine the relative performance of store brands versus national brands.[61] Marketwide information can be made available as well through the electronic data transfer. The Nationally Advertised Brands Scanning System (NABSCAN) tests and reports product data in over 36 market areas.[62]

Developing a coordinated retail information system, which integrates the many operational retailing functions with the planning, auditing, and management functions, is one of the more complex tasks of today's retailer. Although increasing percentages of retailers are employing specialized electronic cash registers and point-of-sale terminals, only seldom is the overall communications system thoughtfully designed. Integrating the management and operational communications and information tasks requires front-end planning that considers the specific needs, organization, and company strategies and objectives.

The specialization and miniaturization of computer systems has brought new technology to channel communications, but can introduce new complications if not properly planned. Minicomputers are so readily available that in some cases nearly every element of an organization will procure its own. This proliferation creates an incompatible and uncoordinated network of data processors rather than an integrated channel communications system. One of the keys to a successful system design is a conscious matching of the company and channel structure and strategy with the proposed information system. For example, depending on the amount of control or coordination desired, a particular channel network or member can decide to utilize a large centralized computer system or it can opt for a distributed data system, which can combine central processing with decentralized information processing and communications capabilities at remote locations.[63]

Promotion Management

The development of new technologies and the vast improvements in the capacity of existing communication technologies have also had far-reaching ramifications for promotional flows and promotion management in marketing channels. *Telemarketing* and *videotex* are prime examples.

Telemarketing.   Telemarketing is "a marketing communication system utilizing telecommunication technology and trained personnel to conduct planned, measurable marketing activities directed at targeted groups of consumers."[64] The internal processes of a telemarketing center are illustrated in Fig. 10–2, and Table 10–2 outlines some of the management reports they generate. Many corporations, such as B.F. Goodrich, IBM, and GTE, have set up telemarketing centers within their companies. Effective applications of telemarketing to im-

---

[61] *Ibid.*

[62] *Ibid.*, p. 65.

[63] Jack R. Buchanan and Richard Linowes, "Understanding Distributed Data Processing," *Harvard Business Review*, Vol. 58 (July-August 1980), p. 153.

[64] Roy Vorhees and John Coppett, "Telemarketing in Distribution Channels," *Industrial Marketing Management* (December 1983), p. 105.

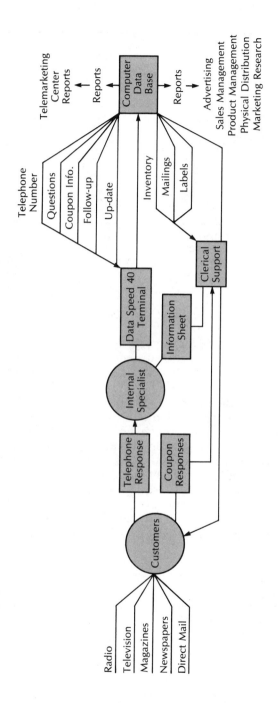

Figure 10–2 The processing system within a telemarketing center

Source: Reprinted by permission of the publisher from Roy Vorhees and John Coppett, "Telemarketing in Distribution Channels," *Industrial Marketing Management* (December 1983), p. 106. Copyright by Elsevier Science Publishing Co. Inc.

Table 10–2 Reports from a telemarketing center to other marketing groups

Advertising	Physical Distribution
Inquiries per advertisement	Consumers' orders
Profiles of respondents	Distributors' orders
Sales conversion rates per advertisement	Tracing and dispatching
Market Management	Shipment requirements
Segment analyses	Inventory requirements
Marginal account identification	Product return needs
Marketing Research	Customer service needs
"Demographic" data	Product Management
Image and attitude studies	Sales per product
Forecasting data	Questions and complaints
	Consumer profiles
	Sales Management
	Lead qualification
	Marginal account status

Source: Reprinted by permission of the publisher from Roy Vorhees and John Coppett, "Telemarketing in Distribution Channels," *Industrial Marketing Management* (December 1983), p. 106. Copyright 1983 by Elsevier Science Publishing Co. Inc.

prove channel communications are many, as illustrated by the following examples.[65]

The B.F. Goodrich Chemical Group uses a telemarketing center for order taking, customer service, and information dissemination. When customers call, a center specialist brings up the customer's file on a data terminal screen, records the order, checks inventory, and, when necessary, talks with production and shipping to schedule the shipment. Field sales personnel are also supported by being provided current inventory data and estimated arrival times. High-volume accounts are scheduled for field visits, which increase the number and quality of contacts between B.F. Goodrich and its best customers.

The 3M Company relies on a telemarketing center to assist customers with equipment trouble. After calling 3M's 800 number, the customer describes the problem to a skilled technician who has access to an on-line computer system. 3M has found that on more than 30 percent of the calls, the equipment difficulty can be solved in minutes without having to dispatch a service technician. This has improved customer service and provided a valuable service at a very reasonable cost to 3M.

Westinghouse Credit Corporation uses telemarketing to qualify leads and develop good prospects for field salespeople. Calls are made from the telemarketing center to determine interest, verify mailing information, and transmit leads to branch offices. Results are used in planning future distribution needs in terms of volumes and locations.

Videotex. *Videotex* is the term used to describe two-way interactive systems in which the user, by means of a telephone line, a two-way cable system, or some combination of diverse telecommunication technologies, can consistently access text and graphic information and a variety of transactional services from remote

[65] *Ibid.*, pp. 106–7. For other examples of the use of telemarketing, see "Making Service a Potent Marketing Tool," *Business Week* (June 11, 1984), pp. 164–70.

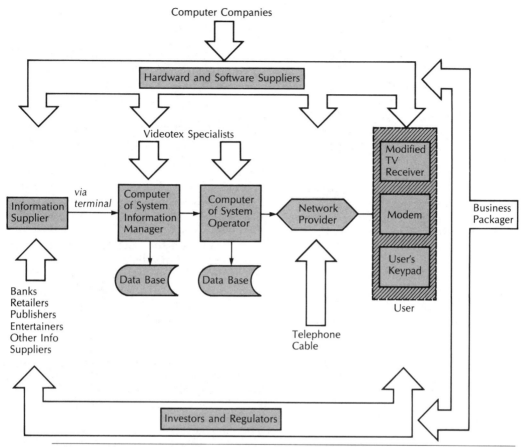

Figure 10–3 Videotex system participants

Source: From John A. Quelch and George S. Yip, "Achieving System Cooperation in Developing the Market for Consumer Videotex," in Robert D. Buzzell (ed.), *Marketing in an Electronic Age* (Boston: Harvard Business School Press, 1985), p. 307. Reprinted by permission.

computers for display on a home computer terminal or a modified television set.[66] A successful videotex operation demands the specialized skills and resources of participants from several different industries and requires different roles to be played by participants, as shown in Fig. 10–3.

The *system operator* is the central role in a videotex system.[67] He links the suppliers of information with their users while being responsible for storage of the information, terminals for updating data, hardware and software developments, interface with customers of services, marketing and distribution of prod-

---

[66] Bill McGee and Lucy Garrick, *The New Electronic Media* (San Francisco: BMC Publications, 1982), p. 3.

[67] This discussion of the participants in a videotex operation is derived from John A. Quelch and George S. Yip, "Achieving System Cooperation in Developing the Market for Consumer Videotex," in Robert D. Buzzell (ed.), *Marketing in an Electronic Age* (Boston: Harvard Business School Press, 1985), p. 306.

ucts and packaging, and control of the mix of services. For these reasons, the system operator may assume the leadership role of the channel.

The *network provider* supplies the communication vehicle linking the user with the system operator. Providers are primarily telephone companies or two-way cable systems. The information supplier provides information or markets products or services through the videotex system. The suppliers create and maintain pages of information to be stored in the system's data base. They are traditional banks, retail outlets, and publishers.

The system *information manager* performs the same functions as the system operator, yet is more specialized. Information managers concentrate on a small segment within the wide range of sources. "The presence of system information managers reduces the number of information suppliers that the system operator has to deal with, and reduces the amount of specialist expertise to be developed."[68] Therefore, a shift in functions and responsibilities will occur.

Finally, the *business packager* (or *promoter*) does not perform an operating role but rather provides the bonds for the entire system by making key business decisions. Frequently the system operator takes on the packager role, but not always. AT&T, a network provider, is an example of a business packager.

Although most roles require the participation of existing channel members, some systems require new channel members—videotex specialists. As can be surmised, the potential impact of videotex on existing distribution channel structures and communications can be profound, as demonstrated by the following examples.

> *CompuSave Corp.* is shipping nearly 300 computer kiosk catalog shopping monitors to grocery and convenience stores. The company warehouses 3,000 items, such as video-cassette recorders, stereos and cameras, and says it sells them at discounts of 25 percent to 50 percent. By the end of 1985, the Irvine, Calif. based firm plans to have 3000 Touch-n-Save models in stores.

> *Southland Corp.* began a two-month test of Touch-n-Save terminals in seven Tyler, Texas, 7-Eleven stores. If the test works out, Southland has an option to buy 6453 more terminals for its stores nationwide.

> *The Marsh Supermarkets chain* in Yorktown, Ind., installed Touch-n-Save terminals in 40 of its 74 supermarkets in 1985. The chain has a one-year exclusive contract to offer the $5000 machines in its area and signed a five-year contract, negotiating the percentage of sales the stores receive.

> *Stop and Shop* terminals also are in 35 Stop-n-Shop grocery stores near Cleveland. "We don't have a mega store. This broadens our sales base," says Charles Rini, executive vice president of Rini Supermarkets, owner of 11 stores. During a Stop-n-Shop customer test, 44 percent used the terminals the first time they saw them, and 6.6 percent made a purchase. Average transaction: $50. Average daily use per machine: 3.2 times.

> *Comp-U-Card International Inc.* is testing The Shopping Machine, a kiosk with 3000 products sold at what is billed as up to 40 percent discounts in several grocery and convenience stores. The kiosk is a smaller version of its on-line shipping consulting service, which offers access to 100,000 products via home computers and telephones. The service has 1.5 million telephone users and 29,000 home computer users. In April 1985, the company, which has no inventory but is only a vehicle for ordering, opened a store in a Lancaster, Pa., mall with four Shopping Machines and three personal computers. Company officials say they expect the store to have

[68] *Ibid.*

about $1 million in sales by the end of 1985. The store kiosk is the first step into what its proponents believe will be a Golden Age of Electronic Retailing, when consumers will be able to order goods through home computer subscriber services.

Sears formed a joint venture with IBM Corp. and CBS Inc. called Trintex to develop a home computer videotex system capable of providing electronic shopping, banking and information services. The company has participated in six tests since 1980, and is one of about 65 suppliers for CompuServe's computerized shopping program, Electronic Mall.

J.C. Penney bought a videotex system in 1983 from a Minneapolis bank and is studying the profitability of the service. The company also uses a computer touch-screen in custom-decorating departments to expand inventory offered in its Minneapolis and Monroeville, Pa., stores.

Montgomery Ward Co. offers merchandise, catalog goods and credit card information through the Chicago-based KEYFAX videotex service. The service was started in November by Keycom Electronic Publishing and is available through home computers and television hook-up terminals.

CompuServe Inc., a home computer service with 800 databases, introduced the Electronic Mall offering products from 65 merchants including Sears, Waldenbooks Co., Record World and Buick Motors. CompuServe's 200,000 subscribers can't buy a car through the Mall, but they can gain information about new models and features.[69]

Implications of EDI for Channel Management

In summary, recent technological developments in marketing channel communications, combined with improved understanding of behavioral and managerial aspects of channel communications, provide new tools for channel management. Several implications of electronic data interchange for channel management are listed below.

First, because EDI systems provide records in a form that permits ease of reconciliation and analysis, the information available to linked distributors and vendors will be more complete and accurate than previous information. The better the quality of information (defined in terms of completeness and accuracy) flowing between two parties in a bargaining situation, the more likely it is that they will come to highly satisfying (e.g., joint profit-maximizing) decisions.

Second, because EDI involves electronic data processing, sales, accounting, finance, legal, and merchandising personnel, it requires contact at various departments and levels between two (or more) organizations. The greater the redundancy of contact, the greater will be the commitment to the interorganizational relationship on the part of the parties, leading to effective and efficient modes of conflict management.

Third, computer-to-computer linkages between organizations require the development of formal rules and procedures to deal with the transmission and receipt of data. The more formalized the relationship becomes (defined in terms of specific rules and procedures), the less flexibility will be available to the parties in dealing with disputes or changes in the environment.

Fourth, EDI will lead to the amassing of more and more data available for analysis. But the trade-off is information overload. Therefore, until the parties assign to subunits the specific responsibility for data analysis, the data will not be utilized to its fullest potential. These subunits may have to be specially created.

[69] "Golden Age of Electronic Selling Seen," *USA Today,* July 5, 1985, p. 1B.

Existing subunits tend to be too myopic for the task; they may also lack the sophistication required to perform penetrating analyses and to draw meaningful inferences.

Fifth, when power is severely imbalanced between a vendor and a distributor, the more powerful party will dictate the type of EDI system and standards to be used. When power is more equally divided among the major vendors and distributors in a given industry, the industry as a whole is likely to become involved and to develop standards which will satisfy all members, even though the standards arrived at will not be optimal for any given member.

Sixth, the larger and more technologically sophisticated the company (in terms of its internal systems), the more likely it is to increase its cost advantages by developing EDI links with its suppliers or customers. Those cost advantages will be realized to the extent the company can integrate EDI and its internal systems.

Seventh, companies with EDI links are slow to recognize other significant aspects of the links beyond the routinization of mundane tasks (ordering, invoicing, shipping, receiving, etc.) when the systems have been initiated, developed, and maintained primarily by data processing personnel.

Finally, at this stage in its development, EDI can be likened to using computers for file and record-keeping purposes. The important relational effects between organizations will be felt when applications analogous to decision support systems are added to EDI systems.[70]

Channel members who effectively use these tools will likely improve their efficiency and secure a more competitive position in the marketplace. Also, the development of an effective EDI will probably result in greater loyalty and commitment of channel members to a particular channel arrangement. Furthermore, the firm that is instrumental in originating and maintaining the system may acquire more power within the channel as the other members become more dependent on the data transmitted. Hence, there is more than one incentive for firms to play an active role in formulating and maintaining a channel communications system.

SUMMARY AND CONCLUSIONS

Inadequate or inappropriate communication, or miscommunication, can lead to wasted resources and stimulate interorganizational conflict. A working information system is a prerequisite to efficient channel coordination. However, an information system will always be imperfect, because its contribution will be impeded by legal, cost, and privacy constraints. Information systems, no matter how carefully developed, are also always subject to distortion, given the perceptual bias inherent in all individuals.

Problems in channel communications generally center in structural and activity issues having to do with channel length, inventory levels, promotion, products, and prices.

The longer the channel, the more highly developed the feedback system available to each channel member must be. Also, there should be mechanisms

[70] Louis W. Stern and Patrick J. Kaufmann, "Electronic Data Interchange in Selected Consumer Goods Industries: An Interorganizational Perspective," in Buzzell (ed.), *op. cit.*, pp. 69–70.

permitting the bypassing of messages in the channel. There is also likely to be a need for the repetition of messages, given the number of links in the channel that can distort message contents.

Inventory management is a channelwide problem and demands channelwide communication. Inventory difficulties are intimately tied to problems associated with ordering, shipping, and delivery. The first step in solving these problems is the development of an effective *intra*organizational information system. Programs using high-speed electronic data processing have revolutionized management's ability to deal with problems of inventory management and control. An especially significant innovation has been the introduction of computerized point-of-sale or front-end systems. These various systems can facilitate the queuing and sequencing of *inter*organizational messages about inventory management and control as well as providing instant feedback throughout a marketing channel. They represent communication breakthroughs whereby a significant amount of noise can be reduced via specialized languages and the alteration of technology. However, the economic, social, ethical, and political issues surrounding the widespread adoption of such systems are profound and must be carefully assessed during the development of such systems.

Coordinated systems involving transportation modes and storage facilities demand appropriate queuing and sequencing of messages if communication noise attending timing problems in physical distribution is to be reduced. The development of specialized languages and the aid of computer technology have been significant for a number of companies in securing on-time delivery and adequate inventory, billing, and shipment information. The application of the concept of shared services also is likely to help reduce redundancy in physical distribution services and communication.

Adequate feedback is critical to the solution of promotion problems. Here, the sales force of channel members—or other personnel operating at the boundary of channel organizations—is in a key position to observe difficulties in promotion and to enhance communication, except, of course, where sales personnel themselves are involved in impeding the information flow. When conflicts of interest are suspected, use should be made of other conflict management strategies, such as channel diplomacy. Clearly, poor communication in promotion results in duplication of effort and dilution of impact.

Although pricing presents continual problems in channels, communication about prices is particularly cumbersome during stagflationary periods. Price lists are often inaccurate, misleading, and/or frequently out of date. However, sharing information in this area is dangerous, because the probability of being accused of conspiring to fix prices is increasing, even if conversations about pricing problems are informal and seemingly innocuous.

The channel management process is incomplete without mechanisms for auditing and assessing the performance of channel members. The development and deployment of such mechanisms assumes the availability of free-flowing and error- and distortion-free information moving through the channel communication system. Whereas this chapter examined the types of problems associated with the gathering and dissemination of channel information, the following chapter deals with the "hard" data necessary for the evaluation of the performance of channel members and channel structures, and the incorporation of this information in channel performance assessment and channel audit mechanisms.

DISCUSSION QUESTIONS

1. It has been suggested that in long channels there is a need for mechanisms permitting the bypassing of messages. Suggest three possible mechanisms that might be used for this purpose. Then discuss how conflict with a "bypassed" channel member might be avoided.

2. In what ways can the computer be used to make communication in marketing channels more efficient and effective? What effect will such data systems have on power relationships in channels? On the roles of channel members?

3. Compare and contrast the problems and opportunities of supermarkets and department stores in installing and utilizing front-end systems. What benefits will each receive from such systems? What difficulties will each face in fully utilizing them?

4. Debate the pros and cons of the adoption of UPC-oriented systems from a consumer perspective and from society's perspective.

5. It has been argued that the major manufacturers of data-processing equipment have embarked on different competitive strategies to further differentiate themselves, create "safe" market niches, lessen the chances for interorganizational hook-ups, and generally confuse users. IBM has even been accused of making word processing so complex that users think they need IBM to help them. Suggest some conflict management strategies that might be used by channel members to alleviate this situation.

6. What is the concept of *shared services*? In what ways might it be applied to transportation and storage problems other than those mentioned in the text? What is the relationship between shared services and efficient intrachannel communications?

7. To deal with false warranty claims from dealers, General Motors now includes in its contract with its dealers provisions requiring them to keep two years of records available for inspection by GM instead of one and permitting GM to provide copies to courts or governmental agencies whenever it decides the information is pertinent. Some dealers have complained that their business privacy is thus being eroded. One dealer in the New York area observed that with these provisions GM has granted itself wider power to investigate its dealers, or to help others investigate them. What problems in communications within the channel is this situation evidence of? What solutions are there to these problems? Do the new contract provisions seem equitable?

8. One author has observed that repositioning, scheduling/synchronization, simplification, access, and scale economies are the most important factors in the emergence and growth of vertical marketing systems. Explain what you believe is meant by each term, using examples. Then explain what effect information systems have had on each factor.

9. A wholesaler conducts a distribution cost study to determine the smallest order for breaking even. After finding this size, should the wholesaler refuse to accept orders below this size? What issues and alternatives should be considered?

CHAPTER ELEVEN

Assessing the Performance of Channel Institutions and Structures

The variety of institutions that form the primary components of channels and the factors that influence the way in which they link up in channel structures have been examined in previous chapters. But the channel management process is not complete without assessment of the performance of the institutions and the channel structures in which they have been housed.

Performance is a multidimensional concept. As shown in Fig. 11–1, the performance of marketing channels and institutions thereof can be assessed on a number of dimensions, including effectiveness, equity, and efficiency. Performance assessment can be made from both a macro, or societal, perspective and a micro, or business, perspective. Often the perspectives overlap, and the macro view provides insights into operational features of individual enterprises. This chapter, while noting the track record of some key channel members (e.g, wholesalers and retailers), will extend its coverage to a number of managerial and channel audit mechanisms that can be used in evaluating channel performance.

CHANNEL SYSTEM EFFECTIVENESS

As indicated in earlier chapters, the marketing flows (physical possession, ownership, promotion, negotiation, financing, risking, ordering, and payment) are organized by institutions and agencies making up commercial channels of distribution in such a way as to provide goods and services in desired quantities (lot size) when needed (delivery time). These goods and services are made available at a number of different locations (market decentralization), at which they are

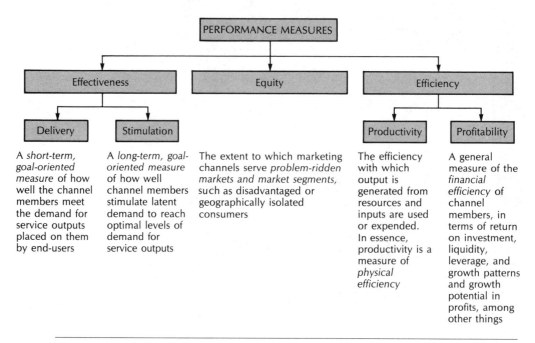

Figure 11–1 Performance measures in marketing channels

displayed and generally combined with complementary and substitutable items (assortment breadth) in accordance with marketplace demand. Therefore, the *output* of a given commercial channel of distribution may be conceptualized as lot size, delivery time, market decentralization, and assortment breadth.[1] Household consumers and industrial and business users are key actors in distribution channels because they participate directly in the marketing flows. However, the lower their degree of participation in the flows, the more work must be done by commercial channel members in providing the output, and thus the higher will be the final price of goods and services. If consumers were willing to increase the amount of search and selection time they devote to purchasing and thus absorb part of the marketing task, prices could probably be reduced.

Unfortunately, there are no quantitative measures that provide an insight into aggregate performance in terms of system output, beyond global estimates of the dollar and physical amounts of goods and services passing through the distribution system.[2] Qualitatively, though, it is possible to point to a number of historical changes.

[1] This model and discussion of system output draw heavily from Louis P. Bucklin, "Marketing Channels and Structures: A Macro View," in Boris W. Becker and Helmut Becker (eds.), *American Marketing Association Combined Conference Proceedings* (Chicago: American Marketing Association, 1973), pp. 32–35. Also see Dale D. Achabal, John M. Heinekey, and Shelby H. McIntyre, "Issues and Perspectives on Retail Productivity," *Journal of Retailing*, Vol. 60, No. 3 (Fall 1984), pp. 107–27; and Charles S. Goodman, "Comment: On Output Measures of Retail Performance," *Journal of Retailing*, Vol. 61, No. 3 (Fall 1985), pp. 77–82.

[2] See the chapters on retailing and wholesaling in this text for relevant statistics on the volume of goods and services passing through the distribution system.

First, there has been a significant increase in the size of the average retail transaction over time.[3] Consumers are therefore buying in larger lots, requiring less marketing flow participation and output from commercial channel systems in this respect. The increase in transaction size permits retailers to buy in larger lots, which in turn reduces the need for wholesaler services. In turn, these developments permit lower distributive costs since commercial channel service outputs are reduced, and thus lower prices to consumers are possible. Similarly, the development of the automobile and improved road networks have, as Bucklin observes, reduced the need for highly decentralized retail systems for *convenience* goods.[4] Offsetting this, however, has been the increase in decentralization for *shopping* items accompanying the emergence of the planned regional shopping center.

Second, there has been no obvious reduction in the willingness of either ultimate household consumers or industrial and business users to accept longer delivery times for the products they desire to buy. Shortages of raw materials may alter this somewhat; in the future, users may have to wait longer to be assured of appropriate supplies.[5] The willingness of consumers to postpone and ration purchases of products in short supply, or to accept longer delivery times, will be rewarded not by lower prices but merely by the ability to secure and consume the scarce commodities.

On the other hand, rising affluence has increased the range of products household consumers would like to buy at a single stop, raising the requirement for broader store assortments and increased speculative inventories within channel systems. Commercial channel output has had to rise here; the increase in store size, for example, has been caused by the expanding number of items being stocked.[6] There are, however, serious problems associated with the increase in available assortments to desirable levels of consumer choice. If one considers number of brands to be an element of assortment, then it is possible that there is "overchoice" in the marketplace. In a study of this problem, Settle and Golden surveyed household consumers on their choice perceptions; ideal and perceived assortment size were compared to the actual choices available at the retail level.[7] It was found that actual choices were greater than perceived and ideal choices.

This overabundance of brands can lead to inefficiencies in the use of resources and higher prices to consumers. Furthermore, consumers are becoming increasingly confused as to which brands and package sizes of various products represent the best buys from a purely economical perspective. This confusion was demonstrated by Friedman in an experiment on consumer choice in which 33 young married women were asked to select the most economical (largest quantity for the price) package for 20 different categories of typically purchased products on sale at a selected supermarket.[8] Among other findings, Friedman

[3] David Schwartzman, *The Decline of Service in Retail Trade* (Pullman, Wash.: Bureau of Economic and Business Research, Washington State University, 1971).

[4] Bucklin, *op. cit.,* p. 33.

[5] See Philip Kotler, "Marketing during Periods of Shortage," *Journal of Marketing*, Vol. 38 (July 1974), pp. 20–29.

[6] Bucklin, *op. cit.,* p. 33.

[7] R. B. Settle and L. L. Golden, "Consumer Perceptions: Overchoice in the Marketplace," in Scott Ward and Peter Wright (eds.), *4th Annual Conference Proceedings* (Association for Consumer Research, 1973), pp. 29–37.

[8] Monroe Peter Friedman, "Consumer Confusion in the Selection of Supermarket Products," *Journal of Applied Psychology*, Vol. 50 (December 1966), pp. 529–34.

reported that the sampled consumers were, on the average, unable to select the most economical package 43 percent of the time. Thus, even though assortment breadth is generally a desirable output of commercial channel operations,[9] there may be threshholds above which more choice becomes dysfunctional or wasteful.

The broader assortments required on the retail level have, to a significant extent, been responsible for the continued growth and survival of wholesalers and have offset, at least partially, the negative effect on the use of wholesalers caused by the increase in retail transaction size. Specialized wholesalers, such as rack merchandisers, who carry broad assortments of limited lines, have, as pointed out in Chapter 3, been especially successful in supplying food stores with nontraditional items (e.g., phonograph records, magazines, and health and beauty aids).[10] In the industrial goods sector, there has also been an increase in demand for wholesaler services, especially because of the growth in sales of items for which wholesaler support has long been relied upon by suppliers and customers, such as machinery, equipment, and supplies. Offsetting this somewhat has been the tendency to move away from "double wholesaling" in the industrial sector as more and more suppliers find themselves capable of absorbing promotional flows for their products. The latter change has had the greatest negative impact on agent middlemen.[11]

If hard evidence is scant for assessing commercial channel output (viewed in terms of lot size, waiting or delivery time, market decentralization, and product assortment), it is virtually nonexistent for assessing how well the heterogeneous production capacity of an industry is fitted by the sorting processes to the heterogeneity of consumer tastes and incomes.[12] There have, however, been some data gathered on this subject in the case of disadvantaged consumers.

EQUITY IN SERVING VARIOUS MARKETS

Given the profusion of wholesaling and retailing institutions in the United States, it is difficult to imagine pockets of the population that are not adequately served by the distributive trades, at least in terms of the availability of goods and services at fairly reasonable prices. Yet it has been carefully documented by a number of scholars that the poor in the United States, especially those living in ghetto areas of major cities and in rural communities, are disadvantaged by the distributive system as well as by other aspects of our economy and society.[13]

[9] For example, Buzzell feels that "most businessmen *and* most academicians would agree that the performance of an industry or company is higher, other things being equal, to the degree that it provides *choice* to customers and to the degree that it manifests *flexibility* in altering its offerings response to changes in demand." Robert D. Buzzell, "Marketing and Economic Performance: Meaning and Measurement," in Fred C. Allvine (ed.), *Public Policy and Marketing Practices* (Chicago: American Marketing Association, 1973), pp. 154–55.

[10] The increase in commercial channel output of such items comes at a cost to the consumer, however, in the form of higher prices.

[11] Bucklin, *op. cit.,* pp. 33–34.

[12] A channel audit, as specified in Chapter 1, might provide a means for criticizing channel performance along these output dimensions. The result should produce insights for social as well as business policy.

[13] See, for example, David Caplovitz, *The Poor Pay More* (New York: Free Press, 1963); Louise G. Richards, "Consumer Practices of the Poor," in Lola M. Irelan (ed.), *Low-Income Life Styles* (Washington, D.C.: U.S. Department of Health, Education, and Welfare, Welfare Administration, Publication No. 14), pp. 67–86; Frederick D. Sturdivant and Walter T. Wilhelm, "Poverty, Minorities, and

While there is some evidence of outright discrimination against minority groups by merchants in their pricing and credit practices,[14] the primary reasons for the absence of broad assortments of reasonably priced merchandise and services seem to be related more to the structure of trade in these areas than to racial or socioeconomic bias. For example, it has been shown that food chain prices do not vary significantly between ghetto and suburban locations within a given trading area, although there is still some controversy as to whether quality differs among outlets of a given chain organization.[15] Rather, it is the absence of food chain and major department store operations in the ghetto and rural areas that prohibits the residents of these areas from obtaining the benefits available to their suburban counterparts. The mobility of the poor is limited, so they must rely on the stores within their communities. While these stores have been known to charge high prices and to extend credit at usurious rates, their profitability is very low, which indicates that their costs of doing business are extremely high.[16] A summary of barriers to successful ghetto distribution cited by retailers is presented in Exhibit 11–1.

A partial explanation of this inequity in distribution is the fact that ghetto retailers in particular are offering "services" of some importance to their constituents, most of whom, according to Goodman, are aware of the high prices being paid. Among these services are high-risk credit, small-lot transactions, convenient purchasing, and a persuasive (often deceptive) rationale to buy goods poor consumers would like to have but cannot really afford.[17] Exhibit 11–2 summarizes factors identified as important in neighborhood store patronage by ghetto residents.

From a competitive perspective, the structure of retailing in ghettos is highly atomistic. There are many small stores offering similar merchandise. Barriers to entry, as Sturdivant points out, are also quite low.[18] Therefore, on the basis of economic theory,[19] one would predict that from a macro perspective,

---

Consumer Exploitation," *Social Science Quarterly*, Vol. 49 (December 1968), pp. 643–50; and Frederick D. Sturdivant (ed.), *The Ghetto Marketplace* (New York: Free Press, 1969).

[14] See Sturdivant and Wilhelm, *op. cit.*

[15] Donald E. Sexton, Jr., "Do Blacks Pay More?" *Journal of Marketing Research*, Vol. 8 (November 1971), pp. 420–26; Charles S. Goodman, "Do the Poor Pay More?" *Journal of Marketing*, Vol. 32 (January 1968), pp. 18–24; Donald F. Dixon and Daniel J. McLaughlin, Jr., "Low-Income Consumers and the Issue of Exploitation: A Study of Chain Supermarkets," *Social Science Quarterly*, Vol. 51 (September 1970), pp. 320–28; and Louis W. Stern and William S. Sargent, "Comparative Prices and Pedagogy: Towards Relevance in Marketing Education," *Journal of Business Research*, Vol. 2 (October 1974), pp. 435–46.

[16] *Economic Report on Installment Credit and Retail Sales Practices of District of Columbia Retailers* (Washington, D.C.: Federal Trade Commission, 1968), p. 18; and Frederick C. Klein, "Black Businessmen Running Ghetto Store Can Be a Survival Test," *Wall Street Journal*, January 31, 1977, pp. 1, 13.

[17] Charles S. Goodman, "Whither the Marketing System in Low-Income Areas," *Wharton Quarterly* (Spring 1970).

[18] Frederick D. Sturdivant, "Distribution in American Society: Some Questions of Efficiency and Relevance," in Louis P. Bucklin (ed.), *Vertical Marketing Systems* (Glenview, Ill.: Scott, Foresman and Co., 1970), pp. 102–3.

[19] See the arguments presented by Joe S. Bain, *Industrial Organization*, 2nd ed. (New York: John Wiley & Sons, 1968); and Richard Caves, *American Industry: Structure, Conduct, and Performance*, 2nd ed. (Englewood Cliffs, N.J.: Prentice-Hall, 1967). These positions have been summarized in Louis W. Stern and John R. Grabner, Jr., *Competition in the Marketplace* (Glenview, Ill.: Scott, Foresman and Co., 1970). Also see John F. Cady, "Competition and Economic Dualism," in Alan R. Andersen, *Marketing: Research Challenges* (Chicago: American Marketing Association, 1977), pp. 56–71.

performance would be higher in ghetto areas than in the suburbs, where there are generally fewer outlets of larger size. The fact that marketing practices and performance are generally unbearably bad in the ghetto calls into question the assumptions of industrial organization economists about the benefits that derive from atomistic competition.[20] In fact, this questioning is supported by the findings of scholars who have studied less highly developed economies where similar structural conditions appear to hold. For example, in their critique of distributive systems for eggs, milk, and produce in sections of South America, Riley, Harrison, Slater, and colleagues concluded that

> excessive atomistic competition hampers productivity improvements by stifling technological innovations and inhibits the agricultural and marketing development process by fostering market uncertainty, high transaction costs and excessive market wastes and by preventing the effective transmission of incentives to firms in the production-marketing system.[21]

While the reluctance of food chains, department stores, and regional shopping centers, among others, to enter the ghetto and poor rural areas can no

---

[20] See Stern and Grabner, *op. cit.*, pp. 36–40, for a summary of the assumed benefits. Bucklin and Carman have, implicitly at least, raised similar questions regarding the performance of the present "atomistic" health care delivery system in the United States. See Louis P. Bucklin and James M. Carman, "Vertical Market Structure Theory and the Health Care Delivery System," in Jagdish N. Sheth and Peter L. Wright (eds.), *Marketing Analysis for Societal Problems* (Urbana-Champaign, Ill.: University of Illinois, Bureau of Economic and Business Research, 1974), pp. 7–39; and Chapter 13 of this book.

[21] Harold Riley, Kelly Harrison, Charles C. Slater, et al., *Market Coordination in the Development of the Cauca Valley Region—Colombia* (East Lansing, Mich.: Michigan State University, Latin American Studies Center, 1970), p. 189.

doubt be traced to high occupancy costs, crime rates, and/or lack of discretionary income to support new, large-scale ventures, the fact remains that these areas are truly disadvantaged relative to other shopping areas and that as long as they remain so there will exist a high degree of inequity in the distributive system.[22] Only the institutionalization of a significant amount of coordination among government agencies, chain organizations, wholesalers, manufacturers, and various facilitating agencies (such as insurance companies) will bring about needed change in this situation. Many solutions on the supply side have been suggested, such as tax incentives for chain organizations entering the ghetto and investment credits,[23] but few have been enacted on a sufficiently large scale to have any major impact. On the demand side, it will obviously be necessary to elevate the incomes and increase the mobility of ghetto and rural residents so that they can have a modicum of bargaining power in their dealings with merchants in their communities.

CHANNEL SYSTEM EFFICIENCY

Productivity

Productivity is a measure of efficiency in using inputs (e.g., labor and capital) to generate outputs (e.g., sales volume, gross margins, and value added). Ideally, productivity is a measure of physical efficiency; therefore, productivity

[22] Shopping areas adjacent to many university campuses may be subject to many of the problems found in ghetto communities. See, for example, Stern and Sargent, *op. cit.*

[23] See Frederick D. Sturdivant, "Better Deal for Ghetto Shoppers," *Harvard Business Review,* Vol. 46 (March-April 1968), pp. 130–39.

Table 11–1   Literature on cross-sectional productivity

Reference	Year of Data	Geographical Scope (number of observations)	Retail Level of Analysis	Productivity Measure[a]	Independent Variables[b]	Observed Sign
Hall, Knapp, & Winsten 1961	1948	U.S.A.: States & District of Columbia (49)	Food stores, Clothing stores	S/L	Y; G (20 yr.); φ; R²	**Food** / **Clothing**: Y +/+; G +/+; φ 0/−; R² .76/.48
George 1966	1961	UK: Towns (160)	Aggregate retailing & 7 industry groups	S/E	Y; S/N; %MC; T; R²	**All Retailing** / **Groceries**: Y +/+; S/N +/+; %MC n.r./+; T +/+; R² .82/.76
Schwartzman 1971	1958	U.S.A.: SMSAs (188)	Eight industry groups	S/L	Y; W; S/N; S/H; S; (S/H)-Gas; R²	**Groceries** / **Groceries**: Y −/−; W +/+; S/N +/+; S/H −/+; S −/−; (S/H)-Gas +/+; R² .78/.78
Bucklin 1978a	1963, 1967, 1964, 1968	USA: States (96) Japan: Prefectures (84) (data pooled for the 2 census yrs.)	Aggregate retailing	S/E	Y; G(4 yr.); N/POP; φ; W; %S-Dept.; Time; R²	**USA** / **Japan**: Y 0/+; G 0/0; N/POP −/−; φ 0/0; W +/+; %S-Dept. −/+; Time +/+; R² .63/.96

[a] S/L = sales per employee
S/E = sales per FTE employee

[b] Y = per capita income
G = growth rate
φ = population density
S/N = sales per store
%MC = % of sales in multiples & co-ops
T = labor market tightness
W = annual wage rate in retail industry

R² = coefficient of determination
S/H = sales per household
S = sales in geographical area
(S/H)-Gas = gasoline expenditures per household
N/POP = number of stores per capita
%S-Dept = % of sales by department stores
Time = 0 in first year, 1 in last year
n.r. = not reported

Source: Charles A. Ingene, "Labor Productivity in Retailing," *Journal of Marketing*, Vol. 46 (Fall 1982), p. 79. Reprinted from *Journal of Marketing*, published by The American Marketing Association.

Table 11—2 Rates of growth of output per hour for all persons

Sector	Average Annual Rate of Growth		Compounded Annual Rate of Change 1980–84			
	1973–79	1979–84	1980–81	1981–82	1982–83	1983–84
Business	0.8	1.0	1.9	0.2	2.7	3.2
Farm	3.2	3.7	16.4	−0.1	−17.5	17.9
Mining	−5.1	0.4	−6.5	−0.5	14.6	0.5
Manufacturing	1.5	2.7	3.1	2.1	4.3	3.6
Wholesaling	0.5	2.8	3.0	1.2	5.2	7.8
Retailing	1.0	1.8	1.5	−0.1	4.7	3.6

Source: "Continued Increases in Industry Productivity in 1984 Reported by BLS," *Bureau of Labor Statistics News* (Washington, D.C.: November 12, 1985), pp. 1–4; Bureau of Labor Statistics special computer runs provided upon authors' request, March 1986.

analysts attempt to remove the impact of price changes on the figures used (e.g., sales volume) by deflating them to generate real outputs. Developing an understanding of productivity in the distributive trades requires scrutiny of the measures of productivity used and an analysis of correlates of productivity in wholesaling and retailing.

In terms of measures of output, productivity analysts rely heavily upon sales volume data. While gross margin or value added would be closer to an ideal measure of output, wide differences exist in average gross margin percentages in the different sectors in wholesaling and retailing. Such differences lead to distortion in results. Additionally, gross margin and value added data are not as available or as easily obtainable as sales volume data.

In terms of measures of input, productivity analysts rely heavily on labor man-hours because the distributive trades are labor-intensive. As a matter of fact, persons engaged in trade represent 22 percent of the labor force in the U.S.[24] Therefore, productivity in the distributive trades is usually measured in terms of sales per man-hour or sales per employee, as shown in Table 11–1, which summarizes the measures used in a number of studies. Most productivity figures are presented as average annual percentage rates of change to allow comparisons between components under study over a period of years. Usually, productivity figures in the distributive trades are compared with those in other sectors in the economy, particularly manufacturing, as shown in Table 11–2.

Productivity increases experienced in the period 1979–84 contrast sharply with those in earlier periods, when the distribution trades trailed other sectors of the economy. During the period 1979–84, the 2.8 percent average increase in wholesaling productivity exceeded growth rates in all sectors of the economy other than farming. Although retailing did not fare as well—a mere 1.8 percent average increase, the compounded annual rates of growth (1980–84) demonstrate that the retailing sector has picked up tremendously in the latter years of the period. The 4.7 percent increase in 1982–83 and the 3.6 percent increase in 1983–84 exceed productivity growth in manufacturing and in the business sector.

[24] Philip Van Ness, *Productivity in Wholesale Distribution* (Washington, D.C.: Distribution Research and Education Foundation, 1980), p. 1.

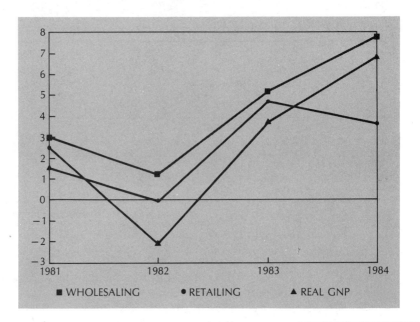

Figure 11–2 Productivity in distribution (relative to GNP growth, 1981–84)

Note: Wholesaling/retailing productivity measured by average annual rates of growth of output per hour for all persons (based on compounded annual rates of change).
Source: "Continued Increases in Industry Productivity in 1984 Reported by BLS," *Bureau of Labor Statistics News* (Washington, D.C.: November 12, 1985), pp. 1–4; Bureau of Labor Statistics special computer runs provided upon authors' request, March 1986.

Also, in the 1980s productivity performance in the distributive trades closely tracked the key general economic indicator, the GNP, as shown in Fig. 11–2. For example, during the 1981–82 recession there were noticeable declines in productivity growth. When the recovery began in 1983, productivity turned around. Most impressive are the 1983–84 increases of 7.8 percent in wholesaling productivity and 3.6 percent in retailing productivity. Some analysts point out that the farm sector's 17.9 percent productivity jump in 1983–84 dwarfs wholesale and retail increases, but such a comparison does not dampen the spirit of distributive trade enthusiasts, for several reasons.

First, wholesaling and retailing, as mentioned, are labor-intensive industries. Man-hours increased in these sectors at a substantially faster rate than in other sectors.[25] Second, there are indications that to improve productivity the distributive trades are more dependent than other sectors upon growth in sales volume. This issue is critical because of the possibility of persistent low growth in constant dollar retail sales.[26] Low growth in sales rates, accompanied by fast rates of increase in man-hours, guarantees lower gains in productivity. Finally, within the agricultural and manufacturing sectors of the U.S. economy, farmers, pro-

[25] *Ibid.,* p. 5
[26] Louis P. Bucklin, "Growth and Productivity Changes in Retailing," a paper presented to the Theory in Retailing Seminar, American Marketing Association and the Institute for Retail Management, New York University, 1980, p. 1.

Table 11–3   Relative productivity performance of five retail types

	Average Annual Rates of Change (Percent)[a]		
	1979–84	1982–83	1983–84
Franchise new car dealers	2.2 [b]	9.0[b]	−0.1 [b]
Apparel and accessory stores	4.9	5.5	6.0
Drug and proprietary stores	1.1	1.7	1.8
Hotels, motels, and tourist courts	−0.3	1.1	7.7
Retail food stores	−0.5	1.8	−1.0

[a] Average annual rates of change, based on linear least squares trends of the logarithms of an index of output per hour of all persons.
[b] 1977 = 100 (base year).

Source: Bureau of Labor Statistics News (Washington, D.C.: November 1985); Bureau of Labor Statistics special computer runs provided upon authors' request, March 1986.

cessors, and industrial firms historically have turned to innovative technology, employing capital inputs more widely. Innovations related to checkout automation, information processing, materials handling, warehouse modernization, packaging, and larger and more productive facilities were adopted in the distributive trades on a large scale only in the 1970s.

Despite the deployment of computer technology in the distributive trades for over a decade, the cost reduction potential of these technologies has only now been realized. This positive impact has been long in coming. At first, it was necessary to overcome customer, labor, and traditional industry resistance to deployment of these technologies.[27] Once introduced, it was necessary for the industry to gain both a facility with the technology and experience in its operations. Now, the benefits have started to outweigh the initial cost of computerization of retail and wholesale operations. Further productivity improvements are anticipated because of the other improvements in management systems introduced in the 1980s, including increased use of telemarketing, more effective use of the sales force, and market development strategies involving extending existing product lines into new markets. Also, an increasing number of wholesaling and retailing firms are moving away from simple data-processing applications of computer technologies to more sophisticated managerial applications involving computerized materials handling and inventory control systems, warehouse space management, delivery routing and scheduling, vehicle load planning, as well as other applications discussed in Chapters 4 and 9.[28]

To gain an accurate profile of productivity trends in the distributive trades, it is necessary to examine performance at the subsector level—that is, at the level of wholesale industry groups and retail institutional types. The complexity of the factors determining productivity leads to productivity growth variations among industry groups and institutional types. For example, productivity growth varied considerably among the retail institutional types presented in Table 11–3. The

[27] Louis P. Bucklin, "Technological Change and Store Operations: The Supermarket Case," *Journal of Retailing* (Spring 1980), p. 13.

[28] The Arthur Anderson study cited in Chapter 3 presents a more detailed analysis of the factors affecting productivity in wholesaling. Interested readers are referred to Arthur Anderson and Company, *Future Trends in Wholesale Distribution: A Time of Opportunity* (Washington, D.C.: Distribution Research and Education Foundation, 1982).

EXHIBIT 11–3   Productivity in apparel stores

Productivity in apparel stores has experienced steady growth between 1979 and 1983. . . . This growth has been influenced by broad trends in general retailing and by changes in industry structure, locational shifts, and technological improvements.

At the industry structure level, there has been a rapid growth in the number and proportion of chain stores. These chains are less labor intensive and provide less personal service than independents. In addition, the industry is experiencing a period of heightened competition as off-price stores, discounters and retail factory outlets enter the market. This virulent competition has led to a shakeout where marginal stores have been forced out of business.

Increased use of computers for store operations has also led to productivity improvements. There is widespread use of point-of-sale technology in the apparel store industry. Although usage varies greatly throughout the industry, the benefits which range from inventory control improvements to speedier credit verification have led to increased productivity. Automated accounts receivable systems have also been introduced. Output per man-hour has improved because computerization has reduced employee hours consumed in the administration of credit and collection procedures. Equally effective are electronic marking and security surveillance systems which have reduced shoplifting and man-hours engulfed in security and surveillance administration and implementation.

Source: Based on U.S. Bureau of Labor Statistics, "Productivity in Apparel Stores," *Monthly Labor Review* (October 1984), pp. 37–42.

---

productivity analysis of apparel retail stores presented in Exhibit 11–3 illustrates the diversity of factors leading to changes in productivity and variations in these changes among retail institutional types.

While productivity studies of the subsectors vary in methodology and in the number and nature of the factors that determine productivity in different industries and institutional types, all analysis points out clearly that productivity is a complex phenomenon resulting from the interaction of a number of variables. For example, a study conducted by Takeuchi reveals that the state of technology, scale of operation, capacity utilization, integration of processing facilities, level of consumer service, product assortment, quality of management, and quality of labor are the critical variables influencing productivity in the supermarket industry.[29]

Some researchers indicate that unless total factor productivity—the impact of labor, capital, and land—is considered, one cannot reach sound conclusions about productivity.[30] This can be particularly true as accelerated adoption of new technology results in massive infusions of capital. Others warn that in many wholesale industries and in retailing, leasing of buildings, vehicles, fixtures, and point-of-sale terminals is commonplace. Therefore, until reliable data on leased property and equipment can be developed and analyzed, it will be difficult to assess the true impact of fixed assets on productivity in the distribution sector of

[29] Hirotaka Takeuchi, "Productivity Analysis as a Resource Management Tool in the Retail Trade," Ph.D. dissertation, University of California, Berkeley, 1977.

[30] See, for example, Van Ness, *op. cit.*, pp. 15–16.

the economy. In another vein, some researchers have documented that productivity depends not only on the performance of distributive institutions but also on the structure of the markets in which they compete.[31] In its turn, structure—for example, in department store retailing—is determined by income per capita, automobile ownership, scale of operation, size of transactions, average wages, density of population, and growth or decline of population in the markets studied.[32] A study by Hise, Gable, Kelley, and McDonald reached similar conclusions.[33] Ingene cautions that

> analysis of retail productivity trends historically have focused on national or statewide statistics. While this approach has been imposed by the available data, it has two crucial limitations. First, retailing is a local activity. Analysis of large data can conceal important differences between local areas. Second, attempts to improve retail productivity must operate within the constraints of the local nature of competition. Thus, it is important to know the determinants of productivity in local areas.[34]

The host of structural and local factors examined in Ingene's study are summarized in Exhibit 11–4.

Setting aside the complexity of productivity analysis and the lack of systematic data on value added and gross margins as alternative measures of output, landmark studies of distribution cost (a surrogate variable for inputs) and value added (a measure of output) do exist. From a distribution cost standpoint, wholesale and retail institutions account for only a portion of total marketing charges incurred in bringing a product from its origin to ultimate consumption. Although their share is the dominant one, accounting for perhaps as much as 75 percent of the total,[35] other institutions (manufacturers, facilitating agencies, and consumers themselves) also contribute significantly to total marketing expenditures.

From a macro perspective, it is obvious to even the most casual onlooker that the cost of distribution in industrialized societies is relatively high. In such societies, progressions in economic development and consumer affluence are accompanied by a shift toward the sales of luxury goods, some of which carry extremely heavy marketing costs. The evolution of industrial goods markets also adds new marketing costs to the system, concomitant with economic growth.[36]

Suspicions about the relatively high cost of distribution have been confirmed by the statistics developed in a number of studies on the subject. For

[31] Louis P. Bucklin, "Structure, Conduct, and Productivity in Distribution," and Johan Arndt, "Exploring Relationships between Market Structure and Performance in Retailing," in Hans B. Thorelli (ed.), *Strategy Plus Structure Equals Performance* (Bloomington, Ind.: Indiana University Press, 1977), pp. 219–46.

[32] Hirotaka Takeuchi and Louis P. Bucklin, "Productivity in Retailing: Retail Structure and Public Policy," *Journal of Retailing*, Vol. 53, No. 1 (Spring 1977), pp. 35–46.

[33] Richard Hise, Myron Gable, J. Patrick Kelley, and James B. McDonald, "Factors Affecting the Performance of Individual Chain Units: An Empirical Analysis," *Journal of Retailing*, Vol. 59, No. 2 (Summer 1983), pp. 22–39.

[34] Charles Ingene, "Labor Productivity in Retailing," *Journal of Marketing*, Vol. 46 (Fall 1982), p. 88.

[35] Louis P. Bucklin, *Competition and Evolution in the Distributive Trades* (Englewood Cliffs, N.J.: Prentice-Hall, 1972), p. 296.

[36] For a thorough analysis of the productivity and performance of retailing and wholesaling in the United Kingdom, see T. S. Ward, *The Distribution of Consumer Goods: Structure and Performance* (London: Cambridge University Press, 1973).

EXHIBIT 11–4   Structural and local factors
               influencing labor productivity
               in retailing

- Capital intensity

  An increase in capital intensity in retailing in a geographical market, when store size and retail space saturation are held fixed, will increase labor productivity.

- Average store size

  As average store size in a geographic market increases, when the capital to labor ratio and retail space saturation are held fixed, labor productivity declines.

- Retail space saturation

  As retail space saturation increases, when the capital to labor ratio and store size are held fixed, labor productivity declines.

- Retail wage rate

  The higher the retail wage rate in a geographical market, the higher will be the level of labor productivity.

- Retail competition

  As the number of "mom and pop" stores per household rise in a geographic area, the productivity of labor in regular grocery stores will rise.

- Average household income

  As average household income in a community rises, labor productivity in retailing will increase.

- Average household size

  The larger the average household size in a geographical area, the higher will be labor productivity.

- Consumer mobility

  As mobility increases due to greater availability of private transportation, labor productivity in retailing will rise. As mobility decreases due to more congestion in a geographical area, labor productivity in retailing will decline.

Source: Based on Charles Ingene, "Labor Productivity in Retailing," *Journal of Marketing,* Vol. 46 (Fall 1982), pp. 75–90. Reprinted from *Journal of Marketing,* published by The American Marketing Association.

example, in a thorough investigation in the 1950s, Harold Barger noted that the combined gross margins of retailers and wholesalers were 37.4 percent.[37] Wholesalers' gross margins were 7.7 percent, retailers' 29.7 percent.[38] More recent studies on distributive costs have focused on value added rather than gross margins. The former excludes from gross margins the costs middlemen pay for services rendered by institutions in other sectors of the economy, such as their expenditures for fuel, electric energy, and transportation. Thus, what remains in the distributive sector are the middleman's own costs, the charges on his capital, his expenditure on labor, and his profits. Value added may constitute as much as 70 to 85 percent of the distributive gross margin.[39]

From a theoretical perspective, value added supposedly indicates the unique contribution of middlemen, yielded by their managerial skills in combining labor, capital, and land in various ways, to the final dollar value of products

[37] Harold Barger, *Distribution's Place in the American Economy since 1869* (Princeton, N.J.: Princeton University Press, 1955), p. 60. Gross margin is always stated in terms of sales; the combined figure for retailers and wholesalers as a proportion of the cost of goods sold would run over 50 percent.

[38] Stanley C. Hollander has provided some appropriate warnings about interpreting cost figures such as these, in "Measuring the Cost and Value of Marketing," in William G. Moller, Jr., and David L. Wilemon (eds.), *Marketing Channels: A Systems Viewpoint* (Homewood, Ill.: Richard D. Irwin, 1971), pp. 373–83.

[39] Bucklin, *Competition and Evolution,* p. 298.

Table 11—4 Value added in marketing of commodities in six sectors
of the economy, 1948, 1958, 1963, and 1967

Sector	Millions of Dollars 1948	%	Millions of Dollars 1958	%	Millions of Dollars 1963	%	Millions of Dollars 1967	%
Transportation	$11,560	19.7	$16,070	16.1	$ 17,582	14.3	$ 23,110	14.1
Retailing	26,440	45.1	44,419	44.5	55,708	45.3	75,214	46.0
Wholesaling	12,949	22.1	24,587	24.7	32,740	26.6	43,051	26.3
Manufacturing	6,934	11.8	13,709	13.7	15,227	12.4	20,103	12.3
Minerals	270	0.5	397	0.4	412	0.3	477	0.3
Advertising	439	0.7	685	0.7	1,185	1.0	1,594	1.0
Total	58,592	100.0	99,867	100.0	122,854	100.0	163,549	100.0

Source: Louis P. Bucklin, "A Synthetic Index of Marketing Productivity," a paper presented to the 58th International Marketing Conference of the American Marketing Association, Chicago, 1975, p. 7.

or services.[40] For the 1964–65 period, the value added by wholesalers and retailers combined was approximately 23 percent; for the retail sector alone it was about 14½ percent, and for wholesaling it was 8½ percent.[41] Since 1949, the percentages have been quite stable.

In a highly innovative study, Bucklin computed the value added in the performance of marketing activities in six sectors of the U.S. economy—transportation, retailing, wholesaling, manufacturing, minerals, and advertising.[42] Although his findings are tentative and subject to error because of the way in which the data were derived, they provide some interesting comparisons, as shown in Table 11–4. Thus, in 1967, the value added in the marketing of commodities by the six sectors totaled $163.5 billion. Approximately 72 percent of the total was contributed by retailing and wholesaling, and another 14 percent by the logistical institutions composing the transportation sector. The large share accumulated by the former two sectors indicates that any advances in their performance and productivity will have a marked effect on performance and productivity in marketing generally.[43]

[40] The concept of value added is truly meaningful only if there is sufficient competition in a market. Otherwise, prices in that market include monopoly or oligopoly profits that are of doubtful "value" to consumers. This weakness in the concept prompted Sturdivant to observe that "the emergence of the value added concept doubtless retarded objective and critical analysis of socially significant questions related to distribution. With . . . a prevailing attitude that marketing costs must equal value or else goods and services would not be purchased, it is little wonder that consumer behavior emerged as the dominant area of interest for marketing scholars." Sturdivant, "Distribution in American Society," p. 98.

[41] Bucklin, *Competition and Evolution*, p. 300. Although Bucklin called his computations *distributive trade-cost ratios*, they are very similar to value-added computations. Furthermore, Bucklin's findings are similar to those presented in a thorough study by Reavis Cox, Charles S. Goodman, and Thomas C. Fichandler, *Distribution in a High-Level Economy* (Englewood Cliffs, N.J.: Prentice-Hall, 1965).

[42] Louis P. Bucklin, "A Synthetic Index of Marketing Productivity," a paper presented to the 58th International Marketing Conference of the American Marketing Association, Chicago, 1975, pp. 4–8.

[43] For an excellent treatment of productivity in marketing, see Louis P. Bucklin, *Productivity in Marketing* (Chicago: American Marketing Association, 1978).

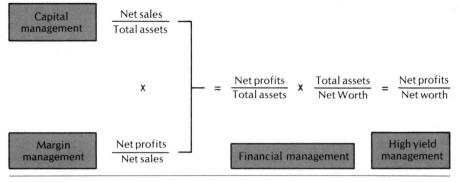

Figure 11–3 The strategic profit model (SPM)

Source: Bert C. McCammon, Jr., "Perspectives for Distribution Programming," in Louis P. Bucklin (ed.), *Marketing Systems.* © 1970 by Scott, Foresman and Company. Reprinted by permission of the publisher.

Profitability

No single measure of performance fully reflects the financial well-being of the firm. The financial performance of wholesalers and retailers is multidimensional, requiring an examination of (1) profitability, or return on investment, (2) liquidity, or the ability of the firm to meet its financial liabilities within a time frame, (3) capital structure, or leverage ratio, (4) growth pattern of sales and profits, and (5) growth potential of sales and profits.[44] Dun and Bradstreet's Key Business Ratios for Retailing and Wholesaling, a sample of which is shown in Tables 11–5 and 11–6, illustrate the types of financial ratios of interest to performance analysts. However, return on investment is accepted as an aggregate performance measure in the retail and wholesale trades.

The strategic profit model has been developed by managerial accountants to evaluate and diagnose profitability problems such as those that confront retailers and wholesalers. Because of the importance of such a model in formulating effective interorganizational strategies as well as in assessing performance in distribution, it is explained in some detail here.

The strategic profit model (SPM) is portrayed in Fig. 11–3. The SPM is basically a product of the insights into financial management generated by the DuPont Company. DuPont was one of the first to explore, in detail, the interrelationship of various financial ratios. In its planning activities, it developed and used DuPont charts (see Fig. 11–4), which illustrated that, for example, asset turnover and net profit as a percentage of sales are related, since the elements contained in them lead to net profits on assets.[45]

[44] Robert F. Lusch and James M. Kenderdine, "Financial and Strategic Trends of Chain Store Retailers; 1974–1975," *Review of Regional Economics and Business* (April 1977), pp. 11–17.

[45] Erich A. Helfert, *Techniques of Financial Analysis,* 3rd ed. (Homewood, Ill.: Richard D. Irwin, 1972), p. 71. For further elaboration on profitability analysis, see Frank H. Mossman, Paul M. Fischer, and W. J. E. Crissy, "New Approaches to Analyzing Marketing Profitability," *Journal of Marketing* (April 1974), pp. 43–48; and Leland L. Beik and Stephen L. Buzby, "Profitability Analysis by Market Segment," *Journal of Marketing* (July 1973), pp. 48–53.

Table 11–5 Key business ratios: Retailing

Line of Business (and number of concerns reporting)	Current Assets to Current Debt (times)	Net Profits on Net Sales (percent)	Net Profits on Tangible Net Worth (percent)	Net Sales to Net Working Capital (times)	Collection Period (days)	Net Sales to Inventory (times)	Fixed Assets to Tangible Net Worth (percent)	Current Debt to Tangible Net Worth (percent)	Total Debt to Tangible Net Worth (percent)	Current Debt to Inventory (percent)
5211	4.5	6.8	24.3	9.7	22.2	9.2	12.1	21.2	28.3	41.2
Lumber & other bldg.	2.4	2.7	12.6	5.3	34.3	5.8	28.0	50.6	71.8	76.1
mtls. dealers (2313)	1.5	1.1	7.0	3.2	50.7	4.0	66.7	119.7	162.8	127.9
5422	3.9	8.4	43.5	14.1	7.6	8.7	10.9	20.7	30.3	48.0
Household appliance	1.9	3.5	17.1	7.3	16.7	5.4	29.2	61.4	83.1	85.4
stores (2342)	1.3	1.0	5.0	3.8	31.0	3.7	67.8	164.5	198.0	120.0
5733	5.1	12.1	35.7	8.2	8.0	5.0	8.5	18.1	26.4	27.7
Music stores	2.4	4.9	16.8	4.3	16.7	5.4	29.2	61.4	83.1	85.4
(1135)	1.5	1.4	5.1	2.4	37.2	2.2	54.8	147.5	181.9	96.3
5912	4.5	7.5	39.5	10.5	7.6	8.2	10.0	23.1	28.6	33.9
Drug, proprietary	2.7	3.8	19.0	6.6	13.5	6.0	24.0	49.5	69.0	56.1
stores (2286)	1.7	1.4	8.3	4.5	22.5	4.6	54.3	112.6	159.0	89.0
5941	6.1	10.8	35.5	8.1	2.9	5.4	9.0	13.6	21.8	21.8
Sporting goods, bicycle	2.8	4.5	16.6	4.5	7.3	3.5	22.7	44.8	65.9	49.4
stores (2062)	1.6	0.9	4.9	2.7	17.1	2.4	57.0	119.4	157.4	80.6
5611	6.6	11.4	31.7	6.2	5.4	5.1	5.9	13.7	18.2	22.1
Clothing & furnishings,	3.1	4.7	13.9	3.8	14.2	3.6	15.1	39.2	52.0	48.2
men's & boys' (1922)	1.9	1.3	4.3	2.4	32.8	2.5	36.1	93.1	128.9	81.2
5621	6.8	12.3	35.5	7.5	5.8	6.6	8.6	11.7	16.3	23.3
Women's ready-to-	3.2	5.5	16.3	4.2	17.1	4.4	22.2	34.2	47.0	49.4
wear stores (2469)	1.8	1.5	5.3	2.5	35.1	2.9	47.5	85.8	112.0	89.5
5992	4.5	12.1	56.8	16.9	14.2	28.4	27.5	13.8	22.5	54.1
Florists	2.2	5.7	25.4	8.7	24.0	14.5	57.2	38.8	64.6	118.1
(1238)	1.2	1.8	8.1	5.0	35.4	7.3	105.4	99.9	155.5	236.1
5732	4.1	11.3	49.1	14.8	4.2	8.3	13.4	17.9	27.6	42.0
Radio & television	1.9	5.5	21.3	6.9	9.8	5.4	35.8	58.8	80.0	81.4
stores (1393)	1.3	1.4	5.1	3.8	22.2	3.5	78.0	151.4	200.8	119.5

Note: In each set of three figures, the center one is the median and the figures above and below it are, respectively, the upper and lower quartiles.

Source: Dun & Bradstreet Industry Norms and Key Financial Ratios, 1985. Reprinted with the permission of *Dun's Business Month*, 1985, Copyright 1985, Dun & Bradstreet Publications Corporation.

Table 11–6 Key business ratios: Wholesaling

Line of Business (and number of concerns reporting)	Current Assets to Current Debt (times)	Net Profits on Net Sales (percent)	Net Profits on Tangible Net Worth (percent)	Net Sales to Working Capital (times)	Collection Period (days)	Net Sales to Inventory (times)	Fixed Assets to Tangible Net Worth (percent)	Current Debt to Tangible Net Worth (percent)	Total Debt to Tangible Net Worth (percent)	Current Debt to Inventory (percent)
5013 Automotive parts & supplies (2016)	4.4	6.2	24.3	8.9	20.4	7.9	9.6	24.3	28.7	39.1
	2.5	3.1	11.5	5.2	30.2	5.1	21.1	53.8	73.8	67.7
	1.6	1.1	4.6	3.3	41.6	3.5	46.3	129.2	173.8	110.8
5064 Electrical appliances, tv and radios (653)	3.0	6.3	26.5	16.9	18.1	12.4	6.9	34.3	44.6	66.3
	1.8	2.4	12.8	8.2	30.6	7.6	16.4	88.6	100.9	112.1
	1.3	0.9	5.7	5.0	42.7	5.0	40.9	217.5	242.1	162.7
5063 Electrical apparatus and equipment (1484)	3.4	7.0	26.2	12.0	29.5	12.5	9.4	30.7	37.3	62.8
	2.1	3.0	12.1	6.7	42.0	7.3	20.5	73.7	91.9	105.2
	1.4	1.0	4.5	3.9	56.9	4.7	48.2	165.1	203.3	176.9
5112 Stationery and supply (838)	3.8	9.6	39.6	16.0	26.4	26.3	10.4	26.5	33.5	66.4
	2.2	3.7	19.5	8.2	37.9	10.6	24.0	66.6	89.9	123.9
	1.4	1.5	6.7	4.6	52.9	6.1	51.7	160.5	198.8	225.2
5012 Autos, remodelled vehicles (679)	2.7	4.7	26.3	19.1	11.6	12.7	10.2	37.5	55.8	69.2
	1.6	2.0	12.7	10.4	20.8	6.6	26.3	114.2	149.7	98.3
	1.2	0.7	3.9	6.0	35.0	4.1	65.0	239.2	297.8	135.8
5065 Electronic parts and equipment (1344)	3.9	9.3	35.6	14.7	22.6	16.5	8.1	24.0	32.4	60.8
	2.1	4.0	16.9	6.9	39.0	8.3	22.0	65.6	86.6	113.4
	1.4	1.2	6.0	3.8	60.2	4.9	53.3	167.9	216.3	199.2
5122 Drugs & proprietaries (450)	3.3	5.7	22.5	15.5	19.9	13.2	8.6	30.3	40.6	65.7
	1.9	2.0	12.7	8.5	32.3	8.0	21.0	80.1	105.0	113.9
	1.4	0.7	5.1	4.4	47.0	5.4	42.2	194.7	235.3	172.6

Note: In each set of three figures, the center one is the median and the figures above and below it are, respectively, the upper and lower quartiles.

Source: Dun & Bradstreet Industry Norms and Key Financial Ratios, 1985. Reprinted with the permission of *Dun's Business Month*, 1985, Copyright 1985, Dun & Bradstreet Publications Corporation.

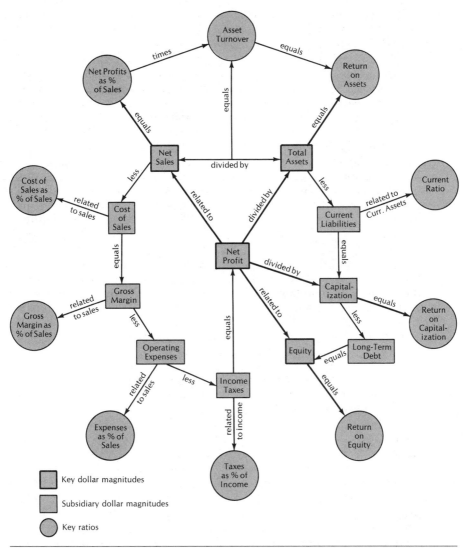

Figure 11–4 An example of a DuPont chart showing key ratios as a system

Source: Erich A. Helfert, *Techniques of Financial Analysis,* 3rd ed. (Homewood, Ill.: Richard D. Irwin, 1972), p. 71.

The SPM involves multiplying a company's profit margin by its rate of asset turnover and its leverage ratio to derive its rate of return on net worth. Let us look briefly at each of the components of the model.

Net Profits/Net Sales (Profit Margin). The relationship of reported net profit to sales indicates management's ability to recover the cost of merchandise or services, the expenses of operating the business (including depreciation), and the cost of borrowed funds from revenues generated during a given period, as well as its adeptness in leaving a margin of reasonable compensation to the owners for providing their capital at a risk. The ratio of net profit to sales essentially expresses the cost/price effectiveness of the operation.[46]

Although the net profit margin shows how well the firm performs given a particular level of sales, it does not show how well the firm uses the resources at its command.[47] The amount of net profit may be entirely satisfactory from the point of view of the sales volume; however, the sales volume may be insufficient in relation to capacity—the amount of capital invested in assets used in obtaining sales.[48]

The ratio of net profits to net sales should also be considered in connection with the turnover of inventory and accounts receivable. Rapid turnovers of inventory and receivables may be a result of reduced sales prices and relatively high rates of cash discounts. When not accompanied by reduced costs and operating expenses, the smaller sales income would result in a lower net profit. A low net profit may be a result of excessive selling and general administrative expenses.[49]

Net Sales/Total Assets (Asset Turnover). The ratio of net sales to total assets is a measure of the effectiveness of management's employment of capital and may show whether there is a tendency toward overinvestment in assets, especially in inventory and receivables in the case of wholesalers and retailers. This ratio (sometimes referred to as the *turnover ratio*) provides a clue as to the size of asset commitment required for a given level of sales or, conversely, the sales dollars generated for each dollar of investment.[50]

Net Profits/Total Assets (Return on Assets). Neither the net profit margin (net profits/net sales) nor the turnover ratio (net sales/total assets) by itself provides an adequate measure of operating efficiency. The net profit margin ignores the utilization of assets, whereas the turnover ratio ignores profitability on sales. The return on assets ratio (ROA), or earning power, resolves these shortcomings. As pointed out by Van Horne, an improvement in the earning power of a firm will result if there is an increase in turnover on existing assets, an increase in the net profit margin, or both.[51] The interrelation of these ratios is shown in the SPM (Fig. 11–3). Two firms with different asset turnovers and net profit margins may have the same earning power. For example, if wholesaler A has an asset turnover of 4 : 1 and a net profit margin of 3 percent and wholesaler B has an asset turnover of 1.5 : 1 and a net profit margin of 8 percent, both have the same earning power—12 percent—despite their vast differences in operating modes. Thus, earning power can be improved by increasing sales revenue

[46] Helfert, *op. cit.*, p. 53.

[47] For an insightful analysis of the weaknesses of the net profit margin as a performance indicator, see Eugene M. Lerner, *Managerial Finance* (New York: Harcourt Brace Jovanovich, 1971), pp. 46ff.

[48] Ralph D. Kennedy and Stewart Y. McMullen, *Financial Statements* (Homewood, Ill.: Richard D. Irwin, 1973), p. 390.

[49] *Ibid.*

[50] It should be noted that, while simple to calculate, the overall asset turnover is a crude measure at best, since the balance sheets of most well-established companies contain a variety of assets recorded at widely different cost levels of past periods. Helfert, *op. cit.*, p. 55.

[51] James C. Van Horne, *Fundamentals of Financial Management*, 2nd ed. (Englewood Cliffs, N.J.: Prentice-Hall, 1974), p. 39.

through higher prices (and probably lower volume) or higher volume (probably at lower prices). This may increase both profit margin and turnover. Costs can be reduced to the point where they do not affect quality, and profit margin can be widened through improved control. The amount of capital employed can be reduced by increasing the turnover of inventory and accounts receivable, and by utilizing the fixed assets more efficiently.[52]

Total Assets/Net Worth (Leverage Ratio).   The ratio of total assets to net worth indicates how reliant a firm is on borrowed funds for both short- and long-term purposes. The lower the ratio, the more the firm is being financially supported by owners' equity as opposed to debt capital. Although a low ratio indicates a high degree of solvency as well as a desire by management to rely on ownership or equity capital for financing purposes, it also indicates that management is probably highly conservative and risk-averse. Debt capital requires fixed interest payments on specific dates and eventual repayment, as well as the threat of legal action by creditors if payments are overdue. On the other hand, dividends on ownership capital are paid at the discretion of the directors, and there is no provision for repayment of capital to stockholders.

Furthermore, equity capital is typically more costly than debt capital. Thus, by retaining an excessive amount of ownership capital relative to debt capital, the company may be foregoing opportunities to trade on its equity (so-called *leveraging operations*) by refusing to borrow funds at relatively low interest rates and using these funds to earn greater rates of returns. Consequently, aggressive management will often rely heavily on debt capital, because if there is a difference between these two rates on a large investment base, management can increase earnings per share without having to increase the number of common shares outstanding.

Net Profits/Net Worth (Return on Investment, or Return on Net Worth).   The main interest of the owners of an enterprise will be the returns achieved by management effort on their share of the invested funds. An effective measure of the return on owners' investment (ROI) is the relationship of net profit to net worth (equity). This ratio reflects the extent to which the objective of realizing a satisfactory net income is being achieved. A low ratio of net profits to net worth may indicate that the business is not very successful because of several possible reasons: inefficient and ineffective production, distribution, financial, or general management; unfavorable general business conditions; or overinvestment in assets. A high ratio may be a result of efficient management throughout the company's organization, favorable general business conditions, and trading on the equity (effective leveraging).[53]

As McCammon has explained, the SPM has four important managerial purposes:

1. The model specifies that a firm's principal financial objective is to earn an adequate or target rate of return on net worth.
2. The model identifies the three "profit paths" available to an enterprise. That is, a firm with an inadequate rate of return on net worth can improve its performance

[52] Donald H. Schuckett and Edward J. Mock, *Decision Strategies in Financial Management* (New York: AMACOM, 1973), p. 122.
[53] Kennedy and McMullen, *op. cit.*, pp. 353–54.

Margin Management		Asset Management		Leverage		Return on Net Worth
$\dfrac{\text{Net Profits}}{\text{Net Sales}}$	X	$\dfrac{\text{Net Sales}}{\text{Total Assets}}$	X	$\dfrac{\text{Total Assets}}{\text{Net Worth}}$	=	$\dfrac{\text{Net Profits}}{\text{Net Worth}}$
Percent		Times		Times		Percent
1968 1.4		2.6		2.3		8.8
1974 1.0		2.6		2.7		7.0
1979 1.7		2.9		2.5		12.3

Figure 11–5 Composite strategic profit model for retailing corporations (1968, 1974, 1979, 1985)

Source: Distribution Research Program, University of Oklahoma.

by accelerating its rate of asset turnover, by increasing its profit margin, or by leveraging its operations more highly.

3. The model dramatizes the principal areas of decision making within the firm, namely, capital management, margin management, and financial management. Furthermore, firms interrelating their capital, margin, and financial plans may be described effectively as engaged in the practice of high-yield management.

4. The model provides a useful perspective for appraising the financial strategies used by different organizations to achieve target rates of return on net worth.[54]

Given the significance of the SPM from a managerial standpoint, we will turn now to the question of the past performance of wholesalers and retailers in terms of high-yield management. The answer is provided in Figs. 11–5 and 11–6, which show composite SPMs for retailing and wholesaling over a 17-year period.

Analysts are hardly enthusiastic about the 1985 results. Although the margin management ratio for retailing corporations is at its highest level, 2.8 percent, this gain was offset by the noticeable decline in the asset management ratio. The result is a return on net worth for retailing corporations in 1985 of 12.9 percent, not significantly different from the 12.3 percent attained in 1979. For wholesaling corporations, the 1985 results are devastating. After a spectacular rise in 1979, margin management, asset management, and return on net worth ratios for wholesaling corporations are back to their lower levels of 1968 and 1974.

Given the generally disappointing results of 1985 and the fact that analysts were also unenthusiastic about the apparent improvements of 1979 over 1974, it is useful to uncover the reasons the results are not better.[55] First, given the

[54] Bert C. McCammon, Jr., "Perspectives for Distribution Programming," in Bucklin (ed.), *Vertical Marketing Systems*, p. 38.

[55] The following analysis is based on a number of sources, including March 1986 communications with Bert C. McCammon, Jr., and September 1980 communications with Robert F. Lusch, Distribution Research Program, University of Oklahoma; Bert C. McCammon, Jr., Jack J. Kasulis,

	Margin Management $\dfrac{\text{Net Profits}}{\text{Net Sales}}$	$\times$	Asset Management $\dfrac{\text{Net Sales}}{\text{Total Assets}}$	$\times$	Leverage $\dfrac{\text{Total Assets}}{\text{Net Worth}}$	$=$	Return on Net Worth $\dfrac{\text{Net Profits}}{\text{Net Worth}}$
	Percent		Times		Times		Percent
1968	1.2		2.9		2.4		8.6
1974	1.1		2.6		2.6		7.5
1979	1.5		3.2		2.9		14.2

Figure 11–6 Composite strategic profit model for wholesaling corporations (1968, 1974, 1979, 1985)

Source: Distribution Research Program, University of Oklahoma.

double-digit inflation in 1979, the return on net worth improvements over 1974 can quickly disappear if return figures are inflation-adjusted to reflect real returns. Given inflationary pressures of the late 1970s, analysts recommended (unadjusted for inflation) a target return on net worth (after taxes) of around 20 percent. The reported 1979 return-on-net-worth figures of 12.3 percent for retailing and 14.2 percent for wholesaling are well below these target returns. While the return to single-digit inflation in the 1980s may somewhat temper these expectations, profitability profiles for high-performance retailers such as the ones listed in Table 11–7 sustain capital market expectations for such high returns on net worth.

Second, the retail and wholesale corporations rely heavily on financial leverage to improve their financial performance. Indeed, wholesale corporations increased their leverage ratio from 2.6 in 1974 to 2.9 in 1979 and 3.0 in 1985. Heavy reliance on leverage is not without its perils. Liquidity is an area of grave concern among financial analysts. Financial leverage reduces liquidity ratios. Analysts recommend that retail and wholesale corporations should strive to improve the quality of their balance sheets by cutting back on financial leverage and improving liquidity. Recommended leverage ratios range from 2.0 to 2.2

and Jack A. Lesser, "The New Parameters of Retail Competition: The Intensified Struggle for Market Share," in Ronald W. Stampfl and Elizabeth Hirschman (eds.), *Competitive Structure in Retailing: The Department Store Perspective* (Chicago: American Marketing Association, 1980), pp. 108–18; Bert C. McCammon, Jr., and William L. Hammer, "A Frame of Reference for Improving Productivity in Distribution," *Atlanta Economic Review* (September-October 1974), pp. 9–13.; Albert D. Bates and Bert C. McCammon, Jr., "Resellers' Strategies and Financial Performance of the Firm," in Thorelli (ed.), *op. cit.*, pp. 146–78; Bert C. McCammon, Jr., "The Changing Economics of Wholesaling: A Strategic Analysis," in Barnett A. Greenberg (ed.), *Proceedings of the 1974 Southern Marketing Association* (Atlanta: Georgia State University, 1975); Bert C. McCammon, Jr., et al., "Strategic Issues in Retailing: A Managerial Analysis" (Norman, Okla.: Distribution Research Program, University of Oklahoma, 1977); and Bert C. McCammon, Jr., "Strategic Issues and Options in Wholesaling," a paper presented before the American Marketing Association Doctoral Consortium, Madison, Wisc., 1979.

Table 11-7 Profitability profile of power retailers, 1984

| | Strategic Profit Model Ratios | | | | |
Retailer	Net Profits ———— Net Sales (percent) ×	Net Sales ———— Total Assets (times) =	Net Profits ———— Total Assets (percent) ×	Total Assets ———— Net Worth (times) =	Net Profits ———— Net Worth (percent)
Price Company	2.5%	4.4×	10.7%	2.6×	28.2%
Home Depot	4.0	2.4	9.8	1.6	15.7
Standard Brands Paint	6.6	1.6	10.6	1.3	13.3
Toys "R" Us	6.6	1.6	10.1	1.9	19.2
Dress Barn	4.6	3.0	13.8	1.8	25.0
Clothestime	3.4	3.9	13.2	2.0	26.9
Syms	6.2	2.7	16.8	1.4	23.7
Claire's	11.0	2.1	22.5	1.9	42.8
Pier 1	10.7	1.8	19.6	1.7	33.1
Herman's	4.0	2.5	10.1	3.8	38.6
Tandy	10.1	1.7	17.1	1.7	28.5
Long's	3.0	3.8	11.3	1.4	16.2
Wal-Mart	4.2	2.8	11.9	2.2	26.6

Sources: Company annual reports; Distribution Research Program, University of Oklahoma, provided by Bert C. McCammon, Jr.

times, in contrast with the reported 1985 figures of 2.5 times for retailing and 3.0 times for wholesaling.

Third, over the years there is either a decrease or no noticeable increase in asset productivity in wholesale and retail trade, despite attempts to improve space and inventory productivity through the deployment of a number of alternative strategies, as discussed in Chapters 2 and 3.[56] Analysts point out that while these strategies may increase sales volume for one corporation, such gains may be achieved at the expense of other retailers or wholesalers. The net impact is shifting patronage from one retailer to another. These shifts, however modest, have a major impact on the retail or wholesale operator, as amply illustrated by the following comment:

> Most retailers operate fairly close to their break-even points. Supermarkets, for example, with their unusually tight margins, have a break-even point that ranges between 94 and 96 percent of their current sales. General merchandise retailers, with more margin latitude, *still* have a break-even point that approaches 85 to 92 percent of the current sales, with the precise relationship depending on the firm's cost structure, managerial style, gross margin, current profitability, and other factors. Because they operate so close to their break-even points, general merchandise retailers, like others, are *unusually* vulnerable to any downturn in sales and market share, i.e., even a modest contraction in volume can convert a profitable store into a break-even or loss operation.[57]

[56] These strategies for retailers include supermarket retailing, store positioning, market intensification, secondary market expansion, and nonstore retailing. Innovative strategies for wholesalers include system selling, multi-level merchandising, inventory and service diversification, total capability supplying, and superspecialization.

[57] McCammon, Kasulis, and Lesser, *op. cit.*, p.110.

Furthermore, improving space and inventory productivity often requires large capital investments. For example, increasing inventory turnover requires comprehensive, accurate, and timely information. This translates into the need for massive investments in point-of-sale data entry terminals and a whole complement of the data-processing equipment necessary to generate timely inventory management and other reports. Indeed, these large capital investments by retailers result in an increase in total assets. In summary, intensified competition results in nominal increases in sales volume, and capital requirements to improve space and inventory productivity result in increasing total assets. This combination of intensified competition and an increase in total assets explains the modest improvements in asset turnover in retailing from 2.6 times in 1974 to 2.9 times in 1979 and its setback to 2.2 times in 1985.

Finally, profit margins in retailing and wholesaling have not increased enough, given the impact of inflation. Indeed, the increase in profit margins for retailing from 1.0 percent in 1974 to 1.7 percent in 1979 and 2.4 percent in 1985 is hardly adequate in view of the fact that the profit margin for retail corporations was 1.4 percent in 1968. Similarly, profit margins for wholesaling increased from 1.1 percent in 1974 to 1.5 percent in 1979, in contrast with 1.2 percent in 1968 and a repeat performance in 1985. What worries analysts even more is that profit margins in distributive trades have traditionally experienced a secular decline. This decline was due primarily to declining gross margins, rising payroll expenses, and increased occupancy cost. Given the continued intensified competition, inflationary labor wages, and ever-increasing construction costs, there is no relief in sight to rid the distributive trade of the prospects of further margin erosions.

From a micro perspective, then, it is difficult to laud the aggregate performance of retailing and wholesaling institutions. There is, however, a curious contradiction in this area between macro and micro viewpoints. While businessmen view low profits as evidence of weak performance, economists and antitrust enforcement agencies often take an opposite position.[58] The latter would tend to attribute low profits to a high degree of competition in the marketplace, which has served to force prices down to levels close to average and marginal costs. Although there is evidence that competition has had some real effect on profits, as pointed out in previous chapters, it would be wrong to make the global assumption that the financial conditions in the distributive trades are solely or even primarily the result of competitive forces. In fact, it would be more logical to assume that lack of innovative, effective, and aggressive management has been as much the cause as any other factor. Organizations such as Wal-Mart, Herman's Sporting Goods, Pier 1, and Tandy, among others mentioned in Table 11–7, are uniquely and skillfully managed from an *inter-* as well as an *intra*organizational perspective, and their profitability reflects this. But such organizations are obviously the exception, not the rule, in distribution.[59]

---

[58] For a discussion of these points, see Stern and Grabner, *op. cit.*

[59] For a financial analysis of some highly successful retailers and wholesalers, see Bates and McCammon, *op. cit.*, pp. 165–78; and Bert C. McCammon, Jr., and James M. Kenderdine, "High Performance Wholesaling," *Hardlines Wholesaling* (September 1975), pp. 17–51. The performance of retail, wholesale, and manufacturing institutions by line of business in terms of SPM ratios is reported annually in Dun and Bradstreet's *Key Business Ratios*. Some trade associations report SPM ratios for classifications of their members and leading member institutions. See, for example, Bert C. McCammon, Jr., and Robert F. Lusch, "The New Economics of Hardware/Home Center Retailing: A Financial Profile of 17 Leading Hardware/Home Center Companies," *Hardware Retailing* (October

1. Total distribution cost per unit
2. Transportation cost per unit
3. Warehousing cost per unit
4. Production cost per unit
5. Costs associated with avoiding stockouts
6. Percent of stockout units
7. Percent of obsolete inventories
8. Percent of bad debts
9. Customer service level by product, by market segment
10. Accuracy of sales forecasts
11. Number of errors in order filling
12. Number of new markets entered
13. Percent sales volume in new markets entered
14. Percent of markdown volume
15. Number and percent of discontinued channel intermediaries (distribution turnover)
16. Number and percent of new distributors
17. Percent of damaged merchandise
18. Percent of astray shipments
19. Size of orders
20. Ability to keep up with new technology—data transmission
21. Percent of shipments—less than truckload (LTL) vs. truckload (TL)
                              —less than carload (LCL—used with rail shipments)
                              vs. carload (CL)
22. Energy costs
23. Number of customer complaints

Source: Adel I. El-Ansary, "A Model for Evaluating Channel Performance," reported in Douglas M. Lambert, *The Distribution Channel Decision* (New York: National Association of Accountants and the Society of Management Accountants of Canada, 1978), p. 40.

OTHER PERFORMANCE VARIABLES

There are a host of other variables that would be meaningful to evaluate in order to arrive at an overall judgment of performance in distribution.[60] From a macro

---

1976). Management consulting firms provide similar information for subscribers and clients. See, for example, Reports of Management Horizons, Inc., of Columbus, Ohio. Also, the Distribution Research Program, College of Business Administration, University of Oklahoma under the direction of Bert C. McCammon, Jr., maintains SPM data banks and produces a number of reports annually for lecture series and conferences.

[60] For discussion of a number of performance variables, see Buzzell, *op. cit.*, pp. 143–59; and John R. Grabner, Jr., and Robert A. Layton, "Problems and Challenges in Market Performance Measurement," in Allvine (ed.), *op. cit.*, pp. 163–82.

perspective, it would be useful to know whether channels and channel institutions have been progressive over time—that is, whether they have been innovative and adaptive, especially with regard to changes in technology. From a social perspective, the effect of various distributive practices on energy consumption, hard-core unemployment, and the quality of the environment should be assessed. On the micro side, an evaluation of the number of stockouts, obsolete inventories, damaged shipments, and markdowns over time, among other operating variables, as listed in Exhibits 11–5 and 11–6 would provide a closer approximation of actual performance.

EXHIBIT 11–6 Qualitative measures of channel performance

1. Degree of channel coordination
2. Degree of cooperation
3. Degree of conflict
4. Degree of domain consensus (role prescription and variation)
5. Recognition of superordinate goals
6. Degree of development of channel leadership
7. Degree of functional duplication
8. Degree of commitment to channel
9. Degree of power locus development
10. Degree of flexibility in functional shiftability
11. Availability of information about:
    a. Physical inventory
    b. Product characteristics
    c. Pricing structure
    d. Promotional data
       i) Personal selling assistance
       ii) Advertising
       iii) Point of purchase displays
       iv) Special promotions
    e. Market conditions
    f. Services available
    g. Organizational changes
12. Assimilation of new technology
13. Innovation in distribution generated within the channel
14. Extent of intrabrand competition
15. Extent of routinization of channel tasks
16. Extent of use of optimal inventory standards
17. Relations with trade associations
18. Relations with consumer groups

Source: Adel I. El-Ansary, "A Model for Evaluating Channel Performance," reported in Douglas M. Lambert, *The Distribution Channel Decision* (New York: National Association of Accountants and the Society of Management Accountants of Canada, 1978), p. 41.

Unfortunately, aggregate measures for these macro and micro performance variables are generally unavailable or are restricted to narrow lines of trade. It is necessary, therefore, at this time to rely basically upon the information about system output, cost, efficiency, profitability, and equity provided thus far in arriving at a judgment about the performance of the distributive trades.

Nonetheless, a landmark study by the National Council for Physical Distribution Management provides comprehensive lists of productivity measures of physical distribution activities, such as transportation, warehousing, order processing, and inventory management.[61] Although the study does not cover empirical analysis of productivity in physical distribution, the availability of comprehensive lists and frameworks for productivity measurement should encourage their application in the future.[62]

MECHANISMS FOR AUDITING DISTRIBUTION CHANNELS

Channel members who desire to evaluate the performance of their individual firms can use a number of auditing mechanisms, including matrix analysis for auditing channel flows; a channel environment, structure, and policy audit; and techniques for assessing the profits and costs of alternative channel relations, including distribution cost analysis and direct product profit (DPP) analysis.

Matrix Analysis for Auditing Channel Flows

The notion that the compensation of a channel member should be based on the extent to which he participates in channel flows has been emphasized previously. Gross margins and functional discounts in most lines of trade are traditionally established, however. Therefore, actual compensation may be at variance from the compensation a channel member is entitled to.

What is needed in these situations where role relationships have not been delineated in an effective and meaningful way is an audit of the flows in the channel in order to determine the extent of participation of the members in each. An audit of this nature will not only permit an adjustment of the compensation structure within the channel, but should also lead to the elimination of cost duplication and thereby result in the lowering of prices to end-users.

The beginning of a channel audit may involve the construction of a matrix of system relationships. Such a matrix describes the channel, permitting precise comparisons of the operations of the various channel components as well as comparisons of one channel system with others. In such a matrix, the institutions and agencies included in any given channel can be portrayed as components of the system. Important elements of the task environment (i.e., the portion of the environment upon which the system depends) can also be shown. Thus, by

---

[61] Kearney Management Consultants, *Measuring Productivity in Physical Distribution* (Chicago: National Council for Physical Distribution Management, 1978).

[62] The extent to which many of the proposed measures are utilized by a cross section of channel members in a number of industries can be found in Douglas M. Lambert, *The Distribution Channel Decision* (New York: National Association of Accountants, 1978), pp. 82–86.

employing a matrix, one can represent the structure of various relationships within the channel system and between system components and the task environment.

A complete matrix would encompass all firms in the channel. However, a channel might contain 500 firms, which would require 250,000 cells—a matrix too complex to portray here. Thus, levels within the channel rather than individual firms are presented in Fig. 11–7. Likewise, it is not feasible to include all components of the task environment, since they are too numerous and not

Figure 11–7 Matrix analysis of marketing flows in a marketing channel for automobiles: A manufacturer's perspective

Source: Adapted from Louis W. Stern and Jay W. Brown, "Distribution Channels: A Social Systems Approach," in Louis W. Stern (ed.), *Distribution Channels: Behavioral Dimensions* (Boston: Houghton Mifflin, 1969), p. 10.

		Commercial Channel				Task Environment			
		Mfr.	Dlr.	Sfc.	Ad. Ag.	Cons.	F.T.C.	N.A.D.A.	Competitors' Channels
		1	2	3	4	5	6	7	
Manufacturer	1		A B C D F	F D	C D			D	D	
Dealer	2	D G F		D H F		A B C D F	D	D	
Sales Finance Company	3	D E F H	D E F H			D E F	D	D	D E F H
Advertising Agency	4	D				C			D
Consumer	5		D G F	D F H					D F G H
Federal Trade Commission	6	D	D					D	D
Nat'l. Auto. Dlrs. Assn.	7	D	D				D		D
Competitors' Channels				D F H	C D	A B C D E F	D	D	

Flow: Direction: Code:
            Mfr.   Cons.

Flow	Direction	Code
Ownership	⟶	A
Phys. Poss.	⟶	B
Promotion	⟶	C
Negotiation	⟷	D
Financing	⟷	E
Risking	⟷	F
Ordering	⟵	G
Payment	⟵	H

always identifiable. Nevertheless, the important components can be easily recognized and are portrayed here, also.

The system matrix in Fig. 11–7 uses the commercial channel for a manufacturer's new automobiles as a relatively uncomplicated example.[63] The channel consists of the manufacturer, his dealers, an advertising agency, and an independent sales finance company that finances both dealers' purchases from the manufacturer and consumers' purchases from dealers. Competitors' channels and consumers represent the most important elements of the task environment. In the history of new-car distribution, other important task environment elements have included the Federal Trade Commission and the dealer trade organization, the National Automobile Dealers Association (NADA).

The meaning of each cell can be demonstrated by the cell in row 1, column 2. This cell shows the nature of the relationship between the manufacturer and the dealer when the manufacturer initiates the interaction. The manufacturer promotes cars to dealers (C), negotiates the terms of sales (D), passes the automobile and its title to dealers (A and B), and, at the same time, accepts certain business risks (F) in his relationship with dealers. The backward flows for the dealer-manufacturer relationship are contained in cell (2, 1). The dealers order from the manufacturer (G), negotiate the terms of sales (D), and accept risk (F). All other cells are analyzed in the same way. The relationships involving the NADA and the FTC are not marketing flow relationships. Since these relationships have been characterized by bargaining, the marketing flow "negotiation" has been used to typify the relationships involving these organizations. Thus, the matrix, as a starting point for an audit of channel relationships and roles, depicts the variety of channel interactions. These include *intra*organizational interactions (within a channel member's firm—e.g., cell 1, 1), *inter*organizational interactions (between channel members—e.g., cell 1, 2), and extrachannel or environmental interactions (between the channel members and the task environment elements—e.g., cell 1, 6).

Channel Environment, Structure, and Policy Audit

A channel member's performance is contingent upon the market environments in which it operates, the behavior and performance of other members in the channel system, and the marketing policies adopted throughout the channel. These relationships are illustrated in Fig. 11–8. It should be understood that the independent variables that influence channel member performance are dynamic. Therefore, a periodic audit of channel environment, structure, and policy is necessary to ensure delivery of performance according to the role specifications and expectations of all members of the marketing channel. A channel audit of this nature is best illustrated by the case study presented in the appendix to this chapter.

Distribution Cost Analysis

Distribution cost analysis is a tool that, when properly employed, can help channel members determine whether the channels in which they participate are

[63] For an application of the system matrix to the pharmaceutical industry, see Mickey C. Smith, Kenneth B. Roberts, and Darego Maclayton, "The Pharmaceutical Industry I: Distribution Channels and Relationships," *M M & M Journal* (January 1976), pp. 32–34.

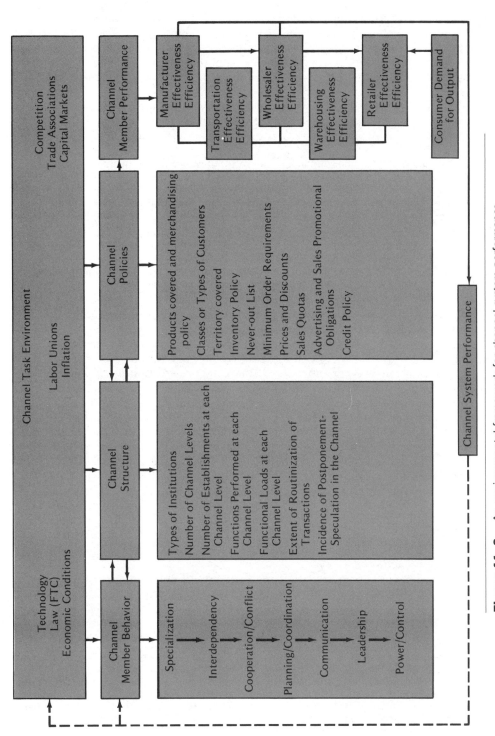

Figure 11–8 An environmental framework for channel system performance

Source: Adel I. El-Ansary, "Perspectives on Channel System Performance," in Robert F. Lusch and Paul H. Zinszer (eds.), *Contemporary Issues in Marketing Channels* (Norman, Ok.: The University of Oklahoma Printing Services, 1979), p. 51.

profitable or whether they need modifications based on a knowledge of the revenues and costs associated with serving them. Generally, a distribution cost analysis would be undertaken by a manufacturer or the original supplier of a particular good or service, because these channel members tend to have the greatest vested interest in the performance of the good or service throughout the channel.

The use of the method rests on the adequacy of accounting data that can be manipulated to provide an assessment of various channels. The benefits of distribution cost analysis can be far-reaching. Here are two examples.

- One manufacturer allocated marketing costs to his four different channels of distribution, and on the basis of the results, one entire channel was eliminated and a number of small customers in another channel were discontinued. In addition, marketing efforts were increased on the remaining profitable channels. In one year, net profits doubled from approximately $150,000 to $300,000.
- Another manufacturer found through a distribution cost analysis that two-thirds of all customers sold direct were responsible for losses ranging from 26 to 86 percent of sales. By transferring unprofitable small accounts to wholesalers, the company has achieved a 40 to 50 percent net reduction in marketing costs and a 25 percent increase in the percentage of net profits.[64]

Thus, there appears to be considerable opportunity to reduce costs and increase profits through analyses of relative costs by channels.

In performing a distribution cost analysis, the accounting data typically available to a firm on its profit and loss statement must first be reorganized and reclassified into marketing function or flow categories.[65] Assume, for example, that Table 11–8 is the profit and loss statement of Harrison Manufacturing Company, a hypothetical producer of plastic towel racks, dish drains, soap dishes, and other kitchen and bathroom accessories. Assume, also, that the expenses listed in Exhibit 11–5 are limited to those associated with the marketing flows of physical possession (storage and delivery), promotion (personal selling, advertising, sales promotion, and publicity), and ordering and payment (billing and collecting). The first step in distribution cost analysis is to show how each of the natural expense items shown in Table 11–8 was incurred through Harrison's participation in each of the flows. A hypothetical breakdown is presented in Table 11–9. For example, it has been determined that most of the salaries went to sales agents and the rest went to an advertising manager, a sales promotion manager, a traffic manager, and an accountant, along with various support personnel in each area.

This simplistic example belies the difficulty of splitting natural expenses into functional cost groups. Generally, careful study is required, along with

[64] These examples were drawn from Charles H. Sevin, *How Manufacturers Reduce Their Distribution Costs*, Economic Series No. 72, U.S. Department of Commerce (Washington, D.C.: U.S. Government Printing Office, 1948), p. 4.

[65] Thorough explanations of distribution cost accounting methods and procedures can be found in J. Brooks Heckert and Robert B. Miner, *Distribution Costs*, 2nd ed. (New York: Ronald Press Co., 1953); and Donald R. Longman and Michael Schiff, *Practical Distribution Cost Analysis* (Homewood, Ill.: Richard D. Irwin, 1955). The discussion of distribution cost analysis here is based largely on Martin Zober, *Marketing Management* (New York: John Wiley & Sons, 1964), pp. 241–67; and Philip Kotler, *Marketing Management: Analysis, Planning, and Control,* 4th ed. (Englewood Cliffs, N.J.: Prentice-Hall, 1980), pp. 639–44; and Patrick M. Dunne and Harry I. Wolk, "Marketing Approach," *Journal of Marketing* (July 1977), pp. 83–94.

Table 11–8 Harrison Manufacturing Company profit and loss statement
(in thousands of dollars)

Sales		$35,000
Cost of goods sold		20,000
Gross margin		15,000
Expenses		
Salaries	$ 3000	
Advertising	2500	
Trucking	500	
Rent	3500	
Insurance	1400	
Supplies	1000	
	11,900	
Net profit		$ 3100

considerable research, before the costs can be allocated equitably. An example of the various means by which natural expense categories may be assigned to various functional categories is provided in Table 11–10. Also, it has been assumed that all of the natural expenses listed in Table 11–8 were directly allocable to the functional (flow) groupings. Clearly, this is an oversimplification, because many of the expenses incurred by a firm do not relate directly to the performance of marketing functions.

The second step in distribution cost analysis as it applies directly to marketing channel decisions involves determining how much of each activity has gone into serving the various channels used by the firm. This step calls for allocating the various costs associated with each functional (flow) category to each channel. Some of the bases available for allocating selected costs associated with various functional categories to different channel or customer groupings are shown in Table 11–11.

Assume that the Harrison Manufacturing Company sells directly to department stores, discount houses, and supermarket chains. Using allocation bases

Table 11–9 Functional (flow) expense breakdown
(in thousands of dollars)

Natural Expenses	Total	Physical Possession		Promotion			Ordering and Payment
		Storage	Delivery	Personal Selling	Advertising	Sales Promotion	Billing and Collecting
Salaries	$ 3000	$ 150	$ 100	$2000	$ 500	$ 200	$ 50
Advertising	2500				1500	1000	
Trucking	500		500				
Rent	3500	2500	50	500	200	100	150
Insurance	1400	1000	350				50
Supplies	1000		500	100	150	150	100
Total	$11,900	$3650	$1500	$2600	$2350	$1450	$350

Table 11–10 Classification of natural expense items into functional (flow) cost groups

Expense Items	Means by Which Natural Expense Items Are Assigned to Functional Cost Groups	Functional Cost Groups to Which Natural Expense Items Are Assigned
Sales salaries and expense	Time study	Order routine and promotion
Truck expense	Direct (to cost group)	Handling (or delivery)
Truck wages	Direct (to cost group)	Handling (or delivery)
Truck depreciation	Direct (to cost group)	Handling (or delivery)
Outside trucking	Direct (to cost group)	Handling (or delivery)
Warehouse wages	Time study (or direct to cost group)	Handling, storage, and investment
Office wages	Time study (or direct to cost group)	Order routine, reimbursement, or other functions
Executive salaries	Managerial estimate	All functional groups
Rent	Space measurement	All functional groups
Storage (outside)	Direct (to cost group)	Storage
Warehouse repairs	Managerial estimate	Storage and handling
Warehouse supplies	Managerial estimate	Storage and handling
Insurance		
Property and equipment	Managerial estimate	All functional groups
Inventory	Direct (to cost group)	Investment
Personnel	Wages	All functional groups
Office expense	Direct (to cost groups and managerial estimate)	Order routine, reimbursement, promotion, or other functions
Utilities	Some direct (to cost groups), others to cost groups via space measurement	All functional groups
Professional services	Managerial estimate	Functions benefited
Taxes, inventory	Direct (to cost group)	Investment
Social Security	Add to wages	All functional groups
Bad debts	Direct (to cost group)	Reimbursement

Source: U.S. Department of Commerce, *Distribution Cost Analysis,* Economic Series No. 50 (Washington, D.C.: U.S. Government Printing Office), p. 17.

similar to those shown in Table 11–11 and applying the results to the Harrison example yield the data in Table 11–12. Thus, it costs Harrison $3.65 per cubic foot of warehouse space to store the merchandise it sells, $0.65 to deliver each case of its merchandise to its retail customers, $47.00 for every sales call made to each of the stores in the various retail chains, and $35.00 for billing and collecting per order. The advertising and sales promotion figures (1.57 × and 1.45 ×) reflect the multipliers that must be applied to each advertising and sales promotion dollar expended by Harrison in each channel. These multipliers permit inclusion of the cost of the support (personnel, rent, and supplies) that has been given to each of these functional areas.

The third step in distribution cost analysis is the preparation of a profit and loss statement for each channel. In Table 11–13, the cost of goods sold has been allocated to each channel in proportion to the revenues that the channel delivers to Harrison. The expense figures are derived from the information in Table 11–12. Although it is clear from Harrison's distribution cost analysis that all channels are returning a net profit (in reality, a contribution to profit, since not all

Table 11–11 Selected bases of manufacturer's allocation of functional (flow) cost groups to channels or customer groupings

Functional Cost Groups	Bases of Allocation to Channels or Customer Groupings
Storage of finished goods	Floor space occupied
Order assembly (handling)	Number of invoice lines
Packing and shipping	Weight or number of shipping units
Transportation	Weight or number of shipping units
Selling	Number of sales calls
Advertising	Cost of space, etc., of specific customer advertising
Sales promotion	Cost of promotions
Order entry	Number of orders
Billing	Number of invoice lines
Credit extension	Average amount outstanding
Accounts receivable	Number of invoices posted

Source: Adapted from Martin Zober, *Marketing Management* (New York: John Wiley & Sons, Copyright © 1964), p. 246. Reprinted by permission of John Wiley & Sons, Inc.

cost figures have been included in this hypothetical example), the return from serving supermarket chains is very low relative to the return from the other two channels. In addition, the return from the department store channel is surprisingly high. Thus, Harrison might consider increasing his business to department stores and/or deemphasizing sales to supermarket chains.

It must be understood that the results of a distribution cost analysis *do not* constitute an adequate informational basis for making explicit moves of the type

Table 11–12 Allocating functional-group costs to marketing channels

Function (Flow) Group	Physical Possession		Promotion			Ordering and Payment
	Storage	Delivery	Personal Selling	Advertising	Sales Promotion	Billing and Collecting
Allocation Bases	Floor Space Occupied in Own Warehouse (000 cu ft)	Number of Shipping Units (000 cases)	Number of Sales Calls (000)	Cost of Advertising Space (000)	Cost of Promotions (000)	Number of Orders (000)
Channel types						
Department stores	200	500	5	$ 150	$ 100	1
Discount houses	450	1000	20	700	400	5
Supermarket chains	350	800	30	650	500	4
Total	1000	2300	55	$1500	$1000	10
Functional-group Cost (000)	$3650	$1500	$2600	$2350	$1450	$350
Number of units	1000	2300	55	$1500	1000	10
Average cost	$3.65	$.65	$47	1.57×	1.45×	$35

Table 11–13 Profit and loss statement for Harrison's channels (in thousands of dollars)

	Department Stores	Discount Houses	Supermarket Chains	Total
Sales	$7500	$15,500	$12,000	$35,000
Cost of goods sold	4400	8800	6800	20,000
Gross margin	3100	6700	5200	15,000
Expenses				
Storage ($3.65 per cu ft)	$ 730	$ 1643	$ 1277	$ 3650
Delivery ($0.65 per case)	325	650	525	1500
Personal selling ($47 per call)	245	940	1414	2600
Advertising (1.57×)	235	1095	1020	2350
Sales promotion (1.45×)	145	580	725	1450
Billing and collecting ($35 per order)	35	175	140	350
Total expenses	$1715	$ 5083	$ 5102	$11,900
Net profit (or loss)	$1385	$ 1617	$ 98	$ 3100
Profit-to-sales ratio	18.5%	10.4%	0.8%	8.9%

suggested. Before a decision is made to emphasize or deemphasize a particular channel or to take *any* corrective action, answers to the following kinds of questions must be generated by management.[66]

- To what extent do buyers buy on the basis of the type of retail outlet versus the brand? Would they seek out the brand in those channels that are to be emphasized?
- What are the future market trends regarding the importance of these three channels?
- Have marketing efforts and policies directed at the three channels been optimal?

It would also be imperative to generate an analysis by product line and to study the interaction effects between channel and product profitability. In isolation, a distribution cost analysis can only indicate symptoms; coupled with a product line analysis, a channel audit, some knowledge of channel members' perceptions of marketing programs, and a strategic profit model analysis, it may lead directly to causes.

Furthermore, the decision to eliminate or deemphasize a channel is far-reaching, affecting every aspect of the business. For example, such a decision would need to be reviewed in light of the possibility that smaller production runs and a reduced scale of production with the same amount of fixed costs would increase the unit manufacturing costs. In addition, a forecast of just what will happen to sales volume over a certain period is needed in order to assess the possible change in distribution policy.[67] It is also necessary to estimate the decrease in total expense that would result from the action. In performing such an analysis, it is important to separate the nonsavable (fixed) costs from the savable costs, because even when decisions to eliminate or deemphasize a channel are made, some of the costs associated with the deemphasized channel are likely to continue.

[66] Kotler, *op. cit.*, p. 642.
[67] Sevin, *op. cit.*, p. 11.

Besides the decision-making dilemma, there is considerable controversy surrounding the allocation methods to be used in distribution cost analysis. This controversy generally revolves around whether to allocate all costs or only direct and traceable costs. If the latter is the case, as it was in our hypothetical example, then the analyst must be satisfied in dealing with a contribution-to-profit figure as his final output, rather than a net profit figure. For marketing channel problems, this approach is acceptable, because it is extremely difficult, if not impossible, to find reasonable ways of allocating indirect, nontraceable common costs (e.g., general management salaries, taxes, interest, and other types of overhead) to alternate channels.[68]

Even with these accounting questions, distribution cost analysis, performed in only a rudimentary fashion, can form the beginning step in the development of a channelwide information system, for in the process of going through the exercise, the manager is forced to consider all of the critical variables making for profitable channel relations. He will, in turn, begin to ask for appropriate information from other departments within his own firm and from other channel members. This process, in and of itself, should lead to more effective communication of common problems and, it is to be hoped, more successful interorganization management.[69]

Direct Product Profit (DPP)

The concept of DPP was developed in the early 1960s by McKinsey and Company for General Foods Corporation.[70] DPP creates an individual profit and loss statement for each product carried. The system measures product performance by:

- adjusting gross margin for each item to reflect deals, allowances, forward-buy income, cash discounts, etc.
- identifying and measuring costs that are directly attributable to that product (e.g., labor, space, inventory, transportation.)[71]

The method is based on transaction cost analysis and requires detailed accounting data. It took the explosion of computerization and modern-day scanning systems to make it a reality.[72]

DPP information provides retailers with more accurate measures of the contribution of a product to their profit than do the traditional measures of value—gross margin, gross profits, and gross profit per unit of space. DPP focuses only on direct costs that are affected by the operating or merchandising

---

[68] Readers interested in pursuing this controversy, as well as a deeper understanding of the details and difficulties associated with distribution cost analysis, are urged to consult Sevin, *op. cit.;* Heckert and Miner, *op. cit.;* and Longman and Schiff, *op. cit.*

[69] In fact, Warshaw has argued that manufacturers *must* assume responsibility for introducing wholesalers to the use of distribution cost analysis if they wish to escape wholesalers' blanket condemnations for inadequate margins. See Martin R. Warshaw, "Pricing to Gain Wholesalers' Selling Support," in Moller and Wilemon (eds.), *op. cit.*, p. 247.

[70] *The Economics of Food Distributors,* McKinsey General Foods Study (New York: General Foods Corporation, 1963).

[71] "Insight Report: Direct Product Profitability in Perspective," *Competitive Edge* (a publication of Willard Bishop Consulting Economists, Ltd.), Vol. 5 (September 1984), p. 1.

[72] *CPDA News* (December 1985–June 1986), p. 14–15.

Table 11-14 Direct product profit example.
The following illustration for two different dry grocery products highlights the key elements of DDP:

	Item A	Item B
Sales revenues	100.0%	100.0%
− Cost of goods	79.5	76.5
Gross margin	20.5	23.5
+ Cash payment discounts	1.6	0.0
+ Deals/allowances	2.0	1.2
+ Forward-buy profits (net)	1.3	0.0
+ Back-haul revenues	0.8	0.0
Adjusted gross margin	26.2	24.7
Warehouse costs		
− Labor	1.1	1.6
− Space	1.0	1.2
Transportation costs		
− Labor/equipment	1.2	1.5
Store costs		
− Stocking labor	2.6	2.9
− Checkout labor	1.7	1.9
− Space (energy, occupancy)	2.2	2.7
Headquarters costs		
− Inventory carrying	0.7	0.4
Total direct product costs	10.5	12.2
Direct product profit	15.7	12.5
− Fixed costs (allocated)	10.5	10.5
Net profit	5.2	2.0

Source: "Insight Report: Direct Product Profitability in Perspective," *Competitive Edge* (a publication of Willard Bishop Consulting Economists, Ltd.), Vol. 5 (September 1984), p. 2.

practices associated with each product, however. Other expenses that are essentially fixed (e.g., indirect labor, headquarters overhead, etc.) are excluded. An illustration for two different dry grocery products is provided in Table 11–14. It shows that the "true" contributions of two different items can vary substantially. It also shows that gross margin can be a misleading indicator of actual performance. Indeed, as Willard Bishop, a well-known consultant to the food industry, points out, "there is oftentimes very little correlation between gross margin and direct product profit."[73] Some of the options available to manufacturers who wish to improve the DPP contribution of their items are listed in Exhibit 11–7.

DPP strikes a practical balance between net profit, which is relatively meaningless for individual products, and gross profit, which ignores direct operating cost and cash discounts. A *Progressive Grocer* study reported in the *CPDA News* agrees:

In fact, if done well, Direct Product Profit could represent a quantum improvement over gross-margin measurements and stand traditional thinking on its head by

[73] "Insight Report: Direct Product Profitability in Perspective," p. 2.

**EXHIBIT 11–7   Manufacturers' options to improve
the DPP contribution of their items**

- Consolidation of retail product sizes
- Streamlining package configurations
- Better utilization of case cube
- Back-haul (customer pick-up) programs
- Drop shipments to stores
- Product line reductions

- Case-pack modularity
- Consolidated shipping programs
- Customized "mixed" pallet ordering
- Smaller case packs (for slow movers)
- Prebuilt display modules

---

disclosing to retailers that products with a high gross margin may actually contribute less to the bottom line than those with a lower margin.[74]

The slim earnings generated by food distributors pose a mandate to boost productivity and reduce cost. DPP data can help distributors reduce their internal costs. DPP methodology forces distributors to learn about the cost behavior of warehouse and storage functions in considerable detail—receiving, moving to storage, paperwork, selecting, checking, loading, and space cost. For small items, shelving and checkout costs must be closely examined; for large items, conserving shelf space is a must.[75] Knowledge of DPP can be especially helpful in improving space management.

The Food Marketing Institute (FMI) has embraced the DPP concept and is coordinating industry efforts to develop a unified DPP model.[76] Such efforts are based on a strong belief that DPP data can be used to foster more and better cooperation between distributors and manufacturers. First, knowledge of DPP can help to identify high-cost products or activities that are susceptible to improvement through manufacturer-distributor joint action, including package size, case size, case and package design, and/or delivery methods. Second, DPP data can help distributors and manufacturers improve distributor profitability by supplementing research-based data on product movements and shelf facings to develop store shelving plans, testing store display methods and locations, and conducting product category profit studies. Finally, understanding DPP can materially affect a manufacturer's sales strategies and programs. By learning more about distributors' costs and how they behave, manufacturers should be able to shape their deals to win greater trade acceptance.[77]

SUMMARY AND CONCLUSIONS

This chapter has focused on assessing the performance of the distributive trades—particularly retailing and wholesaling—in terms of system effectiveness, equity, productivity, and profitability.

[74] *CPDA News.*
[75] *The Economics of Food Distributors*, pp. 37–38.
[76] *CPDA News*, p. 15.
[77] *The Economics of Food Distributors*, pp. 34–35.

System effectiveness was evaluated in terms of the service outputs (lot size, delivery time, market decentralization, and assortment breadth) that the commercial channel provides to ultimate household consumers and to business and industrial users. Historically, there has been an increase in the size of retail transactions, which has generated more direct buying by retailing institutions. As a result, the need for wholesalers' services in the form of large-lot buying has been reduced. On the other hand, there appears to be no slackening in the desire of customers for rapid delivery, although it is possible that such demands may soften somewhat as shortages are experienced both in the United States and abroad.

Market decentralization requirements have been reduced relative to convenience goods due to the development of greater mobility in personal transportation. But decentralization has been increased relative to shopping goods with the emergence of planned regional shopping centers. In addition, the requirements of customers for broader assortments have spurred the movement toward larger retail stores and have, concomitantly, created an increased need for wholesaler services in gathering together diverse merchandise for retail display. A similar development has been witnessed in certain industrial goods markets (e.g., machinery, equipment, and supplies) that have sustained relatively rapid growth and have traditionally relied on a full range of services from wholesalers. On the other hand, the incidence of "double wholesaling" has been declining as manufacturers have become more sophisticated in managing promotional flows for their industrial products.

While there is undoubtedly a great deal of flexibility and choice provided by the variety of available retailing and wholesaling institutions, from both a macro and a micro perspective, inequities in distribution do, in fact, exist, particularly in the servicing of ghetto and rural communities. Although racial, economic, and social discrimination accounts for some of the inequity, the predominant reason for the problem appears to be structural inadequacies, especially in the ghetto marketplace. The atomistic retail market structures present there are not performing as well as industrial organization economists would lead us to expect they should. Incentives on the supply side and improvements on the demand side are required if the inequity is ever to be eliminated.

System productivity, measured primarily by the percentage increases in sales per man-hour, has traditionally lagged in distribution behind other sectors of the economy (e.g., manufacturing and agriculture). A turnaround was experienced in 1983 and 1984, when increases in wholesaling paralleled those in manufacturing and retailing led manufacturing by comfortable margins. Nonetheless, productivity increases in the farming sector dwarfed those of retailing and wholesaling. Although these results may seem disappointing, one must consider the reasons for this lag behind the farm sector. First, man-hours increased in wholesaling and retailing sectors at a substantially faster rate than they did in other sectors. Indeed, retailing and wholesaling are labor-intensive industries. Second, the distributive trades are more dependent than other sectors upon growth in sales volume. Wholesaling and retailing have experienced low growth in constant dollar sales. Finally, the distributive trades did not turn to capital-intensive technological innovations on a large scale until the late 1960s and the 1970s. Meanwhile, farmers, processors, and industrial firms turned to innovative capital-intensive technology much earlier. Subsector analysis of wholesaling industry groups and retail institutional types is more indicative of productivity in distribution; therefore, aggregate analysis must be interpreted with caution.

Productivity and profitability are different though related measures of the efficiency of distributive institutions. While productivity deals with physical efficiency, profitability concerns financial efficiency. Research results confirm a positive relationship between profitability and productivity.[78] The strategic profit model has been employed in this chapter to assess financial efficiency in the distributive trades. Despite the apparent improvement of return on net worth (net profit/net worth), analysts are not enthusiastic about financial performance results in retailing and wholesaling. The 1985 return on net worth of 12.9 percent in retailing and 9.9 percent in wholesaling are hardly adequate if compared with the 20 percent target returns and more prescribed by financial analysts.

Additionally, wholesale and retail corporations rely heavily on financial leverage (total assets/net worth) to generate higher return on net worth. Recommended leverage ratios range from 2 to 2.2 times in contrast with the reported 1985 figures of 2.5 times for retailing and 3.0 for wholesaling. Therefore, retail and wholesale corporations may be compromising on their liquidity. Such compromise is perilous in view of the intensified competition and lower growth in sales volume. Analysts are also unhappy about the marginal improvements in asset productivity (net sales/total assets) in retailing and wholesaling. Despite attempts to improve space and inventory productivity, marginal results materialized as a consequence of the large required increases in fixed assets as well as the limited gains in sales volume. Finally, profit margins (net profit/net sales) in retailing and wholesaling have not increased enough, given the impact of inflation. Analysts are not comforted either by the fact that profit margins in the distributive trades have experienced secular decline. Given the prevalent inflationary pressures, there seems to be no relief in sight to detect margin erosion. In short, it is difficult to laud the aggregate financial performance of retailing and wholesaling institutions.

In general, there is a lack of data to assess other key performance variables, such as progressiveness, ecological and environmental considerations, and operational efficiencies. Thus, it is necessary to rely on the present data in evaluating aggregate performance. On this basis alone, the conclusion must be that the overall picture is not very impressive, although it must be recognized that the standards applied are very high relative to those that might be employed in other parts of the world.

From both a macro and a micro viewpoint, what appears to be needed is more coordination in distributive systems. Suboptimization is likely to occur in the absence of effective coordination. From a management perspective, improved results for retailers and wholesalers are more likely when, working with other commercial channel members, they can simultaneously increase profit margins and rates of asset turnover, especially in light of the fact that retailing and wholesaling organizations are already highly leveraged. On the macro side, it is likely that increased intrachannel coordination will lead to less duplication of efforts within the system and thus greater output at lower or at least stable costs. Furthermore, a resolution of inequities in distribution will, obviously, demand a

[78] Takeuchi, *op. cit.*, pp. 235–45.

synergistic effort on the part of government and commercial channel members. The coordination required can be accomplished through effective interorganization management combined with enlightened government policies and actions.

DISCUSSION QUESTIONS

1. What criteria should be used to evaluate the performance of the distributive trades, other than those addressed directly in this chapter, from a macro (societal) perspective? From a micro (firm) perspective? How would the distributive trades rate on the additional criteria relative to manufacturing?

2. Should different criteria of performance be applied to channels comprising nonprofit or publicly financed organizations? If yes, what criteria would you suggest? If no, explain how the various criteria would have to be modified to fit nonprofit situations.

3. What steps might be taken to increase productivity (output per man-hour) in wholesaling? In retailing?

4. Debate the pros and cons of using value added as a measure of performance of marketing channels.

5. Explain how capital, margin, and financial management are interrelated. What problems pose the largest hurdles to the practice of high-yield management within marketing channels?

6. Describe what you perceive to be the strategic profit models (or the strategies for achieving a high return on investment) for such firms as Neiman-Marcus (a department store catering to middle-class-and-above consumers), A&P, Levitz (a furniture warehouse-showroom chain), Graybar Electric (a wholesaler of major appliances), and McKesson (a drug wholesaling firm.)

7. According to industrial organization economists, when low seller and buyer concentration, little product differentiation, and easy entry exist simultaneously in a market, the chances for good economic performance, from a social welfare perspective, are higher than in the opposite situation. How, then, could they (or you) explain the performance of the ghetto marketplace?

8. What are some likely solutions to the distribution problems in the ghetto marketplace?

9. Overall, how would you characterize the performance of the distributive trades? Is it poor, improving, or strong from a macro perspective? From a micro perspective? If poor, what needs to be done to improve it?

10. Prepare a systems matrix for a candy manufacturer who distributes through rack jobbers to supermarkets.

A Case Study of Channel Environment, Structure, and Policy Audit: Simpson Timber's Columbia Door Division

MARKET ENVIRONMENT

Simpson Timber's Columbia Door Division, a manufacturing facility for wood flush doors used in home and building construction, is located in Southwest Washington. While the major markets for this plant were in California, Oregon, and Washington, it had also penetrated the western areas of the Midwest markets (mostly Mountain States), where no flush door manufacturers existed.

Simpson was realizing major successes in the Midwest market by selling doors to major wholesalers, who supplied many of the retail units and major contractors scattered throughout an eleven-state area. While the wood flush door market was treated by most wholesalers and manufacturers in this area as a commodity market, the wholesalers, given equal treatment by the manufacturers, tended to prefer specific manufacturers like Simpson. This preference presumably arose through "personal" contacts made during the introduction of the products and the contacts made with the wholesalers by the Simpson representatives selling other lines of Simpson specialty products.

Having traditionally treated the flush door market as a commodity market, Simpson had given it minimal attention except for price and delivery. An agent served as the Midwest middleman, providing information to Simpson on competitors' prices and delivery schedules. The agent also took orders from the wholesalers. The agent provided no services to customers other than information processing. The distance between the wholesale centers in the Midwest market and the manufacturing facility made direct visits to these middlemen by Columbia Door marketing personnel an infrequent event. This was deemed unnecessary because the company's share of the product's wholesale market in the region had been substantial, stable, and growing slightly.

THE PROBLEM

However, a new class of middlemen was entering the market in strong enough force to demand direct negotiations with the competitive manufacturers. Previ-

Source: Reprinted from William G. Browne and E. D. (Pat) Reiten, "Auditing Distribution Channels," *Journal of Marketing* (July 1978), pp. 38–42, published by the American Management Association.

ously Simpson's Columbia Door Division had chosen to ignore other types of middlemen and protect the industry's normal channel relationship (manufacturer → wholesaler → retailer, contractor and industrial builder). This policy probably was appropriate earlier in the company's marketing efforts, when only the wholesaler had order sizes large enough to fill complete carloads (the normal lot size delivered from most building supply manufacturers).

With the advent of major industrialized home builders, major component builders and sizeable chain retail lumber yards, there were increasing pressures for the manufacturers to sell directly to these new middlemen.

Simpson Timber, with little information coming from the agent, was having a difficult time tracking the market activities of their competition and potential customers. After a gross picture of the situation was obtained by using many approximations and substantial secondary data sources, management decided to obtain a closer view of the trends and events or conditions that were supporting the trends. Accordingly, a survey was conducted in the market, covering most of the high-volume users.

THE CHANNEL ENVIRONMENT, STRUCTURE, AND POLICY AUDIT

Initially the Columbia Door Division's records were reviewed to develop a list of their customers for the past three years. Volume trends for each of the customers (all of them wholesalers) were established.

Building statistics were obtained from R. C. Mean's Forecasts for home-starts. From these statistics, using standardized conversion multipliers, the number of wood flush doors consumed or to be consumed in the market could be estimated. When these figures were compared with estimates of the number of units handled by wholesalers, they were noticeably larger; and the trend indicated that the gap could become even larger.

Personnel in the door division were concerned as to the accuracy of the secondary sources used in these calculations and wanted confirmation of their initial observations. It became evident that a survey would be necessary to obtain more accurate figures concerning the market impact of the new middlemen purchasing directly from manufacturers. Figures were also needed to obtain better understanding of the impact of new specialty flush doors on the middlemen's purchase intentions. Thus, the survey questionnaire was designed in part to identify the elements of the market most responsive to the specialty type doors.

To identify wholesalers, retailers, major contractors, industrialized home builders, and large component builders who might purchase wood flush doors in sizeable quantities, raw lists were developed from the *Directory of Forest Products Industry; The Bluebook of Major Homebuilders; Dun and Bradstreet, Middle Market Directory; The Yellow Pages* of local phone directories; *Lumberman's Redbook;* and Simpson's own accounting records. Best estimates were that these lists included every possible carload lot purchaser in the market. (It was recognized that a number of entries on the lists did not qualify for carload lost purchases so one of the survey's leading questions focused on purchase sizes.) The lists were consolidated into a master list with duplicate entries eliminated.

The questionnaire was developed with the major goals of obtaining information on:

- Annual wood flush door volume
- The volume of major door subgroups, such as unfinished and prefinished
- The year-to-year increase in purchases of each such group
- The number of suppliers, volume from each supplier, and breakdown of sales per customer type
- Major competitors
- Any major channel and product volume trends that were occurring, including trends for specialty-type subgroups

Telephone interviews were utilized. Responses from the middlemen (wholesalers, retailers, industrial component, and home builders) verified that the historical channel arrangement (until the late 1960s) had been through the wholesaler (see Chart 1).

The data also indicated that there had been a substantial shift in the channel arrangement (see Chart 2). In particular, further expansion of direct purchases from the industrial sector was to be expected.

It was also revealed that the specialty product introduced by Masonite was being accepted readily and uniformly throughout the market. No single class of middlemen was providing for the majority of specialty product distribution. Also most of the middlemen, and especially the larger ones, expected to see substantial growth in the specialty market and were looking for new supplier competition in this part of the market.

Chart 1 Historical channel arrangement: Wood flush door suppliers

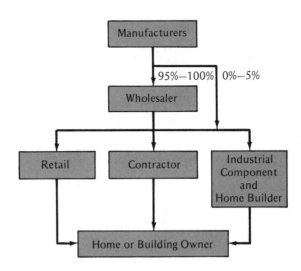

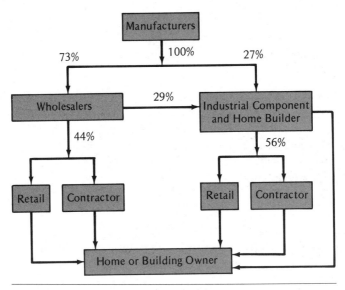

Chart 2 Current channel arrangement: Wood flush door suppliers

CHANGES INSTITUTED

The first change to be considered and instituted was for the company to replace the agent. Simpson feared that the substantial "goodwill" the agent may have created with the company's traditional flush door customers would be endangered.

Also there was concern that the agent's product lines from other manufacturers complemented, in some way, his door offering from Simpson. However, the responses indicated that there was no direct physical connection between the agent's other products and the flush doors. Also, conversations with some of the middlemen who had been cooperative during the questionnaire stages of the project provided data to suggest that these fears should not be of great concern.

Once the decision was made to find a replacement for the agent, it was concluded that the position should be filled internally by opening a sales office in the market. This would mean that there would be a sales position in the region responsible for both the commodity door and the introduction of the new specialty substitute.

RESULTS

Missionary work with larger retailers and contractors improved sales to the wholesalers who were serving these markets. There appeared to be an upsurge in demand, primarily to fill inventory in the retail locations where the salesman had substantial influence because of his previous experiences.

The salesman also opened direct negotiations with selected members of the industrial and retail sectors. These visits were limited to industrial and retail customers who had small, if any, flush door purchases from the company's current wholesale customers. Responses from these negotiations were favorable, with a number of initial orders. Visible concern by the current wholesale customers was not evident.

PART FOUR

CHANNEL MANAGEMENT IN OTHER CONTEXTS

CHAPTER TWELVE

International Marketing Channels

Except for the smallest marketers of goods and services, it is doubtful that any commercial institution can avoid contact with the international marketplace in one form or another, even if such avoidance were somewhat desirable. The opportunities to be gained from trading with foreign companies, serving foreign consumers, or offering assortments of merchandise selected from the world's production are simply too great to pass by.

However, involvement in the international marketplace is becoming more and more complex as dramatic changes take place in the world economy. Basic conditions such as the strong dollar, sluggish growth abroad, and debt problems among the less developed countries have generated trade deficits in the United States over the last several years.[1] Although exports declined to $213.1 billion in 1985, causing a $148.5 billion deficit, the U.S. remains the single largest contributor to world exports, with approximately 13 percent of the total export market.[2]

One of the growth areas for U.S. exports has been the developing countries. Ten of the 20 largest U.S. trade partners in 1984 were developing countries, including Mexico, Taiwan, Korea, Hong Kong, Brazil, Venezuela, Saudi Arabia, Singapore, Indonesia, and China. Table 12–1 provides data on exports to and imports from the 20 largest partners as well as their overall importance to U.S. trade.

U.S. imports, on the other hand, expanded 6 percent in 1985, to $361.6 billion. This figure is significantly less than the 1984 growth rate of 26 percent.[3]

[1] "U.S. Trade Outlook," *Business America* (U.S. Department of Commerce, ITA) Vol. 9, No. 6 (March 17, 1986), p. 3.
[2] *Ibid.*, p. 3, 19.
[3] *Ibid.*, p. 4.

Table 12–1   Twenty largest U.S. trading partners, 1984

	Total Transactions	U.S. Exports ($ billions)	U.S. Imports
Canada	113.4	46.5	66.9
Japan	83.9	23.5	60.4
Mexico	**30.3**	**12.0**	**18.3**
United Kingdom	27.3	12.2	15.0
Germany, Fed. Rep.	26.9	9.1	17.8
Taiwan	**21.1**	**5.0**	**16.1**
Korea, Rep.	**16.0**	**6.0**	**10.0**
France	14.6	6.0	8.5
Italy	12.9	4.4	8.5
Hong Kong	**12.0**	**3.1**	**8.9**
Netherlands	11.9	7.6	4.3
Brazil	**10.9**	**2.6**	**8.3**
Venezuela	**10.2**	**3.4**	**6.8**
Saudi Arabia	**9.6**	**5.6**	**4.0**
Belgium-Luxembourg	8.6	5.3	3.3
Singapore	**7.8**	**3.7**	**4.1**
Australia	7.7	4.8	2.9
Indonesia	**7.1**	**1.2**	**5.9**
China, People's Rep.	**6.4**	**3.0**	**3.4**
Switzerland	5.8	2.6	3.2
Total, Twenty Countries	444.2	167.5	276.6
Total, Ten Developing Countries	131.3	45.5	85.8
TOTAL U.S. TRADE	559.1	217.9	341.2
	(percentages)		
Ten Developing Countries, as a percentage of total U.S. trade	23.5	20.9	25.1

Note: Developing countries in bold type. Export figures are f.a.s. (free alongside ship) transaction values. Import figures are c.i.f. (customs, insurance, and freight).

Source: U.S. Department of Commerce, *Highlights of U.S. Export and Import Trade*, December 1984, Tables E-5 and I-8.

In view of lagging exports, moderate import growth is necessary to correct the large trade deficit.

Regardless of the United State's merchandise trade position, U.S. companies are becoming increasingly involved in and reliant on international business. Within the past 30 years, U.S. companies overall have increased their investment in foreign affiliates from about $25 billion to over $200 billion.[4] Table 12–2 provides data on the largest U.S. multinationals and the importance of their foreign operations to the total performance of the company.

In general the importance of world trade to many economies can be seen in Table 12–3, which illustrates the dependence on world trade of the United States, France, Germany, the United Kingdom, and Japan. With the increased dependence of these countries on world trade has come increased competition. Companies such as Norelco (Holland), Libby (Switzerland), Volkswagen (Ger-

[4] Philip R. Cateora, *International Marketing*, 5th ed. (Homewood, Ill.: Richard D. Irwin, 1983), p. 3.

Table 12–2 The 25 largest U.S. multinationals

Company	Foreign Revenue (millions)	Total Revenue (millions)	Foreign as % of Total	Foreign Operating Profit (millions)	Total Operating Profit (millions)	Foreign as % of Total
Exxon	$69,386	$97,173	71.4%	$2,208	$4,343	50.8%
Mobil	37,778	60,969	62.0	880	1,380	63.8
Texaco	31,118	46,986	66.2	833	1,281	65.0
Standard Oil of Calif	16,957	34,362	49.3	404	1,377	29.3
Phibro-Salomon	16,600	26,703	62.2	218	337	64.7
Ford Motor Company	16,526	37,067	44.6	460	−658	P/D
IBM	15,336	34,364	44.6	1,646	4,409	37.3
General Motors	14,376	60,026	23.9	−107	963	D/P
Gulf Oil	11,513	28,427	40.5	300	900	33.3
E I du Pont de Nemours	11,057	33,223	33.3	488	1,491	32.7
Citicorp	10,865	17,814	61.0	448	723	62.0
ITT	9,824	21,922	44.8	851	1,194	71.3
BankAmerica	8,051	14,955	53.8	253	389	65.0
Chase Manhattan	6,207	10,171	61.0	215	307	70.0
Dow Chemical	5,544	10,618	52.2	143	356	40.2
General Electric	5,490	27,192	20.2	395	1,817	21.7
Sun Co.	4,901	15,739	31.1	54	706	7.7
Standard Oil Indiana	4,862	28,389	17.1	618	1,826	33.8
Occidental Petroleum	4,715	18,527	25.4	345	548	63.0
Safeway Stores	4,380	17,633	24.8	84	160	52.5
J. P. Morgan	4,268	6,885	62.0	283	394	71.8
Eastman Kodak	4,181	10,815	38.7	302	1,860	16.2
Manufacturers Hanover	3,929	7,640	51.4	147	295	49.8
Procter & Gamble	3,737	11,994	31.2	88	777	11.3
Xerox	3,630	8,456	42.9	151	424	35.6

Source: Excerpted by permission of *Forbes* magazine, July 4, 1983, p. 114, © Forbes Inc., 1983.

Table 12–3   Dependence on world trade

	Value of Manufactured Exports, 1985 ($ billions)	Share of World Exports, 1985	Exports as Percent of GNP, 1985
United States	145	12.8	5.3
France	70	5.7	19.9
Germany	152	10.3	29.7
United Kingdom	68	5.8	23.0
Japan	164	10.1	10.2

Source: U.S. Department of Commerce, International Trade Administration, March 1986.

many), and Honda (Japan) are foreign-based companies producing brands familiar to U.S. consumers and causing U.S. producers increased competition.

Meanwhile, the volume of foreign goods carried by U.S. wholesaling and retailing firms has risen significantly since the mid 1950s. Major retailing firms are expanding their operations abroad. Multinational retailers constitute a long list that includes Federated Department Stores in Madrid; Sears in Mexico, South America, and Spain; J. C. Penney in Belgium and Italy; Kresge in Australia; Walgreen in Mexico; Safeway in Great Britain, Germany, and Australia; and Jewel in Belgium, Italy, Mexico, and Spain.[5] These are joined by scores of multinational franchisors, exemplified by McDonald's, Kentucky Fried Chicken, Weight Watchers, Avis, Hertz, and Holiday Inn, to name only a few.[6] The internationalization of retailing is not limited to U.S. retailers, however. For example, Prisunic, Monsprix, and SCOA Trading Company of France; Ahlen & Holm and EPA of Sweden; and Booker McConnell, John Holt & Company, and Hudson's Bay of Britain have tapped worldwide markets, as have certain European franchisors, such as Wimpy and Carrier Cook Shops.[7] In the United States, Saks and Marshall Field's are owned by a British firm, and A&P and Aldi by German firms.

It is possible to postulate that unless a firm is somehow actively participating in the international marketplace—either through support of buying offices, in the case of retailers and wholesalers, or through attempts to sell abroad, in the case of manufacturers, it will suffer a severe competitive disadvantage to those that are.

The purpose of this chapter is to examine the channels of distribution available to organizations that wish to tap foreign markets and to enumerate some of the myriad interorganizational problems associated with trying to use them. Attention is also directed to institutional responses and possible alternatives for overcoming these problems. It is, however, very important to note at the outset that generalizations about international marketing channels are frequently deceptive because of the vast environmental differences from country to

[5] Stanley C. Hollander, "The International Store-Keepers," *MSU Business Topics* (Spring 1969), pp. 13–22.

[6] Bruce Walker and Michael Etzel, "The Internationalization of U.S. Franchise Systems: Progress and Procedures," *Journal of Marketing*, Vol. 37 (April 1973), pp. 38–46.

[7] Stanley C. Hollander, *Multinational Retailing* (East Lansing, Mich.; Michigan State University, 1970), pp. 27–41, 62–70. See also "Inflation and Recession Dampen Profits Worldwide," *Business Week* (July 14, 1975), pp. 71–75.

country. Indeed, the marketing channel has been described as one of the most differentiated aspects of national marketing systems. To a large extent, as was pointed out in Chapter 1, channels are shaped by their environments; therefore, to equate retailing in India, for example, with retailing in Egypt or to make inferences about retailing in the two countries combined would be misleading and erroneous. Although all countries have some semblance of a wholesaling and a retailing structure, the variations within each structure are vast indeed, as indicated in Fig. 12–1.[8]

INTERORGANIZATIONAL PERSPECTIVE OF ALTERNATIVE FORMS OF INTERNATIONAL EXPANSION

The perspective taken in this chapter is basically that of a U.S. manufacturer considering expansion abroad. There appear to be four basic routes to such expansion, although clearly there are numerous possible variations. The simplest form of expansion is through the *exportation* of a company's products to nations with a demand for the products. Exportation can be achieved directly, through the use of foreign distributors or agents, or by establishing overseas marketing subsidiaries. Alternatively, exportations can be achieved through the use of trading companies, domestic export management companies, or piggybacking. Through the last arrangement, one manufacturer uses its overseas distribution channels to sell another company's product along with its own.[9] The benefits from this allied operation derive from the manufacturer's existing system, established contacts, and knowledge of the foreign market.[10] Piggybacking is beneficial for both parties. It provides additional revenue through exports for firms that cannot justify continuing in the market because of small export potential. In addition, piggybacking supplements existing marketing efforts by providing coverage in markets where a manufacturer is not currently represented.[11] Here are some examples of piggybacking:

- Singer Sewing Machine Company distributes products closely allied to its own, such as fabrics, patterns, notions, and thread.[12]
- Sony, the Japanese electronics firm, sells U.S. and European products in Japan. Through Sony International Housewares it distributes for Whirlpool, Schick, Regal Ware, Heath, and other U.S. firms.[13]
- Colgate Palmolive Company buys razors and blades from the Wilkinson Sword Company in Britain and distributes them in the United States, Puerto Rico, Canada, and Scandinavia. Henkel Company of Germany uses Colgate to distribute Putt Glue Stick.

[8] Readers interested in descriptions of distribution channels in different countries may refer to overseas business reports published by the U.S. Department of Commerce.

[9] Vern Terpstra, *International Marketing*, 3rd ed. (Hinsdale, Ill.: Dryden Press, 1983), p. 330.

[10] Ruel Kahler, *International Marketing*, 5th ed. (Cincinnati: Southwestern Publishing Co., 1983), p. 172.

[11] *Ibid.*

[12] Cateora, *op. cit.*, p. 593.

[13] Kahler, *op. cit.*, p. 172.

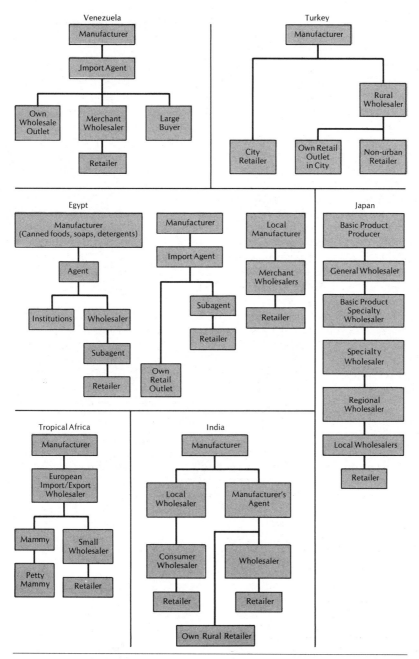

Figure 12–1 Marketing channels in selected countries

Source: George Wadinambiaratchi, "Channels of Distribution in Developing Economics," *The Business Quarterly,* Vol. 30 (Winter 1965), pp. 74–82.

- Borg-Warner markets Hamilton Beach Company's small appliances, McGraw Edison Company's Toastmaster products, and In-Sink-Erator Company's garbage disposals through established channels in Europe.[14]

The advantage of exportation to foreign markets is that it involves minimal investment, and thus the risk of failure will not usually affect the overall activities of the firm. The disadvantage of relying mainly on export agencies, however, is that the company will usually have *little control* over the marketing of its products in foreign markets.

Another form of expansion is *licensing,* whereby the company forges a contractual agreement with a foreign organization to manufacture and/or sell its products abroad with the understanding that a certain percentage of the profits will accrue to each of the parties.[15] The "home" company generally is expected to furnish technical assistance to the foreign firm. The main advantages of this route are the low investment required by the home company and the assurance that at least some form of purposive marketing strategy will be adopted for the firm's products. However, as in the case of simple exportation, there may be *little real control* over the licensee's operation. It is even possible that the licensee will eventually acquire the technical expertise of the home firm, thereby altering the dependency relationship. Thus, *power* in such situations may *rapidly shift* to the foreign firm.

A third and more involved route to expansion is the establishment of *joint ventures,* whereby two or more firms share the investment and risk of the expansionary effort. If the joint venture is forged with a foreign firm, the home firm obviously gains the commitment of the foreign firm to share its skills and its market access. Again, there are problems of control, but they appear to be less than in situations where mutual investment is not involved.

Joint ventures enable U.S. companies to penetrate difficult markets such as Japan. For example:

- Baxter Travenol Laboratories of Deerfield, Illinois, a leading manufacturer of medical-care products, has a successful joint venture with Sumitomo Chemical Company. Sales of the joint venture are reported as increasing at a faster rate than the parent firm's 23 percent annual growth rate.[16]
- Sears Roebuck & Company has a joint venture with Seibu Stores in Japan. The venture operates 80 stores, and significant annual sales increases are reported in appliances and apparel.[17]
- Kentucky Fried Chicken Japan is a joint venture between Heublein and Mitsubishi Corporation. KFC opened its first ten restaurants in 1970. By 1977 the number of stores had grown to 150, with $15.3 million in sales.[18]

Similarly, Japanese companies cracked the U.S. market via joint ventures such as the one formed between TRW and Fujutsu.

If the home company wishes to achieve a high degree of control over the

[14] Terpstra, *op. cit.,* p. 332.

[15] In consumer goods marketing, soft drink companies (PepsiCo, Coca-Cola) have long been engaged in international franchising. More recently, fast-food firms, such as McDonald's, have expanded, using licensing arrangements. See "Europe: A Wolfish Hunger for U.S. Fast Foods," *Business Week* (October 21, 1972), p. 34. Also see Walker and Etzel, *op. cit.*

[16] Mike Thorp, "Drive to Bolster Dollar by Increasing Exports Encounters Obstacles," *Wall Street Journal,* September 20, 1978, p. 20.

[17] *Ibid.*

[18] Mike Thorp, "Marketing in Japan Takes Twisty Turns, Foreign Firms Find," *Wall Street Journal,* March 9, 1977, p. 19.

marketing of its products abroad, it will probably undertake a fourth route—*direct investment*—by establishing a wholly owned subsidiary in a foreign country. If it does this, it must commit itself to learning the mores and nuances of each foreign market it enters. The dollar amount of the investment—in terms of both capital expenditure and management time—is likely to be substantial, and there is always a risk of expropriation and nationalization, particularly in politically unstable countries.[19]

Direct investment has been encouraged by foreign trade restrictions, which have frequently made it difficult or impossible for a U.S. company to compete in a foreign market without having a plant or subsidiary abroad. In addition, Robert Solomon, the Federal Reserve Board's former chief adviser on international finance, has observed that

> an overvalued dollar made it cheap to acquire assets abroad. It also made it unattractive to convert foreign earnings back into dollars and thus tended to encourage reinvestment of profits abroad. In the late 1950s and the early 1960s, the profitability of investment simply was higher abroad than in the U.S.[20]

Thus, by 1983 U.S. direct investment abroad had reached $226.12 billion, compared with $135 billion of foreign direct investment in the United States. The United States is the largest investor abroad, with approximately 50 percent of total direct investment. U.S. investment abroad, however, has been concentrated much more in the developed than in the developing countries. Within slightly more than 20 years, the percentage of American foreign investment in the developed nations has risen from 60.6 percent to 71.7 percent.[21]

Although the United States is a major foreign investor, direct investment in the U.S. is increasing in importance relative to U.S. direct investment in other countries. In 1960 the ratio of U.S. direct investment abroad to foreign direct investment in the United States was 4.6 to 1, but in 1982 the ratio decreased to 2.2 to 1. As a matter of fact, foreign direct investment in the United States doubled between 1978 and 1982.[22] Among the several reasons for this increase are (1) the depreciation of the American dollar against other currencies, (2) lower prices for land, energy, transportation, and work space, (3) political stability, and (4) the large market size and potential of the United States.[23]

As illustrated in Table 12–4, Americans consume the products and use the services of many foreign firms with direct investments in the United States. Examples of some of the most commonly used products and services include Peter Paul candy bars, Pepsodent toothpaste, Hardee's hamburgers, A&P groceries, and Howard Johnson motels and restaurants.[24]

In selecting a foreign market entry method, decision criteria related to the firm, its industry, the foreign market, and the entry method have to be established. Key decision criteria are summarized in Exhibit 12–1.

---

[19] For a complete discussion of these and other expansionary routes, see Cateora, *op. cit.*, Chapter 17. For data on some of the political difficulties encountered in direct investment, see "Multinationals Find the Going Rougher," *Business Week* (July 14, 1975), pp. 64–69.

[20] Quoted in Lindley H. Clark, Jr., "Global Crossroads: Multinational Firms under Fire All Over, Face a Changed Future," *Wall Street Journal*, December 3, 1975, p. 21.

[21] Donald Ball and Wendell McCulloch, Jr., *International Business*, 2nd ed. (Plano, Tex.: Business Publications, 1985), p. 32.

[22] Martin C. Schnitzer, Marilyn M. Liebrenz, Konrad W. Kubin, *International Business* (Cincinnati: Southwestern Publishing Co., 1985), p. 404.

[23] *Ibid.*

[24] *Ibid.* p. 402.

Table 12–4 Fifteen largest foreign investments in the United States

Foreign Investor	Country	U.S. Company	Industry	Revenue ($ million)	Assets ($ million)
1. Seagram Co., Ltd.	Canada	Joseph Seagrams (100%) E. I. duPont (21%)	Spirits and wines Chemicals	$ 1,480 35,173	$ 4,780 24,432
2. Anglo American Corporation	South Africa	Phibro-Salomon (21%) Engelhard (29%) & others	Metal trading and metals	36,653 32,417	43,694
3. Royal Dutch Shell	Netherlands Great Britain	Shell Oil (69%) Billiton Metals (100%) and others	Energy, Metals	20,978	22,169
4. British Petroleum	Great Britain	Standard Oil Ohio (53%) B P North America (100%)	Energy	11,599 N.A.	16,362 N.A.
5. Mitsui & Company	Japan	Alumax (50%) Mitsui & Co. USA (100%)	Aluminum General trading	1,510 8,055E	1,512 2,046
6. B.A.T.	Great Britain	BATUS (100%) Hardee's Food (100%) People's Drug Stores (96%)	Paper, tobacco, retailing Fast food Drug stores	9,545 5,524 807 791 7,122	3,903 364 229
7. Flick Group	Germany	W. R. Grace (28%)	Multicompany	6,219	5,035
8. Tenglemann Group	Germany	Great A&P Tea (51%)	Supermarkets	5,222	1,200
9. Renault	France	American Motors (46%) Mack Truck (46%)	Automotive	3,272 1,212	1,724 973
10. Brascan, Ltd.	Canada	Scott Paper (24%) Noranda, Inc. (100%) MacMillan Bloedel (100%)	Paper products Aluminum Forest products	4,484 2,465 1,023 763 4,251	2,252 N.A. N.A.
11. Philips	Netherlands	North American Philips (59%) Signetics (100%)	Electronics Semiconductors	3,800 450	2,252 N.A.
12. General Occidentale	France	Grand Union (100%)	Supermarkets	3,519	765
13. Volkswagen	Germany	Volkswagen of America (100%) Royal Business Machines (100%)	Automotive Office equipment	2,992 500E 3,492	N.A. N.A.
14. Bayer	Germany	Mobay Chemical (100%) Miles (100%) Agfa-Gervaert (100%) and others	Chemicals Health care Photography	3,445	2,700E
15. Mitsubishi	Japan	Mitsubishi Int'l Co.	Trading Co.	3,165	N.A.

Notes: E—estimated   N.A.—not available

Source: "The 100 Largest Foreign Investments in the U.S.," excerpted by permission of *Forbes* magazine, July 2, 1984, pp. 117–18. © Forbes, Inc., 1983.

EXHIBIT 12–1   Decision criteria for selecting foreign market entry

NUMBER OF MARKETS

Companies have different ambitions in international marketing, including the number of countries they want to enter. Different entry methods offer different coverage of international markets. For example, wholly owned foreign operations are not permitted in some countries; the licensing approach may be impossible in other markets because the firm cannot find qualified licensees; or a trading company might cover certain markets very well but have no representation in other markets. To get the kind of international market coverage it wants, the firm will probably have to combine different entry methods. In some markets, it may have wholly owned operations; in others, marketing subsidiaries; in yet others, local distributors.

PENETRATION WITHIN MARKETS

Related to the number of markets covered is the quality of that coverage. An export management company, for example, might claim to give the producer access to 60 countries. The producer must probe further to find out if this "access" is to the whole national market or if it is limited to the capital or a few large cities. Having a small catalog sales office in the capital city is very different from having a sales force to cover the whole national market.

MARKET FEEDBACK

If it is important that the firm know what is going on in its foreign markets, it must choose an entry method that will provide this feedback. Although in general the more direct methods of entry offer better possibilities of market information, feedback opportunities will depend in part on how the firm manages a particular form of market entry.

LEARNING BY EXPERIENCE

Experience is still the best teacher, and the firm will get more international marketing experience the more directly it is involved in foreign markets. The firm with international marketing ambitions should choose an entry method to help it gain some experience and realize these ambitions. The firm cannot "learn by doing" if others are doing the international marketing.

CONTROL

Management control over foreign marketing ranges from none at all—for example, selling through a trading company—to complete control as in a wholly owned subsidiary. The firm may want a strong voice in several aspects of its foreign marketing, for instance, pricing and credit terms, promotion, product quality, and servicing of its products. The extent to which such control is critical to the firm will bear heavily on its choice of entry method.

INCREMENTAL MARKETING COSTS

There are costs associated with international marketing, no matter who does it. However, the producer's incremental marketing outlays and working capital requirements will vary with the directness of the international marketing channel. For example, with indirect exporting there would be practically no additional outlays by the producer.

PROFIT POSSIBILITIES

Presumably, profit is a major goal of the company. In evaluating the profit potential of different entry methods, the long-run sales and costs associated with each entry method must be estimated. Costs and profit margins are less important than total profit possibilities. For example, one entry method may offer a 25 percent profit margin on a sales volume of $2 million, but another may offer a 17 percent profit margin on a sales volume of $10 million. The latter entry method probably would be more attractive, even though it has lower profit margins, because the total profit available is greater ($1.7 million as opposed to $500,000).

INVESTMENT REQUIREMENTS

Investment requirements are obviously highest in wholly owned foreign operations. Plant investment, however, is not the only consideration; capital also may be required to finance inventories and to extend credit. Since the amount of capital required varies greatly by method of market entry, this financial need will be an important determinant for most firms.

ADMINISTRATIVE REQUIREMENTS

The administrative burdens and costs of international marketing vary by entry method. These include documentation and red tape, as well as the amount of management required. For example, indirect exporting or licensing may involve very little additional burden on management.

PERSONNEL REQUIREMENTS

Not only capital requirements vary by method of entry; so do personnel needs. Generally, the more direct kinds of involvement require a larger number of skilled international business personnel. If the firm is short of "internationalists," it will be constrained in its alternatives.

EXPOSURE TO FOREIGN PROBLEMS

The more directly the firm is involved in foreign markets, the more management will have to deal directly with new kinds of legislation, regulation, taxes, labor problems, and other foreign market peculiarities. If the firm is unable or unwilling to deal with those problems it will choose an entry method that lets someone else handle them.

FLEXIBILITY

If the firm expects to be in foreign markets for the long run, some flexibility in its method of entry is important. Any entry method optimal at one point in time may be less than optimal five years later. Not only do the environment and the market change, so too do the company situation and goals. The firm therefore wants flexibility—the ability to change to meet new conditions. It may wish either to expand its involvement to take advantage of rapidly growing markets, or to contract its operations because of adverse developments.

Although not easy to achieve, this flexibility will be much greater where the firm has planned for it in choosing its method of entry. For this reason, firms sometimes gain experience with limited forms of involvement before committing themselves heavily to a market. However, using distributors and licensees may not always offer the desired flexibility, even though they are limited forms of foreign market involvement.

DESIGNING INTERNATIONAL DISTRIBUTION STRATEGY

Regardless of the expansionary route followed, the international marketer will be faced with the problem of designing and implementing a distribution strategy. The channel system for international marketing, especially for those firms not undertaking direct investment, almost always involves two channel segments, one domestic and the other foreign, as shown in Fig. 12–2.[25] Compared with marketing within one's home country, the international marketing channel is of necessity longer, because it generally involves a large number of intermediaries, which play a major role in facilitating the flow of products from domestic production to foreign consumption. Obviously, this results in increasing the complexity of managing the channel, from an interorganization perspective, because of the idiosyncrasies of international intermediaries, the environments in which they operate, and the lack of effective and economically feasible control over their operations.

In designing international distribution channels and in developing distribution strategy, international marketers focus on common goals, including

1. Adequate market coverage
2. Control over goods in the channel
3. Reasonable distribution costs
4. Continuity of channel relationships and, consequently, continuous presence in the market
5. Desired volume, market share, margin requirements, and return on investment

More likely than not, international marketers find these goals illusory or difficult to achieve because of the idiosyncrasies of international channels, as will become evident as we discuss wholesale and retail linkages and patterns in international markets.

[25] Kahler, *op. cit.,* p. 165.

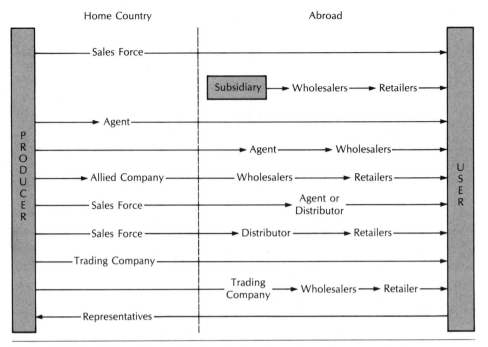

Figure 12–2 Selected international marketing channels

Source: Ruel Kahler, *International Marketing,* 5th ed. (Cincinnati, Ohio: Southwestern Publishing Company, 1983), p. 165.

WHOLESALE LINKAGES TO FOREIGN MARKETS[26]

Figure 12–2 provides some idea of the international channel alternatives available to a domestic producer. Domestic middlemen are located in the producer's home country and provide marketing services from the domestic base. As Cateora points out, they are closer to the manufacturer and are convenient to use, but are removed from their foreign markets and therefore may not be able to provide the kind of market information and representation available from foreign-based middlemen.[27] Table 12–5 summarizes the primary functions performed by the major kinds of domestic middlemen selling to foreign markets. A brief description of a few of the various types of agents follows, based on Cateora's classification scheme:[28]

- *EMC (export management company):* An agent middleman who generally serves a number of principals, each of which has a relatively small international volume, and acts as the international marketing department for the firms he represents. The

[26] The discussion in this section is based largely on the excellent descriptions in Cateora, *op. cit.,* Chapter 18.

[27] *Ibid.,* p. 581.

[28] *Ibid.,* pp. 584–85, 582–83.

main functions performed by the EMC are contact with foreign customers and negotiations for sales. He will usually do business under the principal's name (e.g., using the principal's letterhead), and thus foreign customers seldom know that they are not dealing directly with the export department of the principal. He operates mainly on commission but may also receive fees.

- *MEA (manufacturer's export agent):* An agent middleman similar to the EMC, except that the former does not serve as the producer's export department but has a short-term relationship, covers only one or two markets, and operates on a straight commission basis. Another difference is the MEAs do business in their own names rather than in the names of their principals.
- *Norazi:* An agent who specializes in shady or difficult transactions, such as those involving contraband materials (e.g., radioactive products, war materials), black market currency operations, untaxed liquor, and narcotics.

The "Merchants" category in Table 12–6 refers primarily to merchant wholesale operations. Their functions are almost identical to those of the merchant middlemen described in Chapter 3 except that they sell in foreign countries. Merchant middlemen provide a variety of import and export wholesaling functions involving purchasing for their own accounts and selling in other countries. They bear the majority of trading risks for all the products they handle and receive a profit for the gross margin spread.[29]

Among the most important merchant middlemen in international commerce are trading companies. The origin, functions, and scope of operations of trading companies are discussed in Exhibit 12–2.

Rather than dealing with the home country agents or merchant middlemen, a manufacturer may choose to deal directly with the middlemen located in foreign markets. The advantages of working with foreign-based middlemen are that they provide time and place utility by purchasing and holding the goods at a location relatively convenient to customers; provide credit service; take the risk of price fluctuations; provide varying degrees of sales service; and thus bring the manufacturer closer to markets and shorten his channel. On the other hand, problems may arise due to lack of control. The disadvantages of this type of arrangement are that merchant middlemen select their own selling prices; may have little manufacturer loyalty because they handle large amounts of goods; and are more likely to favor high-profit, high-turnover items. For these reasons it is unwise to rely heavily on foreign middlemen to promote and sell a product aggressively. As with all middlemen, effectiveness depends on the selection of the middlemen and on the amount of control the manufacturer is willing and able to exert.[30] Table 12–6 summarizes the primary functions of foreign-based middlemen. While the functions of the various agent middlemen generally follow the description of U.S. agent middlemen found in Chapter 3, it should be emphasized once again that in foreign commerce there seem to be very few "pure" types. In other words, the functions performed and marketing flows participated in may vary from situation to situation and are generally subject to negotiations. For example, one unique form of agent middleman is the *comprador* or *del credere* agent.

The comprador functions in Far Eastern countries and has historically been particularly important in trade with China. He is essentially a general manager who acts

[29] *Ibid.,* p. 588.
[30] *Ibid.,* pp. 596–97.

Table 12–5   Characteristics of domestic middlemen serving overseas markets

	Agents				
Types of Duties	EMC	MEA	Broker	Buying Offices	Selling Groups
Take title	No	No	No	No	No
Take possession	Yes	Yes	No	Yes	Yes
Continuing relationship	Yes	Yes	No	Yes	Yes
Share of foreign output	All	All	Any	Small	All
Degree of control by principal	Fair	Fair	Nil	Nil	Good
Price authority	Advisory	Advisory	Yes (at market level)	Yes (to buy)	Advisory
Represent buyer or seller	Seller	Seller	Either	Buyer	Seller
Number of principals	Few-Many	Few-Many	Many	Small	Few
Arrange shipping	Yes	Yes	Not usually	Yes	Yes
Type of goods	Manufactured goods and commodities	Staples and commodities	Staples and commodities	Staples and commodities	Complementary to their own lines
Breadth of line	Specialty-wide	All types of staples	All types of staples	Retail goods	Narrow
Handle competitive lines	No	No	Yes	Yes—utilizes many sources	No
Extent of promotion and selling effort	Good	Good	One shot	N.A.	Good
Extends credit to principal	Occasionally	Occasionally	Seldom	Seldom	Seldom
Market information	Fair	Fair	Price and market conditions	For principal not for manufacturer	Good

Note: N.A. = not available

as the representative of a foreign merchant in his operations in a given Oriental country. A comprador is used because of his intimate knowledge of the obscure and enigmatic customs and languages of the importing country.[31]

In many respects, foreign merchant middlemen are also not significantly different, in terms of functions performed, from U.S. merchant middlemen. However, because of the absence of antitrust laws similar to those found in the United States, it is often possible for a U.S.-based producer to exercise greater coercive, reward, and legitimate power over foreign intermediaries. Thus, many foreign distributors have been granted exclusive territorial rights by their suppliers, and relationships with suppliers are frequently formalized through tight franchise or ownership arrangements that might be challengeable in the United States.[32] Another difference is that foreign retailers frequently engage directly in importing for both retailing *and* wholesaling purposes.

[31] *Ibid.,* p. 597.
[32] See "Using Foreign Distributors without Fearing Antitrust," *Business Abroad* (March 8, 1965), p. 28.

Table 12–5 (Continued)

| | Merchants | | | | |
| | | | Buyers for Export | Importers and Trading Companies | Complementary Marketers |
Norazi	Export Merchant	Export Jobber			
No	Yes	Yes	Yes	Yes	Yes
Yes	Yes	No	Yes	Yes	Yes
No	No	Yes	No	Yes	Yes
Small	Any	Small	Small	Any	Most
Nil	None	None	None	Nil	Fair
Yes	Yes	Yes	Yes	No	Some
Both	Self	Self	Self	Self	Self
Several per transaction	Many sources	Many sources	Many sources	Many sources	One per product
Yes	Yes	Yes	Yes	Yes	Yes
Contraband	Manufactured goods	Bulky and raw materials	All types	Manufactured goods	Complementary to line
N.A.	Broad	Broad	Broad	Broad	Narrow
Yes	Yes	Yes	Yes	Yes	No
Nil	Nil	Nil	Nil	Good	Good
No	Occasionally	Seldom	Seldom	Seldom	Seldom
No	Nil	Nil	Nil	Fair	Good

Source: Philip Cateora, *International Marketing*, 6th ed. (Homewood, Ill.: Richard D. Irwin, 1987), p..552.

The combination retailer-wholesaler is more important in foreign countries than in the United States. It is not at all uncommon to find most of the larger retailers in any city wholesaling their goods to local shops and dealers.[33]

From the perspective of interorganization management, control over the activities and operations of marketing channels abroad is generally more difficult to accomplish than it is within the boundaries of the United States, even though antitrust laws may be more lenient in foreign countries. Despite the commonality in functions performed, wholesaling patterns are not as well developed as they are in the United States. It is not unusual to find that manufacturers based in such highly developed economies as Italy[34] are forced to undertake direct shipments to small retailing establishments on a daily or very frequent basis. This kind of distribution obviously eliminates any of the cost advantages of shipping merchandise in large lots as well as prohibiting the accruing of advan-

[33] Cateora, *op. cit.*, p. 598.
[34] Pietro Gennaro, "Wholesaling in Italy," in Robert Bartels (ed), *Comparative Marketing: Wholesaling in Fifteen Countries* (Homewood, Ill.: Richard D. Irwin, 1963), pp. 37–46.

Table 12–6 Characteristics of middlemen located in foreign countries

Type of Duties	Agents					Merchants			
	Broker	Factor	Manufacturer's Representative	Managing Agent	Comprador	Distributor	Dealer	Import Jobber	Wholesaler and Retailer
Take title	No	No	No	No	No	Yes	Yes	Yes	Yes
Take possession	No	No	Seldom	Seldom	Yes	Yes	Yes	Yes	Yes
Continuing relationship	No	Sometimes	Often	With buyer not seller	Yes	Yes	Yes	No	Usually not
Share of foreign output	Small	Small	All or part for one area	N.A.	All one area	All, for certain countries	Assignment area	Small	Very small
Degree of control by principal	Low	Low	Fair	None	Fair	High	High	Low	Nil
Price authority	Nil	Nil	Nil	Nil	Partial	Partial	Partial	Full	Full
Represent buyer or seller	Either	Either	Seller	Buyer	Seller	Seller	Seller	Self	Self
Number of principals	Many	Many	Few	Many	Few	Small	Few major	Many	Many
Arrange shipping	No	No	No	No	No	No	No	No	No
Type of goods	Commodity and food	Commodity and food	Manufactured goods	All types manufactured goods	Manufactured goods	Manufactured goods	Manufactured goods	Manufactured goods	Manufactured consumer
Breadth of line	Broad	Broad (often specialized)	Allied lines	Broad		Narrow to broad	Narrow	Narrow to broad	Narrow to broad
Handle competitive lines	Yes	Yes	No	Yes	No	No	No	Yes	Yes
Extent of promotion and selling effort	Nil	Nil	Fair	Nil	Fair	Fair	Good	Nil	Nil
Extend credit to principal	No	Yes	No	No	Sometimes	Sometimes	No	No	Nil usually
Market information	Nil	Fair	Good	Nil	Good	Fair	Good	Nil	No

Source: Philip R. Cateora, *International Marketing*, 6th ed. (Homewood, Ill.: Richard D. Irwin, 1987), p. 556.

EXHIBIT 12–2   Trading companies

The primary functions of trading companies located within a given country include accumulation, transportation, and distribution of goods imported from other countries. To supplement these activities, other services are frequently offered as well. For example, Japanese companies, in addition to operating in the traditional manner, may provide their clients with services such as market information gathering, development and implementation of marketing plans, and facilities for merchandise handling and wholesaling. Moreover, they often finance imports and exports of merchandise, and either finance or directly invest in distributors and retailers. However, the first function of trading companies is as intermediaries, not only facilitating trade in a variety of products to all parts of the world but also actively looking for and developing new sources of demand.

There are two types of trading companies. The first is located in a developed country and is engaged primarily in selling manufactured goods to developing countries and in return buying their raw materials and unprocessed goods. The second type is typified by the Japanese companies that formed in the 1700s for the purpose of facilitating distribution of goods within the country and subsequently developed import and export operations.

As one can see, trading companies are not a new phenomenon. The Hudson Bay Company and the East India Company are two prime examples of trading vehicles that date back as far as the sixteenth century. Around the turn of this century, the French founded two major trading companies, Cie Française de l'Afrique Occidentale and Ste. Commerciale de l'Ouest Africain. And in 1929, the United Africa Company was formed.

Trading companies continue to be important in modern trade with developing countries. The accelerated economic growth of the Middle Eastern countries, for example, combined with market complexity, cultural differences, and language difficulties, attests to the immense usefulness of these mechanisms in reaching local markets. Many companies local to this region have been built around families who have been merchants for generations. Names such as Alireza, Bugshan, Jomaih, Zahid, Al-Gosaibi, Jameel, Rajhi, and Sharbatly-Soliman are examples of powerful merchant companies that control the import trade in Saudi Arabia. These merchants also own construction companies, hotels, residential properties, transportation companies, supermarkets, and a few light industries. They provide clients with the kind of market access, adequate coverage, and political accessibility and acceptability vital to successful operations. Even the large U.S. industrial companies such as Union Carbide prefer to deal with these strong trading companies rather than venture into a complex market on their own.

Japanese trading companies (*sogo shosha*), on the other hand, operate on a worldwide basis. Although there are approximately 6000 trading companies currently operating in Japan, the ten largest—Mitsubishi, Mitsui, Marubeni, Itoh, Sumitomo, Nisso-Iwai, Toymenka, Kanematsu-Gosho, Ataka, and Michimen—account for more than half of all Japanese imports and exports, one-fifth of Japan's domestic wholesale trade, one-third of Japan's GNP, and over 5 percent of the world's export trade. In the Japanese fiscal year ending March 1984, the nine largest trading houses, led by Mitsubishi and Mitsui, had combined sales of more than $350 billion. Although the original purpose of *sogo shosha* was to serve Japanese companies only, nowadays a substantial part of their activities consists of imports and exports of goods on behalf of manufacturers and commodity buyers in other countries. They derive their business philosophy from the Confucian cultural tradition, which emphasizes harmony and community. Rather than quick profits on single deals, they prefer to build long-lasting relationships with their business counterparts. Needless to say, this strategy has met with much success.

In Brazil, trading companies are highly favored by the government because they are efficient in international trade and they often encourage small producers to enter international markets. In the early 1970s, the Brazilian government passed legislation giving trading companies a variety of tax advantages. Additionally, the government provides loans to the companies for the purchase of goods from local producers, which are in turn marketed abroad. It appears that this kind of government encouragement has shown favorable results. By 1978, there were 40 Brazilian trading companies in operation.

In the United States, some firms have developed in-house trading companies to improve their trade performance. These units provide a variety of functions. They can act as the company's export department, limit the parent company's liability, perform piggyback operations, facilitate countertrade arrangements, and establish a worldwide information system.

Sources: Philip R. Cateora, *International Marketing,* 5th ed. (Homewood, Ill.: Richard D. Irwin, 1983), pp. 590–93; Ruel Kahler, *International Marketing,* 5th ed. (Cincinnati: Southwestern Publishing Co., 1983), pp. 170–72; Alexander K. Young, *The Sogo Shosha: Japan's Multinational Trading Companies* (Boulder, Colo.: Westview Press, 1979); Don T. Dunn, Jr., "Agents and Distributors in the Middle East," *Business Horizons* (October 1979), pp. 71–72; and Mike Thorp, "Marketing in Japan Takes Twisty Turns, Foreign Firms Find," *Wall Street Journal,* March 9, 1977, pp. 1, 19. See also Masayoushi Kanabayashi, "Japan's Big and Evolving Trading Firms: Can the U.S. Use Something Like Them?" *Wall Street Journal,* December 17, 1980, p. 48; Roger Schreffler, "Renovations for Japan's Trading Houses," *Distribution* (October 1984), pp. 17–25; and Ruel Kahler *International Business* (Cincinnati, Ohio: Southwestern Publishing Co., 1983), pp. 171–72.

tages from an efficient division of labor within the channel. Furthermore, a recurring pattern in foreign countries is that huge middlemen and tiny middlemen predominate.[35] This means that the supplier seeking to tap international markets must either give over control to economically and often politically powerful distributors or must develop his own system. For example,

> in Malaya, . . . fewer than a dozen merchant houses (European) handle over half of the import trade, while hundreds of local trading companies handle the balance. In Israel, there are some 1,500 wholesalers, most of whom are small. Contrast these with Hamashbir Hamerkazi, a giant wholesaler who handles all kinds of products and has full or partial ownership in 12 major industrial firms. In the early 1960's they reportedly handled approximately 1/5th of all the wholesaling volume of that country. . . . In India, . . . outside companies may have a hard time gaining distribution because the large wholesalers have such an entrenched position that by providing the package of financial and marketing services, they are able to obtain monopsonistic power. Japan's zaibatsu (trading and financial combines) finance subwholesalers, retailers, and manufacturers as well, making a completely integrated link centering around the strongest middlemen.[36]

Wholesale Linkages

The status and role of wholesalers as well as the size of wholesaling operations vary from country to country,[37] as illustrated in Table 12–7. In developing countries, wholesalers play a crucial role by handling imports as well as products

[35] For a thorough description of wholesaling in a variety of countries, see Bartels (ed.), *op. cit.*

[36] Cateora, *op. cit.,* p. 623; and Philip R. Cateora and John M. Hess, *International Marketing,* rev. ed. (Homewood, Ill.: Richard D. Irwin, 1971), p. 826.

[37] Subhash C. Jain, *International Marketing Management* (Boston: Kent Publishing Co., 1984), pp. 439–440.

Table 12–7 Wholesaling in selected countries, 1980

	Number of Wholesalers	Number of Wholesale Employees	Employees per Wholesaler	Retailers per Wholesaler	Population per Wholesaler
United States	383,000	4,397,000	11	5	575
Ireland	2,495	32,200	13	14	1,668
Austria	12,026	153,500	13	3	624
Sweden	21,132	178,600	8	2	393
West Germany	—	1,133,000	—	—	—
Belgium	56,289	177,400	3	2	174
United Kingdom	80,104	1,087,000	14	3	698
Israel	4,862	36,900	8	8	782
Japan	369,000	3,688,000	10	5	314
India	116,000	—	—	32	5,612
Turkey	22,650	65,500	3	8	1,951
Iran	17,601	53,000	3	12	2,096
Chile	620	23,400	38	2	17,581
Brazil	41,123	300,000	7	14	2,886
Korea	20,260	93,700	5	19	1,856
Ghana	460	1,100	2	5	24,565
Italy	120,366	547,000	5	8	473
Egypt	1,506	40,100	27	1	27,224
Yugoslavia	1,110	138,100	124	70	20,000

Sources: United Nations Statistical Yearbook; 1979/80 (New York: United Nations, 1981); and *Statistical Abstract of the United States, 1980.* Reprinted in Subhash C. Jain, *Marketing Management* (Boston: Kent Publishing Company, 1984), p. 439. © by Wadsworth, Inc. Reprinted by permission of PWS-KENT Publishing Company, a division of Wadsworth, Inc.

of small domestic manufacturers, and also finance the flow of goods between producers and retailers.

Several trends in the wholesale market have important implications for international marketers. One worldwide trend in wholesaling is the move toward more vertical integration from the wholesale or retail level back to the manufacturer.[38] This development is of concern to marketers who have been dependent on a wholesaler to handle their products, because they often find the channel is blocked by the wholesaler handling his own custom-manufactured products.[39]

Another development in the wholesale market that tends to concentrate distribution power in the hands of a relatively small number of wholesalers is the emergence of voluntary chains, resident buying offices, and buying pools, sponsored by wholesalers.[40] A voluntary chain is a group of retailers assembled by a wholesaler-supplier who agrees to provide certain services in return for purchase commitments.[41] The formation of wholesaler chains is a reaction to the emerging trend toward vertical integration and is in an attempt to streamline by limiting the areas of operation and strictly controlling them.[42]

Perhaps one of the most fascinating examples of the problems of achieving effective wholesale distribution abroad is the story of Levi Strauss's efforts to gain a large market share for its clothing products (jeans, pants, and shirts) in

[38] Cateora, *op. cit.*, p 624.
[39] *Ibid.*
[40] *Ibid.*
[41] V. H. Kirpalani, *International Marketing* (New York: Random House, 1984), p. 456.
[42] Jain, *op. cit.*, p. 440.

Europe in the late 1960s and early 1970s. According to a *Fortune* report on its problems, the company made "a fast grab for the European market without sufficient control on inventory and distribution."[43] The upshot was a debacle that cost Levi Strauss at least $12 million and left the company with a deficit of over $7 million in the fourth quarter of 1973. Some of the relevant facts of the debacle are detailed in the following paragraphs.[44]

Because demand in Europe was far outrunning supply, there seemed, from management's perspective, to be no pressing need for inventory controls. In 1970, Levi Strauss Europe (LSE)'s inventory turned over seven times (about four is normal for apparel), and the main warehouse in Antwerp had to be fully replenished an incredible 19 times. Independent distributors were buying LSE's merchandise without any careful planning as to future demand. Learning that a shipment was arriving, distributors would send trucks to Antwerp and buy anything they saw.

To improve Levi's distribution within Europe as quickly as possible, LSE acquired the firms that had been its national distributors in ten countries and turned them into sales subsidiaries. This move was made rather than bringing in Levi Strauss salesmen, who were experienced in domestic apparel markets but unfamiliar with marketing in Europe. Close relationships between manufacturers and retailers are vital in the apparel business, and management believed that LSE's distributors and their sales staff would provide that tie, enabling the company to keep attuned to changes in each national market. However, meshing the acquired firms with LSE proved unexpectedly difficult. Their presidents were long-established businessmen in their own countries, and they resisted changing their methods. In Britain, one former owner resisted proposals for warehouse consolidation and other managerial changes so strongly that the company shifted him into another job.

In keeping with well-established Levi Strauss policy, each national manager retained full autonomy and profit responsibility. At first, LSE received only quarterly balance sheets—outdated information. Moreover, each new subsidiary operated differently, with its own accounting and inventory-control systems. Only in Switzerland was the operation computerized, but its system did not fit with LSE's. Furthermore, several of the firms did not have accurate information about their inventories. Their reports were often so lacking in details (about sizes and styles, for example) as to be meaningless.

Almost three-quarters of the pants the company sold in Europe were imported from plants located outside the continent. Once the goods did reach Europe, LSE could not keep track of them. Moreover, the ever-increasing volume of pants overwhelmed the efforts of clerks to keep adequate records of the movements. As a result, warehouse workers often did not know where to find goods stacked in the bins. Incredible as it seems, if a retailer returned a shipment, LSE's warehouse had no means of reentering the goods into inventory.

On top of all this, fashion changes swept Europe and compounded what already was a major catastrophe in the making. Further evidence of LSE's lack of control was found when one distributor who had not been acquired requested a particular style, which LSE declined to produce. Rather than accepting LSE's decision, the distributor flew to Hong Kong and ordered two million pairs of the style he wanted directly from the Levi Strauss manufacturing subsidiary there.

[43] Peter Vanderwicken, "When Levi Strauss Burst Its Britches," *Fortune* (April 1974), p. 131.
[44] These details were reported in *ibid.*, pp. 133–35.

Although one might argue that even with the lack of control LSE was able to accomplish its objective because it eventually captured the largest share of the European market for jeans,[45] there can be little doubt that the European experience was a traumatic one that Levi Strauss would not like to repeat. The fact remains that the European wholesalers were, to a very large extent, the root cause of LSE's major problems and that even vertical integration was ineffective in securing the needed control over their operations. One lession is therefore abundantly clear: if adequate distribution and effective interorganization management were so difficult for a sophisticated U.S. manufacturer and marketer to secure in a developed, highly industrialized market like Europe, they are likely to be even more difficult to secure in less developed economies. In international marketing channels, nothing can be taken for granted.

As is so clearly evident in the Levi Strauss case, the need to develop functioning and meaningful information systems is absolutely crucial. Above anything else, this facet of international marketing may be the most arduous problem, given the current state of foreign distribution and the power held by the middlemen in those markets. As Fayerweather has observed,

> secretiveness is one of the prominent characteristics of the independent trader in any society. The ability to outbargain and outmaneuver competitors in the marketplace often depends upon keeping your own counsel and playing a lone wolf game. So the . . . merchant . . . is thoroughly imbued with a philosophy quite at odds with the concept of transmitting information to producers. It is rank heresy by his standards, for example, to tell a manufacturer how much inventory he has, one of the key pieces of information that can help the producer. . . .
>
> Individualistic peoples are more inclined (than group-oriented societies) to look on others as antagonists and to think, especially, in work relations, in terms of competing and outmaneuvering those around them rather than cooperating. The cultures of Latin America, the Middle East, and Far East generally lean in this direction. Clearly, group-oriented attitudes (such as exist in the U.S.) facilitate the transmission of information, while merchants in an individualistic culture find their natural disinclination to communicate reinforced.[46]

RETAILING IN INTERNATIONAL MARKETS[47]

As frustrating as it must sound to someone looking for information about international distribution channels, the structure of retailing in foreign markets is even more diverse than the structure of wholesaling. This diversity is demonstrated, for example, in Table 12–8, which documents size differences in foreign retailing. Retailing is in many respects a localized activity, deeply influenced by prevailing social and cultural norms as well as by government controls.[48]

---

[45] It has been shown that companies that have achieved the highest market shares in various industries also have the highest returns on their investments. See Robert D. Buzzell, Bradley T. Gale, and Ralph G. M. Sultan, "Market Share: A Key to Profitability," *Harvard Business Review*, Vol. 53 (January-February 1975), pp. 97–106.

[46] John Fayerweather, *International Marketing*, 2nd ed. (Englewood Cliffs, N.J.: Prentice-Hall, 1970), pp. 71–72.

[47] The discussion in this section is based largely on Fayerweather, *op. cit.*, pp. 60–79. See also Terpstra, *op. cit.*, pp. 377–85; and Jain, *op. cit.*, pp. 441–45.

[48] Jain, *op. cit.*, p. 441.

Table 12–8 Retail patterns in 16 countries

Country	Population (millions)	GDP per Capita	Consumption per Capita	Number of Retailers
Belgium	10	$4,725	$3,257	128,989
Colombia	23	1,117	845	547,000
France	53	4,692	2,883	569,000
West Germany	61	4,741	2,512	344,752
Hungary	10	2,741	1,729	35,346
India	548	383	260	3,760,000
Iran	34	1,762	1,008	214,063
Italy	54	2,950	2,060	927,372
Japan	112	3,960	2,248	1,548,000
Kenya	15	383	262	4,756
Republic of Korea	35	921	633	320,471
Malaysia	10	1,233	748	7,036
Netherlands	13	4,282	2,569	n.a.
Phillipines	42	738	535	320,400
United Kingdom	56	3,789	2,632	262,501
United States	203	6,205	4,288	1,855,018

Source: Statistical Yearbook 1979/1980 (New York: United Nations, 1981), Table 165, pp. 705–6; Table 18, pp. 69–74; Table 134, pp. 404–15.

Any institutional framework in a country is a function of its environment.[49] Thus, as industrial progress increases, retailing is for the most part performed by larger and larger units.[50] For example supermarkets have been found to be much more common and retail outlets much larger in countries with relatively higher GNPs per capita.[51] As established in Chapter 2, food retailing in the United States is dominated by the larger supermarket. However, as Fayerweather points out,

> in Europe, supermarkets are progressing, but over 80 percent of the food trade is still in the hands of small merchants with modest stores. In India, food is still mainly sold through thousands of individual tradesmen squatting in open markets, hawking their goods from door to door, or selling from tiny hole-in-the-wall shops.[52]

Furthermore, time lags in the development of retailing innovations and improvements appear similar in length to lags in environmental development.[53] The European experience appears to be paralleling the historical development of food distribution in the United States. Certain European marketers appear to have benefited markedly by the U.S. experience in the sense that as they develop new modes of food distribution, there is a high degree of concern with increased productivity. Thus, in West Germany and Switzerland, food discounting operations that provide limited assortments of merchandise have achieved remarkable performance records. These stores carry only dry groceries, are relatively small (compared to U.S. standards), lack frills, rely on bulk merchandising (as contrasted with shelf display of individual items), use a minimum number of person-

[49] *Ibid.*, p. 443.
[50] Fayerweather, *op. cit.*, p. 61. See also Johan Arndt, "Temporal Lags in Comparative Retailing," *Journal of Marketing*, Vol. 36 (October 1972), pp. 40–45.
[51] Fayerweather, *op. cit.*, p 61.
[52] *Ibid.*, p. 62.
[53] *Ibid.*

nel, emphasize private label merchandise at remarkable values, and are located in densely populated areas. They served as the models for the "box" stores established by Aldi, Jewel, and A&P's Plus Stores in the late 1970s in the United States.

The diversity between Europe and India in food retailing just cited is found in various merchandise categories in other countries as well.

> In some countries, such as Italy and Morocco, retailing is composed largely of specialty houses carrying narrow lines. In other countries, such as Finland, most retailers carry a rather general line of merchandise. Retail size is represented at one end by Japan's giant Mitsukoshi Ltd., which today continues to set an unparalleled standard of excellence of goods, fair prices, and superior service, and enjoys the patronage of more than 100,000 customers every day. The other extreme is represented in the market of Ibadan, Nigeria, which has some 3,000 one- or two-man stalls.[54]

While the size of retail establishments appears to vary with economic development, so does the level of service that retailers provide to both manufacturers and consumers. Thus, large retail houses generally carry inventory, render financial help, display and promote merchandise, and furnish market information. On the other hand, a smaller retailer would depend on the manufacturer or wholesaler to provide these functions.

An international marketer would have difficulty dealing directly with smaller retailers. Thus, in nations where retailing is a mom-and-pop business, the wholesaler becomes vitally important. By the same token, new ideas and innovations overseas can be successfully introduced only at the retail level in countries that have large retail houses.[55]

The reasons for these differences in service and specialization can be explained, in part, in terms of consumer behavior. The lack of mobility, refrigeration, and other amenities, combined with the desire for social interaction, supports the present fragmented retailing systems in many low- and middle-income countries. On the other hand, the investment required in both facilities and education to enter retailing in developing nations is extremely low.[56] For some, retailing—of one form or another—represents the only avenue to earning a living. Thus, from both a demand and a supply side, the existing system is reinforced.

Unfortunately for such nations the cost of such a system is extremely high, both for consumers and for retailers. From the standpoint of consumption, there are no opportunities to shop at outlets where distribution economies have been achieved, and lower prices can be gained only by effective bargaining and exhaustive search. On the supply side, tradesmen have an extremely low status in their societies; in fact, shopping expeditions represent for some consumers a way of being able to support their self-esteem, because during such expeditions they can interact with someone of lower status. In fact, improvements in retail distribution have been seen by some as a primary means for elevating a develop-

[54] Cateora, *op. cit.*, p. 625.

[55] Jain, *op. cit.*, p. 442.

[56] For analytical discussion of some of these issues, with particular reference to Greece, see Lee E. Preston, "Marketing Organization and Economic Development: Structure, Products, and Management," in Louis P. Bucklin (ed.), *Vertical Marketing Systems* (Glenview, Ill.: Scott, Foresman and Co., 1970), pp. 116–33; and Arieh Goldman, "Outreach of Consumers and the Modernization of Urban Food Retailing in Developing Countries," *Journal of Marketing*, Vol. 38 (October 1974), pp. 8-16.

ing country, because through lower prices, gained through better distribution methods, the real income of the population will increase, and thus there is a greater likelihood for a long-term savings-investment cycle to commence.[57]

One interesting method of retailing is illustrated by the Japanese department stores, or *depatos,* as they are conveniently called in Westernized Japanese.[58] The emphasis in all major Japanese department stores is on variety, service, and quality. Within one store customers can find fancy foods, pet shops, restaurants, kimonos and fabrics, beauty salons, travel and concert ticket agencies, and florists. In addition, a variety of services are provided ranging from ordering a car, to courses in flowering arranging or tea ceremony, or even to securing a loan.

Moreover, Japanese department stores are designed as places for the entire family to visit, with rooftop playgrounds, in-store baby-sitting services, and free parking. These *depatos* are organized according to the "trickle-down" theory of marketing: lure the family to a top-floor exhibition area and then let them slowly make their way down through the floors, each area appealing to a certain family member.

Developments and innovations in retailing such as those in the Japanese department stores symbolize the active change in retailing that has been occurring for some years. The rate of change appears to be directly related to the stage and speed of economic development in the countries concerned, but even the least developed countries are experiencing dramatic changes.[59] Some of the coming trends in retailing include the growth in self-service retailing, discount houses, automatic vending, and mail-order and direct sales, as well as the franchising of fast foods.

The major changes in British retailing over the past two decades, for example, have been the development of the supermarket and, more recently, the superstores, which have at least 25,000 square feet or better. They offer one-stop shopping for both food and nonfood items on a single level, supported by parking areas.[60]

Developments such as consolidation of middlemen, larger store size, self-service, and discounting have not gone unnoticed by small merchants. As the structure of retailing evolves, distribution is becoming enmeshed in a battle between politically powerful independent retailers and wholesalers and economically powerful chain, discount, and department stores. This battle will likely continue as international retailing progresses.[61]

INTERNATIONAL MARKETING CHANNELS FOR COUNTERTRADE

Barter, or countertrade, is one of the most rapidly growing elements of world trade.[62] *Countertrade* is any business arrangement in which payment is made

[57] This point has been developed by Charles C. Slater, "Market Channel Coordination and Economic Development," Bucklin (ed.), *op. cit.,* pp. 135–56.

[58] Peat Marwick, "Inside a Japanese Department Store," *World,* No. 4 (1983), pp. 40–43.

[59] Cateora, *op. cit.,* p. 626.

[60] Peat Marwick, "What's New in International Retailing," *World,* No. 4 (1983), p. 33.

[61] Cateora, *op. cit.,* p. 630.

[62] Kirpalani, *op. cit.,* p. 493.

other than on a cash-for-goods basis.[63] The growth of this trade arrangement is paralleling the increase in sales to Eastern European countries, the Soviet Union, the People's Republic of China, and many developing countries. The growth of countertrade can be seen by the increase from the 28 percent use of counter-trade in East-West contracts in 1976 to the 50 percent use of countertrade agreements in 1984. Private trade experts have estimated that nearly one-third of all world trade, or more than $700 billion, are countertrade arrangements.[64] Reasons for the increased use of countertrade include financial problems occurring in developing economies that limit a country's credit, cash shortages due to large debt-servicing payments, the strength of the dollar versus the inconvertability of other currencies, poor marketing channels and marketing expertise, and import restrictions designed to limit foreign exchange drain.[65]

One of the largest barter deals made to date was Occidental Petroleum Corporation's agreement to ship superphosphoric acid to the Soviet Union in exchange for ammonia urea and potash under a 20-year, $20 billion deal.[66] In this "simple" barter arrangement there was a direct exchange of goods between two parties. More complicated forms of countertrade include compensation deals, counterpurchase, and product buy-back agreements.

Compensation deals involve partial payments in both goods and cash. For example, a seller delivers lathes to a buyer in Venezuela in exchange for a payment of 70 percent convertible currency and 30 percent tanned hides and wool. The advantage of a compensation deal over barter is the immediate cash settlement of at least a portion of the transaction, with the remainder of the cash being generated after the goods have been successfully sold.[67]

Counterpurchase, the most frequently used type of countertrade, requires that two contracts be negotiated. In the first contract the seller agrees to sell a product at a set price to a buyer and receives payment in cash. However, the first contract is contingent on a second contract, which is an agreement by the original seller to buy goods from the buyer for the total monetary amount involved in the first contract or for a set percentage of that amount. The advantage of this arrangement over a compensation deal is the greater flexibility it offers the seller.[68]

In a *product buy-back* arrangement, a company barters technological knowledge needed to build, or actually builds, a plant in return for partial payment in the form of a certain portion of the plant's output. For example, General Motors Corporation bought automobiles from Brazil in partial payment for building an automobile manufacturing plant there.[69]

Countertrade arrangements are complicated and take a long time to negotiate, and thus most U.S. companies prefer to avoid them. In addition, problems arise over the quality and types of goods offered, the value of the goods, and the financial strain placed on the company because capital is tied up longer than it would be for a normal transaction. Because of the special nature of counter-trade, the problems associated with these transactions, and their growing impor-

[63] Martha B. Mast, "Some Businesses Are Turning to Barter in Trading," *Foodstuffs* (July 30, 1984) pp. 5, 53–54.
[64] *Ibid.*
[65] *Ibid.*
[66] Cateora, *op. cit.,* p. 455.
[67] *Ibid.*
[68] *Ibid.*
[69] *Ibid.*

tance in world trade, marketing channels in countertrade deserve special mention.

Special channels have developed to handle countertrade, such as the following:

1. The selling responsibility of the goods may be turned over to specialists known as barter houses, switch traders, intermerchants, or trading houses. (Also, Japanese trading companies engage in nonmoney trading.) These specialists are located in London, Vienna, Zurich, Munich, and Hamburg, and trade virtually in anything.

2. Some multinational corporations have established in-house countertrade units. An example is Northrop's offset program. When Northrop sells aircraft to many countries, part of the payment is received as the transaction is concluded. The balance is paid when the offset program has successfully sold goods and services of the country that bought the aircraft to third-party countries.

3. Some multinationals look to other multinationals to help sell the products they acquire in countertrade. For example, when Pullman-Kellogg agreed to receive fertilizer in payment for designing and building a plant in Nigeria, it turned to International Mineral and Chemicals and Transcontinental Fertilizers to market the Nigerian fertilizers.[70]

4. The product received may be sold through the companies' regular marketing channels. For example:

   When the Soviet Union agreed to allow PepsiCo to ship its syrup from the United Kingdom, bottle it in the U.S.S.R., and sell it in small quantities, it was agreed that PepsiCo would take back Soviet products for its pay. Stolichnaya vodka had never sold well in the United States, partly because it must compete with American vodka and vodka coming from countries that enjoy most-favored nation treatment. Still, PepsiCo took Stolichnaya for its pay and agreed that the amount of Pepsi Cola that would be bottled would be a function of Soviet vodka sales in the United States. Fortunately for PepsiCo, the vodka fit neatly into one of Pepsi's channels. It became part of the product line of Monsieur Henri, a subsidiary of PepsiCo that imports and distributes liquor and wines for the American market.[71]

5. The product or raw material received may be used in the company's own production processes. For example, Cadbury-Schweppes (U.K.) markets its products in Eastern Europe and takes back canned fruits in payment. The fruits are shipped to England, where they are used as flavoring for Schweppes' bottled drinks.[72]

Naturally, the last two channel alternatives are the shortest and easiest. However, they are the exception rather than the rule in countertrade.

PROBLEMS IN ESTABLISHING AND MANAGING INTERNATIONAL MARKETING CHANNELS

Although it may appear redundant to emphasize further problems in establishing foreign distribution, since numerous difficulties have been highlighted

[70] Robert E. Weigand, "Barter and Buy-Backs: Problems for the Marketing Channels," in Richard P. Bagozzi (ed.), *Marketing in the 1980's: Changes and Challenges* (Chicago: American Marketing Association, 1980), pp. 256–58.

[71] *Ibid.*

[72] *Ibid.*

throughout this chapter, it is essential that the marketing manager be aware of most of the major obstacles prior to initiating international trade. Careful planning is crucial if a company is to obtain the lucrative benefits possible from serving foreign markets. Only through a knowledge of likely problem areas can such planning be undertaken.

First, it is not always easy to find out which middlemen may be available to handle a company's merchandise. Several directories have been published that may aid in this task.[73] Other sources, suggested by Cateora, include foreign consulates, Chamber of Commerce groups, middlemen associations, business publications, management consultants, and carriers.[74]

Although it may be difficult to find qualified representatives and middlemen in foreign markets, rigorous selection criteria must be applied. Four selection criteria have proven to be particularly important, especially in the Middle East: (1) the representative's financial strength; (2) his connections; (3) the number and kind of other companies he represents; and (4) the quality of his local personnel, facilities, and equipment. The problem is that such information about agents and distributors may not be readily available.[75] Careful selection for foreign middlemen cannot be overemphasized. When middlemen do not perform, it may be necessary to terminate relationships. This task is formidable in many countries. Middlemen have legal protection that makes it difficult to terminate relationships. For example, in Norway a manufacturer cannot change agents without proof of negligence. Also, personal and family connections remain very important, particularly in the Middle East. Terminating a powerful middleman can result in the expulsion of the foreign firm from the country in extreme cases. Indeed, it has been observed that while international marketers may switch from local agents and distributors by developing their own marketing subsidiaries in foreign markets, in some foreign markets, particularly in the Middle East, the agent and distributor are retained permanently.[76]

Second, the international marketer may be constrained in the kinds of channels available, due to host-country trade practice concerning the distribution of particular products; the economic structure of the host country as pertains to private versus state-controlled markets; and cultural conditions that might militate against the utilization of a particular type of channel.[77]

Third, it is likely that a relatively larger proportion of a company's advertising budget will have to be devoted to channel communications than in the United States, because there are so many small middlemen who must be reached.[78]

Fourth, access to markets may be blocked by existing financial and other tie-in arrangements with middlemen often not available to companies in the United States. In Japan, for example, manufacturers are one of the primary

[73] See the U.S. Department of Commerce *Trade List* and *World Trade Directory Reports* as well as the commercially published *Trade Directories of the World* and *A Guide to Foreign Business Directories.*
[74] Cateora, *op. cit.,* pp. 636–37.
[75] Don T. Dunn, Jr., "Agents and Distributors in the Middle East," *Business Horizons* (October 1979), p. 74.
[76] *Ibid.*
[77] Jain, *op. cit.,* p. 431.
[78] Cateora, *op. cit.,* pp. 601–2. It should be noted, however, that there are even increasingly higher hurdles to overcome with respect to advertising. See "Curbs on Ads Increase Abroad as Nations Apply Standards of Fairness and Decency," *Wall Street Journal,* November 25, 1980, p. 48.

sources of financial assistance to the middlemen with whom they deal.[79] Such assistance solidifies trade relations in that country, and, given the emphasis on the accomplishments of the group rather than the individual (e.g., Japanese manufacturers are more likely than American executives to look upon their resellers as members of their "group"), it may be extremely difficult for an "outsider" to break into an established channel system. This is true for other countries as well. For example, United Fruit Company found that the only way in which it could adequately gain satisfactory distribution in Europe was to purchase distributors.[80] The seriousness of this problem is reflected in the fact that some of the largest multinational corporations maintain 80 to 90 percent of their subsidiaries abroad solely for the purpose of distribution.[81]

In fact, difficulties encountered in establishing international marketing channels account for the worldwide trend toward increased backward vertical integration into manufacturing on the part of the middlemen and forward vertical integration into wholesaling and retailing on the part of manufacturers.[82] Such a trend may provide additional barriers to new entrants to foreign markets, given the capital requirements for integration. The situation is being further aggravated by the desire of large foreign wholesalers and retailers to develop their own private branding programs.[83] Evidence of such a movement is provided by the efforts of a large voluntary chain, Spar International, which comprises 200 wholesalers and 36,000 retailers in 12 Western European countries, to place greater and greater emphasis on its own labels.[84]

A fifth trouble area is that, because middlemen in less developed countries are distinctly less venturesome than those in more advanced ones and therefore are less willing to accept innovation risk, companies seeking to market to such countries must assume a greater burden of demand development than they must in the United States. This is particularly true of a country like India. Furthermore, as Fayerweather observes,

> the small-merchant structure is very likely to result in gaps in market coverage. At the extreme, companies selling small expendable items—toothpaste, flashlight batteries, and razor blades—find in a country like India that only 10 percent or so of the thousands of little merchants are stocking their products. The cost of inventory is one deterrent, but even discounting that, the small operator wants to limit his line to keep it within the bounds of his personal control both physically and from a management point of view.[85]

Cateora underscores this problem by stating that

> the high cost of credit, danger of loss through inflation, lack of capital, and other concerns cause foreign middlemen in many countries to carry inadequate invento-

[79] Robert E. Weigand, "Aspects of Retail Pricing in Japan," in Louis W. Boone and James C. Johnson (eds.), *Marketing Channels* (Morristown, N.J.: General Learning Press, 1973), p. 320.

[80] "United Fruit Purchases Distributors to Gain Common Market Entry," *Wall Street Journal,* November 2, 1962, p. 21.

[81] C. Hederer, C. D. Hoffman, and B. Kumar, "The Internationalization of German Business," *Columbia Journal of World Business* (September-October 1972), p. 43.

[82] For examples of outright ownership of foreign wholesaling and retailing firms, see Vern Terpstra, *American Marketing in the Common Market* (New York: Frederic A. Praeger, 1967), p. 98. See also Lars-Gunnar Mattsson, *Integration and Efficiency in Marketing Systems* (Stockholm, Sweden: Economic Research Institute, 1969).

[83] Cateora, *op. cit.,* p. 621; and Terpstra, *International Marketing,* p. 392.

[84] Terpstra, *International Marketing,* p. 384.

[85] Fayerweather, *op. cit.,* pp. 68–69.

ries, causing out-of-stock conditions and loss of sales to competitors. Physical distribution lags intensify this problem so that, in many cases, the manufacturer must provide local warehousing or extend long credit to encourage middlemen to carry large inventories.[86]

Sixth, motivating middlemen in foreign markets can be a formidable task. Agents and distributors in the Middle East are influenced by thousands of years of bazaar trading. Marketing to them means to "sit on the product" and wait for the customer to come to them. A common attitude among merchants is that they do not sell, but people buy. The "carrot and stick" philosophy of motivating agents and distributors in the United States and Europe fails in the Middle East. Financial incentives may not motivate them to push the product aggressively if the process is complex and long. If they are making money today, they are not particularly motivated by making more. The following comment underscores these attitudes:

> We told our representatives about a special sales promotion that could increase profits by at least $50,000. Our German distributor would kill himself for that, but many of our Middle Eastern people basically yawned. They would rather go skiing in Switzerland.[87]

Finally, the myriad of problems associated with maintaining adequate distribution can be summed up in the term *control*. Securing some semblance of control may be absolutely necessary if the international marketer is going to achieve any success in foreign markets. Because power may reside in the hands of large wholesalers, it may be necessary to use some form of contractual arrangement (e.g., franchising) and make broad concessions in order to convince the wholesalers to monitor the marketplace and to engage in effective marketing practices. The control gained may come to the supplier through osmosis, but at least there will be some assurance (although probably not a great deal) that one's product is receiving adequate care and attention throughout the channel. Distribution in foreign locales through intermediaries always entails compromise. The compromise involves the loss of control over foreign marketing operations in exchange for relatively low-cost representation.[88] The manufacturer-exporter must compare his goals with those of the foreign distributor and decide whether or not a suitable compromise will be reached.

These problems can be more readily understood and effectively dealt with when international marketers develop a better understanding of the traditions, customs, and evolution of the marketing channels in the countries in which they operate. Exhibit 12–3 provides a summary of the Japanese philosophy and environment, and their impact on the structure and policies of the traditional Japanese marketing channel. It illustrates the type of constructive analysis that international marketers must engage in if they are to function successfully in a foreign market. The analysis underscores the fact that foreign distribution channels, structure, and practices are environmentally and culturally determined. Their roots are embedded in the basic philosophies of the culture. Therefore, environmental and cultural sensitivity is a must for successful dealing with distribution problems in international marketing.

[86] Cateora, *op. cit.,* p. 639.
[87] This example and the preceding discussion are from Dunn, *op. cit.,* pp. 76–77.
[88] Jain, *op. cit.,* p. 436.

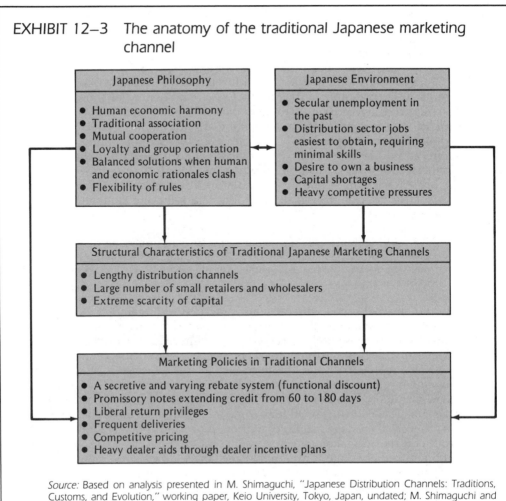

EXHIBIT 12–3   The anatomy of the traditional Japanese marketing channel

Japanese Philosophy

- Human economic harmony
- Traditional association
- Mutual cooperation
- Loyalty and group orientation
- Balanced solutions when human and economic rationales clash
- Flexibility of rules

Japanese Environment

- Secular unemployment in the past
- Distribution sector jobs easiest to obtain, requiring minimal skills
- Desire to own a business
- Capital shortages
- Heavy competitive pressures

Structural Characteristics of Traditional Japanese Marketing Channels

- Lengthy distribution channels
- Large number of small retailers and wholesalers
- Extreme scarcity of capital

Marketing Policies in Traditional Channels

- A secretive and varying rebate system (functional discount)
- Promissory notes extending credit from 60 to 180 days
- Liberal return privileges
- Frequent deliveries
- Competitive pricing
- Heavy dealer aids through dealer incentive plans

Source: Based on analysis presented in M. Shimaguchi, "Japanese Distribution Channels: Traditions, Customs, and Evolution," working paper, Keio University, Tokyo, Japan, undated; M. Shimaguchi and Larry Rosenberg, "Demystifying Japanese Distribution," *Columbia Journal of World Business* (Spring 1979), pp. 32–41; and M. Shimaguchi and William Lazer, "Japanese Distribution Channels: Invisible Barriers to Market Entry," *MSU Business Topics* (Winter 1979), pp. 49–62.

INTERNATIONAL PHYSICAL DISTRIBUTION

So far our discussion has focused on the "transaction" flow in international channels. International physical distribution channels are as complex as transaction channels and more complex in the world marketplace than in domestic markets. Here are some examples:

- Mattel owns manufacturing and distribution facilities in the United States, Canada, Hong Kong, Taiwan, Mexico, England, West Germany, Italy, Australia, Belgium, Japan, and Venezuela.[89]
- Eaton produces in 43 countries and the United States. Its products are exported to 100 countries through a worldwide Swiss-based marketing organization.[90]
- Texas Instruments stocks materials in 16 world market areas. These distribution facilities are hooked up with a global computer-teletype-telephone communication network.[91]

The complexity of international physical distribution emanates from a number of factors, including:

1. The complexity of the transport modes: the transfer from one mode to another affords multiple opportunities for damage, pilferage, and delay.
2. The distance and duration of movements increase the cost of transportation and the cost of money invested in the goods in transit.
3. Exposure to varied climatic conditions often necessitates different packaging and storage arrangements.
4. More documentation is required in moving across national boundaries.[92]

Multinationals find it beneficial to centrally plan and control physical distribution. In this manner, they can maintain stable and efficient production levels at plants in different countries, lower distribution cost by consolidating smaller orders into larger shipments, and provide faster customer service.[93]

The exporter has to decide what level of service to provide in the foreign market and plan the physical distribution accordingly. The principle here is that physical distribution decisions must be linked to marketing goals.[94]

International physical distribution affects the international marketer's ability to compete effectively, for two reasons. First, customer service level (e.g., delivery time, availability of parts) is dependent upon the speed and efficiency of physical distribution. Second, physical distribution cost is one of the major cost elements in international markets.[95] In addition to tariffs and customs duties, import-export license fees, and the cost of adjusting to local content, labeling, packaging, and safety laws, the cost of documentation runs very high for international distribution. International shipping documents include the export declaration, ocean bill of lading, packing list, *pro forma* commercial invoice, final commercial invoice, dock receipt, delivery instructions, insurance certification, shipping instructions, delivery permit, letter of transmittal, and possibly tens of other documents, depending on the nature of the goods shipped.[96] One study

[89] Bernard J. Hale, "The Problems of Managing an International Distribution System," in James C. Johnson (ed.), *Readings in Contemporary Physical Distribution*, 2nd ed. (Tulsa: PPC Books, 1977), p. 219.

[90] Terpstra, *International Marketing*, 3rd ed., p. 384.

[91] *Ibid.*, p. 385.

[92] Kirpalani, *op. cit.*, p. 459.

[93] Terpstra, *International Marketing*, 3rd ed., p. 385.

[94] Kirpalani, *op cit.*, p. 459.

[95] Terpstra, *International Marketing*, 3rd ed., p. 398.

[96] Ronald H. Ballou, *Business Logistics Management Planning and Control* (Englewood Cliffs, N.J.: Prentice-Hall, 1985) pp. 236–37.

reported that the average export shipment requires about 36 man-hours of documentation. Similarly, import shipments require 27 man-hours. In fact, it is estimated that paperwork costs account for close to seven percent of U.S. international trade.[97] Naturally, reducing these costs means improving the profit potential of international marketing and enhancing the competitiveness of the firm.

In addition to the high cost of international distribution, the international marketer is faced with a number of other problems, among them the following:[98]

1. Shipping rates and charges may vary. Although water carrier conference members are not allowed to vary rates, a shipper may obtain lower rates from nonconference carriers. However, the shipper should be prepared to pay penalties on any conference-carrying shipping he might do in the same geographic area. Also, water shipping rates are determined on basis of weight and measurement. The cubic displacement of a shipment must be carefully watched. The following example illustrates.

   One logistics department was able to save over $7 million in transportation charges for its company by using the ocean rate structure to its advantage. It was responsible for shipping 30-inch pipe and cement supplies to a foreign country that was to build a pipeline. The low weight–space ratio of pipe meant high shipping costs. Working with pipeline engineers, the logistics department was able to get the engineers to accept half of the pipe in 31-inch diameter, because it had little effect on pipeline operation. The 30-inch pipe was shipped inside the 31-inch pipe and the cavity filled with bags of cement needed for the pipeline construction. A substantial savings in freight charges resulted.[99]

2. The liability for loss and damage in international shipping is less than in domestic shipping. This means an additional burden on the shipper to provide adequate insurance coverage and extra protective packaging.
3. The physical distribution manager has to deal with a vast number of legal requirements and regulations imposed by governments of countries with which the company deals.
4. Containerization is a logical solution used by international shippers to offset expensive packaging costs and loss because of damage and pilferage. However, containerization adds its own costs, including extra loading fees and container rental fees.

The important managerial concept is to control international physical distribution as a system. When one considers the life cycle of a product from material source through processing or manufacturing to the consumer, the greatest portion of that life cycle or time is often spent in movement or storage.[100]

Modern technology, including supertankers, jumbo jets, better refrigeration, freeze-drying, and intermodal coordination, discussed in Chapter 4, can contribute to the reduction of international distribution cost and the resolution of some of the other problems referred to earlier. Also, international marketers should avail themselves of free-trade zones to overcome legal and tariff barriers, and to reduce distribution cost by taking advantage of proximity to markets and/or low-cost labor. Over 40 nations have established free-trade zones where inter-

[97] "Reducing Paperwork," *Transportation and Distribution Management* (November 1971), p. 15.
[98] Hale, *op. cit.*, pp. 219–22.
[99] Ronald H. Ballou, *Basic Business Logistics* (Englewood Cliffs, N.J.: Prentice-Hall, 1978), pp. 447–48.
[100] Kirpalani, *op. cit.*, p. 459.

national marketers can establish manufacturing, assembly, or distribution facilities. Imported goods or materials may be left in a free-trade zone for storage, assembling, further processing, or manufacturing and later shipped out of the zone to another country without customs formalities, tariffs, and other controls imposed by the government of the foreign country where the zone is located.[101]

Finally, the international marketer should keep in mind that the goal of effective physical distribution is not just reduction of costs but also increases in profits through greater sales due to improved customer service.[102]

SUMMARY AND CONCLUSIONS

In this chapter, we attempted to examine channel alternatives in international markets and the myriad interorganizational problems associated with their deployment. These problems can be dealt with through effective channel management. The concepts embodied in channel management theory and in the analysis of domestic marketing channels are equally applicable to international channels.

International marketing can be very lucrative, as evidenced by the increased world dependence on trade. In addition, participation in the international marketplace may be a requirement if a company is to continue to survive and grow; effective distribution increasingly seems to demand a global view.

In seeking to describe channels serving foreign markets, it is essential to understand that generalizations must be treated cautiously and even with suspicion. The differences in the basic structures of distribution from country to country may not be vast, but the nuances and variations within the structures are significantly different.

The perspective taken in this chapter is basically that of a U.S. manufacturer considering expansion abroad by either exporting, licensing, engaging in joint ventures, or direct investing. As a company moves from one expansion route to the next, the amount of control increases, as does the amount of investment required by the home company. In this respect, the choice and the consequences of the various routes are not far different, conceptually, from those associated with forming conventional, administered, contractual, and corporate channel systems on a domestic basis. Regardless of the expansionary route followed, the international marketer will be faced with the problem of designing and implementing a specific distribution strategy. This generally involves assessing two channel segments—one domestic and the other foreign. Each segment is composed of agent and merchant middlemen whose functions are not widely different from those performed by comparable middlemen in the United States. However, because of the mores and other environmental characteristics of international markets, the outcomes achieved by given channel arrangements may be far different from those predicted for U.S. channels. For example, control problems are more severe on an international basis because of the polarity of wholesale trade. This is true even though antitrust laws may not be as stringent as they are in the United States. Furthermore, all relationships are subject to intensive negotiations, and thus variations among and within channels abound.

[101] Terpstra, *International Marketing*, 3rd ed., p. 399.
[102] *Ibid.*, pp. 397–98.

In order to remain reasonably close to developments in international markets and to secure relevant and timely information, it is likely that firms seeking expansion abroad will have to rely heavily on foreign-based, as opposed to domestically based, middlemen. Even with the market contact that such middlemen allow, difficulties can easily arise, as was evidenced in the case of Levi Strauss, which could not develop adequate distribution and inventory controls even though it had vertically integrated a number of foreign wholesaling firms.

Retailing presents as much, if not more, diversity to the international marketer as wholesaling—and many of the frustrations. The polarity of wholesale trade is mirrored by a similar polarity on the retail level. With economic development there is increased evidence of larger retail units, but the small shop still predominates in lower- and middle-income countries and even throughout much of Europe. Consumer cooperatives have emerged in Europe to exert a countervailing pressure on some of the inefficiencies of traditional retail distribution. In developing nations, however, the retailing systems seem uniquely suited to consumer behavior and the level of affluence and mobility, but the cost to both consumers and traders is high, especially in terms of economics for the former and in terms of status for the latter. Improvements in distribution may produce far-reaching benefits for these countries, because such improvements will probably lead to increases in real income for individual consumers.

Several problems can be highlighted in the establishment of international marketing channels. First, it may be difficult to determine just which middlemen are available or willing to provide adequate distribution for a particular supplier. Second, considerable intrachannel promotion will be required in order to obtain adequate attention. Third, access to particular channels may be blocked because of existing arrangements, some of which would be illegal if practiced in the United States. Fourth, middlemen, especially in developing economies, may be less willing to accept the risks of innovation that come with the marketing of new products. In addition, they may be less willing to assume inventory burdens (as compared with U.S. middlemen), and thus may force much of the effort associated with the flow of physical possession back onto suppliers. Finally, the securing of at least some semblance of control within an international channel is likely to be critical, and in international marketing, reliance may have to be placed on foreign middlemen as the controlling agents or channel leaders.

DISCUSSION QUESTIONS

1. Compare and contrast the routes to expansion abroad—exportation, licensing, joint ventures, and direct investment—with the conceptual foundations, institutional arrangements, strengths, and weaknesses of conventional, administered, contractual, and corporate vertical marketing systems, respectively.

2. Discuss the reasons for the increase in foreign direct investment in the United States and U.S. increased direct investment abroad. What impact does the latter have on the U.S. economy and in particular on the U.S. balance of payments?

3. Analyze the international distribution strategies of two major multinational corporations (select them from different industries). Comment on whether the strategy is appropriate or inappropriate, and why.

4. According to an article in the *Wall Street Journal* (March 13, 1985), some major companies are being forced to become international traders of many different products in order to do business overseas. Because so many countries have big

debts and bad credit, these companies increasingly have to help their foreign customers pay for products or else miss getting sales. For example, Coke beat out Pepsi and won the use of a new Polish bottling facility by agreeing to export one million cases of Polish beer within five years. Of course the most direct way to do business with cash-short clients is to barter, or exchange goods for goods. But barter is so difficult to coordinate that many companies are turning to more sophisticated forms of countertrade.

Explain the difficulties in arranging barter agreements. What are some more favorable forms of countertrade? What are the advantages and disadvantages of these countertrade arrangements?

5. It has been stated that "from an interorganization management perspective, control over the activities and operations of international marketing channels is generally more difficult to accomplish than it is within the boundaries of the United States." Do you agree? Why?

6. Explain Levi Strauss's European problems in behavioral terms (e.g., power, conflict, conflict management, roles, etc.). Applying an interorganizational analysis, suggest some solutions that would enable the company to avoid similar situations.

7. Explain how and why distribution channels are affected by improvements in a country's economic stage of development. Comment specifically on each member in the channel (wholesaler, retailer, distributor, etc.).

8. In an article in *Distribution* (October 1984) on Japan's trading houses, the future of the *shosha* is portrayed as insecure. Although these gigantic, long-established companies have been providing valuable services for over a century, the combined effects of worldwide recession and structural change within the Japanese domestic economy have negatively affected them. American general trading companies may be affected by similar problems.

Describe what trading companies are, how they operate, and what services they provide. What changes are occurring in the structure and composition of trading companies? What is the impact of these changes on the structure of export-import marketing channels in Japan and the United States?

CHAPTER THIRTEEN

Marketing Channels for Services

Among the characteristics distinguishing goods from services, none is more important for marketing channel strategy than the intangibility of services. As Upah points out,

> because of intangibility, services cannot be stored or transported, nor can they be produced in one place and then shipped to another for sale by [wholesalers or] retailers. As a result, many services must be sold through multiple local . . . outlets combining promotion and production activities. Consider, for example, the number of local "production outlets" required for such services as hair styling, dry cleaning, banking, roadside lodging, and minor repair services.[1]

A critical aspect of service marketing, therefore, is how services are to be made widely available so that end-users can avail themselves of them without expending enormous amounts of resources. The answer to this question can be answered only by focusing on marketing channel strategies and tactics, which involve decisions about the number and type of "retail" outlets to employ, the kinds of "middlemen" to use, and the extent of the reliance placed on facilitating agencies. For nonprofit organizations, this question is compounded by the fact that two separate distribution systems must be established, one dealing with resource *allocation* and the other with resource *attraction*. In any case, whether a service is provided by a for-profit or not-for-profit organization, a major issue is the availability of something intangible.

---

[1] Gregory D. Upah, "Mass Marketing in Service Retailing: A Review and Synthesis of Major Methods," *Journal of Retailing*, Vol. 56 (Fall 1980), pp. 60–61.

The basic principles of interorganization management espoused throughout this text apply to the marketing of services when there are units that can be isolated as "wholesalers" and "retailers," as in the financial services and travel industries. In other situations, where production and sale take place simultaneously (e.g., dentistry, restaurants, barber shops), there are very few purely "vertical" (multi-level) marketing channel problems. Here, special attention must be given to location issues, because the provision of time and place utilities is a major way in which such services generate value for end-users. Location decisions for services are very similar to retail location decisions, and therefore the discussion in Chapter 2 on that topic will not be repeated here. In fact, the marketers of services can learn a great deal by studying what has been going on in retailing generally; therefore, the whole of Chapter 2 should be relevant to them. However, it is important to point out that there are a number of potential management problems associated with the retailing of services stemming from differences between services retailing and goods retailing. These differences and their managerial implications are summarized in Table 13–1.

Table 13–1 Potential management problems associated with the retailing of services

Services as Compared with Goods	Managerial Changes Needed for Services Retailing
a. Measuring Performance	
Capital expenditures vary widely for different services	Return on net worth may not be the most important measurement of the value of a service to the retailer
Little or no inventories are required to offer services	Turnover, mark-down controls, and other goods-related controls are not appropriate
Higher labor costs	Profit after labor costs replaces the gross margin of goods retailing
Some services support the sale of goods	Sales-supporting services should be evaluated differently from revenue-producing services
Cost accounting is more important	Job-specific records will be required to assess the profitability of each sale
b. Store Organization	
More specialized supervision	Separate management for service areas will be required
More specific search for service employees	Nontraditional sources for identification of employees must be used
Lower employee turnover	Frequent salary and performance reviews must be carried out
Higher pay for skilled craftspeople than for merchandising personnel	Pay levels will need to be adjusted upward over periods of longevity for service employees
c. Service Production	
More involvement in manufacturing of the service	Production skills will need to be obtained by supervisors
More emphasis on quality control	Supervisors must be able to assess the quality of a service performed for a customer
More need to monitor consumer satisfaction	Need for research with prior customers to measure their satisfaction with the service
More need to refine scheduling of employees	Maximizing the service employees' time requires matching consumer purchasing to ability to produce the service

Table 13–1 (Continued)

Services as Compared with Goods	Managerial Changes Needed for Services Retailing
Quality must be consistent among all outlets	Standards for consistency of the service must be established and continually evaluated; central training may be required for craftworkers in multiple branch operations
d. Pricing	
Services vary in cost; therefore, pricing is more difficult	Prices may be quoted within a range instead of an exact figure before the purchase
More difficulty in price competition or promotion based upon price	Services should be promoted on the basis of criteria other than price
e. Sales Promotion	
Value is more difficult for consumers to determine	Consumers need to be convinced of value through personal selling
Difficult to display within store	In-store signing or a service center are required to notify customers of service's availability
Visual presentation is more important	Photographs of before-and-after may be possible with some services
	Testimonials may be possible with other services
Cross-selling with goods is important	A quota or bonus for goods salespersons who suggest services will lead to increased service selling
More difficult to advertise in catalogs	Conditions for the sale and away-from-the-store performance must be specified
f. Complaints	
More difficult to return a service	Policies must be established on adjusting the service purchased with a dissatisfied customer
A customer is more sensitive about services involving the person	Specific guarantees and policies about adjustments must be established; new types of insurance must be added to cover liabilities
g. Controls	
Greater opportunity to steal customers	Employee assurance of loyalty must be established
	Protection of store loyalty must be obtained

Source: J. Patrick Kelly and William R. George, "Strategic Management Issues for the Retailing of Services," *Journal of Retailing,* Vol. 58 (Summer 1982), pp. 40–42.

Several examples of how the marketing channels for specific services have been organized make up the substance of this chapter. The examples indicate the potential for applying the framework implicit in the previous twelve chapters of this text to the services area, even though a number of these examples relate more to horizontal (same-level) interorganization management issues than they do to vertical issues. The reason for isolating a discussion of the channels for services in a separate chapter is that services represent a very large and increasing proportion of the gross national product in the United States. Their importance is so great that they deserve special attention.[2]

[2] See James L. Heskett, *Managing in the Service Economy* (Boston; Harvard Business School Press, 1986).

CHANNEL CONFIGURATIONS

The dominant channel configurations in the service sector, as isolated by Rathmell, are depicted in Fig. 13–1. Intermediaries in the form of agents or brokers often appear in service industries.

> Their essential function is to bring performer and consumer or user together. They represent either of the primary channel components, and the longest service channel results where agents and brokers representing both seller and buyer intervene. Examples include the following. Rental agents represent the owners of rental housing and office space. Travel agents represent all types of travel services: surface and air transportation, hotels and motels, and packaged tours. Insurance agents and brokers are probably the most widely known service in-

Figure 13–1   Dominant channel configurations in the service sector

Source: John M. Rathmell, *Marketing in the Service Sector* (Cambridge, Mass.: Winthrop Publishers, Inc., 1974), p. 110. Reprinted by permission of the publisher.

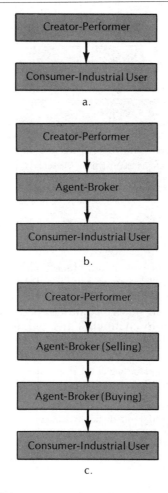

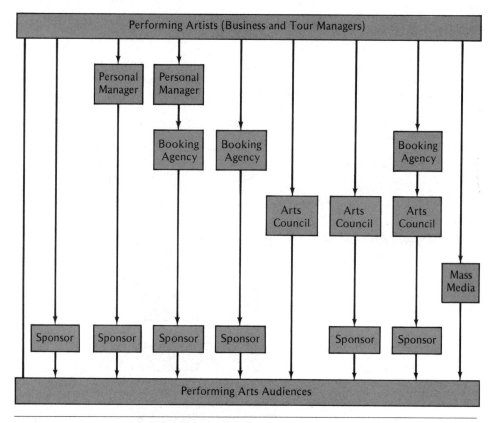

Figure 13–2 The marketing channels for the performing arts

Source: John R. Nevin, "An Empirical Analysis of Marketing Channels for the Performing Arts." From *Marketing the Arts,* edited by Michael P. Mokwa, William M. Dawson, and E. Arthur Prieve. Copyright © 1980 by Praeger Publishers. Reprinted by permission of Praeger Publishers.

termediaries. . . . Artistic performers and entertainers are represented by agents.[3]

The marketer of services is usually faced with a number of alternative channels, direct and indirect, as shown in Fig. 13–2.

It is difficult to typify the functions performed by the various agents and brokers who appear in service channels, because the duties performed vary so widely from channel to channel. Thus, agents who represent entertainers are similar to sales agents, while rental agents are mainly processors of transactions

[3] John M. Rathmell, *Marketing in the Service Sector* (Cambridge, Mass.: Winthrop Publishers, 1974), pp. 109–10. Donnelly has argued that "any extra-corporate entity between the producer of a service and prospective users that is utilized to make the service available and/or more convenient is a marketing intermediary for that service." Thus, under this definition, when an employer is authorized by his employees to deposit their pay directly into their checking accounts and when the employer agrees to participate in a bank's "direct pay deposit" plan, the employer becomes an intermediary in the distribution of the bank's service. See James H. Donnelly, Jr., "Marketing Intermediaries in Channels of Distribution for Services," *Journal of Marketing,* Vol. 40 (January 1976), pp. 55–70.

rather than decision makers. Clearly, however, service agents and brokers are, like their counterparts in other fields, involved primarily with the flows of promotion and negotiation. For some services, such as automobile repair and restaurants, merchant wholesalers play an important role in providing the basic supplies needed in their performance. The actual service, however, originates at the retail level. Franchising is extremely important in the marketing of a wide variety of services, such as automobile rentals, carpet cleaning, dry cleaning, temporary office help, and motels. In fact, any *standardized* service is an appropriate candidate for franchising.

Marketing channels for services, like those for goods, often resist change, especially if the channel is composed of small, entrepreneurial firms. The following examples of the changing relationship in the distribution channel for air travel illustrate:

- In early 1980, Pan Am was considering selling large blocks of tickets on scheduled flights at wholesale prices to contractors or middlemen who would assume the risk and responsibility of pricing and marketing the tickets as they saw fit. Travel agents spoke out in opposition to the plan. They felt that the plan positioned them in direct competition with their own supplier, the airline. Also, they pointed out that the already bewildering fare structure could be further muddied by the diversity of prices offered by contractors (the wholesalers). They feared that the plan would allow nontravel-related merchants the possibility of retailing airline tickets at their wholesale cost as a promotional tool for their basic line of merchandise.[4]

- Traditionally, airlines paid a fixed-rate commission of 7 percent for point-to-point domestic ticket sales. In return for creating conditions that made the travel agency profitable, airlines have always been able to write the rules governing agency competition. A Civil Aeronautics Board rule, effective May 1980, abolished the fixed-rate commission and ordered carriers to propose new plans for compensating travel agents. Officials of the agency indicated that the intent was to promote retail price competition and encourage new alternative retail outlets.

  United Airlines was the first to respond, proposing to pay a flat $8.50 per ticket. Travel agencies reacted by diverting traffic to other airlines offering higher commissions. United suffered a 14 percent sales drop in one month as a result, in part, of the new commission. Finally, United withdrew the plan and offered a sliding-scale plan paying travel agents from $7.50 to $37.50, depending on the distance flown. Other airlines offered different plans. For example, Eastern proposed a commission ranging from 8 to 11 percent, Frontier Airline's plan called for 10 to 11 percent, and American Airlines' plan was so complex that most agents indicated that they could not understand it.[5]

- Via computer links, organizations can make their own airline reservations. For example, Ohio State University's athletic department sometimes books as many as 50 flights a week; the availability of an on-line system has saved the department an enormous amount of time and a significant amount of money. Some travel agents, however, fear that automation, by giving travelers more direct control, could eventually make agencies dispensable. For their part, the airlines recognize that the changes are raising sensitive issues. Some admit privately that they do want more control over the distribution of their tickets. But airline executives vigorously deny

[4] Josh Levine, "Pan Am Seeks Ticket Wholesaling," *Advertising Age* (January 23, 1980), pp. 1, 84.

[5] "The Fracas over Who Will Sell Airline Tickets," *Business Week* (April 28, 1980), p. 107; "United Air to Pay Travel Agents Flat Fee, Replacing Commissions Based on Fares," *Wall Street Journal*, February 5, 1980, p. 5; "United Air, Responding to Complaints, Alters Travel Agent Compensation Plan," *Wall Street Journal*, February 19, 1980, p. 8.

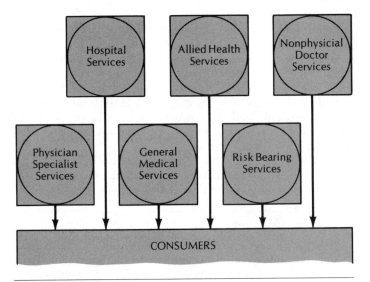

Figure 13–3 The flat nonintegrated structure for the delivery of health care services

Source: Louis P. Bucklin and James M. Carman, "Vertical Market Structure Theory and the Health Care Delivery System," in Jagdish N. Sheth and Peter L. Wright (eds.), *Marketing Analysis for Societal Problems* (Urbana, Ill.: University of Illinois Bureau of Economic and Business Research, 1974), p. 23.

that their intention is to bypass travel agents entirely. In fact, carriers are in most cases marketing their on-line systems through travel agents, and any reservations made with them are routed to the agents, not to the airlines.[6]

APPLYING CHANNEL CONCEPTS
TO SERVICES: FIVE EXAMPLES

Health-Care Services[7]

Four different market structures for the delivery of health-care services may be isolated, although a number of others also exist. The first, the flat nonintegrated structure (see Fig. 13–3), is the archetype of the present private-practice, fee-for-service system in which every hospital, each physician, and all other health-care providers sell directly to consumers. The organizations involved in this system undertake no effort to coordinate their activities; any

[6] Francis C. Brown III, "Automation Brings Travel Services Right to the Traveler's Doorstep," *Wall Street Journal*, August 7, 1986, p. 21.

[7] The discussion of health care services is drawn from an excellent and innovative essay by Louis P. Bucklin and James M. Carman, "Vertical Market Structure Theory and the Health Care Delivery System," in Jagdish N. Sheth and Peter L. Wright (eds.), *Marketing Analysis for Societal Problems* (Urbana, Ill.: University of Illinois Bureau of Economic and Business Research, 1974), pp. 7–39.

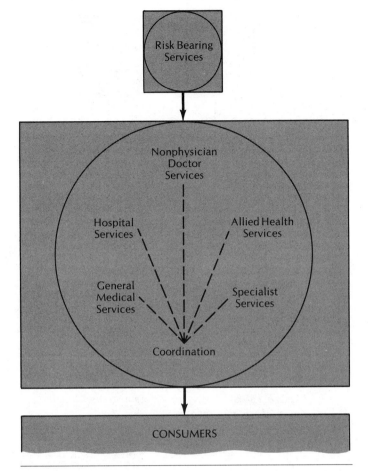

Risk Bearing
Services

Nonphysician
Doctor
Services

Hospital
Services

Allied Health
Services

General
Medical
Services

Specialist
Services

Coordination

CONSUMERS

Figure 13–4   The vertically integrated structure for the delivery
of health care services

Source: Louis P. Bucklin and James M. Carman, "Vertical Market Structure
Theory and the Health Care Delivery System," in Jagdish N. Sheth and Peter L.
Wright (eds.), *Marketing Analysis for Societal Problems* (Urbana, Ill.: University
of Illinois Bureau of Economic and Business Research, 1974), p. 25.

coordination that does take place comes from market pressures emanating from
consumers.[8]

The second is a vertically integrated structure where coordination of the
activities of all providers is shifted to a comprehensive health-care institution,
such as the Kaiser Permanente, which provides for all potential patient health
needs within a single establishment.[9] Although there are a number of variations,
Fig. 13–4 is representative of a major form of these so-called health maintenance

[8] *Ibid.*, p. 23.
[9] *Ibid.*, p. 24. Kaiser employs 5200 physicians. For a discussion of the changing face of health
care in the U.S., see Anne B. Fisher, "The New Game in Health Care: Who Will Profit?" *Fortune*
(March 4, 1985), pp. 138–43; "The Big Business of Medicine," *Newsweek* (October 31, 1983), pp. 62–
74; and "Rx: Competition," *Business Week* (February 8, 1982), pp. 58–64.

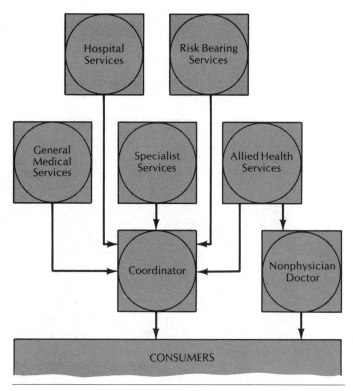

Figure 13–5 The vertical, nonintegrated structure for the delivery of health care services

Source: Louis P. Bucklin and James M. Carman, "Vertical Marketing Structure Theory and the Health Care Delivery System," in Jagdish N. Sheth and Peter L. Wright (eds.), *Marketing Analysis for Societal Problems* (Urbana, Ill.: University of Illinois Bureau of Economic and Business Research, 1974), p. 27.

organizations (HMOs). Coordination among activities is achieved through an internal control mechanism. Payments are received from consumers on a capitation basis, and each consumer belongs to only one group.

In the third structure, coordination is achieved by means of the control exerted by one health provider or by a middleman (see Fig. 13–5). In this nonintegrated arrangement, consumers make annual capitation payments to the coordinator of their choice. It is then the responsibility of the central coordinator—a pure middleman, a general practitioner individual or group, a pediatric individual or group, or a general practice community clinic or hospital—to buy specialized services from other types of providers or to undertake to perform these internally.

The fourth type of arrangement is the long, vertical nonintegrated structure (see Fig. 13–6), characterized by multiple modes of coordination. According to Bucklin and Carman,

general financial support and insurance services are provided through a nonprofit foundation for a complete health package. Individual providers would similarly

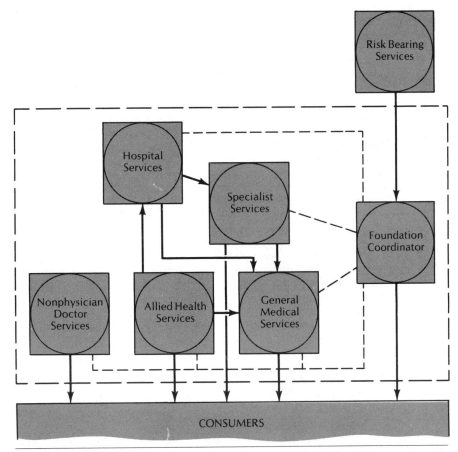

Figure 13–6 The long, vertical nonintegrated structure for the delivery of health care services

Source: Louis P. Bucklin and James M. Carman, "Vertical Market Structure Theory and the Health Care Delivery System" in Jagdish N. Sheth and Peter L. Wright (eds.), *Marketing Analysis for Societal Problems* (Urbana, Ill.: University of Illinois Bureau of Economic and Business Research, 1974), p. 28.

belong to the foundation which would reimburse the former on a fee-for-service basis. The foundation would develop its own techniques, such as peer review, to control the use of providers and their charges for service. All consumers within a given area, such as a county, would be members of the foundation.[10]

Under this system, as in the previous two, consumers would make an annual capitation payment, but in this case their payment would go to the foundation.

In their analysis of these four arrangements, Bucklin and Carman have relied heavily on Bucklin's theory of channel structure, which was discussed in Chapter 1 of this book. Thus, their basic conclusions about the arrangements are

[10] Bucklin and Carman, *op. cit.,* pp. 26–27.

couched in terms of service outputs and costs. Some of their conclusions are as follows:[11]

1. Consumer search for information and the need for seller promotion appear to be greatest in the flat nonintegrated structure. The least seller promotion and consumer search cost are provided by the vertically integrated structure.

2. The flat nonintegrated structure is the one that is likely to adapt best to consumer needs in terms of providing facilitating outputs. It is also the one that allows consumers the greatest opportunity to select that health service they perceive as best suiting their needs.

3. The flat nonintegrated structure is likely to be the one that incurs the greatest waste of resources, is least efficient, and provides the greatest degree of discrimination among consumer groups. Wealthy consumers may be able to cope handily with the system. Impoverished consumers may literally fail to survive.

4. The vertically integrated system (HMO) is likely to result in better use of existing health supply resources and to be more efficient. It also provides the basis for evenhanded care for all people.[12] On the other hand, there is likely to be minimal adjustment of facilitating outputs to consumer needs, problems in effecting community control in the absence of competition, and a tendency over time for bureaucratic rigidities to accrue. Consumers have the least choice of specific providers.

5. The vertically nonintegrated structures provide a middle ground, involving characteristics of both ends of the spectrum. Consumer choice opportunities are improved, but the possibilities for some discrimination in resource use also appear likely. Both vertically nonintegrated systems also provide maximum opportunity for the entry of new types of structures and hence incentive for innovation.

Any analysis of health-care services must recognize, implicitly or explicitly, the significance of effective interorganization management in the organization of health care delivery systems. Each of the structures just enumerated varies the extent of role specification, centralization of power, and potential for conflict management that might be expected. In fact, the typology here is very similar to that developed throughout this book for conventional, administered, contractual, and corporate channels. The application of the concepts from vertical market structure theory and from interorganization management theory can, therefore, be combined to provide prescriptions for improving health-care systems.[13]

An extreme example of what is happening in health-care delivery can be found on a 40-acre campus in Delray Beach, Florida, where National Medical Enterprises (NME), the nation's second largest (to Humana) health-care services company, is testing what amounts to an enormous shopping mall for health care. The complex includes (1) Delray Community Hospital, a 211-bed general acute-care hospital; (2) Hillhaven Convalescent Center of Delray, a 120-bed skilled-care nursing home; (3) the Fair Oaks Hospital of Boca/Delray, a 72-bed psychiat-

---

[11] *Ibid.*, pp. 29, 35.

[12] Recent evidence indicates that HMOs have a positive competitive impact in health care. They provide service at lower cost. See, for example, "FTC Staff Report Says HMOs Have Competitive Impact," *FTC News Summary* (August 1977), p. 1; "HMOs Can Hold Down Health Care Costs," *Wall Street Journal*, August 5, 1977, p. 5; and "Unhealthy Costs of Health Care," *Business Week* (September 4, 1978), pp. 58–68.

[13] For further discussion of this point, see Louis W. Stern and Frederick D. Sturdivant, "Discussion," in Sheth and Wright (eds.), *op. cit.*, pp. 39–41; and Donald E. L. Johnson, "University Hospitals Will Anchor Vertical Systems," *Modern Health Care* (December 1979), pp. 50–54.

ric hospital that specializes in substance abuse; and (4) a 60-bed rehabilitation hospital to treat victims of spinal cord injuries and stroke. Nearby is a shopping center, on company-owned land, containing everything from a health-food store to a bank to a pharmacy as well as three medical buildings containing condominium offices sold to physicians by NME. NME claims that it saves money on operating costs from having neighboring facilities that can pool purchasing dollars and even share medical facilities. The proximity also improves medical care, because doctors find it easy to check up on a nursing patient as long as they are at the neighboring hospital. This physician convenience promotes cross referrals that boost NME's business.[14]

Population Control and Family Planning Services[15]

The topic of population control and family planning is highly controversial. Population control refers to the *control* of births, whereas family planning refers to the spacing of births and the limiting of family size to some number of children *desired* by a couple. Population control advocates are highly critical of the family planning approach to the world's population problem.

Without engaging in this debate, it is possible to observe that the present system in the United States for distributing birth control services to the population is quite fragmented and highly decentralized. Medical birth control services (e.g., abortion, the IUD, sterilization, and birth control pills) may be distributed through private or public health practice. In addition, they may be offered through clinics established solely for this purpose and staffed by personnel possessing the required level of medical expertise. The channels for nonmedical methods (e.g., condoms, chemical preparations, and information on so-called natural methods of contraception such as the rhythm system) are largely identical to those for the medically dependent techniques, except for one important exception—the addition of traditional commercial channels, including retail drug outlets and vending machines.

Anyone interested in seeking improvements in the dissemination of birth control devices and information—either for population control or family planning purposes—must focus on reducing the costs of the physical, temporal, and psychic distances separating individuals from the agencies providing the services or mechanisms. Private medical practitioners have, on the whole, historically been hesitant to *initiate* the subject of birth control with their established patients. Presumably, they would be even more reluctant to become active agents in any channel whose sole function is the providing of such services. It is expected that if this group is to assume a more active role, two steps must be taken. First, the program must remunerate physicians. Second, the norms of the medical profession must support such activities.

Enrolling the physician as an active participant would definitely increase the availability of birth control services to the more affluent. However, as pointed out in the discussion of the present flat nonintegrated structure in

[14] Michael L. Millenson, "Health Care's 1-Stop Shopping," *Chicago Tribune*, February 9, 1986, section 7, p. 3.
[15] The discussion of population control and family planning services is drawn from an unpublished term paper by Raymond Neil Maddox, "Distribution and Social Problems," Ohio State University, 1973.

health-care delivery, among the problems confronting the less fortunate is the limited availability of medical services of any type. Therefore, this suggestion would be, at best, of limited utility in raising the level of accessibility for these groups.

An innovative approach in solving the problem of accessibility has been adopted in Louisiana. As reported by El-Ansary and Kramer, a major component of the so-called Louisiana model was an improvement in clinic site selection and service level determination.

> To reduce travel time, strategic locations were selected for the program's clinic satellites. Also, clinic layout was planned to reduce the time consumed in information and physical flows. The areas assigned for waiting rooms were limited to force faster customer flows. Bottlenecks in the system were identified and eliminated. It was realized that improving the service level would result not only in a higher percentage of kept appointments and active customers but also in better utilization of physical facilities and human resources.[16]

Although heavy reliance on clinics to provide birth control services may be functional in parts of the United States, it is not always the best distribution approach, especially in underdeveloped countries. As Farley and Leavitt point out,

> a complete reliance upon clinics as outlets is questionable, especially when one considers their high cost per client visit and the relatively poor revisit rates they achieve. Several problems contribute to this situation:
>
> - Medical resources, especially personnel, are expensive and generally in short supply . . .
> - Red tape may be substantial because of overly complex control systems . . .
> - Clinical systems may bias a program's emphasis to the exclusion of [nonmedical types of contraception] . . .
> - As a distribution network, clinics tend to be sparsely dispersed . . . . [Also,] a visit to a clinic may involve substantial waiting time . . .
> - Clinics lack anonymity . . . .[17]

However, in both developed and underdeveloped economies, the commercial distribution of nonmedical means seems to offer the greatest potential for rapidly expanding the number and availability of birth control mechanisms.

> Most cultures have a functioning distribution structure which delivers basic commodities to even the most remote areas of the countryside. The network is intensive and provides relatively anonymous outlets which are physically close to the customer. Wholesalers and retailers know how to deliver goods to customers, and distributors know how to stimulate consumer demand. It is possible that the retail structure could be utilized to provide distribution outlets for contraceptive materials, thus helping resolve the logistical problems facing the clinic system . . . .

[16] Adel I. El-Ansary and Oscar E. Kramer, Jr., "Social Marketing: The Family Planning Experience," *Journal of Marketing*, Vol. 37 (July 1973), p. 3.

[17] Reprinted from John U. Farley and Harold J. Leavitt, "Marketing and Population Problems," *Journal of Marketing*, Vol. 35 (July 1971), p. 31, published by the American Management Association.

Other channels, such as mail order, could be used in some nations to supplement the clinic system's distribution of certain items.[18]

Indeed, if food and variety stores, as well as pharmacies, were engaged as distributors of point-of-purchase information, contraceptive chemicals, and contraceptive devices, the increase in the number and accessibility of outlets would be tremendous. In India, for example, the government engaged the distribution services of some of the largest packaged-goods companies in the country, including Hindustan Lever, ITC, and Brooke Bond, because of their reach into the remotest areas. In fact, the government eventually elected to work with health clinics, barbers, field workers, retail stores, and vending machines.

A major advantage in using traditional commercial channels for the distribution of birth control services is that they tend to help reduce psychic distance—that is, the hesitancy to seek birth control services owing to the intimate nature of the product and the modesty or shyness associated with its use. Medical channels, including public agencies, no matter how available, are separated from certain segments of the population by major psychological barriers.[19] A consumer's basic familiarity with commercial retail outlets is an important means of reducing this distance.

There is a close correspondence between the marketing of birth control services and the marketing of "normal" products, because most contraceptive devices are tangible items. While there are numerous services (such as counseling) that attend population control and family planning, a major problem in this area is the availability and accessibility of the devices themselves. Thus, thinking in terms of traditional marketing approaches seems to be a natural course. The principles of interorganization management seem as relevant here as they are to the marketing of all forms of packaged goods.

Recycling Services[20]

The recycling of waste products has become a subject of considerable notoriety as increased concern has been voiced over environmental quality. Considering the low prices paid currently for waste materials (bottles, cans, paper, etc.) and the high costs involved in the collecting, sorting, and transportation of these objects to recycling plants, industry is relying heavily on civic and community groups, who use volunteer help primarily in the collection process. Normal business costs are usually absent when these groups handle the collection, because labor and vehicles are generally donated. However, one of the problems in relying on these groups is that their efforts are generally very sporadic, at best. Furthermore, the problem is growing faster than the membership of ecology-minded groups.

[18] Reprinted from John U. Farley and Harold J. Leavitt, "Marketing and Population Problems," *Journal of Marketing*, Vol. 35 (July 1971), p. 31, published by the American Management Association.

[19] See Gerald Zaltman and Ilan Vertinsky, "Health Service Marketing: A Suggested Model," *Journal of Marketing*, Vol. 35 (July 1971), p. 26.

[20] The discussion of recycling services is drawn primarily from an unpublished term paper by Sam B. Dunbar, Jr., "The Recycling of Waste Products: Effects on Distribution Channels and Marketing," George Washington University, 1978.

Traditional distribution channels have been used in some recycling efforts. During the immediate post–World War II years and before, distribution of soft drinks, for example, was specifically tied to the use of the returnable bottle. From the bottler's point of view, the returnable bottle was desirable because its use reduced his production costs. He found it more economical to clean existing bottles and reuse them than to buy new bottles. Middlemen, such as retail food stores, cooperated because the system was the most convenient for the producer involved, and he could bring pressure to bear on the middlemen to secure their cooperation. Currently, however, returnable bottles account for less than 50 percent of the soft drink industry's business, because both retailers and consumers resisted the returning and handling of empty bottles. Supermarkets directly influenced bottlers to introduce soft drinks in one-way bottles as early as 1948.[21] While one-way containers have increased the bottler's costs, these costs have been passed on to the consumer. The response of the consumers has been demonstrated by their willingness to pay higher prices for the convenience afforded by these containers. Thus, the recycling problem in this area has multiplied.

If recycling is to be a feasible solution to waste disposal, some means must be developed to channel these wastes back to firms for further use. But traditional channel concepts must be reversed because, in the case of soft drinks especially, the consumer is the *producer* of the waste materials that are to be recycled. Thus, the consumer becomes the first link in the recycling channel of distribution rather than the last. The recycling of waste materials is, therefore, essentially a "reverse-distribution" process.[22]

The contrast between forward and reverse channels is illustrated in Fig. 13–7 and Table 13–2. The reverse-direction channel returns the reusable waste products from consumer to producer.

> Conceptually, reverse distribution is identical to the traditional channel of distribution. The consumer has a product to sell, and in essence, he assumes the same position as a manufacturer selling a new product. The consumer's (seller's) role is to distribute his waste materials to the market that demands his product.[23]

However, the consumer, in most instances, does not consider himself to be the producer of waste materials. Therefore, he is not readily concerned with planning a marketing strategy for his product, which would be reusable wastes. When the producer is unaware of or indifferent to the fact that he is the producer, then the problem becomes acute.

So far, many recycling channels eliminate the middleman, unless that middleman is a voluntary group. That there are generally no established middlemen in these backward channels between the producer and the consumer of waste products is unfortunate. It causes the producer (consumer) a number of inconveniences. Foremost is the accumulation of waste materials on his part, without adequate storage facilities, as well as an absence of facilities to transport them.

---

[21] William G. Zikmund and William J. Stanton, "Recycling Solid Wastes: A Channels-of-Distribution Problem," *Journal of Marketing*, Vol. 35 (July 1971), p. 36.
[22] *Ibid.*, pp. 34–35.
[23] *Ibid.*, p. 35.

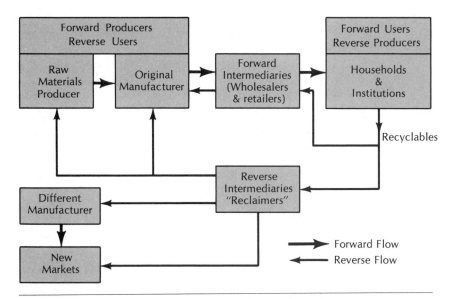

Figure 13–7 Forward and reverse channels of distribution

Source: Joseph Guiltinan and Nonyelu Nwokoye, "Reverse Channels for Recycling: An Analysis of Alternatives and Public Policy Implications," in Ronald C. Curhan (ed.), *1974 Combined Proceedings* (Chicago: American Marketing Association, 1975), p. 341.

Table 13–2 Forward versus reverse channels: Some key distinctions

Forward Channels	Reverse Channels
Products:	
High unit value	Low unit value
Highly differentiated	Little or no differentiation
Much product innovation	Little or no innovation
Few producers	Many originators
Markets:	
Routinized transactions established	Routinized transactions not established
Many final users	Few final users
Varied customer demands	Standardized demands
Supply often less than or equal to demand	Supply typically greater than demand
Large assortment discrepancy	Small assortment discrepancy
Key Functions:	
Assorting	Sorting
Allocation	Accumulation
Heavy promotional effort	Low promotional effort
Speculative inventories	Few speculative inventories
Packaging	Collection

Source: Joseph Guiltinan and Nonyelu Nwokoye, "Reverse Channels for Recycling: An Analysis of Alternatives and Public Policy Implications," in Ronald C. Curhan (ed.), *1974 Combined Proceedings* (Chicago: American Marketing Association, 1975), p. 342.

Barnes believes that recruiting intermediaries to help in the recycling process is essential:

> In order for this backward flow to occur with any degree of efficiency, intermediaries . . . must occupy positions between the many heterogeneous producers of waste and the firms wishing to consume these wastes. The intermediaries seem to perform traditional middlemen activities, with sorting as the most important function . . . . These middlemen must be capable of working with large quantities of refuse and must be able to economically sort out dissimilar wastes and accumulate large masses of waste products into homogeneous quantities.
>
> Channel conflicts must be resolved if a firm's recycling program is to be successful. Traditional middlemen must be willing to cooperate. But historically, middlemen in this reverse role have found cooperation unprofitable. The activities included in recycling (counting, sorting, storage, paying consumers, etc.) take time away from activities deemed more important so that the recycling effort is usually pushed aside.[24]

On the other hand, in the area of trash recycling, private and municipal trash collection systems provide the collection and storage functions. The buyer of the collected wastes may be a power plant, a metals company, a fertilizer company, and the like. This channel is a convenient one for the individual household. However, trash collection by basic trash collection agencies may not be the ultimate answer to the recycling problem. Trash needs to be sorted and then routed to storage centers for ultimate transportation to recycling centers, and most municipalities are unwilling to incur the costs associated with these tasks.

If an effective reverse channel of distribution is to become a reality, the ultimate consumer must first be motivated to start the reverse flow. In addition, a greater degree of cooperation has to be achieved among channel members. A barrier to increased cooperation and coordination is the lack of profitability. In the absence of legislation mandating recycling efforts (or taxing noncompliers), improved recycling efforts may depend on a higher order of social responsibility by middlemen, given the lack of profits. Several new types of intermediaries may emerge to facilitate recycling processes. One of these is the reclamation or recycling center, a modernized "junk yard" placed in a convenient location for the customer, who would be paid an equitable amount for his waste goods. Initial processing of the waste materials, when collected, might be accomplished at these centers. For example, aluminum producers, can makers, and beverage distributors have set up more than 2000 recycling centers across the United States. Some producers send trucks to neighborhoods to pick up cans.[25] In addition, central processing warehouses may be developed by existing middlemen in traditional channels, where trash can be stored and where limited processing operations on waste material may be performed. For example, aluminum can producers are equipping beverage distributors with can flatteners, shredders, compactors, and truck trailers to encourage them to accept empties for recycling.[26] Transportation costs would likely represent a major barrier to such recycling efforts, however. Other possibilities include such reverse channels

---

[24] James H. Barnes, Jr., "Recycling: A Problem in Reverse Logistics," *Journal of Macromarketing,* Vol. 2 (Fall 1982), pp. 33–34.

[25] "Recycling Ease Gives Aluminum an Edge over Steel in Beverage-Can Market Battle," *Wall Street Journal,* January 2, 1980, p. 28.

[26] *Ibid.*

as manufacturer-controlled recycling centers, joint-venture resource recovery centers, and secondary dealers.[27]

The development of solid waste reverse channels of distribution has been influenced by federal, state, and local legislation directed at all phases of the environment. For example, reverse channels have been given considerable impetus in states enacting bottle bills, which ban nonreturnable drink containers. Oregon, Vermont, Michigan, Massachusetts, and South Dakota, among several other states, have enacted such laws. The Oregon Minimum Deposit Act is the most comprehensive recycling law, requiring retailers and distributors to accept and pay refunds on all empty cans and bottles of the kind, size, and brands sold by them. As more states, counties, and localities enact similar laws, reverse distribution channels will become a permanent part of the distribution structure in the United States.[28]

Lodging Services[29]

Marketing channels in the lodging industry (hotels, motels, motor inns, tourist courts, etc.) are becoming increasingly complex and sophisticated. While hotels throughout the world tend to be small (e.g., over 40 percent of U.S. hotels and motels are too small to have even one paid employee), there is an increasing amount of economic concentration in the lodging industry, due in part to the development of interorganizational communication systems, franchised networks, and corporate vertical marketing systems. The various channels of distribution in the lodging industry are shown in Fig. 13–8. Direct channels of distribution among hotels, motels, and other lodging operations and their customers are concerned mainly with the sales function. That is, an individual hotel's salesmen concentrate on:

1. Maintaining sales contact with channel intermediaries such as tour operators, travel agents, representatives and transportation companies
2. Maintaining sales contact with community firms and organizations in an attempt to obtain lodging and function business
3. Following the leads furnished by other sources[30]

Indirect channels, however, are more significant to lodging providers than are direct channels. Intermediaries in these channels include travel agents, hotel representatives, tour operators, space brokers, airlines, and the centralized reservation and sales operations of franchised or chain hotels.

- *Travel agents* may contract for rooms on a customer's behalf, but they more frequently deal through other intermediaries who hold blocks of rooms or otherwise act as agents for the hotels.

---

[27] For a discussion of these latter channels, see Joseph Guiltinan and Nonyelu Nwokoye, "Reverse Channels for Recycling: An Analysis of Alternatives and Public Policy Implications," in Ronald C. Curhan (ed.), *1974 Combined Proceedings* (Chicago: American Marketing Association, 1975), pp. 343–44; and Zikmund and Stanton, *op. cit.,* p. 38.

[28] Peter M. Ginter and Jack M. Starling, "Reverse Distribution Channels for Recycling," *California Management Review* (Spring 1978), pp. 77, 78.

[29] The discussion of lodging services is drawn from William H. Kaven, "Channels of Distribution in the Hotel Industry," in Rathmell, *op. cit.,* pp. 114–21.

[30] *Ibid.,* p. 116.

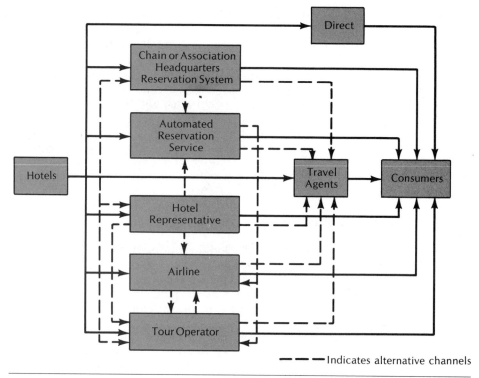

Figure 13—8   Marketing channels for lodging services

Source: William H. Kaven, "Channels of Distribution in the Hotel Industry," in John M. Rathmell (ed.), *Marketing in the Service Sector* (Cambridge, Mass.: Winthrop Publishers, Inc., 1974), p. 118. Reprinted by permission of the publisher.

- *Hotel representatives* act as sales and reservation agents for a number of noncompeting hotels, such as resorts.
- *Automated reservation services,* such as American Express Space Bank, maintain for a fee in their computers an inventory of available hotel rooms from around the world so that travel agents can buy rooms for their customers.
- *Airlines* maintain an inventory of room availability to accommodate customers and travel agents who prefer to make complete arrangements with but one phone call for flight and room reservations.
- *Centralized reservation and sales operations* of associated, franchised, or chain hotels/motels facilitate the flow of room availability information to potential consumers and promote, sell, and accept reservations for space.[31]

With the increased dependence of many hotel and motel operators on these intermediaries, power has shifted in the channels for lodging services. The intermediaries can maintain a wide number of alternatives and can mediate considerable rewards for lodging providers. Thus, in part as a reaction to the changing character of the power relationships, a considerable movement within the industry to form vertical marketing systems has been initiated not only by

[31] *Ibid.,* pp. 116–17.

hotel and motel owners but by organizations closely connected with the industry, such as airlines. Either through contractual or ownership arrangements, these systems permit control over all channel flows, especially those associated with information processing.

Clearly, the move to vertical marketing arrangements, such as those forged by Holiday Inn and others, has been motivated by other reasons as well. Such arrangements permit greater economies of scale in promotion, increased speed and economy in the flow of information, and in increased closeness to consumers when they are making their purchase decisions. The use of nationwide toll-free hotel reservation numbers, for example, has made the desired closeness to consumers a reality for many lodging organizations. In addition, these kinds of systems frequently lead to economies of scale in purchasing and operations. Most important, vertical systems that effectively employ interorganization management principles and techniques present to the public the image of a national or regional company of high standards with whom customers can deal with confidence.

One of the outstanding practitioners in the lodging industry is Marriott Corporation. Marriott, which claims its business is to manage hotels and not to own them, has been more aggressive than its rivals in selling hotels to investors and operating them under the Marriott name. This vertical arrangement has paid off handsomely for the company. Typically, Marriott puts up its money to build a hotel and then sells it to a group of investors—an insurance company, limited partnership, or real estate investment trust—that gets the tax breaks and some of the hotel's cash flow. Marriott then manages the property in return for about 5 percent of the hotel's revenues and 20 percent of its operating profits. In 1985, about 43,000 of Marriott's 61,000 rooms operated under this arrangement, more than its rivals. (Roughly 10,000 rooms were franchised to others and 7900 were owned by Marriott outright.) Its management system uses as its foundation a multivolume *Book of Knowledge* containing tens of thousands of instructions. Marriott relies on it to institutionalize friendliness and consistency. The idea is for customers to find the same pleasurable experience in every one of Marriott's hotels. Because of its system, Marriott has been the most successful lodging operation in the United States over the last decade.[32]

Property and Casualty Insurance Services[33]

Although there are two main segments of the insurance industry—life and health insurance *and* property and casualty insurance—attention is focused here on the latter, because the channels are somewhat more complex and dramatic changes are taking place within them. Over the past 35 years, the typical fragmented pattern of marketing property and casualty insurance—the so-called American agency system—has been consistently losing ground to centrally coordinated systems—so-called direct-writing or direct-selling systems, which now

[32] See Leslie Wayne, "Marriott Stakes Out New Territory," *New York Times*, September 22, 1985, section 3, p. 1; David Elsner, "No Room for Error at Marriott," *Chicago Tribune*, February 2, 1986, section 7, p. 1; and "Bill Marriott's Grand Design for Growth: Upscale and Down in the Lodging Market," *Business Week* (October 1, 1984), pp. 60–61.

[33] The discussion of property and casualty insurance services is drawn from Michael Etgar, "The Effects of Forward Vertical Integration on Service Performance of a Distributive Industry," *Journal of Industrial Economics* (March 1978), p. 249.

control more than a quarter of the overall property and casualty market and close to half of the automobile insurance market.[34]

Under the American agency system, insurance representatives are commission-compensated *independent agents* who may and usually do represent several insurers. Independent agents sell only for insurers who are willing to permit them to retain ownership and control over policy and expiration records.[35] This means that if an independent agent terminates his relationship with a particular insurance company, he customarily has the legal right to retain all agency records and to receive commissions on unexpired policies with the insurer in question. The independent agent's accounts cannot be assigned to other agents, but he may sell to another agent his right to seek renewal of policies sold. The historical roots of the American agency system go back to the second half of the nineteenth century. In order to serve a widely dispersed population and at the same time diversify their risk portfolios, insurance companies designed a distributive system that allowed them to have representatives in many population centers.[36]

The direct-writing system, on the other hand, comprises a variety of modes of distributing property and casualty insurance. In many cases, the distributor for a direct-writing company has no ownership rights in renewals and represents only one company. Compensation for the representatives of a direct-writing company may be in the form of commissions, salaries with bonuses, or a combination of these methods. When commissions are paid, the representatives are usually paid reduced commissions on renewed policies. The representatives are employees of the insurance company (e.g., Allstate) and not independent contractors.

Another form of the direct-writing system is found in certain companies that typically develop out of an association with farm bureau organizations. These firms are represented by exclusive representatives who are independent contractors. The most prominent insurance companies that operate this way are those that belong to the State Farm Mutual Insurance Group and the Nationwide Mutual Insurance Group. The larger exclusive agency insurers have made tremendous increases in their sales of automobile insurance in the last 15 years and more recently are showing substantial gains in fire, homeowners, and even life and health insurance.[37]

A few insurers solicit business directly by mail. The most prominent insurance company that operates in this manner is the Government Employees Insurance Company (GEICO). Although GEICO was initially established to sell insurance to employees of the federal government, it now sells insurance to all. The applications that are received as a result of mail promotions are handled by company employees in headquarters and branch offices.

In a sense, the three modes of direct-writing distribution represent a continuum of centralized coordination and control. On one end of the spectrum is the channel that is closest in form to the independent agency—that is, distribution of property and casualty insurance by exclusive representatives who are

[34] David L. Bickelhaupt, *General Insurance,* 9th ed. (Homewood, Ill.: Richard D. Irwin, 1974), p. 128.

[35] *Ibid.,* p. 251.

[36] James L. Athearn, *General Insurance Agency Management* (Homewood, Ill.: Richard D. Irwin, 1965), p. 10.

[37] Bickelhaupt, *op. cit.,* pp. 128–29.

independent contractors. In the middle is the commissioned employee system, and at the far end is the mail-order system. The latter two are examples of corporate vertical marketing systems.

According to Bickelhaupt, the main advantage of the direct-writing system is lower cost through reduced commissions or decreased expenses due to centralization of some functions, such as policy writing, records keeping, billing, training, advertising, and sales.[38] On the other hand, the American agency system offers the advantage of a wide variety of independent entrepreneurs who provide an assortment of options, in the form of the companies they represent, to potential consumers.

Given the threat posed by the increasing trend toward contractual and corporate direct-writing marketing systems, there is evidence that the American agency system has begun to incorporate some features of the former systems. Several of the largest insurance companies using independent agents (e.g., Insurance Company of North America, Chubb Insurance Group, and Royal-Globe Group) began during the early 1970s to issue exclusive agency contracts for their regular clients.[39] In addition, billing arrangements have been routinized in a manner similar to that for direct-writing companies. On the other hand, some direct-writing insurers have granted their larger and more successful exclusive agents certain rights similar to the ownership rights that independent agents have to renewals and records. Under these agreements, the established exclusive agent, if he terminates his relationship with the insurer or retires from business, would be paid by the insurer for his book of business.[40]

In general, however, it is likely that the independent agency system is going to have to move closer to the direct-writing system (rather than vice versa) in order to remain competitive. The advantages that the latter are securing are similar to those that have been gained by vertical marketing systems in other fields.[41] There is, however, always the tradeoff between benefits of increased efficiencies in operation and the attractiveness to consumers of providing large assortments. In fact, direct-writing companies have begun to develop a wide line of "products," under different brand names, in order to serve the variety of segments in the market for insurance, and thus are showing a willingness to sacrifice some of their efficiencies for even deeper market penetration.

SUMMARY AND CONCLUSIONS

The location and type of "retail" outlets through which services are to be dispensed are critical decisions in ensuring the availability and accessibility of these services. The process involved in the creation of time and place utilities is even more important in the marketing of services than it is in the marketing of

---

[38] *Ibid.*, p. 129.

[39] *Ibid.*, p. 130.

[40] *Ibid.*

[41] For an empirical study of the power relationships in the channel for property and casualty insurance, see Michael Etgar, "Effects of Administrative Control on Efficiency of Vertical Marketing Systems," *Journal of Marketing Research* (February 1976), pp. 12-23; and Michael Etgar, "Channel Domination and Countervailing Power in Distributive Channels," *Journal of Marketing Research* (August 1976), pp. 254–62.

tangible products. In addition, problems in establishing marketing channels for certain services are often compounded by the need of some organizations to attract resources from groups that are different from those to whom their services are provided.

Marketing channels for services are generally very short; direct marketing (between service creator or performer and end-users) is the norm. Franchising is, however, becoming an increasingly important form of channel organization in the profit-oriented service sector.

Services are also becoming more widely dispersed and decentralized, and thus the need for interorganizational cooperation and coordination has increased. In addition, redundancies, inequities, and inefficiencies are especially prevalent in the provision of many social welfare services. These deficiencies can be reduced considerably through the application of interorganization management principles. However, for the most part, the emphasis must be placed on interorganizational coordination at the "retail" level of distribution, because many services are both produced and distributed at the local level and do not involve the kind of extensive vertical networks that are found in the marketing of tangible commodities. Services do not generally pass through the hands of intermediaries. Attention must, then, be concentrated on developing effective combinations of the *retailing* marketing mix elements (hours of operations, facilitating services, assortments, location and facilities, expense management, promotion, and the like).

Although there are literally hundreds of service industries to which channel concepts have been or might be applied, the bulk of this chapter has been devoted to providing only five examples. Similar examples should be developed for other service industries as well, because the process involves a rethinking of the roles of the agencies and institutions participating in the various channels and may thereby lead to a restructuring and reappraisal of the way in which a number of services are provided.

DISCUSSION QUESTIONS

1. Is it appropriate to apply interorganization management concepts developed in connection with the marketing of tangible goods to the marketing of services? What are the basic differences between the marketing of goods and the marketing of services that make a transfer of concepts difficult? What concepts from interorganization management of channels appear to be most relevant to an analysis of services?

2. What is the difference between availability and accessibility? How might a health systems manager go about making health services more available? More accessible?

3. For a religious organization (church, crusade, etc.), isolate two separate distribution systems—one dealing with resource *allocation* and the other dealing with resource *attraction*. Which interorganization management concepts, if any, appear to apply to the two systems?

4. Why is it that "the process involved in the creation of time and place utilities is even more important in the marketing of services . . . than it is for the marketing of tangible commodities"?

5. Relate the discussion in Chapter 2 of location decisions to the marketing of services. Which aspects of the former discussion seem to be most pertinent to the marketing of services, and which appear to be least pertinent?

6. Under which of the various health system structures outlined under "Health-Care Services" is the consumer likely to be better off (if there is no government payment for health insurance)? Under which will the physician be better off? Which health system is likely to be most effective over the long run? Which most efficient?

7. Does one set of institutions or agencies appear to be the logical focus of channel control in the distribution of population control and family planning services? If so, what role should this set play in the channel—in other words, how could it manage the channel more effectively to achieve the goal(s) of the channel?

8. Diagram the specific flows (physical possession, ownership, etc.) involved in the channels for recycling services. Which institutions or agencies within these channels are likely to participate most heavily in each of the flows?

9. Analyze the role of travel agents in the marketing channels for lodging services. How much power do they have? What are the bases of their power? What types of conflicts are they likely to be involved in? Should they assume the role of channel managers?

Index

AUTHOR

A

Abrams, Bill, 63n, 84n, 340n
Achabal, Dale D., 478n
Agins, Teri, 346n
Albion, Mark S., 423
Alderson, Wroe, 5, 7n, 20, 33, 102, 196n, 197, 219n
Alexander, Ralph S., 116n
Allvine, Fred C., 480n, 502n
Alsop, Ronald, 274n
Anand, Punam, 301n
Andersen, R. Clifton, 24n
Anderson, Alan R., 481n
Anderson, Erin M., 212n, 275n
Anderson, James C., 131n, 269n, 273n, 297n, 299n, 365n, 413n
Applebaum, William, 51n, 52n
Appleby, Harrison J., 147
Arbeit, Stephen P., 72n
Arndt, Johan, 260n, 489n, 548n
Arrow, Kenneth J., 308n
Artle, Ronald, 219n
Assael, Henry, 296
Athearn, James L., 582n

B

Bacharach, Samuel B., 309n
Bagozzi, Richard P., 225n, 268n, 273n, 552n

Bain, Joe S., 481n
Balderston, Frederick E., 219n, 467n
Baldwin, David A., 270n, 388n
Baligh, Helmy H., 219n, 249n
Ball, Donald, 533n
Ballou, Ronald H., 153n, 155n, 161n, 162n, 170n, 180n, 188n, 557n, 558n
Banerji, Shumeet, 304n
Barger, Harold, 490
Barmash, Isadore, 110n
Barnes, James H., Jr., 578n
Barnes, Peter W., 318n
Bartels, Robert, 541n, 544n
Bass, Stephen J., 74n, 75, 77n
Bates, Albert D., 40, 46, 47n, 55n, 63n, 65, 67n, 68n, 70n, 74n, 75, 77n, 78–79, 333, 344, 499n
Baum, Dan, 274n
Bavelas, Alex, 455n
Beak, Joel, 222n
Bearden, William O., 62n
Becker, Boris W., 478n
Becker, H. G., 159n
Becker, Helmut, 478n
Becker, Robert J., 221n, 257n
Beier, Frederick J., 267n, 432–33
Beik, Leland L., 492n
Bellew, Patricia A., 27n
Bennett, Amanda, 352n
Bennett, Peter D., 22n, 219n

SUBJECT

Grocery chains, countervailing power and, 271, 272
Grocery Manufacturers of America, 291–92
Grocery retailing, 64, 121
  formats of, 41, 43–44
Gross margin, 131–32
  definition of, 100
Gross margin of profit, 96
Gross margin return on inventory (GMROI), 46–47
  definition of, 96
Gymboree exercise centers, 344

H

Hallmark, 207–8
Hardware, intertype competition and, 69, 70
Health and beauty aids, intertype competition and, 69, 70
Health-care services, 568–73
Health maintenance organizations (HMOs), 569–72
Hertz, 287
Hierarchical preference ordering method (sequential elimination), 216–18
Hilton Hotels, 339
Holcomb, J. L., Manufacturing, 126
Home Depot, 70
Home Shopping Network (HSN), 59
Honeywell, 287–88
Horizontal combinations or conspiracies, 405–6
Horn & Hardart Company, 275
Hospital Corporation of America, 130
Hotel industry, 579–81
Household good warehouses, 158
House-to-house selling, 43
Humana, 130
Hypermache (hypermarket), 80
Hypermarkets, 54, 55

I

I-Am-Me's, 66
IBM, 3, 4, 203, 207, 271–73, 335–37, 366
  World Trade Distribution Center (WTDC) of, 160
Ikea, 70
Illinois Tool Works (ITW), 204
Image positioning, 65, 67
Image projection, 65
Incentives
  for resellers' employees, 392
  in Zusman-Etgar model, 309–10
Incomes, retailing and, 60–61
Independent Grocers Alliance, 293
India, 544, 549
Inducement-contributions balance channel conflict and, 289
Industrial goods, wholesalers and, 124–31
Information. *See also* Communications
  secrecy of, 448

sources of, 452–55
wholesalers and, 103
Zusman-Etgar model and, 308–9
Information impactedness, 213
Information power, 276n
Information-processing technology, wholesalers and, 121–23
Information Resources, Inc. (IRI), 449
Initial markup (mark-on), 95
Inland Steel, 320
Inner-directed consumers, 65
In re Chock Full O'Nuts Corp., Inc., 379
Installation and repair services, distribution strategies and, 210
Institutional life cycle
  consumer focus and, 76, 87
  management activities in, 75, 77
Institutional life cycles, 73–78
Insurance, property and casualty, 581–83
Integrateds, 67
Intensive distribution, pitfalls of, 205–8
Intensive distribution strategy, 205–8
Intermediaries, 31. *See also* Physical distribution systems; Retailers; Wholesalers
  definition of, 5
  as independent markets, 28–29
  rationale for, 5–9
  service outputs and, 19–20
  sorting function of, 6–9
    accumulation, 7, 9
    allocation, 9
    assorting, 9
    sorting out, 7, 9
Internal expansion, vertical integration by, 403
Internal Revenue Service (IRS), bribery and, 392
International marketing channels, 32, 526–60
  alternative forms of international expansion, 531–37
    direct investment, 533
    exportation, 531
    joint ventures, 532
    licensing, 532
    piggybacking, 531–32
    selecting a foreign market entry method, 533, 535–37
  for countertrade, 550–52
  distribution strategy, 537–38
  physical distribution, 556–59
  problems in establishing and managing, 552–56
  recent trends, 526–31
  retailing, 547–50
  wholesale linkages to foreign markets, 538–47
    comprador (del credere agent), 539–40
    export management company (EMC), 538–39
    foreign middlemen, 539, 542

trading area measurement and evaluation and, 50–51
Location clause, 389
Lodging services, 579–81
Lofino's, 72
Logistics. *See* Physical distribution systems
Lot size, 18–19
Lynn, Frank, & Associates, 112–13, 136–37

M

McCrory Corporation, 274
McDonald's Corporation, 214, 275, 332, 337, 339
McGuire Act (1952), 384
McGuire-Staelin model, 249–55, 309n
  first-level games in, 251–54
  second-level games in, 254–55
McKesson Corporation, 121–24, 136
McKinsey and Company, 513
Macy's, 65, 72
Mail-order houses, 42, 54, 55, 63, 80
Maintained markup (margin), 95
Maintenance, repair, or operating (MRO), 117
Malaya, 544
Malls, 55–57
Malone & Hyde, 121, 329
Management. *See also* Legal constraints; Management (leadership) of channels; Management science
  asset, 132–34
  definition of, 195
  industrial goods distributors and, 129
  institutional life cycle and, 75, 77
  margin, 131–32
  materials, 144–45
  physical distribution, 149. *See also* Physical distribution systems
Management (leadership) of channels, 27–31, 195–99, 298–301, 410–39. *See also* Coordination, channel; International marketing channels; Organization of marketing channels; Planning, channel
channel member satisfaction and, 418–19
climate of the channel and, 419–20
coercive and noncoercive power and, 414–16
communication problems and. *See* Communications
economic and noneconomic power and, 416–17
electronic data interchange (EDI) and, 473–74
environment and, 411, 413–14
framework for, 29, 30, 410, 412
intrachannel conflict and style of, 417–18
literature on, 441–44
by manufacturers, 421–25
in office furniture industry, 436–39
perceptions of channel members and, 420–21

performance control and audit system and. *See* Performance assessment
by physical distribution agencies, 432–34
by retailers, 428–32
wholesalers and, 136–38, 425–28
Management science
channel coordination and, 304–11
  Jeuland-Shugan model, 304–8
  Zusman-Etgar model, 308–11
channel planning and, 248–59
  Corstjens-Doyle model, 255–58
  McGuire-Staelin model, 249–55
Manufacturers, 6, 31
channel management by, 421–25
industrial goods distributors as viewed by, 129
Manufacturers' agents, 105–7, 110–11, 142
Manufacturer's export agent (MEA), 539
Manufacturers' sales branches and offices, 105, 107, 108, 110
Margin (maintained markup), 95
retailing and, 41–47
Margin management, 46, 131–32
Markdowns, 96, 99
Marketing
direct, 63–64
retailing's significance in, 63–64
Marketing channels, 1–37. *See also specific topics*
boundaries, 15
collective goals and, 196
competition and, 27–29
components of, 35–194. *See also* Physical distribution systems; Retailers; Wholesalers
composition of, 10–14
  channel member specialization, 13–14
  functions and flows, 10–14
cooperative relationship in, 196
definition of, 3
delivery and, 4
design strategies for. *See* Planning, channel
division of labor in, 196
emergence of, 197
explicit rules and policies in, 196–97
intermediaries and, 28–29, 31. *See also* Physical distribution systems; Retailers; Wholesalers
management of. *See* Management (leadership) of marketing channels
as network of systems, 14–18
  commercial, 14–15
  consumer, 14–15
  environment, 15–17
  systems theory framework, 17–18
as open system, 17
organization of. *See* Organization of marketing channels
retailing consequences for, 83–88
for services. *See* Services, marketing channels for
structure of, 3–37

Norwalk (Ohio) Furniture Corporation, 325
Nynex, 203

O

Occidental Petroleum Corporation, 551
Office furniture industry, channel leadership in, 435–38
Off-retail, 96
Off-voice allowances, 467
Oil embargo of 1974, 79
OKG Corporation, 402
Open-to-buy, definition of, 100
Opportunistic behavior, 212–13
Opportunity cost (transfer of cost), 41
Ordering, wholesalers and, 103, 140–43
Order level, 165
Order processing, 174–75, 461–62
Organizational rigidity, 26
Organization of marketing channels, 31, 32, 315–69
   administered systems, 319–26, 351
   advantages of vertical marketing systems, 358–60
   contractual vertical marketing systems, 326–48
      franchise systems, 332–48, 367–69
      voluntary and cooperative groups, 327–32
   conventional, 315–19, 358–60
   corporate vertical marketing systems, 348–58
      advantages and disadvantages of, 353–58
      backward vertical integration, 349
      compared to other systems, 350–53
      forward vertical integration, 348–49
   legal restrictions and constraints on. *See* Legal constraints
   operational definition of, 196
Original equipment manufacturers (OEMs), 204
Original retail, 95
Osmark Industries, 174
Outputs, marketing channels and, 18–20
Ownership, 211–14
   wholesalers and, 103, 139–43

P

Pan Am, 567
Parcel post services, 185
Participative leadership, 281, 418
Pathological conflict, 289–90
Pay-back period, 219
Penney, J. C., 65, 473
PepsiCo, 291, 353, 552
Perceptions
   channel conflict and, 288–89
   of channel members, channel control process and, 420–21
Performance assessment, 198–99, 477–515
   auditing distribution channels and, 504–15
      channel environment, structure, and policy audit, 506, 519–23
      direct product profit (DPP), 513–15
      distribution cost analysis, 506–13
      matrix analysis, 504–6
   effectiveness, 477–80
   efficiency and, 483–502
      productivity, 483–91
   equity in serving various markets and, 480–83
   profitability and, 492–501
      net profits/net sales (profit margin), 495–96
      net profits/total assets (return on assets), 496–97
      net sales/total assets (asset turnover), 496
      strategic profit model (SPM), 492, 496–98
   qualitative measures and, 503
Petrie Stores, 47
Pharmaceutical card system, 123
Physical distribution systems (logistics), 31, 36–37, 145–94
   components of, 145, 146
   concept of, 149–51
      cost tradeoffs, 150, 151, 152, 161–64
      total cost perspective, 150, 161
      total system perspective, 151
      zero suboptimization, 150
   continuous–review reorder–point models, 186–94
      controlling stockouts, 193–94
      how much to reorder, 188–91
      when to reorder, 191–93
   customer service standards and, 151–54
   as cycle, 145–48
   definition of, 144
   flows within, 148
   hidden costs and, 149
   international, 556–59
   inventory management and control and, 162–69
      distribution requirements planning systems, 165–66
      forecasting, 166–68
      how much to reorder and when to reorder, 164–65
      materials requirements planning (MRP), 171–73
      stockouts, controlling, 168–69
   management and, 149
   materials management cycle and, 144–45
   operational elements of, 145, 147
   order processing and related information system flows, 174–75
   pipeline, 157
      rail, 155–56
      truck, 156
      water, 156
   production control and materials, 169–74
      just-in-time logistics systems, 172–74
   retailing and, 120

Weighted factor score method (linear averaging; expectancy value method), 215–16
Welch Foods, 201
Wendy's, 127
Western Auto, 121
Westinghouse Credit Corporation, 470
Wheel of Retailing, 73–74
White Motor Co. v. *U.S.*, 390
Wholesaler-franchisors, 426
Wholesalers (wholesaling), 6, 31, 36, 101–43
  average return for, 121
  channel management and, 136–38, 425–28
  definition of, 101–2
  full-function, 10
  future trends of, 135–36
  limited-function, 10
  marketing as viewed by, 124
  marketing flows and, 139–43
  modern, emergence of, 102–4
  other names for, 101
  pressure on, 104
  selecting and using, 111–31
    business users, 115–19
    consumer goods, 120–24
    criteria of choice, 113, 114
    hard-nosed assessment, 119–31
    industrial goods, 124–31
    retailer services, 113–15
    supplier services, 112–13
  strategic management of, 131–34

asset management, 132–34
  margin management, 131–32
  structure of, 36, 104–11
    agents, brokers, and commission merchants, 105–8, 110–11, 142–43
    customer categories, 109n
    limited-function wholesalers, 106
    manufacturers' sales branches and offices, 105, 107, 108, 110
    merchant wholesalers, 105–9, 139–40
    retailer-sponsored cooperatives, 106
  vertical marketing system and, 121
Wholesaler-sponsored voluntary groups, 327–28, 426
Woolworth, 47
Working wives, 58, 62
World Trade Distribution Center (WTDC), 160
Wrigley, William, Jr., Company, 321

Y

Yuppies (young, urban, upwardly mobile professionals), 59–61

Z

Zero suboptimization, 150
ZIPS, 174
Zusman-Etgar model, 308–11